# Landlord and Tenant
# in Colonial New York

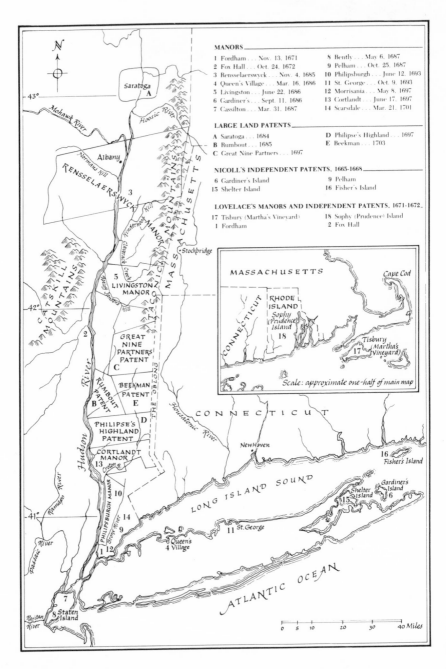

**Manors of Colonial New York and Large Land Patents on the East Side of the Hudson River.** Also showing Governor Nicholl's Independent Patents, 1665–1668, and Governor Lovelace's Manors and Independent Patents, 1671–1672. Based on the map by Max Mayer in Montgomery Schuyler, *The Patroons and Lords of Manors of the Hudson* (New York, 1932), 3–4. (Drawn by Richard J. Stinely.)

# Landlord and Tenant in Colonial New York

## Manorial Society, 1664–1775

by Sung Bok Kim

Published for the Institute of Early American History and Culture
Williamsburg, Virginia
by The University of North Carolina Press
Chapel Hill

The Institute of Early American History and Culture
is sponsored jointly by
The College of William and Mary in Virginia
and The Colonial Williamsburg Foundation

Library of Congress Cataloging in Publication Data

*Kim, Sung Bok, 1932 –*
   *Landlord and tenant in colonial New York.*

   *Bibliography: p.*
   *Includes index.*
      *1. Landlord and tenant—New York (State)—*
*History.   2. Manors—New York (State)—History.*
*I. Institute of Early American History and*
*Culture, Williamsburg, Va.   II. Title.*
*HD211.N7K55      333.5'4'09747      77-24423*
*ISBN 0-8078-1290-0*

To Robert E. Brown
and B. Katherine Brown

# Preface

The distinctive hallmark of New York in the colonial period was the string of great baronial estates that dominated its landscape. Carved out in the last quarter of the seventeenth century and the first decade of the following, these estates—about thirty in number—together occupied more than two million acres of the fertile province land. Approximately half of these estates were manor grants with lordship privileges; the rest were nonmanorial patents. While some of the grants, like Cortlandt Manor, were early broken up by sale, other huge domains, such as Rensselaerswyck Manor, Livingston Manor, Philipsburgh Manor, Philipse's Highland Patent, and Beekman Patent, remained in the hands of the proprietary families throughout the colonial period.

For the development of their estates, landlords relied on the labor of agricultural tenants, which resulted in the emergence of a large tenant population in New York unrivaled by any other colony in North America. By 1776 there were at least six or seven thousand tenant farmers in New York.[1] In a society where ownership of land was a primary source of status, and in an economy where wheat and timber products were staple goods, the great proprietors inevitably became "elites" in the broadest sense of the word. Among them and their relatives were the Van Rensselaers, Livingstons, Van Cortlandts, Philipses, Beekmans, De Lanceys, Morrises, and Smiths. Whether active or not, the presence and influence of these prominent families were felt in almost every nook and cranny of provincial politics and society.

Recent scholarship on colonial New York has made us much more

---

1. John Watts's proposal in the *Pennsylvania Ledger: or the Weekly Advertiser*, Oct. 29, 1777.

knowledgeable about the political behavior of the landed gentry at the provincial level. But this is hardly the case with respect to the development, conditions, and problems of the great domains that helped to shape the gentry's character and outlook. This is not to say that no previous study has been done of the provincial land system and related topics. Since the publication in 1886 of Edward F. DeLancey's remarkable essay, "The Origin and History of Manors in New York, and in the County of Westchester," a number of monographs, pamphlets, and essays have touched on various aspects of this complex subject. Some of them are no more than nostalgic evocations of the manorial grandeur of the great families. The most noteworthy scholarly works are: Charles W. Spencer, "The Land System of Colonial New York" (1917); Julius Goebel, Jr., *Some Legal and Political Aspects of Manors in New York* (1928); Samuel Nissenson, *The Patroon's Domain* (1937); Irving Mark, *Agrarian Conflicts in Colonial New York, 1711–1775* (1940); Harry C. Melick, *The Manor of Fordham and Its Founder* (1950); and Patricia Bonomi's essay, "New York Land System," in her work *A Factious People: Politics and Society in Colonial New York* (1971).

Unfortunately, Goebel, Nissenson, and Melick did not take their studies beyond the seventeenth century. Mark's work is by far the most comprehensive investigation of New York agrarian society. Though limited in chronological coverage, it reflects a concern with fundamental issues—tenant-landlord relations, social and political dominance of the landed class, and persistent conflicts between the landed and landless. The breadth of his research is impressive, as is suggested by the profuse footnotes in the book, which nearly match the main text in length. Briefly stated, his main theses are as follows. Lease terms for tenants on both the manors and nonmanorial patents were onerous, oppressive, and degrading. Through the domination of the courts and key political offices at various levels, and with the help of real property law, the "landed aristocracy" were able to safeguard their corruptly and fraudulently obtained land titles and continually to exploit the helpless tenants. The engrossment of land by the few had a "discouraging effect on the development of a small farmer class" and accounted for the "relative underpopulation" of the province. All these factors conspired to turn agrarian society into a seething kettle of discontents, with occasional armed uprisings by the aggrieved landless farmers.[2] Historians have generally accepted Mark's

2. Irving Mark, *Agrarian Conflicts in Colonial New York, 1711–1775* (Port Washington, N.Y., 1965 [orig. publ. New York, 1940]), 65, 66, 72, 195; Mark, "Agrarian Conflicts

interpretations. For this reason, no one interested in New York colonial society and its problems can be oblivious to the weight of his scholarship.

As I will show in this volume, Mark's view requires considerable revision. He erred in some crucial details and interpretations, not because he adopted a Marxist approach to the subject—an approach that has, after all, yielded great returns in the past—but because he did not use it properly. His error was in relying too much on lease deeds and the "land law"—or, to use the Marxist jargon, on the skeleton of legal superstructure—to determine the nature and dynamics of tenant-landlord relations. It was a serious mistake, for the legal framework concealed as much of the true picture as it revealed. Real estate law in the first half of the eighteenth century was in a state of anarchy. Its language still retained archaic feudal vestiges, and lease contracts bore little relationship to what landlords and tenants actually did or did not do. Laws and contracts often tell us more about how things should be than about how they are. I might add that other scholars beside Mark have discussed lease structure and actual practice as though they were one and the same.[3]

Mark appears also to have been swayed by the phenomenon of violent disturbances on some of the estates in the mid-eighteenth century and even in the 1840s. Eager above all to explain the rioting of the landless, he was impelled to emphasize every possible cause of strain in New York agrarian society. At the same time, he chose to disregard the good and positive features of tenant-landlord relationships that insured order and prosperity on these baronial estates for many years until 1751. He thus failed to account for the fact that, even during the decades of violence, most of the large estates remained quiet—even though the prevailing lease conditions on these estates were almost the same as those of their trouble-torn neighbors—and that most riots were extremely localized events in the areas adjoining the New England colonies of Massachusetts and Connecticut. Needless to say, the history of New York

in New York and the American Revolution," *Rural Sociology*, VII (1942), 275–293.

3. Charles Worthen Spencer, "The Land System of Colonial New York," New York State Historical Association, *Proceedings*, XVI (1917), 150–164; Stephen L. Mershon, *The Power of the Crown in the Valley of the Hudson* (Brattleboro, Vt., 1925); S. G. Nissenson, *The Patroon's Domain*, New York State Historical Association Series, No. 5 (New York, 1937); David Maldwyn Ellis, *Landlords and Farmers in the Hudson-Mohawk Region, 1790–1850* (Ithaca, N.Y., 1946); George Dangerfield, *Chancellor Robert R. Livingston of New York, 1746–1813* (New York, 1960); Ulysses Prentiss Hedrick, *A History of Agriculture in the State of New York* (Albany, N.Y., 1933); Don R. Gerlach, *Philip Schuyler and the American Revolution in New York, 1733–1777* (Lincoln, Neb., 1964), app. C; Staughton Lynd, *Anti-Federalism in Dutchess County, New York: A Study of Democracy and Class Conflict in the Revolutionary Era* (Chicago, 1962).

agrarian society was no more the story of tenants preparing all the time for armed uprisings than the history of the American colonies was continuously the story of the colonists conspiring for independence.

Apart from methodological shortcomings, another factor has led historians astray: our ingrained ideological animus against landlordism. An inevitable corollary is the worship of yeomanry. The concept of the independent and virtuous freeholder has been a traditional darling of Anglo-Saxon and American social theorists. A system built on the concentration of landed wealth by the few, which appeared to impede the growth of middling yeomen farmers, was anathema to populist historians. Frederick Jackson Turner could not pass by the colonial New York land system without condemning it.[4] Mark dubbed it "inequitable" and "fraudulent."[5] Staughton Lynd, a more recent New York historian, saw fit to put "notorious" and "disdainful" before "landlords" without bothering to explain why they deserved such epithets.[6] He perhaps did not have to explain because the landlords, in his perception, could not be anything but disreputable. Regrettably, the addiction to yeoman ideology deprived historians of the capacity to examine objectively the development and conditions of the great landed estates.

This book is a study of the rise, structure, and functioning of the four largest manors in colonial New York—Rensselaerswyck (1,000,000 acres), Livingston (160,000 acres), Cortlandt (86,000 acres), and Philipsburgh (92,000). The first two were located in the frontier county of Albany and the last two in Westchester County north of New York City. Because of the sheer size of the manors—together occupying more than half of the total acreage of the large developed estates of the colony—and because of their geographic distribution, this book is in fact a study not only of manorial society but also of New York agrarian society as a whole where tenancy prevailed. My claim to comprehensiveness is based also on the fact that in the course of the first three decades of the eighteenth century the distinction between manors and nonmanorial patents, as far as their internal governance was concerned, became negligible. The economic and social forces affecting manorial tenants were practically the same as those affecting nonmanorial tenants.

---

4. Frederick Jackson Turner, *The Frontier in American History* (New York, 1950 [orig. publ. 1920]), 80–83.

5. Mark, *Agrarian Conflicts*, 50.

6. Staughton Lynd, "Who Should Rule at Home? Dutchess County, New York, in the American Revolution," *William and Mary Quarterly*, 3d Ser., XVIII (1961), 335, 337; Lynd, "Abraham Yates's History of the Movement for the United States Constitution," *WMQ*, 3d Ser., XX (1963), 224.

The first three chapters of my work examine the questions of how and why the manors came into being, what brought about the subsequent demise of the manorial lordship, and what eventually took its place. Chapters 4 through 6 are concerned with the economics of land and landlordism, landlord-tenant relationships, and the problem of tenantry. Regarding the last two subjects, which make up the core of the volume, the following questions guided me. How onerous or satisfactory were lease terms? Did the specifics of lease contracts coincide with the actual practice? How did a tenant typically relate himself to the landlord? How did he cope with the problems of weather, soil, and topography? How did he perceive his socioeconomic environment, and what did it mean, both economically and psychologically, to be a tenant? Were his chances for economic advancement blocked? How did his life and his property holdings compare to those of freeholders? Finally, chapters 7 and 8 narrate and analyze the violent disturbances on some of the great domains in the third quarter of the eighteenth century.

I consider this book to be a result of my cumulative educational experience since I came to the United States in 1960. Countless thoughtful persons taught me the discipline of history, encouraged me to persist in it when my morale was sagging, and cared about my well-being when I was in trouble. Some of them, to be sure, played no direct role in the making of this particular book. But without the good training I received from them, I would have been intellectually and emotionally unprepared to cope with the often frustrating process of research.

I wish to thank Professor David S. Lovejoy of the University of Wisconsin, under whose guidance I painfully learned the elementary lessons of graduate study in history. He was a rigorous taskmaster, never content with a mediocre performance from any of his students. Yet a warm affection always tempered his attitude toward me. No less inspiring was Professor Merle Curti of the same university, who allowed me, despite my being a master's candidate, to attend his lively seminar for doctoral students in American intellectual history; there I became aware of various issues and methodological problems inherent in American history. I am also grateful to some of his students, namely, John Livingston, John Tomsich, and Jackson Raymond Wilson, for exposing me to bad as well as to good aspects of American life, apart from their good intellectual companionship. My personal contact with them was beneficial to me at the crucial stage of my acculturation.

I do not know how to express my gratitude to Professor Robert E.

Brown and his wife, B. Katherine Brown. He was my mentor at Michigan State University and first called my attention to the pressing need for an in-depth study of a New York colonial manor. My doctoral dissertation, "The Manor of Cortlandt and Its Tenants, New York, 1697–1783" (1966), was done under his direction. When I consulted the Browns about my plan to investigate all the major manors in the province, their response was enthusiastic. Hearing that I had completed the first draft of my new study, they drove from East Lansing, Michigan, to Guilderland, New York, to talk with me about it, and they spent considerable amounts of their precious time to read it and comment on its content and style. They are not just teachers in the ordinary sense of the word. They have taken care of me all these years in a manner that only true parents would. Thus I dedicate this book to them.

This present work began in earnest with a three-year postdoctoral fellowship (1968–1971) at the Institute of Early American History and Culture, Williamsburg, Virginia. In an age when the nebulous syndrome of "publish or perish" prevails, this fellowship is a splendid anomaly. It provided me with the opportunity to grope and mature, without which, I am sure, I could never have finished the project. For that, I am thankful to those concerned in the fellowship program, particularly to Lester J. Cappon and Stephen G. Kurtz, the former directors of the Institute. Benefits from my association with several past and present Institute staff members—Norman S. Fiering, Larry R. Gerlach, James H. Hutson, Herbert A. Johnson, Bernard W. Sheehan, John E. Selby, and Thad W. Tate —are more than I can specify here. The regular Monday lunch of the staff was not just a social gathering, but, at least for me, a scholarly bull session. Other Institute colleagues—Joy Dickinson Barnes, Patricia Blatt, Patricia Higgs, Mary Anne O'Boyle Leary, and Donna C. Sheppard—all supported my research with good offices and cheer. In particular, Joy and Norman, my editors, have done a conscientious and expert editorial job with their provocative queries, suggestions, and corrections. Any mistakes in the book, however, are my exclusive responsibility. Edward P. Crapol and Richard Maxwell Brown of the College of William and Mary were always willing to listen to my half-baked ideas and to prod me with pertinent questions.

While I was at the writing stage, several people helped me in different ways. John R. Dahl, Robert M. McColley, Winton U. Solberg, and Clark C. and Mary Lee Spence, my colleagues at the University of Illinois at Champaign-Urbana, extended to me their encouragement and friendship in the aftermath of a tornado that badly damaged our homestead shortly after we settled in that prairie country. Kendall Birr of the History Department, State University of New York at Albany, gave me a lighter burden of teaching in return for my promise to concentrate on writing. Harry S. Price, Thomas Beck, G. J. Barker-Benfield, and John Monfasani of the same institution read the entire manuscript and offered valuable criticisms.

Special thanks are due to the staff members of various manuscript depositories. The most helpful were Arthur J. Breton and Thomas Dunnings of the New-York Historical Society, who, in addition to being patient with a stream of requests for more material, often alerted me to uncataloged and hitherto unused materials that they thought might be useful to my study. I am also obliged to Peter Kristoff and James Corsaro of New York State Library, Albany; Robert Wheeler and Patricia Smith, formerly of Sleepy Hollow Restorations Library, Tarrytown, N.Y.; A. K. Baragwanath of the Museum of the City of New York; John Dann of the William L. Clements Library, University of Michigan, Ann Arbor; the staff of the Manuscript Division of the New York Public Library; and the staffs of the county clerk's offices of Albany, Dutchess, and Westchester counties.

Finally, I express my profound gratitude to my aging parents, younger brothers and sisters, and relatives living in Korea, who have endured my absence from home for a long time. I deeply appreciate my younger brother Sung Bong's devotion and sacrifice in looking after our family welfare so that I could indulge in my dreams. It goes without saying that my wife, Leda, merits a special citation for her steady support of me and my work. My children, Briana, Cortland, and Blakeley, particularly the twin boys, have surely delayed my work, but by doing so they inadvertently gave me more time to think.

# Contents

# Maps and Sketches

# Tables and Graphs

# Short Titles

| | |
|---|---|
| Blathwayt Papers | William Blathwayt Papers (microfilm), Colonial Williamsburg Foundation Research Department, Williamsburg, Va., which also owns the originals. |
| *Colden Letter Books* | *The Colden Letter Books, 1760–1775* (New-York Historical Society, *Collections*, IX–X [New York, 1876–1877]). |
| *Colden Papers* | *The Letters and Papers of Cadwallader Colden* (New-York Historical Society, *Collections*, L–LVI [New York, 1917–1923]). |
| *Doc. Hist. N.Y.* | E. B. O'Callaghan, ed., *The Documentary History of the State of New York* (Albany, N.Y., 1849–1851). |
| Duane Papers | James Duane Papers (microfilm), published by the New-York Historical Society, New York, which owns the originals. |
| Livingston-Redmond MSS | Livingston-Redmond Manuscripts (microfilm); originals at Franklin Delano Roosevelt Library, Hyde Park, N.Y. |
| Loyalist Transcripts | American Loyalists, Examinations in London and New York, Audit Office Transcripts, New York Public Library. |

| | |
|---|---|
| *N.Y. Col. Docs.* | E. B. O'Callaghan and B[erthold] Fernow, eds., *Documents Relative to the Colonial History of the State of New-York . . .* (Albany, N.Y., 1853–1887). |
| *N.Y. Col. Laws* | *The Colonial Laws of New York from the Year 1664 to the Revolution* (Albany, N.Y., 1894–1896). |
| N.Y. Col. MSS | New York Colonial Manuscripts, New York State Library, Albany. |
| N.Y. Land Papers | New York Colonial Manuscripts, Land Papers, 1642–1803, New York State Library, Albany. |

# Landlord and Tenant
# in Colonial New York

# CHAPTER I

≈≈≈≈≈

# The Rise of the Manors, 1664-1687

### The Heritage of New Netherland

Every institution has historical roots. The New York manorial system that evolved in the last quarter of the seventeenth century was no exception. It has been claimed that the manors were the product of the "illegal" and "corrupt" practices of greedy English governors, notably Thomas Dongan (1682–1688) and Benjamin Fletcher (1692–1698), who were fond of taking bribes for lavish land grants.[1] The manors seem to have had much more complicated origins, however. This likelihood is suggested by the appearance before 1674 of several rudimentary manors that later turned into full-fledged examples of the institution. Thus, it is necessary to examine the political and economic circumstances of the English administration inherited from Dutch New Netherland, as well as the governors' problems, in order to trace the background of and uncover the reasons for the establishment of manors.

The States General of the United Netherlands declared in the preamble to the charter given to the West India Company in 1621 that the prosperity of the nation must be maintained by trade and navigation. In founding New Netherland, the commercial company fulfilled the intentions of the States General to the letter, establishing a colony that was, in effect, a fur-trading operation. The excessive dependence of the colony on the fur trade had both positive and negative effects. The venturesome

1. Mark, *Agrarian Conflicts*, 19.

3

Dutch traders and colonists, encouraged by the easily navigable rivers and spurred on by rivalry with the English to the east and by the lure of furs, penetrated deep into the Indian country. Thus, the colony that the English conquerors acquired in 1664 was, like New France to the north, geographically much more extensive than any contemporary English colony in North America. Its territory on the mainland stretched 150 miles along the Hudson River corridor northward from Manhattan to Fort Orange (Albany) and 30 or 40 miles along the Raritan and Delaware rivers. However, the remarkable geographical expansion—already accomplished in the middle of the 1630s—was not accompanied by substantial settlement, with the result that the colony remained sparsely peopled.

At the end of the Dutch period, New York's settlement toward the interior was not contiguous. It was concentrated in three population centers—New York, Kingston, and Albany (formerly New Amsterdam, Esopus, and Beverwyck). The entrepôt of the colony, New York City with a population of fifteen hundred, was a replica of burgeoning, modern Amsterdam, built mostly of "brick and stone, covered with red and black tiles" presenting "a pleasing Aspect to the spectator." But this city did not spread beyond the present Wall Street, where its fortification ended, although the settlement of a small peripheral village, Harlem, was taking place without fanfare. The major part of Manhattan Island was still pasture and common for roaming livestock.[2] Then there was Long Island, stretching 180 miles parallel to the mainland, where toward the west were a half-dozen agricultural villages of Dutch origin and toward the east another small group of villages of English origin. The island was relatively well settled and growing rapidly from the steady immigration of land-hungry New England farmers; together with New York City, it accounted for more than half of the colony's population. Midway up the Hudson River was Kingston, a collection of widely scattered villages with about a hundred settlers who were slowly recovering from the ravages of the intermittent Esopus War of 1658–1664. The town of Albany, about 60 miles further up the Hudson, built upon barren, sandy soil and stockaded with logs and boards, had no more than two hundred inhabitants, all of whom had come there solely for Indian trade. Their commerce extended as far as the Great Lakes and the Seneca country on the Susquehanna River. Albany's satellite village 16 miles to the north-

2. Daniel Denton, *A Brief Description of New-York* (1670), with a bibliographical note by Victor H. Paltsits, Facsimile Text Society, Publication No. 40 (New York, 1937), 3.

west, Schenectady, had just been settled by fourteen families under Arent Van Curler. Dispersed around these two frontier posts were some forty thatched houses on the manor lands of Rensselaerswyck in which about two hundred persons drew their livelihood from farming and tapping the Indian trade. David Pieterszoon De Vries's observation in 1639 that every Dutch "boor," or peasant, was also "a merchant" probably still held true even thirty years later.[3]

The rest of the country was dominated by Indian culture, with the possible exception of Oost-dorp, or Easttown (present Westchester), with fewer than thirty houses huddled together in the pattern of a Connecticut town. Elsewhere the occupants of crude huts managed a forlorn existence. Most of these isolated settlers did not have land titles, nor did they bother to obtain even rudimentary governance except when they were threatened by Indian attack. Miles of land between Manhattan and Albany, purportedly consisting of "barren mountain hills, not improveable by human industry," were left undisturbed by Europeans.[4] The Delaware and Raritan areas were not much better inhabited. In August 1665, when Philip Carteret with an entourage of thirty persons arrived to take up the first governorship of New Jersey at the site that would later become its capital of Perth Amboy, he found only a cluster of four cabins waiting for him. An observer of the New Jersey scene commented in 1671 that there were several villages on the ocean side near the entrance of the Raritan River, but that there was not even one for about a sixty-mile stretch between the entrance to the Raritan and the Delaware Bay. Struck by the primitive state of settlement in the region, he declared, "This Countrey is Peopled onely with wild Beasts."[5] New Netherland, though it had a government, never developed into anything more than a congeries of trading posts under a commercial directorate.

The painfully slow settlement of the colony was caused by a number of factors. One was the exclusively commercial orientation of the Dutch West India Company, which saw no advantage in extensive immigration. The company feared that more immigrants would mean tougher compe-

3. "From the 'Korte Historiael ende Journaels Aenteyckeninge,' by David Pietersz. de Vries, 1633–1643 (1655)," in J. Franklin Jameson, ed., *Narratives of New Netherland, 1609–1664*, Original Narratives of Early American History (New York, 1909), 207.

4. E. B. O'Callaghan and B[erthold] Fernow, eds., *Documents Relative to the Colonial History of the State of New-York* . . . (Albany, N.Y., 1853–1887), III, 798, hereafter cited as *N.Y. Col. Docs.*

5. [George Lockhart], *A Further Account of East-New-Jersey* (Edinburgh, 1683), 5; George Bancroft, *History of the United States from the Discovery of the American Continent* (New York, 1883–1896 [orig. publ. Boston, 1834–1874]), I, 522.

tition for the peltries it wanted to monopolize. Suffering from an acute financial deficit, however, the company made modest attempts in 1629 and again in 1640 to attain the twin goals of increasing population and of shifting the burden of investment in agriculture from the company to private capital.[6] It promised generous land grants and privileges to any stockholder who would undertake the planting of fifty families in the colony. Specifically, the planter was to receive land lying along a navigable stream for sixteen miles on one side or eight miles on both sides and extending into the interior for an infinite distance. He was also to hold supreme administrative and judicial power over his people, except in cases involving a capital offense or more than 50 guilders. However, the company reserved the fur trade monopoly for itself. This was the famous patroonship scheme of colonization. Kiliaen Van Rensselaer, an Amsterdam merchant and company stockholder, availed himself of the offer and in 1630 established a vast colony around Fort Orange. Subsequently, seven more men took up a patroonship.

But the patroonship was not a thriving institution. The company's commitment to colonization proved to be lukewarm at best, for it did not provide adequate transportation for immigrants, cattle, and provisions. When the patroons challenged the company's traditional rights, it was only too eager to harass them.[7] In addition, the patroons found it difficult to procure colonists. Prospective tenants were unwilling to submit to feudal control when there was plenty of free land available both in New Netherland and in neighboring provinces. By the end of the Dutch period, none of the patroonships except the Van Rensselaers' had survived.

Commercialism and shortsighted profit-seeking were endemic, affecting almost every colonist as well as the Dutch West India Company. Despite their allegations to the contrary, the patroons were more interested in furs than in colonizing. As Kiliaen Van Rensselaer acknowledged in 1633, "the main cause" of conflict between the patroons and the company was "nothing but the trade in furs and the question by whom it shall be conducted."[8] The farmers under the patroons also realized that trade with the Indians was a quicker way to a fortune than the drudgery of tilling the soil. This was particularly true of the tenants in Rensselaerswyck. Although they ostensibly came there for farming, easy accessibility

6. Van Cleaf Bachman, *Peltries or Plantations: The Economic Policies of the Dutch West India Company in New Netherland, 1623–1639* (Baltimore, 1969), 124, 96.
7. "From the 'New World,' by Johan de Laet, 1625, 1630, 1633, 1640," in Jameson, ed., *Narratives of New Netherland*, 30.
8. Cited in Bachman, *Peltries*, 124.

to a source of peltry was probably the most important reason for their settlement.[9]

Unlike the English, who equated ownership of land with status and wealth, well-to-do Dutch merchants did not try to buy social position by acquiring a country estate. The possibility that, with an increase in population, these lands would someday become valuable failed to steer them to land speculation. The wealth of most affluent New York Dutch in the 1650s and 1660s consisted in the ownership of boats, buildings such as mills and breweries, and well-located lots on Manhattan Island.[10] The determined campaign by the town of Beverwyck (Albany) to corner the northern fur trade exclusively for its burghers was simply a local manifestation of the attitude of the company. To insure an uninterrupted flow of furs to the town merchants, they resisted westward settlement tenaciously and often successfully.

A major discouragement to the settlement of the colony was the destructive Indian wars of 1643–1644 and 1658–1664, which terrorized the outlying colonists. In 1643 Pavonia on Staten Island and many budding hamlets north of Manhattan were wiped out. In 1663 a recently built village at Esopus (Kingston) was burned to the ground, and most of its inhabitants were either killed or taken prisoner. Contributing to these outbreaks and their intensity was the unrestrained traffic in arms and liquor long engaged in by the traders and the company representatives in the colony.[11] In the face of aggressive expansion by New England colonists from the east, nothing was more harmful to the colony's security than the decimation of its settlers. Peter Stuyvesant, the last governor of New Netherland, knew that time was running out for the colony unless it

9. Samuel G. Nissenson, *The Patroon's Domain* (New York, 1937), 80.

10. Here I have in mind the five wealthiest men in New York City in 1674: Frederick Philipse, Cornelis Steenwyck, Nicholas De Meyer, Oloff Stevense Van Cortlandt, and Jeronimus Ebbingh. They were all merchants, and variously drew their fortunes from trading, brewing, manufacturing wampum, moneylending, or shipping. For their property holdings, see Hugh Hastings, ed., *Ecclesiastical Records, State of New York* (Albany, N.Y., 1901–1916), I, 641–643. For their occupations, see Jaspar Dankers and Philip Sluyter, *Journal of a Voyage to New York and a Tour in Several of the American Colonies in 1679–80*, trans. and ed. Henry C. Murphy (Long Island Historical Society, *Memoirs*, I [Brooklyn, N.Y., 1867]), 353; Edward Hagaman Hall, *Philipse Manor Hall at Yonkers, N.Y.: The Site, the Building, and Its Occupants* (New York, 1912), 50–55; *The Journal of the Reverend Silas Constant, Pastor of the Presbyterian Church at Yorktown, New York . . .* (Philadelphia, 1903), 424–425; will of Cornelis Steenwyck, in *Abstracts of Wills, on File in the Surrogate's Office, City of New York* (New-York Historical Society, *Collections*, XXV–XLI [New York, 1892–1908]), II, 414, hereafter cited as *Abstracts of Wills*; will of Nicholas De Meyer, *ibid.*, I, 203; will of Jeronimus Ebbingh, *ibid.*, 26.

11. Allen W. Trelease, *Indian Affairs in Colonial New York: The Seventeenth Century* (Ithaca, N.Y., 1960), 168; *N.Y. Col. Docs.*, XIII, 228–229, 237–238, 245, 256–257.

was revitalized through a large infusion of Dutch immigrants.[12] But the heavy hand of traditional commercialism that dominated the Dutch settlement could not be easily overcome; New Netherland surrendered to British military power without firing a single shot. The reliance on trade and commerce that had so greatly boosted the Dutch nation at home had undermined one of her colonies.

## Ducal Scheme versus "Independent" Local Jurisdictions

Six months before the quiet conquest of New Netherland took place, Charles II in March 1664 granted his brother James, the duke of York and Albany, a vast territory extending from "the west side of Connecticut river to the east side of Delaware bay" and including Long Island (most of which had been previously given to Connecticut under her charter of 1662), Nantucket, Martha's Vineyard, and the eastern part of Maine. But the actual land mass assigned to Richard Nicolls, deputy governor, was much smaller, since James had already conveyed the region of present-day New Jersey to his favorites, John, Lord Berkeley, and Sir George Carteret. It was further reduced by the transfer, in 1681, of the Delaware region to William Penn and, in 1691, of Martha's Vineyard, Nantucket, and eastern Maine to Massachusetts.

Although the province of New York had shrunk, the English governors had a difficult job of presiding over and assimilating a polyglot population of about eight thousand into a proprietary scheme. It was reported that the Dutch constituted nearly three-fourths of the inhabitants, English dissenters nearly one-fourth, and other nationalities the remainder. Further complicating the matter was the problem of defending the colony against Dutch reconquest and against the continual threat of Indian attack.[13] Both objectives, assimilation of the population and defense, demanded a policy that would reconcile traditional local practices and privileges with the overriding imperative of establishing a strong proprietary government.

As for the Dutch inhabitants, Nicolls had already promised in the articles of capitulation to confirm titles in property, freedom of conscience, and "their own customs concerning inheritance." Nicolls quickly

---

12. Introduction to "The Journal of Van Ruyven, Van Cortlant, and Lawrence, 1663," in Jameson, ed., *Narratives of New Netherland*, 428; Trelease, *Indian Affairs*, 173.
13. Richard Nicolls to duke of York, [two letters, n.d.], and to Lord Arlington, Apr. 9, 1666, *N.Y. Col. Docs.*, III, 105–106, 114; Gov. John Winthrop to Arlington, Oct. 25, 1666, *ibid.*, 137.

sensed the political wisdom of appeasing the Dutch and perceived that promoting trade would answer this end as well as make the province profitable to the duke of York.[14] Furthermore, he probably had good reason to believe that the Dutch, who had compelled Stuyvesant to accept what was inevitable in 1664 and had never been tainted with anti-Stuart ideology, would prove much "better subjects" in the long run than the New England colonists and would "support this government better then can be reasonably expected from new comers of our owne nation." Earlier, Nicolls had written to the duke that he would try to "put the whole Government into one frame and policy," but he was sympathetic to Dutch law and local institutions.[15] The same conciliatory spirit guided his successor, Colonel Francis Lovelace (1667–1674). When English laws were introduced to the Dutch town of Esopus at the inhabitants' own request, the governor in council in September 1673 ordered that only those who were of the Reformed religion and "well inclined towards the Dutch nation" be nominated for the town offices.[16] This gentle encouragement to the Dutch to fit their system of governance gradually into the English framework would continue for some years to come.

It was not the Dutch but the New England settlers on Long Island and in Westchester that most worried Nicolls and his successors. Deeply attached to Connecticut, from which most of them had come, and jealous of their local self-government, the settlers were not happy with the ducal scheme. When Nicolls wrote in 1666 that "Democracy hath taken so deepe a Roote in these parts, that the very name of a Justice of the Peace is an Abomination," he certainly had in mind the thirteen English towns in the colony.[17] For these early New York governors, seasoned with autocratic Stuart doctrines, republicanism and local autonomy were altogether incompatible with the imperatives of the Restoration at home and, more particularly, with the proprietary form of government in the colony. Consequently, one of Nicolls's first official acts was to curb sharply those aspects of town life that were irreconcilable with his consolidation policy. The governor promulgated the so-called Duke's Laws and compelled representatives from the Westchester area and the Long Island towns to ratify them in the spring of 1665. Under these statutes,

14. *N.Y. Col. Docs.*, II, 250–253.
15. Nicolls to Lord Arlington, Apr. 9, 1666, *N.Y. Col. Docs.*, III, 114; Nicolls to earl of Clarendon, Apr. 7, 1666, N.-Y. Hist. Soc., *Colls.*, II (1869), 119; Nicolls to duke of York, Nov. 1665, *ibid.*, III (1870), 104.
16. *N.Y. Col. Docs.*, XIII, 471, 475.
17. Nicolls to earl of Clarendon, Apr. 7, 1666, N.-Y. Hist. Soc., *Colls.*, II (1869), 119.

the election of town magistrates, constables, and overseers was made contingent upon the governor's approval, and the traditional independent town court was replaced by a system in which the justice of the peace, the governor's appointee, was the central figure. The justice was authorized to "preside as chief in any of the Towne Meetings within the Jurisdiction where he lived, if he pleased to do so," and thus was in a position to influence their proceedings. He, together with other justices sitting as a court of sessions, would be empowered not only to review appeals from the lower court of constables and overseers but also to try all criminal matters and civil cases involving less than £20.[18] In addition, the court of sessions determined and allocated the tax quota for each town. These same justices, with the exception of the governor and his council, constituted the highest tribunal in the colony, the court of assizes, which exercised the supreme legislative and judicial power. Although "collected out of the Lawes of the other [New England] Colonyes," the Duke's Laws undoubtedly put an end to the full-fledged local self-government New Englanders had known. In fact, Nicolls considered these codes, which were "not contrived so Democratically" as those of other colonies, as an instrument to "revive the Memory of old England amongst us" and lay in the "foundations of Kingly Government in these parts so farre as is possible, which truely is grievous to some Republicans."[19]

If local community self-government was anathema to Nicolls, so too was the feudal patroonship of the Van Rensselaers. The governor was familiar with the patroon's persistent, though futile, efforts to undercut New Netherland government control of the fur trade and of Beverwyck (Albany). He could see the danger of the mammoth domain growing into a local power strong enough to challenge his government. It was therefore imperative that the patroonship be reduced.

Nicolls's first antipatroon measure took the form of a rejection of the Van Rensselaers' claim to the town of Albany, which was based on a patent that the States General had given the family in 1641. The governor could not afford to let Albany, the second major town of the province and the hub of one of its most important revenue-producing areas, slip

18. *The Colonial Laws of New York from the Year 1664 to the Revolution* (Albany, N.Y., 1894–1896), I, 44, hereafter cited as *N.Y. Col. Laws*.
19. Nicolls to earl of Clarendon, Apr. 7, 1666, N.-Y. Hist. Soc., *Colls.*, II (1869), 119. For the New England influence on the Duke's Laws, see Morton Pennypacker, *The Duke's Laws: Their Antecedents, Implications, and Importance* (New York, 1944); George L. Haskins and Samuel E. Ewing, "The Spread of Massachusetts Law in the Seventeenth Century," in David H. Flaherty, ed., *Essays in the History of Early American Law* (Chapel Hill, N.C., 1969), 186–191.

out of his control, even if the family's pretension were legally valid. Besides, like his Dutch predecessors Peter Minuet and Peter Stuyvesant, Nicolls probably looked upon the prospering Dutch burghers of the town as a valuable counterpoise to the power and wealth of the patroonship. Thus, in October 1664, Nicolls assured the town of Albany of its independence from the patroonship and its continued monopoly of the Indian trade, both of which it had enjoyed since 1652. This was a blow to the Van Rensselaers. Their only consolation was a letter of "confirmation" from the governor authorizing them to exercise their traditional rights within the limits of the domain. But the letter of confirmation further stipulated that Jeremiah Van Rensselaer, the domain director, must procure a new English patent within a year and pay fifty beavers and a thousand planks of lumber annually in time of peace.[20]

A year later, Nicolls dealt a more shattering blow when he stripped the patroon of his traditional right to appoint and maintain a local court. Jeremiah Van Rensselaer's power was reduced to nominating three men for a new consolidated court of Albany, Rensselaerswyck, and Schenectady. The governor would choose two of the three men for the six-member court.[21] This meant in effect that Van Rensselaer could influence only two votes in the court. Upset at the diminution of his authority, he complained that "there is nothing left of our high, middle and low jurisdiction of the colony."[22] The new arrangement put an end to the patroon's use of the court to enact ordinances for the domain and to punish infractions of them.[23]

Nevertheless, the Van Rensselaers hoped to get some relief from England; they expected that Nicholas Van Rensselaer, Jeremiah's younger brother, who had attracted the attention of Charles II during his exile in

20. As of 1660 the patroonship was owned by five families, the heirs of Kiliaen Van Rensselaer (a two-fifths share), Jan De Laet (one-fifth), Toussain Muyssart (one-fifth), and Samuel Blommart and Adam Bessels (together one-fifth). Because they owned a double share of the domain, the Van Rensselaers took sole management of it and refused to make an account of its affairs to the others until the partnership was liquidated in 1685. For this reason and to avoid confusion, I will discuss the patroonship as if it belonged only to the Van Rensselaer family. For the distribution of the shares, see Nissenson, *Patroon's Domain*, 318–328; and A. J. F. van Laer, trans. and ed., *Correspondence of Maria Van Rensselaer, 1669–1689* (Albany, N.Y., 1935), 151–152, 158–159, hereafter cited as *Maria Van Rensselaer Correspondence*.

21. *Maria Van Rensselaer Correspondence*, 362, 365; Joel Munsell, ed., *The Annals of Albany* (Albany, N.Y., 1850–1859), VII, 97–98.

22. Jeremiah Van Rensselaer to Oloff Stevense Van Cortlandt, Sept. 12, 1665, and to Jan Baptist Van Rensselaer, Aug. 8, 1668, A. J. F. van Laer, trans. and ed., *Correspondence of Jeremias Van Rensselaer, 1651–1674* (Albany, N.Y., 1932), 382, 411, hereafter cited as *Jeremias Van Rensselaer Correspondence*.

23. Nissenson, *Patroon's Domain*, 272–273.

Holland by predicting the restoration of the Stuarts, would soon secure from the king or the duke a patent that would include Albany. In December 1666, a highly incensed Nicolls wrote to Jeremiah Van Rensselaer: "I perceive that you conclude the Towne of Albany to be part of Renzelaerwick; I give you freindly advice not to grasp at too much authority. . . . If you imagine there is pleasure in titles of Government I wish that I could serve your appetite. . . . Sett your hearth therefore at rest to bee contented with the profitt not the government of a Colony, till we heare from His Royall Highness."[24] This blunt letter well summed up the governor's determination not to countenance a competing power in the province. Political and administrative control even at the local level was to be reserved almost exclusively for the governor, not for anyone else.

Nicolls's policy of strengthening the central power did not rely only on curtailing the autonomy of patroon lords and self-governing communities. He also took the positive step of establishing government enclaves in strategic areas (see the frontispiece map). Variously styled "independent patents," "governorships," or "manors," they were David Gardiner's Isle of Wight (October 1665),[25] Constant and Nathaniel Sylvester's Shelter Island (May 1666),[26] Thomas Pell's Pelham (October 1666),[27] and John Winthrop, Jr.'s, Fisher's Island (1666).[28] According to their patents, each locality would be regarded as an "intire infranchised Townshipp Manor and place of itself"—not in any way to be "subordinate or belonging unto . . . any riding or towne or townshipps, place or jurisdiction"—and each should be controlled in "all matters as to Government accordingly by the Governor and Councell and General Court of Assizes only." Conspicuously absent from these patents was any reference to a manorial lordship. Nothing was said of any form of administrative and judicial authority for the grantees. In defining jurisdictional matters for the patents, the governor seemed less concerned about what kind of power and function the patentees had than he was about making the patents antithetical to townships of the New England type. These patents

---

24. Nicolls to Jeremiah Van Rensselaer, Nov. 6/16, 1666, N.Y. Col. Docs., III, 143–144, and in Jeremias Van Rensselaer Correspondence, 389. For the Dutch governors' attitude toward the patroonship, see Nissenson, Patroon's Domain, 253.

25. Patent Book I, 22–23, Office of the Secretary of State of New York, Albany. The patent for Gardiner took the form of confirming a deed of 1639 from the earl of Sterling to Lyon Gardiner, father of David.

26. New York Colonial Manuscripts, XXXVIII, 155, New York State Library, Albany, hereafter cited as N.Y. Col. MSS; Benjamin F. Thompson, History of Long Island; Containing an Account of the Discovery and Settlement . . . (New York, 1839), 234.

27. Deed Book A, 240–243, Westchester County Clerk's Office, White Plains, N.Y.

28. M. L. Woolsey, The Winthrop Manor of Fishers Island . . . (Baltimore, 1927).

were also quite distinct from feudal-style manors, which typically came equipped with civil and criminal authority. For the grantees, the major benefit lay in immunity from possible political interference and taxation by neighboring towns, a benefit that the patentees would increasingly appreciate.

The geographic distribution of Nicolls's four independent patents revealed his other motive in granting them. Except for Fisher's Island, they were all situated in areas sharply disputed between New York and Connecticut. Despite the settlement in 1664 fixing the southern boundary between the two colonies at Mamaroneck and thence running northward in a continuous line twenty miles at all points from the Hudson River, Connecticut did not leave its territorial ambitions at rest. Shelter Island and Gardiner's Island were at the east end of Long Island, where New England settlers, dissatisfied with ducal rule, were talking openly about joining Connecticut. They were also the strategic points at which Nicolls feared the Dutch might attempt an invasion. Pell's patent, lying between Mamaroneck and Westchester, occupied part of the area that in 1663 Connecticut had commissioned Pell to purchase from the Indians. He had already settled there with a few farmers.[29] Nicolls shrewdly maneuvered for Pell's allegiance for New York by giving him a large tract of land (about two thousand acres) that he could not possibly hope to obtain from the township-oriented Connecticut government. It is difficult to explain, however, why Nicolls granted Fisher's Island to John Winthrop, Jr. The governor probably felt the need to reward Winthrop for his distinguished service during the English conquest of New Netherland and to moderate Winthrop's zeal for the expansion of Connecticut.

By establishing these independent patents, Nicolls was trying to fortify New York's territorial claims against Connecticut. In view of the chaotic condition of nearly all the colonial boundaries, his concern is understandable. In this early period, a boundary was whatever was claimed, occupied, and forcibly held. Amidst the scramble for land, no measure appeared to Nicolls more effective in widening jurisdiction over the area

---

29. Benjamin Trumbull, *A Complete History of Connecticut, Civil and Ecclesiastical, from the Emigration of Its First Planters, from England, in the Year 1630, to the Year 1764* . . . (New London, Conn., 1898 [orig. publ. 1818]), I, 257–276, app. 16; "Appendix 'G.' Colonial Records of the State," in *Second Annual Report of the State Historian of the State of New York* (Albany, N.Y., 1897), 143–144. As Sir John Werden, the duke's secretary, wryly put it, Connecticut's boundary might "extend to all as far as Virginia as to what they now clayme," because her patent was so vaguely drawn. Werden to Gov. Edmund Andros, Jan. 28, 1676, *N.Y. Col. Docs.*, III, 236. (Note that throughout this study, dates in the months January to March have been converted to the New Style calendar.)

of conflict than settling the country with the right kind of people and then setting up preemptive rights against a rival colony.[30] Some of these "independent" patents would be transformed later into manors of full stature. And the same considerations that led to the establishment of these patents—encouraging settlement, protecting territorial prerogatives, providing for military security, and advancing political-ideological goals—would also operate together to make a strong impetus for the creation of the manorial system.

Governor Francis Lovelace, who succeeded Nicolls in August 1667, went a step further by gradually developing a much more elaborate system of local political units directly under his authority. Faithfully following the duke of York's claim, as interpreted by Nicolls, to "all the Islands except Block Island from Cape Codd to Cape May,"[31] Lovelace in July 1671 granted to Thomas Mayhew a patent for most of the island of Martha's Vineyard and at the same time appointed Mayhew "Governor or Chiefe Magistrate" for life of that island and Nantucket (see the frontispiece map for this and Lovelace's other patents). Mayhew was further designated as president of a court, composed of himself and three assistants elected annually by two towns on the island, which would have jurisdiction over cases involving less than £5. In this arrangement, Mayhew would have a double vote.[32] A year later, Lovelace not only granted to John Paine, a Boston merchant, a patent for Prudence Island (also called Sophy) by Narragansett Bay but also gave Paine a life governorship over the patent with authority similar to Mayhew's, a move that greatly alarmed the Rhode Island magistrates.[33] Lovelace's efforts at expanding and fortifying the bounds of his master's domain were short-lived, however, as Massachusetts soon annexed Martha's Vineyard, and Rhode Island took over Prudence Island.

While extending the duke's power to the outlying islands, Lovelace was also active in laying out power bases on the mainland. He established

---

30. Julius Goebel, Jr., *Some Legal and Political Aspects of Manors in New York*, Order of Colonial Lords of Manors of America, New York Branch, *Publications*, No. 19 (Baltimore, 1928), 12.

31. Nicolls to Thomas Mayhew, Jan. 3, 1667, *N.Y. Col. Docs.*, III, 170.

32. See the documents in the section titled "Thomas Mayhew, Jurisdiction of Martha's Vineyard, Nantucket and Other Islands, etc.," in Victor Hugo Paltsits, ed., *Minutes of the Executive Council of the Province of New York: Administration of Francis Lovelace, 1668–1673* (Albany, N.Y., 1910), I, 365–370, hereafter cited as *Executive Council Minutes*. See also Herbert Alan Johnson, "The Advent of Common Law in Colonial New York," in George Athan Billias, ed., *Law and Authority in Colonial America* (New York, 1970 [orig. publ. New York, 1965]), 83–84.

33. See the documents in "Prudence Island—Controversy over Jurisdiction and John Paine," in *Executive Council Minutes*, II, 725–736.

two "manors," Fordham and Fox Hall. In November 1671, a year and a half after he had authorized one John Archer to settle sixteen families upon a tract of land called Fordham, adjacent to the Harlem River, Lovelace granted him a patent turning the lands into a semi-independent local jurisdiction responsible only to the governor.[34] Except for a minor point obliging Archer to maintain a church minister, the patent contained nothing new, although Lovelace thought in the following years that he had granted "the priveledge of a Mannor" to Archer and used the alluring term "manor" in later describing the patent.[35] Further up the Hudson, the Fox Hall Manor patent (October 1672) consisted of a mansion house and adjacent tract of about 230 acres owned by Thomas Chambers, justice of the peace and captain of a militia company at Kingston.[36]

The Fox Hall patent was unique for two reasons. First, it explained clearly Lovelace's motive for granting it; second, for the first time the word "manor" was specifically attached to a patent. It acknowledged Captain Chambers's service "in the time of the warrs against the Indyans," his accomplishment in making the mansion "defensible against any sudden Incursion of the Indyans or others," and his having "acquired a considerable Estate" by his industry. In transforming Chambers's real estate into an independent government preserve, Lovelace was concerned with military security against the Indians, whereas the original impulse for the Fordham patent stemmed from the governor's desire to increase settlement.[37] However, both patents were silent on concrete administrative and judicial functions for the grantees.

Lovelace believed that shielding the patents, by their independent status, from possible harassment by nearby local governmental units was

---

34. About two months before the patent was issued, the mayor's court of New York had ordered Archer to "behavie himselfe" towards the inhabitants at Fordham, who complained that Archer had tried to "Ruel and Governe over them by Rigur and force." Making an independent political unit out of Archer's settlement would, the governor probably figured, free the landlord from the court jurisdiction. Berthold Fernow, ed., *The Records of New Amsterdam from 1653 to 1674 Anno Domini* (New York, 1897), VI, 324–326; "Proceedings in the Mayor's Court. Differences between Harlem and Fordham," Sept. 8, 1671, *N.Y. Col. Docs.*, XIII, 459. For the full text of the Fordham patent, see J. Thomas Scharf, ed., *History of Westchester County, New York, Including Morrisania, Kings Bridge, and West Farms* (Philadelphia, 1886), I, 159–160.

35. Lovelace to Archer, June 28, 1672, *Executive Council Minutes*, II, 700–701; Lovelace, "An Order about the Mannor of Fordham . . . ," Apr. 20, 1673, *N.Y. Col. Docs.*, XIII, 471 (quoted).

36. For Chambers's landholding at Esopus, see "Colonial Records," in *Second Annual Report of the State Historian*, 266–267; *N.Y. Col. Docs.*, XIII, 446.

37. "A Priviledge Granted to Capt. Thomas Chambers, for the Erecting Fox Hall into a Mannor," Oct. 16, 1672, *N.Y. Col. Docs.*, XIII, 468, and in *Executive Council Minutes*, II, 759–760.

a sufficient reward to the proprietors for their contributions in various causes. Even this reward was graded according to the degree of actual and potential service one could and did render to the colony. A case in point was the grant of a favor in August 1670 to one Isaac Bedlow, who had earlier received from Nicolls a patent for Oyster Island near New York. "For an Encouragement" to Bedlow "in his further manuring and Improvement" of the island, Lovelace gave the island the new name of "Love Island" and designated it "a Priviledged place Where no warrant of Attachment or arreast shall be of force or be served unlesse it be by the peace of Criminall matters," thus immunizing Bedlow from any outside interference involving a civil case.[38] This sort of privilege constituted a "semi-independent" status as compared to the full-blown independence of the other proprietors. In return, the governor expected patentees and other clients to render material and moral service in government causes.[39]

It was not until April 1673 that Lovelace first moved to equip a "manorial" patent with some semblance of judicial authority. Having taken account of Archer's being the "principall Proprietor" of Fordham and recognizing the impracticality of holding a court there, as ordinary townships did, under the jurisdiction of the constable and overseer to determine cases of debt and trespass between the proprietor and his tenants or between one tenant and another "in their New Settlement," Lovelace ordered the establishment of a court for Archer's manor. This court was to be held quarterly or more frequently and would handle civil cases; a manor steward, the proprietor's man, would preside with the assistance of the constable and one or two other inhabitants of the manor. It should be noted that the governor's action in introducing a court system similar to the English manorial court baron was prompted directly by Archer's request and indirectly by the circumstance of the patent's being independent of any other township, and that the order bestowing this favor upon the proprietor came separately from his patent. Since the new privilege to Archer was not an integral part of the patent, the governor would be called upon from time to time to order an official of Fordham to hold the court and would appoint a steward for the purpose.[40] Valuable as the privilege might have been to Archer, the Fordham patent was not yet fully "manorialized" and was a far cry in its structure

---

38. *N.Y. Col. Docs.*, XIV, 639. This island is presently known as Bedlow (or Bedloe) Island, where the Statue of Liberty now stands.

39. Lovelace to Archer, June 28, 1672, *Executive Council Minutes*, II, 700–701.

40. Lovelace, "Order about Fordham," Apr. 20, 1673, *N.Y. Col. Docs.*, XIII, 471; N.Y. Col. MSS, XXX, 125, XXXI, 42.

from the prototypical English manor, for there is no evidence that Archer had been provided with the power to hold courts leet or had been given criminal jurisdiction over his patent. In addition, the other independent patents were still left with unclear legal and governmental responsibilities.

Like his predecessor Nicolls, Lovelace pursued a policy designed to reduce the privileges of Rensselaerswyck. In August 1671 he upgraded the town of Albany by giving it a third commissioner for the court of Albany, Rensselaerswyck, and Schenectady (Rensselaerswyck had two; two more came from the outlying areas). The quorum being four, the governor's excuse for this action was that the frequent absence of the Rensselaerswyck members impeded court operations. Whatever the reason, the outcome was that Albany could now often dominate the court, and the Van Rensselaers' influence on local affairs was considerably reduced.[41]

We can safely conclude, I believe, that feudal manors did not exist in New York before 1673. There were several independent administrative units, diverse in origin and purpose, but conceived mainly to enhance the duke of York's territorial and political interests. At this early stage, the governors rejected the idea of using the Dutch patroonship or any feudal example such as the Palatinate of Durham as a model for the settlement and local administration of the colony. The governors' fear of diluting the central authority in the province led them to curtail the authority of both "feudal" and "democratic" (community townships) local units on the mainland. Nevertheless, Lovelace's order in 1673 creating a court baron at the Fordham patent marked a notable departure from Nicolls's policy and Lovelace's earlier measures and constituted an important step forward in the development of New York's manorial system.

The process of manorialization, if such it may be called, was arrested during Major Edmund Andros's administration (1674–1682), for he neglected to establish a single independent patent or manor. Judging from Andros's background—soldier, lord of the seigneury of Saumarez in Guernsey, and landgrave in Carolina (1672) under the feudal Fundamental Constitutions—he might have been expected to lean toward organizing the colony according to the semifeudal model with which he was familiar. Furthermore, the situation of New York at his arrival was little changed from that which had confronted his predecessors. The chief

41. *Executive Council Minutes*, II, 548–550. Jeremiah Van Rensselaer mistakenly thought that Lovelace granted Albany two additional commissioners for the court instead of one. Van Rensselaer to Johan Van Wely, Sept. 27, 1671, *Jeremias Van Rensselaer Correspondence*, 443; Nissenson, *Patroon's Domain*, 280.

problems at hand were ancient boundary disputes with Connecticut, rebellious towns at the east end of Long Island refusing to recognize his authority and reaffirming their connection with Connecticut, and the French menace from the north resulting from the escalation of commercial rivalry over the fur trade.[42] These political ingredients could have persuaded him to continue the pattern set by his predecessors of creating independent patents. Why did he not do so?

Part of the answer lay in the duke of York's instructions of July 1674, in which Andros was given specific guidelines for granting land. The duke ordered him to observe as closely as possible "the rules and propositions given to planters by those of New England and Maryland," so that immigrants "may have equall encouragement to plant" in New York as in any other neighboring colonies.[43] In picking New England and Maryland as examples, James was either ignorant of, or not bothered by, the fact that their practices were diametrically opposed. Land policy in the New England colonies was evolving around a highly communal and egalitarian township system, while in Maryland manorial grants, at least until 1675, were the principal instrument of colonization.[44] But it seems that what caught the duke's eye was not their divergence in modes of colonization and social structure but their flourishing population in contrast to his vacant domain. The selection of "republican" New England colonies as a model for his governor clearly indicated that if James, duke of York, and his advisers had ever dreamed of transplanting a palatinate state to the New World, that dream had been gravely shaken by the dynamics of competition for settlers among the English colonies.[45]

Thus, a wide range of policy options was open to Andros. In the end he chose neither of the examples suggested in his orders. In August 1675, his council passed a resolution promising to any prospective free immigrant from Europe sixty acres, plus fifty acres per head for his wife and

---

42. For these problems, see *N.Y. Col. Docs.*, XIV, 688–689, 690, 722–723, 724, 763–764, III, 215 (Andros's commission, July 1, 1674), 223, 230–231, 235, 272–273, XIII, 531–532.

43. *Ibid.*, III, 216, 218 (quoted).

44. Harry Wright Newman, *The Flowering of the Maryland Palatinate* (Washington, D.C., 1961), 61–67; Newton D. Mereness, *Maryland as a Proprietary Province* (New York, 1901), 52.

45. The depth of the duke's involvement in the intercolonial competition for settlers can be measured by his principal adviser's order in 1676 to a New York official: "You may receive and give all incourage to any inhabitants that will come with their fameyles and goods, of whatsoever kind or country they be, from any of the other plantacions, to dwell with you at New Yorke." Sir John Werden to William Dyer, collector at New York, Nov. 30, 1676, *N.Y. Col. Docs.*, III, 245.

children, and the like amount for a servant after the expiration of his contract. And he had the resolution disseminated in England and other places.[46] This headright system was soon accompanied by grants of larger amounts of land to single individuals. Whereas the lord proprietor of Maryland erected every grant of more than a thousand acres into a manor with baronial privileges, Andros did not. Lord Baltimore heavily relied on adventurers, who bore the major burden of transporting people to his colony, and rewarded them with privileges in return for their service, but under the conditions prescribed by the New York council resolution, Andros had no settlement promoters to reward. It is also probable that Andros made no manorial grants simply because he disliked the method of consolidating central authority through these independent patents.

The governor's view on private independent jurisdictions within the colony manifested itself in his handling of the Van Rensselaer patroonship. In 1674 the Van Rensselaers sought to obtain a royal patent securing their property rights and jurisdictional privileges, administrative and judicial, not only in the domain but also over the town of Albany. They claimed to have enjoyed these rights and privileges before 1652. Their petition was addressed to the duke of York, who ordered Andros in July 1674 to look into the affair and to make a report thereof "as favorably for them as justice and the laws will allow."[47] With the order came an unusual recommendation that must have made Andros well aware of the family's weight and standing in York's circle. It concerned Nicholas Van Rensselaer, part owner of Rensselaerswyck, who had been ordained as an Anglican priest. James told Andros to "signify" to the local Dutch churches that their acceptance of the Van Rensselaer clergyman would be construed as "a mark of their respect and good inclinations towards" the duke himself.

Andros arranged for Nicholas Van Rensselaer to be invited by the Albany Dutch Reformed Church as associate minister, but he deliberately ignored the order to provide information and proof regarding Rensselaerswyck's status.[48] In March 1678, during his brief visit to London, he was summoned before the duke's council to comment on the case of Rensselaerswyck. Somehow Andros managed to be noncommittal with respect to the Van Rensselaers' claim to Albany, although he took note of

46. *Ibid.*, XIII, 485.
47. *Ibid.*, III, 224, 225.
48. *Ibid.*, 225; Hastings, ed., *Ecclesiastical Records of N.Y.*, I, 684.

"their Great charge and Trouble and Hazard" in settling their domain.[49] Implicit in Andros's stand was his disapproval of the Van Rensselaers' effort to swallow up the important town.

Soon thereafter Andros was called upon to make what was probably the most crucial decision in his career as governor of New York. In July 1678, upon a report of his council, the duke of York decided to accept almost every fundamental claim of the Van Rensselaers—their right to Albany, except its fort, and the restoration of the ancient privileges and immunities that the patroonship had enjoyed prior to 1652—and sent an order to Andros to issue a royal patent for the domain.[50] Andros was put in a dilemma. To carry out the order would mean the loss of an area that was of pivotal importance to the government and to private individuals, to say nothing of the loss of revenue. But refusing to comply would be a high breach of trust. It seemed to Andros to be an absolute political necessity that he reassure the Albanians—who were shocked at the news of the duke's decision—of the integrity of their town. He wrote to them in October that the duke intended to give the Van Rensselaers their former rights, "but without wronging any Others of which all Care and Regard Shall bee had."[51] This interpretation, however, was not strictly in accord with James's intentions, for his directive had conveyed no such words of conciliation; nor did it allow room for Andros's maneuvering. The order specifying the legitimate right of the Van Rensselaers to the town and to the burghers' future rent payment was an explicit one. Andros decided to serve the best interests of his master, who had failed to keep himself abreast of the colony's affairs, by ignoring his words. So the case of Rensselaerswyck remained unresolved during the rest of Andros's tenure in New York.[52]

## The Rise of the Manors: "Wee Are Cooped Up"

Perhaps no governor's policy better exemplifies the lack of a consistent pattern in the organization and settlement of New York than that of Colonel Thomas Dongan (1682–1688). Arriving in the colony in August

---

49. "The case of the Colony of Rensselaerswyck 27 Apr. 1678" and "The Report on the Petition by his Counsell, John Churchil and Keneay Finch, London June 4, 1678," Miscellaneous Manuscripts, Rensselaerswyck, New-York Historical Society, New York City. See also Munsell, ed., *Annals of Albany*, VII, 266–267.

50. *N.Y. Col. Docs.*, III, 269–270.

51. Andros to the magistrates of Albany and Schenectady, Oct. 31, 1678, *ibid.*, XIII, 533.

52. Andros's attitude did not seem to have much to do with the Van Rensselaers' being

1683, the new governor erected many manorial lordships during his tenure. In setting up independent patents, his predecessors had been parsimonious in granting privileges, but Dongan was lavish, giving manorial proprietors the authority to hold courts baron (civil jurisdiction) and courts leet (criminal and administrative jurisdiction) and the power of advowson to nominate a church minister within their domain. These lordship courts, patterned after manors established in Ireland and Scotland in the mid-seventeenth century, were supposed to function independently of any outside authority except that of the governor. The Dongan manors, in terms of form and land tenure, were not the same as the old English manors, which had imposed military obligations on the manorial lords. Such military tenure had been abolished in favor of free and common socage—freehold tenure with quitrent obligation—by a statute passed under Charles II in 1660.[53] But in many respects they were similar. In any event, the quantities of land Dongan attached to the manors were prodigious: one grant exceeded a million acres. In addition, he made several large nonmanorial grants.

Evidence pertaining to Dongan's motivation is sketchy and circumstantial. But, on the basis of the little that is known, we can speculate that his manorial policy was the result of various difficulties, some economic, some territorial, some political—difficulties created by both his own and his predecessors' decisions.

Let us first examine the economic and territorial problems. All the provincial governors had been eager to encourage settlement in the colony. They looked upon the settlers as if they were bees bringing pollen to a hive. Immigration was the means of making the country self-sufficient, of adding military manpower, and of expanding the duke's territorial claims. Consequently, the governors had distributed promotional tracts in Boston, England, Europe, and Barbados promising generous assistance to settlers.[54] The governors were most receptive to petitions for licenses to purchase lands from the Indians for the sake of "Speedy

---

of Dutch origin. He was often accused by his critics of favoring Dutch settlers over English in the colony. Sir John Werden to Andros, May 24, 1680, *ibid.*, III, 283–284.

53. Eric Kerridge, *Agrarian Problems in the Sixteenth Century and After* (London, 1969), 19; C. H. Firth and R. S. Rait, eds., *Acts and Ordinances of the Interregnum, 1642–1660* (London, 1911), II, 883–884; Goebel, *Legal and Political Aspects of Manors*, 14; Montgomery Schuyler, *The Patroons and Lords of Manors of the Hudson*, Order of Col. Lords, N.Y. Branch, *Pubs.* (New York, 1932), 13–14.

54. Woolsey, *Winthrop Manor of Fishers Island*, and also Aaron Leaming and Jacob Spicer, *The Grants, Concessions, and Original Constitutions of the Province of New-Jersey* . . . (Philadelphia, [1752]), 661–663; letter from Lovelace to governor of Bermuda, concerning immigration, June 3, 1669, *N.Y. Col. Docs.*, XIII, 424–426.

Improvement." Sometimes they authorized certain individuals who had an influence with the Indian proprietors to buy the lands for the government.[55] As part of the promotion, quitrents were not always imposed upon the grant of a patent, leaving the matter to future adjustment, although the Duke's Laws required the reservation of 2s. 6d. sterling per one hundred acres.[56] Both Nicolls and Lovelace were so concerned about the defense and settlement of the frontiers that they turned soldiers who were dispatched there into farmers and banned the soldier-farmers from selling their farm lots for three years from the time of the grant, in order to make them steady inhabitants. For the same reason, anyone neglecting to settle and improve his patent by a certain date was threatened with its forfeiture and a stiff fine.[57]

Despite the promotional activities of the governors, however, settlement of the colony progressed slowly. In describing the state of the colony in 1678, Andros estimated that only about twenty thousand acres in New York proper were newly taken up and patented. If this was true—and there is strong reason to believe it was—the twenty thousand acres were perhaps barely enough to accommodate the demand arising from natural population increase in the province.[58] New York's lagging rate of settlement was underscored also by the absence of any dramatic change in its demography. According to several contemporary observers, the population of eight thousand in 1664 had increased to only ten thousand by 1678, the year Andros made the above report.[59]

Contributing to the slow growth of population and equally sluggish process of settlement were the almost complete (but predictable) cessation of immigrants from Holland after the English takeover, the desolate landscape of mainland New York, and, especially, the uncertainty surrounding Indian intentions. An English resident of Long Island, Daniel Denton, was not alone when he claimed in 1670 that one of the reasons

---

55. E. B. O'Callaghan, ed., *The Documentary History of the State of New York* (Albany, N.Y., 1849–1851), I, 87, hereafter cited as *Doc. Hist. N.Y.*; *N.Y. Col. Docs.*, III, 188, XIII, 569 (quoted); "Order of Gov. Andross (regarding) Lands," Nov. 16, 1677, Van Cortlandt Papers, VA 566, Sleepy Hollow Restorations Library, Tarrytown, N.Y.

56. "Mr. [John] Lewin's Report on the Government of New-York," 1681, *N.Y. Col. Docs.*, III, 303; *N.Y. Col. Laws*, I, 44, 81; N.Y. Col. MSS, XLII, 107.

57. *N.Y. Col. Docs.*, XIII, 416, 418, 457; "Colonial Records," in *Second Annual Report of the State Historian*, 273–274.

58. *Doc. Hist. N.Y.*, I, 90.

59. Evarts B. Greene and Virginia D. Harrington, *American Population before the Federal Census of 1790* (New York, 1932), 88–89; United States Bureau of the Census, *Historical Statistics of the United States, Colonial Times to 1957* (Washington, D.C., 1960), 743.

for the sparsely settled state of the province was the lack of assurance of "safety from the Indians."[60] Garrisoning the major frontier settlements like Esopus (Kingston) against the hostile Indians was deemed essential to the survival of settlements. The threat of the Indians was such that the English governors continued the Dutch regulations whereby individuals were discouraged from seating themselves in "remote places," for whatever purpose, because officials feared that stragglers and lone houses in open country would be easy prey to the "fury of the Heathen."[61] The Indian menace thus led the governors to restrain frontier individualism, but at the same time they were unable to obtain, like the New England colonies, collective planting by cohesive groups. Moreover, although New York was not directly exposed to the ravages of King Philip's War (1675–1676), the ferocity with which the Indians vented their wrath, and tales about the slaughter of at least one-twentieth of the New Englanders, must have had an inhibiting effect upon New York settlement.[62]

Not wholly unrelated to fear of Indian attack as a deterrent to settlement was the location of the province. The farther a settlement was removed from the coastal population centers, the more minatory were the Indians. From a geographic viewpoint, New York, lying west of the New England colonies, was the latter's hinterland and frontier. Frontier conditions, namely, hostile environs and a primitive existence for the pioneers, could, of course, discourage settlement. That the New Englanders' movement in the middle of the seventeenth century had been directed primarily toward safer Long Island, rather than the interior, demonstrates this point. Furthermore, without a good transportation system eastward to provide access to markets for farm produce, agricultural settlement in the interior was a serious economic drawback.

The real and perceived qualities of New York's soil and topography also diminished the province's attractiveness for colonization. To the farmer, the soil, terrain, and location of an area were all-important.[63] The elongated province was chopped up by two mountain chains, the Catskill Mountains to the west and the Taconic Mountains to the east of the Hudson River, both running hundreds of miles in a north-south

---

60. Denton, *Brief Description*, 15–16.
61. Gov. Lovelace's report on the state of New York, 1670(?), *N.Y. Col. Docs.*, III, 188; Capt. Brockholls to Francis Skinner, May 10, 1683, *ibid.*, XIV, 769. For the Dutch regulations on settlement, see *ibid.*, XIII, 53; Trelease, *Indian Affairs*, 144–146.
62. Douglas Edward Leach, *Flintlock and Tomahawk: New England in King Philip's War* (New York, 1958), 10, 243.
63. Herman Beukema, "The Role of Geology in the History of the Hudson Highlands," *New York History*, XXXIII (1952), 268–269.

direction and surrounded by steep hills. Impressed by the unfriendly physical features of Ulster and some parts of Orange and Dutchess counties northeast of Peekskill, New Yorkers called these locales "highlands," perhaps by analogy to the Highlands of Scotland. The mountainous terrain of the Hudson River valley fostered a belief that the land contours and soil of most parts of the province were unfit for cultivation.[64] In 1691 New York officials reported home that Kingston consisted of five small towns that "have not above 3,000 acres of manureable land; all the rest being hills and mountains, not possible to be cultivated."[65] To the problem of barrenness was added even an alleged climatic adversity. Governor Nicolls wrote in the summer of 1665 that the area between the Hudson and the Connecticut rivers was so cold that "few or none will bestow their labours" there.[66] Of course, he was mistaken. But the result of these imagined and actual handicaps to development was that many governors argued for annexing the fertile neighboring colonies in order to augment New York's poor resources.

Dongan may not have been aware of all these reasons for the slow pace of New York's settlement, but he certainly knew of his predecessors' vain attempts to improve the situation. In 1686 he reported that, except for Long Island, where the population was rapidly expanding to the point that people were beginning to "complain for want of land," the province had not been able to recruit more than an average of three English, Scottish, or Irish families a year from 1678 to 1685. The alleged surplus population of Long Island, he feared, would move to a neighboring colony, even though the lands in the upper, unpopulated part of New York were going begging.[67]

The urgency to increase immigration to the province never seemed greater than in the 1680s. For one thing, boundary disputes with the

64. Thomas Dongan's report on New York, 1687, N.Y. Col. Docs., III, 397.

65. Ibid., 797; John Miller, New York Considered and Improved, ed. Victor Hugo Paltsits (Cleveland, Ohio, 1903), 44.

66. Nicolls to duke of York, July 30, 1665, N.-Y. Hist. Soc., Colls., II (1869), 77.

67. Dongan's report on New York, 1686, N.Y. Col. Docs., III, 399. Historians of colonial New York have attributed the colony's slow settlement and development to the early concentration of lands in the hands of a few, arguing that the settlers, eager to obtain a freehold, went to those colonies where a liberal land system prevailed. It should be remembered, however, that many people avoided or left New York even when most of its lands were yet to be appropriated by the great proprietors. For the traditional viewpoint on the subject, see Turner, Frontier in American History, 80–83; Mark, Agrarian Conflicts, 73–74; David M. Ellis, Landlords and Farmers in the Hudson-Mohawk Region, 1790–1850 (Ithaca, N.Y., 1946), 11–12; Ruth L. Higgins, Expansion in New York (Columbus, Ohio, 1931), 24–25. Compare Sung Bok Kim, "A New Look at the Great Landlords of Eighteenth-Century New York," WMQ, 3d Ser., XXVII (1970), 581–614.

neighboring colonies remained unabated. In late 1683 Dongan was distressed to learn that Connecticut laid claim to the land "within 16 or 17 miles" of New York City and "to Esopus and Albany allso." Although the colonies soon reached an agreement on the boundary line, he was suspicious of Connecticut's intent. There was no guarantee that it would honor this agreement after it had persistently "abused" the earlier one.[68] The expansionist Massachusetts Bay Colony also cast covetous glances on the land "betweene Conecticut and Hudson's River," claiming all land to the "south sea," as Connecticut did.[69] Simultaneously, New York was plagued by East Jersey's claim to Staten Island. To lay the groundwork for an eventual annexation of the island, an agent of the East Jersey proprietors was endeavoring to buy up Captain Christopher Billop's plantation at the southwest end of the island. Threats from the hostile Indians to scattered settlements and plantations continued.[70] To the north, the rapidly growing French power under Lefebvre de la Barre and his successor, the marquis de Denonville, became more bellicose than ever.

At the base of the conflict between French Canada and New York lay the Indian trade.[71] The far Indians—like the Illinois, Ottawas, Miamis, and Hurons—who controlled major sources of furs, were under French protection. But the flow of furs toward Montreal was drastically reduced once the pro-English Iroquois in 1680 launched an invasion of the Illinois country and committed depredations against the French traders and priests. Thereafter, the French objective was the total destruction of the Iroquois, which Dongan was eager to prevent. Though he himself was a Roman Catholic, and though peace reigned between his master and the French king whose cause he had once served as a soldier, he was a pugnacious English imperialist determined to wrest the fur trade from the French.[72] Dongan completed what Andros had started: the establishment of a formal protectorate over the Iroquois confederation, or the Five Nations. Dongan increasingly appreciated their role as a shield

68. N.Y. Col. Laws, I, 1039–1043; Daniel J. Pratt, ed., Report of the Regents of the University, on the Boundaries of the State of New York ... (Albany, N.Y., 1884), II, 237–251.

69. Dongan to Sir John Werden, Feb. 18, 1685, N.Y. Col. Docs., III, 356.

70. Dongan to earl of Perth, Feb. 13, 1685, ibid., 353–354. See also ibid., III, 348, 350, XIII, 554.

71. Dongan to Father Lamberville, May 20, 1686, and to Lords of Trade, Mar. 1687, W. Noel Sainsbury et al., eds., Calendar of State Papers, Colonial Series ... (London, 1860– ), XII (America and West Indies, 1685–1688), 328, 432, hereafter cited as Calendar of State Papers, Col. Ser.; N.Y. Col. Docs., III, 394, 398, 428–430.

72. Sir John Werden to Dongan, Nov. 1, 1684, N.Y. Col. Docs., III, 352; Trelease, Indian Affairs, 260.

against the French as well as a supplier of animal skins. Thus, an attack on the Five Nations became an attack on the English king. Moreover, Dongan, like Andros, extended the northern boundary of New York to include the entire territory south of Lake Ontario. As a symbolic act to assert English sovereignty there, Dongan put the arms of the duke of York (now King James II) upon "all the Indian Castles near the Great Lake." He also encouraged the Iroquois to make peace with the far Indians, so as to channel furs eastward to Albany. These measures only escalated the tension on the frontier. The French frequently sent expeditions, small and large, to punish the tribes.[73] Although the expeditions failed, the French menace was ever present, and Dongan became chronically suspicious of French intentions, despite their professions of good faith, and alarmed about the security of the province. Indeed, it was during his governorship that New York, of all the British colonies in North America, became the focal point of the struggle between the two European powers.[74]

In short, the province was hemmed in and continually harassed and preyed upon by neighbors from all directions. Dongan's apprehension about the situation was most dramatically expressed in February 1686 when he wrote home that "wee are cooped up."[75] He could not fail to see that the plight of New York was due partly to underpopulation and sparse settlement. To Dongan, who was perhaps New York's most aggressive and expansionist-minded colonial governor, it was obvious that something had to be done quickly to settle the province and fortify its territorial claims. The headright system (granting land piecemeal to small yeoman farmers) was rejected because it had failed miserably under Andros between 1674 and 1681. Dongan's solution was to grant large tracts of land to single individuals or small groups, with the expectation that they would undertake to promote the settlement of their patents. The feasibility of such a method was suggested by some historical precedents. In the Middle Ages the German *Landesherr* set up numerous *Gutsherrschaft* (manors) to open for agriculture the frontier marshlands northeast of the Elbe River. Recent Dutch patroonships and Lord Balti-

---

73. Dongan's report, 1687, *N.Y. Col. Docs.*, III, 393; Dongan to Secretary William Blathwayt, Apr. 11, 1685, *ibid.*, 363, also 428–430, IX, 236–239, 242–248, 269; Lefebvre de la Barre, governor of Canada, to Dongan, June 15, 1685, *Doc. Hist. N.Y.*, I, 99.

74. Dongan was also worried about Pennsylvania's northward expansion toward the upper Susquehanna River for the purpose of diverting furs from New Yorkers. *N.Y. Col. Docs.*, III, 394.

75. *Ibid.*, 397.

more's manors had medieval prototypes in origin and function. The great manorial estates created in Ireland and Scotland in the first half of the seventeenth century were probably familiar to Dongan, who was of Irish extraction. It is perhaps not too much to suppose that he had in mind transplanting to New York some of the useful functions of the traditional manor. On at least one occasion he justified making a 160,000-acre manorial grant on the grounds that it would be "Encouraging the future Settlement" of the land.[76]

Dongan's land policy coincided with, and was undoubtedly influenced by, a significant change in the economic orientation of the province. For many years the province's economy had almost wholly depended on the fur trade, but during the 1670s and 1680s the volume of the trade declined steadily. From a peak volume of 46,000 beavers moving in both 1656 and 1657 from Fort Orange to New Amsterdam, the trade tapered off until it reached only 9,000 in 1686, partly because the northern Indians were frequently diverted from hunting by fighting among themselves.[77] This depression in furs created a problem in capital adjustment for the mercantile community.[78] Simultaneously, from abroad came an increasing demand for grain, in particular from the West Indies—a development that provided the merchants with a substitute export commodity to which they could divert their capital from the slackening Indian trade. As early as 1671 the exportation of grain had increased so much that the government feared there would not be enough to feed the inhabitants, and a ban on such exports was in effect for a year, over the strong protests of Long Island farmers and New York City traders.[79] In the late 1670s the yearly export of wheat was about 60,000 bushels. The New York City magistrates contended in 1684 that "the manufacture of flour and bread . . . hath been and is the chief support of the trade and traffic to and from this city and maintenance of its inhabitants in all degrees." So important had the new food industry become by 1686 that New York added the flour barrel to the official seal of the province.[80]

76. See the Livingston Manor patent of June 22, 1686, Doc. Hist. N.Y., III, 625.

77. David Arthur Armour, "The Merchants of Albany, New York, 1686–1760" (Ph.D. diss., Northwestern University, 1965), 24; Trelease, Indian Affairs, 131.

78. This decline can be traced to several sources, including the French penetration into the area south of the Great Lakes and the resulting interception of furs bound for Albany, and the Iroquois' diversion from hunting because of their involvement in war with the French and her Indian allies. See Dongan to Lord President, Sept. 28, 1687, N.Y. Col. Docs., III, 428–430.

79. "Colonial Records," in Second Annual Report of the State Historian, 172–173, 179–180.

80. Ostensibly for the sake of insuring the quality of the farm produce and its reputa-

The emergence of the grain trade compelled New York merchants to reconsider the value of rural land ownership. As the demand for produce increased, the great economic potential of the land, notwithstanding its wildness, seemed no longer in doubt. As a side effect, the influx of new settlers attracted by the prospect of commercial farming in New York would raise land values. Under these circumstances, some merchants, like Frederick Philipse, Stephanus Van Cortlandt, Robert Livingston, and others, lost no time in expanding their activities to include milling grain and acquiring land in the countryside.[81] The absence of economic specialization at this early stage in American history made it easy for merchants to diversify in this fashion. In sum, Dongan's unprecedented granting of manors and large patents was also in part a response to unprecedented demands for agricultural land.

## The Rise of the Manors: Political Motives

If Dongan's only concerns had been settling the colony, extending its territorial claims, and responding positively to changing economic opportunities, he would have been content to grant large tracts of land without other privileges attached. But he went further and equipped some of the grants, small and large, with lordship privileges that were unrelated to economic and territorial imperatives. This suggests that in making these grants, he had in mind functions for their proprietors other than serving merely as agents for settlement.

Indeed, the manorial aspect of Dongan's land policy was a reflection of the turbulent politics of the 1680s. Significantly, the governor created these provincial lordships at the very time when popular agitation against the ducal system of government finally bore fruit in the establishment of

tion in the overseas market, New York City tried to get a monopoly of bolting and casking of flour and of making bread for export. The privilege, granted in 1680, brought a good deal of business to the city. N.Y. Col. MSS, XXIX, 29, 84, 184, XXXI, 109, 134, 144, XXXIII, 6. See also Curtis P. Nettels, *The Roots of American Civilization: A History of American Colonial Life* (New York, 1938), 343; David M. Ellis *et al.*, *A Short History of New York State* (Ithaca, N.Y., 1957), 81–82; "Answers of Gov. Andros to Enquiries about New York; 1678," *Doc. Hist. N.Y.*, I, 90.

81. Fernow, ed., *Records of New Amsterdam*, XII, 115, 124–125; Dankers and Sluyter, *Journal of a Voyage to New York in 1679–80* (Long Island Hist. Soc., *Memoirs*, I), 344, 253; Hugh Grant Rowell, "The Story of the Philipse Castle Restoration," *N.Y. History*, XXIV (1943), 326–334; Philipse Papers, PX2225, Sleepy Hollow Restorations Lib.; J. Hammond Trumbull and Charles J. Hoadly, eds., *The Public Records of the Colony of Connecticut . . .* (Hartford, Conn., 1850–1890), III, 313; E. B. O'Callaghan, ed., *Calendar of Historical Manuscripts in the Office of the Secretary of State, Albany, New York* (Albany, N.Y., 1865–1866), II, 507.

the General Assembly in New York, and when the royal government under James II (the former duke of York) was endeavoring everywhere to strengthen the powers of the colonial governors at the expense of the colonial legislatures. Judging from this provincial and imperial political context, it seems probable that Dongan, unlike Andros, was attempting to make allies of the provincial elite and in that way solidify the foundations of royal prerogative in the colony.

Popular opposition to the ducal government first took the form of an antitax movement. Since the late 1670s, most of the Long Island towns had persistently refused to pay what they called "heavy taxes" without their consent.[82] After November 1680 the New York merchants refused to pay excise taxes and trade duties, the major sources of income for the support of the administration, on the grounds that the duke's tariff ordinance had expired. William Dyer, collector, member of the council, and mayor of New York City, who attempted to collect the duties without direct authorization from the duke, was sued the following year in the mayor's court by Samuel Windsor of Long Island for "high Treason" and later indicted by the grand jury in the court of assizes on the same count. Both the grand jury in its bill against Dyer and the court of assizes in its petition to the duke inveighed against the heavy burden of taxation imposed without popular consent and argued that an "assembly of the people," the "undoubted birth right" of the king's subjects, was one of the remedies for it.[83]

Simultaneously, the excise tax was also challenged. In 1681 John De Lavall, a prominent merchant in New York, refused to pay Robert Livingston, the Albany excise collector, the tax on 510 gallons of rum. When De Lavall was required in court to account for his conduct, he used the occasion to discuss the constitutionality of the tax by questioning whether or not the power of taxation belonged to the king or to the governor and the king's subjects. His answer was that taxation without the consent of the subjects was illegal. He proposed to the court that the excise collector, by acting in a way unwarranted by law, "be deemed to be a disturber of his Majesty's peace." The people watched the case with keen interest. However, the members of the court excused themselves from passing a verdict on it and referred it to the "supreme authorities at

---

82. David S. Lovejoy, "Equality and Empire: The New York Charter of Libertyes, 1683," *WMQ*, 3d Ser., XXI (1964), 501.

83. *N.Y. Col. Docs.*, III, 288–289; "Proceedings of the General Court of Assizes Held in the City of New York, October 6, 1680, to October 1682," N.-Y. Hist. Soc., *Colls.*, XLV (1912), 10–11.

New York." In the meantime, excise payments ceased, and ships came and went without paying customs.[84] This cessation was a mortal blow to government finance, because the duke in 1681 had already relinquished his rights to customs duties and to control of trade in New Jersey, which was estimated to constitute one-third of the New York trade. In the eyes of Anthony Brockholls, who was in charge of the administration as Andros's deputy during the latter's absence, the government appeared to be "wholly over thrown and in the Greatest Confusion and Disord'r Possible."[85]

Underlying the popular objection to the taxes and tariffs was the long-cherished aspiration of obtaining a controlling voice in the fiscal affairs of the province. This aspiration, the provincial "whigs" believed, could be fulfilled only by the establishment of a representative assembly in the image of those in the neighboring New England colonies. Faced with a critical financial situation in his domain, the duke had to overcome his scruples against a representative system, his bête noire, or the bankruptcy of his government would be unavoidable. In January 1683 he instructed Dongan to call an assembly upon his arrival in New York.[86] As a result, on October 17, 1683, less than two months after Dongan arrived, the first New York General Assembly, consisting of eighteen deputies from different parts of the colony, met at Fort James.

The assembly, which sat until August 1685, passed many measures and acts, but its foremost achievement was the famous "Charter of Libertyes and Priviledges," which was written probably by Matthias Nicolls, the speaker, formerly secretary of the province under Governor Nicolls, twice mayor of New York City, and a lawyer by training. The charter, a potpourri of Magna Carta, the Petition of Right of 1628, and other English constitutional documents, was designed to lay down the basic framework of government for the province. Supreme legislative power, subject to the veto of the king and the duke of York, was declared to be vested forever in a governor, his council, and "the people mett in General Assembly." Representing the executive branch, the governor and council

84. A. J. F. van Laer, ed., *Minutes of the Court of Albany, Rensselaerswyck and Schenectady, 1668–1685* (Albany, N.Y., 1926–1932), III, 153–155; Anthony Brockholls to Robert Livingston, Jan. 13, 1682, Livingston-Redmond Manuscripts (microfilm), Roll 1 (originals at Franklin Delano Roosevelt Library, Hyde Park, N.Y.), hereafter cited as Livingston-Redmond MSS.

85. Brockholls to Andros, Sept. 17, 1681, *N.Y. Col. Docs.*, III, 289. The best account of the revenue situation in this period is Lovejoy, "Equality and Empire," *WMQ*, 3d Ser., XXI (1964), 495–501.

86. *N.Y. Col. Docs.*, III, 230, 235, 317.

should govern "according to the Lawes established." The charter also defined in uncompromising terms what the colonists considered to be the indispensable rights of Englishmen, namely, the guarantee of certain individual liberties, the protection of property, and the right to assent to legislation and taxation.[87] Falling under the rubric of individual liberties were habeas corpus, trial by jury, limitations on excessive bail, and the immunity of private homes from the quartering of troops in time of peace. Not content with leaving the calling of the assembly to a governor's discretion, as ordered by the duke in the instructions, the charter provided for triennial meetings, a right that even Parliament did not enjoy at the time. It also divided the province for administrative and other purposes into counties and reapportioned representation by county, allowing two deputies for each. In addition, New York City and County were allowed to send a total of four delegates, while the town of Albany could send one.

Having delineated the fundamental principles of government, the deputies took up the task of applying them. The assembly, in compliance with Dongan's request, passed a revenue bill granting the duke "duties and Customs hereafter Specified."[88] Significantly, in passing the bill the assembly asserted its exclusive right to originate money bills, as if the governor and council had nothing to do with them, though they were to be legislative partners according to the charter. Challenges to the gubernatorial authority did not stop there. In their effort to bring the entire province under the purview of general laws, the assemblymen by such measures as "An Act to settle Courts of Justice" (passed in November 1683) destroyed the privileges of the independent patents and manors. Similarly, in 1683 the assembly annexed Gardiner's Island to the town of East Hampton, which eliminated the privileges of Gardiner's patent.[89] All the other independent patents met a similar fate. These legislative acts were a direct infringement of the governor's prerogative to specify the kind of local government he wanted on patented land.

Surprisingly, Dongan and his council consented to all the measures and acts of the assembly in spite of their unpalatable features. Perhaps the governor deemed it politically expedient to pass the problem to his master for a decision, or perhaps Dongan had been influenced by the handsome grant of money voted earlier by the assembly for his "great

87. N.Y. Col. Laws, I, 111–116.
88. Ibid., 116–117.
89. Ibid., 125–128, 143–144.

many favours." The duke, after deliberating on the charter and the various bills for several months, signed and sealed them in October 1684, but they never left England.[90]

Although Dongan was personally flattered by the assembly's generosity and by the adequate appropriation of money for the government's expenses, he had every reason to believe that the going would be rough for him in the future. He knew all about the assertive behavior of the New England assemblies, whose example the New York deputies were imitating.[91] He had also tasted the upsurge of whiggish principles, culminating in the assembly's extensive inroads into his prerogative. There was no indication in the temper and deeds of the assembly that its members would abate their zeal and be less assertive or act in any way differently from their counterparts in the other colonies. In practical terms, the governor would be restricted in the use of revenue from duties, excises, and other taxes. Even his salary and personal emoluments would be dependent upon the whims of the deputies.

Evidently, the assembly's encroachment on the governor's power started Dongan searching for a scheme to bolster his standing or at least to create a countervailing agency that would arrest the drift of the colony toward a sort of provincial parliamentary supremacy. He could count on the loyalty of the council, composed mostly of local gentlemen, as a check on the lower house. In addition, he seems to have desired an aristocratic bastion at the local level responsive to his command. We can discern his quest for allies and for a new political base in his handling of the case of Rensselaerswyck.

Rensselaerswyck in 1683 was officially under the directorship of Stephanus Van Cortlandt, a member of the council and a wealthy merchant of New York. Because of his involvement in political and business activities in the city, actual management of the domain affairs was left to his sister who lived on the premises, Maria, widow of Jeremiah Van Rensselaer. The Van Rensselaers hoped through Van Cortlandt's access to the governor to get what they had long failed to obtain—the recovery of Albany, restoration of their former feudal privileges, and secure title to their holdings. In the first several months after his arrival, the governor

90. *Ibid.*, 137–138; duke of York to Thomas Dongan, Aug. 26, 1684, *N.Y. Col. Docs.*, III, 348, 357–359; *Historical Magazine and Notes and Queries . . . of America* (Dawson's), VI (1862), 233; *Calendar of State Papers, Col. Ser.*, XII, 279, 282–283.

91. Gov. Andros believed that the American colonies, though independent of each other, were "most influenced by the Massachusetts, both in state and religion." "Governor Andros' answer to Enquiries of the Council of Trade," 1678, *N.Y. Col. Docs.*, III, 264.

repeatedly assured both Van Cortlandt and Maria Van Rensselaer that he would settle the case for good and grant a new patent for Rensselaerswyck. Beyond that, he was negative. The governor's attitude led Van Cortlandt to report to his sister in November 1683: "I have no doubt but that we shall get a patent for the colony, but not such privileges as [the Van Rensselaers] had formerly."[92]

In September 1684, Van Cortlandt went through the usual procedure of filing a petition to the governor for a patent. To strengthen the Van Rensselaers' position, Van Cortlandt reminded Dongan of the warrant of June 7, 1678, from the duke of York to Andros, which had ordered Andros to issue a patent for the domain including Albany and to restore the family's ancient privileges. If such a comprehensive title was impossible, Van Cortlandt asked Dongan first to grant a patent "without Albany," leaving the weightier question of "Albany and the other privileges" to the judgment of the duke.[93] Dongan quickly referred the problem home for instructions. Sir John Werden, the duke's secretary, replied on November 1, 1684, with a brief note that practically gave Dongan a free hand in the matter. The note did not go into specifics, but advised Dongan to "make any agreements with them [the Van Rensselaers] for the Duke's advantage, which they will consent unto, but not hurt their possessions and rights." Dongan, like Andros, judged it "not for his Majesty's interest that the second town" of the province, bringing "soe great a revenue," should be placed in the hands of "any particular men."[94] Aside from his own reservations about the Van Rensselaers' claim to Albany, Dongan knew that there was formidable Albanian opposition to falling under the control of a private family.

A complication further stalled immediate action on the matter. During the preceding few years, bitter controversy had raged over several competing claims to Rensselaerswyck. One of the disputants was an ambitious Scot named Robert Livingston. In January 1675, Livingston, just turned nineteen, had come from Rotterdam to Albany after a short stay in Boston. He brought with him little money but a combination of rare talents—proficiency in both Dutch and English, skill in penmanship, and knowledge of bookkeeping—that made him a valuable addition to

92. Stephanus Van Cortlandt to Maria Van Rensselaer, [end of Aug. 1683], Oct. 20, 1683, and [Nov. 1683], and Maria to Richard Van Rensselaer, [Oct. 1683], *Maria Van Rensselaer Correspondence*, 118–119, 120–121, 134, 127.

93. Richard Van Rensselaer to Maria Van Rensselaer, [Sept.] 1684, *ibid.*, 162, 163; Nissenson, *Patroon's Domain*, 298.

94. *N.Y. Col. Docs.*, III, 351; Dongan to the Committee of Trade, 1687, in Munsell, ed., *Annals of Albany*, II, 61–62.

the Dutch-speaking frontier community that had come under English rule. Impressed by Livingston's abilities, Dominie Nicholas Van Rensselaer, then director of Rensselaerswyck, had hired him in August 1675 as secretary of the domain.[95] A month later he had been made clerk of the town of Albany as well. Before the year was over, Andros had appointed him secretary to a board of Indian commissioners that the governor had set up to coordinate Indian affairs. Though the post was without salary for twenty years, Livingston made good use of it. He managed to turn it from the dull job of translator and copier of transactions (mostly in Dutch) into that of key adviser on Indian policy.[96] The official and unofficial meetings with the Indian sachems not only afforded him an advantage over others in the fur trade but also enabled him to acquire expert knowledge of Indian problems, which were increasingly preoccupying the attention of Andros and his successors. At Nicholas Van Rensselaer's death in 1678, Livingston's advancement in officialdom and trade had received a fillip. In July 1679 he had married his former employer's widow, Alida, daughter of Philip P. Schuyler, founder of that prominent family in New York. Through this marriage Livingston also had become linked with Stephanus Van Cortlandt, the husband of the former Gertrude Schuyler, Alida's sister (see the genealogies of the Van Rensselaer and Livingston families in appendix 1).[97]

Soon after the marriage with Alida, Livingston had hatched a scheme to acquire Nicholas Van Rensselaer's share (10.4 percent) of Rensselaerswyck on the pretext that Alida's deceased husband had owed him a substantial sum of money before he died.[98] Livingston demanded to be reimbursed by a partition of the domain. He had no difficulty in enlisting moral support from Rensselaerswyck's other owners, such as the heirs of

95. Jonathan Pearson, trans., and A. J. F. van Laer, ed., *Early Records of the City and County of Albany and Colony of Rensselaerswyck*, University of the State of New York, New York State Library History Bulletins 8–11 (Albany, N.Y., 1916–1919), III, 441–442.

96. Lawrence H. Leder, *Robert Livingston, 1654–1724, and the Politics of Colonial New York* (Chapel Hill, N.C., 1961), 15–16; John A. Krout, "Behind the Coat of Arms: A Phase of Prestige in Colonial New York," *N.Y. History*, XVI (1935), 49–50.

97. Livingston's spectacular rise can be measured by the following events. In 1682, when still a young man of 26, he was presented by the Dutch Reformed Church in Albany with a pew on its newly built gallery "as a reward for his trouble in getting contributions." Only two years before, he had been appointed collector of customs and excise of Albany. In this office he was to get a shilling for every pound he collected. Munsell, ed., *Annals of Albany*, I, 104; Stephanus Van Cortlandt and Peter Delanoy to Richard Pretty, Nov. 1, 1680, Livingston-Redmond MSS, Roll I.

98. *Maria Van Rensselaer Correspondence*, 100, 115, 125–126, 128, 168–169; Nissenson, *Patroon's Domain*, 386–387.

Toussain Muyssart and Adam Bessels residing in Holland, who were said to have received no profit or account from the Van Rensselaers for the past five decades and were naturally disgruntled with the family.[99] Philip P. Schuyler, Livingston's father-in-law and a powerful figure in local and Indian affairs, also favored the dissolution of the plantation, with the hope of converting his several lease farms in the domain into a fee simple estate.[100]

On October 29, 1683, Livingston submitted a petition to the governor for a division of Rensselaerswyck. Opposing him were Richard Van Rensselaer, the family head as the surviving son of the first patroon, and his sister-in-law Maria Van Rensselaer, both of whom were determined to preserve the domain's integrity. Stephanus Van Cortlandt found his position in this feud most uncomfortable, because he was both Maria's brother and Livingston's brother-in-law by his marriage to Gertrude, sister of Van Cortlandt's wife, Alida. At the same time, his kinship position brought him an unusual opportunity to serve as arbitrator between the contestants. Van Cortlandt realized that as long as Livingston, who had "the governor on his side," persisted in his demand, no new patent for the domain could be procured.[101] With the help of the Schuylers, he seems to have worked out a compromise, upon which the governor issued an order on June 15, 1685, officially putting an end to the dispute. The compromise, signed four days later in the presence of the governor by Livingston and Peter Delanoy, attorney for Richard Van Rensselaer, stipulated that Livingston no longer be responsible for Nicholas's unpaid debts, that he be rewarded 800 schepels of wheat, and that in return he release all the domain lands he had seized and withdraw his objections to a new patent for Rensselaerswyck. Meanwhile, Richard Van Rensselaer and his nephew Kiliaen Van Rensselaer[102] had in the spring of 1685 bought a two-tenths share of the heirs of both Adam Bessels and Samuel Blommart, another proprietor. By this purchase, the dissolution of the

99. Nicholaes Van Beeck to Rev. Godfredius Delius, May 29, 1684, *Maria Van Rensselaer Correspondence*, 151–152. At this time, the Muyssarts and the Besselses each owned a tenth of the domain. Nissenson, *Patroon's Domain*, 328n.

100. On Schuyler's farms and his alignment with Livingston, see *Jeremias Van Rensselaer Correspondence*, 59, 94, 128, 133, 135, 144, 169–173. Philip Schuyler died in May 1683, and his wife Margaret then pursued his plans.

101. Maria Van Rensselaer to Richard Van Rensselaer, Nov. 12, 1684, *ibid.*, 169.

102. This Kiliaen Van Rensselaer (d. 1687), son of Johannes, should not be confused with Kiliaen Van Rensselaer (d. 1719), the eldest son of Maria. In July 1685, Richard Van Rensselaer appointed Johannes's son director of the domain and sent him to New York. Nissenson, *Patroon's Domain*, app. C.

original nominal partnership in the domain, except for a share of Muys-sart's, was almost accomplished.[103]

After all this delay, Dongan on October 17, 1685, granted a patent to Kiliaen Van Rensselaer, son of Maria, and Kiliaen Van Rensselaer,[104] son of Johannes. The patent, in addition to investing the domain with the title "Lordship and Manor of Rensselaerswyck," furnished the Van Rensselaers with feudal privileges, including the right to a seat in the General Assembly. About a million acres, much larger than the original Dutch grant of 1629, were contained in the new grant, which consisted of two widely separated tracts. The first, about 850,000 acres, began at the southern end of Beren Island and ran northward for twenty-three miles along the Hudson River and inland twenty-four miles from both sides of the river; it also included all the islands in the Hudson. The second, commonly known as the Claverack part of the manor, the boundaries of which were vague, started from what is now Four Mile Point and ran southward for some ten miles along the east side of the river and twenty-four miles into the woods. Excluded from the manor were the town of Albany and a sixteen-mile strip of land from Albany to Schenectady (see the map of Rensselaerswyck on p. 37).

The patent was at best a mixed victory for the Van Rensselaers. It thwarted their traditional dream of annexing Albany, but it gave them for the first time a secure English title to their expanded landholdings against many local pretenders, a means of control over the domain inhabitants, and independence from the Albany County jurisdiction.[105] The right to send a deputy to the assembly conferred representation of their interests at the provincial level, to say nothing of boosting their prestige. More important, the manorial patent, the first of its kind ever granted, had political implications far beyond its familial and local significance. It clearly showed that Dongan's reservations about granting feudal privileges to the Van Rensselaers, which Stephanus Van Cortlandt had noticed during the closing months of 1683, had vanished in the course of two years. Indeed, a momentous shift can be discerned in Dongan's attitudes, in no small degree due to his apprehension that the assembly was gaining too much power at his expense. By granting the

103. Patent Book 7: 135, Office of N.Y. Sec. of State; *Maria Van Rensselaer Correspondence*, 86, 99–101, 117, 157. For a fuller account of the disputes and compromise, see Leder, *Livingston*, 24–32.

104. See note 102 above. Kiliaen Van Rensselaer (son of Johannes) was naturalized on Oct. 31, 1685, probably a month after his arrival from Holland. Patent Book 7: 152, Office of N.Y. Sec. of State.

105. *Maria Van Rensselaer Correspondence*, 18.

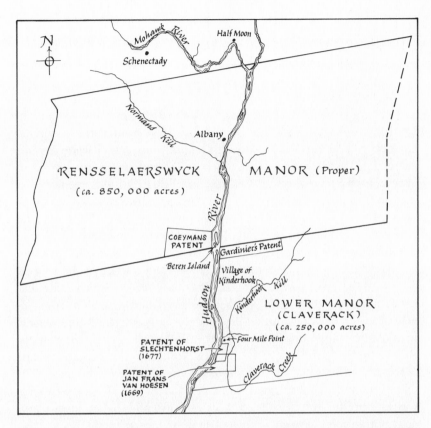

**Rensselaerswyck Manor, 1685.** Adjusted from John R. Bleeker's map of 1767 and Cadwallader Colden's map of Claverack, 1771, in E. B. O'Callaghan, ed., *The Documentary History of the State of New York* (Albany, N.Y., 1849–1851), III, 916, and New York Colonial Manuscripts, Land Papers, 1642–1803, XXIX, 56, New York State Library, Albany. (Drawn by Richard J. Stinely.)

manor the medieval courts baron and courts leet, the governor did violence to the judicial act passed by the assembly in October 1683. There is no evidence that Dongan ever tried to get the assembly to agree with this fait accompli. His antiassembly bias was further shown by his reversal of the 1683 annexation of Gardiner's Island to the town of East Hampton, and his creation on September 11, 1686, of the "Lordship and Manor of Gardiner's Island." Though the "manorializing" of the island was done in response to a petition of David Gardiner praying to be reinstated to his former privileged status, the governor must have acted with a clear knowledge that he was undoing the assembly's repudiation of what might be called the extraterritorial status of the island.[106]

Dongan's counteroffensive against the popular branch was in keeping with, and undoubtedly encouraged by, a move at the Court of St. James toward tighter imperial control of the American colonies. The move, which had been in agitation since 1675, was initiated in the fall of 1684 by the revocation of the charters of the Bermuda Company and the Massachusetts Bay Colony. In the following few months, the charters of Connecticut, Rhode Island, Maryland, and Pennsylvania were, in rapid succession, earmarked for prosecution by the court officials. After some letup caused by the death of Charles II in February 1685, the tempo of the campaign against the charter governments increased under James II, who had long been convinced that the little commonwealths were inimical to the development of a sound colonial administration.[107] Soon *quo warranto* proceedings against these colonies and others were instituted. On March 3, 1685, the Lords of Trade in the presence of the king reexamined the New York Charter of Liberties of 1683, which James had once approved, and concluded that the government of New York "be assimilated to the Constitution that shall be agreed on for New England, to which it is adjoining." Although the official message disallowing the charter probably did not arrive in New York until late August or early September 1686, Dongan might have surmised from the prolonged delay that his master was displeased with it.[108] And he probably foresaw what was in store for the province and its new assembly when most of the neighboring colonies were being systematically disciplined.

In any case, Dongan's actions suggest that he had anticipated the new imperial policy, although his granting Rensselaerswyck the political privilege of representation in the assembly in addition to the usual manorial rights seems to indicate that as late as October 1685 (the date of the Van Rensselaer patent), he still held the view that the assembly was there to stay for some time to come.[109] Independently of the crown, Dongan

---

106. "Report to Surveyor General, 1797," Land Book 5: 54, Bureau of Waterways, New York State Department of Transportation, Albany; Robert David Lion Gardiner, "Gardiner's Island," *N.Y. History*, XIV (1933), 53–60.

107. Philip S. Haffenden, "The Crown and the Colonial Charters, 1675–1688: Part I," *WMQ*, 3d Ser., XV (1958), 297–311; Lovejoy, "Equality and Empire," *ibid.*, XXI (1964), 510–514.

108. *N.Y. Col. Docs.*, III, 357–359, 360, 370; *Calendar of State Papers, Col. Ser.*, XII, 8, 242.

109. The first assembly lasted until Aug. 13, 1685. The second met on Oct. 20, but sat only one session, which passed six bills. On Oct. 29 Dongan found "important reasons" for

was engaged in steering a course of action against provincial whiggism. With the establishment of the first New York manor, therefore, Dongan's own counterrevolution—if one may be allowed to call the rise of the assembly and its measures in late 1683 and 1684 a peaceful revolution—was set in motion. His goals clearly paralleled those of the hard-line imperial reorganization of the colonies.

Dongan went on to grant five more manorial patents to various men of stature. These patents, each styled as "Lordship and Manor," were Lloyd's Neck for James Lloyd (March 16, 1686), Livingston Manor for Robert Livingston (July 22, 1686), Cassilton for John Palmer (March 31, 1687), Bentley for Christopher Billop (May 6, 1687), and Pelham for Thomas Pell (October 20, 1687). Pelham, like Gardiner's Island, had originally been an independent patent. These grants ranged in size from the 160,000 acres of Livingston Manor to the several hundred acres of Lloyd's Neck, and were scattered in different parts of the colony. Although the lords were not given the right to representation in the assembly, they were furnished with the usual medieval judicial and administrative authority, indicating that Dongan hoped that the manor would be a convenient local administrative and political unit.[110] By early 1686 the General Assembly had become practically nonexistent. It was continually prorogued by the governor, who now regarded it as an absurdity in the light of the king's offensive against charter governments and their parliamentary attributes. It is plain that Dongan expected the manorial proprietors to support the royal cause.

As one student of New York history has pointed out, it is quite possible that the patent for Livingston Manor, situated south of Rensselaerswyck and on the east side of the Hudson River, was partly the governor's reward for Livingston's surrender of his claims against Rensselaerswyck (see the map on p. 40).[111] That Livingston, a favorite of the governor, so readily agreed to the apparently unfavorable compromise of July 1685 after years of bitter quarreling with the Van Rensselaers further

---

proroguing it until Sept. 25, 1686. However, it never met again until it was finally dissolved by the governor's proclamation in the following Jan. *N.Y. Col. Laws*, I, 173–177; *Minutes of the Common Council of the City of New York, 1675–1776* (New York, 1905), I, 166–167.

110. The Manor of Lloyd's Neck (or Queen's Village) was given the privilege of holding courts leet but not courts baron. It is impossible to determine what caused this discrimination. *Papers of the Lloyd Family of the Manor of Queens Village, Lloyd's Neck, Long Island, New York, 1654–1826* (N.-Y. Hist. Soc., *Colls.*, LIX–LX [New York, 1926–1927]), I, 72–77, hereafter cited as *Lloyd Papers*.

111. Leder, *Livingston*, 35.

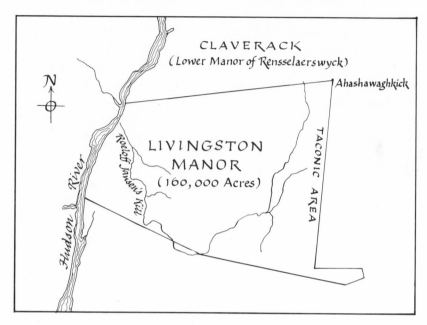

**Livingston Manor, 1686.** Adjusted from John Betty's survey map, 1714, in E. B. O'Callaghan, ed., *The Documentary History of the State of New York* (Albany, N.Y., 1849–1851), III, 690. (Drawn by Richard J. Stinely.)

underscores such a possibility, as does the timing of the patent, about a year after the compromise and seven months after the Rensselaerswyck patent.[112]

Though devoid of the power of lordship, the nonmanorial land patents also seem to have been an intricate part of Dongan's overall antiwhig policy. These included Saratoga Patent (about 150,000 acres north of Albany), granted in 1684 to Dr. Cornelis Van Dyke and six others;[113] Rumbout Patent (256 square miles in Dutchess County), granted

112. *Doc. Hist. N.Y.*, III, 611–627; Pearson, trans., and Van Laer, ed., *Early Records of Albany and Rensselaerswyck*, II, 189–192, 281–283. In 1702 Livingston argued that this patent gave him a tract of 16 miles long and 24 miles broad. Earl of Bellomont to Board of Trade, Jan. 2, 1702, *Doc. Hist. N.Y.*, III, 629.

113. The six other associates of the patent (dated Nov. 4, 1684) were Peter Philips Schuyler, John Bleecker, Johannes Wendell, Dirck Wessells (Ten Broeck), David Schuyler, and Robert Livingston, all prominent merchants in Albany connected with Indian affairs. Patent Book 5: 159–165, Office of N.Y. Sec. of State.

to Francis Rumbout, a wealthy New York merchant, and two others;[114] Catskill Patent (about 40,000 acres) for Elizabeth Van Dyck and others;[115] three patents for Frederick Philipse, the wealthiest merchant of the province and a member of the governor's council, altogether about 50,000 acres in Westchester County along the east side of the Hudson River;[116] and a patent to Stephanus Van Cortlandt for two tracts of land (several thousand acres at and around Haverstraw and Verplanck's Point).[117] The grants of the last two, it should be noted, were transformed into manors in the following decade. The granting of patents to leading figures in local and public affairs indicates that Dongan hoped to bind these men to the governor and the king.

Why did Dongan offer two types of grants—manors and patents? It appears that when a patent was granted to a group of individuals belonging to different families, as was the case with a number of patents, a lordship title was out of the question because the honor could not be collectivized. Philipse and Van Cortlandt seem to have decided against soliciting this privilege during the Dongan administration since they were still in the process of expanding their landholdings to adjacent areas. If they had wanted the manorial proprietorship, they could easily have gotten it because of their political influence with the governor, which was unrivaled by any other provincials at the time.

Dongan's essentially political motives were further revealed by his charging only trivial quitrents on these new patents, in variance with the Duke's Laws, which fixed 2s. 6d. annual rent per hundred acres. For instance, the Rumbout patentees were required to pay a rent of only 6 bushels of winter wheat; Livingston, 28 s. (about 7 bushels of wheat); the Saratoga patentees, 20 bushels; Van Cortlandt, 2 bushels. Rensselaerswyck's rent, which had been assessed at 150 bushels of wheat since

114. Jacobus Kipp and Stephanus Van Cortlandt were the two other patentees. The patent was dated Oct. 17, 1685. *Ibid.*, 206–210.

115. "Cadwallader Colden's Map" (1725?), in Justin Winsor, ed., *Narrative and Critical History of America* (Boston and New York, 1884–1889), V, 237.

116. Deed Book A, 50, 55, 62–63, 150–151, 163–172, Deed Book B, 8, 201–222, 233, F, 2, 435, Westchester Co. Clerk's Office.

117. This patent was dated Mar. 16, 1685. Patent Book 5: 306–309, Office of N.Y. Sec. of State. Also there were two other large grants. One was the so-called Hosick Patent (4 square miles) along the Hosick River granted in 1688 to Maria Van Rensselaer, Hendrick Van Ness, Gerrit Teunissen (Van Vechten), and Jacobus Van Cortlandt. See the advertisement for a division of the patent in *New-York Gazette; and the Weekly Mercury*, Apr. 18, 1771. The other was a patent granted in 1686 to Philip Philipse, son of Frederick. The tract lay north of Frederick's estate. New York Colonial Manuscripts, Land Papers, 1642–1803, II, 149, N.Y. State Lib., hereafter cited as N.Y. Land Papers.

Governor Nicolls's time, was reduced to 50 bushels under the new manor patent. These rates were indeed low for the amount of land involved, even if we make allowances because the land was almost totally unimproved. The rates appear even more absurd when we consider that during this period Dongan was calling in other patents, particularly those of whiggish towns, to ascertain the amounts of land purchased from the Indians and to compel the patentees to renew their patents with a larger quitrent.[118] This policy was clearly intended to recoup government revenue by drawing upon the proprietary land that lay beyond the assembly's interference. This apparent contradiction in Dongan's actions supports the conclusion that, in creating the manors and patents, he chose to forsake revenue in order to gain political advantage.[119]

The manorial system in New York evolved in stages. At the hand of Dongan, it finally took a mature form comparable to that of old England. His manorial and nonmanorial grants were designed for multiple purposes: promoting settlement, extending territorial rights, facilitating economic diversification, and consolidating antiwhig forces for the sake of executive and royal authority in the province. Dongan appears to have been influenced by the fear of local oligarchical power that had obsessed his predecessors, but if at any point he had such a fear, it was swept away by the more dangerous specter of legislative hegemony. Whatever the external differences between the manors and the independent patents, the motives for granting both were almost the same. That two of the independent patents, Pelham and Gardiner's, were later transformed into manors supports this point. With the establishment of seven manors and several large nonmanorial patents, New York was now set on the road toward a legally stratified society.

But the granting of manorial lordships and large amounts of land

118. Dongan's report, 1686, N.Y. Col. Docs., III, 401; warrant to Benjamin Collier, sheriff of Westchester County, Mar. 16, 1685, HM786, Henry E. Huntington Library, San Marino, Calif.; warrant to Richard Pretty, sheriff of Albany County, the same date, N.Y. Col. MSS, XXXIV, 46; warrant to Samuel Winder of Richmond County, Mar. 8, 1684, ibid., 11.

119. Julius Goebel argued wrongly that the manors were created partly to obtain revenue. Goebel, Legal and Political Aspects of Manors, Order of Col. Lords, N.Y. Branch, Pubs., No. 19, 16–17. However, Dongan did receive substantial fees for the patents he issued. The record reveals that the Van Rensselaers paid £200, the magistrates of Albany £300 for the city charter, the Hempstead town patentees £60 in cattle, and New York City £300 for its charter. We may assume that Dongan took varying sums for other patents. These fees were regarded as a gubernatorial perquisite. N.Y. Col. Docs., III, 495.

did not end with Dongan. The process continued in subsequent years, particularly during the governorship of Benjamin Fletcher. It was he who established five more manors, including the Philipsburgh and Cortlandt manors, and several nonmanorial grants. Their rise and related events will be the story of the next chapter.

# CHAPTER II

# Threats to the Manor Lords, 1688-1701

### Leisler's Rebellion and Landed Interest

In addition to its long-range impact on New York provincial society, Governor Thomas Dongan's policy of "manorialization" and of giving profuse land grants to a few individuals had some immediate political consequences. It coalesced the beneficiaries of the policy into a special interest group friendly to the existing government, while it embittered those who had not acquired land and drove them into opposition. This latter group included merchants like Jacob Leisler and Jacob Milborne of New York City. Dongan thus laid the material foundations for the formation of the first political factions in the history of the province. The ensuing struggle between these two factions largely set the tone and provided the dynamics of provincial politics for some years to come. Leisler's Rebellion (1689–1691) was only one of several effects of that struggle. A clear understanding of the long-term conflict is of utmost importance because the fortunes of the manorial proprietors, the Van Rensselaers, and Robert Livingston, and of those soon-to-be manor proprietors, Frederick Philipse and Stephanus Van Cortlandt, were deeply involved in it.

As part of the policy of introducing firmer royal control and greater administrative centralization to the American colonies, Edmund Andros in 1686 was appointed governor-general of the Dominion of New England. Two years later, New York, along with the Jerseys, was annexed to the dominion, and at the same time, Dongan was superseded by Andros. In July 1688, Captain Francis Nicholson, who was thoroughly military-minded and contemptuous of representative government, assumed the post of lieutenant governor under Andros.[1] Although Dongan had long argued for a consolidation of the colonies, he was "highly dissatisfied at the Sudden change," obviously because he had lost his job as a result of the absorption of the province into the larger unit.[2] Many other New Yorkers, particularly Long Islanders, were extremely unhappy with the turn of events, but for a different reason. To them, membership in the dominion carried with it a formal death warrant for the languishing assembly and foreboded the restoration of an executive government that they identified with tyranny. One of the consequences, they felt, would be higher taxation for the inhabitants already "oppressed by heavy taxes" due to the increasing cost of defense against France.[3] Furthermore, there was a fairly widespread belief, though unfounded in fact, that the officials of the dominion were either outright papist or "pretended protestant"—pro-Catholic—and were conspiring to sell out and enslave the English nation to the Catholic interest.[4] A noisy party at the governor's fort in August 1688 celebrating the birth of a son to the Catholic James II deepened these suspicions. The perpetuation of a Catholic dynasty now seemed certain, a prospect disturbing enough to set in motion a revolutionary force at home. Tension permeated the air. Nicholson's display of temper and arrogance and his disparaging attitude toward the New Yorkers, whom he was reported to have defined as "a conquered people," certainly did not alleviate the tension between the ruling group and the ruled. Explosive ingredients were all there, and only a spark was needed to touch them off.[5]

The Revolution of 1688 in England against King James II supplied that catalyst. In Boston the restless Puritans, upon receiving the report, quickly arrested and jailed Governor Andros. On April 26, 1689, New

1. For Nicholson's career, see Stephen Saunders Webb, "The Strange Career of Francis Nicholson," *WMQ*, 3d Ser., XXIII (1966), 513–548.
2. Edward Randolph to William Blathwayt, Aug. 19, Sept. 12, 1688, William Blathwayt Papers (microfilm), Roll 1, Colonial Williamsburg Foundation Research Department, Williamsburg, Va. (which also owns the originals), hereafter cited as Blathwayt Papers.
3. Randolph to Blathwayt, Aug. 19, 1688, *ibid.*, Roll 1; Bernard Mason, "Aspects of the New York Revolt of 1689," *N.Y. History*, XXX (1949), 169–174.
4. "Address of the Militia of New-York to William and Mary," June 1689, *N.Y. Col. Docs.*, III, 584; Stephanus Van Cortlandt to Edmund Andros, July 9, 1689, *ibid.*, III, 592.
5. Webb, "Nicholson," *WMQ*, 3d Ser., XXIII (1966), 522; Leder, *Livingston*, 60; Stephanus Van Cortlandt to Edmund Andros, *N.Y. Col. Docs.*, III, 593–594; N.-Y. Hist. Soc., *Colls.*, I (1868), 295.

Yorkers heard of the overthrow of the dominion government, and on May 4, Long Islanders, especially of Queens and Suffolk counties, who had never been reconciled with the Stuart monarchy, raised the banner of revolution. Groups in Westchester County followed suit. Almost all the magistrates and military officers in these areas were "put out," and new ones were chosen by the people. On May 6 a rumor that a thousand French troops and a great number of their Indian cohorts were advancing south threw the population into a panic.[6] At this critical juncture, Nicholson appeared to his enemies to be reluctant to take strong measures against the French menace, which lent credence to the idea that a Catholic plot was afoot. Nothing could calm the people, as they were "so possessed with jealousyes and fears of being sold, betrayed," wrote one of the frustrated members of the dominion council. Finally, the citizens of the city of New York rose up and, on the last day of May, took over the governor's fort without encountering any resistance. The dominion government in New York collapsed.[7]

The rebellion, led by Jacob Leisler, militia captain of the city, had no positive program of its own, at least in the beginning. It was basically anti-Stuart and anti-Catholic; its leaders had the simple objectives of ousting those officials associated with the dominion system and, to a lesser degree, of preserving the province for King William and Queen Mary. In quick succession, the rebels proclaimed the king and queen as their new rulers, established a committee of safety as an interim government for the province, named Leisler the commander of the fort, and put the city in defensive readiness. To finance the defense measures, the committee appointed Peter Delanoy as collector of the customs. In August, before adjourning for the winter, the committee gave Leisler the "power and Authority of a Commander in Chief" of the province.[8] In the meantime, Leisler not only stopped the functioning of those city magistrates with commissions from the old regime but also tried to impress his authority and extend the "revolution" everywhere. All these actions were taken in the belief that a new governor would soon come from England and would approve the actions of the rebels.

6. Nicholson and his council to the Board of Trade, May 15, 1689, N.Y. Col. Docs., III, 574.
7. Hendrick Cuyler's deposition, June 10, 1689, N.-Y. Hist. Soc., Colls., I (1868), 270–271; "A Declaration of the Inhabitants Soudjers . . . ," May 31, 1689, Doc. Hist. N.Y., II, 10.
8. N.Y. Col. Docs., III, 596; Doc. Hist. N.Y., II, 14–15, 16–39.

But the originally temporary status of the Leislerian government took on a different coloration when, on December 8, 1689, a royal courier brought two letters from the home government. Both were addressed to Nicholson or "to such as for the time being take care for Preserving the Peace and administring the Lawes" in New York. One letter appointed Nicholson or his alternate "Lieutenant Governor and Commander in Chief" of the province. By this time, Nicholson, taking counsel from his fear of the mob, had fled to England.[9] Leisler was confronted with two alternatives: he could surrender to Frederick Philipse and Stephanus Van Cortlandt, members of the dominion council of New York, to whom Nicholson had entrusted the government, or he could appoint himself as Nicholson's successor in order to carry on the anti-Stuart revolution in the province. He chose the latter course and on January 10, 1690, declared that he was the new lieutenant governor.[10] Once dressed in the garments of legitimacy, Leisler set out to administer the province. He appointed council members and new justices of the peace, ordered new elections of local officials, established the courts, and enforced the collection of customs.

Unlike the revolution in the New England colonies, where the fall of the dominion was received as everyone's salvation, the changeover in New York ran into stiff opposition from various sources. The most serious antagonists were those great commercial-landed tycoons who had been favored by Andros and Dongan with land, honor, and office. Almost without exception, they were Dutch Reformed in religious belief, situated in the urban centers of either New York or Albany, and linked with one another by intermarriage. Typical of this group of anti-Leislerians were Stephanus Van Cortlandt, Nicholas Bayard, Frederick Philipse, Robert Livingston, and Peter Schuyler.

Van Cortlandt's career was representative of the way the system worked.[11] At the age of thirty-four, he had been appointed by Governor Andros to the mayorship of New York, which was just the beginning of his political preferment. In 1680, when he was thirty-seven, he had been taken into the influential governor's council. Van Cortlandt returned these favors with his unwavering loyalty to Andros. When Captain John

9. N.Y. Col. Docs., III, 605, 606, 673.

10. Stephanus Van Cortlandt to William Blathwayt, Dec. 18, 1689, Blathwayt Papers, Roll 2.

11. Gertrude Van Cortlandt to William Blathwayt, May 17, 1701, *ibid*. He is described here as being "soft and malleable in temper."

Lewin was sent to New York in 1681 by the duke of York to inquire whether "anyone has any complaints" against Andros, Van Cortlandt had strongly advised his sister Maria Van Rensselaer to "admonish Mr. Marten Gerrits . . . not to say anything to the deteriment of Sir Edmund, but to say that all he did was for the best interest of [the] entire province." The reciprocity of favors between Andros and Van Cortlandt undoubtedly cemented their political partnership, despite their different religious affiliations.[12] From 1683 to 1689, Van Cortlandt's officeholdings expanded to include the first judgeship of the Admiralty Court, customs collector, master of the chancery court, deputy for William Blathwayt (receiver general of the colonies), and deputy secretary of the province. A rich trader, brewer, and gristmill owner, he also had acquired, with the help of Andros and Dongan, large landed estates in the northern part of Westchester County.[13] All these advantages, plus his kinship with the best families in Albany, the Schuylers, Livingstons, and Van Rensselaers, afforded him formidable influence in the political and economic affairs of the colony.

No less important a figure was Nicholas Bayard, a prominent merchant in New York and a nephew of Peter Stuyvesant. In February 1687, he became a member of Dongan's council. Though he was not endowed with land grants like some of the other councilmen, he took his council job seriously enough to take a stand against a man he called "the Grand Robber Jacob Leisler."[14] Another councillor, Frederick Philipse, the richest merchant-landowner, had received many favors from the governor and was rumored to have had a secret trade partnership with Andros. Outwardly compromising with the Leislerians, he secretly worked for the conservative group.[15]

With the vigorous support of Bayard, Van Cortlandt assumed the leadership of the anti-Leislerian faction in New York City, where he had been the chief magistrate. When Leisler shut down the mayor's court— equivalent to a county court of general sessions and common pleas—

12. Stephanus Van Cortlandt to Maria Van Rensselaer, Apr. 1681, *Maria Van Rensselaer Correspondence*, 48.

13. N.Y. Col. MSS, XXXIV, 8a, 12, XXXV, 10, 37, XXXVIII, 50; Van Cortlandt Papers, VX1995, Sleepy Hollow Restorations Library, Tarrytown, N.Y.; Stephanus Van Cortlandt to William Blathwayt, Dec. 18, 1689, Blathwayt Papers, Roll 2.

14. N.Y. Col. MSS, XXXV, 37.

15. George W. Schuyler, *Colonial New York: Philip Schuyler and His Family* (New York, 1885), II, 292; *N.Y. Col. Docs.*, III, 302–315, 610, 634, 649.

Van Cortlandt's house itself became a city hall, from which he conducted government business and corresponded with anti-Leislerian elements elsewhere.[16] Among these correspondents were Peter Schuyler, the first mayor of Albany, militia colonel, and a leading fur trader, and Robert Livingston, secretary to the commissioners of Indian affairs and holder of many local offices. They were both brothers-in-law of Van Cortlandt and beneficiaries of Dongan's land policy. Then there was Kiliaen Van Rensselaer (d. 1719), the young proprietor of Rensselaerswyck, a justice of the peace, a nephew of Van Cortlandt, and another of Dongan's favorites.[17] At the end of June 1689, Bayard took refuge in Albany and reported on the abuses to which he, Van Cortlandt, and others had been subjected by the Leislerians. Schuyler, Livingston, and Van Rensselaer, because of their familial ties to the New York opposition, were enraged at Leisler and his clique.[18]

The Albany leaders first responded to the revolt in New York City by organizing the Albanians into a convention and turning down Leisler's call for unity under his banner. This anti-Leisler attitude was surprising only in that the city of Albany needed all the help it could get to defend itself from "such Eminent Danger Threatened by the French . . . and there Praying Indians."[19] Like Van Cortlandt and his followers, the Albany convention declared its allegiance to the new English sovereign and swore its anti-Catholicism but categorically rejected Leisler as a usurper and charged that his authority extended at best only to the city and county of New York. Extremely tired of the Leislerian "threats, insolencies, abuses, falsities and lyes, unlawful actings and mischeeffs," Van Cortlandt joined Bayard in Albany in the middle of August 1689. From this time on, Albany became the stronghold of the anti-Leislerian faction, making the Leislerian revolt merely a local phenomenon of New York City and vicinity.[20]

Apart from their kinship with Van Cortlandt, the Albanian leaders had another reason for resisting Leisler. They saw some serious implications in Leisler's repudiation of any commissions, rights, and privileges granted by James II. If they were to accept Leisler's position, it would

---

16. Stephanus Van Cortlandt to Andros, June 22 and July 9, 1689, N.Y. Col. Docs., III, 595–596, 593; "Journal of Nicholas Bayard," ibid., 599–604.
17. N.Y. Col. MSS, XXXIII, 53, 197; Doc. Hist. N.Y., II, 119.
18. N.Y. Col. Docs., III, 594.
19. Doc. Hist. N.Y., II, 88, 92–93, 99–100, 102, 103, 119.
20. Leisler and council to the bishop of Salisbury, Jan. 7, 1790, ibid., III, 655.

mean the loss not only of their offices but also of the Albany city charter of 1686, including its traditional monopoly of the fur trade.[21]

But then a tragic event shattered the Albanian resistance to Leisler. On the night of February 8, 1690, 200 French and Indians fell suddenly upon the sleeping and snow-covered village of Schenectady, killing 62 people, carrying off 27 more, and burning almost all the houses. The panic generated by the attack and the impending disaster it foreboded to nearby areas were too real for the convention to ignore. They knew, however, that they could not combat the "Power of Canida" without adequate money and men at their disposal.[22] The convention sent Livingston and Captain Gerrit Teunissen Van Vechten to the New England colonies and one Reynier Barents to Ulster County and New York City to seek soldiers, ammunition, and provisions. Barents's instructions, dated February 27, ordered him to "wait on the Governor if he be arrived, otherwise on the authority there," meaning Leisler, and, more important, to beseech the Leislerians to "lay aside all animosities and divisions and that every one exert his power to crush the Common Enemy."[23] Albany's dire predicament gave Leisler a chance to fulfill his ambition of ruling the entire country. He lost no time in dispatching 160 men under three commissioners, instructing them to demand that the convention recognize his authority as the condition for their assistance. Early in March, the convention, forlorn and broken, their hoped-for aid from the neighboring colonies unrealized, decided to accept the condition. Thus, the last bastion of the anti-Leislerians finally crumbled.[24]

This victory did not put an end to Leisler's prosecution of political opponents. As a conciliatory gesture, he kept Peter Schuyler, Kiliaen Van Rensselaer, and others in their respective offices for a while.[25] But his mind was set on punishing those who were most obnoxious to his regime. On January 7 or 8, 1691, his agents captured Bayard, chained him with iron bars, and kept him prisoner in this condition until the overthrow of Leisler. The same fate befell William Nicolls, lawyer and staunch anti-Leislerian. Warrants of arrest were issued for Van Cortlandt, Livingston,

21. See "Journal of the Albany Convention," entry on Nov. 10, 1689, *Doc. Hist. N.Y.*, II, 120–121.

22. *Ibid.*, 157, 155, 176; *N.Y. Col. Docs.*, III, 599.

23. *Doc. Hist. N.Y.*, II, 174.

24. Massachusetts politely refused to help the convention. Connecticut's attitude was still in doubt at this time, although it would eventually agree to send about 200 soldiers to Albany. Robert Livingston to Edmund Andros, Apr. 14, 1690, *N.Y. Col. Docs.*, III, 708; *Doc. Hist. N.Y.*, II, 191.

25. *Doc. Hist. N.Y.*, II, 194, 304, 353.

Thomas Dongan, and many others. Van Cortlandt took flight to New England, the Jerseys, and Philadelphia.[26] Livingston, who was blamed by Leisler for Albany's flouting of his authority, successfully eluded Leisler's posse in New England. Both he and Van Cortlandt were not idle in exile; they kept themselves abreast of conditions in New York and tried to discredit Leisler and his followers by writing to politically influential men in England.[27]

The Leislerian revolt had more than a political dimension. It also reflected a social and economic conflict between the landed and landless merchants of New York. This division within the mercantile community itself can be seen through an examination of the leadership of the two factions.

As noted above, opposing the Leislerians were such men as Philipse, Van Cortlandt, Livingston, and Peter Schuyler, all merchants with large undeveloped landed estates, and Kiliaen Van Rensselaer.[28] Around this group was clustered a coterie of lesser commercial-landed men, like David and Brant Schuyler, Dirck Wessells Ten Broeck, John Bleecker, and Johannes Wendell, all of Albany; Lewis Morris (a member of Governor Dongan's council) of Westchester County; and John Pell, lord of Pelham Manor.[29] They had enjoyed exalted social and political status and disdained their opponents as social and economic inferiors. They often referred to Leisler's faction as "lowly," "weak," "poor," and "illiterate," while designating themselves as "considerable men," "men of sense and estate," and "principal men."[30]

Although their estates were not equal to the most wealthy of their opponents, the Leislerian leaders were by no means poor and unrespectable. Consider, for example, Leisler himself and some of those whom the anti-Leislerians most hated—Jacob Milborne, Peter Delanoy, Gerard

26. N.Y. Col. Docs., III, 657; N.Y. Col. MSS, XXXVI, 134, 138, 142; Stephanus Van Cortlandt to Francis Nicholson, Apr. 6, 1691, Blathwayt Papers, Roll 2; Doc. Hist. N.Y., II, 35, 42–43.

27. Jacob Leisler to Capt. Benjamin Blagge and others, Mar. 1, 1690, Doc. Hist. N.Y., II, 179; Leder, Livingston, 68–74; Robert Livingston to earl of Nottingham, Mar. 27, 1690, Livingston-Redmond MSS, Roll 2; Livingston to Robert Ferguson, Mar. 27, 1690, N.Y. Col. Docs., III, 699; Van Cortlandt to Andros, May 19, 1690, ibid., 715–719.

28. This Kiliaen Van Rensselaer was the son of Maria.

29. Abstracts of Wills, on File in the Surrogate's Office, City of New York (N.-Y. Hist. Soc., Colls., XXV–XLI [New York, 1908]), II, 267–268, hereafter cited as Abstracts of Wills; Doc. Hist. N.Y., II, 263; N.Y. Col. Docs., III, 656; Doc. Hist. N.Y., II, 330–331; N.Y. Col. MSS, XXXVIII, 81.

30. N.Y. Col. Docs., III, 585, 665, 717; Stephanus Van Cortlandt to Blathwayt, Dec. 18, 1689, Blathwayt Papers, Roll 2; Albany Convention to Col. Henry Sloughter, Jan. 20, 1690, Livingston-Redmond MSS, Roll 2.

Beekman, Samuel Staats, and Samuel Edsall, all members of the rebel council.[31] Leisler, a trader, was the wealthiest man in New York City in 1674 and two years later tied for second place. Through his marriage in 1663 to Elsje Tymens, the widow of the rich merchant Cornelisen Van der Veen, he was remotely related to the distinguished families of the colony, including the Van Cortlandts, Loockermans, and Bayards. Yet he was never accepted by the social elite or accorded any government office, except for a captaincy of the city militia.[32]

Leisler had much in common with the New Englanders. He adhered to a rigid Calvinist orthodoxy and disliked the navigation laws, high duties, and the dominion government. Thus, he was popular with Long Islanders, particularly those of Suffolk County, which was inhabited wholly by English settlers from New England. In the late 1680s Suffolk often chose Leisler to present their petitions to the government.[33]

Milborne, Leisler's son-in-law after 1690, the brother of a Baptist preacher in Boston, and a trader, considered himself worth at least £1,000 sterling in 1676. If this claim is to be believed, he was certainly a well-to-do man. He was also apparently hot-tempered and rebellious: he was once beaten and imprisoned briefly by Andros for scurrilous remarks about the governor and government and "incouraging others to be mutinous."[34] Milborne was never able to ingratiate himself with the dominant socioeconomic group and remained a social outcast.

Unlike Leisler and Milborne, Peter Delanoy had originally been accepted by his opponents. In the early 1680s Delanoy had the good fortune of being treasurer of the city and collector. Merchant by occupation and called "an honest, Godfearing man" by Maria Van Rensselaer, he had also been on good terms with the Van Cortlandts and the Van Rensselaers, the latter having chosen him as their attorney in their dispute against Robert Livingston. But he fell out of grace with Dongan and his associates when he was suspended in 1686 from the collectorship under suspicion of dishonesty. If not rich, he seems to have managed a comfort-

---

31. N.Y. Col. Docs., III, 684.

32. Jerome R. Reich, Leisler's Rebellion: A Study of Democracy in New York, 1664–1720 (Chicago, 1953), 58–59; Lawrence H. Leder, "The Unorthodox Domine: Nicholas Van Rensselaer," N.Y. History, XXXV (1954), 173–174.

33. For Leisler's personal differences with the Van Cortlandts, Bayards, and Van Rensselaers, see Leder, "Unorthodox Domine," N.Y. History, XXXV (1954), 173–174; Reich, Leisler's Rebellion, 58–59; Leder, Livingston, 59; N.Y. Col. Docs., III, 637; "Leisler's Warrant and Instructions to Johannes Provost, etc.," Aug. 1689, N.-Y. Hist. Soc., Colls., I (1868), 296; N.Y. Col. MSS, XXXIII, 50, XXXV, 45b–d.

34. Van Laer, ed., Minutes of the Court of Albany, Rensselaerswyck and Schenectady, III, 146–148; "Case of Milborne against Andros," [1681], N.Y. Col. Docs., III, 300–301.

able living.[35] His father-in-law, Samuel Edsall, was a rich hatmaker and Indian trader whose political base was in New Jersey.[36]

Other Leislerian leaders had similar backgrounds. Gerard Beekman, a surgeon, had been a justice of the peace and a captain of militia in King's County. Like his brother Henry in Ulster County, he seems to have had modest means and enjoyed a respectable standing in the locality.[37] Staats, well known for his anti-English bias, was also a surgeon. He and his brother Joachim of Albany, who was appointed by Leisler as the commander of Fort Orange succeeding Peter Schuyler, were wealthy enough in January 1688 to buy three large farms in Rensselaerswyck from Richard Van Rensselaer, a Dutch shareholder of the manor, for 10,500 guilders. But they were not allowed to occupy the farms for several years because of the objections of Maria Van Rensselaer and her son Kiliaen, who were determined to appropriate the domain in its entirety for themselves. This incident undoubtedly angered the Staats against Kiliaen Van Rensselaer and his chief mentor, Van Cortlandt.[38]

Though comfortable, and in some cases quite wealthy, none of these rebel leaders owned a landed estate in the countryside. The same was true of such of their associates as Robert Walters, Abraham Gouverneur, and Cornelius Pluvier, all merchants.[39] The wealth of the Leislerian merchants consisted exclusively of real estate in the metropolitan area and of commercial capital. This was their most distinct characteristic in contrast to their antagonists. In a way, the Leislerians were economic

35. Maria Van Rensselaer to Richard Van Rensselaer, Jan. 1683, *Maria Van Rensselaer Correspondence*, 86; Stephanus Van Cortlandt and Peter Delanoy to Richard Pretty, Nov. 11, 1680, Livingston-Redmond MSS, Roll 2; Mrs. [Mariana Griswold] Schuyler Van Rensselaer, *History of the City of New York in the Seventeenth Century* (New York, 1909), II, 314; Joel Andrew Delano, *The Genealogy, History, and Alliances of the American House of Delano, 1620–1899* . . . (New York, 1899), 63–64.

36. *New York Genealogical and Biographical Record*, XXVII (1896), 58.

37. Philip L. White, *The Beekmans of New York in Politics and Commerce, 1647–1877* (New York, 1956), 122–131, 73–77. Henry Beekman at first supported Leisler, but soon turned against him.

38. *Doc. Hist. N.Y.*, II, 51–52; "Affidavit of Kiliaan Van Rensselaer" (trans. from the Dutch), Sept. 1692, N.-Y. Hist. Soc., *Colls.*, I (1868), 328–331; deposition of Mrs. Magdalena Claas and Niclaas Dirksen, Aug. 30, 1691, MS N358, Sleepy Hollow Restorations Lib.; Maria Van Rensselaer to Richard Van Rensselaer, [Sept.] 19?, 1688, *Maria Van Rensselaer Correspondence*, 185–188; Nissenson, *Patroon's Domain*, 340–343.

39. Samuel Edsall and his wife owned a 500-acre tract north of Manhattan Island, but they sold it off for £140 in 1668. Lucy D. Ackerly, *The Morris Manor*, Order of Col. Lords, N.Y. Branch, *Pubs.* (New York, 1916), 6. For information on the Leislerian leaders, see Stephanus Van Cortlandt to Blathwayt, Dec. 18, 1689, Blathwayt Papers, Roll 2; Monroe Johnson, "The Gouverneur Genealogy," *N.Y. Gen. and Biog. Rec.*, LXX (1939), 135–138; David T. Valentine, *History of the City of New-York* (New York, 1853), 79–80; W. P. Belknap, *De Peyster Genealogy* (Boston, 1956), 89.

misfits unable to join in the diversification occurring in the colony from 1670 to 1688, in which land and its produce were becoming sources of profit as important as peltry. While Livingston, Philipse, the Schuylers, Van Cortlandt, Ten Broeck, and Wendell were developing agriculturally related businesses as well as their commerce and getting richer as New York entrepreneurs of a new type, the fortunes of the Leislerian leaders were on the wane in relative terms. Leisler, for example, might still have been "a merchant of good Estate" in 1689, but his wealth about this time, as a commentator put it, was definitely "decaying."[40]

The composition of the two factions was at least partly the result of the widening socioeconomic gap between landed and landless mercantile men. Leisler's group was generally infected with jealousy of and hatred for the Van Cortlandt-Livingston party. The Leislerian attitude in turn made the landed men apprehensive of the potential harm the landless rebels might do to their patents and manorial privileges. Material evidence of that possibility was furnished when, at the outset of the revolt, the Leislerians repudiated all the commissions, rights, and privileges issued in the name of James II. In fact, Milborne openly declared in November 1689 that the Albany city charter was invalid with the dethronement of the king. The question of whether the rebels ever actually attempted to destroy the large patents is irrelevant. The landed interest held and expressed the fear that all the large land titles would become "null and void" in due course, and the Leislerians did nothing to alleviate or remove this concern.[41] It therefore persisted throughout the rebellion. It is no wonder that not a single landed man joined the rebel ranks. Significantly, one of the first acts of the anti-Leislerian assembly after the suppression of the revolt was to pass a bill (May 6, 1691) confirming "Grants Patents and Rights" of the "Cityes Townes Mannours and Freeholders." The legislation, in the judgment of the solons, was "absolutely necessary for quieting and satisfieing" the uneasy inhabitants.[42]

The importance of the socioeconomic differences between the two factions becomes more evident when we realize that they did not disagree on some fundamental issues. They both declared their loyalty to the newly

40. "Affidavit of George Dolstone," Feb. 19, 1691, N.-Y. Hist. Soc., *Colls.*, I (1868), 317–318, 321; John Miller, *A Description of the Province and City of New York; with Plans of the City and Several Forts as They Existed in the Year 1695*, ed. John Gilmary Shea (New York, 1862), 52; Van Rensselaer, *History of New York City*, II, 372.

41. *Doc. Hist. N.Y.*, II, 120–121.

42. *N.Y. Col. Laws*, I, 224–225; *Journal of the Legislative Council of New-York, 1691–1765* . . . (Albany, N.Y., 1861), I, 5–6.

established political order in England; they both were anti-Catholic; and they both were committed to defense against the French. It is true that the Leislerians twice convoked the assembly, once at the end of February and again in August 1690, but their motive was not so much a profound faith in popular institutions as a desperate need for a defense fund.[43] It is also true that Leisler and his council consented to the assembly's rule that "all towns and places would have equal freedom to boult and bake and to transport any thing their places afford, and that one place should have no more priviledges, than the others," not because they believed in the doctrine of free trade, which in practice would seriously undermine the economic position of New York City, their stronghold, but because they considered it politically expedient to garner support in the countryside for their precarious regime.[44]

The successful revolution in England and in Massachusetts provided the discontented in New York with an occasion to attack the political and economic establishment in the colony. But, because the cleavage within the old commercial interests originally occurred during the administrations of Andros and Dongan, particularly the latter, it appears that government land policy in the 1680s played as much a role in the course of Leisler's Rebellion as did British and provincial politics. As if to underscore this point, the land question would again emerge as a burning political issue between the Leislerians and anti-Leislerians several years later when the former became dominant in the provincial government.

## Governor Fletcher and the Rise of Philipsburgh and Cortlandt Manors

Leisler's political dominance did not last long, for King William, in whose name he took the reins of the New York government, recognized him only as a captain of the provincial militia and a plain merchant who had now become notorious. If Leisler had dealt the coup de grace to French power in the north or had done other memorable things for the

43. Stephanus Van Cortlandt to Edmund Andros, May 19, 1690, *N.Y. Col. Docs.*, III, 717; *Doc. Hist. N.Y.*, II, 282, 290, 355–357; N.Y. Col. MSS, XXXVI, 118; Reich, *Leisler's Rebellion*, 106; *N.Y. Col. Laws*, I, 218–219.

44. *N.Y. Col. Docs.*, III, 717. Recent discussions of Leisler's Rebellion are David S. Lovejoy, *The Glorious Revolution in America* (New York, 1972), and Thomas J. Archdeacon, "The Age of Leisler—New York City, 1689–1710: A Social and Demographic Interpretation," in Jacob Judd and Irwin H. Polishook, eds., *Aspects of Early New York Society and Politics* (Tarrytown, N.Y., 1974), 63–82.

glory of the empire, his self-appointed role might have been received by the king and his council with appreciation. Unfortunately for Leisler, an intercolonial expedition against Canada, organized under his leadership, came to nothing. And Joost Stol, a dram seller and ensign in Leisler's militia company, whom Leisler had sent to London to work for the rebels' interests, was too much of a rustic figure to neutralize the powerful influence of William Blathwayt, Andros, Nicholson, Randolph, and others of anti-Leislerian persuasion at the court.[45]

The royal instructions of January 31, 1691, to the new governor, Henry Sloughter, clearly reflected the strength of the anti-Leislerians and the failure of Stol's mission. The governor was ordered to call to his council twelve men who were almost all foes of Leisler—Philipse, Van Cortlandt, Bayard, and Nicolls among them.[46] The governor himself considered Leisler a usurper. Subsequent to Sloughter's arrival on March 19, 1691, Leisler and several of his followers were tried by a hastily formed special court of oyer and terminer and found guilty of treason and other crimes. On May 16, 1691, Leisler and Milborne were hanged as an "exemplary punishment"; the others were reprieved.[47] The execution relieved some vengeful anti-Leislerians of their anxiety about a possible royal pardon for the culprits. The climate of hate was such that some of the Leislerians felt compelled to take refuge in other colonies.

With the change in the political tide, the anti-Leislerian leaders quickly recovered their former eminence, and some obtained further political preferment. Robert Livingston, now returned from exile, received from Sloughter a lucrative job as the commissary for victualing the garrison in New York and Albany, in addition to being confirmed in the local offices he held before. To handle his business in New York City, he took in his brother-in-law Van Cortlandt as a partner.[48] Philipse, who had betrayed his weakness in the face of Leislerian intimidation, was nevertheless still regarded as the elder statesman of the party claiming loyalty to legitimacy. Subsequently, the governor appointed him and Bayard to

45. N.Y. Col. Docs., III, 597.

46. The others were Gabriel Minvielle, William Smith, Thomas Willett, William Pinhorne, Chidley Brooke, Joseph Dudley, Nicholas De Meyer, Francis Rumbout, and John Haines. Reich, Leisler's Rebellion, 112–113.

47. Stephanus Van Cortlandt to Blathwayt and Francis Nicholson, May 7, 1691, Blathwayt Papers, Roll 2; "Answer to the Memorial presented by Captain Blagge to the King," 1691, N.Y. Col. Docs., III, 766; "Governor Sloughter to the Committee," May 7, 1691, ibid., 763.

48. Deposition of Robert Livingston and Stephanus Van Cortlandt, June 1698, Livingston-Redmond MSS, Roll 2; Leder, Livingston, 78–79.

serve as "Commanders in Chief" during the governor's absence.[49] Van Cortlandt, who as deputy auditor of the province retained a close tie with William Blathwayt, was made a justice in the newly created Supreme Court. His social standing rose a notch when, in May 1691, his brother Jacobus, after several years of courtship, married Eva Philipse, a step-daughter of Frederick Philipse.[50] The young Kiliaen Van Rensselaer, lord of Rensselaerswyck, became a member of the new assembly.

But it was not domestic politics or its polarization that engrossed the manorial proprietors and the governors in the last decade of the seventeenth century.[51] Rather, the old problem of defending the province against the French in Canada and their Indian allies demanded attention. The cold war of mutual surveillance between England and France burgeoned into a hot war. The nature of the conflict also changed. It was no longer merely over peltry but over the fate of British North America. King William's War (1689–1697) was the beginning of what Francis Parkman called the "Half-Century of Conflict." New York was to play a crucial role in this conflict because of her strategic importance, which was recognized by foe and friend alike.[52]

The destruction of Schenectady in February 1690 and the killing of eight or ten settlers at the neighboring village of Conestoga in May clearly indicated what the French could do and meant to do. War phobia gripped the frontier people, causing them to desert their outlying plantations. "Reports of the coming of the French and Indians" made the farmers of Ulster County "fly" into Kingston from all directions. One contemporary observer noted that "most of the Albany woemen" were now at New York City.[53] In 1692 Robert Livingston's wife, Alida, wrote from Albany, "Families leave here with every sloop," and "the enemy will find an open door as the Places above have been deserted." The town authority and the governor tried in vain to stop the exodus of able-bodied men from the frontier county and to induce the return of those

49. Henry Sloughter to Col. Townly, May 1691, N.Y. Col. MSS, XXXVII, 90, 165.

50. Minutes of May 15, 1691, in New York Council Minutes, VI, 26, N.Y. State Lib., hereafter cited as N.Y. Council Minutes; Stephanus Van Cortlandt to Francis Nicholson, May 7, 1691, Blathwayt Papers, Roll 2.

51. The execution of Leisler and Milborne shocked their followers into political paralysis for a while.

52. Edward Randolph to Blathwayt, Boston, Sept. 17, 1692, Blathwayt Papers, Roll 1; Miller, Description of New York, 113–114 (editor's note); "Representation of the Lords of Trade to the Lords Justice," Oct. 4, 1700, N.Y. Col. Docs., IV, 701.

53. Extract of council minutes of Feb. 5, 1694, in "New York and the New Hampshire Grants," N.-Y. Hist. Soc., Colls., II (1869), 407; Stephanus Van Cortlandt to Edmund Andros, May 19, 1690, N.Y. Col. Docs., III, 716–717.

who had fled. As a result of the war, the county population was reduced from the high point of 2,144 in 1687 to 1,476 in 1698.[54]

At the same time, the Five Nations were restive. They resented English neglect of their welfare while they were exposed to French depredations during the Leislerian disorder. Moreover, the show of panic on the part of the frontier inhabitants made the Indians skeptical of the English as their potential military ally. It was feared that the Iroquois might make peace with the French, a collusion that would have been disastrous for English America from Maine to Virginia.[55]

Defense measures entailed heavy expenditures of money. Maintaining troops (two English companies and local militia), supplying gifts and arms for the Iroquois Confederation, repairing forts, paying for the governor's frequent trips to Albany, as well as meeting other incidental expenses, cost the provincial government £6,000 annually. But the yearly revenue dropped from £5,162 in 1687 to an average of £3,500 in the following decade,[56] due to the escalating effect of the war. The war lessened the volume of furs reaching Albany and depressed the Indian trade, which in turn led to a decline in government tax revenue. The frontier farmers neglected husbandry either because they were frightened away from their farms or because they were mustered into active duty.[57]

---

54. *Doc. Hist. N.Y.,* II, 193; governor's proclamation, Mar. 19, 1692, N.Y. Col. MSS, XXXVIII, 85; Alida Livingston to Robert Livingston, Apr. 7, 1692 (Dutch), Livingston-Redmond MSS, Roll 2, quoted in Leder, *Livingston,* 83; "Return of the Population of the city and county of Albany . . . ," Mar. 27, 1687, N.Y. Col. MSS, XXXV, 75; *N.Y. Col. Docs.,* IV, 420; "List of the names and number of Inhabitants in the City and County of Albany, July 31, 1698," Abraham Yates, Jr., Papers, 1607–1825, New York Public Library.

55. Edward Randolph to Blathwayt, Boston, Sept. 17, 1692, Blathwayt Papers, Roll 1; memorial of Chidley Brooke and William Nicolls to the Lords Justice of England, May 19, 1696, Livingston-Redmond MSS, Roll 2; extract of council minutes, Sept. 4, 1693, in "N.Y. and the N.H. Grants," N.-Y. Hist. Soc., *Colls.,* II (1869), 404; N.Y. council to Lords of Trade, Nov. 23, 1696, *N.Y. Col. Docs.,* IV, 245.

56. Benjamin Fletcher to Messrs. Brooke and Nicolls, Dec. 20, 1696, *N.Y. Col. Docs.,* IV, 249; earl of Bellomont to Lords of Treasury, May 25, 1698, enclosing an "Account of the King's revenue from all sources in the Government of New York, 1687," and a "Comparative statement of the revenue of New York, from 1692 onwards," with the following figures:

| 1687 | £5,162 | 1695 | £3,601 |
|------|--------|------|--------|
| 1692 | £3,371 | 1696 | £3,184 |
| 1693 | £2,972 | 1697 | £3,603 |
| 1694 | £4,333 | | |

*Calendar of State Papers, Col. Ser.,* XVI, 240; "Account of the Revenue of New York from 1690 to 1696," *N.Y. Col. Docs.,* IV, 173.

57. L. Van Schaick and Dirck Wessells Ten Broeck to the speaker of the assembly, 1692, *N.Y. Col. Docs.,* III, 817–818; *Journal of the Votes and Proceedings of the General*

To make matters worse, the government pressed heavy taxes on the already impoverished people. The combination of high taxes, military service, decline in trade, and fear of war together drove as many as two or three hundred families to join the Leislerian émigrés in removing mostly to Pennsylvania and Maryland and, to some extent, to New England.[58] All these factors further thinned the government tax base.

Although the General Assembly was restrained in voting money for frontier defense, the painful plight of the inhabitants crippled even moderate tax collections. A special tax voted by the legislature was honored by the people with scorn and delinquency.[59] Replying to an urgent appeal by the new governor, Benjamin Fletcher, for punctual collection of taxes in Westchester County, Colonel Caleb Heathcote, a member of the council and resident of the county, wrote in 1693: "We have taken all necessary Care therein, nor shall any threats be wanting them to a complyance, but Scarce one in twenty have bread for their familys and were the Rivers not furnished with clams and oysters in a year we should scarse have 10 men left in the County."[60] If the people in the relatively secure areas were so reduced, it is not hard to imagine how desperate the situation of the frontier people must have been. Rumor had it that Long Islanders, distressed by "continual Impressment in money and man," would "willingly" give up half of their estate to the New York government if they were allowed to be under Connecticut's jurisdiction.[61] Some of the landed tycoons were also apparently distressed financially. Kiliaen Van Rensselaer, lord of Rensselaerswyck, petitioned the governor in 1693 to waive

---

*Assembly of the Colony of New York, 1691–1765* (New York, 1764–1766), I, 21; "The City Records," Munsell, ed., *Annals of Albany*, II, 128, III, 15–16.

58. "Information furnished by the Reverend Mr. Miller respecting New York, 1696," *N.Y. Col. Docs.*, IV, 183. The desertion of the Leislerians from the province had been serious enough to cause the provincial government to assure an immunity for those returning Leislerians from all the "vexatious suits unlawful and unjust." "Proclamation by Governor, Council and the House of Representatives," May 19, 1691, N.Y. Col. MSS, XXXVII, 116.

59. *Journals of Legislative Council*, I, 15–16; Benjamin Fletcher to the assembly, Aug. 17, 1692, N.Y. Col. MSS, XXXVIII, 102b, 168; David Jamison to Robert Livingston, Feb. 23, 1692, Livingston-Redmond MSS, Roll 2; Stephanus Van Cortlandt to Blathwayt, May 29, 1696, Blathwayt Papers, Roll 2.

60. Caleb Heathcote to Fletcher, May 4, 1693, N.Y. Col. MSS, XXXIX, 49a. Dissatisfied with heavy taxes and continuous impressment, Rye and Bedford attempted in 1697 to secede from New York. *Ibid.*, XLI, 36, 45, 56, 59; *N.Y. Col. Docs.*, IV, 276. See also the receiver general's warrant to Robert Livingston, May 1694, Livingston-Redmond MSS, Roll 2.

61. Deposition of Samuel Smith, Oct. 30, 1693, N.Y. Col. MSS, XXXIX, 104; Fletcher to the Committee of Trade, Oct. 9, 1693, *N.Y. Col. Docs.*, IV, 56.

his quitrent (fifty bushels of wheat) for the previous year on the ground
that the war and an "extraordinary flood of rain" had so damaged his
manor "that it could not afford him Sustenance."[62]

In this precarious situation, aid from the London government and
the neighboring colonies was not without some drawbacks. To be sure,
the home government stationed two regular companies in New York, but
it took the position that the charges for supporting the troops and building forts at Albany, Schenectady, and other places should be borne by the
province.[63] The sister colonies, though willing to be sheltered by New
York from the ravages of French and Indian attacks, were too provincial-
minded to see the war in the context of imperial interests. From 1691 to
1695, Connecticut, the Jerseys, Maryland, and Virginia together contributed about £3,000 for defense; but New York alone spent over
£30,000.[64] Pennsylvania—until late 1696—and Massachusetts refused
to assist at all. Meanwhile, Pennsylvania, the Jerseys, and Connecticut
not only welcomed army deserters and refugees from New York but also
lured trade away by charging no customs duties on imports and exports.[65]
Governor Fletcher exploded: "Whilst we have the burthen they have the
Trade and profit, which will draw people after it when the other drive
them." He warned in 1693 that New York could not then "muster 3000
militia formerly five thousand."[66] All of these problems added to New
York's miseries and further weakened its defense capability.

As might be expected, the debts of the provincial government spiraled. As of November 1692, it owed £4,850 and in 1694, £7,890.[67]
Governor Fletcher saw that his administration was heading toward bank-

62. "Council meeting July 20, 1693," Miscellaneous Documents, Box 8, "Van Rensselaer," Albany Institute of History and Art, Albany, N.Y.; petition of Kiliaen Van Rensselaer, June 10, 1697, N.Y. Col. MSS, XLI, 82; Henry Beekman to Fletcher, Aug. 16, 1697,
ibid., 103.

63. N.Y. Col. Docs., III, 689.

64. Memorial of Chidley Brooke and William Nicolls to Lords Justices of England,
1696, ibid., IV, 172, 233, 243; James Graham to Robert Livingston, Sept. 25, 1692,
Livingston-Redmond MSS, Roll 2; Alice Davis, "The Administration of Benjamin Fletcher
in New York," N.Y. History, II (1921), 216–218.

65. Benjamin Fletcher to William Blathwayt, Feb. 14, 1693, Blathwayt Papers, Roll 2;
Fletcher to Blathwayt, Aug. 18, 1693, in "N.Y. and the N.H. Grants," N.-Y. Hist. Soc.,
Colls., II (1869), 406; Fletcher to Lords of Trade, Oct. 9, 1693, and June 10, 1696, and
Fletcher to Blathwayt, Aug. 15, 1693, N.Y. Col. Docs., IV, 55–56, 84, 159; Fletcher to
Blathwayt, July 1694, N.Y. Col. MSS, XXXIX, 171; N.Y. council to Lords of Trade, Dec.
15, 1696, C.O. 1039/5, 265, Public Record Office.

66. Fletcher to Committee of Trade, Oct. 9, 1693, N.Y. Col. Docs., IV, 55.

67. Fletcher to Blathwayt, Sept. 10, 1692, ibid., III, 846; "Report of Stephanus Van
Cortlandt, Nov. 1, 1692," and "A List of Debts of the Government, 1694," N.Y. Col. MSS,
XXXIX, 8a, 135.

ruptcy. He also knew that the country had to be defended at whatever cost, for otherwise something worse than bankruptcy would result. He regularly appealed to his superiors and to the neighboring colonies for help, arguing that if New York fell, the others would fall also and that New York's resources alone were inadequate.[68] His appeal elicited many words of sympathy but little material assistance. Often his treasury was empty when the enemy was marching south, a predicament that called for instant action and ready funds. At such critical moments, the governor had only one recourse: turning to the wealthy councillors.

In this period, the governor's council was not merely an executive, legislative, and judicial branch of government. It functioned also as a private lending agency from which the governor could borrow money to carry out his responsibilities. Because the councillors extended loans or rendered themselves as security for loans from others, the New York government avoided bankruptcy, and the colony was spared from ruin. The vital role of the council was typically demonstrated at a council meeting on July 31, 1696:

His Excellency did communicate to the Council intelligence from the Frontiers that the Enemy are upon their March. . . .
His Excellency did desire their opinion what is to be done being there is no Money in the Coffers. . . .
His Excellency did declare his readyness to go provided they will find money to answer the necessary charge. Coll Cortlandt profferred his personal credit for £200 towards the expedition. Coll Bayard offered the same. Fred Phillips offers the same Lt. Coll Monville the same, Coll Heathcote the same.[69]

Interest on loans was generally 10 percent, or rarely 8 percent, which were of course exorbitant rates by London standards (6 percent) but were common in the colony, where money was scarce.[70] At first victualing the troops and lending money to the government were thought

---

68. Fletcher to Blathwayt, Sept. 10, 1692, and Fletcher's instructions to Col. Lodwick, June 13, 1693, N.Y. Col. Docs., III, 848, IV, 33; "Memorial to Commrs. of Trade and Plantations," Jan. 12, 1696, N.Y. Col. MSS, XLI, 13; "Memorial of Brooke and Nicolls to the Lords Justice of England," May 19, 1696, Livingston-Redmond MSS, Roll 2; extracts of council minutes of Feb. 15, 1692, July 11, 1695, and Sept. 6, 1695, in "N.Y. and the N.H. Grants," N.-Y. Hist. Soc., Colls., II (1869), 399–400, 423–424, 427.

69. Extracts of council minutes of July 31, 1696, Sept. 19, 1693, Mar. 14, 1695, and Apr. 16, 1695, in "N.Y. and the N.H. Grants," N.-Y. Hist. Soc., Colls., II (1869), 430 (quoted), 404–405, 419–420, 422–423; Calendar of State Papers, Col. Ser., XIII, 702, XIV, 322; Dixon Ryan Fox, Caleb Heathcote, Gentleman Colonist: The Story of a Career in the Province of New York, 1692–1721 (New York, 1926), 18–19; council minutes, Mar. 17, 1693, C.O. 1183/5, 304.

70. In 1695 one Peter Jacobs Marius advanced £100 to the government at 8 percent interest, but it was probably the only incident where the interest was that low. Extract of

to be a lucrative business. But once it was known that the certificates or warrants issued by the governor in return for a cash advance were not likely to be promptly and regularly redeemed, many moneyed men recoiled from such undertakings. For example, it took Livingston and Van Cortlandt six or seven years of pleading, and a trip across the Atlantic by Livingston, before some of their loans (£2,484 8s. 1½d.) were repaid.[71] In one instance, Van Cortlandt had to pay 8 percent interest on a loan of £110 that he had taken from Frederick Philipse. But he was pleased with even that high rate, writing to Livingston that he "could not obtain the same anywhere else."[72] Despairing of quick compensation, their pockets often empty, and pressed by their own creditors for payment, Livingston and Van Cortlandt more than once expressed a desire to quit victualing, but each time they were dissuaded from doing so by the council's "earnest request."[73] All in all, both army contracting and making loans to the debt-ridden government entailed great risk as well as great profit.

Preoccupied with the defense problem quite as much as Dongan had been, Governor Fletcher could not but be impressed by the readiness with which the gentlemen of the council advanced money "out of their own Fortunes." He was most appreciative of those who "answered an emergency when money was not in Treasury." In an age when the line between public service and the pursuit of private profit was undefined, and in a situation where failure or success in obtaining money meant the difference between the death and the survival of the province, it was natural for Fletcher to view these advances, though exorbitant in interest, as forms of public service.[74] He was not the only one who thought this way. As early as 1689, the officers of the two English companies camped in Albany and New York City declared that they had "never rec'd any pay, subsisting only through the Kindness of Mr. Stephanus Courtland

council minutes of Mar. 14, 1695, in "N.Y. and the N.H. Grants," N.-Y. Hist. Soc., *Colls.*, II (1869), 419–420.

71. Leder, *Livingston*, 81; "Memorandam of John Povey"(?), Jan. 1696, and Stephanus Van Cortlandt to Blathwayt, Jan. 7, 1692, both in Blathwayt Papers, Roll 2.

72. Stephanus Van Cortlandt to Robert Livingston, Oct. 5, 1691 (Dutch), Livingston-Redmond MSS, Roll 2.

73. Council minutes, Mar. 17, 1693, C.O. 1183/5, 304; Leder, *Livingston*, 83, 87, 91; minutes of May 7, 12–14, 1694, N.Y. Council Minutes, VI, 92, 94–97.

74. Benjamin Fletcher to Blathwayt, Feb. 14, 1693, Blathwayt Papers, Roll 2. It should be pointed out that Fletcher, like Henry Sloughter, received from the victualers 10 shillings per soldier as a gubernatorial perquisite. The record shows that from Oct. 1692 to Oct. 1694 Fletcher's income from this source amounted to £219 3s. 11½d. See "Memorandum of Steph: Van Cortlandt and Robt Livingston," June 1698, Livingston-Redmond MSS, Roll 2.

... and others who supply'd these necessities during their continuance there."[75] Van Cortlandt, who bought presents for the Indians, clothed and fed soldiers, provided beds and fire buckets for a garrison in the fort on Manhattan, paid New Jersey troops, and lent money to the government, was officially thanked several times by his colleagues in the council.[76]

On the political front, too, Fletcher was well satisfied with the performance of most of his councillors. He was especially fond of Van Cortlandt. The councillor stood by the governor and maintained good humor, at least in public, even when his pecuniary interest conflicted with the latter's policy. In this instance, as in others, his father's advice "not to quarrel with one's superiors" stood him in good stead.[77] Fletcher's major political problem was a bitter feud with Robert Livingston, brother-in-law of Van Cortlandt. Here, the political agility of Van Cortlandt was severely tested, but in the end, he emerged not only unscathed but amply rewarded. Since that quarrel had so much impact on both political development in the colony and the fortunes of the manorial proprietors, it merits our consideration.

Although the governor's failure to repay past loans was primarily at issue, the Fletcher-Livingston feud also involved other differences. Livingston was angry because the governor had diverted to defense uses money that had originally been appropriated by the assembly for repaying him and other creditors of the colony. He was also angry because in 1695 the governor had seized the brigantine *Orange* and its cargoes, of which he was part owner, for alleged violation of the Navigation Acts. Despairing of ever getting his certificates for debts amounting to £2,917 redeemed by Fletcher, he sailed for England to plead his case.[78] Once he arrived in London in July 1695, he quickly made a liaison with the Whig politicians who were gaining influence with the king. One of them was Richard Coote, earl of Bellomont, who was publicly known to be convinced of Leisler's innocence. With encouragement from Bellomont, Livingston seized every opportunity to denounce Fletcher before the authorities for maladministration, corruption, and dereliction, and he at-

75. Officers' petition to Commissioners for Trade and Plantations, Nov. 11, 1689, N.Y. Col. MSS, XXXVI, 133, 134.
76. N.Y. Council Minutes, VI, 209, VII, 220, 224. For Van Cortlandt's activity, see *ibid.*, VI, 138, 152, 157, 175, 192, VII, 25, 110, 117, 171, 178, 182, 220, 224, VIII, pt. 1, 4; "A List of Debts of the Government, 1694," N.Y. Col. MSS, XXXIX, 135, XXXVIII, 160; memorial of Stephanus Van Cortlandt, July 9, 1695, *ibid.*, XL, 38.
77. *Maria Van Rensselaer Correspondence*, 140.
78. *N.Y. Col. Docs.*, IV, 127–144.

tributed Fletcher's financial trouble to his mismanagement of funds.[79]

Fletcher, whose political affiliation was with the Tories, was furious with Livingston. Unable to control his rage, he wrote to two of his councillors who were on their way to London to represent the province. Beginning as a bookkeeper, said Fletcher, Livingston had "screwed himself into one of the most considerable estates in the province. . . . [I] hope you'll endevour to keep a man of such vile principles from sucking any more the blood of the Province, for he had a very spunge to it. . . . He had rather be called knave Livingston, then poor Livingston."[80]

Nevertheless, in August 1696, Livingston returned to New York triumphant, armed with a royal order commanding the governor to satisfy his "claims and demands" and with royal commissions of life appointment as collector of quitrents, receiver of excises, clerk of the peace and court of common pleas of the city and county of Albany, and secretary to the commissioners of Indian affairs. Together, these positions promised a yearly salary of £100.[81] In addition, Livingston presented to Fletcher a letter from Charles Talbot, duke of Shrewsbury, urging the governor to pay what was due to Livingston. Talbot was secretary of state for the Northern Department, a prominent leader of the Whigs, and a patron of the earl of Bellomont, and in Fletcher's mind, his letter was clear evidence of collusion between Livingston and the Whig politicians —an unforgivable treachery.[82] Spurning the royal orders, Fletcher and the council in September 1696 stripped Livingston of his local offices on the grounds that the man was "an aliene borne" and appointed instead Colonel Peter Schuyler, a member of the council and brother-in-law of Livingston. Fletcher also refused to satisfy the credit claim.[83]

The bitter feud between the governor and Livingston put Van Cortlandt in an extremely difficult position. As his brother-in-law's partner in

79. On Apr. 30, 1695, Parliament reversed the attainders and convictions of Leisler and Milborne. For Livingston's contact with Bellomont, see Leder, *Livingston*, 102–103.

80. Benjamin Fletcher to Messrs. Brooke and Nicolls, Dec. 20, 1696, *N.Y. Col. Docs.*, IV, 251.

81. Copy of minutes of the Privy Council meetings, Nov. 21, 1695, and Jan. 16, 1696, Livingston-Redmond MSS, Roll 2.

82. Benjamin Fletcher to William Blathwayt, Aug. 22, 1696, Blathwayt Papers, Roll 2; duke of Shrewsbury to George Harris, Feb. 11, 1690, and to Maj. Wyth, Feb. 15, 1690, William J. Hardy, ed., *Calendar of State Papers, Domestic Series, of the Reign of William and Mary, 1689–1690, Preserved in the Public Record Office* (London, 1895), 456, 464; John C. Rainbolt, "A 'great and usefull designe': Bellomont's Proposal for New York, 1698–1701," *New-York Historical Society Quarterly*, LIII (1969), 334.

83. Council minutes, Sept. 10, 15, 17, 1696, N.Y. Col. MSS, XL, 195, 197, 197b; "Account of the Excise from the 25th day of March 1696 to the 17th day September following," Livingston-Redmond MSS, Roll 2.

victualing and trade, Van Cortlandt had prayed that Livingston would attain the objectives of the trip, that is, a settlement of their victualing account.[84] But it was probably a disappointment to him that Livingston had involved himself in the morass of partisan politics. As a leader of the anti-Leislerians, Van Cortlandt could not approve of his brother-in-law's sudden political turnabout, which appeared to be merely for business interests. He therefore joined Fletcher and his colleagues in condemning Livingston. The governor reported, "The Gentlemen of the Council here particularly his brother in Law the Deputy Auditor (Van Cortlandt) were much surprized at [Livingston's] proceedings" and "Coll: Cortland is ready to testify that I ow'd him [Livingston] not a farthing when he left this place."[85] Van Cortlandt's demeanor at the expense of a blood tie obviously impressed the governor.

There were several others who in different capacities ably served the governor. The most distinguished among them was Colonel Peter Schuyler, an anti-Leislerian. As commander of the Albany County militia, Schuyler rallied the friendly Indians and led many expeditions against the enemy.[86] Another impressive figure was Dirck Wessells Ten Broeck. During the Dongan and Andros administrations, he made three trips to Canada on official business, indicating that he was active in English diplomacy. Together with Kiliaen Van Rensselaer, he supported the garrison at Albany during the Leislerian revolution. His expenses ($£1,105$ 2s. 9d.) in these undertakings remained unpaid throughout Fletcher's governorship.[87] Nevertheless, the governor found him always ready to promote the imperial cause. No measure was more illustrative of Fletcher's confidence in these three local leaders than his entrusting them in 1696 with plenary power to spend allocated funds and to deploy three companies of regular troops as they saw fit for the frontier defense.[88]

Godfredius Delius, minister of the Dutch Reformed Church at Al-

84. Stephanus Van Cortlandt to Blathwayt, Dec. 3, 1694, Blathwayt Papers, Roll 2. In this letter Van Cortlandt asked Blathwayt to help Livingston. For Van Cortlandt's trade partnership with Livingston, see Stephanus Van Cortlandt to Francis Nicholson, Apr. 6, 1691, ibid.; Leder, Livingston, 90; "Invoice of Eight bundles Dear and bar Sins and one case with Beaver and Peltry . . . ," Sept. 7, 1695, Livingston-Redmond MSS, Roll 2; May 22, 1695, entry in journal of Livingston's voyage, ibid.

85. Benjamin Fletcher to Blathwayt, Aug. 22, 1696, Blathwayt Papers, Roll 2; Fletcher to Blathwayt, July 13, 1696, N.Y. Col. Docs., IV, 165.

86. Benjamin Fletcher to House of Representatives, Mar. 29, 1697, N.Y. Col. MSS, XLI, 53.

87. Petition of Dirck Wessells Ten Broeck and Kiliaen Van Rensselaer, Mar. 14, 1695, ibid., XL, 11; petition of Ten Broeck, 1691, ibid., XXXVII, 131; "A List of Debts of the Government," 1694, ibid., XXXIX, 135.

88. N.Y. Col. Laws, I, 369–371; N.Y. Col. Docs., IV, 59–62.

bany, also served the governor well. The remarkable success of the French in extending their influence among the Indians had been very much due to the proselytizing activity of Jesuit missionaries.[89] This lesson was driven home to the New York governors, who, beginning with Sloughter, took "more interest" in missionary diplomacy. The spiritual conversion of the Indians to Protestantism, it was hoped, would be accompanied by their attachment to the English interest, thus undercutting French strength in the frontier. Delius met this imperial need by translating portions of the Bible into the Indian language, by converting two hundred Indians, mostly Mohawks, to Christianity, and, more important, by providing intelligence on the situation of the French and the hostile Indians to the governors.[90] Fletcher, who looked upon the fidelity of the Five Nations as the pillar of the security of the province, recognized Delius's usefulness and often consulted him on defense matters. On August 8, 1696, the governor appointed Delius, Ten Broeck, Schuyler, and Evert Bancker, an Indian trader, to be the commissioners of Indian affairs.[91]

When these prominent provincial leaders came forward with petitions for land grants, Fletcher naturally obliged. As long as the war was on and as long as he wanted to engage them further "in his interest," it was absolutely necessary for the governor to reward them.[92] Under the circumstances, land and privileges were the best prizes he could dispense. He also reasoned, as his predecessors had, that the granting of frontier land would help extend English territory toward the French, which in turn "might prevent the French from destroying Schenectady, as they had done before, and so turne to his Majesty's account." Some of the land applicants, who were familiar with the governor's thinking, noted this in their petitions.[93]

89. David Schuyler to earl of Bellomont, Aug. 17, 1700, Hastings, ed., *Ecclesiastical Records of N.Y.*, II, 1374–1376.

90. Henry Sloughter to William Stoughton, Dorchester, Eng., 1691, N.Y. Col. MSS, XXXVII, 160; "Order on Robert Livingston," June 11, 1691, *ibid.*, 163; report of Stephanus Van Cortlandt and Nicholas Bayard, Aug. 16, 1693, *ibid.*, XXXIX, 91a; Godfredius Delius to Benjamin Fletcher, Jan. 12, 1692, and May 24, 1695, N.Y. *Col. Docs.*, IV, 78–79, 125, also, 88, 92–96; Hastings, ed., *Ecclesiastical Records of N.Y.*, II, 1007, 1010–1011, 1038–1039, 1055, 1065–1066, 1305–1306, 1309.

91. Benjamin Fletcher to Godfredius Delius, Apr. 9, 1700, Hastings, ed., *Ecclesiastical Records of N.Y.*, II, 135; N.Y. *Col. Docs.*, IV, 175, 177, 363.

92. "Report of the Board of Trade on the Affairs of the Province of New-York," Oct. 19, 1698, N.Y. *Col. Docs.*, IV, 392.

93. Fletcher's answer to the charges against his extravagant grants, Dec. 24, 1698, N.Y. *Col. Docs.*, IV, 447–448; petition of Caleb Heathcote and Augustin Graham for land upon the Hudson River, Feb. 20, 1696, N.Y. Col. MSS, XL, 132; Stephanus Van Cortlandt's petition for a manor patent, June 17, 1697, N.Y. Land Papers, II, 245; Godfredius Delius

In addition to reasons of political patronage, Fletcher turned to land grants because, like his predecessors, he faced the difficult task of peopling the colony. Moreover, he was mortified to witness that, in spite of his appeals, New York inhabitants steadily deserted by the hundreds in order to avoid the war and heavy taxes. The prospect of recruiting colonists for the wild frontier was more dismal than ever.[94] The imperatives of defense called for the kind of farmers who were willing to stay and defend their community. Yet, given the exhausted state of public finances, promotion of settlement under direct government auspices seemed out of the question. Fletcher's alternative, then, was to depend on private land developers for the essential task. In 1694 Captain John Evans, commander of the British warship *Richmond*, argued in his petition for land that he "hath brought over onto this province a Considerable Estate which Hee is inclined to employ for the settlement and cultivation of vacant and Unappropriated Land . . . for which end He is Intended to send for a considerable Number of Poor familyes from Ireland." That Evans's petition was granted on the basis of this argument is suggestive of the nature of the governor's land policy.[95]

During his governorship from 1692 to 1698, Fletcher made what his political opponents called "extravagant" grants of land to a number of individuals. These grants amounted to several million acres. Significantly, almost all of the beneficiaries either were members of his council or were men closely associated with his war efforts, such as Van Cortlandt, Philipse, Bayard, Schuyler, Delius, Ten Broeck, and Captain Evans. The bulk of the lands in question were situated in the northern and western frontiers exposed to French incursion, and in some instances, as we shall see, the grantees had purchased much of the property prior to their being awarded the total grant. Fletcher, like Governor Dongan, used two forms of patents: one a manorial lordship patent and the other a common land patent.

One of the five manorial patents the governor issued was Philipsburgh (June 12, 1693) in Westchester County (see the map on p. 68).[96]

---

to the classis of Amsterdam, Oct. 21, 1700, Hastings, ed., *Ecclesiastical Records of N.Y.*, II, 1416–1417; Frederick Philipse's petition for a manor patent, 1693, N.Y. Col. MSS, XXXIX, 26.

94. The Reverend John Miller, Anglican chaplain of the two British Companies of Foot, observed in 1695 that "the outparts of the Province (where the best land is) towards Canada are so harrassed by the French and their Indians that men are fearfull to plant and dwell there." Miller, *Description of New York*, 45, 54.

95. John Evans's petition, Mar. 3, 1694, N.Y. Col. MSS, XXXIX, 137.

96. Four other manors were: St. George (Oct. 2, 1693) for Col. William Smith, a

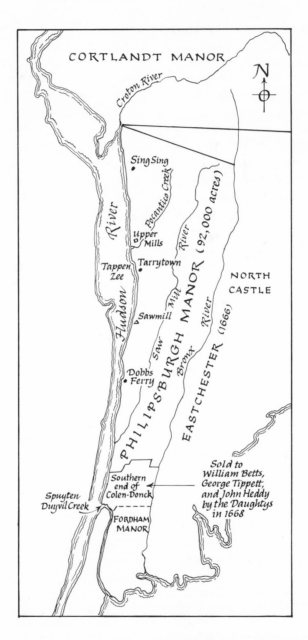

**Philipsburgh Manor, 1696.** Adjusted from "A plan of the Manor of Philipsburgh" (1783) in J. Thomas Scharf, ed., *History of Westchester County, New York, Including Morrisania, Kings Bridge, and West Farms* (Philadelphia, 1886), I, 161. (Drawn by Richard J. Stinely.)

Philipsburgh was created out of a series of purchases that Frederick Philipse had made over the years.[97] His investment in land began in 1672 with the purchase, in partnership with two others, of the land in what was then known as Youncker Van der Donck's patroonship at Yonkers. From this base, he expanded his holdings northward and southward as opportunity presented. In 1680 he secured from the Indians the lands around Pocantico creek in present-day north Tarrytown; the next year, adjacent land southward in Mount Pleasant; in 1682, another tract toward the Weghqueghsick (Dobbs Ferry), and still another southward to the great rock called "Mochkeurisckassin" joining the northern boundary of the lower Yonker Plantation that belonged to several settlers.[98] These were all confirmed and granted by a royal patent in December 1684. In the next two years, he bought off his partners' shares in the former Van der Donck property. Three years later, he secured from his eldest son Philip a two-mile-long tract called Sincksink (Sing Sing), which lay between the Croton River and the land he had already bought. In 1687 and again in 1692 he acquired several hundred acres at Tappan on the west side of the Hudson River for the purpose of establishing a ferry across the river.[99] All these tracts contained in total about 92,000 acres. The Philipsburgh Manor patent of 1693 incorporated the lands into a lordship domain with the privileges of court leet and court baron and of advowson for its proprietor. The patent also gave Philipse additional land, approximately a hundred acres called Paparinemo at Spuyten Duyvil creek, with authority to erect a drawbridge and collect tolls from its users.

A second manorial grant in Westchester County, the Manor of Cortlandt, consisted partly of several purchases Van Cortlandt had made since 1683, but mostly of newly patented land granted in 1697. In the

councillor; Fletcher (Sept. 6, 1694) for Capt. John Evans; Morrisania (Dec. 9, 1694) for Col. Lewis Morris, merchant; and Kingsfield (Dec. 12, 1695) for Nicholas Bayard, a councillor. N.Y. Council Minutes, VII, 19, 109, N.Y. State Lib.; N.Y. Col. MSS, XXXIX, 101, 113, 154.

97. Petition of William Merrit, Frederick Philipse, and Daniel Whithead, Mar. 1, 1694, N.Y. Col. MSS, XXXIX, 138.

98. This Yonker Plantation (about 2,500 acres) was sold by Elias Doughty to William Betts, John Heddy, and George Tippett on July 6, 1668. About 10 families owned the tract when the Manor of Philipsburgh was granted. See "A Plan of the Manor of Philipsburg in the County of Westchester in the State of New York ... 1785, with the addition of the Southern end of Colen-Donck," Scharf, ed., History of Westchester County, I, 161; petition of Samuel Hitchcocks and two others, [1691?], N.Y. Col. MSS, XXXVIII, 55.

99. N.Y. Col. MSS, XXIX, 26; "Abstract of the Boundarys of Fredrick Philips his patent according to the Several Indian Deeds, for which it was granted, 1704," "Real Estate, 3198," 38, 189, 43, Museum of the City of New York; Deed Book B, 201–222, 233, Westchester County Clerk's Office, White Plains, N.Y.

previous chapter we noted Van Cortlandt's acquisitions of land from the Indians around and at Haverstraw, Verplanck's Point, and Salisbury Island, which were confirmed by Governor Dongan in 1685.[100] His holdings were expanded a decade later when he bought from Major Hugh MacGregor of New York City lands in the vicinity of Peekskill.[101] Sometime before the manor patent was issued, he obtained from an Indian a tract "in the rear" of his domain on the Croton River. In addition, in 1689 Van Cortlandt had bought another piece of land south of the river. These several tracts were not contiguous. However, the manor patent overcame the gaps by extending the domain due east twenty miles from both Anthony's Nose and the northern bounds of Philipsburgh into the woods to the "supposed" Connecticut boundary. This rectangular-shaped manor in the northern part of Westchester County contained about 86,000 acres (see the map on p. 71). The manor proprietor, his heirs, or his assignees were granted the right to send a representative to the assembly beginning twenty years after the date of acquisition, in addition to the usual lordship privileges of courts leet and baron and of advowson.[102]

The four manors under study—Rensselaerswyck, Livingston, Philipsburgh, and Cortlandt—owed their rise to a peculiar conjunction of political, economic, and defense conditions in New York. In a frontier society where a transplanted authority was not fully integrated with the populace, the governors found it convenient to govern through local men of wealth and prominence. This method of governance was perhaps the only available option, because the province contained much conquered area and many alien inhabitants who, though legally assimilated into the English empire, were still far from being emotionally committed to the proprietary or royal authority in the last quarter of the seventeenth century. Moreover, the province was threatened from within by the whiggish proclivities of the people and from without by the French and by neighboring colonies. The governors needed assistance from the Van Rensselaers, the Philipses, the Schuylers, the Livingstons, the Van Cortlandts, and the like. The creation of the manors and the granting of great patents

100. For Stephanus Van Cortlandt's land purchases up to 1685, see Deed Book A, 128, Westchester Co. Clerk's Office; Van Cortlandt Papers, V1694, Sleepy Hollow Restorations Lib.; Patent Book 7: 177–190, and Patent Book 5: 306–309, Office of the Secretary of State of New York, Albany.

101. The deed is dated July 13, 1695, Patent Book 9: 351, Office of N.Y. Sec. of State. Originally, the land was bought by Maj. Hugh MacGregor on July 12, 1688. Cortlandt Manor Papers, Van Cortlandt Family Papers, N.-Y. Hist. Soc.

102. N.Y. Land Papers, II, 245; Patent Book 7: 165–169, Office of N.Y. Sec. of State.

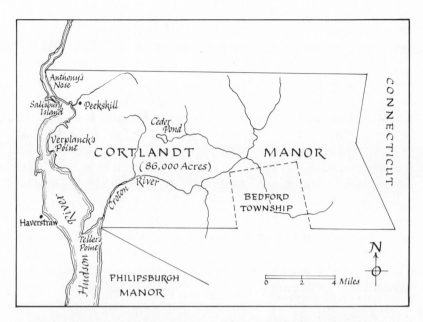

**Cortlandt Manor, 1697.** Adjusted from a map in the Cadwallader Colden Papers, New-York Historical Society, New York. (Drawn by Richard J. Stinely.)

were expected to answer the imperatives of defending and governing the colony and to engage distinguished families further in the prerogative interest.

## The Earl of Bellomont and the "Extravagant" Grants

In the middle of 1697 the manorial proprietors were full of hope for better days ahead. King William's War visibly tapered off, and in September 1697 the Treaty of Ryswick restored peace to the frontiers. Refugees from the war were trickling back to their devastated plantations. Peace was expected to attract immigrants to the colony, and land values would accordingly soar—a delightful prospect for the landowners. The mercantile community, too, shared this euphoric note. Thanks to Governor Fletcher's late connivance at privateering to Madagascar and Curaçao and his relatively tolerant attitude toward violations of the navigation laws (despite the *Orange* case), New York City had become a bustling nest for privateers. In the three years from 1696 through 1698, its trade volume quadrupled, the number of merchants expanded, and the population as a whole grew considerably. Edward Randolph, a roving eye of British mercantilism, was amazed at the contrasts between the city he saw in 1698 and the city he remembered in 1689.[103]

But the expectations of both landed men and merchants were soon shattered by political developments following the dismissal of Fletcher in 1697. The earl of Bellomont, new governor of New York, Massachusetts, and New Hampshire, arrived in New York City on April 2, 1698. Jacob Leisler, Jr., also returned from London about the same time with an act of Parliament exonerating his father of attainder and treason. The appearance of the two men alarmed the anti-Leislerians, who had controlled the previous administration. Predictably, the Leislerians were jubilant and revengeful. So were the trimmers like Robert Livingston, a victim of political ostracism during the preceding two years.[104]

For a month Bellomont did nothing except familiarize himself with the state of affairs. On April 10 he commissioned Van Cortlandt and Bayard to inspect the fort on Manhattan and to make a report—an indication that Bellomont was not yet embroiled in factionalism. But he soon concluded that he could not get "any assistance" from the anti-Leislerian councillors, who were known to be caballing daily at Fletcher's lodging. Although at the council meeting of May 17 the governor proposed to increase the number of assemblymen from the current nineteen to thirty, presumably "in order to put it out of the power of any future Governor to make a party," he had by then clearly become as zealous a Leislerian partisan as the Leislerians themselves. Now he saw provincial politics in Manichaean terms, a struggle between the "sober, virtuous" Leislerians and the evil-minded anti-Leislerians.[105] In his report of May 8 to the Board of Trade, he spelled out his intentions. He would stamp out illicit trade and privateering and dismiss those councillors who were breaking the Navigation Acts.[106]

Stemming partly from his reformist impulses and partly from his personal pique against Fletcher, Bellomont's campaign produced radical changes in the council and in local governing units, increasing the Leislerian influence. His first victims were Captain John Evans, a man enjoy-

103. Edward Randolph to Blathwayt, Sept. 12, 1698, Blathwayt Papers, Roll 2; earl of Bellomont to Lords of Trade, May 8, 1698, N.Y. Col. Docs., IV, 302.

104. Leder, Livingston, 126–127; Edward Randolph to Blathwayt, May 12, 1698, Blathwayt Papers, Roll 2.

105. Bellomont to Lords of Trade, May 25, 1698, Calendar of State Papers, Col. Ser., XVI, 235; Bellomont to Lords of Trade, Sept. 21, 1698, N.Y. Col. Docs., IV, 375.

106. Bellomont to Lords of Trade, May 8, 1698, N.Y. Col. Docs., IV, 302.

ing "the great friendship" of Fletcher, and William Nicolls, a member of the council. In early May, both were clapped in jail, the skipper upon suspicion of harboring pirates on board the *Richmond*, and the councillor on the charge that he had acted as a broker between Fletcher and some pirates five years before.[107] They were then stripped of their offices. Fletcher, too, was accused of protecting pirates at a fee of £100 per head, and Bellomont ordered that the evidence against the ex-governor be sent home with him for a hearing.[108] Bellomont steadily widened the purge, so that by the end of September a majority of Fletcher's thirteen councillors were removed. In their stead, he swore in two anti-Leislerians turned Leislerians, Robert Livingston and James Graham, the attorney general, and three die-hard Leislerians, Samuel Staats, Abraham De Peyster, and Robert Walters. To root out the tory (anti-Leislerian) influence even at the local level, he replaced almost all the justices and sheriffs who held commissions from Fletcher. He seized and condemned several ships and their cargoes for violations of the trade laws. All these actions, according to Van Cortlandt, "cocked up" the enemies of the previous administration.[109]

One of the victims of the Leislerian ascendancy was Frederick Philipse, the oldest member of the council and the richest merchant-landowner in the province. Philipse followed the unfolding of Bellomont's policy with dismay, for it threatened to ruin his maritime commerce, which rested on a flotilla of ten ships, to say nothing of his political prominence. The evidence, though fragmentary, indicates that he and his son Adolph were heavily involved in illicit trade for pirated goods.[110] They thus joined the "mutinous" merchants complaining against Bellomont that they were "Free born" and would not pay custom duties.[111] As the enmity of the governor toward the anti-Leislerian councillors

107. Bellomont to Lords of Admiralty, May 18, 1698, *Calendar of State Papers, Col. Ser.*, XVI, 229–230.

108. Stephanus Van Cortlandt to Blathwayt, May 28, 1698, Blathwayt Papers, Roll 2; *N.Y. Col. Docs.*, IV, 304, 307–309, 314–315, 318, 320–322.

109. Stephanus Van Cortlandt to Blathwayt, July 18, Oct. 27, 1698, Blathwayt Papers, Roll 2; Edward Randolph to Blathwayt, Sept. 12, 1698, *ibid.*; Bellomont to Lords of Trade, June 22, Oct. 21, 1698, *N.Y. Col. Docs.*, IV, 321, 398–399.

110. Frederick Philipse to Capt. Adam Balldridge at St. Mary, Feb. 25, 1695, and Philipse's order to Capt. Samuel Burges, June 9, 1698 (typescripts), Philipse Papers, Sleepy Hollow Restorations Lib.; "Copy of the Examinations of the Masters and Mariners of the Frederick (belonging to Frederick Philipse) seized at Hambrough" and "Copy of Several Depositions relating to a Ship belonging to Mr. Fredk Philips of N. Yorke," received by the Board of Trade, Sept. 12, 1698, C.O. 1040/5, 68–69; Board of Trade to Lords Justices, Oct. 1, 1698, *N.Y. Col. Docs.*, IV, 390–391.

111. Edward Randolph to Blathwayt, Sept. 12, 1698, Blathwayt Papers, Roll 2.

mounted, Frederick Philipse found his presence on the council increasingly uncomfortable. When Bellomont fired Bayard and four others from the council, Philipse expressed his wish also to be dismissed, which the governor quickly granted.[112]

Possibly due to Livingston's influence, Van Cortlandt and Schuyler were spared from the purge. Van Cortlandt, though a staunch anti-Leislerian and brother-in-law of Frederick Philipse,[113] not only was spared the purge during these early months of Bellomont's regime but was given the highly remunerative post of receiver general in June 1698. A similar favor was bestowed on Schuyler, although he too had been a favorite of Fletcher. That both Van Cortlandt and Schuyler, two out of three holdover councillors, were brothers-in-law of Livingston suggests that Livingston had a hand in their "good luck."[114] At one time, the governor declared, "the Government has no small obligation to Mr. Livingston, for were it not for him, the four Companys here had deserted long since. . . . I find nobody willing to subsist the companies but Mr. Livingston, who purely to serve the government and prevent the disgrace of the soldiers desertion did undertake it. . . ." The governor's laudatory opinion of the merchant-landowner was to be expected in view of their common hostility toward Fletcher and, perhaps more important, of their joint investment in Captain William Kidd's privateering against the pirates.[115] Thus advantaged, Livingston seems to have managed to shelter his relations from disgrace.

Other factors contributed to Van Cortlandt's success with the new governor. Generally, he acted in a temporizing manner, at least outwardly: he was too timorous to make noises even when he was angry with Bellomont's political witch-hunting and enforcement of the trade

---

112. Minutes of Sept. 29, 1698, N.Y. Council Minutes, VIII, 64; Stephanus Van Cortlandt to Blathwayt, Oct. 27, 1698, Blathwayt Papers, Roll 2.

113. In 1692 Frederick Philipse married Catherine Van Cortlandt, sister of Stephanus. This was the second marriage for both. D. T. Valentine, *Manual of the Corporation of the City of New-York* (New York, 1865), 605.

114. When Bellomont shuffled the Indian commissionership, Schuyler and Livingston were put in the place of Dirck Wessells Ten Broeck and Godfredius Delius. Bellomont to Schuyler and Livingston, Aug. 1, 1698, *Calendar of State Papers, Col. Ser.*, XVI, 432–433; "General Account of Victualling his majesties forces," May 1, 1698–Nov. 1, 1700, Livingston-Redmond MSS, Roll 2; minutes of Oct. 6, 1698, N.Y. Council Minutes, VIII, 67–68; Leder, *Livingston*, 137.

115. Bellomont to Lords of Trade, Oct. 21, 1698, *N.Y. Col. Docs.*, IV, 399; articles of agreement among Bellomont, Livingston, and Kidd, Oct. 10, 1695, *ibid.*, 762–765; "Articles of Agreement made Feb. 7, 1695/6" among Livingston, Kidd, and Richard Blackham, Livingston-Redmond MSS, Roll 2; Maurice Cranston, *John Locke: A Biography* (New York, 1957), 421.

laws. Together with another opportunist, James Graham, he fed Bellomont damaging information against Fletcher. He also tried to persuade
Bayard to mend his fences with the new governor. Yet, in private he
vigorously defended his former superior and denounced the new governor
for dismissing all "the fittest," "best experiencest," "qualified," "good,"
and "honest" people from offices.[116] This two-faced posture enabled him
to float on the political vortex. Furthermore, Bellomont probably thought
it prudent to keep Van Cortlandt as an ally, for the New Yorker had good
connections in London. Van Cortlandt had been the deputy auditor of
the province since 1688 for William Blathwayt, auditor-general of the
plantations and a member of the Board of Trade. Blathwayt's influence
had declined because of his Toryism, but he was still a powerful official
to be reckoned with. He highly appreciated Van Cortlandt's services and
expert knowledge in revenue matters.[117] As long as Van Cortlandt served
ably in that role, Bellomont perhaps could not afford to mistreat him and
irk Blathwayt as well.

For the anti-Leislerians, the worst was yet to come. Not content
with political purges and crackdowns on illicit trade, Bellomont soon let
loose his vengeance against the "extravagant" land titles granted by the
preceding governors. Started originally as a response to the request of a
local government and as a political measure to punish a few of Fletcher's
favorites, Bellomont's land policy gradually blossomed into what he called
a "great and usefull designe" to restructure provincial society.[118] As might
be expected, it drove every landed man, including the manorial lords,
into the opposition camp. The ambitious design of the new governor was
the first and probably the greatest challenge the landed interests ever
encountered during the colonial period.

The initial impetus for the move to destroy the great patents came
from the Albany burghers. Jealous of their traditional monopoly of the
fur trade, the Albanians always guarded against any scheme that might
chase away the trading Indians—the source of peltry—from the Albany

---

116. Bellomont to Lords of Trade, Nov. 8 and 12, 1698, *N.Y. Col. Docs.*, IV, 418–421,
427–428; Stephanus Van Cortlandt to Blathwayt, May 28, July 18, Sept. 21, Oct. 27,
1698, Blathwayt Papers, Roll 2.
117. Thanks to Van Cortlandt's efforts, in Mar. 1693 the council resolved to allow
Blathwayt 5 percent of the whole revenue of the province. In return Blathwayt allowed Van
Cortlandt two-fifths of his salary for auditing the province's revenue. Edward Randolph to
Blathwayt, Oct. 20, 1692, and Chidley Brooke to Blathwayt, Mar. 7, 1693, Blathwayt
Papers, Roll 1; Van Cortlandt to Blathwayt, Dec. 3, 1694, *ibid.*
118. Rainbolt, "A 'great and usefull designe,'" *N.-Y. Hist. Soc. Qtly.*, LIII (1969),
341.

area. They opposed settlement westward and northward of Albany because they feared it would hinder the flow of native goods to the city.[119] As early as January 1698, several months before Bellomont's arrival, the Albanians protested Governor Fletcher's late patenting of two hundred square miles of Mohawk land, about fifty miles north of Albany, to Delius, Ten Broeck (mayor of Albany), Schuyler, and two others. The common council of the city sought in vain to persuade the grantees to surrender these lands to it. In February 1698 the city petitioned Fletcher against the patent, complaining that it would bring "utter Ruine to the general trade and commerce of this Citty." But nothing came of the petitioning. In early May they tried again, this time by sending Jan Janse Bleeker, recorder of the city, and Robert Livingston on the same mission to the new governor. Almost simultaneously, they opened negotiations with Henry Van Rensselaer, brother of Kiliaen Van Rensselaer (lord of Rensselaerswyck), to obtain for the city the release of his patent of six square miles at Schaghticoke, which adjoined five hundred acres of city property located about ten miles north of Albany. When this negotiation became deadlocked over a minor difference, the city quickly instructed the agents to procure the revocation of the Schaghticoke patent.[120]

Meanwhile, the city succeeded in inducing two of the alleged Indian proprietors of the Mohawk land, called Hendrick and Joseph, to depose before Bellomont and Graham that they had conveyed the land to no one. When questioned about their marks and seals on a bill of sale of the land dated July 8, 1697, the natives asserted that they were "cheated out." Further, the Indians complained about Kingsfield Manor patent, some twenty-four miles northwest of Schenectady and granted to Nicholas Bayard in 1695, on the grounds that they had "never sold" the tract in question.[121] The city also had the Albany County representatives to the assembly write a memorial (dated June 6, 1698) to the governor. In this memorial they turned an essentially local interest into an imperial issue, arguing that the grants of the frontier lands would compel the Mohawk nation to desert New York and "fly to the French," with disas-

---

119. Robert Livingston to Lords of Trade, May 13, 1701, *Doc. Hist. N.Y.*, IV, 873.
120. Schaghticoke Patent was granted in Dec. 1697. N.Y. Land Papers, II, 262. For the proceedings of the Albany city government in these affairs, see the "City Records" of Albany, Jan. 26, 28, Feb. 4, 7, 17, Apr. 11, May 7, 9, 1698, in Munsell, ed., *Annals of Albany*, III, 30–34.
121. "Deposition of Henry and Joseph two of the Maquase nation," May 31, 1698, *N.Y. Col. Docs.*, IV, 345–346. For Nicholas Bayard's landjobbing see petitions, Sept. 28, and Dec. 12, 1695, N.Y. Col. MSS, XL, 75, 113; Hastings, ed., *Ecclesiastical Records of N.Y.*, II, 1318.

trous consequences to the trade, revenue, and security of the province.[122]

The timing of the Albany protest could not have been more propitious, for Bellomont was then busily collecting evidence against Fletcher, and die-hard Leislerians like Staats, De Peyster, Walters, and Abraham Gouverneur were at the same time bent on destroying their antagonists, who invariably held large landed estates. Sympathy from the new governor was assured also because the predicament of the city closely paralleled one of his own. He held a grudge against his predecessor for having rented away the gubernatorial perquisites of the "King's Farm" and part of the "King's Garden," the former to Trinity Church in New York City and the latter to Caleb Heathcote, an ex-councillor. Misguided by distorted information furnished by Graham and Leislerian partisans, Bellomont saw in the leases and the extravagant grants nothing but Fletcher's malicious and premeditated vendetta against himself. In other words, he imagined that Fletcher had made these grants only after he learned of the appointment of Bellomont and that his purpose had been to "engage a considerable part of men in his interest" and deliberately to render the government of New York "so much more uneasy" to his successor.[123] Here Bellomont was not entirely correct, for the majority of the grants had been made long before May 1697, when Fletcher was advised of Bellomont's appointment.[124] Bellomont's propensity to perceive the situation in personal and partisan terms was undoubtedly encouraged by the vindictive Leislerians, which unfortunately blinded the new governor to the military, political, and economic context of his predecessor's land policy.

By July 1698, Bellomont had made up his mind to destroy all the Fletcher grants. He placed this task "above all others" in his governing policy. Although the decision to vacate the titles originated from personal and partisan motives, his official explanation based it on a combination of legal, political, and public welfare considerations. First, Bellomont claimed, the patents had been issued by his predecessor in violation of

---

122. Memorial of Jan Janse Bleeker and Ryer Schermerhoorn, June 6, 1698, *N.Y. Col. Docs.*, IV, 330–331.

123. James Graham to Bellomont, June 30, 1698, *Calendar of State Papers, Col. Ser.*, XVI, 304–306; Bellomont to Lords of Trade, July 1, 1698, and Lords of Trade to Lords Justice, Oct. 19, 1698, *N.Y. Col. Docs.*, IV, 334–335, 392.

124. The sequence of events leading to Bellomont's appointment was as follows: On Mar. 16, 1697, the duke of Shrewsbury, secretary of state for the Northern Department, wrote the Lords of Trade directing them to prepare a commission and instructions for Bellomont as governor of New York, Massachusetts, and New Hampshire. On June 18 the king issued the commission. *N.Y. Col. Docs.*, IV, 261, 266–273, 284–292.

procedural rules, that is, without consulting the attorney general of the province. Second, because of the extravagant grants, he and his successors would have no more land with which to reward "the services of subjects in peace or War."[125] Bellomont was obviously unmindful of Fletcher's desperate need to reward those who had served British interests in time of war. His third and perhaps most interesting justification was that the oligopolistic ownership of the huge tracts would keep the province from being settled.[126] Implicit in this reasoning was the idea that immigrants would be unwilling to settle unless they could possess a freehold estate. Politically whiggish and intellectually Harringtonian, Bellomont apotheosized the virtues of freeholders and their beneficial effect on political culture.[127] He expressed his presuppositions unmistakably when he wrote:

If it were not for Collonel Fletcher's intolerable corrupt selling away the lands of this Province, it would outthrive the Massachusets Province and quickly outdoe them in people and trade. The people are so cramp'd here for want of land that several families . . . remov'd to the new country (a name they give to Pennsylvania and the Jersies;) for, to use Mr. Graham's expression to me and that often repeated too, what man will be such a fool to become a base tenant to Mr. Dellius Collonel Schuyler, Mr. Livingston (and so he ran through whole role of our mighty landgraves) when for crossing Hudson's river that man can for a song purchase a good freehold in the Jersies?[128]

Though he himself was the owner of the 77,000-acre Kenmare estate in Ireland, which he had acquired as a political spoil in 1696, Bellomont felt no qualm or sense of inconsistency in condemning the great landed estates in New York as an impediment to the public welfare. At any rate, his projected campaign received a strong endorsement from the Lords Justices.[129]

125. Bellomont to Lords of Trade, July 1, Oct. 19, Nov. 28, 1698, *ibid.*, 334, 391–392, 434. Bellomont reported that Fletcher had granted away three-fourths of the province, or approximately seven million acres. His attorney general, James Graham, stated that Fletcher "granted away every foot of Land that was to be disposed of in the Government." Thomas Weaver, a Leislerian member of the council, said exactly the same. Needless to say, they all exaggerated the situation. "Mr. Weaver's Statements to the Board of Trade," Sept. 27, 1698, *ibid.*, 384.

126. Bellomont to Lords of Trade, July 1, 1698, *ibid.*, 334.

127. A good account of the "independent yeoman" ideology expounded by Harrington and others can be seen in J. G. A. Pocock, "Machiavelli, Harrington, and English Political Ideologies in the Eighteenth Century," *WMQ*, 3d Ser., XXII (1965), 547–583. Regarding Bellomont's yeoman rhetoric, see Lords of Trade to Lords Justice, Oct. 19, 21, 1698, *N.Y. Col. Docs.*, IV, 393, 397.

128. Bellomont to Lords of Trade, Nov. 28, 1700, *N.Y. Col. Docs.*, IV, 791.

129. Bellomont received this estate as a result of the Whig redistribution of Irish lands

Sometime between July 1698 and April 1699, however, Bellomont's attitude changed significantly. He stopped thinking of his campaign purely in partisan terms and began to consider it more and more as a wise economic, social, and defense design. Underscoring this change was his inclusion in his blacklist of all the great patents above two thousand acres, regardless of the political affiliation of the patentee.[130] His plans for indiscriminate assault on the large landed estates seem to have been spurred by two considerations. One was an instruction from the Board of Trade calling for the procurement of naval stores for the British navy, which, Bellomont figured, could be accomplished through the exploitation of the lands toward Canada. He proposed a scheme in which British soldiers would play a central role: in time of peace about a thousand troops would be placed on the northern frontier, where they would be employed in production of naval stores.[131] Upon termination of military service, the soldiers would be granted varying sizes of freeholds according to their ranks—four hundred acres for captains, two hundred acres for lieutenants, and fifty acres for corporals—on the condition that the lands were unalienable except to the crown. For the rest of the province, he hoped to create a middling yeoman society at the expense of the large landed estates.[132] He deplored that the "whole Province is given away to about thirty persons in effect." To prevent like occurrences in the future, he proposed "a restriction on all Governors never to grant above 1000 acres to any man whatsoever without particular leave from His Majesty" with reservation of a quitrent of 2s. 6d. per hundred acres.[133]

This projected land reform, however, did not envision any political liberalization, such as retailoring the relationships between the central and local governments in favor of the latter. Rather, its political objective was to destroy the influence of the landed magnates and to fragment land

---

forfeited from supporters of James II in the Glorious Revolution. John G. Simms, *The Williamite Confiscation in Ireland, 1690–1703* (London, 1956), 86–97; Lords Justice to Bellomont, Nov. 10, 1698, *N.Y. Col. Docs.*, IV, 375.

130. Bellomont to Lords of Trade, May 3, 1699, C.O. 1042/5, 139.

131. Lords of Trade to Bellomont, Feb. 23, 1698, and Bellomont to Lords of Trade, May 25, 29, 1698, *N.Y. Col. Docs.*, IV, 298, 314–315, 529; Bellomont to Col. Abraham De Peyster, Jan. 9, 22, Feb. 5, 19, Mar. 17, Aug. 3, Oct. 30, 1699, in Frederic De Peyster, *The Life and Administration of Richard, Earl of Bellomont, Governor of the Provinces of New York, Massachusetts, and New Hampshire, from 1697 to 1701* (New York, 1879), app., i–vi, xi.

132. Bellomont to Lords of Trade, Apr. 17 and Aug. 24, 1699, *N.Y. Col. Docs.*, IV, 502–505, 553; Rainbolt, "A 'great and usefull designe,'" *N.-Y. Hist. Soc. Qtly.*, LIII (1969), 339–341.

133. Bellomont to Lords of Trade, Oct. 21, 1698, and Aug. 24, 1699, and to Lords of Treasury, Oct. 27, 1698, *N.Y. Col. Docs.*, IV, 397, 554–555, 537.

ownership to such an extent that the colonists would be more amenable
to executive control. Only in this context can we understand Bellomont's
acute displeasure when he learned that Fletcher had granted to Westchester Borough the privilege of electing its own mayor—a privilege that
New York and Albany did not have—as well as other rights of self-
government comparable to those enjoyed by the New England towns.[134]

As a test case or, as Bellomont put it, "as an essay" to find out how
his scheme would "relish with the people," he singled out for attention
several grants to leading anti-Leislerians like Bayard, Delius, Evans, and
Heathcote. If he succeeded in this, he reported in April 1699, he then
would move on to "breake the rest."[135] The second targets included,
among others, the manors of Rensselaerswyck, Livingston, Cortlandt,
and Philipsburgh. Predictably, the landed men in general were alarmed.
When the governor introduced in the council in early May a bill aimed at
the first targets, he found the councillors divided equally—Livingston,
Van Cortlandt, and William Smith of St. George Manor voting nay, and
three others, De Peyster, Staats, and Walters, all Leislerians, aye. He
could effect its passage with his casting vote. Needless to say, he was

---

134. Bellomont had become so revengeful and bitter toward Fletcher that he made a
wild and absurd charge that Westchester Borough "has greater priviledges than any town in
America" and that the "major part of [its] inhabitants are felons upon record." Bellomont
to Lords of Trade, Nov. 12, 1698, and Lords of Trade to Bellomont, Aug. 21, 1699, *ibid.*,
427, 548.

135. *N.Y. Col. Laws*, I, 412–417. The Fletcher grants in the first category to be
revoked were:

| Grantee | Date of Grant | Location | Quantity |
|---|---|---|---|
| G. Delius | Sept. 1, 1696 | Albany County | 840 sq. miles |
| G. Delius<br>P. Schuyler<br>D. W. Ten Broeck<br>E. Vancker<br>W. Pinhorne | July 30, 1697 | Mohawk country | 100 sq. miles |
| N. Bayard | Dec. 12, 1695 | Albany County | ? |
| J. Evans | Sept. 20, 1694<br>Aug. 9, 1694 | Ulster County<br>near King's Farm<br>on Manhattan Island | 300,000 acres<br><br>70 acres |
| C. Heathcote | Apr. 2, 1696 | Part of King's<br>Garden | |
| Trinity Church | Aug. 19, 1697 | Lease of King's<br>Farm for seven<br>years | |

See also "A List of New Grants of land by Coll. Fletcher . . . ," C.O. 1049/5, 439.

furious with the defiant councillors—manorial proprietors who were mindful of the ominous implications of Bellomont's plan to the security of their own estates. The bill at first fared no better in the assembly, although the popular body was dominated by a Leislerian majority of sixteen over the six anti-Leislerians. It took a second ballot and hard arm twisting on the part of the governor, and even an infringement of parliamentary rules such as denying the speaker his right to vote, to pass the bill by a margin of only one.[136]

Bellomont had completely miscalculated the mood in the province. He had expected a ground swell of enthusiasm for the bill because he believed the grandees were "generally much hated" by the populace.[137] But, as it turned out, its reception by the legislature was disappointing. The measure stirred up intense "fury" and "implacable hatred" against him. Even James Graham, attorney general and speaker of the assembly, who had initially advised the governor to destroy the patents, opposed the bill "with all his might."[138] Graham argued that the property of Evans and Bayard should not be condemned without a hearing and during their absence from the colony, and that vacating titles would debase the "Great Seal" and the "public faith of England."[139] Besides these legalistic scruples, the speaker's turnabout was probably caused mainly by the urging of his closest friends, Livingston and Van Cortlandt, and by his own increasing concern for the future of Morrisania Manor (1,920 acres), which had been granted in 1697 to Lewis Morris, his son-in-law.[140]

Even the Leislerian-dominated Seventh General Assembly (March 2,

---

136. Godfredius Delius to the classis of Amsterdam, Oct. 21, 1700, Hastings, ed., *Ecclesiastical Records of N.Y.*, II, 1405–1406; Bellomont to Lords of Trade, May 12, 1699, *N.Y. Col. Docs.*, IV, 510–511; Nicholas Bayard to Bridgewater, Oct. 16, 1699, Ellsmore Collection, EL 9775, Henry E. Huntington Library, San Marino, Calif., and photostats at Sleepy Hollow Restorations Lib. Peter Schuyler and Dirck Wessells Ten Broeck had already given up their respective interests in the Delius grant of July 30, 1697. On Aug. 2, 1698, Henry Van Rensselaer agreed to surrender his Schaghticoke patent to Albany city. Munsell, ed., *Annals of Albany*, III, 55–56; deed of conveyance from Van Rensselaer to Albany, Aug. 30, 1699, Drawer No. 1, Albany Institute of History and Art, Albany, N.Y. For factional alignment in the assembly, see Bellomont to Lords of Trade, Apr. 27, 1699, *N.Y. Col. Docs.*, IV, 509; *Journal of Legislative Council*, I, 137, 140.

137. Bellomont to Lords of Trade, Apr. 17, 1699, *N.Y. Col. Docs.*, IV, 506–507.

138. Bellomont to Secretary William Popple, Nov. 29, 1700, and "Notes of what passed between Mr. Graham and the Earl of Bellomont about the Bill for breaking some of Coll: Fletcher's extravagant grants of land, May 4, 1699," *ibid.*, 812–813.

139. James Graham to Blathwayt, Morrisania, July 3, 1699, Blathwayt Papers, Roll 2; *N.Y. Col. Docs.*, IV, 813. Because of his opposition to the vacating bill, Graham lost the speakership to Abraham Gouverneur. *Journal of Legislative Council*, I, 141–142.

140. Ackerly, *Morris Manor*, 7–8, 19–20.

1699–June 1, 1701) showed reluctance to support Bellomont's overly ambitious project. With the exception of the committed Leislerians, many of the solons were, as he aptly pointed out, "landed men, and when their own interest came to be touched, 'tis more than probable they will flinch." Kiliaen Van Rensselaer, lord of Rensselaerswyck and a member of the assembly, observed that "nothing will be done [in the assembly] that will amount to anything, for the gentlemen have met together, but could not agree, because most of those who made the greatest ado" about the Delius patent had some interests in other great patents "under fictitious names."[141] Exactly who Van Rensselaer meant by "most of those" is unknown. It is probable that he was talking about the former anti-Leislerians, like Graham, who now were siding with the Leislerians, and some members from Albany County.

Bellomont's difficulty lay also in the antipathy of some Leislerians to the idea of land reform as a means of social change. They had supported Bellomont's first vacating bill in the hope that the recovered land would be distributed among them as political spoil, just as the English Whig politicians had recently done with the Tories' Irish estates. Like their opponents, they looked upon politics in no other terms than as a vehicle for acquiring mundane privileges and benefits. When Bellomont refused to accommodate their wishes, they turned their backs on his land policy. In August 1699, for example, Ryer Schermerhoorn, a Leislerian assemblyman from Albany County, asked the governor to grant to himself and Hendrick Hansen, another Leislerian assemblyman from the county, a tract of land six miles long and two miles wide toward Canada. The governor exploded with rage and urged his confidant to "chide" Schermerhoorn and Hansen for their "disrespect to the King, and disingenuity to me." "Besides," he continued, "I have complain'd to the King of Coll. FLETCHER's extravagant Grants [of] Lands—and shall I commit the same fault and absurdity myself, that I have accu'd FLETCHER."[142] Bellomont was remarkably consistent here, but to the local politicos, consistency was irrelevant if it was divorced from interest. Significantly, several days after these exchanges, Bellomont expressed to the Board of Trade skepticism that he had "strength enough" in the assembly to break the rest of the large grants.[143]

---

141. Kiliaen Van Rensselaer to Godfredius Delius, [late June 1699], Letters, 1674–1700, No. 997, in Rensselaerswyck Manuscripts, N.Y. State Lib.

142. Bellomont to Abraham De Peyster, Aug. 21, 1699, De Peyster, *Life of Bellomont,* app., viii.

143. Bellomont to Lords of Trade, Aug. 24, 1699, *N.Y. Col. Docs.,* IV, 553.

Yet, Bellomont persisted in his original objectives. He appealed to the home authorities to give him a complete mandate, "a peremptory order from the King," that would sanction his endeavor, for he feared that nothing short of it would be sufficient to deal with the council and assembly.[144] "Till these grants of land have had their doom," Bellomont pleaded, "these people are irreconcileable." Later he proposed that Parliament should take upon itself the business of breaking the grants. On another occasion, he asked the Lords of Trade to send able lawyers for the offices of attorney general and chief justice, since the present officeholders, Graham and Smith, were both truculently uncooperative.[145]

Individually and collectively, the manorial proprietors took appropriate measures to subvert Bellomont's scheme. They joined other "angry" landholders in financing a trip to England by Delius for the purpose of dissuading the king from ratifying the first vacating act.[146] To the embarrassment of the governor, in June 1699 Kiliaen Van Rensselaer and his brother Henry successfully prevailed upon Hendrick and Joseph, the two Mohawk Indians, to recant their depositions against the grants to Delius and others.[147] Adolph Philipse (son of Frederick), whose Highland Patent in Dutchess County was earmarked for destruction, and Johannes Van Cortlandt, the eldest son of Stephanus, along with twenty-nine other prominent merchants of New York City, signed a memorial to the king denouncing what they called the "maladministration" of Bellomont. One of their charges against him claimed that his policy was a "discouragement to the labour and industry of the Planter and Husbandman."[148]

Stephanus Van Cortlandt and the governor soon were at odds with each other. Bellomont reported to a correspondent that following the vote in the council on the first vacating bill, Van Cortlandt was depressed and pouty and acted as though he expected to be dismissed at any moment. In letters to Blathwayt, Van Cortlandt criticized the governor's

144. Bellomont to Lords of Trade, June 22, 1699, *ibid.*, 533; Nicholas Bayard to Bridgewater, June 23, and Oct. 16, 1699, Ellsmore Coll., EL 9765 and 9775.

145. Bellomont to Lords of Trade, Aug. 24, 1699, *N.Y. Col. Docs.*, IV, 549; Bellomont to Lords of Trade, May 29, 1699, Oct. 17, Nov. 28, May 25, 1700, C.O. 1042/5, 139; *N.Y. Col. Docs.*, IV, 725, 785, 644, 647; Bellomont to Bridgewater, May 12, 1699, Ellsmore Coll., EL 9764.

146. Bellomont to Lords of Trade, June 22, 1699, *N.Y. Col. Docs.*, IV, 533.

147. Kiliaen Van Rensselaer to Godfredius Delius, [late June 1699], Letters, 1674–1700, No. 997, Rensselaerswyck MSS; "Recantation of Joseph and Hendrick, Before the Magistrates of Albany," June 8, 1699, Hastings, ed., *Ecclesiastical Records of N.Y.*, II, 1318.

148. Bellomont to Lords of Trade, Aug. 24, 1699, "Petition of Sundry Merchants of New York to the king," Mar. 1700, *N.Y. Col. Docs.*, IV, 554–555, 624.

dilatory payment of military contractors and his clumsy management
of Indian affairs. Bellomont of course reciprocated by calling Van Cortlandt a "brute" and by threatening to throw him out of public office.[149]
Van Cortlandt then took the unusual step of contracting a new deed with
the Indians for various of his manor lands, four months after the first
vacating bill was passed. The lands he bought this time lay within the
limits of the manor patent, but had not been included in his previous
purchases.[150] His action was obviously aimed at eliminating the kind of
title defects that had rendered the patents of Delius and others assailable.

Among the manorial landgraves, Livingston was the only one who
maintained friendly relations with the governor. To be sure, he and Bellomont had their differences with regard to the land reform. Bellomont
often mentioned the small population of Livingston Manor as an example of why the great patents should be destroyed.[151] And Livingston did
vote against the first vacating bill. Yet, they had certain common interests
that overshadowed their differences. Livingston was in deep trouble in
the middle of 1699 because his partner Captain William Kidd, who was
supposed to prey upon the roving pirates in the western Atlantic and the
Red Sea, was accused by the British Admiralty of having turned pirate
himself. Bellomont, also a partner in the enterprise, was embarrassed.
Anxious to prove his innocence and to disassociate himself from the
messy affair, Bellomont quickly arrested the captain and sent him home
to be tried. Livingston was frightened at the possibility that he might be
implicated in the charge of piracy and his bond of £10,000 sterling to
Bellomont for Kidd's good performance forfeited. Under the circumstances, he was well aware that his fortune depended on the goodwill of
the governor.[152]

Political and business considerations also influenced Livingston's attitude. Despite his anti-Fletcher activities, he was never trusted by the die-
hard Leislerians for his part in the deaths of Leisler and Milborne. He
was also disliked by the Tories for his desertion from their ranks and his
hobnobbing with their vindictive opponents. The lonely man therefore

149. Stephanus Van Cortlandt to Blathwayt, Oct. 16 and Dec. 8, 1699, Blathwayt
Papers, Roll 2; Bellomont to Lords of Trade, May 13, 1699, N.Y. Col. Docs., IV, 517; De
Peyster, Life of Bellomont, app., xiii.

150. Indian deed of Aug. 8, 1699, Van Cortlandt Papers, V1694, Sleepy Hollow
Restorations Lib.

151. Bellomont to Lords of Trade, May 3, 1699, C.O. 1042/5, 139; Bellomont to
Lords of Trade, Jan. 2, 1701, N.Y. Col. Docs., IV, 822–823.

152. N.Y. Col. Docs., IV, 762–765; James Graham to Robert Livingston, Mar. 18,
1700, Livingston-Redmond MSS, Roll 2; Bellomont to Somers, Mar. 7, 1700, quoted in
Leder, Livingston, 148. Regarding the Kidd affairs, see ibid., 142–145.

had only the governor and his brothers-in-law for aid and comfort. Often the Leislerian assembly was swayed to his advantage only through the governor's intercession.[153] Besides, Livingston found compelling the advice of his friend Graham to be "very obsequ[i]ous" to Bellomont, so that his large credit (about £7,000) from military contracting would have a chance for early redemption by the government.[154]

For Bellomont's part, he appreciated Livingston's service in the victualing of troops and in Indian affairs. The manor proprietor was frequently consulted and called upon by the governor to attend conferences with the Iroquois, over whom Livingston and Peter Schuyler exerted a strong influence. At one time, Bellomont confided to a Leislerian leader, "I am obliged to Mr. LIVINGSTON, and would not willingly put any slight upon him." Indeed, Bellomont tried hard to minimize Livingston's culpability in the Kidd affair, perhaps because he felt that his partner was as much an innocent victim as he was himself.[155]

In any event, all the signs from London in the summer and fall of 1700 were encouraging to the manorial interests and disheartening to Bellomont. For one thing, the first vacating bill had yet to receive royal approval more than a year after its submission. For another, a confidential report from one Montague, a solicitor hired by the anti-Bellomont faction in the province, stated that the solicitor general of England was strongly opposed to the bill and that the king would surely reject it. Still another sign was the rumor that Fletcher was coming back to the province as governor. This last greatly frightened the Leislerians. At least one or two of them were reported to have bolted ranks.[156]

The royal government's foot-dragging on provincial land reform, and the various reports of a reversal in policy, were occasioned by the political controversy at home over the large Irish estates that King William had distributed in 1696 mostly among Whig favorites. From 1698 to 1700, owners of these estates came under a mounting chorus of attack from the Tories and the disaffected Whigs in Parliament who wanted to restore the lands to the crown and use the proceeds from their sale to pay

153. Minutes of General Assembly, May 5, 10, 11, 12, 13, 1699, Journal of the General Assembly, 1698–1705, 55, 57–58, 59, 61–62, N.-Y. Hist. Soc.; minutes of May 15, 1699, N.Y. Council Minutes, VIII, 109; Journal of Legislative Council, I, 136.
154. Bellomont to Lords of Trade, Feb. 28, 1700, N.Y. Col. Docs., IV, 608–609; James Graham to Robert Livingston, Jan. 16, 1700, Livingston-Redmond MSS, Roll 2.
155. Bellomont to Abraham De Peyster, Apr. 5, 1700, De Peyster, Life of Bellomont, app., xiv–xv; James Graham to Robert Livingston, Feb. 20 and Mar. 18, 1700, Livingston-Redmond MSS, Roll 2; Leder, Livingston, 142, 143, 148–149.
156. Bellomont to Lords of Trade, Oct. 17, 1700, N.Y. Col. Docs., IV, 713.

the war debt. Whig beneficiaries of the Irish grants vigorously opposed this resumption measure. They were thus put in a dilemma: they could not morally uphold the vacating bill and other land reform programs for New York and at the same time defend their own extravagant landholdings in Ireland.[157]

But the dilemma of his Whig colleagues in England did not trouble Bellomont. Later piqued by Parliament's breaking all of the Irish grants, including his, Bellomont argued that for the sake of fairness Parliament should "not hesitate a minute to break all the grants made by Collonel Fletcher." "There's a world of difference," he continued, "between grants made immediately by the King. . . . I mean where the Grantees had done faithful services to the crown, and grants of almost a whole Province by an upstart corrupt Governour."[158] It was a facile but absurd distinction. Being basically a fierce partisan, Bellomont was incapable of imputing to men of opposing political credos a sense of public service or even good morals.

In the crosscurrents created by the good news from London on top of Bellomont's continued threat, Stephanus Van Cortlandt grew "crazy and infirm" and died on November 25, 1700. The frustrated governor followed him in death only four months later.[159] With Bellomont gone, his "great and usefull" design also fizzled. The other manorial proprietors congratulated one another over their relief from the nightmare that had haunted them for the past three years.

157. Rainbolt, "A 'great and usefull designe,'" *N.-Y. Hist. Soc. Qtly.*, LIII (1969), 346–350.
158. Bellomont to Lords of Trade, Nov. 28, 1700, *N.Y. Col. Docs.*, IV, 785, 791.
159. Bellomont to Lords of Trade, Oct. 17 and Nov. 28, 1700, *ibid.*, 713–714, 725, 796; Gertrude Van Cortlandt to Blathwayt, Nov. 26, 1700, Van Cortlandt Family Papers, N.-Y. Hist. Soc.

# CHAPTER III

# The Privileges of Lordship and the Governance of the Manors

### Destruction of the Manorial Lordship

After successfully overcoming the political challenges to their manorial land titles, the Van Rensselaers, Livingstons, Philipses, and Van Cortlandts would continue to possess their vast estates throughout the colonial period. But they were not so fortunate with the privileges of manorial lordship, which had been designed to equip them not only with a feudal means of governance for their domains but also with immunities from county and local jurisdictions. These privileges were what differentiated the colonial manors from ordinary land patents. In the course of the first two decades of the eighteenth century, however, this feudal power was destroyed, blurring the distinction between the two types of grants.

The governance of the manors has intrigued historians. Yet there has been no consensus among them on as basic a question as whether the proprietors enjoyed the feudal privileges of holding courts baron and courts leet. Some scholars, notably E. Wilder Spaulding, have asserted that "all the true manors enjoyed some kind of jurisdiction in the form of courts-baron for civil and courts-leet for criminal cases."[1] Others, like

---

1. Spaulding, *New York in the Critical Period, 1783–1789* (New York, 1932), 59 (quoted), 61, 65; Stephen L. Mershon, *The Power of the Crown in the Valley of the Hudson*

Irving Mark, have maintained that these courts never actually functioned, except possibly during the early years of English administration.[2] But historians have altogether neglected to investigate the process through which the lordship disintegrated. This study will endeavor to explain that process and also to clarify a number of other questions regarding the power of the manorial proprietors. We will see that the evolution of landlord-tenant relations, the institution of tenancy, and the quality of life in general in these manors were much affected by the power or lack of it at the disposal of the grandees.

One means by which the local power of the lordship was undermined was through the inheritance of property, as is illustrated by the case of the Manor of Cortlandt. On April 14, 1700, Stephanus Van Cortlandt, the manor founder, left a detailed will regarding the disposition of his real and personal estate.[3] First, he ordered that a tract within the manor called Meanagh (presently Verplanck's Point) be separated from his estates and given to his eldest son, Johannes, after the death of his wife, Gertrude. Second, he willed that all of his real and personal property be equally divided among his eleven children, male and female, or be held in common among them after his wife's death. The decision as to when it should be divided after his wife's death was left to several appointed guardians. He also stipulated that in the case of the death of any of his sons before the age of twenty-one, or the death of any unmarried daughters before that age, their share should devolve upon the surviving children.

The most striking aspect of Van Cortlandt's will is that primogeniture was slighted. Verplanck's Point, the tract of 915 acres that was given to Johannes as heir, was an inconsiderable portion of the immense property Van Cortlandt bequeathed. At his death, Stephanus held, besides his manor and personal estates, one-third of the Rumbout Patent of sixteen square miles in Dutchess County, 15,000 acres in Orange County, 40 acres with gristmills and sawmills on the Rahway River in East Jersey (valued at £345 in 1730), the Bowman's Farm of 1,200 acres in Sussex County,

---

(Brattleboro, Vt., 1925), 88. A slightly modified view while admitting that the manor proprietors exercised lordly rights is seen in Carl L. Becker, *The History of Political Parties in the Province of New York, 1760–1776* (Madison, Wis., 1909), 10; E. Marie Becker, "The 801 Westchester County Freeholders of 1763 and the Cortlandt Manor Land-Case Which Occasioned Their Listing," *N.-Y. Hist. Soc. Qtly.*, XXXV (1951), 297.

2. Mark, *Agrarian Conflicts*, 57–58; Patricia U. Bonomi, *A Factious People: Politics and Society in Colonial New York* (New York, 1971), 189–190.

3. Stephanus Van Cortlandt's will, Museum of the City of New York.

Pennsylvania, and nineteen lots and two houses (valued at £3,770) in New York City.[4] Even the special consideration he gave Johannes of making the first choice in the division of the estate was mitigated by the provision that the division must be made "equall in worth one to another."

That the testator granted in fee simple the real estate including the manor to all of his children was of great consequence for the future of the manor. Had Stephanus been keenly interested in the perpetuation and integrity of his manorial lordship, he would have entailed the entire manor to his eldest son, thereby insuring its descent and the descent of the lordship according to the rules of primogeniture. The expected fragmentation of the manor among the devisees left no room for any possible pretensions to lordship by his eldest son: Johannes's inheritance of 915 acres at Verplanck's Point, along with his equal sharing of the manor with his brothers and sisters, was hardly sufficient to make him the lord over a vast domain in the way his father had allegedly been. Furthermore, the absence of any reference to the lordship in the will suggests that Stephanus had no intention of passing it on. But why did Stephanus dispose of his manorial estate in a way that practically abandoned the lordship less than three years after he got it? He was a man of business acumen, political agility, and, above all, aristocratic mentality; as his career clearly demonstrates, he was well acquainted with political and judicial matters in the province. It is inconceivable that such a man would so easily give up this hard-won prize if he attached much significance to it. The evidence shows that Van Cortlandt let it die under duress, for before his death the lordship had come under attack from several sources that cast grave doubts on its compatibility with the development of other institutions and with the political and cultural proclivities of the colonial population. His action reflected what had already happened and would continue to happen in the course of the early eighteenth century.

The legal underpinning of the lordship was the power of a manorial lord, his heirs, and assignees to hold and keep in the manor "one Court

---

4. Patent Book 5: 206–210, Office of the Secretary of State of New York, Albany; "Writs of Partition of Roumbout Patent in 1707," Van Cortlandt Papers, V1974, Sleepy Hollow Restorations Library, Tarrytown, N.Y. Regarding his estates in East Jersey, New York City, and elsewhere, see Van Cortlandt Family Papers, Case for Oversized Manuscripts, New-York Historical Society, New York; "Real Estate of Stephanus Van Cortlandt, Appraisment of the lott houses at York and Mils at raway," Letters, etc., 1716–1819, Van Cortlandt-Van Wyck Papers, New York Public Library; Stephanus Van Cortlandt to William Blathwayt, Dec. 7, 1694, Blathwayt Papers, Roll 2; Van Cortlandt Papers, V1704, Sleepy Hollow Restorations Lib.

Leete and one Court baron" as often as he or they should see fit. In old English usage, the court leet enacted the manorial administrative ordinances and prosecuted offenders against manorial regulations; the court baron tried civil actions between tenants and the lord and handled matters relating to land tenure. Together, the courts baron and leet were authorized to receive "all fines issues and Amerciaments," to issue the customary writs, and, for the rents, services, debts, and so on, to distrain goods if necessary and all or part of the leasehold premises in question. In the case of Rensselaerswyck, the lord was by the patent of 1685 authorized to receive all the "fines issues and Amerciaments" to be forfeited or imposed not only at his own courts but also at the courts of assizes, of oyer and terminer, and of sessions of the peace if they were ever held within his manor. In addition, all manorial lords were granted advowson, the right to nominate a clergyman in their domain.[5] If the lords had actually been allowed to exercise these powers, they would have been as formidable as any baron of the English Middle Ages.

The manorial lordship could be operative only if it enjoyed independent administrative and judicial status free from any outside interference and was accountable solely to the governor and council. Primarily as a counterpoise to the "republican" tendencies of local governmental units and partly as a supplement to the local administration of justice, Governor Thomas Dongan envisioned this autonomy for the manors when he granted the privileges of lordship. Because of their aristocratic and feudal features, such lordships were anathema to the colonists and became involved in bitter struggles with local governments and the General Assembly. Once a manor lost its independent status to a neighboring town, to the county in which it was situated, or to the assembly, the privileges of lordship were doomed.

Such challenges from competing jurisdictions came early. They generally took the form of disputes between manors and adjoining towns over local ordinances and taxation. In May 1687, barely a year and a half after the Rensselaerswyck patent was granted and a year after Albany was incorporated, the two clashed over the right of licensing a public tavern. Jealous of the vast manor surrounding the city, the burghers were always on guard against erosion of their authority. On this occasion, the city warned Hendrick Lansing, a tenant of the manor, to stop selling beer and rum at his dwelling house, because he did not have a license from the

5. See the patent of 1685 for the Manor of Rensselaerswyck in Nissenson, *Patroon's Domain*, app. D. The quotation is from p. 383.

mayor, who alone was "Impowered to graunt Lycences to sell Liquor by Retail" in the county of Albany, according to the city charter of 1686. When this warning did not avail, the city brought the case into the county court of sessions. In this instance, as in many others to follow, the city had an overwhelming advantage over other towns in the county and over the manor. Because its charter empowered the mayor, recorder, and aldermen (at this time six) of the city to sit as justices of the peace in a mayor's court of common pleas and also in "the court of sessions, or [any] courts, and court of Oyer and terminer" for the county of Albany, the city was able to dominate by sheer force of numbers the judicial and administrative arms of the county government.[6] As might be expected, the court of sessions ordered Lansing to "keep no more any Common Tiplinghouse or sell any wine Beer or Strong Liquor . . . upon his peril," even though he possessed a license dated May 30, 1687, from the manor lord, Kiliaen Van Rensselaer.[7] The incident shows that the manor lord, armed with his patent, had tried to establish an administrative sanctuary independent of the city and county. This quarrel with the city, however, was merely a pinprick to what Kiliaen Van Rensselaer had to endure from Albany County and from the General Assembly in the following decades.

How weak the lordship was and how impossible the task of maintaining the legal and administrative powers of the manorial patents were well attested by the fate of others with similar powers. In July 1688, Hendrick Selyns, the proprietor of the Manor of Fordham, petitioned the governor's council for protection of his manorial independence, which had been grossly impaired by the town of Westchester. He pleaded:

Yor peticioner being seized of the Manor of Fordham to which Mannor among others it is granted a priviledge that itt shall not belong to or to under the jurisdiccion of any other town Rideing or place but as to itts government to be ruled by the Governr and Councill only notwithstanding which the Inhabitants of the towne of Westchester have not only Exercised Jurisdicion over the inhabitants of the said Mannor but have forcibly Entered within the same and . . . still continue under Colour of the said Township to disturb Yor petitioner in his peaceable and quiet possession of the said Mannor . . . in contempt of this

---

6. The Albany city charter is in *N.Y. Col. Laws*, I, 195–216.
7. This Kiliaen was the son of Maria. The other Kiliaen, the first manor lord under the English patent, son of Johannes Van Rensselaer, died in Feb. 1687. Nissenson, *Patroon's Domain*, 340. For the dispute between Albany and Rensselaerswyck over Hendrick Lansing's tavern, see the Minutes of Court of Sessions, 1685–1689, 35–36, Albany County Clerk's Office, Albany, N.Y.

honable board [council] under whom alone the said Mannor ought to be according to its constitucion.[8]

This episode illustrates the extent to which the manor had been degraded from the initially proud enclave created by Lovelace. There is no evidence, however, that anything was done to relieve Selyns. Nor did Lieutenant Governor Richard Ingoldsby in 1692 do much about the case of Shelter Island, an independent patent that theoretically had certain privileges analogous to those of the Manor of Fordham, when its proprietors appealed to him to prevent the "overthrowe" of the patent by Suffolk County officials. Even Fletcher, while lavishly granting large manors with considerable privileges, did not want to be bothered with it, referred the problem to the assembly, and let it suffer oblivion there.[9]

Much of the difficulty experienced by the manorial patentees was due to the absence of an adequate definition of lordship, particularly in relation to neighboring towns and to larger local units like counties. In the 1670s and 1680s, when the governor held the upper hand in every aspect of government, it was not anticipated that jurisdictional conflicts would develop between the different local governments; even if disputes did arise, their resolution was considered to be within the competency of the governor, since he had no other rival authorities with which to contend. But once the assembly began legislating county administrative apparatus and functions in the province, the status of the manors became ambiguous. The governor by his prerogative could create and incorporate cities by charter and both town and manors by patent, but the assembly took upon itself the authority of organizing these local units, superimposing a county over them, prescribing their relationships, and assigning their respective functions. In 1683 and 1691, the legislature established twelve counties in the place of the old local units, shires and ridings. The

---

8. Selyns's petition, July 26, 1688, N.Y. Col. MSS, XXXV, 167.
9. On the basis of the patent of 1666, the second-generation proprietors of Shelter Island claimed that the island was "freed from having any reliance or dependance upon Long Island but [was] a Township and Manor of its Selfe subject in matter of Government to" the governor and council only, and even from taxes under a separate arrangement. Despite this privilege, the justices of the peace and collectors of Suffolk County tried to "overthrowe" and "infringe" upon the island patent by "threatening to impose dues and demand the paymt of rates and taxes towards the charge of their County." The proprietors nevertheless expressed their willingness to contribute money directly to the governor "as much as their neighb[o]r and as fully and largely as if the same were be assessed" by the county officials. They further argued that once they submitted to the county taxation, it would constitute a precedent to encroach further upon their "Privileges and Immunityes." See "Petition of Giles, Nathaniell and Peter Sylvester," July 16, 1692, N.Y. Col. MSS, XXXVIII, 155; *Journal of General Assembly*, I, 77–79.

government of each county was placed in the hands of a semiannual court of general sessions composed of justices of the peace from the towns. Although they were appointed by the governor, the justices had in common with the assembly an animus against private manorial jurisdictions.[10] The officials' bias stemmed largely from their eagerness to expand county tax bases by extending their jurisdiction over the manors.[11] In the last decade of the seventeenth century, the manors of Rensselaerswyck and Livingston north of Roeloff Jansen's Kill comprised about two-thirds of Albany County, while the manors of Cortlandt and Philipsburgh constituted about a half of Westchester County. The manors were usually too valuable a tax resource for a county to ignore, especially at a time when the colonists were laboring under heavy taxation. Indeed, the issue of taxation was the wedge that helped crack manorial lordship.

In 1691 manors were incorporated into a uniform provincial administrative system under "An Act for the defraying of the publique and necessary charge throughout this Province and maintaining the poor and preventing Vagabonds." This act required each town—including the manors—to elect a supervisor whose responsibility was to meet annually with supervisors of other towns in his county, in order to "supervise and examine and allow the contingent public charges of each county," and also to act as the chief executive officer of each town.[12] This measure did not interfere with the administrative control that the county court of general sessions exercised over such elective local officials as supervisor, collector, assessor, and constable. The court still held vital power over raising county taxes and also established the distribution of tax quotas for subcounty jurisdictions. However, the long-term effect of the 1691 legislation was to reduce the manor to a part of county government and to replace the lord with an elected supervisor as administrative head.

Kiliaen Van Rensselaer attended the county court of sessions as a justice of the peace in 1698 and agreed to the tax quota for his manor toward paying the debt of the city and county of Albany. Moreover, Nicolas Dow and Marte Cornelise, the two assessors from the manor, participated in the court deliberations to raise the county quota ($£120$) to pay for a gift voted by the assembly for Bellomont and John Nanfan,

---

10. N.Y. Col. Laws, I, 121, 125–128, 143–144, 226–231, 267–268.
11. John Cuyler, a justice from Albany city, proposed that a tax should be imposed on all lands "as well unimproved as Improvd rated according to the value of the Estates." This proposal of course aimed at the unimproved baronial estates in the county of Albany, but nothing came of it. Philip Livingston to father, Robert, Jan. 8, 1724, Livingston-Redmond MSS, Roll 2.
12. The act was dated May 13, 1691, N.Y. Col. Laws, I, 237–238.

the lieutenant governor. According to the report of one of the manor justices of the peace, in 1701 Van Rensselaer was elected as supervisor for his manor and attended the county supervisors' meeting.[13] Yet, despite this involvement of his manor in county affairs, he later seized every opportunity to resist assembly action that might subordinate the manor to the county. Van Rensselaer of course was not alone among many lords in insisting on an extracounty status.[14]

Complaints by officials of some counties against refractory manors increased. As early as 1691, recognizing that "several Manors and Jurisdictions within the respective Countyes" had neglected or refused to choose assessors and collectors, the assembly ordered the justices of the peace of the counties in which such manors lay to appoint the tax officials for them. This order was a rider to an act designed to procure a defense fund necessitated by King William's War, then underway. In 1692 a similar rider was added to an act raising a gift of money for Fletcher.[15] In fact, the assembly had to insert the same antimanorial provision in practically every revenue act from 1691 to 1711,[16] which evidences the obstinacy of some manor owners in defying the county ordinances. Tucking antimanorial measures in revenue acts was an obvious maneuver by the deputies to overcome possible objections from the governors. The executives simply could not refuse the material benefits of a defense appropriation or a sumptuous gift solely for the sake of the lofty principles of manorial independence. Even though they might discern the strategem of the assembly and greatly value the unqualified support that the manorial proprietors gave to his prerogative, typically the governors were too money-minded to do much for the manors.[17] This is another example of how assembly control of revenue measures was used to paralyze the

13. Minutes of Court of Sessions, 1685–1689, 1717–1723, and 1763–1782, all in three volumes, Albany Co. Clerk's Office; court of sessions minutes for Westchester County, 1657–1697, in Deed Book D, 17–139, Westchester County Clerk's Office, White Plains, N.Y.; Court of Sessions Minutes, Dec. 28, 1698, N.Y. Col. MSS, XLII, 67 (11); Munsell, ed., *Annals of Albany*, III, 54–55, IV, 122.

14. Isaac Arnold and five other justices of Suffolk County to Gov. Benjamin Fletcher, 1694, N.Y. Col. MSS, XXXIX, 124. The justices reported that "some of the Islands dependencyes of this County refuse to be within the said County."

15. N.Y. Col. *Laws*, I, 259–260, 309–312; N.Y. Col. MSS, XXXIX, 12a.

16. N.Y. Col. *Laws*, I, 258–262, 272–273, 275–276, 277–278, 317–321, 369–375, 398–399, 446, 495, 746–747.

17. The manorial proprietors, especially the Van Rensselaers, were fervent supporters of the prerogative. Unlike the assembly representatives from other districts, they defined the legislature's role primarily as one of assisting the governor. "The Mannor of Renslaar Wyck, Debt to Richard Brewer and Rutger Bleecker," Aug. 25, 1710, Staats Family Archives, Box 3, N.Y. State Lib.

colonial governors. It was probably this coordinated attack by the counties and the assembly, and the governors' desertion of manorial causes, that accounts for Van Cortlandt's early surrender of his pretension to lordship.[18] It might also be the reason why Frederick Philipse, the first proprietor of the Manor of Philipsburgh, by will in 1700 divided his manor in fee simple between his son, Adolph, and his grandson Frederick, an action that undermined the integrity of the lordship and anticipated eventual fragmentation of its land title.[19]

The controversy between the assembly and the manors over administration within the manors was eventually settled in favor of the assembly. With the passage of the assembly act of 1691, the administrative side of manor lordship became a dead privilege. Acting on the general principles outlined in that law, the lower house passed in August 1705 an act establishing a detailed administrative structure specifically for Rensselaerswyck, the most ancient and populous of the New York manors. It required the manor freeholders to elect annually a supervisor, treasurer, assessor, and collector for the domain, who would have the same authority and functions as the respective officers of other towns and be liable to the same penalties.[20] However, Kiliaen Van Rensselaer still refused to comply with these acts and insisted on a status separate from Albany County. By the following year, the county and assembly apparently had had enough of Van Rensselaer's intransigence. In 1706 the legislature passed a bill that spelled out the nature of the conflict between the manor and the county. In addition to defining more clearly than ever the functions of manor supervisor at the manor and county level and expanding the number of assessors and collectors from one to three each, the act denounced "all shifts and tricks" contrived by the proprietor to "evade the force of this or any former Act" and declared with a view to preventing their future recurrence that "the Mannor . . . can by no reasonable construction be intended to be Divided from [Albany] County."[21] No stronger language could have been found to chastise the obstinate

18. If Benjamin Fletcher's concern for the manors was neutralized by his need for war financing, Bellomont's avowed antimanorialism was, of course, a boon to the antimanorial forces in the province.

19. Frederick Philipse's will, Oct. 26, 1700, Philipse Papers, PA815, Sleepy Hollow Restorations Lib.

20. For the purposes of the suffrage, a man holding a lifetime lease or longer was regarded as a freeholder.

21. "An Act for the better raising, Levying and defraying the necessary Charge of the Mannor of Renslaerwick in the County of Albany," passed Oct. 21, 1706, *N.Y. Col. Laws*, I, 603–604.

manorial lord. More important, this action brought to an end the pro-tracted controversy over the administrative relationship between Rensse-laerswyck Manor and Albany County. Governor Edward Hyde, Viscount Cornbury (1702–1708), and his council approved the bill without objec-tion.[22]

The reduction of Rensselaerswyck to a mere township in Albany County, however, did not automatically entail the reduction of the other manors as well. At least another decade of wrangling passed before all the manors were completely incorporated into a county system under assembly supervision. In the first decade of the eighteenth century, as in the previous ten years, the manors of Livingston, Philipsburgh, Cortlandt, and their proprietors simply refused to elect the designated tax officials and also neglected to join with neighboring towns in electing supervisors. In the case of Philipsburgh and Cortlandt manors, the Westchester court of sessions usually appointed assessors and taxed them anyway.[23] In 1710 the tenant-residents on the Westchester manors, who were mostly Dutch, despite "many Reiterated and Sharp orders" from the county justices of the peace, refused to make a return of the names and number of people on the manors from sixteen to sixty years of age. In the words of Sheriff John Clapp, the people gave for their noncompliance "no other reason but a dread of the Consequences that might Insue: Like David's numbering of the people."[24] It is more than likely that the biblical allusion was a cloak for their fear that a census return would lead to detested taxation. It is also possible that the manor inhabitants were hinting at their extracounty status, for they alone in the county were delinquent. If such was the case, their behavior was undoubtedly instigated by Philip Van Cortlandt and Adolph Philipse, the second-generation proprietors of their respective manors. Nevertheless, the Westchester manors were as yet sparsely settled—in 1712 only 87 white inhabitants lived at Cortlandt Manor, and 309 at Philipsburgh—self-contained, isolated agricultural units on the outskirts of the county, and the manorial settlers there were probably as wary as their landlords of an elaborate county administrative machinery, the benefits from which seemed marginal.[25]

22. Journal of Legislative Council, I, 244.
23. Dixon Ryan Fox, ed., The Minutes of the Court of Sessions (1657–1696), West-chester County, New York (Westchester County Historical Society, Publications, II [White Plains, N.Y., 1924]), 93–94.
24. John Clapp to Sec. George Clarke, Oct. 10, 1710, N.Y. Col. MSS, LIV, 77; Doc. Hist. N.Y., III, 945; Gov. Hunter to Lords of Trade, June 12, 1712, N.Y. Col. Docs., V, 339.
25. "Census of Westchester County, 1712," Doc. Hist. N.Y., III, 949.

Annoyed at the subterfuge of the inhabitants and proprietors of the manors but unable to coerce them into obeying county orders, the justices and supervisors of Westchester County in October 1711 solicited the intervention of the General Assembly in the matter. The response of the popular body was, as expected, prompt and favorable; a month later it passed a punitive measure against the manors empowering the assessors and collectors of a town adjacent to any delinquent manor to assess and collect public taxes in the manor.[26] In commenting on the meaning of the assembly measure, Governor Robert Hunter (1710–1719) stated simply that it was to "remedy some inconveniences that have arisen from the neglect of some manors in that County to Elect supervisors and collectors."[27] The legislation seems to have had the desired effect: the Manor of Cortlandt for the first time in 1712 sent a constable, and in 1714 an assessor and a collector, to the borough of Westchester, the county seat.[28]

There is no reason to believe, on the one hand, that the Westchester manors elected or shared a supervisor with a Westchester town or, on the other hand, that the manor lords or their assignees necessarily took on the public function of administrative head for their manors. Indeed, a manor lord or his assignees had no place, or recognition of a place, in the provincial government until 1722, when a law was enacted to increase the number of supervisors in Westchester County. Under this law, a manor with more than twenty inhabitants might choose its supervisor annually, but if the manor inhabitants neglected to choose the officer, the "owner" or his deputy on the manor would be regarded as its supervisor with the same authority as those elected by virtue of the law.[29] This last provision, viewed in the context of Hunter's remarks in 1712 about the customary neglect of the manors to choose their supervisors, was obviously a belated recognition by the assembly that no one other than the manor proprietor or his deputy could effectively represent domain affairs. To the eighteenth-century mind, property and representation were one and inseparable. At this nascent stage of manorial development, it is

26. *Journal of General Assembly*, I, 302, 304, 306; "An Act to oblige the Mannors in the County of West Chester to pay their Arrears of Taxes," Nov. 24, 1711, *N.Y. Col. Laws*, I, 752.

27. Robert Hunter to Lords of Trade, Jan. 1, 1712, *N.Y. Col. Docs.*, V, 299.

28. Minutes of the Westchester County court of sessions, 1697–1712, in Deed Book D, Westchester Co. Clerk's Office.

29. *N.Y. Col. Laws*, II, 130–131. According to this law, the owner of a manor with fewer than 20 inhabitants would automatically become the supervisor of the manor. The provision was probably designed for Scarsdale Manor, which was perhaps the only manor with fewer than 20 people. *Doc. Hist. N.Y.*, III, 94.

inconceivable that the tenants thought otherwise. The assembly act of 1691 and the new act of 1712 ordering the election of a supervisor, therefore, probably sounded incongruous to these tenants when they already had a supervisor in the person of their landlord, whose right to the domain and its administration could not have been challenged. However, whatever reasons the tenants or the manor proprietor might have had for avoiding the election of a supervisor, the 1722 law would henceforth compel one or the other to bear the burden of county government. Either way, the new law infused some order into the hitherto chaotic manor administration and helped tighten the county's jurisdictional control over the manorial districts.[30]

Nothing in the history of the manors is as revealing about the causes and nature of disputes involving original manorial privileges, particularly administrative ones, as the case of the Manor of Livingston. The manor straddled both Albany and Dutchess counties—the section north of Roeloff Jansen's Kill was part of the former, and the section south, part of the latter (see the map on p. 40). This anomaly developed partly as a result of imprecise geographical knowledge of the area and partly because the manor was carved out of the counties after they had already been established in 1683.[31] Notwithstanding the potential dangers to the estate from the two counties, Robert Livingston, armed with the manor patent of 1686 granting him lordship and other privileges, presumed himself reasonably secure. For a time, his case was supported by the eclipse and subsequent demise of assembly power and by the embryonic features of county administrative machinery during the three-year period before the Leislerian Rebellion in the years 1687 to 1689. Livingston's situation, however, altered radically following the rise and increasing assertiveness of county and assembly government and the corresponding decline of executive authority.

The seeds of conflict nurtured in the aspirations of the Livingston Manor lordship did not begin to blossom for three decades after the manor patent was issued. In the meantime, about ten tenant families, scattered mostly along Roeloff Jansen's Kill and at the foothills of the Taconic Mountains, engaged in simple agricultural pursuits.[32] According

30. Special legislation for the administration of Cortlandt Manor was passed in 1737 when the manor was ordered to elect yearly one supervisor, one treasurer, two assessors, and one collector. *N.Y. Col. Laws*, II, 960–962; *Journal of General Assembly*, I, 683–684, 687–688, 695, 719, 720, 721, 723.

31. *N.Y. Col. Laws*, I, 122, 268.

32. "List of Livestock" distributed among the tenants, Jan. 27, 1707–Aug. 25, 1709, Livingston-Redmond MSS, Roll 2.

to the survey map drawn by John Betty in 1714, there were two roads starting from the manor house on the Hudson River: a wagon path that went southward along the kill and a road called Kings Highway that led toward Massachusetts. Most of the manor land was completely forested except for the roads and the cultivated areas.[33] Occasionally a manor steward would inspect the crop on the fields, and periodically tenants would go to the manor store to procure merchandise or to pay rent. Otherwise, life was exceedingly routine. At this pioneering stage, the manor, at least until 1710, was so quiet, and the number of tenant families so few, that the county governments, Albany as well as Dutchess, probably did not think it was worthwhile to interfere with it in either taxation or administrative matters. The assembly had passed two bills concerning the manor, one in 1703 for general application and the other in 1709 especially for several families in the northern part of the domain. The latter bill directed these families to unite in one precinct with those of Catskill and Coxsackie precincts, and with all those living to the south of Rensselaerswyck on the west side of the Hudson River, and elect a supervisor and tax officials.[34] It appears that the manor residents quietly ignored the directives and that the county indulged them in their refractoriness.

Then two notable events occurred that had significant consequences for county-manor relations. In the short period from 1710 to 1718, the manor population jumped from about seventeen to fifty families,[35] an increase prompted by the migration of about a thousand Palatines to the six-thousand-acre tract in the southwestern part of the manor that Livingston had sold to Governor Hunter in 1710. New tenants moved into the manor proper with an eye on the Palatines as a captive market.

Another event of significance was that Livingston in October 1715 secured from the governor a confirmatory patent for his manor. This new patent contained three important features. First, it corrected the ambiguities of the manor's original boundaries by replacing the Indian and natural landmarks with "courses and distances" according to the survey performed by John Betty in 1714. Second, the manor freeholders were authorized to send a representative to the General Assembly. Finally, the

---

33. *Doc. Hist. N.Y.*, III, 690; Edwin Brockholst Livingston, *The Livingstons of Livingston Manor . . .* (New York, 1910), 110.

34. *N.Y. Col. Laws*, I, 539–542, 705.

35. "List of Debtors," Jan. 20, 1710, to Mar. 5, 1718, Livingston-Redmond MSS, Roll 3; "A list of the Inhabitants and Slaves in the City and County of Albany, 1714," N.Y. Col. MSS, LIX, 19.

new patent confirmed both the lordship privileges and the inhabitants' right to choose assessors as provided for in the 1686 patent, adding collectors and two constables to the list of elected officials. Though Governor Hunter hoped the manor representation would increase his partisan following in the assembly, it certainly would also have the effect of enhancing the political influence of the manor proprietor in county and provincial affairs.[36] Furthermore, the confirmation of the lordship plus the manor's right to elect its own officials was a direct rebuff to the provincial law of 1709 requiring manor inhabitants to join the other towns. The new patent somewhat clarified and elevated the manor's status, but it was far from the goal to which Livingston and his old friend and a prominent manor resident, Dirck Wessells Ten Broeck, aspired. Their ultimate design for the manor seems to have been its independence from both Albany and Dutchess counties, which could be attained only by turning it into a county itself.[37]

Ensconced in the new patent, Livingston soon seized an opportunity to assert his manorial privileges. In January 1716, Francis Salisbury, assessor of the combined district of Catskill, Coxsackie, and part of the manor lying in Albany County, came down to the manor to assess the county tax on certain of the manor inhabitants who had had no part in his election. This was the first instance in which Albany County tried to collect taxes in the manor. Perhaps the county believed that the increased population there was too valuable a revenue source to remain untapped and that the new confirmatory manor patent, granted just three months earlier, seriously threatened to disturb the existing administrative arrangement between the county and the manor. Livingston, interpreting his new patent broadly, rebuked Salisbury and the county by declaring that he had "the Privilege to choose assessors in his own manor and that he had accordingly caused the freeholders and Inhabitants to choose one." In the meantime, the manor proprietor had written to his son Philip, clerk of the city and county of Albany, to acquaint the justices of the peace in the court of sessions with the privilege granted by Governor Hunter. The county officials were incensed at Livingston's remarks. His

36. Robert Hunter's order to David Jamison, attorney general, Oct. 1, 1715, *Doc. Hist. N.Y.*, III, 689–691, 695, 696. See also a copy of the new confirmatory patent, Miscellaneous Manuscripts, Livingston, R-W, N.-Y. Hist. Soc. In the same year, Hunter gave Dutchess County another seat in the assembly, in hopes of strengthening his control of the legislature. See White, *Beekmans*, I, 162.

37. Dirck Wessells Ten Broeck to Robert Livingston, May 18, 1717 (Dutch), quoted in Leder, *Livingston*, 242.

nephew, Robert Livingston, Jr., mayor of Albany and thus a justice of the peace, despite his blood tie, seems to have peremptorily told Salisbury to go back and assess the manor, although the poor assessor pleaded that it was "a great trouble" for a collector to go to so distant a place in order to collect the tax, and that it was also "hard for him or anybody" who was unfamiliar with the "circumstances" of the manor people to assess them. In an unusual assertion of local authority, John Cuyler, a justice of the peace and a wealthy Indian trader, declared at the court that "it was not in the Governours Power" to grant such a privilege to Robert Livingston, that only the assembly had that power, and that the county would have "nothing to doe" with Livingston's pretension.[38]

The Dutchess County justices of the peace were also hostile. In early 1717 they boycotted the manor assessors who were sent down to the county seat to represent the part of the manor lying in Dutchess, on the grounds that the oath administered by a manor official (Dirck Wessells Ten Broeck) to the assessors did not "conform to the act of Assembly."[39] It is hard to say precisely what irregularities were in the oath, but it did invoke the new manor patent and not the assembly act as the legal basis for the assessors' authority, which was probably the basis for the justices' objection. Both Cuyler and the Dutchess County justices struck right at the heart of the old controversy between the governor and the assembly, and between the counties and the manors, over the issue of the manors' status in county administration. As in many other similar cases, the counties again took the initiative in challenging manorial power, this time in the name of and with the support of the assembly, and in the face of gubernatorial intentions.

As the first test of his patent had been a resounding defeat for Livingston, he was prompted to reconsider the whole question of the manor's relationship with the counties. He was no stranger to local and provincial politics, as his career as clerk of the city and county of Albany, member of Bellomont's council, and member of the assembly in 1709 attests.[40] With this rich and diverse background, Livingston understood the assembly's natural inclination to "incroach as often" and "as far as" it could upon the executive prerogative. By the 1710s the assembly had acquired sole authority over money bills, and, henceforth, almost nothing

38. Teunis Van Slyk's deposition, Feb. 29, 1716. Frances Salisbury's deposition, Mar. 22, 1716, and Philip Livingston's certificate of notice to the Albany County justices, 1716, Livingston-Redmond MSS, Roll 3.

39. Henry Beekman to Robert Livingston, Mar. 21, 1717, *ibid.*

40. *Journal of General Assembly*, I, 239.

important in the province could be done without its approval.[41] Livingston must also have been aware of how sensitive the assembly had been to any attempt to diminish its power and how protective it had been toward the counties, which were its creation, whenever a manor, which was a gubernatorial establishment, posed a problem. He thus became convinced of the futility of expecting sympathy for his cause from the assembly, though he was himself a member, or from the governor, who, like his predecessors, was willing to grant lordly power on paper but unwilling to be aggressive in implementing and supporting it.[42]

In this unpromising situation, Livingston debated with himself and others the various alternatives. His friend Ten Broeck proposed the creation of a separate county out of the manor, but this scheme, with which Livingston himself had once toyed, seemed unrealistic because neither the assembly nor the counties affected would ever accept it. The options ultimately narrowed down to one: that of choosing between the counties, Dutchess and Albany—the former "poor" and the latter "oppressive" —in order to minimize the tax burden on the manor and to make its administration uniform in every section. For reasons unknown, Livingston picked Albany County.[43] On May 14, 1717, just four days after he was admitted to the assembly, Livingston introduced a bill to unite the two parts of the manor with the county, which the assembly quickly passed according to an earlier understanding between him and some members from the Hudson River counties.[44] The act, approved by the governor and council, specified that the manor "shall be and forever Remain and be Annexed to the County of Albany," and that the "Inhabitants" (there is no reference to the freeholders) were authorized to elect "one Super-

41. Lord Cornbury to Charles Hedges, July 15, 1705, *N.Y. Col. Docs.*, IV, 1150–1156; "Reasons of the council showing their right to alter and amend money bills," Nov. 16, 1711, and "The Opinion of the assembly to the governor," Nov. 23, 1711, N.Y. Col. MSS, LVI, 173–174, 187, LVII, 2; *Journal of Legislative Council,* I, 328; Lords of Trade to Gov. Hunter, Jan. 12, 1712, Livingston-Redmond MSS, Roll 3; *Journal of General Assembly*, I, 86, 186–189, 307, 309, 333.

42. The only help Livingston obtained from Hunter in implementing the new patent was the latter's effort to persuade some members of the assembly not to oppose Livingston's admission to the popular body. But Hunter was indifferent to the local controversies aroused by the manor lordship. As for the issue over Livingston's admission to the assembly in 1717, see Robert Livingston to his wife, Alida, May 13, 1717 (Dutch), quoted in Leder, *Livingston*, 239, 241–242.

43. Ten Broeck to Livingston, May 18, 1717 (Dutch), quoted *ibid.*, 242; Philip Livingston to father, Robert, May 20, 1717, Livingston-Redmond MSS, Roll 3; John Livingston to father, Robert, May 29, 1717, *ibid.*

44. *Journal of General Assembly*, I, 395, 396–398. For a good discussion of the manor status and Livingston's strategy, see Leder, *Livingston*, 236–240, 241–243.

vizor, one Treasurer, one Assessor and one Collector" for the manor.[45] Curiously, Philip Livingston, son of Robert, somehow understood the bill for annexation to be a stratagem on his father's part to have the domain "freed from both [the counties of Albany and Dutchess] in time," for the sake of "the manor Inhabitants and Tenants."[46] However that may be, this law brought the manor under the uniform provincial administrative norms, and the supervisor form of government formally replaced that of the lordship.

The metamorphosis of Livingston Manor is clearly illustrated by two tenants' lease deeds, one from 1708 and one from 1732, which contain quite different descriptions of administrative practices in the manor. A printed lease for Andrew Gardner in 1708 stipulated that the tenant and his heirs "shall be subject and obedient to the Laws rules and jurisdiction which is or shall be hereafter made and Established in and by a court Leet and Court baron when the same shall be Erected and the power thereof Exercised and used within the said Manor."[47] The indenture does not say whether the manorial courts were in actual operation at the time the deed was drawn, but it suffices to show Livingston's intention to establish them sometime in the future. However, a printed lease agreement with Evert Evertse in 1732 for a small lot on the manor had a provision entirely different from Gardner's with regard to manor administration. It stated that Evertse, his wife, and their heirs and assigns, "every one of them . . . at all Times hereafter, be Subject unto, observe, do and obey all reasonable Orders, Rules and Agreements as shall at any time hereafter be made by the Majority of the Inhabitants of the Mannor of . . . Philip Livingston."[48] Conspicuously lacking in this deed was a reference to the manorial courts. This significant change toward a more democratic system, at least in form, which took place sometime before 1732, is a concrete testimony to the success of the counties of Albany and

45. "An Act for Annexing that part of the Mannor of Livingstone, which now Lies in Dutchess County, into the County of Albany," May 27, 1717, *N.Y. Col. Laws,* I, 915–916.
46. Philip Livingston to father, Robert, May 20, 1717, Livingston-Redmond MSS, Roll 3. Robert Livingston, Jr., a grandson of the first Robert and the third lord of Livingston Manor, seriously thought about trying to have the law repealed for some reason, but nothing came of it. Robert Livingston, Jr., to James Duane, Nov. 22, 1763, James Duane Papers (microfilm), Roll 1. All references to the Duane Papers are to the microfilm edition published by the New-York Historical Society, New York, which owns the originals.
47. Lease to Andrew Gardner, Mar. 25, 1708, Livingston-Redmond MSS, Roll 3.
48. Lease to Evert Evertse and his wife, May 1, 1732, *ibid.,* 6. From this time on, all the printed leases contained no reference to the court leet and court baron. The only exception was a lease deed, dated Apr. 14, 1748, for Solomon Shute (*ibid.*). It seems that Philip Livingston mistakenly used the old form of lease for this tenant.

Dutchess and the assembly in imposing on the manor and its owner the same principles of local government that the other towns were then practicing.

A similar fate befell the judicial privileges of the manors. Each of the manorial proprietors was equipped, as we noted above, with the lordly power to police within his domain by virtue of his manor patent. If any cases arose in his manor concerning rent, debt, trespass, and land tenure, the lord was supposed to hold a court baron. But we find that these cases between landlord and tenant and between tenant and tenant were adjudicated not by the lord and his assigns but by duly constituted courts of sessions, courts of common pleas, and higher courts.

Records on this matter are scanty and piecemeal, but the few extant documents shed enough light on the malfunction of the judicial system of the lordship. As early as 1686 Kiliaen Van Rensselaer was resorting to the provincial judiciary rather than to a manorial court, as is shown by his ejectment suit brought against his tenant Gerrit Teunissen Van Vechten in the court of oyer and terminer.[49] William Brown, a tenant of the Manor of Cortlandt, was sued in 1759 by Stephen Van Cortlandt, the third "lord" of the manor, on a trespassing charge in the supreme court.[50] Another case involved Frederick Philipse and his tenant at will Uriah Travis in the Manor of Philipsburgh. In May 1769 Philipse sued Travis in the court of common pleas for Westchester County in order to recover two years' rent that was in arrears (an annual rent for Travis's lease was £6 4s. 6d.). Of utmost importance is Philipse's specific acknowledgment in his declaration filing the suit that his manor was "within the jurisdiction of the court."[51] If the court had jurisdiction over the manor for rent and land tenure, then where was the court baron? Why did the manor "lord" not convene his handy court for his own material advantage?

Not only Philipse, but the residents and tenants on all these manors also invariably referred disputes involving themselves to a court other than the manorial court. In 1705, one Melzert Abrahamse Van Deuse

49. "Kiliaen Van Rensselaer vs. Garret Tewnison," May 16, 1686, N.Y. Col. MSS, XXXIV, 5.

50. "A writ of the Supreme Court to the Sheriff of Westchester County, Nov. 10, 1759," Van Cortlandt Papers, VX1617, Sleepy Hollow Restorations Lib. For a similar case of trespass, see "Henderick Van Rensselaer vs Art Middoch," in the court of common pleas for Albany County, Mar. 11, 1740, Misc. MSS, Livingston, N-P. In this case, the declaration stated that the cause lay "within the Jurisdiction of this court."

51. "Frederick Philipse against U. Travis for arrears of rent," May 1769, in the Westchester court of common pleas, Philipse Papers, Huguenot Historical Association, New Rochelle, N.Y.

of Rensselaerswyck brought an action in the mayor's court of Albany against his fellow manor tenant Cornelis Van Vechten for the latter's alleged delinquency in repaying a £15 debt. After some debate over the competency of the court in the case, the court with the assistance of the jury proceeded and found the defendant not guilty.[52] Again, a trespass and damage suit involving two tenants on Cortlandt Manor, Lawrence Haff and Moses Knap, was tried in 1759 and 1760 by Joseph Sherwood, a justice of the peace, with a jury.[53] Even a disputed election of a constable in the Manor of Rensselaerswyck was dealt with by the court of sessions.[54] In at least one instance, a tenant on the Manor of Livingston, Melgart Shutselaer, turned in 1749 to a justice of the peace of Albany County, Henry Van Rensselaer of Claverack, rather than to his landlord, in order to settle a difference with a neighbor, Johannis Michiel, over the course of a road.[55]

That rent, debt, and some petty disputes were tried in the provincial and county courts rather than the manorial court is hardly irregular in view of the judicial system set up by the province. The law establishing courts of judicature for the province in 1691 specified in detail the respective jurisdictions of various courts. According to the law, a justice of the peace was empowered to handle with or without a jury, depending on the wishes of both plaintiff and defendant, cases of debt and trespass to the value of 40 shillings. This justice of the peace's court was a revision of the town court of three commissioners established under "An Act to settle Courts of Justice" in 1683.[56] (In 1754, the competence of the justice was upgraded, enabling him to take cognizance of all causes from £2 to £5 except when, as before, the king's affairs or the title of lands were concerned.[57]) The law of 1691 also established in every county a court of common pleas to try all actions or suits to the value of £20 and "tryable at the Common Law of whatever nature, . . . except [any] thing relating to title of land." The Supreme Court of Judicature was to try causes

---

52. Munsell, ed., *Annals of Albany*, V, 114–116.

53. Haff's charge against Joseph Sherwood, Mar. 13, 1760, N.Y. Col. MSS, LXXXVIII, 12; writ of Philip Livingston, Jr., clerk of the city and county of Albany, Jan. 13, 1740, Misc. MSS, Livingston, N-P.

54. Court of sessions, Oct. 14, 1701, Munsell, ed., *Annals of Albany*, IV, 144–145.

55. Philip G. Livingston to Henry Van Rensselaer at Claverack, Apr. 12, 1749, Van Rensselaer-Fort Papers, 1729–1789, N.Y. Pub. Lib.

56. *N.Y. Col. Laws*, I, 125–126, 226–231, 303–308, 359–360, II, 964–967.

57. *Ibid.*, III, 1011–1016, IV, 296–301, 736–737; James De Lancey to Lords of Trade, Dec. 15, 1754, *N.Y. Col. Docs.*, IV, 929; John Tabor Kempe's commonplace book, John Tabor Kempe Papers, Miscellaneous, Box 5, N.-Y. Hist. Soc.

valued at over £20 and also was to sit on appeals from the lower courts.[58]

The legislative records pertaining to the structure of the colonial judiciary in New York contain no reference whatever to the manorial court baron. No stipulation was made, for example, as to the causes and amounts with which the court baron was to deal. The letter and tenor of the legislation concerning the judiciary make it clear, just as in the area of administration, that the laws were to be applicable to every "town, manor, precinct and county" in the province.[59] Therefore, it is logical to conclude that the manors never enjoyed judicial autonomy for either the court leet or the court baron. Illustrating this point is a letter that Robert Livingston, Jr., the third "lord" of the Manor of Livingston, wrote in 1763 to both his son Peter and his son-in-law James Duane asking about the feasibility of "establishing a court" in the manor.[60] His inquiry was probably prompted by the inconvenience that he and his tenants had experienced in traveling some forty miles to the county seat, where the court of sessions and the court of common pleas were held, in order to obtain justice. That the inquiry was ever made testifies indisputably to the nonexistence of a manorial court there.

The act of 1717, drafted by Robert Livingston and approved by the assembly, that annexed the Dutchess County part of his manor to Albany County, confirmed to the "proprietor" of the manor, "his Heirs and Assigns all such Franchises, privileges, and Immunities, which have from time to Time been granted to him, his Heirs and Assigns, from his present Majesty King George, and his Royal Predecessors, Kings and Queens of England." In 1751 and again in 1752, the deputies, for the first time in the legislative annals of New York and in one of their rare moments of humor, called Robert Livingston, Jr., "Lord" and passed an act authorizing him or a justice of the peace, with the assistance of two freeholders, to assess the damages that should be charged against the owners of roving animals in his manor.[61] The assembly's declaration of respect for the lordly privileges was, of course, entirely hollow, for the counties had obstructed, and the deputies many years earlier had killed forever, most of those rights essential to the functioning of the manor lordship. Deprived of its vital powers, the lordship came to represent more the shadow than

58. These lower courts included the court of sessions or general sessions with jurisdictions over criminal and administrative matters.

59. *N.Y. Col. Laws*, III, 1011, also I, 481–682, II, 964.

60. Robert Livingston, Jr., to James Duane, Nov. 22, 1763, Duane Papers, Roll 1.

61. *N.Y. Col. Laws*, I, 916, III, 882.

the substance of a feudal institution. On one occasion close to the end of the Dutch period, depressed over the steady erosion of the patroonship, Jeremiah Van Rensselaer, director of the Van Rensselaer colony, stated: "One may think oneself to be a great lord, but it does not amount to much, as you well know."[62] Under English rule, the legal power of the manor lord amounted to equally little.

## The Authority and Power of the Manor Landlords

It would be a mistake, however, to suppose that the castration of the manor lordship left the proprietors politically powerless. Though most of the legal authority derived from their patents was gone, the mere fact that these men owned vast tracts of land and had great wealth put them at the top of the provincial class hierarchy and brought them a variety of respectable public offices, which in turn gave them considerable influence.[63]

A cursory survey of the officeholding of a few proprietors reveals the extent of their political influence. Kiliaen Van Rensselaer, the second lord of Rensselaerswyck, seems to have been a justice of the peace for thirty-four years, from 1684, when he was a young man of twenty-one, to his death in 1719. During most of this time, his career was divided between serving as assemblyman from his manor from 1692 to 1703 and as councillor from 1703 to 1719.[64] Jeremiah, son of Kiliaen, followed in his father's footsteps. A member of the House of Representatives for the manor from 1726 to 1743, he was nominated for a seat in the council in 1744 but not appointed.[65] Robert Livingston, the founder of his family in the colony, was a provincial councilman (1698–1701); an assemblyman briefly from the city and county of Albany (1709–1710); and for a longer period an assemblyman from his manor (1716–1725). He occupied the house speakership for eight years until his retirement. Mean-

---

62. Jeremiah Van Rensselaer to John Baptist Van Rensselaer, Oct. 17, 1661, *Jeremias Van Rensselaer Correspondence*, 269–270.

63. Cadwallader Colden's classification of the provincial class hierarchy in "State of the Province of New York," Dec. 6, 1765, *The Colden Letter Books, 1760–1775* (N.-Y. Hist. Soc., *Colls.*, IX–X [1876–1877]), II, 68–69, hereafter cited as *Colden Letter Books*.

64. *Journal of General Assembly*, I, 20, 32, 37, 54, 86, 92, 118, 129, 144; Minutes of the Court of Common Pleas, 1698–1699, N.Y. Col. MSS, XXXIII, 53, 197, XXXIV, 77, XLII, 67; "List of Officers in New-York and Their Salaries," Apr. 20, 1693, N.Y. Col. Docs., IV, 26. Kiliaen Van Rensselaer also appears as one of the judges of the court of common pleas in 1713 and 1714. N.Y. Col. MSS, LVIII, 119, LIX, 40.

65. *Journal of General Assembly*, I, 545, 557, 573, 574, 704, 749; George Clinton to Lords of Trade, Oct. 9, 1744, N.Y. Col. Docs., VI, 261.

while, he probably retained the justiceship during most of his political
life.[66] In the same year that the elder Livingston left politics, his son
Philip was appointed to the council (1725–1749), while another son,
Gilbert, represented the manor in the assembly from 1726 to 1736.
Robert Livingston's grandson, Robert, Jr., was also an assemblyman,
from 1737 to 1752.[67] Adolph Philipse, bachelor proprietor of the northern part of the Manor of Philipsburgh after the death of his father, Frederick, was a councilman from 1705 to 1720, sometime justice of the
supreme court, and speaker of the house for all but two years from 1725
to 1746.[68] No less extensive was the officeholding record of Adolph's
nephew Frederick Philipse II, proprietor of the southern part of the
manor, who was both a representative from Westchester County continuously from 1726 to 1751 and also a justice of the supreme court (1728–
1751).[69] Finally, Philip Van Cortlandt, the second "lord" of Cortlandt
Manor, was a justice of the peace for Westchester County in 1710—
while he lived in New York City—and a member of the council from
1729 until his death in 1746.[70]

At the local level, a proprietor considered the retention of a justiceship of the peace desirable for several reasons. Apart from its prestige,
the office offered its holder an opportunity to represent his domain's
interest at the court of general sessions, which was the highest county administrative authority and the place where such local concerns as roads,
taxes, fencing, and the county levy were discussed and decided upon.

66. For Robert Livingston's activities in the assembly, see Journal of General Assembly,
I, 239, 243, 271, 381, 395, 413, 513; Leder, Livingston, 205, 239–240, 247, 257–258,
280, 282–283. As for Livingston as a justice of the peace, see the deposition of Elizabeth
Taat, Jan. 16, 1722, Livingston-Redmond MSS, Roll 4; Robert Livingston's warrant against
Dirck Wessells Ten Broeck, Jr., of Albany, Aug. 24, 1713, ibid., Roll 3; "List of Persons for
whom Commissions [justice of the peace] are made out in the County of Albany," July 25,
1710, N.Y. Col. MSS, LV, 40, LIX, 40.

67. William Burnet to Lords of Trade, Nov. 26, 1720, Dec. 1725, N.Y. Col. Docs., V,
580, 772; Journal of General Assembly, I, 545, 557, 573, 574, 704, 749, II, 1, 63, 222,
275, 329. Philip Livingston also appears as a justice of the peace of the city and county of
Albany, Misc. MSS, Albany, Box 3, N.-Y. Hist. Soc.

68. Stanley Katz, Newcastle's New York: Anglo-American Politics, 1732–1753 (Cambridge, Mass., 1968), 152; Journal of General Assembly, I, 513, 545, 557, 573, 574, 702,
717, 749, II, 1–2, 63; Lord Cornbury to Lords of Trade, Feb. 25, 1705, and William
Burnet to Lords of Trade, Nov. 26, 1720, N.Y. Col. Docs., IV, 1137, V, 578–579. For
Philipse's seat in the supreme court, see Deed Book G, 250, Westchester Co. Clerk's Office.

69. Journal of General Assembly, I, 545, 557, 573, 702, 749, II, 1, 63, 222, 275. In
1728 Frederick Philipse was one of the judges of the court of common pleas for Westchester
County. Deed Book F, 255, Westchester Co. Clerk's Office.

70. "List of civil officers of the County of Westchester," June 25, 1710, N.Y. Col. MSS,
LIV, 20, 40. Van Cortlandt's appointment, Feb. 3, 1729, ibid., LXVIII, 145.

Service as a justice also enabled the proprietor to keep in close touch with county politics. Moreover, the office could be used to maintain order among the tenants. Acting as a member of the justice of the peace court either by himself or with the assistance of a jury, a proprietor could try petty disputes and, in one landlord's words, "quiet noisy people, and turn off such as would chuse to be troublesome."[71] When a landlord did not himself hold a justiceship, he usually picked loyal tenants to be appointed to the office. Sometimes he served in the office together with one or two tenants.[72] The same area might have several justices. At the provincial level, membership either in the council or in the assembly opened up for the manorial lord the possibility of greater political influence, plus higher social standing. These offices placed him in a position to keep a protective watch on his land title as well as to promote his personal interest. For some proprietors, public service at the provincial level offered a vent for soaring ambition and the chance to exercise noblesse oblige.

Some proprietary families, notably the Philipses, the De Lanceys, and the Livingstons, exerted a tremendous impact on eighteenth-century New York politics. As opposition leaders, they were often able to thwart gubernatorial policies they disliked; as court party leaders, their support was highly regarded and sought by almost every governor.[73] By contrast, their influence at the local (county) level was not as impressive as their officeholdings might suggest. A manor owner as justice of the peace could issue a warrant to a county sheriff or a local constable authorizing the arrest of a disturber of the peace. But as an individual justice, he was entirely helpless when civil action involved more than £5 or when he was a party to a cause. Furthermore, since he was usually merely one of several justices in his neighborhood, a tenant who happened to dislike

71. Abraham Lott to David McCarty, Apr. 7, 1775, McCarty Papers, N.Y. Pub. Lib.; Robert Livingston, Jr., to Abraham Yates, Jr., Apr. 14, 1755, Abraham Yates, Jr., Papers, 1607–1825, Box 1, ibid.

72. Fragmentary records indicate that Jacob Vosburgh and Tobias Ten Broeck, tenants in Livingston Manor, were justices of the peace in 1709, 1720, and 1721. Minutes of Court of Sessions, 1717–1723, 15, 17, Albany Co. Clerk's Office. In Philipsburgh Manor, the tenants John Harmense in 1709, Abraham Devoe in 1713, Abraham Martlinghs in 1747, and Gilbert Drake in 1770 held the justiceship. "List of officers in the Manor of Philipsburgh," Tarrytown Argus, Apr. 18, 1903; Deed Book D, 17, Westchester Co. Clerk's Office; petition of Richard Budd to Daniel Horsmanden, Mar. 28, 1770, Kempe Papers, Law Suits (A–B).

73. Katz, Newcastle's New York, passim; Bonomi, Factious People, 89–99, 146, 156–165.

the landlord could turn to another justice for adjudication of a dispute with a fellow tenant.[74] This circumstance made it difficult for a manor justice to behave arbitrarily. By the same token, at the meetings of the county justices (court of sessions or otherwise), the manor owner could regularly be outvoted by his colleagues. The number of justices in a given county varied over time. In 1710 Westchester County had a total of sixteen justices, including two from the manors of Philipsburgh and Cortlandt. In 1711 Albany County had about the same number.[75] Since majority rule prevailed at these meetings, the justices from the manors, being two or three at most, were a desperate minority, a status that they had to endure throughout the colonial period.

In the case of Albany County, the principal power was the city of Albany, whose justices (mayor, recorder, and aldermen), by using their superiority in numbers, which was augmented by the frequent nonattendance of the justices from the countryside, were able to dominate county government and run it as the city's interests dictated.[76] Even juries, in both criminal and administrative cases, tended to be dominated by the members from the city when impaneled.[77] In 1721, Andrew Coeymans, assemblyman from Rensselaerswyck Manor, expressed disgust with the city's customary way of bending everything and every other town to its own advantage. Referring specifically to the tax assessment of the county, Coeymans wrote, "If any precinct brings in their Estimate [the city justices] outvote them and make that precinct pay as they please, taking off one less and putting so much as they please on [the other]. Some precincts

74. Philip Livingston to Henry Van Rensselaer, Apr. 12, 1749, Van Rensselaer-Fort Papers.
75. "List of civil officers of the County of Westchester," June 25, 1710, N.Y. Col. MSS, LIV, 40; "List of the Justices for the City and County of Albany," Dec. 27, 1711, Livingston-Redmond MSS, Roll 3. For the composition of the justices' court, see Minutes of Court of Sessions, 1717–1723, 1763–1782, Albany Co. Clerk's Office. See also N.Y. Col. MSS, XLII, 67 (1–9), XLIX, 95.
76. Philip Livingston to father, Robert, Jan. 8, 1724, Livingston-Redmond MSS, Roll 4.
77. A list of jurors in 1687 for the Albany County court of sessions shows that of the 16 jurors impaneled, 10 were from Albany city, 2 from Schenectady, 2 from the Manor of Rensselaerswyck, 1 from Half-Moon, and 1 from Conestoga. Another list of 12 jurors in the same year had 7 from Albany, 2 from Catskill, 1 from Schenectady, and 2 from the manor. Unfortunately, lists of jurors in subsequent years are not available, but the pattern of jury distribution in that county is not likely to have changed. Writs of venire and lists of jurors, Apr. 10, 1687, N.Y. Col. MSS, XXXV, 80b, 81b. The Albany city magistrates as justices of the peace also sat on the court of oyer and terminer, which had a high criminal jurisdiction. Joel Munsell, ed., Collections on the History of Albany, from its Discovery to the Present Time (Albany, N.Y., 1865–1871), I, 216.

they have raised above half in 2 years and threaten next time to make them pay more."[78]

What was true of Albany's control in county tax affairs was also true in other matters. When Philip Livingston, son of the first Robert and an official of Albany city, called Albany County "oppressive," he must have had in mind the magistrates of Albany city, because they were in fact identified with Albany County.[79] They were vigilant over their privileges and even their pride. Once Robert Livingston, speaker of the assembly, a justice of the peace, elder statesman of the county of Albany, and supervisor of his manor, seized an occasion to advise the county justices on some courthouse problem. They rebuffed him by saying that "they did not want [his] advice nor Instructions in That affair."[80] Watching at close range this and other incidents, such as the court of sessions fining two justices from Livingston Manor six shillings each for no apparent good reason, Philip Livingston had enough of their abusiveness. In a rare outburst of sarcasm, he wrote to his father: "They would needs have you to pay to drink your health which I could hardly deny to pay Since they are but seldom in that humour."[81]

Kiliaen Van Rensselaer had no better luck with the Albany magistrates. In 1712 he communicated to them that the twenty-one-year privilege of the city residents to cut timber or firewood on his manor, as provided in its charter, had long since expired and urged them to negotiate with him for renewal. Henceforth, he said, he would prosecute anyone cutting the wood without a license. The reaction of the magistrates was belligerent. They resolved that in case Van Rensselaer prosecuted any of the city residents, "We make our selves defend'ts for him."[82] Behind this resolution was undoubtedly their confidence that they would try the case anyway and give the verdict in favor of the accused at the court of sessions, which they controlled. Given that a man of stature like Livingston or Van Rensselaer received this kind of rude treatment from Albany

78. "Memorial of Andrew Coeymans one of the Representatives for the Mannor of Renselaerswyck in the County of Albany to Governor Wm Burnet and the Council," July 13, 1721, Livingston-Redmond MSS, Roll 2; Philip Livingston to father, Robert, Feb. 15, 1722, Jan. 8, 11, 1724, and Aug. 9, 1724, *ibid.*, Roll 4.
79. Philip Livingston to father, Robert, May 20, 1717, *ibid.*, Roll 3.
80. Thomas Williams to Robert Livingston, Jan. 28, 1721, *ibid.*, Roll 4.
81. Philip Livingston to father, Robert, Feb. 8, 1721, *ibid.*
82. Munsell, ed., *Annals of Albany*, VI, 279–280, 280–281, 284–285; Philip Livingston to father, Robert, Jan. 15, 1713, Livingston-Redmond MSS, Roll 3; deed of agreement between Albany city and Kiliaen Van Rensselaer, Feb. 18, 1717, Deed Book 5: 361–363, Albany Co. Clerk's Office.

officials, and that a manor justice was just one of many in the county, we have reason to believe that the "lord's" influence as a local officer was quite marginal. For the same reason, a manor owner could not take for granted that he could safely abuse his power—if that ever happened—on the manor.[83]

The preponderance of the city of Albany in county affairs, however, was due not only to its charter right and the effective use of that right but also to the city's important economic and social functions. It was the "central-place" in the frontier county, to use the terminology of historical geography.[84] Because of Albany's traditional monopoly of the Indian trade (though often infringed upon by interlopers), its superior fortifications, and its common use as the embarkation point for military expeditions against enemy Indians and French Canada, those seeking the lucrative trade with the natives and the garrisons at the fort gravitated to it. Along with these commercial interests came service industries and craftsmen such as blacksmiths, carpenters, bricklayers, masons, and brewers, as well as tavern keepers and innholders. The growth of farming villages in neighboring areas, spurred on particularly in the early decades of the eighteenth century by the extraordinary demand for wheat and flour, further contributed to the town's prosperity. The farmers sold their produce to the shopkeepers in exchange for merchandise and borrowed money from the merchants. In the city, wheat and flour were certified, packed, and often exported directly to overseas markets. For most of the frontier inhabitants, Albany was the entrepôt for goods and the main link with the outside world. The farmers also came to town to settle litigation at the courts that met each spring and fall and to register their deeds with the county clerk. This enviable political and economic position continued even after the Indian trade monopoly was broken partially in 1722 and completely in 1726.[85] For, once started, the growth of

83. Abraham Yates, Jr., active in Albany County politics since 1750, stated in his manuscript, "History of Albany" (not dated), that "from the date of the Charter (Albany) the politicians of the Patroons have purused the Plan to get such a number of members in the Corporation [of Albany] as were sufficient to frustrate the measures necessary to support [Albany's] rights and to get the body into such measures as to humor the Patroon's interest." But evidence indicates that Albany city was always able to frustrate the scheme of the Van Rensselaers and the Livingstons. Abraham Yates, Jr.'s, "History," Yates Papers, Box 4.

84. On central-place theory, see, for example, James T. Lemon, "Urbanization and the Development of Eighteenth-Century Southeastern Pennsylvania and Adjacent Delaware," *WMQ*, 3d Ser., XXIV (1967), 501–533.

85. *N.Y. Col. Docs.*, IV, 753, V, 572, 682; *Journal of General Assembly*, I, 441; Henry Holland to Robert Livingston, June 16, 1721, Livingston-Redmond MSS, Roll 5; *N.Y. Col. Laws*, II, 8–12, 98–105, 197; Minutes of Supreme Court of Judicature of New

the city became self-generating, even after the primary cause of that growth had long since disappeared. Furthermore, the city of Albany still retained influence in Indian affairs. Until 1747, when William Johnson replaced them,[86] Albany officials, under authority granted by Bellomont, served as commissioners of Indian affairs. The commissioners adroitly employed their authority and prestige with the natives to obtain furs and land for themselves and their friends.[87]

Before 1722 one had to be a freeman of Albany in order to trade with the Indians; in fact, freemanship was a prerequisite for any business within the city before and after that date. Frederick Philipse, based in New York City, had a house in Albany and alternated his residence between the two towns in the 1670s and 1680s. Two generations of the Livingstons, Robert and Philip, kept a townhouse there for trade and other purposes,[88] as did the Rensselaerswyck proprietors, Kiliaen, Jeremiah, Stephen, and Stephen, Jr., and others, like Henry Van Rensselaer, the owner of the Claverack part of Rensselaerswyck after 1704.[89] Associating with and befriending the city's powerful officials was the golden path to economic advancement. Precisely for this reason, Philip Livingston chose to stay in Albany, though he detested the hubbub of commerce and longed for country living. Similarly, many of the manorial proprietors and their kinsmen sought an office in city government.[90]

Aside from economic and political advantages, Albany had certain other attractions. Though dusty in the dry season and muddy in the rainy —for its streets, unlike the city of New York's, were not paved, and its low-lying area near the river was regularly flooded in the early spring—it had a certain glamour for the landlords. It was a place where society

---

York, 162, 170, 172, 221, Hall of Records, New York. An excellent discussion of the Albany monopoly of Indian trade is found in Armour, "Merchants of Albany," 4–7, 139, 147–149, 152, 155–156.

86. Armour, "Merchants of Albany," 253.

87. "Copy of Caveat for the Corporation of Albany for land in the Mohawk country, 1719," "Uncatalogued Livingston Manuscripts," N.-Y. Hist. Soc.

88. Van Laer, ed., *Court Minutes of Albany, Rensselaerswyck and Schenectady,* II, 9, 10–12, 106, 130, 396, III, 430; Philip Livingston to father, Robert, Mar. 25, Apr. 10, 1724, Livingston-Redmond MSS, Roll 4; Robert Livingston, Jr., to father, Robert, Jan. 25, 1714, *ibid.,* Roll 3.

89. "Journal of Isaac Norris, during a Trip to Albany in 1745 . . . ," in *Pennsylvania Magazine of History and Biography,* XXVII (1903), 24–25.

90. Henry Van Rensselaer, brother of Kiliaen, was alderman of the city in 1699. Philip Livingston was its mayor from 1722 to 1723, clerk of the city and county of Albany, and secretary to the commissioners of Indian affairs for many years after 1721. Munsell, ed., *Annals of Albany,* IV, 98, VIII, 276; N.Y. Col. Docs., IV, 567; commission for the office of clerk, Jan. 30, 1721, Livingston-Redmond MSS, Roll 4.

gathered; lawyers, merchants, and other men of means lived there, and nicely dressed, perfumed ladies were seen in its few narrow streets. It was also a place where one enjoyed lively entertainment and small talk and celebrated a friend's birthday at one of its several taverns. At least one manor proprietor defined a trip to Albany as "to go a pleasureing."[91] The landlords might primarily reside at their rustic country mansions, but their hearts and their fantasies were tied to the city. In this small, homogeneous, Dutch community of no more than three hundred families before the large influx of New Englanders in the 1750s, everyone knew everyone else, and their relationships were bound to be personal.[92] Albany was a social setting in which the landlords, it seems, were concerned as much about their social acceptability and standing among their peers as about their economic position and the pursuit of profit. Defiance of accepted norms or an addiction to excess in any form could mean social ostracism.

Dyspeptic Robert Livingston, Jr., a man who had spent most of his youth in New York City and, of all the Livingstons, had the least connection with Albany, nevertheless betrayed extreme sensitivity to the opinion of the Albanians. After putting down the rioters in the eastern part of his manor bordering Massachusetts, he wrote in May 1757 from his manor seat to Abraham Yates, Jr., his friend and sheriff of the city and county of Albany: "Pray Inform me what the People in your City Say of it and how its relished by the better Sort, I think I did my duty; but p[e]rhaps I am not a proper Judge as its in my owne case, if you have any news communicate it." After he received the good news in July that the grand jury had indicted the rioters, he hoped the "better Sort of people do not condemn me for proceeding in the manner I do, and I certenly can at pr[e]sent have no other remedy." He was still concerned that his peers might not approve of him. On another occasion, he insisted to Yates that "you vindicate my character . . . in every Company you hear it mention'd that I may not lay under the Imputation of telling falsehoods."[93] These comments are clear manifestations of the ways in which peer-group pressure could constrain a landlord's conduct.

Equally revealing, though not directly related to Albany, was the

91. John Lindsay to Jeremiah Van Rensselaer, Mar. 19, 1737, Letters, 1700–1749, Rensselaerswyck Manuscripts, N.Y. State Lib.; Robert Livingston, Jr., to Abraham Yates, Jr., June 8, 1759, Yates Papers, Box 1.

92. Henry Van Drissen's report to earl of Loudon, June 2, 1757, Loudon Papers, LO3774, Huntington Lib.; Nov. 1755 entry in Copy Book and Journal of Abraham Yates, June 1754–Sept. 1758, Yates Papers, Box 3.

93. Robert Livingston, Jr., to Abraham Yates, Jr., May 18, July 19, 1757, Aug. 6, 1759, Yates Papers, Box 1.

attitude of Oliver De Lancey, one of the proprietors of Cortlandt Manor. In 1755, defending his tardiness in collecting overdue rents, debt, and the interest on loans, De Lancey advised his sister Susannah Warren, the widow of Sir Peter, to be patient, explaining that, "it will take some time to Call in the Money due unless I take such harsh Measures as would bring on Me some Disesteem in the Country I am always to live."[94] The concern for reputation, coupled with the political and economic power of Albany city, seems to have forced the landlords to a moderate course in the management of their country estates.

As the example of De Lancey suggests, there is no reason to think that the proprietors of the manors of Cortlandt and Philipsburgh behaved any differently, for they were exposed to almost the same combination of pressures as the northern manorial proprietors. Although Westchester County did not witness the development of a town as powerful as Albany, the landlords had to contend with the strong collective power of the towns in the county, and suffered the lot of minority representation at county governmental proceedings whenever county interests came into conflict with the manors.[95] On at least one occasion, even the assembly admitted that a manorial proprietor and his people had been overtaxed by the county to the benefit of the other towns, a practice that, as we have seen, was not peculiar to that county alone.[96] Thus, because of the superior political power of the towns, the county could become the overseer of the landlords and undercut their local authority.

## The Internal Aspects of Manorial Governance

Ironically, the deterioration of the power of the manorial proprietors was partly the result of their privilege (derived from their patents) of

94. Oliver De Lancey to Susannah Warren in London, Feb. 1, 1755, and Dec. 25, 1755, Gage Papers in Gage Additional Manuscript 1201, on microfilm at Sleepy Hollow Restorations Lib. and N.-Y. Hist. Soc. (originals at Sussex Archaeological Society, Lewes, Sussex, England), hereafter cited as Gage Papers.

95. In the first two decades of the 18th century, Westchester Borough served as the county seat, but it was basically a farming community. So was every other town in the county throughout the colonial period. Since there was no population center as such, the county justices had difficulty in agreeing on the location of a county court and jail. Even the polling place for the county election for the assembly moved from one town to another at different times, first at Rye, then at East Chester, and finally at White Plains in 1751. N.Y. Col. Laws, II, 6, III, 847–849; Benjamin Collier to James Alexander(?), Apr. 9, 1697, James Alexander Papers, Box entitled "Westchester County," N.-Y. Hist. Soc.; Henry B. Dawson, "Westchester-County, New York during the American Revolution," in Scharf, ed., History of Westchester County, I, 177.

96. N.Y. Col. Laws, I, 130–131.

sending a representative to the assembly. This privilege, granted to Rensselaerswyck in 1685, Cortlandt Manor in 1697 (to be effective twenty years after the patent date), and Livingston Manor in 1715, was intended by the governors to augment conservative power in the assembly.[97] At the same time, it was thought that the proprietors would employ their access to the popular branch of the government, together with their other lordly rights, to solidify their aristocratic hold at the local level. However, the original intention behind manorial representation was eventually frustrated on both counts. Without exception, manorial representatives, initially attached to the governors' interests in the 1720s and 1730s, later became the most outspoken antiprerogative and whiggish members, constituting a force that the conservative elements in the province endeavored to suppress in subsequent years, particularly during the Revolutionary era. Thus, ironically, the manorial privileges originally granted to enhance the crown's prerogative ultimately produced a force against this very prerogative.[98] Equally ironic, the privilege of representation contributed to the weakening of the proprietors' natural aristocratic tendencies in their respective domains.

The provincial government enacted laws in 1683, 1699, and 1701 that defined suffrage qualifications for general elections. The law of 1683 stipulated that only freeholders in the county and freemen in "any Corporation" should have the vote and defined a freeholder as everyone who was "Soe understood according to the Lawes of England." In England a voter in Parliamentary elections was, from the middle of the sixteenth century, an adult male who drew an annual income of 40 shillings from either a life leasehold or a freehold estate. The laws of 1699 and 1701 added a provincial touch to the earlier practice, establishing that a voter must have either a £40 freehold estate "free from all Encumbrances" or an "Estate of freehold during his Life, or for and dureing the Life of His

---

97. In 1734 Lewis Morris feared that Gov. Cosby would fall upon the scheme of "makeing a majority" of the court party in the General Assembly by creating new manors with representation privilege. His fear was grounded in the rumor that the Cortlandt Manor proprietors, at the instigation of the governor, would invoke the manor patent right of representation and claim a seat in the legislature. Indeed, Philip Verplanck, a grandson of the manor founder, returned to the assembly that year and, along with his uncle, Philip Van Cortlandt (a Cosbyite councilman), became an influential supporter of the governor. Lewis Morris to Cadwallader Colden, Jan. 17, 1734, *The Letters and Papers of Cadwallader Colden* (N.-Y. Hist. Soc., *Colls.*, L–LVI [New York, 1917–1923]), II, 100, hereafter cited as *Colden Papers*; *Journal of General Assembly*, I, 663, 664, 667. Robert Livingston's pro-Hunter and pro-Burnet politics is a familiar story.

98. Cadwallader Colden to earl of Dartmouth, Apr. 4, 1775, *N.Y. Col. Docs.*, VIII, 565; *N.Y. Col. Laws*, V, 874–875.

Wife," to the value of £40, which he had possessed three months before the date of a writ for election.[99] Conforming to the general sense of English law, these laws converted the lifetime leasehold (or longer), which was improved to £40 value, into a freehold for purposes of voting, whereas the leasehold for a fixed term of years, no matter how long it might be, and the leasehold at sufferance or at the will of a landlord, no matter how valuable it might be, was not defined as a freehold. The rationale for giving freehold status only to the lifetime leasehold was obviously that the possessor of such an estate would have a great enough sense of security and freedom to exercise personal judgment in elections independently of the will of his landlord.

These laws necessitated that the manorial proprietors create a considerable number of freeholders in their manor so that an election could be held to choose an assembly representative. Selling land in fee simple without any encumbrances whatsoever would have been one sure way of accomplishing this purpose, but the partial or total breakup of the manor estate was not attractive to most of the landowners. The alternative was conveying the land in perpetuity at a fixed rent, a type of landholding that had evolved in Europe and that was different from "feudal tenurial holding," or leasing it for one, two, or three lives. In general, the Van Rensselaers adopted the former, and the Livingstons and Van Cortlandts the latter.[100] The emergence of such relatively secure lease tenures was due to a number of factors, but it would not have been introduced at the time it was, or possibly would not have been introduced at all, if these suffrage laws had not been enacted. The beneficial impact of these laws upon the lease system in the manors is exemplified by the dramatic shift in the Van Rensselaers' policy, which roughly coincided with the time the laws were enacted. Their leases from about 1650 to 1690 were for a short term, varying from one to a maximum of twelve years; but these gave way to the perpetual or hereditary lease about the time the suffrage laws were passed. Several small tracts had been granted on perpetual term in the earlier decades, but only in isolated instances. General use of the new lease came only in the late 1680s and thereafter.[101] Of course,

99. N.Y. Col. Laws, I, 112, 405–408, 452–454. For English practice, see Chilton Williamson, American Suffrage from Property to Democracy, 1760–1860 (Princeton, N.J., 1960), 7; Don R. Gerlach, Philip Schuyler and the American Revolution in New York, 1733–1777 (Lincoln, Neb., 1964), app. C, 327–331.

100. For a fuller discussion of lease terms in the different manors, see chap. 5.

101. "A list of Indentures, 1696–1734[44?]," Rensselaerswyck MSS. Samuel Nissenson attributed the introduction of the perpetual lease to the "increasing demand for the land and the disinclination [on the part of the manor proprietor] to part with it absolutely."

the landlord was not legally bound to offer every tenant a perpetual lease and make him a voter. But once a precedent was set, the landlords felt that it was inexpedient to deny others the same popular terms, lest they be charged with discrimination. The frequent invocation of "custom and usage" in lease deeds shows that precedents indeed bore heavily on these contracts.[102] With this significant change in lease terms, most of the Rensselaerswyck tenants became freeholders qualified to vote in assembly elections.

On the Manor of Philipsburgh, on the other hand, which did not have the right of sending a representative to the assembly, the tenants held the least secure tenure—"lease at will" of their landlord—and were disenfranchised. The situation there in all probability would have been different if the manor had been able to send a member to the assembly. Thus, a privilege originally designed in part to strengthen a manor proprietor's aristocratic grip paradoxically resulted in the granting of a secure lease title for the majority of tenants and, as a corollary, in rendering them potentially independent of the landlord's power and influence.

Manorial seats in the assembly were generally monopolized by the proprietors and their relatives throughout the colonial period, provoking one unhappy provincial official to remark that they "are become Hereditary Members" (see table 3.1). As noted above, for a manor district to elect a representative other than the landlord himself or his nominee would have seemed downright absurd to the landlord and probably to his tenants as well.[103] This was particularly true in a political society in which the representative system was territorial in nature and a stake in property was considered the precondition for political participation. Furthermore, the landlord, by dint of his enormous wealth, enjoyed the greatest prestige and respect in the domain.[104] The combination of these

---

However, both reasons would have disposed him to adhere to the traditional short-term lease or impose a much less favorable one on the prospective settlers. Nissenson, *Patroon's Domain*, 57.

102. Gerrit Teunissen Van Vechten's deed, Deed Book 4: 69–70, Albany Co. Clerk's Office; deed between Jonas Douw and Andries Douw, Oct. 8, 1711, *ibid.*, 5: 165–166; deed between Kiliaen Van Rensselaer and Samuel Staats, Sept. 7, 1697, Drawer No. 1, Albany Institute of History and Art, Albany, N.Y.; will of Evert Wendell, July 23, 1749, Wills, XIX, 40–45, Queens College Library, New York.

103. Cadwallader Colden to Lords of Trade, Sept. 20, 1764, *Colden Letter Books*, I, 363–364; "Observations upon the act to explain and amend an act entitled, An Act for regulating the Elections of Representatives in General Assembly made and passed the 8th of May in the Eleventh of King William the third," probably written by Peter R. Livingston in 1769(?), Livingston-Redmond MSS, Roll 11. The author stated that "it must surely appear to be absurd to disqualify the Lord himself from representing his own Tenants and Estate."

104. A contemporary observer made the following remarks about power, prestige,

Table 3.1.  The Manorial Representatives, 1691–1776

### RENSSELAERSWYCK

| | |
|---|---|
| Kiliaen Van Rensselaer | 1691–1700, 1702–1703 |
| Andrew (Andries) Coeymans | 1701–1702, 1715–1726 |
| Henry Van Rensselaer | 1705–1714 |
| Jeremiah Van Rensselaer | 1726–1743 |
| John Baptist Van Rensselaer | 1743–1760 |
| Abraham Ten Broeck[a] | 1761–1776 |

### LIVINGSTON MANOR

| | |
|---|---|
| Robert Livingston | 1716–1725 |
| Robert Livingston, Jr.[b] | 1726–1727 |
| Gilbert Livingston | 1728–1736 |
| Robert Livingston, Jr. | 1737–1758 |
| William Livingston | 1759–1760 |
| Peter R. Livingston | 1761–1769, 1774–1776 |

### CORTLANDT MANOR

| | |
|---|---|
| Philip Verplanck[c] | 1734–1767 |
| Pierre Van Cortlandt | 1768–1776 |

[a] Ten Broeck was the husband of Elizabeth Van Rensselaer, sister of Stephen Van Rensselaer, the fourth "lord" of Rensselaerswyck.

[b] This Robert, Jr., was the second son of Robert, the founder of the manor, and should be distinguished from both Robert, Jr., a nephew of Robert, and Robert, Jr., son of Philip.

[c] Verplanck was the son-in-law of Johannes Van Cortlandt, the eldest son of Stephanus.

circumstances resulted in the remarkable absence of contested elections in the manors except on only two known occasions.

Even in contested elections, rival candidates came from the two different but related landlord families—never from outside. The only deviation from the pattern was the interregnum of Andrew Coeymans, a proprietor of the Coeymans patent within the jurisdiction of Rensselaerswyck and a confidant of Kiliaen Van Rensselaer. Coeymans's debut as a manor representative in 1701 was occasioned when the incumbent, Kiliaen Van Rensselaer, an anti-Leislerian, was expelled from the Leislerian-dominated assembly. However, beginning with the return of

---

respect, and influence due to wealth: "Every one who is Rich is look'd upon to be a Superior to a Poor Man"; "Riches gives a Man an Air of Authority and Grandeur, which command our Respect to him"; "Another Reason assignable, not for the Rise, but for the Continuance of the Practice of Reverencing the Rich, is, That the World has always accustomed itself to pay a sort of Veneration and Homage to them." "R. T. to William Bradford," *New-York Gazette*, Sept. 1739.

Kiliaen in 1702, the manor seat would stay with the Van Rensselaer family during the next decade. In 1715 Coeymans again returned to the assembly, and this time he was to serve until 1726, when Kiliaen's eldest son, Jeremiah, who several months before had reached the legal age of twenty-one, claimed and got the manor seat.[105] The sequence of the election returns makes one suspect that Coeymans was the nominee of the Van Rensselaers and that his service was contrived by the family as a sort of interim arrangement until Jeremiah came to adulthood. The practices of the other manors reinforce this suspicion.

There were two contested elections. The first was at Rensselaerswyck in 1759 when the incumbent, John Baptist Van Rensselaer, third son of the second lord, Kiliaen, was challenged in vain by his nephew Henry, son of Henry Van Rensselaer, the first proprietor of the Claverack part of the manor.[106] The second was the contest in the Manor of Cortlandt in 1768 between Pierre Van Cortlandt, second son of Philip Van Cortlandt (the second lord of the manor), and his nephew Colonel James Verplanck, whose father, Philip Verplanck, retired that year after thirty-four years of public service as the manor representative. Pierre won with the handsome plurality of 116 votes over his opponent's mere 27. Yet, of all the manorial elections, this was probably the only one in which the candidates campaigned vigorously, and its outcome was reported to have been "doubtful."[107] The rest of the elections seem to have been run in a "merry" atmosphere with the votes generally unanimous ("Nemine Contradicente").[108]

Since the tenant electors chose their landlord or his nominee in every election, it seems logical to suppose that they acquiesced in the notion that ownership of the manor gave the landlord an a priori claim to repre-

105. Jeremiah Van Rensselaer was born on Mar. 18, 1705, and took the seat in the assembly on Sept. 27, 1726. "Family Record of the Van Rensselaer from the Dutch Bible, Jan. 1, 1719," translated by H. Bleecker, Miscellaneous Documents, Box 8, "Van Rensselaer," Albany Inst. of Hist. and Art; *Journal of General Assembly*, I, 118, 129, 144, 195, 218, 271, 289, 298, 332, 366, 381, 545.

106. A badly scorched manuscript on the election returns shows that John Baptist Van Rensselaer received 113 votes, mostly from the Manor of Rensselaerswyck proper, and that Henry received 45 votes exclusively from his and his brother's tenants in Claverack (Lower Manor). "Election Poll, Jan. 19, 1759," "Miscellaneous Documents," Rensselaerswyck MSS.

107. James Duane to Abraham Ten Broeck, Mar. 1768, Ten Broeck Family Papers, Box 3, Albany Inst. of Hist. and Art; "Votes Taken at an Election in Manor of Cortlandt, March 10, 1768," Van Cortlandt Papers, V1645, Sleepy Hollow Restorations Lib.

108. Philip Livingston to father, Robert, Apr. 25, 1717, Livingston-Redmond MSS, Roll 3; Gaine's *New-York Gazette; and the Weekly Mercury*, Mar. 14, 1768, on the Rensselaerswyck election.

senting them and that they accepted this leadership as natural. To the modern mind, the election records in these manors seem to point to the hollowness of the elections as a democratic device. Yet, the mere fact that an election was held exerted a subtle influence on the landlord-candidate's behavior. It forced him to submit himself to his constituents and to project himself in a favorable light. For there was always a possibility, however remote, that the constituents might reject him at the polls, a testing ground for his popularity among the tenants. To be rejected by one's own tenants would have been an unacceptable social disgrace. Theoretically, the tenant voters could combine themselves, nominate their own candidate, and defeat their landlord. One landlord seasoned in politics observed that "sometimes alterations [could] happen very Surprisingly and unexpected in Elections."[109] In Dutchess County in 1768, "all the tenants" of Henry Beekman and Robert G. Livingston easily defeated at viva-voce election their landlords' candidate, Robert R. Livingston, despite "all the pains" the landlords took "that could be thought necessary."[110] Thus, the electoral process served as another element in the erosion of the landlord's power.

There is evidence that some manorial landlords did not take elections for granted. Instead, they went to some lengths to ingratiate themselves with the electorate and preferred the carrot to the stick. Philip Livingston, the second "lord" of Livingston Manor, while reporting to his son Robert, Jr., of the latter's election from his manor for the assembly, stated in 1739 that the "freeholders in our mannor would be glad if you sent them . . . the last Certificate for [your] past service in the assembly" and confessed that in return for the tenants' support, he had asked the manor clerk, Dirck Van Veghten, to give "bond" pledging to the electors that his son would serve in the assembly without receiving compensation (10 shillings a day) from them. After having said this, he again expressed his hope that Robert, Jr., would send certificates "to satisfy these people."[111] A few years later, Philip wrote and again asked Robert, Jr., to forward his "last Indenture for assemblyman" and his certificate

109. Robert Livingston, Jr., to Abraham Yates, Jr., Feb. 4, 1761, Yates Papers, Box 1.
110. Robert Livingston to Philip Schuyler, Feb. 27, 1769, Schuyler Papers, Box 23, N.Y. Pub. Lib.; James Duane to Abraham Ten Broeck, Mar. 1768, Ten Broeck Family Papers, Box 3. For this and other assembly elections, see Bonomi, *Factious People*, 255–256; Milton M. Klein, "Democracy and Politics in Colonial New York," *N.Y. History*, XL (1959), 221–246.
111. Philip Livingston to son Robert, Jr., Mar. 24, 1739, Livingston-Redmond MSS, Roll 7. Regarding wages for the assemblymen, see *N.Y. Col. Laws*, II, 116–118. The declaration by a candidate for the assembly that he did not desire any wages for his service

of service to "show people at the Election," which would be held soon. In the same letter, Philip touched on the subject of inviting a minister to his manor church and of finding a method for maintaining him. The landlord hoped henceforth to "oblige the Tenants to pay part" of the minister's salary, departing from the traditional practice, but he was afraid such a proposal would cause him "a Vast deal of trouble." With a view to averting any unexpected complications damaging to his son's chance of reelection, he would, stated he, let the troublesome issue rest until the "Ensueing Election is over."[112]

Notwithstanding the many forces circumscribing them, the manorial proprietors were still predominant in their respective domains, not because of their legal power, which as we have seen was not great, but because of their status as landlords. The owners of these manors, except those of the Manor of Cortlandt, referred to themselves as "lord" or "lord proprietor," drawing on their ancient patent title, but the title had lost its substantive meaning.[113] In the case of Rensselaerswyck, the designations "lord" and "patroon"—or even "the Lord Patroon" on formal occasions—were used interchangeably by the proprietor himself, his tenants, his friends, or even Albany city officials.[114] Sometimes these titles were misapplied. For example, John Van Rensselaer, son of Henry of Claverack, was addressed as "lord" or "patroon" by his tenants, although he was not of the main family lineage of Rensselaerswyck and thus was not entitled to lordship.[115] This social practice denoted not only the proprietors' love for a title but also the measure of high esteem the tenants accorded to their landlords and the high social distinction the latter enjoyed.

Inevitably, a manorial proprietor was expected to perform public

---

seems to have been one of the popular vote-getting devices employed in the 1740s and thereafter. See the announcement of the candidates, Adolph Philipse and three others in New York City and County election, Zenger's *New-York Weekly Journal*, Oct. 24, 1743.

112. Philip Livingston to son Robert, Jr., June 1, 1745, Livingston-Redmond MSS, Roll 7.

113. "Town Book of the Manor of Philipsburgh, 1742–1766," 8, N.-Y. Hist. Soc.; "Sale of improvements," Apr. 11, 1760, Misc. MSS, Livingston, R-W, *ibid.*

114. Sir William Johnson to Sir Jeffery Amherst, June 19, 1763, *N.Y. Col. Docs.*, VII, 524; John Rutherford to Cadwallader Colden, Apr. 22, 1745, *Colden Papers*, III, 112; Adoniah Schuyler to Edward Collins, June 7, 1745, Letters, 1700–1749, Rensselaerswyck MSS; Wills, XXXVII, 37–38, XIX, 40–45, XXXVIII, 13–15, Queens College Lib.; Kiliaen Van Rensselaer's will, Feb. 22, 1687, Wills, AVI, *ibid.*; Stephen Van Rensselaer's will, June 24, 1747, Townsend Collection, Box 1, Albany Inst. of Hist. and Art; Munsell, ed., *Collections on History of Albany*, I, 143.

115. As for the examples of the tenants calling John Van Rensselaer "Patroon" or "Lord," see Wills, XVI, 409–411, XXIX, 468, XXXIII, 312, 312–314, and AV39, AM74,

functions appropriate to his status. Just as the tenants repeatedly chose the landlord or his nominee as their representative to the assembly, they usually voted him or his nominee into the supervisorship of the manor. The "Town Book of the Manor of Philipsburgh, 1742–1766" reveals that Adolph Philipse acted in that capacity until his death in 1750. Two years later, Frederick Philipse III, the sole proprietor and great-grandson of the manor founder, was elected to the post. It was only in 1772 that his tenant, William Davids, replaced his landlord and continued to hold the position until the outbreak of the Revolution. Fragmentary records of the officeholding in Rensselaerswyck, however, present a somewhat different picture. From 1701 to 1734, besides the Van Rensselaer family, at least three tenants, namely, Jonas Douw, Hendrick Douw, and Philip Schuyler, occasionally served in the office.[116] But these aberrations seem to have occurred with the prior consent of the proprietor.

Once in a while, when occasion arose for some community action, the tenants got together and assigned a specific responsibility to their landlord or members of his family. In March 1750, for example, the tenants in the Claverack portion of Rensselaerswyck agreed to raise money for the purpose of destroying wolves and elected Henry Van Rensselaer, a younger son of Henry (the Claverack proprietor), "Colector and pay master General" of the funds.[117] A manor proprietor might be nominated as a commissioner of the highways running through his district, and find himself with the responsibility of laying out and maintaining roads.[118] He might be consulted by the government about the appointment of militia officers and justices of the peace in his district, and be given a rank sufficiently high to hold the command of its militia. He could be called upon by a justice of the peace and the inhabitants in his bailiwick for aid and counsel in minor local, familial, and personal disputes.[119] These functions and roles were aristocratic obligations more than solicited offices.

The landlord had to assume these local responsibilities because they

AF13, all at Queens College Lib. Kiliaen Van Rensselaer, "lord" of Rensselaerswyck, referred to his brother Henry, the proprietor of Claverack, as "yeoman" in a deed. Deed Book 4: 359–360, Albany Co. Clerk's Office.

116. "Town Book of the Manor of Philipsburgh, 1742–1766," 8, N.-Y. Hist. Soc.; "A list of Officers of the Manor of Philipsburgh, 1689–1779," *Tarrytown Argus*, Apr. 18, 1903; Staats Family Archives, Boxes 3 and 4.

117. "Resolution of a Claverack Town meeting," Apr. 3, 1750, Van Rensselaer-Fort Papers, 1729–1789.

118. *N.Y. Col. Laws*, I, 532–538, II, 153–155, 515–523, IV, 895–897, V, 383–390, 715–716.

119. Robert Livingston, Jr., to James Duane, 1771, Duane Papers, Roll 1; John Ten Broeck to John Tabor Kempe, Oct. 9, 1769, Kempe Papers, Letters, A–Z, Box 1.

required time, money, and efforts that men of ordinary means and seasonal pursuits generally could not afford to give, and because the orderly
management of his estate called for his close attention. Besides, the tenants typically were concerned mostly about their immediate needs. Scattered over vast tracts of the domain and separated from one another by
distances ranging from one mile to twenty, the tenants did not relish the
idea of traveling to a place near or at the manor house to attend such
affairs as militia drilling, road repairing, or in general anything that had
to do with government.[120] From the perspective of their self-contained
world, "government" meant trouble and taxation; they seemed to prefer
to be left alone. Occasionally, they were awakened from their individual-
istic hibernation by visible common problems and dangers, such as rampaging hogs and cattle, marauding wolves, or threatening French and
enemy Indians. They lacked the impulse to seek power and the sense of
community that is a prerequisite for collective action.

    Tenant apathy was expressed in a number of ways. For example,
they frequently failed to choose local officials, and those elected often
failed to attend the county meetings.[121] One landlord tried to induce
his tenants to come to the polls for the election of petty local officers,
like overseers and viewers of fence, by amply supplying liquor for the
occasion.[122] In 1701 Peter Coeymans, tenant in Rensselaerswyck, angry
with the "disadvantage of . . . being chosen as Constable" of the manor,
charged the former constable Hendrick Douw, also a tenant, with deliberately neglecting to give an "advance warning [of the election] unto
several Inhabitants" in the district, a neglect that he said caused the
election result.[123] Apparently, neither tenant wanted to bear the burden
of public service. A similar incident occurred in the neighboring Manor
of Livingston. In organizing the manor militia in 1745, Philip Livingston

---

120. Philip Livingston to John D'Witt, Feb. 13, 1741, Livingston-Redmond MSS,
Roll 9.
121. N.Y. Col. Laws, II, 130–131. The records of the Albany County court of sessions
are full of resolutions fining those officials for their absence from the public meetings.
Minutes of Court of Sessions, 1685–1689, 1717–1723, 1763–1782, passim, Albany Co.
Clerk's Office.
122. Philip Livingston to John D'Witt, Mar. 17, 1741, Livingston-Redmond MSS,
Roll 9.
123. Recognizing the validity of Coeymans's charge, the court of sessions fined Douw
20 shillings, but declared Coeymans elected "by majority of votes." Munsell, ed., Annals of
Albany, IV, 144–145. Tenant reluctance to assume public duties persisted in the later
period. Benjamin Thompson, tenant of James Duane, though grateful to the landlord for
procuring him the justiceship of the peace, politely declined it on the grounds that it would
detract from his farming, since he was poor and unable to hire a person to work for him.
Thompson to Duane, Nov. 27, 1791, Duane Papers, Roll 3.

obtained blank commissions and spent almost half a year in negotiating with some of his tenants. But two of them, namely Dirk Spoor and Joachim Radclif, turned down the respectable commission of a lieutenancy, a rebuff that infuriated the landlord. "I shall not," Livingston declared, "recommend any native this time as officers but Germans or a N. England men to be over them our people are hoggish and brutish." The refusal, of course, had to do not so much with beastly qualities (it does, however, show something of their independence of mind) as lack of interest in the office, the performance of which would necessarily result in the neglect of their occupation for at least three or four days a year.[124]

The degree of a tenant's political participation and even interest was closely related to his distance from the public meeting place. The farther away a tenant was, the less likely he would be to involve himself in public affairs. County political leaders, understanding this, asked the assembly to change the location of elections and meetings of county officials to more densely populated areas in order to obtain a maximum turnout of voters. Those who were adversely affected by the assembly's order protested it on grounds of "inconvenience and expence."[125]

Sparse and scattered settlements were not conducive to the growth of social kinship and to a sense of community such as distinguished New Englanders and Long Islanders in their compact settlements. The apathy of manorial tenants, however, had a cause perhaps deeper than the settlement pattern. It was, we may speculate, their land tenure, no matter how lengthy it might be (for one, two, or three lives), that deprived them of a feeling of belonging to the community in which they lived. Improvements they bought or made on the leased land belonged to them, but title to the soil did not. They had property rights, but these were less than complete in contrast with the absolute ownership of freehold. Thus, leaseholding injected an element of transiency into a tenant's life.[126]

This situation imposed expanded responsibilities upon the landlord. His position was tantamount to a trusteeship, by the tenants' default

---

124. Philip Livingston to Robert Livingston, Jr., Jan. 30 and June 1, 1745, Livingston-Redmond MSS, Roll 7.

125. *N.Y. Col. Laws*, II, 6, III, 847–849; petition by several of the freeholders and inhabitants of Rensselaerswyck Manor, *Journal of the Votes and Proceedings of the General Assembly of the Colony of New York, from 1766 to 1776* (Albany, N.Y., 1820), Nov. 29, 1769, hereafter cited as *Journal of General Assembly, 1766 to 1776*.

126. The pervasive political apathy of leaseholders contrasted sharply with the active participation of freeholders in local government in 18th-century Kingston, N.Y. See Patricia U. Bonomi, "Local Government in Colonial New York: A Base for Republicanism," in Judd and Polishook, eds., *Early New York*, 43–44, 47–48.

and with their tacit consent. No evidence exists to show that the tenants were dissatisfied with the landlord's assumption of the active role. But it should be emphasized that modesty characterized his management of the manor, which, in any case, had the simplicity of a rural society. The rudimentary character of the manor governance was reflected in the business conducted at the town meetings of a manor. The inhabitants of Philipsburgh held an annual meeting at which they elected local officials like town clerk, constables, collectors, assessors, overseers of roads, and fence viewers, and usually spent the rest of the session discussing the roads in the manor. No ordinance was issued; nor was any other administrative problem ever brought to the town's attention. A matter that engrossed most of the town clerk's time, and much of the time of the manor population in general, was the registering of earmarks of livestock on the common pastures and of strays in the pounds. Occasionally the clerk recorded the bonds that the tavern keepers rendered to a justice of the peace for their good performance.[127] Although town meeting records of the other manors are not available, it is doubtful that they differed substantially from that of Philipsburgh.

The strikingly narrow range of the town meeting activities of the manors was supplemented by the expanded role of the landlord. Apart from his duties as a supervisor or a justice, and his moral influence, he performed many of the basic leadership functions of this agrarian society through the private lease deeds he drew up with tenants, which detailed their obligations. These obligations, which collectively had the effect of a regulatory ordinance, concerned the building and maintenance of houses, fences, orchards, gardens; the use of the commons; and the cutting of timber in the domain.[128] Lease contracts in Livingston Manor in the late 1760s even dealt with the supposed conduct of a tenant toward "vagrant strangers."[129] Some of the ordinances pertaining to petty local matters on the manors were issued by the General Assembly, in addition to the assembly's laying down general administrative rules and the overall framework. The interference of the assembly, originally necessitated when the manors were integrated into the provincial system, became a matter of course and was sometimes even sought by the proprietors as an aid in coping with certain of their manor problems. In 1712 the assembly

127. "Town Book of the Manor of Philipsburgh," N.-Y. Hist. Soc.
128. See chap. 5.
129. Lease from Robert Livingston, Jr., to William Lowry, Apr. 14, 1769, Livingston-Redmond MSS, Roll 8.

ordered the Rensselaerswyck inhabitants to elect another assessor for the manor to replace one Captain Jonas Douw, who probably refused to serve.[130] It passed a bill reprimanding the manor residents' carelessness "about their swine, in suffering them to run at large."[131] Again, in 1769, the representative body ordered the transfer of the place of election for the manor supervisor from the east side to the west side of the Hudson River, to the "great inconvenience" of the east side inhabitants in the manor.[132]

The problems to which the legislature addressed itself could easily have been managed, it should be pointed out, by the county court of sessions or by the manor town meeting. These legislative actions were all initiated by the manor representative presumably at the request of its proprietor, if they were not the same person. Such frequent resort to the assembly by the manor landlord would have been unnecessary had he been autocratic enough to run his manor business single-handedly or had the inhabitants cared enough about self-governing their community without the paternalistic intervention of the central government. It could also have been that the landlord wanted to let the assembly deal on his behalf with touchy problems, thus obtaining the advantage of legislative sanction for what he hoped to achieve and letting the solons rather than himself take the onus of blame if opposition should develop in his manor. This diplomatic and circuitous way (via the assembly) of conducting business was far different from the authoritarian procedures of a martinet that have sometimes been ascribed to the New York "patroons."

In sum, though the governance of the manors was in the hands of the proprietors, the power and authority with which they governed were derived from their wealth, prestige, and, more important, their position as landlords of the domain—not from the feudal privileges of lordship, which suffered a quick death in New York. Instead of the lordship, a proprietor acquired a justiceship of the peace, but because of the office's limited range of authority under the law and because he was only one of many justices in a given county, he was much restrained. At the same time, a number of other forces, mostly extralegal, were at work in compelling a landlord to be moderate in the exercise of his power over his tenants: these were, first, peer-group pressures and, second, the laws and the process governing the election of manorial representatives. Thus,

130. N.Y. Col. Laws, I, 777–778.
131. Ibid., IV, 872–874, III, 882; Journal of General Assembly, II, 331, 789.
132. Journal of General Assembly, 1766 to 1776, Nov. 29, 1769.

Robert R. Livingston of the Clermont portion of Livingston Manor could boast in the middle of the eighteenth century that "by the goodness of [New York's] civil Constitution the tenant is preserved from Oppression."[133] Though undercut in his power, a landlord still had to administer the manor, because it belonged to him and because the tenants were indifferent to the affairs of the community as a whole and were willing to entrust the responsibilities of governing to him. He therefore met the administrative requirements of his manor mostly by way of the lease contracts and partly by the use of the omnipresent assembly. The governance of the manors, an integral part of the provincial system, thus took on the same character as the governance of the large nonmanorial land patents, and the manorial lords' behavioral patterns approximated those of any ordinary landlords in the province.

133. Beverly McAnear, ed., "Mr. Robert R. Livingston's Reasons against a Land Tax," *Journal of Political Economy*, XLVIII (1940), 89.

# CHAPTER IV

❧❧❧❧❧

# The Economics of Land
# and Landlords

### Economic Opportunity in Colonial New York

The New York manors were not a closed community; they were an integral part of American colonial society. The nature and development of the manors were closely entwined with the growth of the colonies in general and of New York in particular. It would be futile to describe the economic and social status of manorial tenants without taking into account the general economic opportunities that were available to settlers in the province. How did New York compare with other areas in terms of the availability and price of land? How did the persistent scarcity of labor affect land ownership and the economy? What were the economic goals and career patterns of the manorial landlords? How did they perceive the land and its uses? These are some of the questions we will explore in this chapter.

For Governors Thomas Dongan and Benjamin Fletcher, one of the purposes of creating the large manors was to facilitate settlement of the colony, which their predecessors' promotional schemes had failed to achieve. In return for these grants of land and privileges, the proprietors were expected to bear the burden of developing their estates. Their wealth, credit, and influence were thought to be adequate for such an undertaking. A corollary to the new policy was that the provincial government would relinquish its function as an active promoter of settlement. The headright system, in use under the pre-Dongan administrations, was abandoned, since it was incompatible with the very rationale behind the manorial grants. Encouraging each immigrant with an offer of so many acres of free land would have seriously competed with the proprietors' efforts to recruit settlers. The role of the government henceforth was the passive one of prodding the landed men to develop their estates. In late 1698 the governor issued an edict requiring a new patentee to improve at least three acres for every hundred granted, and in 1761 another rule required the settlement of one family for every thousand acres within three years after the land grant. But these regulations were never strictly enforced, for obvious reasons.[1]

The task confronting manor landowners was formidable. Apart from the difficulties and deterrents to settlement that the seventeenth-century governors had faced, there was another problem peculiar to a manorial plantation economy: the widely held and deeply embedded aspiration to farm a piece of land absolutely one's own. This psychology of yeomanry had brought thousands of men and women to America. To the newcomers from England, ownership of unencumbered land appeared to be the most reliable shield against a racking landlord and the terrors of dispossession that they and their forefathers had experienced. To the immigrants from Europe, the manorial system was an instrument of oppression and exploitation, which offered only marginal security from abject poverty. The obverse of yeoman psychology was hatred of the elements of leaseholding—landlords and rent. Daniel Denton, an Englishman on Long Island, aptly spoke for the antirentism of his fellow settlers when he wrote in 1670 in his *Description of New York* that the "Dutch gave . . . bad Titles to Lands," and exacted "the Tenths of all which men produced off their land."[2] In 1671 Jeremiah Van Rensselaer, director of Rensselaerswyck, vouched for the colonists' aversion to tenancy—"it is no longer possible to get any tenants for the farms"—and complained that "if a farmer does not pay his rent, one can not eject him, for no others who are better can be obtained." As the situation got worse several years later, he had to "beg a tenant to stay on the farm and do his bidding."[3]

However strong a newcomer's aspiration to become a yeoman might have been, it could not have sustained itself for long had there not been

1. Lords Justice to earl of Bellomont, Nov. 10, 1698, *N.Y. Col. Docs.*, 425; Robert Hunter to Lords of Trade, June 24, 1710, *ibid.*, V, 168; John Tabor Kempe's note, June 22, 1761, John Tabor Kempe Papers, Box Misc., New-York Historical Society, New York.
2. Denton, *Description of New York*, 15–16.
3. Jeremiah Van Rensselaer to John Van Wely and Jan Baptist Van Rensselaer, Sept. 27, 1674, and to J. B. Van Rensselaer, [Mar. 27], 1674, June 29, 1674, *Jeremias Van Rensselaer Correspondence*, 444–445, 454, 461.

abundant opportunity for him to obtain a livelihood by means other than tenancy. In 1710 Governor Robert Hunter asserted that the land developers' hopes of improving their lands with hired hands would never materialize "in a Country where . . . Property may be had at so easy Rates."[4] Skeptical of the wisdom of renting land as a business, Goldsbrow Banyar, secretary of the province, commented in 1761 that "in a country where there is such plenty of unsettled lands I am sensible, People, who can afford it, would rather purchase than be burthen'd with a Perpetual Rent even tho low."[5] Perhaps no contemporary comments are more expressive of the fundamental conflict between yeoman and landlord aspirations than Oliver De Lancey's. A landed magnate in his own right, he was at the same time the agent for Sir Peter and Susannah Warren's estates in New York and other areas for almost two decades. At least on one occasion, bitterly complaining about the "profuse practice of granting land," which seemed to threaten the vested landed interests, he declared that it was "very difficult to settle tenants as every person can be at an easy rate a freeholder." On another occasion, he remarked that the "estate of Sir Peter has suffered already and will more" from this situation.[6]

Economic opportunity consisted of two ingredients, high wages and cheapness of land. The scarcity of labor in the colony boosted its value. It was reported that in order to meet the demand for labor, New Yorkers were "constrained to import Negroes" from Africa for all kinds of services. A bill introduced by Governor Bellomont for facilitating the conversion of Indians and Negroes to Christianity was violently opposed by members of the General Assembly on the grounds that the Africans, once converted, would free themselves from slavery and thus deprive the whites of the only source of servants.[7] Due to this pressing labor shortage, the earl of Clarendon, ex-governor of the province, could declare in 1711: "No person that has his Limbs, and will work, can starve in that

---

4. Robert Hunter to Lords of Trade, Nov. 14, 1710, and Nov. 12, 1715, *N.Y. Col. Docs.*, V, 179–180, 459. See also Bellomont to Lords of Trade, Nov. 28, 1700, *ibid.*, IV, 791.

5. Goldsbrow Banyar to Samuel Dunlop, Aug. 28, 1761, Goldsbrow Banyar Papers, Lands, Box 6, N.-Y. Hist. Soc.

6. Oliver De Lancey to William Skinner in London, June 10, 1772, and to Fits Roy, William Skinner, and Lord Abington in London, Apr. 10, 1772, Gage Papers, G/Am/133, on microfilm at Sleepy Hollow Restorations Library, Tarrytown, N.Y., and N.-Y. Hist. Soc. (originals at Sussex Archaeological Society, Lewes, Sussex, England), hereafter cited as Gage Papers.

7. William Smith, [Jr.], *History of the late Province of New-York, from its Discovery to the Appointment of Governor Colden, in 1762* . . . (New York, 1830 [orig. publ. London, 1757]), I, 327; Bellomont to Lords of Trade, May 12, 1699, *N.Y. Col. Docs.*, IV, 510–511.

country."[8] Despite the steady influx of immigrants and a natural increase in population in subsequent decades, the problem was never completely solved in the colonial period. Numerous contemporary observers attributed the retardation of manufacturing to the shortage and high price of labor.[9]

Already in 1691 the governor's council spoke of the need for restraining the "Extravagancy of tradesmen and labourers wages," but no legislative wage fixing ever occurred.[10] The wage scale was therefore determined by the rule of supply and demand. Discussing the difficulties of raising two companies of foot soldiers for frontier defense, Sir William Johnson, superintendent of Indian affairs in North America and a long-time resident in New York, reported in 1763 that "the small pay of the officers in a country where People are accustomed to high wages . . . will greatly retard their [mustering]."[11] From about 1690 to 1730, common and unskilled labor commanded from 2s. 3d. to 3s. New York money per day. There were slight deviations, however. In 1699, for example, John Carter charged Robert Livingston 4s. for shoveling snow out of the yard of the latter's town house in Albany. During the same period, skilled workmen, such as blacksmiths, joiners, carpenters, masons, saddlers, bricklayers, millwrights, cordwainers, wheelwrights, and thatchers, earned at least 5s. a day.[12] In subsequent decades, the wage scale for both common and skilled laborers seems to have gone up, though not as high as the inflation in the price of farm produce.[13] Rhapsodizing over the economic

8. Earl of Clarendon to Lord Dartmouth, Mar. 8, 1711, *N.Y. Col. Docs.*, V, 196. Bellomont's ambitious project for building public workhouses to employ "the poor and also vagabonds" elicited only ridicule from the assemblymen when it was introduced. He confessed that he was at first ignorant of the economic conditions in the colony and that indeed "there is not a richer populace any where in the King's dominions than in this Town." Bellomont to Lords of Trade, Apr. 27, 1699, *ibid.*, IV, 511.

9. Cadwallader Colden, "On the Trade of New York, 1723," *Doc. Hist. N.Y.*, I, 716–718; Colden to Micajah Perry, *Colden Papers*, II, 31–32; Henry Moore to Lords of Trade, Jan. 12, 1767, *N.Y. Col. Docs.*, VII, 88; *The Remarkable Case of Peter Hasenclever, Merchant* . . . (London, 1773), 1–12. On the shortage of labor in the American colonies, see Richard B. Morris, *Government and Labor in Early America* (New York, 1946), 45–46.

10. *Journal of Legislative Council*, I, 5; Morris, *Government and Labor*, 84–85.

11. William Johnson to Cadwallader Colden, Oct. 24 and Dec. 30, 1763, *Colden Papers*, IV, 265–266, 271; William Polhampton to Lords of Trade, Mar. 3, 1711, *N.Y. Col. Docs.*, V, 194.

12. Robert Livingston to Lords of Trade, May 13, 1701, and earl of Clarendon to Lord Dartmouth, Mar. 8, 1710, *N.Y. Col. Docs.*, IV, 871, 588–589, V, 196; John Carter's account with Robert Livingston, Jan. 1, 1699, and Robert Livingston's account with Henry Francis and Samuel Johnson, Aug. 11 and 19, 1719, Livingston-Redmond MSS, Rolls 2 and 4.

13. Wholesale price indexes of major farm products almost doubled between the years 1739 and 1766. Bradford's *New-York Gazette*, Oct. 29 to Nov. 26, 1739, and Jan. 7, 1766;

opportunity the colony offered, James Murray, a recent immigrant from Ireland, wrote in 1737 to his old parish minister back home that a common laborer got 4s. 6d. a day, a carpenter and mason 6s.[14] In 1746 Philip Livingston paid 6s. 6d. for one day's work with a wagon.[15] Elias Pelletreau paid a man 3s. for mowing in 1765 and 4s. for sowing in 1772. John Lloyd occasionally paid 4s. for farm work in 1765.[16] It is probably safe to argue that wages for common workmen fluctuated between 3s. and 4½s. a day. As for the skilled, Francis Dominick, a carpenter who was engaged by Abraham Martin to build a house in New York City, charged Martin 7s. 6d. per day for each of his nine skilled workmen in 1767.[17] In 1762 Philip Schuyler of Albany had to pay a carpenter as much as 8s.[18] The cordwainers were paid less, roughly 6s.[19] It appears that the unskilled, if they worked regularly except Sundays, earned an annual income of £46 to £67, and the skilled £70 to £90. Assuming that the basic living costs per year were somewhere around £25 for a family of five in New York City and somewhat less in the country, the workingmen, if hard-working and thrifty, could have lived comfortably.[20]

When contemporary observers said that wages in New York were high, they generally meant in relation to England. John Woolman, the Quaker preacher, observed in London in the early 1770s that laborers near the city earned 10d. (in sterling), or 1s. 3d. in New York currency, only about half as much as the lowest wage for the colonial worker.[21]

---

John Van Cortlandt to Archibald Armstrong, Nov. 4, 1772, Letterbook and Note Book of John Van Cortlandt, N.-Y. Hist. Soc. As for the continuous increase of wages, see James De Lancey's speech, Dec. 7, 1757, in *New-York Mercury* (changed to *New-York Gazette; and the Weekly Mercury* in 1768), Dec. 19, 1757.

14. James Murray to the Reverend Baptist Boyd, published in *N.-Y. Gazette*, Oct. 31, 1737.

15. Wynant Weber's account with Philip Livingston, Nov. 25, 1746, Livingston-Redmond MSS, Roll 6.

16. Account Book of Elias Pelletreau, New York Public Library; Journal (c) of John Van Cortlandt, 1764–1772, *ibid.*; *Lloyd Papers*, II, 531; Van Cortlandt Papers, V1661 and V1689, Sleepy Hollow Restorations Lib.; *N.-Y. Mercury*, Aug. 7, 1758.

17. Goldsbrow Banyar Papers, Misc., Box 16; Gilbert Livingston's "Building Account Book for Workmen," Miscellaneous Manuscripts, Livingston, A-T, *ibid.*

18. "A Compte of Men's Time in the year 1762 Employed at Capt. Schuyler hous in Albany," Schuyler Mansion Papers, I–1–1, New York State Library, Albany.

19. Van Cortlandt Papers, V1661, Sleepy Hollow Restorations Lib.

20. Beverly McAnear, "The Place of the Freeman in Old New York," N.Y. *History*, XXI (1940), 429–430. This broad generalization on the average annual income for workers does not take into consideration any seasonal market fluctuation and economic recession in the colony. But, in light of the available qualitative evidence quoted in the text, underemployment in mid-18th-century New York did not seem to be a chronic problem or serious enough to affect the labor income.

21. Amelia N. Gummere, ed., *The Journal and Essays of John Woolman* (New York,

The comparatively good lot of the colonial laborer was further enhanced by a lower cost of living than in England. Lewis Morris, a fairly well-to-do man by New York standards, touring with his son in England in the mid-1730s, had to squeeze his pocketbook to pay for the exorbitant price of almost everything there. "We can't Lodge so cheap as four times the Price of New York," he grumbled.[22] While the price for one bushel of wheat in England in the 1770s, according to Woolman, was 8s. (in sterling), or 12s. in New York currency, it was on the average only 7s. (New York currency) on this side of the Atlantic.[23]

The high wages in the colony owed much to the availability of cheap land, which absorbed settlers and prevented a glut in the labor market. This rustication process was, of course, impelled partly by the workingman's penchant for acquiring land on which he could stake his economic future. "Every one is able to procure a piece of land at an inconsiderable rate and therefore is fond to set up for himself rather than work for hire," Cadwallader Colden, surveyor general of New York, noted in 1723.[24]

It was difficult, however, for a new immigrant or any poor individual to obtain land directly from the provincial government in eighteenth-century New York, not only because of the preemption of the choice lands by the oligopolistic few in the previous century but also because of the complicated procedure of land granting. An applicant was required first to locate the land and then to obtain from the government a license to purchase it from the Indian owners. If his negotiation with the natives was successful, he would then petition the governor and council for a patent, submitting to them his Indian deed.[25] But in 1736 a new regulation was introduced whereby no Indian deed would be accepted unless the land applied for was first surveyed by the surveyor general or his

---

1922), 305. Richard B. Morris estimated that the colonial workers' wage was 30 to 100 percent higher than that of the English workers. Morris, *Government and Labor*, 45. As for the exchange rate between the New York currency (first issued in 1709) and the British pound sterling, £1 sterling in 1710 equaled about £1 10s. of New York money. *N.Y. Col. Docs.*, V, 171; *N.Y. Col. Laws*, I, 666. This exchange rate seems to have continued to the end of the colonial period. Memorandum Book of Philip Van Cortlandt, 1775, Van Cortlandt Family Papers, N.-Y. Hist. Soc.

22. Lewis Morris to James Alexander, Feb. 24, 1735, Rutherford Collection, II, 116, N.-Y. Hist. Soc.

23. Gummere, ed., *Journal of Woolman*, 206; Alex Ellis to James Duane, July 1, 1772, Duane Papers, Roll 1.

24. Cadwallader Colden, "On the Trade of New York, 1723," *Doc. Hist. N.Y.*, I, 718; Henry Moore to Lords of Trade, Jan. 12, 1767, *N.Y. Col. Docs.*, VII, 88; Morris, *Government and Labor*, 48–49.

25. *N.Y. Col. Laws*, I, 149; Robert Hunter to Lords of Trade, July 7, 1718, *N.Y. Col. Docs.*, V, 511.

deputy in the presence of the natives.[26] Convoluted as it seems on paper, the procedure was still worse in practice. First, only a few government functionaries, namely, those officials associated with Indian affairs, and traders in native goods had access to the Indian tribal chiefs. The privileged few kept this advantage to themselves and their close associates.[27] Second, the expense and the time spent in negotiating with the Indians, surveying, traveling, and taking out a patent was prohibitive for men of ordinary means. For every thousand acres the basic fees alone for the governmental officials—the governor, his secretary, the clerk of the council, the surveyor general, and others—ran to approximately £25. The attorney general, who wrote letters patent, separately charged a £3 fee for each applicant.[28] Surveying and compensating the Indians were additional burdens. In 1771 Sir William Johnson, while working for a client, calculated these costs to be at least £10 10s. per thousand acres.[29] Moreover, one had to worry about the annual quitrent of 2s. 6d. (in sterling) per hundred acres.[30] This and other considerations persuaded Lewis Morris, onetime chief justice of the province, to conclude in 1733 that it was not worth the effort, even for those few who could afford the expense and time, to procure lands through the government.[31]

In the first half of the eighteenth century, the governors had orders limiting the size of grants per patentee to 2,000 acres and subsequently to

26. William Smith, [Jr.], *History of New-York* (1757 ed.), 244; Goldsbrow Banyar to William Johnson, May 18, 1751, James Sullivan *et al.*, eds., *The Papers of Sir William Johnson* (Albany, N.Y., 1921–1965), I, 334–335, hereafter cited as *William Johnson Papers*; *N.-Y. Gazette*, Nov. 29, 1736.

27. This avenue of land acquisition was further narrowed in 1763 when the crown prohibited private individuals from buying lands from the Indians except through the governor and Indian superintendent. Ruth L. Higgins, *Expansion in New York* (Columbus, Ohio, 1931), 30.

28. Goldsbrow Banyar to William Johnson, May 9, 1754, *William Johnson Papers*, I, 401–402; "Fees on Grants of Land" prepared by Goldsbrow Banyar, Jan. 27, 1772, C.O. 1103/5, 211–212, Public Record Office. William Smith, Jr., computed the expense to be £18 or £20 sterling per 1,000 acres. Smith, "Information to Farmers and Mechanics intending to remove from Europe to America," [176–?], William Smith Papers, Box 3, N.Y. Pub. Lib.

29. William Johnson to Lord Adam Gordon, Feb. 18, 1771, *William Johnson Papers*, XII, 894.

30. Gov. Edmund Andros first instituted the imposition of 2s. 6d. sterling annual quitrent per 100 acres. But after his administration no instruction regarding the quitrent was given to either Gov. Henry Sloughter or Gov. Benjamin Fletcher; so they were left at liberty to grant lands at very trivial rent. It was not until the appointment of Robert Hunter in 1709 that the yearly quitrent was reestablished. *N.Y. Col. Docs.*, IV, 392, V, 179–180; Cadwallader Colden's report, 1732, *Doc. Hist. N.Y.*, I, 251; Henry M Cullock to John Selwyn, July 30, 1751, Morristown Historical Park Collection, on microfilm, Roll 33, Morristown, N.J.

31. Lewis Morris to Lords of Trade, Aug. 27, 1733, *N.Y. Col. Docs.*, V, 953.

only 1,000 acres.[32] But the time-consuming and expensive process of land patenting, coupled with innate human greed, pressured landjobbers to acquire larger amounts of acreage than were allowed officially. Despite the restriction, or rather because of it, buyers resorted to borrowing the names of friends and acquaintances when petitioning for a patent, with the understanding that the names would not signify a genuine claim. In 1751 Goldsbrow Banyar, deputy secretary of the province, advised William Johnson to "follow the Custom" of filing a petition for land "in the Names of some Friends in Trust for you and in whom you can confide." Several years later, a bit concerned about the qualifications of those listed in Johnson's petition, Banyar asked Johnson to check if they were unnaturalized or minors, and "if so change them for others."[33] Cadwallader Colden was no less shameless in abusing the official regulation.[34] The officials' attitude was just a reflection of the widespread use of dummy names by other individuals. In 1728 James Alexander, a prominent lawyer, employed the names of Andires Marshalk and John Spratt to get a patent for 3,000 acres in the resumed Evan's Patent.[35] In 1733 Philip Livingston, proprietor of Livingston Manor, borrowed Arent Bradt's name.[36] Alexander Colden, son of Cadwallader, acquired an unspecified amount of land by using the name of George Harrison.[37] In 1765 John Tabor Kempe, James Duane, and Walter Rutherford, all lawyers in New York, used twenty-four Schenectady residents of various occupations and two Rensselaerswyck tenants to obtain a patent of 26,000 acres (Princeton township) and paid £100 for the dummies' good offices.[38] In this

32. *Ibid.*, IV, 549, 553–554, V, 54, 140–142, 652–653; N.Y. Land Papers, XV, 89; N.Y. Col. MSS, LXXXI, 91.

33. Goldsbrow Banyar to William Johnson, May 18, 1751, July 23, 1754, and Johnson to Banyar, Jan. 5 and Sept. 4, 1769, Apr. 27, 1770, *William Johnson Papers*, I, 334–335, 408, XII, 684–685, 751, 817–819.

34. Cadwallader Colden to William Johnson, Nov. 29, 1769, *ibid.*, XII, 756.

35. James Alexander's will, Mar. 30, 1745, Wills, XIX, 437–446, Queens College Library, New York; "State of the case concerning 2000 acres of land in the Mohawks Country," James Alexander Papers, Box 15, N.-Y. Hist. Soc.

36. Arent Bradt's agreement with Philip Livingston, Nov. 20, 1730, Sanders Papers, Box 6, N.-Y. Hist. Soc.

37. Cadwallader Colden's will, Sept. 24, 1773, Wills, XXIX, 257–264, Queens College Lib.

38. Deed Book 8: 217–224, Albany County Clerk's Office, Albany, N.Y. For other comments on the practice of circumventing the restriction on the size of a grant, see John Jay to Henry Outhoudt *et al.*, Sept. 5, 1784, Bureau of Waterways, New York State Department of Transportation, Albany; earl of Hillsborough to William Tryon, Dec. 4, 1771, and Tryon to Hillsborough, Apr. 11, 1772, *N.Y. Col. Docs.*, VIII, 285–286, 293; Gen. Thomas Gage to earl of Shelburne, Apr. 5, 1767, Clarence Edwin Carter, ed., *The Correspondence of General Thomas Gage with the Secretaries of State, 1763–1775* (New Haven, Conn., 1931–1933), I, 131–132.

way, most of the large grants first went to "a certain classe of Men"— government officials, men of means, and their friends.[39]

For a man of little fortune and influence, a common avenue to land acquisition was through private purchase from the original patentees. Many landed men were willing and sometimes obliged to part with their holdings for a number of reasons. Every colonist anticipated a steady inflation in land values, keeping pace with an equally steady population growth and with the mounting demand for foodstuffs for export.[40] Yet only a few grandees could afford to retain a large wild tract of land for a long time while waiting for the right price. The yearly quitrent of 2s. 6d. per hundred acres strained many patentees when the land remained undeveloped and tied up a good deal of capital.[41] Throughout the colonial period, officials constantly complained about the landowners' tardiness —sometimes their outright refusal—to pay the quitrent. Their complaints suggest that men in the land business did not regard this cost lightly.[42] While trying in the 1730s to get a patent directly from the king for several hundred thousand acres along the Mohawk River, Philip Livingston of Livingston Manor asserted that the profitable development of the real estate was feasible "if the quit rents be but moderate," or "about £10 or £15" annually for the whole, that is, much lower than the official rate.[43] Even the rich patroon Kiliaen Van Rensselaer, though required to pay a rent of only fifty bushels of wheat a year for his million-acre manor, found it necessary in 1687 and 1703 to petition the governors for its remittance because of his distress owing to tenant desertion from the domain during wars.[44] It is easy to imagine how badly off a speculator of moderate means would have been in a similar situation.[45] Consequently, patentees without a large reservoir of capital, like the father of Edward Collins of Albany, were disposed to sell idle land as fast as they could.[46]

39. Lewis Morris to Lords of Trade, Aug. 27, 1733, *N.Y. Col. Docs.*, V, 953.

40. Philip Livingston to father, Robert, Feb. 15, 1722, Livingston-Redmond MSS, Roll 4; Robert C. Livingston to Robert Livingston, Jr., Jan. 29, 1770, *ibid.*, Roll 8.

41. Cadwallader Colden to James Alexander, Mar. 27, 1732, James Alexander Papers, Box 2, N.-Y. Hist. Soc.

42. *N.Y. Col. Docs.*, IV, 378, 392, V, 180, 299, 357–358, 561, 900–901, VI, 313, 396, 928.

43. Philip Livingston to Messrs. Storke and Gainsborough in London, May 18, Oct. 23, 1734, Mar. 25, 1736, Miscellaneous Manuscripts, Vol. 5, N.Y. State Lib.

44. Kiliaen Van Rensselaer's petition, June 10, 1697, N.Y. Col. MSS, XLI, 82; petition, June 13, 1702, N.Y. Land Papers, III, 68, N.Y. State Lib.

45. Petition from the freeholders of Ulster County, Sept. 8, 1702, petition from the inhabitants of Schenectady, Feb. 5, 1703, and petition from John Van Loon, Mar. 29, 1705, N.Y. Land Papers, III, 79, 112, IV, 43.

46. Edward Collins to Cadwallader Colden, July 2, 1727, *Colden Papers*, I, 199. In

No less important a factor in the patentees' willingness to sell their grants was the rules of 1698 and 1761 concerning land development. Even though these rules were never enforced, the possibility of forfeiture as a result of noncompliance weighed on the landowners. That their apprehension was genuine is suggested by the various precautionary steps they took. In 1708 Ebenezer Wilson and John Abeel petitioned Governor Edward Hyde (Viscount Cornbury) for additional time in which to settle the area granted to them because the "lands lyes so remote on the borders of the French." In the 1720s James Alexander was obliged to rent out certain portions of his land in order to barely meet the requirement. Concerned about his title to vast unimproved tracts in the Mohawk valley, the politically powerful Sir William Johnson inquired in 1765 of John Tabor Kempe, attorney general, whether he should take the rules seriously.[47]

One possible alternative to selling lands was leasing them. But many landowners discovered both the difficulty of recruiting a sufficient number of tenants and also the marginal profitability of renting as compared to investing in commerce and trade. Land in New York, when unimproved, yielded no rent and, when improved, seldom returned a rental income equal to the interest one could earn by lending the money invested in the land.[48] In 1767 Stephen Skinner, who owned a good deal of land in both New York and New Jersey, bitterly complained that a farm worth £2,000 (New York currency) brought him but £13 a year, whereas the annual interest accrued from £2,000 on loan would have been £140.[49]

---

this letter, Collins, a surveyor, mentioned his father's recent sale of land in Cannojohary and guessed that the burden of quitrent on the land lying idle was one of the reasons for his father's action.

47. Petition from Ebenezer Wilson and John Abeel, Aug. 30, 1708, petition from Wilson and others, Sept. 9, 1708, and petition from Rip Van Dam and others, Sept. 15, 1708, all in N.Y. Land Papers, IV, 149, 150, 135; James Alexander to Cadwallader Colden, Aug. 12, 1729, *Colden Papers*, I, 294; Alexander to John Myndertse, Nov. 6, 1725, and to Isaac Ross, Apr. 2, 1746, Alexander Papers, Boxes 16 and 62; John Tabor Kempe to William Johnson, July 22, 1765, Letters, A–Z, Box 1, Kempe Papers; John Sanders to Henry Jordice in London, Nov. 26, 1768, Letterbook of John Sanders, 1749–1779, Sanders Papers.

48. Poor rental return was a function of poor income from farming. It was estimated that a farmer in the 1720s gained yearly 4 percent of the value of his farm. In the same period, profit from overseas trade was generally 50 to 100 percent of investment. One contemporary observer argued that English imports in New York in the 1690s yielded 100 to 400 percent profit. But, risk in trade was, I believe, as high as profit. Cadwallader Colden, "On the Trade of New York, 1723," *Doc. Hist. N.Y.*, I, 719; Miller, *Description of New York*, 45; Fox, *Heathcote*, 9–10; Edward Collins to Colden, July 7, 1727, *Colden Papers*, I, 199; N.Y. *Col. Laws*, IV, 494; McAnear, ed., "Mr. Robert R. Livingston's Reasons," *Jour. Pol. Economy*, XLVIII (1940), 82.

49. Stephen Skinner to William Skinner, Oct. 23, 1763, Warren Papers, A/Am, Sleepy Hollow Restorations Lib.; John Watts to Robert Watts, Apr. 10, 1786, Robert Watts Pa-

However, his grumblings did not mention the prospects that capital in the form of land could appreciate partly from the improvements of the tenants and partly from the pressure of population increase, while capital in loans remained static. In any event, those proprietors who conceived of no other return from their lands but the receipt of yearly rents were therefore disappointed with the dismal realities and were eager to dispose of their holdings at the first opportunity. "Great quantities in small parcels," according to Cadwallader Colden, were "continually ready to be sold."[50]

The price of land varied and fluctuated both due to such common factors as soil quality, terrain, location, and the terms of sale and also in response to political, military, and economic conditions at any given time. No general criteria can be used to determine land values in all cases and at all times; no two tracts of land, even if contiguous, would necessarily be evaluated by the same measure. There were instances in which lands located at a distance from navigable rivers turned out to be, for some reason, more valuable than lands on a river.[51] Nevertheless, it is possible to glean clues from diverse sources as to the general prices paid for patented lands.

In the first three decades of the eighteenth century, a hundred acres of land of good quality located on the Hudson River about forty miles from New York City were sold for no more than £10 and no less than £5.[52] Influenced by the large influx of immigrants, the natural increase in the population, and the spread of settlements northward, land prices steadily spiraled upward in subsequent years. Yet, in the 1740s Schoharie and Mohawk land close to densely settled farming communities and undisturbed by French and Indian incursions was advertised for as little as £20 to £30 per hundred acres.[53] Even the land near Fishkill in

---

pers, Box 3, N.-Y. Hist. Soc.; John Cockran to Philip Schuyler, Mar. 25, 1772, Schuyler Papers, 1758–1798, Box 24, N.Y. Pub. Lib.; *N.Y. Col. Laws*, III, 988, IV, 494.

50. Cadwallader Colden to Lords of Trade, Jan. 8, 1761, *Colden Letter Books*, I, 54; Peter Silvester to William and Robert Bayard and Joseph Read, May 15, 1771, Silvester Papers, fol. 1, N.-Y. Hist. Soc.

51. "Copy of a letter to Mr. Hugh Gaine," from Henry Remsen(?), ca. 1786, Auditor Office 12, 94/23–26, 45, P.R.O., on microfilm at Library of Congress.

52. Deed from William Skinner to John Beasley, Jr., May 21, 1736, Land, Box 1, in Van Cortlandt-Van Wyck Papers, N.Y. Pub. Lib.; James Murray to Baptist Boyd, *N.-Y. Gaz.*, Oct. 31, 1737. In 1710 Albany city could dispose of its frontier land at Schaghticoke at the rate of £1 and more per acre. The value of the city property probably had not so much to do with the quality of soil as with its possible future as a fur-trade center. Albany city to Symon Daniels of Schenectady, July 15, 1710, Munsell, ed., *Annals of Albany*, VI, 245–246. All the amounts referred to here are in New York currency.

53. Nicholas Bayard, John Grosbeck, and Adoniah Schuyler to Johann Frederick Ries,

Dutchess County was sometimes sold for £30 per hundred acres in the same decade, when the area was undergoing rapid settlement by people from Connecticut.[54] One royal official experienced in land speculation observed that before the French and Indian War the wild frontier lands, "good in quality and not disadvantageous in situation," were bought at the rate of £10 to £20 for a hundred acres. The same lands, however, rose in value to £40 to £50 at the war's end, partly because of the "plenty of money brought into the Province" by the British war effort and the high price of New York farm produce, but mainly, it seems, because of the anticipation of an unbridled expansion of the colonial frontier to the north and west after the elimination of the French menace.[55] But, with the lavish granting of land immediately following the war by both the king and the provincial government, the speculators' dreams of an exorbitant profit were shattered, as land prices fell to a £10 to £30 level.[56]

Prices alone do not tell us whether land at any given time was regarded as expensive or cheap, for these are subjective terms. Most observers—Colden, Banyar, and De Lancey, and the provincial governors—thought that it was cheap. William Smith, Jr., an attorney in New York, was perhaps the only dissenter from the general consensus, asserting that the great landlords "rated their lands exorbitantly high."[57] But it is unclear whether his comment referred to well-improved or to newly patented land. In either case, we still must allow for the possible gap between the proprietors' paper evaluations of their estates and the amounts for which they were actually able and willing to sell land. Significantly, in

---

Oct. 17, 1749, Nicholas Bayard Papers, N.-Y. Hist. Soc.; Cadwallader Colden to James Alexander, Nov. 2, 1744, Rutherford Collection, II, *ibid.*

54. Deed, Stephen Van Rensselaer to Gideon Ver Viele, May 20, 1740, Deed Book II, 169, Dutchess County Clerk's Office, Poughkeepsie, N.Y.; Henry Beekman to Gilbert Livingston, Jan. 19, 1737, Beekman Papers, N.-Y. Hist. Soc.

55. Goldsbrow Banyar to Major Edward Clarke, Feb. 16, 1763, Goldsbrow Banyar Papers, Lands, Box 6, N.-Y. Hist. Soc.; "Warren Johnson's Journal, June 29, 1760–July 3, 1761," *William Johnson Papers*, XIII, 187.

56. William Tryon to earl of Hillsborough, Apr. 11, 1772, *N.Y. Col. Docs.*, VIII, 293. See also "Sale of Forty Thousand Acres of Land near Cherry Valley the Property of George Croghan Esqr.," July 13, 1774, Goldsbrow Banyar Papers, Box 6. In this instance, 100 acres of land were sold for £10. The same source indicates that Belvedere Township of about 10,000 acres was auctioned off at the same rate. For further information on the price of land, see John Lyne to John Chamber, Sept. 14, 1757, John Chamber Papers, Box 1, 68–69, 90, 91, N.Y. State Lib.; Isaac Vrooman to James Duane, Nov. 16, 1762, Duane Papers, Roll 1; Francis W. Halsey, ed., *A Tour of Four Great Rivers, The Hudson, Mohawk, Susquehanna and Delaware in 1769, Being the Journal of Richard Smith of Burlington, New Jersey* (New York, 1906), 48–49.

57. William Smith, [Jr.], *History of New-York* (1830 ed.), I, 276.

1749 Nicholas Bayard and his two partners believed that the sale price of £20 per hundred acres for their Schoharie land—surveyed and platted out—was reasonable, in fact "much cheaper" than Pennsylvania land. They were certain that their price was competitive enough to counter the Penn proprietors' official land grant price since 1732, £15 10s. of Pennsylvania money (its value almost equaled that of New York currency) for a hundred acres with a quitrent of a halfpenny sterling per acre and other charges involved in obtaining a warrant and surveying. They wrote to the Reverend Johann Frederick Ries, a Lutheran minister in Pennsylvania, asking him to send along "such people as have mony to forward their Settlements and the greatest number of grown Children, for their assistance, to clear their lands."[58] If £20 per hundred acres in New York in the late 1740s was a good price for land in comparison with the prices in a sister colony with a reputation for a liberal land policy, then it seems plausible that New York was a more attractive place to settle than we have been led to believe.

For New York landowners, competition for settlers came particularly from Pennsylvania and the Jerseys and, to a lesser degree, from Virginia, Maryland, South Carolina, New Hampshire, and even the Floridas in the 1760s and 1770s. Publicity about the best features of the land policies of these colonies reached New Yorkers through pamphlets, letters, and word of mouth.[59] Many Yorkers responded positively to these appeals, a situation that disturbed New York officials and raised fears of a population drain.[60] Of course, no single factor was responsible for every case of Yorker desertion. Noting in 1696 the movement of two to three hundred families from the province "chiefly" to Pennsylvania and Maryland and "some" to New England colonies, an Anglican minister named Miller at-

58. Nicholas Bayard et al. to Johann F. Ries, Oct. 17, 1749, Bayard Papers. For the Penn family's land policy, see William Robert Shepherd, History of Proprietary Government in Pennsylvania (New York, 1896), 34–35. For the exchange rate of New York and Pennsylvania currencies, see William Johnson Papers, XIII, 186.
59. Advertisement by the proprietors of Kennebeck Purchase, N.-Y. Mercury, Jan. 2, 1764; advertisement by William Byrd of Virginia, ibid., Mar. 25, 1767; advertisement by John Semple of Maryland, ibid., May 5, 1766; advertisement on lands in Mobile and Pensacola, ibid., Mar. 4, 1765; proclamation by Gov. James Grant of East Florida, Oct. 11, 1762, ibid., Jan. 21, 1765; advertisement on lands in South Carolina, ibid., Oct. 11, 1762; advertisement on lands on the Mississippi River by Jacques Rapalje, N.-Y. Gaz.; and Wkly. Mercury, supplement, Dec. 27, 1773. On the Penns' successful promotional campaign, see Gov. Cosby to Lords of Trade, June 10, 1735, and George Clarke to Sec. William Popple, May 28, 1736, N.Y. Col. Docs., VI, 29–30, 56–62; Walter Allen Knittle, Early Eighteenth Century Palatine Emigration: A British Government Redemption Project to Manufacture Naval Stores (Philadelphia, 1936), 217–218, 221; Halsey, ed., Journal of Richard Smith, 56.
60. N.Y. Col. Docs., IV, 791, V, 180, 459, 480, 514, 953.

tributed the migration to New York's higher taxes occasioned by defense expenditures. In 1708 Governor Cornbury, upset over the recent move of young people from Long Island to East Jersey, blamed it on the proximity of the attracting colony, plus the good quality of the soil and the lack of taxes there. For many others, the availability of cheap land in the Jerseys and Pennsylvania was as important a consideration.[61]

Many New Yorkers and recent immigrants, however, were not lured away and, for whatever reasons, chose to stay in the colony. Close to the end of the colonial period, Governor William Tryon believed the steady population increase in New York was due to the "high price of labor and the plenty and cheapness of land fit for cultivation."[62] An examination of the demographic growth of New England and the middle colonies from 1696 to 1775 indicates that New York grew as fast, if not faster, than New Jersey and Connecticut, and much more rapidly than Massachusetts. Compared with Pennsylvania, though, growth was markedly slow, with an increase of only tenfold against the latter's seventeen times. Still, New York's record of nearly doubling its inhabitants every twenty-five years was about par for the course.[63]

The intercolonial competition for immigrants was bound to make a colonist conscious of his own worth. More important, this competition had a great impact on the development and structure of manorial society.

## Occupational Patterns and Economic Goals of the Landlords

The avowed reluctance of farmers to accept leasehold tenure in the midst of abundant economic opportunity posed formidable problems for manorial proprietors interested in developing their estates. We have already noted Jeremiah Van Rensselaer's lamentation over the difficulty of recruiting and keeping tenants in Rensselaerswyck in the 1670s. By 1740 these problems were largely resolved, as will be seen. In the meantime, it was imperative that proprietors offer to potential tenants settlement conditions that would help moderate their dislike of tenancy and would insure contentment after they settled. These promotional measures entailed

61. *Ibid.*, IV, 183, V, 56; "Capt. Samuel Mulford's Representations against the Government of New York, 1717," *Doc. Hist. N.Y.*, III, 368; Andrew Burnaby, *Travels through the Middle Settlements in North-America, in the Years 1759 and 1760* ... (London, 1775), 81; "Rough Draft of Address to the Queen," n.d., Livingston-Redmond MSS, Roll 6.

62. Gov. Tryon's report on the province of New York, June 11, 1774, *N.Y. Col. Docs.*, VIII, 450.

63. Evarts B. Greene and Virginia D. Harrington, *American Population before the Federal Census of 1790* (New York, 1932), *passim.*

certain concessions and capital outlay on the landlord's part. A landlord's willingness and capacity to bear such burdens were dependent on his financial and familial circumstances and on his conception of land use. It is, therefore, necessary to discuss the personal and economic goals of the first- and second-generation manor landlords, who largely determined the course of development of their domains.

As we noted earlier, the founders of these manors, with the exception of Kiliaen Van Rensselaer, were basically commercial in orientation. Yet they were ever ready to diversify their business operations as much as their capital resources allowed. The concept of economic or business specialization was totally foreign to these colonists, so that the acquisition of vast tracts of lands in the late seventeenth century failed to convert them into sedentary country gentlemen. Robert Livingston neglected to build a manor mansion for almost fifteen years after his manor patent was issued.[64] Both Frederick Philipse and his neighbor Stephanus Van Cortlandt passed away without one, although the former had erected a sawmill, two gristmills, and crude living quarters nearby, and the latter probably built a hunting cottage on his land. By 1690 former carpenter and wampum-maker Philipse had established a great commercial network with ten oceangoing vessels linking him to the major trading areas of England, Holland, the West Indies, Africa, and Virginia.[65] He dealt with such diverse goods as cereals, flour, brandies, wine, rum, molasses, slaves, tobacco, Holland linen, iron pots, bricks, stockings, and whatever else could be profitably disposed of. At the same time, he continually expanded his real estate holdings in New York City and other areas.[66] Though their activities were smaller in scale, Van Cortlandt and Livingston each operated two or three ships that traveled to the harbors of Madagascar, the West Indies, Virginia, Dover, and Amsterdam and that carried goods for others as well as for their owners.[67] The cargoes were as varied as those shipped by Philipse. In addition, individually or in

64. Land Papers, Book 5: 37, N.Y. Bureau of Waterways.

65. Exchequer 190/668, 18, 190/669, 4, P.R.O., on microfilm at Sleepy Hollow Restorations Lib.; *Court Minutes of Albany, Rensselaerswyck, and Schenectady*, III, 125; "Ships belonging to Frederick Philipse" (typescript), Philipse Papers, Sleepy Hollow Restorations Lib.

66. Frederick Philipse's will of 1700 shows that he owned 13 houses and several lots including his residence, a bolting house, a cooper's house, and two warehouses. Besides, he owned lands and tenements at Tappan across the Hudson River, in Ulster County, and in Bergen, N.J. Sleepy Hollow Restoration, Inc., *Philipsburg Manor* (Tarrytown, N.Y., 1969), 14; Edward Hagaman Hall, *Philipse Manor Hall at Yonkers, N.Y.: The Site, the Building, and Its Occupants* (New York, 1912), 97–99.

67. Stephanus Van Cortlandt to Francis Nicholson, Apr. 6, 1691, Blathwayt Papers, Roll 2; Leder, *Livingston*, chap. 3, especially p. 90; C.O. 5, 1042/139.

partnership with others, these two were heavily involved in military contracting for provincial and British troops in New York, an enterprise that occupied their attention more and more in the last decade of the seventeenth century.[68] A tax record of 1699 shows that Livingston, though based in Albany, had two waterfront houses in New York City assessed at £250. Van Cortlandt owned at least four houses, including a slaughterhouse worth more than £420, mortgages on several houses, and tracts in and outside the city.[69] In the early 1690s Van Cortlandt bought for £500 a sawmill with some land on the Rahway River in East Jersey with the intention not only of supplying lumber for building ships, army barracks, and houses in his hometown but also of erecting a gristmill and residence house for one of his children.[70] It is not surprising that, for all their large landed estates and manorial titles, these landgraves often called and styled themselves as "merchant" throughout their adult lives.

Of the manor founders, Kiliaen Van Rensselaer (1663–1718) was an anomaly. He had been brought up in the highly commercial environment of Albany and was once apprenticed to a silversmith. Through his mother and his marriage to Maria, daughter of Stephanus Van Cortlandt, he was connected with many prosperous merchant families. He held influential governmental offices—member of the General Assembly from his manor (1691–1700, 1702–1703), member of the governor's council (1703–1719), and commissioner of Indian affairs—any of which could have been put to good use for certain business ends. After the final liquidation of his Dutch partner's interest in the domain, he, like his ancestors, could have exploited the resources of his manor by cornering the produce of its inhabitants and supplying their necessities. But in spite of all these advantages, he never developed an entrepreneurial attitude. To be sure, he sold logwood, timber, and boards that were cut and sawed at his manor, as well as flour, hides, and pitch tar. He sent wheat to New York merchants and dabbled in victualing troops on the frontier.[71] But

---

68. "Memorial of Mr. Livingston to the Board of Trade," Dec. 28, 1696, N.Y. Col. Docs., IV, 252; N.Y. Col. Laws, I, 938, 957, 985, 986; "Petition of Ch. Lodwick," May 3, 1706, Livingston-Redmond MSS, Roll 2; N.Y. Council Minutes, VI, 138, 175, 192, VII, 25, 80, 111, 138, 171, 178, VIII, pt. 1, 4.

69. "Tax Roll, Nov. 29, 1699" (typescript), Sleepy Hollow Restorations Lib.; Van Cortlandt's interest in mortgages and other evidence indicate his extensive moneylending business. N.Y. Col. MSS, XXXIX, 20.

70. Stephanus Van Cortlandt to William Blathwayt, Dec. 7, 1694, Blathwayt Papers, Roll 2.

71. Petition of Peter Schuyler et al., Apr. 2, 1703, O'Callaghan, ed., Calendar of Hist. MSS, 309; Kiliaen Van Rensselaer's accounts with various New York merchants, Miscellaneous Accounts, 1700–1720, in Rensselaerswyck Manuscripts, N.Y. State Lib.; Jeremiah

this was the utmost extent of his trading. Following in the footsteps of his ancestors, he operated a large gristmill at Watervliet several miles north of Albany, primarily for the purpose of obtaining tolls for grinding rather than for the farm produce itself to supply foreign markets. These were typical of the activities of a landed squire in the old tradition. Thus Van Rensselaer styled himself as either a "gentleman" or a "patroon."

The same was true of his young brother Henry (d. 1740), who received in 1704 as his share of the family property the Claverack land (later called the "lower manor") from Kiliaen with a nominal yearly obligation of twenty-five bushels of wheat rent.[72] Before this family property settlement, Henry owned a fourth interest in the brigantine *Orange* with three other partners, Robert Livingston, Peter Schuyler, and Cornelius Jacobs, and engaged mainly in the West Indian trade. He also ran a general store in Albany. But he suffered a severe loss in 1695 when the ship and its cargo were charged with violation of the navigation acts and condemned by the supreme court of the province. The aggrieved party's efforts to recover some portion of the ship and its cargo proved to be futile because of the worsening feud between Governor Fletcher and Livingston. This misfortune was apparently followed quickly by "considerable losses" from fire at his storehouse, which put an end to his overseas trade venture and probably to his retail business as well.[73] He was politically active as an alderman of the town in 1699, occasionally acted as a commissioner of Indian affairs, and was an assemblyman from Rensselaerswyck from 1705 to 1714. But he seems to have long since chosen the life-style of a squire, living alternately at his Greenbush country home called Crailo and at a town house in Albany.[74] The only busi-

---

Dummer to Kiliaen Van Rensselaer, Boston, June 14, 1708, _____ to Kiliaen Van Rensselaer, Oct. 11, 1708, Letters, 1700–1749, Rensselaerswyck MSS.

72. The Claverack land title and its boundaries were confirmed by a royal patent in 1717, but it is impossible to ascertain how large the tract was. The Van Rensselaer family of Claverack claimed that it contained 250,000 acres, whereas Cadwallader Colden believed it to be only 23,000 acres. Deed, June 2, 1704, Deed Book 5: 26–27, Albany Co. Clerk's Office; deed from Kiliaen Van Rensselaer to brother Henry, Mar. 10, 1715, and deed, Henry Van Rensselaer to Jonas Douw *et al.*, Oct. 12, 1712, Drawer 1, Albany Institute of History and Art, Albany, N.Y.; Patent Book 8: 161, Office of the Secretary of State of New York, Albany; Colden to Lords of Trade, May 31, 1765, *Colden Letter Books*, II, 8–12.

73. N.Y. Col. MSS, XL, 18, 111, 153; Paul M. Hamlin and Charles E. Baker, eds., *Supreme Court of Judicature of the Province of New York, 1691–1704* (New York, 1952–1959), I, 163–164. See also Leder, *Livingston*, 94–95, on the *Orange* case.

74. *N.Y. Col. Docs.*, IV, 567, 570–572; "At a Meeting of the Commissioners of Indian Affairs," June 6, 1707, Livingston-Redmond MSS, Roll 3: Helen Wilkinson Reynolds, *Dutch Houses in the Hudson Valley before 1776* (New York, 1965 [orig. publ. New York, 1929]), 113–114.

ness he had outside the plantation was a share in a brewery at "Wolven hook" in the manor.[75] He showed no great zest over personal management of his Claverack estate, as is evidenced by his neglect during his lifetime to build a residential house there. As an absentee landlord, he even let a middleman collect and dispose of wheat rent from his tenants, a practice quite in contrast with that of the commercially oriented landlords in the province.[76]

The male heirs of the manor founders generally followed the occupations of their fathers. Adolph Philipse (1665–1749), the only surviving son of Frederick, was described in 1700, when his father was still alive, as "a gentleman in the first rank of our trade and of the chiefest Interest and substance in our province."[77] Like fellow merchants of the day, he held a huge tract of land later known as "Philipse's Highland (or Upper) Patent" (about 200,000 acres) in Dutchess County. His fortune, built largely upon a partnership with his father, expanded further in 1702 when he inherited five houses and a warehouse in New York City, all of the so-called Upper Manor north of the present town of Dobbs Ferry (including the two gristmills at Pocantico, now Tarrytown), fifteen Negroes, a half of the livestock at the mills, a ship, and a fourth part of his father's personal estate. In the 1720s he enlarged the establishments at the Upper Manor (or Mills) by adding a third set of millstones and doubling the size of a small house for his overseer.[78] These improvements reflected his efforts to add agricultural products to his overseas trade. His ships, seven or eight in number, carried slaves from the west coast of Africa, furs for England, English goods for the Amerindian trade, and products in intercolonial traffic. But, as the century wore on, his trade gravitated more and more to the West Indies and the Madeira Islands and was especially heavy in foodstuffs (flour and biscuits), lumber, sugar, molasses, and wine.[79] Like his father, Adolph's flourishing commerce was matched by his political activism. He served on the governor's council from 1705 to 1720. His leadership in opposing Governor William Burnet's efforts to

75. Lease deed, Henry Van Rensselaer to Jonas Douw, Oct. 12, 1717, Drawer 1, Albany Inst. of Hist. and Art.

76. Philip Livingston to father, Robert, Feb. 18, 1714, Mar. 25 and Apr. 24, 1724, Livingston-Redmond MSS, Rolls 3 and 4.

77. James Graham to Blathwayt, Aug. 2, 1700, Blathwayt Papers, Roll 2.

78. Sleepy Hollow Restorations, *Philipsburg Manor*, 31.

79. "Ships belonging to Adolph Philipse" and "Philipse Shipping Records files," Philipse Papers, Sleepy Hollow Restorations Lib.; Ex. 190/677, 15, and 190/841, 1. Adolph Philipse sold guns to New York expeditionary forces against Canada in 1709. Robert Livingston, "Camp at the Wood Creek Reviewed, August 16, 1707," Livingston-Redmond MSS, Roll 5.

stop New Yorkers from trading with Canada and to reestablish the chancery court, which the landed men in the province viewed as a threat to land titles, turned him to popular politics. He was first elected to the assembly in 1722 and several years later was made its speaker. In that capacity he championed the causes of the commercial and landed interests until his retirement from public life in 1745.[80]

Of the three surviving sons of Robert Livingston, only Philip (1686–1749) and Robert, Jr. (1688–1775), concern us here, because of their connection with Livingston Manor. Though trained in law, both Philip and Robert, Jr., pursued merchant careers after they came of age.[81] Under his father's tutelage, Philip soon converted his small retail store in Albany into a great commercial establishment. He had "very good success" in European trade and, around 1724, began to try his fortune in the West Indies, keeping with the shifting pattern in the colony's trade. He also provisioned garrisons on the northern frontier and supplied his father's manor store with foreign imports.[82] His political preferment was no less impressive. In 1707 Philip was appointed his father's deputy in the offices of secretary of Indian affairs, town clerk, and clerk of the peace of the court of common pleas of Albany; in 1721 he assumed, following his father's resignation, the sole responsibility of these offices, which he was to hold until his death. Thanks to his father's influence with Governor Burnet, he was appointed in 1722 mayor of Albany for a year and, three years later, was admitted to the council. Much as he loved political power, Philip refused to seek a seat in the assembly—although he could have easily gotten one—for fear that his business would suffer; trade was his primary interest.[83] Records on his younger brother Robert, Jr.,

80. N.Y. Col. Docs., IV, 1137, 1180, V, 124, 458, 459, 471, 494, 573, 578–579, 768, 847–848; Journal of General Assembly, I, 513, 545, 557, 573, 574, 717, 749, II, 1, 2, 63. George Clarke noted in 1725 that with the election of Adolph Philipse to the speakership, the assembly became "mercantile interest oriented paying much more attention to tonnage duty and others dealing directly with the trade." Clarke to Mr. Walpole, Nov. 24, 1725, N.Y. Col. Docs., V, 768. However, it would be wrong to suggest that Philipse was indifferent or hostile to the landed cause. As mentioned before, he owned large tracts of land and could not possibly do anything to hurt his land-related business. There was no specialized landed interest as such that could be set apart from broad commercial interests in the first half of the 18th century; indeed, there was no fundamental conflict and political polarity between the two interests, since merchants were landowners as well.

81. "License" for Philip Livingston, Dec. 31, 1719, N.Y. Col. MSS, LXII, 58; Joan Gordon, "The Livingstons of New York, 1675–1860: Kinship and Class" (Ph.D. diss., Columbia University, 1959), 45.

82. Philip Livingston to Robert Hunter, Nov. 13 and Dec. 4, 1711, N.Y. Col. MSS, LVI, 166, LVII, 13; Philip Livingston to father, Robert, Mar. 27 and July 8, 1717, Apr. 21, 1724, Livingston-Redmond MSS, Rolls 3 and 4; N.Y. Col. Laws, II, 44.

83. Munsell, ed., Annals of Albany, V, 152, VIII, 276; "Royal Commission," June 30,

are very scant, but they show that he engaged in trade on a modest scale as an agent of his brothers and father and that he occasionally practiced law to supplement his income.[84] When the manor founder died in 1728, Philip came into possession of the bulk of the domain land (about 141,-000 acres), and Robert, Jr., inherited a tract of 13,000 acres known as Clermont estate on the Hudson River south of Roeloff Jansen's Kill.[85]

The Livingstons' inheritance of this entailed real estate did not change their occupational outlook or their residence. Rather, it offered them, especially Philip, the opportunity and resources to diversify their economic endeavors as their father had done. Philip continued to stay at his Albany house, referring to it as his "home," and considered the city his legal residence. He managed his mercantile and landed concerns from Albany until 1744.[86] Day-to-day administration of the manor was left in the hands of his clerks, but under his meticulous supervision.[87] In the 1730s he owned several ships in part and in whole. His fleet shipped enormous amounts of New York products—mostly foodstuffs—to England, Holland, France, Ireland, Newfoundland, Boston, South Carolina, Barbados, and other Caribbean islands, and imported rum, molasses, wine, slaves, and European goods, which he sold at his stores in Albany, in the manor, and in Schenectady.[88] In late 1741 he took up iron manufacturing at Ancram in the eastern part of his domain, an operation that he estimated would require an initial outlay of £6,000.[89] Deeply involved as he was in these extensive business activities, he still managed to acquire many thousands of acres of land near his manor and on the

1721, Livingston-Redmond MSS, Roll 6; Philip Livingston to father, Robert, Mar. 25 and Apr. 10, 1724, *ibid.*, Roll 4; *Colden Papers*, IV, 94.

84. Robert Livingston, Jr., to father, Robert, Feb. 11 and Mar. 28, 1714, June 25, 1717, Livingston-Redmond MSS, Roll 3; Robert Livingston, Jr., to brother Philip, Oct. 12 and Nov. 7, 1716, *ibid.*, Roll 6.

85. Robert Livingston's will, Feb. 10, 1723, *ibid.*, Roll 4.

86. Philip Livingston to Henry Van Rensselaer, Jr., July 5, 1731, Misc. MSS, Livingston, N-P, N.-Y. Hist. Soc.

87. Philip Livingston to John D'Witt, June 28, Aug. 7, and Sept. 6, 1740, Livingston-Redmond MSS, Roll 9.

88. Philip Livingston to son Robert, Jr., Sept. 12 and Dec. 3, 6, 1740, Oct. 29, 1741, *ibid.*, Roll 7. Occasionally, Philip Livingston also exported peltries, which his agent Henry Van Rensselaer, Jr., bought at Schenectady. Philip Livingston to Henry Van Rensselaer, Jr., June 15, 1732, Misc. MSS, Livingston, N-P; Philip Livingston to son Robert, Jr., Mar. 3, 1741, Livingston-Redmond MSS, Roll 7; for Philip Livingston's ownership of ships, see Gordon, "Livingstons of New York," 98–99.

89. Philip Livingston to Jacob Wendell, Mar. 25, 1741, Livingston Papers, Museum of the City of New York; "Bond of Robert Livingston, Jr., to his brothers and sisters, Nov. 25, 1741," Livingston-Redmond MSS, Roll 7; Irene D. Neu, "The Iron Plantations of Colonial New York," *N.Y. History*, XXXIII (1952), 4–5.

frontier for either speculative or development purposes.[90] His official connection with Indian affairs, his wealth, and his council membership all made it easier for him to satisfy his insatiable hunger for land. Philip Livingston was thus, in the words of one historian, "a comprehensive genius" among colonial entrepreneurs,[91] and few could rival him in combining the careers of lawyer, landlord, foreign and domestic merchant, politician, and iron manufacturer.

Robert, Jr., continued to live in New York City for some twenty years after he inherited the Clermont estate. As before, his preoccupation was with commerce, but he was never able to develop his business into anything comparable to his brother Philip's. He appears to have been aloof, querulous, and arrogant, personality traits hardly conducive to the cultivation of goodwill from others.[92] More important, he failed to receive the sort of political help his father had extended to Philip, with the result that he held no public office except briefly that of representative from Livingston Manor (1726–1727). Nor did he put his law practice to good advantage. The paucity of documents, private and public, concerning his activities suggests how limited his business and social intercourse was. One extant record shows that in 1734 he exported sugar, pitch, and precious metals valued at £724 to London, and another that he sent foreign imports to Henry Van Rensselaer, Jr., in Schenectady. Meanwhile, a good number of tenants had settled on his Clermont estate, which was managed for him by an overseer. In 1743 he at last decided to retire to his country land, hoping to live comfortably on rentals from the tenants and tolls from his mills.[93] Yet he did not, it appears, completely

90. N.Y. Land Papers, XII, 8, 19, 59, 126; Patent Book 11: 54, 314, 488, and Patent Book 12: 83, Office of N.Y. Sec. of State; Philip Livingston to Henry Livingston, Dec. 14, 1734, Misc. MSS, Livingston, N-P; Philip Livingston to Philip Verplanck, Mar. 31, 1739, and deed between Philip Livingston and Elisha Noble, Livingston-Redmond MSS, Roll 6; Colden Papers, II, 188, 223. See also Livingston's voluminous correspondence with Jacob Wendell of Boston, Livingston Papers, Museum of City of N.Y., and with Messrs. Storke and Gainsborough of London, Misc. MSS, Box 5, N.Y. State Lib.

91. Virginia D. Harrington, "The Place of the Merchant in New York Colonial Life," N.Y. History, XIII (1932), 368.

92. I have deduced this conclusion about Robert, Jr.'s, personality from two sources. One is his argument with his brother Philip over a trivial matter in 1713, and the other is his bitterness against his father's friends in New York City for their alleged inhospitality to him. Philip Livingston to father, Robert, Jan. 25, 1713, and Robert Livingston, Jr., to father, Robert, Jan. 25 and Mar. 28, 1713, Livingston-Redmond MSS, Roll 3.

93. "Invoice of Goods to Messrs. Storke and Gainsborough," Dec. 5, 1734, Robert Livingston, Jr., to Henry Van Rensselaer, Jr., May 12, 1743, Misc. MSS, Livingston, N-P. Unspectacular though his trade was, Robert Livingston, Jr., had made an effort to develop his Clermont land so that by 1762 he and his son Robert R. could boast a handsome yearly income of £850 from the real estate. Robert, Jr., owned a sloop, which was employed in

cut himself off from mercantile activities until about 1750.[94] In addition to the Clermont estate, he had a substantial interest in the 1,500,000-acre Hardenbergh Patent, which comprised most of the present Ulster, Delaware, Sullivan, and Greene counties. It was this frontier land that Livingston, together with his associate Gulian Verplanck of New York City, tried in the 1750s to improve with tenants.[95] He began the sedentary life of a landlord, which was most characteristic of the third-generation proprietors, in the second half of the eighteenth century.

The second-generation proprietors of Cortlandt Manor were of diverse backgrounds. As noted earlier, the manor founder, Stephanus Van Cortlandt, had willed in 1700 that the domain be divided equally among his eleven heirs, male and female, in fee simple when they came of age or married. When the land was finally partitioned about three decades later, there were ten heirs (reckoning husband and wife as one party) to the estate. Of these, only two, Philip and Stephen Van Cortlandt, were male issues of Stephanus; the others had married Van Cortlandt women. William Skinner, John Milns, Andrew Johnston, Samuel Bayard, Stephen De Lancey, John Schuyler, Jr., and Henry Beekman were sons-in-law of the manor founder, and Philip Verplanck was the husband of Gertrude, the only daughter of Johannes Van Cortlandt, the deceased eldest son of Stephanus.[96] Many of them were scions of the most illustrious families in colonial New York. Despite this diffusion of the manor ownership, all of the proprietors except two conformed to the occupational pattern of the Livingstons and the Philipses.

Philip Van Cortlandt (1683–1746), the family head after his brother Johannes died in 1702, was an eminent merchant of the metropolis, keeping throughout life the commercial stamp of his father and of his

---

the transportation business between Clermont and New York City. Robert R. Livingston to father, Robert, Jr., Mar. 17, 1762, Robert R. Livingston Collections, Box 1, N-Y. Hist. Soc.; Robert, Jr.'s, "account with John Maile, 1753–58," in "Uncatalogued Livingston Manuscripts," N.-Y. Hist. Soc.

94. As of Dec. 1749, Robert, Jr., designated New York City as his legal residence and gave "merchant" for his occupation. See "Advertisement to be sent to Scotland from Verplank and Livingston to encourage the Setlement of their Lands," Dec. 20, 1749, "Uncatalogued Livingston MSS"; deed of reversion between Robert Livingston, Jr., and his tenants, Mar. 24, 1744, *ibid.*

95. In 1750 Robert Livingston, Jr., and Gulian Verplanck held one-eighth interest in the patent, but their respective shares are unknown. Deed, James Graham to Robert Livingston, Jr., Feb. 26, 1741, "Uncatalogued Livingston MSS"; "General Account of the Several Tracts of Land Peter Fauconnier is concerned, 1702–1770," MSS No. 38.189.29, Museum of City of N.Y.; Robert Livingston, Jr., to brother Gilbert, Mar. 5, 1746, Misc. MSS, Livingston, N-P.

96. See Sung Bok Kim, "The Manor of Cortlandt and Its Tenants, 1697–1783" (Ph.D. diss., Michigan State University, 1966), 89–102.

father-in-law, Abraham De Peyster, wealthy merchant. His appointment to the governor's council in 1730, succeeding Lewis Morris, Jr., of Westchester, was a measure of the influence and prominence he held in the mercantile community.[97] His business records from 1731 to 1741 show that he traded most heavily with the West Indian islands and to a lesser extent with Dover, Madeira, Amsterdam, Boston, South Carolina, Rhode Island, and Perth Amboy. His exports consisted mainly of flour, biscuits, meat, beer, fruit, and lumber.[98] In addition, he owned two inns, a brewery, and a bolting house in New York City. However, in view of the large amount of debt (£5,050 including interest) he incurred, he appears not to have been so successful a businessman as Adolph Philipse or Philip Livingston. Nor was his land acquisition and its development impressive. His speculative activity brought him 5,146 acres of frontier land in five different areas, and he received 7,210 acres of Cortlandt Manor (worth £1,305 as of 1733) and a few thousand acres of Rumbout Patent in Dutchess County as his share of the inheritance.[99] But their benefits remained more potential than real; the frontier lands were inaccessible because of the French threat, and the manor land had remained undivided for more than three decades after his father's death. In 1746, the year he died, there were only six tenants on his manor property, and probably none on his other country lands.

Not much is known about Stephen Van Cortlandt (1695–1756), Philip's brother. Sometime in the 1720s, Stephen made what would become a permanent move to the family property at Second River (now Belleville), Essex County, New Jersey. In 1730 his title to this property was formerly confirmed by his brothers and sisters. It consisted of sawmills and gristmills, a bolting house, a bake house, and other tenements

97. De Peyster's "Account with Robert Livingston," Apr. 21, 1718, to Apr. 10, 1719, Livingston-Redmond MSS, Roll 2; N.Y. Col. MSS, LXXIII, 45, 145; "Account against the estate of Philip Van Cortlandt, dec'd, 1722–1761," Van Cortlandt Papers, V1837, Sleepy Hollow Restorations Lib.; John Montgomerie to Lords of Trade, June 30, 1729, N.Y. Col. Docs., V, 882.

98. Philip Van Cortlandt owned two vessels in partnership with several others. C.O. 5/1225, passim; Letterbook of Philip Van Cortlandt, Van Cortlandt Family Papers, N.-Y. Hist. Soc.; invoice of goods shipped to Thomas Fareweather, Nov. 9, 1729, Sedgwick Papers, II, Massachusetts Historical Society, Boston; N.Y. Col. MSS, LXII, 116, 134.

99. Philip Van Cortlandt's will, Aug. 21, 1746, Van Cortlandt Papers, V1837, Sleepy Hollow Restorations Lib.; I. N. Phelps Stokes, comp., The Iconography of Manhattan Island, 1498–1909 (New York, 1915–1928), IV, 466, 481. Regarding his debts and estates, see "Minutes of the estate of Philip and Stephen Van Cortland Esqrs decd, 1760," BV, N.-Y. Hist. Soc.; Philip Van Cortlandt to uncle Pierre Van Cortlandt, Dec. 12, 1759, Van Cortlandt Papers, V1883, Sleepy Hollow Restorations Lib.; "The Estate of Father Philip Van Cortlandt, 1738–1758," ibid., V1837; N.Y. Land Papers, XV, 143; N.-Y. Mercury, Nov. 28, 1757, and Apr. 2, 1759.

with about 40 acres of land.[100] In the next few years he also received, as his portion of the estate settlement, 7,530 acres of the manor and a few thousand acres of Rumbout Patent. According to a land deed he contracted in 1726, he was a merchant by occupation, but it is impossible to determine exactly the nature of his commercial activity.[101] Being just a few miles from Manhattan Island, the entrepôt for New York and eastern New Jersey, his agricultural and related industrial establishments were advantageously situated. In all probability, Stephen was in the business of buying wheat from neighboring farmers and turning it into flour, biscuits, and bread. But in 1749 he completely disassociated himself from this business by renting the facilities out to three of his sons. He also entrusted the management of his manor land—all together twenty-one farms—to the hands of his son John. At the age of fifty-four he joined the ranks of Robert Livingston, Jr., of Clermont and Henry and Kiliaen Van Rensselaer in the pursuit of a gentlemanly life-style.[102]

Although he belonged genealogically to the third generation, Philip Verplanck (1695–1770) should be mentioned at this point, because he was a party to the first partition of Cortlandt Manor and was closely associated with the domain's history as the only resident landlord until 1749. Verplanck's life can be divided into two periods. He was in Albany trading in Indian goods and surveying until 1730, when he was found guilty by a local court of violating the Canadian trade laws and fined £300.[103] Possibly it was this misfortune and Verplanck's subsequent financial predicament that contributed to the sudden expediting of the division of the manor between 1730 and 1734. Verplanck served the Van Cortlandt heirs as the surveyor for the property, and it was partitioned on the basis of his survey and appraisal of the respective parcels of lands. His move in 1730 to Menagh (later renamed Verplanck's Point) at the northwestern corner of the manor and his family's land inheritance

---

100. Stephen Van Cortlandt to Kiliaen Van Rensselaer, Sept. 2, 1718, Letters, 1700–1749, Rensselaerswyck MSS; Stephanus Van Cortlandt to Blathwayt, Dec. 7, 1694, Blathwayt Papers, Roll 2; "Release of the Parties to Stephen Van Cortlandt," Nov. 12, 1730, Case for Oversized MSS, 1730, Van Cortlandt Family Papers.
101. Deed, Lewis Morris, Jr., and Andries Coeymans to Stephen Van Cortlandt et al., July 19, 1726, Deed Book XII, 183, Office of N.Y. Sec. of State.
102. "Agreement among Stephen Jr., Samuel and Philip Van Cortlandt as Co-partners in the mill at Second River, June 12, 1749," Case for Oversized MSS, 1749, Van Cortlandt Family Papers.
103. Philip Livingston to father, Robert, Jan. 8, 1726, Livingston-Redmond MSS, Roll 4; Rutger Bleecker et al. to sheriff, Mar. 2, 1730, Van Schaick Papers, Box 1, N.Y. Pub. Lib.; Armour, "Merchants of Albany," 177; Verplanck's commission as a deputy surveyor for Cadwallader Colden, Sept. 21, 1721, Philip Verplanck Papers, New York Genealogical and Biographical Society, New York.

(8,500 acres in the manor) did not, however, make him forsake his early occupation. He ran a general store on the premises, a ferry between Menagh and Haverstraw, and a gristmill, and engaged in the carrying trade on the Hudson River with a sloop, the *Clinton*. As the only resident proprietor, he was naturally expected to look after his relatives' interests in such matters as collecting rents and laying out the manor roads. By the same token, he continuously represented the district in the General Assembly for thirty-four years after 1734.[104]

The most successful and opulent merchant of the Cortlandt Manor proprietors was Stephen De Lancey (1663–1741). His career was an example of what the New World could offer a young ambitious immigrant who combined a little money with talent and hard work. A persecuted Huguenot from France, De Lancey arrived in New York in 1686 with £300. Fourteen years later, at the age of thirty-seven, when he married twenty-six-year-old Anne Van Cortlandt, he had firmly established himself in metropolitan commercial circles.[105] His record of capital accumulation was indeed dazzling. Calling himself one of the leading "money'd men" who were rushing for "the prize cocoa," he confessed to Robert Livingston in 1711 that he had invested more than £3,000 in that merchandise alone. In 1728 he was known as "one of the richest men of the Province." By the end of his life he had acquired, as a local obituary put it, "a plentiful fortune" of "about £100,000."[106]

De Lancey's wealth was built on trade as extensive as that of the Philipses, Philip Livingston, and Philip Van Cortlandt and also on investments in real estate, of which the city property was the most valuable. As a busy supplier of the West Indian market, he needed country lands in order to keep available an abundant supply of wheat, the colony's principal staple crop.[107] But a good part of the fertile lands in the Hudson River valley had already been preempted by others in the previous century. Even his Cortlandt Manor share (8,289 acres) and some of the

104. William Edward Ver Planck, *The History of Abraham Isaacse Ver Planck and His Male Descendants in America* (Fishkill Landing, N.Y., 1892), 127–131; N.Y. Land Papers, XIV, 1–3, 8.

105. Edward F. De Lancey, "Memoir of the Hon. James De Lancey," *Doc. Hist. N.Y.*, IV, 1035–1059; Scharf, ed., *History of Westchester County*, I, 862–864; *N.Y. Col. Docs.*, IV, 532.

106. Stephen De Lancey to Robert Livingston, Feb. 14, 1711, Livingston-Redmond MSS, Roll 3; *N.Y. Col. Docs.*, V, 857; Zenger's *New-York Weekly Journal*, Nov. 23, 1741; Harry Yoshpe, "The De Lancey Estate: Did the Revolution Democratize Landholding in New York?" *N.Y. History*, XVII (1936), 167–177.

107. *N.Y. Col. Docs.*, IV, 1133; Bonomi, *Factious People*, 64–65; N.Y. Col. MSS, LV, 164.

Rumbout land came into his possession too late to be of much help. He was thus forced to turn to the two other sources for agricultural produce, country farmers and the city grain market. A Rensselaerswyck account book shows that De Lancey supplied the Van Rensselaers with import goods like London shalloon, cotton cloth, and garter linen and always received in return—perhaps gladly—flour instead of cash.[108]

Involved in business as he was, De Lancey was not indifferent to political matters in the assembly, where such vital issues as custom and tonnage duties and the terms of the Canadian trade were decided. From 1702 to 1737 he was a continuous member of the representative body from New York County, except for one short term, and while he was in office he jealously guarded, together with Adolph Philipse, commercial and landed interests. His political influence and status, however, can be best illustrated by the meteoric ascent of his eldest son, James, in official preferment. In 1729, at the age of just twenty-six, James, trained at Cambridge and Lincoln's Inn, was appointed to the governor's council; in 1731 he was second judge of the supreme court, and two years later chief justice replacing Lewis Morris. Indeed, the very foundations of the De Lancey power, a force that largely accounted for the turbulence of mid-century New York politics, had been laid by Stephen De Lancey.[109]

Another proprietor who deserves special notice is Henry Beekman (1688–1776), the sole male heir of Henry Beekman of Kingston (1652–1716), a large landowner in Dutchess County. His second marriage in 1726 to thirty-eight-year-old Gertrude Van Cortlandt would bring more lands (8,751 acres of Cortlandt Manor and some of Rumbout Patent) to his vast holdings composed primarily of two patents, Rhinebeck (21,766 acres) and Beekman (about 84,000 acres), which his father had conveyed to him. Mostly because of his official duties as sheriff (1728–1733) of the city and county of New York and assemblyman (1724–1758) from Dutchess County, he generally stayed in the bustling metropolis.[110] At his country seat at Rhinebeck he operated sawmills and gristmills and other agricultural processing businesses, usually under the management of his

---

108. Kiliaen and Maria Van Rensselaer's account with Stephen De Lancey, Apr. 1716, June 19, 1719, and Oct. 21, 1721, and Jeremiah Van Rensselaer's account with De Lancey, Apr. 15, 1732, "Miscellaneous Accounts," Rensselaerswyck MSS.

109. Edward F. De Lancey, "Memoir," *Doc. Hist. N.Y.*, IV, 1040–1041; Bonomi, *Factious People*, 145; Milton M. Klein, "Politics and Personalities in Colonial New York," *N.Y. History*, XLVII (1966), 11; Katz, *Newcastle's New York, passim*.

110. *N.Y. Gen. and Biog. Rec.*, LXVIII (1937), 219–220; his obituary in *N.-Y. Gaz.; and Wkly. Mercury*, Feb. 12, 1776; N.Y. Land Papers, VII, 234; White, *Beekmans of New York*, 92–93, 162–163, 169, 206.

agents. Always finding wheat rent from his tenants inadequate, he eagerly bought grain from farmers and sold it, either raw or processed, to the city market. A typical letter of his went as follows: "Give such pris from time to time as others shall," he instructed one of his country agents; "I want the wheat as much as yu can well git Even to 2,000 Bushel at the pris of 5/4."[111] Despite this evidence, his economic orientation was basically that of a country squire, with much involvement in community and provincial affairs. In contrast to the commercial landlords, he was never in the import and export trade, although he had the capital and agricultural resources to sustain such a venture. Nor did he, unlike Philip Livingston, show a great interest in iron manufacturing, although there was, according to his own description, "a fine Furnace all fitted for blasting" with four "large Beds of good Iron Ore within 2 miles of the Furnace" on his Cortlandt Manor land; in 1745 he advertised to lease these industrial facilities, which had been built and run by one Ephraim Hayward and Company since the late 1730s. Judging from his legislative behavior, he was an agrarian localist.[112] He resisted the drive by the governors to establish the chancery and equity court; he opposed the Canadian trade in which the Philipses and the De Lanceys were heavily involved; and he fought against bills giving the metropolis a monopoly in flour milling and packing at the expense of the country millers.[113]

As for the five other remaining manor proprietors, a detailed discussion of their careers and economic orientation is impossible, simply because of the scarcity of records. A case in point is John Miln, the second husband of Maria Van Cortlandt. He was the rector of St. Peter's Church in Albany from 1728 to 1737 and subsequently of a church at Shrewsbury in New Jersey. Apart from his association with holy orders, he occasionally practiced medicine and was appointed (in 1747) as a surgeon to the provincial troops at Albany. A man of experimental cast, he once spent a large sum of money in some agricultural "projects" but reaped "little profit."[114]

---

111. Henry Beekman to Henry Livingston, Jan. 17, Feb. 17, May 6, 1752, Feb. 19, 1750, Jan. 30, 1753, Beekman to Gilbert Livingston, Jan. 21, 1747, Beekman Papers, N.-Y. Hist. Soc. Beekman occasionally joined others in supplying the frontier garrisons with provisions. *Journal of General Assembly*, II, 84.

112. Beekman's advertisement in *New-York Gazette: or, the Weekly Post-Boy*, June 17, 1745.

113. *Journal of General Assembly*, I, 521, 571–572, 576–577, 663; *N.Y. Col. Docs.*, V, 847–848, 882–888, 947; Smith, [Jr.], *History of New-York* (1757 ed.), 132, 172, 173, 253; Henry Beekman to Henry Livingston, Feb. 19, 1751, Beekman Papers; White, *Beekmans of New York*, 165–169, 204–205.

114. Carl Bridenbaugh, ed., *Gentleman's Progress: The Itinerarium of Dr. Alexander*

Another Cortlandt Manor proprietor, John Schuyler, Jr. (1697–1741), husband of Cornelia Van Cortlandt, is known mostly through the reputations of his son Philip, a Revolutionary general, and of his father John, Sr., who built the family plantation at Saratoga. For a while in the late 1720s and early 1730s John, Jr., tried his fortune as a merchant in New York City, but his business did not fare as well as he had hoped, and he was back in his native town by 1734. There he operated the family store, frequently served as an alderman and, in that capacity, as a commissioner of Indian affairs, and he occasionally engaged in victualing troops at forts. All these efforts, however, seemed so unproductive that one historian of the family has aptly commented: "Perhaps his most significant contribution to the family fortunes was his marriage to Cornelia."[115] Samuel Bayard (d. ca. 1750), the only son of Nicholas, who was the most hated enemy of the Leislerians, and husband of Margaret Van Cortlandt, was a trader in the metropolis specializing in European goods and an assemblyman from the city for two terms (1713–1715).[116] Beyond this, little is known about him. Equally obscure were the lives of William Skinner (1687–1758) and Andrew Johnston (1694–1762), both of Perth Amboy, New Jersey. Skinner, the husband of Elizabeth Van Cortlandt, was the first rector of St. Peter's Episcopal Church of that city. Johnston, married to Catherine, was a merchant by occupation and seems to have been politically active at one time or another as speaker of the New Jersey assembly and a member of the governor's council of that province.[117]

Both Jeremiah Van Rensselaer (1705–1745), the eldest son of Kiliaen of Rensselaerswyck proper, and John Van Rensselaer (1708–1782), the eldest son of Henry of Claverack, assumed economic roles similar to their fathers'. They were basically local squires with incomes mainly from their plantations. There is evidence that one Richard Miles of Ma-

---

*Hamilton* (Chapel Hill, N.C., 1948), 48–49, 53, 68, 221; "Release of the Parties to Stephen Van Cortlandt," Nov. 12, 1730, Case for Oversized MSS, Van Cortlandt Family Papers; N.Y. Council Minutes, XXI, 28. Maria Van Cortlandt's first husband was Kiliaen Van Rensselaer, the second lord of Rensselaerswyck.

115. A partition deed for John Schuyler, Jr., and his wife, Oct. 27, 1734, MS No. 12248, N.Y. State Lib.; *N.Y. Col. Laws*, II, 798, 908, III, 108, 804. The quotation comes from Gerlach, *Philip Schuyler*, 6. As for Schuyler's landholdings, see *ibid.*, 319–322.

116. Bayard's account with Robert Livingston, Aug. 26 and Oct. 1724, Livingston-Redmond MSS, Roll 4; Bayard to Kiliaen and Maria Van Rensselaer (in Dutch), Oct. 29, 1708, Letters, 1700–1749, Rensselaerswyck MSS.

117. Deed between Andrew Johnston and John Parker, Feb. 14, 1726, Parker Family Additional Papers, MG19 (add.), New Jersey Historical Society, Newark, N.J.; *The Journal of the Reverend Silas Constant, Pastor of the Presbyterian Church at Yorktown, New York* . . . (Philadelphia, 1903), 427–428.

deira Island tried to interest Jeremiah, who had just turned fifteen, in trading with the island, but nothing seems to have come of it.[118] John Van Rensselaer supplied firewood and candles for the military garrisons at Albany, Schenectady, and Fort William in the mid-1740s. But the commercial activity of these men was of a dabbling sort, hardly comparable in constancy and extent to their younger brothers, Stephen (1707–1747), who later became the patroon upon Jeremiah's premature death, and Henry, Jr. (1712–1793), who like Stephen was a prominent merchant in Albany County.[119] Each seems to have possessed neither the large personal estate nor the drive and capability for business that so distinguished the careers of Adolph Philipse and Philip Livingston. Only Jeremiah, because of his role as assemblyman from his manor from 1726 to 1743, had a reputation that transcended the local. Even here, his record was mediocre. William Livingston, a rare lawyer-intellectual of the province, wrote in 1755 about Jeremiah that the late patroon, though possessed of the great manor, was "scarce ever worth a groat in cash" and that "he murdered his days with gamesters and Debauchers, and as he lived without a Fame, died without a Memory, or what is worse with an indifferent one."[120] The same can be said of his cousin John.

For most of the manorial proprietors, the development of their lands with tenants offered important benefits and opportunities. Aside from boosting land values and bringing in the rental return, it generated a

118. Richard Miles to Jeremiah Van Rensselaer, Apr. 27, 1720, Letters, 1700–1749, Rensselaerswyck MSS. Like his father, Jeremiah operated the family mills at Watervliet and sold foodstuff and boards in the Albany and New York City markets. Henry Beekman to Jeremiah Van Rensselaer, Feb. 15, 1738, Van Rensselaer to Samuel Heath, Nov. 2, 1737, and Van Rensselaer to Enock Stevenson, Nov. 23, 1741, "Misc. Accts, 1700–1720 [misdated]," Rensselaerswyck MSS.

119. George Clinton to John Van Rensselaer, Aug. 27, 1745, Letters, 1700–1749, Rensselaerswyck MSS; *Journal of General Assembly*, II, 410, 432; N.Y. Col. MSS, LXXIX, 21. John Van Rensselaer's will, dated May 25, 1782, shows that he had a house and lot in Albany. Wills, XXXVI, 45–52, Queens College Lib. For information on the commercial career of Stephen Van Rensselaer and Henry Van Rensselaer, Jr., see *N.-Y. Gaz.*, Nov. 4, 1734; *Journal of General Assembly*, I, 784, II, 83; Philip Livingston to Henry Van Rensselaer, Jr., Nov. 14, 1730–July 27, 1737, Misc. MSS, Livingston, N-P; Van Rensselaer-Fort Papers, N.Y. Pub. Lib.; Account Book [of Henry Van Rensselaer, Jr.], Claverack Papers, N.-Y. Hist. Soc.; Philip Livingston to son Robert, Jr., Sept. 5, 1740, Livingston-Redmond MSS, Roll 7; Johannis Ten Broeck, Miscellaneous Manuscripts, N.-Y. Hist. Soc.

120. William Livingston to Peter R. Livingston, Nov. 10, 1755, William Livingston Papers, Letterbook, 1754–1770, on microfilm, Mass. Hist. Soc., which also owns the originals. Another observer stated in 1744, "The Patroon is a young man of good mein and presence. He is a batchllor, nor can his friends perswade him to marry. By paying too much hommage to Bacchus, he has acquired a hypochondriac habit." Bridenbaugh, ed., *Itinerarium of Dr. Alexander Hamilton*, 62. For further information on Van Rensselaer's life-style, see John Lindsay to Jeremiah Van Rensselaer, Mar. 19, 1737, and _____ to Jeremiah Van Rensselaer, Dec. 16, 1742, Letters, 1700–1749, Rensselaerswyck MSS.

supply of farm produce, particularly wheat. Wheat and foodstuffs were the major export items from eighteenth-century New York with which traders could earn coveted hard cash or bills of exchange for foreign goods. Mercantile success in no small degree depended on one's ability to command as large an amount of wheat as the market called for. In pursuit of the cash crop, bakers, bolters, merchants, brokers, and their agents from New York City and Albany crisscrossed the grain-producing countryside. So did some of the manor landlords. Most active in this scramble for wheat were the Livingstons, judging from the available documentary evidence. Both Robert Livingston and his son Philip had at least four or five wheat procurement agents; they served on their manor and at Schenectady, Albany, Kingston, Kinderhook, and Half-Moon.[121] The Philipses relied on the metropolitan grain market in addition to their plantations. The Van Cortlandt proprietors, if they were interested in the crop, procured it wherever and whenever it was available. Because of the delay in the manor partition, they were compelled to go beyond their own domain. Even after the partition, they continued the practice, since none of the proprietors had more than a relatively small share. Generally, the merchant-landlords cherished the land as a source of wheat more than as speculative property or even as rental property. It was partly because of this commercial orientation that certain manor proprietors required tenants to pay their yearly rents in "merchantable" winter wheat and also insisted on the right of first refusal on the purchase of grain beyond the tenants' domestic needs. Agrarian enterprise for these land-lords was definitely auxiliary to their commerce.

High on the list of benefits derived from a large tenant population was the profitable operation of gristmills and sawmills and other related economic endeavors. Though expensive to construct, the mills offered several long-term advantages, the obvious one being income from tolls for grinding and sawing. William Johnson, who was developing lands in the Mohawk valley in the 1730s, counted on an annual income of "at least" £30 from a sawmill he planned to build.[122] A mill owner also could employ his equipment to produce timber boards for market, as the Van Rensselaers did, and wood for flour barrels and casks. A gristmill could yield a "handsome profit" of £40 to £500 a year depending on its operating capacity, toll rates, and the number of customers it at-

121. Kim, "New Look at the Great Landlords," *WMQ*, 3d Ser., XXVII (1970), 598.
122. William Johnson to Goldsbrow Banyar, June 28, 1770, *William Johnson Papers*, XII, 829–830.

tracted.[123] More important, the facility was a magnet that drew grains to it, particularly if it was the only one available in the neighborhood and was conveniently situated. A mill's usefulness for grain procurement was understood by contemporaries. One owner graphically described this indirect benefit: "The Situation of this Mill is very convenient for purchasing of wheat, as large Quantities are brought down the Delaware from Minisink, and must pass by this Mill. There is also plenty of wheat to be bought in the Neighborhood, as it is a plentiful wheat Country." Petrus D'Witt, a clerk at Livingston Manor in the 1730s, in one of his reports to Philip Livingston illuminated another of the advantages of milling—as a leverage to obtain wheat: "I ask'd Mr. Dirk W. Ten Broeck for his wheat. He told me [he] intended to get some boulted at his uncle Renselaers Mill. I told him he could get that done here if we could have the rest of his wheat. He was glad of the opportunity, for being so much nigher; I think we may reather do it for him, than to let the wheat go."[124] With a view to the revenue from tolls and the excellent prospect of wheat purchase, most landlords operated gristmills and, as a precaution against possible competition, made the watercourse their exclusive jurisdiction. A typical example is Kiliaen Van Rensselaer, the second "lord" of Rensselaerswyck. Granting in 1704 to his brother Henry a lease for several hundred acres of land at Greenbush, he specifically prohibited the tenant from erecting a gristmill while allowing the "Liberty to Build a Saw Mill" thereon.[125]

Settling lands with tenants offered another business possibility to the commercially oriented landowner—it created an instant demand for daily necessities. Meeting this demand generally devolved upon the land-

123. The estimation of the yearly toll income is based on the following sources: William Johnson to Peter Warren, May 10, 1739, *ibid.*, I, 4–5; advertisement of a mill for sale, Zenger's *N.-Y. Wkly. Journal*, Jan. 3–June 24, 1743; Robert R. Livingston to father, Robert, Jr. (of Clermont), Mar. 17, 1762, Robert R. Livingston Coll., Box 1; Robert Livingston, Jr., to James Duane, Nov. 30, 1765, Duane Papers, Roll 1; Robert R. Livingston's gristmill account, Mar. 25, 1775, to Feb. 9, 1776, Livingston Account Book, Clermont, 1761–1781, N.-Y. Hist. Soc.; Beverly Robinson's memorial, Dec. 11, 1783, A.O. 12/21/161, P.R.O.; Abraham Ten Broeck to Philip Livingston, Oct. 26, 1775, Letterbook of Abraham Ten Broeck, 1753–1783, in Rensselaerswyck MSS. The last source reveals that the gristmill at Watervliet in Rensselaerswyck returned a net profit of £225 in 1771, £270 in 1772, £500 in 1773, £400 in 1774, and £290 in 1775.

124. Advertisement for the sale of gristmills and sawmills at Coryell's Ferry, *N.-Y. Mercury*, Aug. 13, 1764; D'Witt to Philip Livingston, Jan. 23, 1749, Livingston-Redmond MSS, Roll 6.

125. "A list of Indentures, 1696–1744," Rensselaerswyck MSS; Richard Van Rensselaer to Maria Van Rensselaer, May 11, 1684, *Maria Van Rensselaer Correspondence*, 149.

lord, who was delighted to set up general stores that gave him profit from the sale of merchandise to the farmers and also the opportunity to acquire farm produce in exchange for merchandise. At the same time, the store itself was an inducement for people to settle in the area.[126] It was this calculation that in 1710 prompted Robert Livingston to part with 6,000 acres of his manor for the Palatines whom Governor Robert Hunter had brought into the colony. Livingston's son-in-law, Samuel Vetch, informed of the transaction, remarked, "I am glad . . . you have gott so many Palatines settled upon your Mannor which must be a mighty advantage to you both with regard to your trade and making Land more valuable."[127] Cadwallader Colden, surveyor general of New York, was aware of the beneficial effect that a store had upon the land economy when he wrote his friend James Alexander in 1729: "I was in hopes you would have join'd with us in the store as well as in the land [near Newburgh] for unless a storehouse be built the land will neither grow in its value nor anyway answer the purpose for which it was purchased."[128]

It should be noted, however, that not every manor landlord was able to create on his plantation the linked activities of wheat growing, milling, commercial trading, and operating stores. Some combined two of these activities, some three, some all four, and others none at all, depending on the proprietor's circumstances, his economic orientation, his financial resources, and some other variables. The Van Rensselaers of Rensselaerswyck proper simply could not have established and run a store on their domain in competition with the Albany stores, which fully met the commercial needs of inhabitants in the surrounding areas. Nor did they have sufficient capital and ambition to branch out into overseas trade, although they owned the largest landed estate in the province. Compared to the Van Rensselaers, the first- and second-generation landlords of Livingston and Philipsburgh manors were far more versatile, engaging in every conceivable commercial and agricultural activity and organizing them in such a way that they augmented each other. The wheat brought by their farmers to their gristmills and stores was made

126. Armour, "Merchants of Albany," 189–190; Daniel Campbell's advertisement in *N.-Y. Gaz.; and Wkly. Mercury*, supplement, May 2, 1774.

127. Samuel Vetch to Robert Livingston, Jan. 25, 1714, Livingston-Redmond MSS, Roll 3; Leder, *Livingston*, 212–214, 246; *Doc. Hist. N.Y.*, III, 644–651, 656. Kiliaen Van Rensselaer and Peter Schuyler out of the same motive had offered their lands to Gov. Hunter for the Palatine settlement. *Ibid.*, 651–652.

128. Cadwallader Colden to James Alexander, Dec. 12, 21, 1729, Apr. 18, 1732, Alexander Papers, Box 2; Maj. Philip Skene to John Tabor Kempe, June 24, 1766, Letters, A–Z, Box 1, Kempe Papers.

into flour, bread, and biscuits, which were in turn packed in barrels made of their lumber and were shipped on their sloops for overseas market. They also saw in their tenants a captive market for imported goods.

The Cortlandt Manor proprietors, however, fell far below par in this regard. Until the early 1730s, they were all barred from effectively exploiting their property because of its common ownership. Even after the division of the manor, many of them were ill-prepared and not well situated to attempt large-scale land development. There were several reasons for their sluggishness. First, when the division came, the Van Cortlandt heirs were middle-aged and already firmly fixed in their respective occupations. Moreover, most of them lived far away from the manor. To move to the newly acquired wild land in order to overcome the drawbacks of absenteeism was an unsettling proposition for them. Coupled with these difficulties was the fact that the heirs, with the exception of De Lancey, Beekman, and Philip Van Cortlandt, were not well endowed financially. To most of the manor proprietors, the lands were objects either to be sold quickly or to be kept for their posterity rather than a means for diversifying their economic activity.

Thus, the manor proprietors differed considerably in their economic goals and activities. The first-generation landowners, except for the Van Rensselaers, were basically commercial in orientation, engaging in trading, military contracting, and, to a lesser extent, in moneylending. In the course of the eighteenth century, their sons, particularly the Livingstons and Philipses, became more interested in commercial agriculture and the advantages of grist- and sawmilling and acquiring wheat. In this respect, the land operation of the merchant-landowners was more or less subsidiary to their mercantile activities. But this pattern did not hold true for many of the Van Cortlandt heirs, or for the Van Rensselaer heirs, who were not merchants in the first place. Moreover, there was a trend in mid-century toward a reduction of the external commercial activities of the landowners, with more of them deciding to settle down as rentiers and sedentary country gentlemen. As shall be shown, this change took place only after the number of tenants on their land grew and rental income correspondingly increased enough to support a retired life-style.

# CHAPTER V

# Lease Structure and
# Leasing Practices

## Promotional Measures

Modern scholarship in dealing with the New York colonial land system has generally viewed leaseholding as a "feudal" or "quasi-feudal" institution, the implication being that it was onerous, degrading, oppressive, exploitive, and a blight on individual initiative and normal human aspirations. The New York land system has been portrayed as the nemesis of the Anglo-American dream of a free and virtuous yeomanry, obedient to the imperatives of economic growth and the stuff of a sturdy militia.[1] Thus, the populist historian Frederick Jackson Turner was outraged at what he called "feudal land tenure," "manorial practices," and "undemocratic restraint," which "exploited" settlers on these New York manors.[2] We can trace the ideological ancestry of this view to the works of Thomas Fuller, William Shakespeare, Francis Bacon, Sir Henry Spelman, James Harrington, David Hume, and Thomas Gray in England, and Thomas Jefferson and John Adams in America, some of whom apotheosized an Edenic Anglo-Saxon society of free and independent farmers that was supposed to have existed before the Norman Con-

---

1. Thomas Hutchinson, *The History of the Colony and Province of Massachusetts-Bay*, ed. Lawrence S. Mayo (Cambridge, Mass., 1936), II, 314; R. H. Gabriel, "Crevecoeur, An Orange County Paradox," *Quarterly Journal of the New York State Historical Association*, XII (1931), 45–55.
2. Turner, *Frontier in American History*, 80–83.

quest.[3] But Turner and some other, more recent historians, imprisoned by the historical yeoman frame of reference, have seen only what they expected to find rather than what really existed in the provincial lease system.[4] It was perhaps inevitable, given their prejudices, that any positive aspects of tenancy evolving in the colony would have eluded them. Before we can characterize the landlord-tenant relationship as feudal, exploitive, or undemocratic, we must find out both what it was in principle and how it worked. What was the lease structure? Did the leases accurately reflect the practices?

The various benefits that tenants could reap from the manorial economy all hinged on the proprietor's need for settlers. Developers could not offer onerous lease conditions, because none but the most desperate potential settlers would have accepted them. Both landowners and tenants understood this elementary logic. Prospective tenants were well aware of the economic opportunity in North America, the proprietors' need to improve the land, and the paucity of farmhands, and they made good use of the situation.

It was not uncommon for a potential tenant or buyer to dangle the bait of rapid settlement before a proprietor in order to obtain a favorable bargain.[5] John Watts, a loyalist, looking back to his experience as a land speculator, testified in 1784 that "almost all the lands in New York have been settled originally by Intruders." Landowners, Watts claimed, "were glad that others should set down on their lands." Although a landlord embroiled in a serious title dispute and nervous about possible encroach-

3. I owe my knowledge of the Anglo-American yeoman ideology to H. Trevor Colbourn, *The Lamp of Experience: Whig History and the Intellectual Origins of the American Revolution* (Chapel Hill, N.C., 1965), 31–32, 146–147, 162–163, 176–177; A. L. Rowse, *The England of Elizabeth: The Structure of Society* (New York, 1962), 230–231; and Henry Nash Smith, *Virgin Land: The American West as Symbol and Myth* (Cambridge, Mass., 1950), 140–146.

4. For the antitenancy bias in public policy, see, for example, A. Whitney Griswold, *Farming and Democracy* (New Haven, Conn., 1952 [orig. publ. New York, 1948]), introduction, 18–46, 47, 50, 142–144. The historical writings that found no merit in the New York leasehold system are: Mark, *Agrarian Conflicts*; Ellis, *Landlords and Farmers*; Higgins, *Expansion in New York*; George Dangerfield, *Chancellor Robert R. Livingston of New York, 1746–1813* (New York, 1960); Ray Allen Billington, *Westward Expansion: A History of the American Frontier* (New York, 1949); Lynd, *Anti-Federalism in Dutchess County, New York*.

5. George Coventry to John Van Rensselaer, May 27, 1761, Van Rensselaer-Fort Papers, 1729–1789, New York Public Library; John G. Leake to Robert W. Leake, Nov. 24, 1774, and William Wills to Mrs. Robert Leake, Aug. 19, 1775, Land Papers, Book VII, 127, 143, Bureau of Waterways, New York State Department of Transportation, Albany; Allan MacDonnell to William Johnson, Nov. 14, 1773, *William Johnson Papers*, XII, 1041–1042.

ment on his land might not have spoken so optimistically about the squatters, Watts's view was not wide of the mark.[6] No less revealing was the enthusiastic reception Philip Livingston accorded to seventeen Scottish families coming to his manor in 1741. The anticipated capital outlay was stupendous. In addition to their transportation cost, there was the further expense of feeding these Highlanders for some time and of providing a cow and a horse for each of the families. But Livingston declared to his manor clerk that he was "glad" to bear the burden, because "its no Easy matter to gett 17 families at once." Livingston's reaction was typical. Several years earlier he had ransomed two German indentured families for £42, given generous lease terms, and supplied each of them with provisions for a year and three horses and two cows.[7] Peter Warren, who was eager to develop his Mohawk valley land in the 1730s, wrote in 1738 to his nephew William Johnson, manager of his estates: "I wou'd have you by all means incourage setlers for that is all that's wanting. and Especialy those Germans that one of the Tenants are gone for. . . ." For a plan of settlement, Warren allocated £600 to be spent over a three-year period. Another landlord advised his agent in 1765: "I dare say you will take pains to please tenants, as the prosperity of my settlement will depend a good deal on their Being satisfied."[8] These few samples of the colonial land developers' frame of mind provide some clues as to what potential tenants could expect from their landlords.

The promotional schemes to attract settlers took many forms and varied from one landlord to another and from time to time. They generally were of two types: those offering material help and those offering good lease terms. Naturally, both types were dispensed most generously by manor proprietors who were equipped with abundant capital and were pressed for tenants. The less fortunate landlords counted on good lease terms, and others simply relied on the advantageous location of a tract. The greatest inducement, however, was material assistance, for

6. John Watts's testimony, 1784, American Loyalists, Examinations in London and New York, Audit Office Transcripts, XL, 596–600, N.Y. Pub. Lib., hereafter cited as Loyalist Transcripts.

7. Philip Livingston to Petrus D'Witt, Mar. 5, 11, 1741, Livingston-Redmond MSS, Roll 9; Livingston to Jacob Wendell, Oct. 17, 1737, Feb. 27 and May 10, 1739, Livingston Papers, Museum of the City of New York. The tenants were expected to pay back the landlord's advances "when they are able."

8. Peter Warren to William Johnson, Nov. 20, 1738, William Johnson Papers, XIII, 1–3 (2, quoted); William L. Stone, Life and Times of Sir William Johnson, Bart. (Albany, N.Y., 1865), I, 62–64; James Duane to Isaac Vrooman, Jan. 20, May 5, 1765, Duane Papers, Roll 1. A good discussion of Duane's promotional activities is Edward P. Alexander, A Revolutionary Conservative: James Duane of New York (New York, 1938), chap. 4.

freehold tenure necessarily lacked that provision. Some landlords figured that once a certain area was well settled with people, this settlement would itself become a magnet, luring others who were principally concerned with the conveniences of a developed community, such as good roads, security, and social amenities. Thus, landlords tended to give the first settlers better terms than those who followed.[9] For this reason and also because of the problems inherent in the pioneering tasks, the promotional burden fell more heavily on the first-generation proprietors and those initiating settlement than on the successive generations.

One advantage of owning gristmills and sawmills that has not yet been discussed was their importance as a promotional device. Landlords and settlers agreed that mills were one of the "Articles of the greatest Importance" to farming and therefore a "great inducement" to settling lands. Without a sawmill nearby, it was very difficult, if not impossible, to build a residential house, barn, and outhouses, and without a gristmill, both subsistence and commercial farming were easily liable to fail. One Martin Betting, who was negotiating for a lease in the Manor of Rensselaerswyck, wrote: "It is to[o] hard yet for us poor people to go on our places in Canajoherry, as there is no saw Mills to git boards build with."[10] The celebrated author Crèvecoeur observed that it was "often the want of mills" that prevented poor back settlers "from raising grain."[11] In the 1710s about fifty poor Palatine families in the Schoharie valley, after several years of hard struggle, had to abandon their primitive settlement because they could not sustain it without the aid of mills.[12] It was not uncommon for the value and attractiveness of a farm to be measured by its distance from grist- and sawmill sites. At the initial stage of settlement a new township composed of modest freeholders usually considered the establishment of mills as one of the most essential business items for the town meetings and took pains to search for someone with financial means

9. [An Albanian] to Mr. Fancounier, Apr. 4, 1714, Bleecker, Collins, and Abeel Papers, Box 2, N.Y. Pub. Lib.; Robert Livingston, Jr., to James Duane, Nov. 9, 1764, Duane Papers, Roll 1; Philip Livingston to Jacob Wendell, May 10, 1739, Feb. 27 and Mar. 4, 1740, Livingston Papers, Museum of City of N.Y.; Abraham Lott to John Wendell, Aug. 15, 1770 (photocopy), Wendell Family Papers, Box 1, N.Y. Pub. Lib.

10. William Johnson to Goldsbrow Banyar, June 28, 1770, Allan MacDonnell to Johnson, Nov. 14, 1773, *William Johnson Papers*, XII, 829–830, 1041–1042; Martin Betting to Abraham Ten Broeck, May 21, 1783, Letters, 1767–1794, Rensselaerswyck Manuscripts, New York State Library, Albany. In 1739 Philip Livingston stated that "a saw mill . . . ought to be the first thing without which we can't Pretend to setle." Livingston to Jacob Wendell, Oct. 19, 1739, Livingston Papers, Museum of City of N.Y.

11. J. Hector St. John [Michel Guillaume St. Jean de Crèvecoeur], *Letters from an American Farmer* . . . (London, 1782), 228.

12. Knittle, *Palatine Emigration*, 217–218, 221.

to undertake the task. To attract such a man, the community often offered many concessions and privileges.[13]

Farmers intending to lease land, however, did not have to worry about the problem that vexed the freeholders. Most New York landlords felt "obliged" to erect mills "for the use" of their tenants, and once established, they became the concern of everyone in the community.[14] Instead of being the instrument of a landlord's exploitive impulses, a mill was an institution upon which the common economic welfare and even the survival of the community rested. In April 1690 the Leislerian commissioners in charge of northern frontier defense during King William's War ordered the immediate fortification of the mill belonging to the anti-Leislerian patroon at Watervliet. The structure was to be protected "against any attack or invasion," and the commissioners "strictly required" all Albany County residents "to be aiding therein with their Persons . . . as they will answer the contrary at their utmost Perill."[15] This public mobilization could have been justified only in the name of communal interest, which the mill at that juncture represented. Philip Livingston entertained the same notion of his mills. Distressed about the suspension of gristmill operation in his manor in the early spring of 1741 due to ice around the dam, he urged his clerk to "gett all our neighbours [tenants] will be willing to assist in a thing which will be for their benefit and Ease as well as ours."[16]

At the beginning of its settlement, Philipsburgh had two gristmills, each with one pair of grindstones; by 1750, two more pairs of the stones had been added. The facilities were twelve miles from each other, one at Yonkers called "Lower Mills" and the other at the Pocantico. Each was equipped to handle grinding, bolting, and packing flour. One of the mills also had an attached sawmill, which was consumed by fire in 1759 but was soon rebuilt.[17]

13. For the proceedings of various towns in Westchester County with respect to mills, see Deed Book E, 244, and Deed Book F, 150–155, Westchester County Clerk's Office, White Plains, N.Y.; Amos Canfield, comp., "Westchester County, N.Y., Miscellanea . . . ," N.Y. Gen. and Biog. Rec., LX (1929), 259; Fox, Caleb Heathcote, 56.
14. James Duane to Isaac Vrooman, Mar. 4, 1765, Duane Papers, Roll 1; Duane to Robert Livingston, Jr., Jan. 5, 1767, Livingston-Redmond MSS, Roll 8.
15. Doc. Hist. N.Y., II, 218–219; N.Y. Col. MSS, XXXVI, 56; Joseph Pixley's deposition, May 30, 1755, ibid., LXXX, 168.
16. The community concept of mills was exemplified in the procedure by which they were licensed by the provincial government. Gov. Robert Hunter gave his permission for building the facilities in a community only after he consulted its inhabitants. William Britton of Richmond County to Hunter, Jan. 29, 1713, and Nathaniel Britton to Hunter, Feb. 23, 1713, N.Y. Col. MSS, LVIII, 88, 94, 114.
17. N.Y. Col. Docs., XIII, 546; Deed Book A, 150–151, Westchester Co. Clerk's

There is no indication that the Manor of Livingston had been furnished with mills before 1699, when Robert Livingston built along with his manor mansion a sawmill with twelve saws and possibly a gristmill. His long delay in establishing these industries was perhaps due to a lack of working capital, much of which he had tied up in victualing troops and other trade ventures, for the cost of setting up two mills of moderate size would have been at least £700 or £800.[18] In the 1710s, in response to the increasing influx of farmers, he built another gristmill at the southeastern corner of the manor near the Palatine settlements. Since until 1719 no other mills existed within a twenty-mile radius of the manor seat on the Hudson, the operation of his mills was not only monopolistic but also a great boon to his tenants and the people in adjacent areas.[19] In that year Claverack acquired both a sawmill and a gristmill, and another gristmill went up to the south of the manor, but they do not seem to have affected Livingston's interest.[20] His son Philip, the most aggressive of all the Livingstons and probably of all the manorial proprietors in promotional activity, erected both kinds of mills at Ancram, since there was evident need for them in the area due to the establishment of iron manufacturing there in the late 1730s and early 1740s. Robert Livingston, Jr., of Clermont ran two gristmills in the 1750s, one at his seat and the other in the "Camp" (the Palatine towns), but he sold the latter to one Jonas Tomes, probably in 1760.[21]

Kiliaen Van Rensselaer, son of Maria, enjoyed one unique advantage over the other manorial proprietors. When he became the sole patroon of

---

Office; Fernow, ed., *Records of New Amsterdam*, VII, 115, 124–125; *New-York Gazette: or, the Weekly Post-Boy*, Jan. 6, 1752, Sept. 24, 1753, Oct. 15, 1759; *N.-Y. Mercury*, May 28 and Oct. 22, 1759; "An Estimate of the Losses of Frederick Philipse," Philipse Papers, PA808, and lease deed to William Pugsley, June 2, 1761, *ibid.*, PA249, both in Sleepy Hollow Restorations Library, Tarrytown, N.Y.

18. "Duncan Campbell's account of the Iron work for the Mills," Mar. 15, 1699, Livingston-Redmond MSS, Roll 2; James Duane to Robert Livingston, Jr., Jan. 5, 1767, *ibid.*, Roll 8; earl of Bellomont to Lords of Trade, Jan. 2, 1701, *N.Y. Col. Docs.*, IV, 825; Alexander, *Revolutionary Conservative: James Duane*, 65; Beverly Robinson's expenses in building mills, A.O. 12/21, 161, Public Record Office.

19. Deed of lease, Henry Van Rensselaer to Robert Van Deusen, Sept. 10, 1718, Deed Book 5: 422–423, Albany County Clerk's Office, Albany, N.Y.; Hendrick Harmans's advertisement in *N.-Y. Gaz.; and Wkly. Mercury*, Sept. 10, 1770.

20. Garret Van Deusen's deposition, Oct. 19, 1744, on his father Abraham's gristmill, "Uncatalogued Livingston Manuscripts," New-York Historical Society, New York; Deed Book 5: 422–423, Albany Co. Clerk's Office.

21. "Suggestions Relating to my couzn: Building a Griss Mill on Roelif Jansens Kill in the Manor," n.d., Livingston-Redmond MSS, Roll 7; Robert R. Livingston to father, Robert, Jr., Mar. 17, 1762, Robert R. Livingston Collection, Box 1, N.-Y. Hist. Soc.; Livingston Account Book, Clermont, 1761–1781, *ibid.*; Robert Livingston, Jr.'s, payment of tax for the mill in the Camp, Aug. 1759, "Uncatalogued Livingston MSS."

Rensselaerswyck in 1687, the domain was a little over a half-century old and had all the necessary agricultural-processing industries. He was spared having to start from scratch; he had inherited the main mills at Watervliet and several sawmills at scattered places. The only gristmills and sawmills that he constructed were those at Schodack, about eight miles south of Albany, which he probably expected to service his tenants and possibly even the inhabitants of Kinderhook to the south. Van Rensselaer managed the Watervliet and Schodack establishment directly but rented out at least three sawmills that were operated with the assistance of his black slaves. As of 1764 Rensselaerswyck proper had seven sawmills and three gristmills. Of these, six sawmills and two gristmills were on lease.[22] Judging from the bitter protest registered by a gristmill leaseholder against the erection of another mill within eight miles, the patroon seems to have followed a policy of promising mill lessees that none would be built closer than eight miles apart.[23]

When Henry Van Rensselaer of Claverack obtained his estate he had neither his brother Kiliaen's good fortune nor the capital to build mills by himself. Consequently, pressed to develop his lands, he took the extraordinary step of letting out to one Robert Van Deusen a watercourse at Claverack and had the tenant erect sawmills and gristmills on it. The contract provided that Van Deusen operate them for a term of twenty-five years for the small rent of £3 10s. 6d. and for grinding a hundred schepels of wheat a year for the landlord. At the expiration of the lease, the buildings and utensils were to be appraised by two "indifferent persons," and Van Deusen would "have the Refusal if the same is to be let again to a stranger." This bargain was quite favorable to the tenant, because the lease term was exceptionally long for such a profitable enterprise and because the landlord was explicitly restricted on the vital matter of the disposition of the mills at the expiration of the lease. The episode clearly shows the dear price a landlord of lesser means might have had to pay in order to make his lands attractive for settlement.[24]

22. Kiliaen Van Rensselaer's will, June 18, 1718, Townsend Collection, Box 1, Albany Institute of History and Art, Albany, N.Y.; Stephen Van Rensselaer's will, June 24, 1747, Wills, XVI, 190, Queens College Library, New York; Abraham Ten Broeck to "Sir _____," Feb. 16, 1764, Letters of Abraham Ten Broeck, 1753–1783, in Rensselaerswyck MSS. At least half of the expenses for building gristmills and sawmills on the "Fifth Kill" had been borne by a tenant named Van Vechten. Abraham Ten Broeck to Philip Livingston in Philadelphia, Sept. 22, 1775, *ibid.*

23. Robert Woodworth to [the patroon], n.d., No. 987, Letters, 1674–1700, Rensselaerswyck MSS. This letter was apparently misfiled, since Woodworth was first mentioned as a tenant in 1768. Rensselaerswyck Rent Ledger, 1768–1789, 118, *ibid.*

24. Lease to Van Deusen, Sept. 10, 1718, Deed Book 5: 422–423, Albany Co. Clerk's

A 1732 survey map of the Manor of Cortlandt drawn by Philip
Verplanck shows a mill at what is presently known as Furnace Brook,
near Verplanck's Point. Whether this was a sawmill or a gristmill and
whether it was built by Stephanus Van Cortlandt or his widow, Gertrude,
is unknown. Whatever the case, as far as mill construction was concerned, the performance of the second- and third-generation Van Cortlandts was poor. Verplanck and Pierre Van Cortlandt (son of Philip) were
the only landlords who built and ran mills, while the Beekmans, like
Henry Van Rensselaer, had them constructed through the means of leasing mill sites.[25] Several reasons for this state of affairs come to mind. We
have already noted the proprietors' weak financial position, their absenteeism, and the lateness of the first partition of the manor. By 1734, when
the first partition took place, a number of mills already existed in surrounding townships and patents, and these welcomed customers from the
manor. Equally important, the original division of the lands, which allocated each heir four lots many miles apart from one another instead of
being contiguous, impeded the development of an integral plantation
system with mills and other facilities.[26]

Some landlords went far beyond the establishment of mills in their
efforts to attract settlers. Direct material and financial help was given to
tenants who were destitute, which they mostly were in the early stages of
manorial settlement.[27] The nature and volume of the first aid varied in
relation to a number of obvious factors—developers' needs, generosity,
and financial ability, and tenants' circumstances.[28] The Livingstons and

---

Office. John Van Rensselaer, who inherited the Claverack estate in 1740, adopted a similar
policy of leasing mill sites. See deposition of Joseph Pixley, a tenant of Van Rensselaer,
May 30, 1755, N.Y. Col. MSS, LXXX, 168. It appears that Henry Van Rensselaer, Jr.
(second son of Henry), who settled in Claverack in 1741, operated Van Deusen's mills
himself, probably after the termination of the lease. He opened a general store and operated
the gristmills and sawmills there, while his brother John was loafing at Greenbush. "Abraham Fonda's Estate account with Henry Van Rensselaer, 1749–1762," and John H. Wendell to Henry Van Rensselaer, Jr., Feb. 20, 1741, Van Rensselaer-Fort Papers, 1729–1789;
Account Book of [Henry Van Rensselaer, Jr.], Claverack Papers, N.-Y. Hist. Soc.

25. The map of Cortlandt Manor in 1732, Sleepy Hollow Restorations Lib.; Antoinette
F. Downing, *Interpretive Paper of the Restoration of Van Cortlandt Manor at Croton-on-
Hudson, New York* (Williamsburg, Va., 1959), 401; Philip Verplanck's will, Oct. 23, 1767,
Wills, XXVIII, 128, Queens College Lib.; Pierre Van Cortlandt's account, 1752–1753,
V1689, Sleepy Hollow Restorations Lib. The Beekmans gave 15-year leases to Peter Calvill
in the 1740s, Jury Brewer in 1746, and Caleb Barton in 1757, all of whom agreed to build
and operate sawmills and gristmills. Van Cortlandt Papers, V1960, *ibid.*; lease to Barton,
Van Cortlandt-Van Wyck Papers, Box 1, N.Y. Pub. Lib.

26. See the sketch on p. 183.

27. This point will be elaborated in chap. 6.

28. William Smith, Jr., to Mr. Thom, Nov. 14, 1774, William Smith Papers, Box 4,
N.Y. Pub. Lib.

probably the Philipses were most forward and generous in dispensing such aid, while the other proprietors were less so. The amount of material help seems to have been in proportion to the poverty level of the recipient: the poorer he was, the more he received. As the wilderness receded under the thrusting hands of labor, and the soil afforded an improved sustenance to the cultivator, the occasions for such benefactions correspondingly decreased. For example, such help was seldom offered to a tenant who bought another tenant's lease and improvements.[29]

The most common assistance consisted of provisions for tenant families for the first year, farming equipment, and livestock (cows, sheep, hogs, and horses). There were two arrangements under which the landlord supplied these animals. One was the so-called half-increase, whereby he and his tenant would equally share the increase of the stock; the other required the tenant to compensate for the animals when he could afford to do so.[30] The half-increase, first used in New York perhaps by Kiliaen Van Rensselaer, the Dutch founder of Rensselaerswyck, became quite popular with colonial landlords and tenants alike. A farmer named Willem Teller called it in 1679 "the praiseworthy custom" of patroonship.[31] However, it was discontinued in the domain in the late 1680s, a change that coincided with the introduction of a perpetual lease (in fee) replacing traditional tenure of years. The Van Rensselaers at the time probably felt that no further assistance for tenants was needed beyond offering the best available lease terms. Robert Livingston, who, as the secretary of Rensselaerswyck, had experience in administering the half-increase, also applied it to his own manor, which suggests that he was persuaded of its merit as a promotional device. In the fall of 1714 he wrote to his son Philip in Albany asking him to purchase twenty cows the next spring "for the people" he was planning to settle on the manor. His

---

29. For the incidents of material assistance by colonial landlords, see William Corry to George Clarke, Dec. 5, 1740, June 12 and Oct. 8, 1756, N.Y. Col. MSS, LXXIII, 28, LXXXII, 160, LXXXIII, 133; Philip Skene to John Tabor Kempe, June 24, 1766, Letters, A–Z, Box 1, John Tabor Kempe Papers, N.-Y. Hist. Soc.; William Edmeston to Passafor Carr, Aug. 31, 1771, and Apr. 9, 1772, Passafor Carr Papers, New York State Historical Association, Cooperstown, N.Y.; Gerlach, *Philip Schuyler*, 46–60; N.Y. Land Papers, XI, 134, 188, XII, 8, 43, 93, 100, 145, 155–156, 164, XIII, 26, 39.

30. "Novum Belgium by Father Isaac Jogues, 1646," in Jameson, ed., *Narratives of New Netherland*, 260.

31. Lease, William Teller to Claes Willemsen Coppernol, Apr. 12, 1679, Pearson, trans., and Van Laer, ed., *Early Records of Albany and Rensselaerswyck*, III, 472–473, 488–490, 507–508, 508–510, 558–559, 581–582; a landlord's advertisement for Palatine or Welsh settlers in *N.-Y. Wkly. Journal*, July 15, 1734; N.Y. Col. Laws, II, 206; Nissenson, *Patroon's Domain*, 70–71.

accounts show that, in addition to cows, he provided horses and hogs.[32] Philip Livingston, however, broke with his father's policy and, rather than using the half-increase, simply credited against his tenants what he gave them, which sometimes included one cow and horse and several months' provisions to each tenant family, plus feed for their livestock.[33] Records for the Philipses and the Van Cortlandts are not available, but there is no reason to suppose that practices on their manors differed significantly from what was common at the others.[34]

To these aids, some manorial proprietors hitched a variety of other encouragements as well. Robert Livingston and Stephen Van Cortlandt of New Jersey built houses for their tenants, generally with a short-term lease.[35] Philip Livingston obliged many tenants when he gave them "apple trees for the first planting" for their orchard. Most manor landlords initially bore the expenses of opening back roads that linked with the main highways and various sections of the plantation.[36] In 1718 Kiliaen Van Rensselaer willed his heir not to lease any of his lands "fit to make hay" lying within two miles of the Hudson River on the north side of the Fifth Kill; he intended that "they should remain for a common encouragement of new settlers."[37] Minor though it seems, this instruction underscored his concern for the development of his estate and, what was inseparably related to it, the welfare of his tenants.

No less important was the initial rent-free period for tenants. Defer-

32. Robert Livingston to son Philip, Oct. 29, 1714, Livingston-Redmond MSS, Roll 6; Robert Livingston's instruction to Joseph Aplin, Mar. 18, 1719, and Mar. 15, 1721, Aplin to Robert Livingston, Mar. 18, 1720, *ibid.*, Roll 4.

33. That Philip Livingston became a procurement agent for his manor tenants was evidenced in one of his letters to Henry Van Rensselaer, Jr., of Schenectady. He wrote, "I wish you could get 100 [schepels] small pease for the use of our farmers who must feed wheat to their hogs." Livingston to Van Rensselaer, Feb. 23, 1737, Miscellaneous Manuscripts, Livingston, N-P, N.-Y. Hist. Soc. It is also worth noting that he advanced transportation expenses for the Scottish Highlanders coming to his manor and ransom money for two German families who had agreed to become his tenants. Philip Livingston to Jacob Wendell, Oct. 17, 1737, May 10 and Feb. 27, 1739, Livingston Papers, Museum of City of N.Y.

34. Bellomont observed in 1701 that Philipsburgh Manor had "about 20 families of those poor people," Bellomont to the Lords of Trade, Jan. 2, 1701, *N.Y. Col. Docs.*, IV, 823.

35. George White's receipt, July 17, 1719, Livingston-Redmond MSS, Roll 4; Oliver De Lancey and John Van Cortlandt to Tobias Lent, Sept. 11, 1762, Letterbook of John Van Cortlandt, N.Y. Pub. Lib.

36. Philip G. Livingston to Philip Livingston, May 9, 1748, Livingston-Redmond MSS, Roll 10; Abraham Ten Broeck's payment of £20 to Levi Peas, Nov. 12, 1770, Abraham Ten Broeck's Accounts of the Manor, 1763–1787, Rensselaerswyck MSS.

37. Kiliaen Van Rensselaer's will, June 18, 1718, Townsend Coll., Box 1.

ral of rent, a necessity of frontier farming as well as a lure for settlers, helped cushion the financial burden of the tenant in the pioneering stage. William Smith, Jr., a noted jurist, commented that the length of the rent-free period was determined by the "situation and quality of the land, and the generosity, ability or views of the landlord."[38] In these manors, it ranged from a minimum of nine months to a maximum of twelve years, which was also the range of rent deferrals found among common, that is, nonmanorial, landlords in New York.[39] The grace period generally corresponded to the time a tenant needed to develop the virgin soil and thus to be in a position to support his family and also pay regular rent. From the late 1690s to 1768, Rensselaerswyck tenants with perpetual leases were free of rent payment for the first ten years, provided that they settled on rough and wild land.[40] From 1768 to 1783, when perpetual leases were no longer given, deferral periods were very unpredictable, one tenant receiving a one-year exemption for a fourteen-year lease, another nine years for the same, and still a third, eleven years for a twelve-year lease.[41] In the years 1737 through 1739 Philip Livingston offered a free-rent period of nine years and afterwards three to six years, while his son Robert, Jr., demanded only the payment of two fowls and two days' work from his tenants during the first nine months to five years.[42] Similarly, the Beekmans of Cortlandt Manor usually asked only two fowls a year during the first two to four years, but the Bayards collected no rent of any kind during the first seven years. The others, like Stephen and John Van Cortlandt, allowed some tenants to pay "nothing but improvements in lieu of the rent" for the first half of the lease period.[43]

38. William Smith, Jr., to Mr. Thom, Nov. 14, 1774, William Smith Papers, Box 4.

39. Goldsbrow Banyar to Samuel Dunlop, Oct. 18, 1762, Mar. 17, 1773, Goldsbrow Banyar Papers, Box 6, N.-Y. Hist. Soc.

40. Lease, Robert Livingston, Jr., to Philip Couchman, Mar. 26, 1771, Livingston-Redmond MSS, Roll 8; Livingston Manor Rent Ledger, 1767–1784, 60, N.-Y. Hist. Soc.; Rensselaerswyck Rent Ledger, 1768–1789, 81, Rensselaerswyck MSS. One exceptional case was the free-rent period of 40 years given to William Rogers of Rensselaerswyck. See "Agreement, Sept. 3, 1767," Ten Broeck Family Papers, Box 3, Albany Inst. of Hist. and Art.

41. Rensselaerswyck Rent Ledger, 1768–1789, 69 on John Sullivan, 98 on Edmund Tift, 160 on Othneal Gardner, Rensselaerswyck MSS.

42. Philip Livingston to Jacob Wendell, Oct. 17, 1737, Feb. 27 and May 10, 1739, Livingston Papers, Museum of City of N.Y.; lease to Michael Stoppelbeen, June 15, 1745, Livingston-Redmond MSS, Roll 9; lease to Francis Sale, ·Apr. 23, 1748, and lease to Hendrick Stiver, Apr. 19, 1748, ibid., Roll 6. For Robert Livingston, Jr.'s, policy, see lease to John P. Lawrey, Mar. 1760, ibid., Roll 7; lease to Hendrick Tiel, Mar. 25, 1771, ibid., Roll 8.

43. Leases, Samuel Bayard to Philip Linnebecker and Peter Win, 1732, Bayard-Campbell-Pearsall Collections, 1732–1827, N.Y. Pub. Lib.; lease to Joseph Purdy, Dec. 30, 1737, Van Cortlandt Papers, V2194, Sleepy Hollow Restorations Lib.; lease to Gabriel Carman,

Leaseholding had some unpalatable features, however, particularly if the lease was for a term of years or at the will or sufferance of the landlord, both of which undoubtedly inhibited settlement. Suppose a man of twenty-one years of age held a lease for a twenty-year term—he would, by the time of its expiration, be "old and spent" and yet face the possibility of eviction. Moreover, he could take none of his improvements with him if he wanted to start over somewhere else.[44] One observer familiar with the disposition of the people in the Albany area stated in 1727 that the hiring of land under this condition is "what the people hereabouts do not care to do."[45] In theory, a lease at the will or sufferance of the landlord was likely to subject a lessee to the whims of the lessor and tended to breed a sense of insecurity in the former. The desire on the part of potential tenants for more durable and secure tenure was publicly known.[46] Some landlords believed that meeting this wish was the best possible promotional scheme. Others felt differently and relied exclusively on material encouragements without the accompaniment of a tenurial modification. In the course of the first half of the eighteenth century, however, most tenants on these four manors, including even the "at-will" tenants, enjoyed a secure tenure. Obviously, lease terms were not entirely of a promotional nature. They contained provisions defining the obligations as well as the privileges of tenants in relation to their landlord. The rest of this chapter will explore the evolution and character of the lease terms upon which tenant-landlord relationships were founded.

## Lease Tenure

Among the four manors under study, Rensselaerswyck offered, from the late 1680s on, the most secure tenure, variously called a "durable lease," "perpetual or forever lease," or "lease in fee." It was a conveyance

Nov. 2, 1767, and Receipt Book of John Van Cortlandt, 1766–1771, *passim*, Van Cortlandt Family Papers, N.-Y. Hist. Soc.

44. John Sanders to Henry Jordice in London, Nov. 26, 1768, Letterbook of John Sanders, 1749–1779, N.-Y. Hist. Soc.

45. Edward Collins to Cadwallader Colden, July 7, 1727, *Colden Papers*, I, 197; Isaiah Ross to James Alexander, Mar. 26 and June 14, 1746, James Alexander Papers, Box 62, N.-Y. Hist. Soc.; Philip Harmanse to Henry Beekman, Feb. 25, 1774, "Uncatalogued Livingston MSS"; Oliver De Lancey to William Skinner, Jan. 7, 1775, Warren Papers, G/Am, Sleepy Hollow Restorations Lib.; Thomas Tillotson to Robert R. Livingston, Dec. 12, 1781, Robert R. Livingston Coll., Box 6.

46. A fine discussion of the disadvantages of a short-term lease as compared with a life or perpetual lease is in "A Memorandum Book of Business . . . [by] John G. Van Schaick, Albany March 29th 1782," Van Schaick Family Papers, 1715–1831, N.Y. State Lib.

of title to the land "in full ownership" to a lessee and his heirs forever with the reservation of a perpetual rent.[47] Sometimes, but not always, "consideration" money was demanded of a lessee when the transaction took place. In 1689 Margaret Schuyler, widow of Philip, obtained Schuyler Flats for 5,000 guilders and an annual rent of twenty bushels of wheat or corn and four hens.[48] In 1705 Volkert and Gerrit Teunissen Van Vechten paid to the patroon "some English money" for their lease with a yearly rent.[49] But Andries and Albert Andries Bratt in 1707 paid no consideration money for their 120-acre perpetual lease, nor did Jacobus D'Lametre for his lease of 128 acres in 1709.[50] As far as the form was concerned, these tenure arrangements with the Van Rensselaers were virtually the same as those in an ordinary freehold patent with a quitrent, the only difference being that in the former case the land was granted by a private person and in the latter by the government. We have already seen Jeremiah Van Rensselaer's difficulties in recruiting and keeping tenants in the 1670s partly because of a short lease term, generally six years. As early as 1660, Jeremiah had proposed to the coproprietors in Holland that the lease policy be changed and some lands let out in fee.[51] We might also recall that Kiliaen Van Rensselaer, after the issuance of the English patent, needed to create freehold voters in his manor so that the election of a manor representative to the General Assembly could be held. For this particular purpose, the offer of a life term to the settlers would have been sufficient, according to the provincial franchise laws. But the proprietor in fact gave a much better tenure, which suggests that his new lease had promotional as well as political motives.

When Kiliaen Van Rensselaer died, it looked as though perpetual lease tenure would not survive him. In his will of June 18, 1718, he stipulated that his heirs should not lease to "any person" and that "such leases so to be made in writing" should terminate "upon the death of the

47. Robert Ludlow Fowler, *History of the Law of Real Property in New York: An Essay Introductory to the Study of the N.Y. Revised Statutes* ... (New York, 1895), 118; Mark, *Agrarian Conflicts*, 63–64.

48. Lease, Kiliaen Van Rensselaer to Margaret Schuyler, Sept. 1689, and lease to Gerrit Teunissen Van Vechten, Oct. 15, 1694, Deed Book 5: 51–54, and Deed Book 4: 69–70, Albany Co. Clerk's Office; Kiliaen Van Rensselaer to Richard Van Rensselaer, [May 1687], *Maria Van Rensselaer Correspondence*, 180–181.

49. Deed Book 5: 146, Albany Co. Clerk's Office.

50. Lease to the Bratts, 1707 (half-scorched), Miscellaneous Manuscripts, I, No. 11, N.Y. State Lib.; Deed Book 5: 104, 424, and Deed Book 6: 104–106, 225–227, Albany Co. Clerk's Office.

51. Nissenson, *Patroon's Domain*, 61; *Jeremias Van Rensselaer Correspondence*, 226.

grantor upon forfeiture of [his] manor . . . to the next heir in taile."[52] But despite this testament, his heirs continued to grant perpetual leases, as did his brother Henry of Claverack.[53]

Without doubt, tenants liked this sort of agreement, and they vigorously objected to any proposals to alter it. Their attitude was dramatically revealed in an incident involving John Van Rensselaer, the eldest son of Henry, and his tenants. John, who was holding the Claverack estate in fee tail, was told by his lawyers in 1762 that the perpetual leases the tenants "had from his father, where [were] at present, of no force, nor that those he [himself] had given would be of any consiquence to the people after his decease," because such a lease was in violation of the entailed status of the estate. On the last day of November that year, he communicated the lawyers' opinion to his assembled tenants and announced his position in the matter. "He was Sorry," he said, that "he had not known it before for if he had he would never have done it and he would then go break the Intale and give them new Deed for all they now have agreable to their present Leases." These were indeed reassuring words, but his remarks, according to one attending the gathering, put the tenants "in a great flustration," and they were reported to have decided to "send some persons to New York" to consult lawyers about it.[54] A year later, the landlord successfully docked the entail and gave them perpetual leases with a minor modification, although he was at the time advised by his son-in-law Philip Schuyler and many other friends "not to continue [the lease] practice so injurious to the Interest of his Family."[55]

52. Kiliaen Van Rensselaer's will, June 18, 1718, Townsend Coll., Box 1.

53. "A list of Indentures, 1696–1744," and "Leases granted by Stephen Van Rensselaer Esquire and his ancesters for lands," Sept. 1, 1790, both in Rensselaerswyck MSS; lease papers, Van Rensselaer-Fort Papers, 1729–1789; Claverack Papers, fol. 1; "Lease," Bethlehen, Albany Inst. of Hist. and Art. Occasionally, the Van Rensselaers departed from this ancient practice: in the 1760s, two leases were for three lives and one for 100 years. Jacob W. Vrooman's lease of 121 acres, Aug. 21, 1769, Rensselaerswyck Rent Ledger, 1768–1789, 187, Rensselaerswyck MSS; lease, John Van Rensselaer to Henry Cuyler, Apr. 26, 1766, Harmanus Bleecker Papers, Box 2, 1752–1805, N.Y. State Lib.; lease to Bastian H. Visscher, Deed Book 11: 217, Albany Co. Clerk's Office.

54. Robert Livingston, Jr., to Abraham Yates, Jr., Dec. 2, 1762, Abraham Yates, Jr., Papers, 1607–1827, Box 1, N.Y. Pub. Lib. The opinion of Van Rensselaer's lawyers was probably correct. A holder of an estate in fee tail may not convey it to another, for the grantee would take a life estate, measured by the life of the grantor—in law known as an estate *per autre vie*. Similarly, a lease in perpetuity, extending beyond the life of the lessor, would necessarily terminate with his death. Hence, the need to dock the entail and then execute new perpetual leases.

55. Docking the entail took the form of "a common recovery" of the estate from a fictitious trespasser in the suit of ejectment in the supreme court of New York. Deed, Jan.

A few months later, Stephen Van Rensselaer, the proprietor of Rensse-laerswyck proper, finding himself in the same dilemma, also docked the entail in order to legalize the durable lease.[56]

Yet some of the Van Rensselaer heirs in mid-century were not entirely happy with the perpetual lease. One Albanian knowledgeable in domain affairs noted that they "much repented" the tenurial concessions their ancestors had made, although they fully understood the motive behind them, that is, the recruitment of settlers. They were dissatisfied because perpetual tenure deprived the landlord of "any advantages" from the land except a fixed "trifle" rent while it imposed an obligation upon him to protect the leased land for the tenants.[57] Moreover, the landlords probably suspected that the arrangement fostered a spirit of indepen-dence in the tenantry. Anne Grant, a longtime resident of Albany County before the American Revolution, observed the temper of the manor ten-ants: "You may suppose the tenants did not greatly fear a landlord, who could neither remove them, nor heighten their rents. Thus, without the pride of property, they had all the independence of proprietors. They were like German Princes, who, after furnishing their contingent to the Emperor, might make war on him when they chose."[58] What to the early patroons seemed a golden opportunity to promote settlement had be-come a liability and unpleasant burden for their descendants.[59] Follow-ing the death of Stephen Van Rensselaer II (1742–1769), the trustees of the manor—Philip Livingston, Stephen's father-in-law, and Abraham Ten Broeck, Stephen's brother-in-law—granted many short-term leases ranging from one to fifteen years. But these were merely an interim arrangement during the adolescent period of his eldest son, Stephen III (1764–1839). Arriving at his majority in 1785, Stephen III resumed the traditional policy.[60]

---

15, 1763, Deed Book 7: 155, Albany Co. Clerk's Office. For new leases given by John Van Rensselaer after the docking, see Deed Books 8: 386, 9: 66–68, and 10: 259; Philip Schuyler's testimony on the Claverack lease practice, Mar. 8, 1787, A.O. 12/30, 125–126.

56. Entry on Sept. 13, 1763, Abraham Ten Broeck's Accounts of the Manor, 1763–1787, Rensselaerswyck MSS.

57. "A Memorandum Book of Business," by John G. Van Schaick, Mar. 29, 1782, Van Schaick Family Papers; Schuyler's testimony on Claverack lease, Mar. 8, 1787, A.O. 12/30, 125.

58. [Anne] Grant, Memoirs of an American Lady: With Sketches of Manners and Scenery in America, As They Existed Previous to the Revolution (New York, 1809), 7, 264.

59. The Van Rensselaer heirs did not take corrective steps because of their regard for precedents. "Leases granted Stephen Van Rensselaer Esquire and his ancesters for Lands," Sept. 1, 1790, Rensselaerswyck MSS.

60. From 1769 to 1783, the trustees granted altogether 95 leases, of which one was for three lives and the rest for years. Abraham Ten Broeck to Philip Livingston, Oct. 26, 1775,

Tenure practices at Livingston Manor were radically different from those at its northern neighbor. Well acquainted with the settlement problems of a frontier society, Robert Livingston must have weighed the advantages and disadvantages of Kiliaen Van Rensselaer's recourse to perpetual tenure and its applicability to his estate. Instead of rushing into one set of practices at the outset, he decided to experiment with different tenurial terms. Fortunately, until the new confirmatory patent was issued in 1715, he was spared the political necessity of turning his tenants into voters, a problem that the Van Rensselaers had encountered earlier and that would have forced him to grant at least a life-term lease. The records, though not complete, indicate that initially some of his tenants held a perpetual lease and some, more commonly, were under an "at-will" lease with livestock on the half-increase basis.[61] Livingston soon found perpetual leases disagreeable. For example, in 1718 he compelled Andrew Gardner, his sloop master and holder of a fee (perpetual lease) farm of 122 acres, to surrender the original deed for a certain compensation and to accept a concurrent, two lives (husband and wife) term instead.[62] Significantly, this event occurred in the same year that Kiliaen Van Rensselaer by his will enjoined his heirs not to offer perpetual leases. This important change in lease policy seems to have been prompted by several considerations. In the first place, fee tenure ran counter to the landlord's desire to entail his lands as he saw fit. With a concurrent life lease, the landlords could count on a modest profit from what was called an "alienation fee"—commonly a year's rent—upon the transfer of a lease from father to son, whereas the perpetual contract forever removed such an advantage. Moreover, the landlords probably feared, as we have noted, the tendency of the fee arrangement to breed a princely disposition in the tenantry, thus making it difficult for them to exercise decisive control in manorial affairs.

Robert Livingston's reversal of Gardner's lease seems to have set the precedent for his heirs to follow. Of 106 leases in the Manor of Livingston from 1718 to 1775, one was for "forever," 3 for three lives, 75 for two concurrent lives, 19 for a life, and 8 for a term of years.[63] The figures

---

Letters of Abraham Ten Broeck, 1753–1783, and Rensselaerswyck Rent Ledger, 1768–1789, *passim*, both in Rensselaerswyck MSS; William B. Fink, "Stephen Van Rensselaer: The Last Patroon" (Ph.D. diss., Columbia University, 1950), 31–36.

61. Lease to Andrew Gardner of Perthshire, Scotland, Mar. 25, 1708, Livingston-Redmond MSS, Roll 3; Robert Livingston's will, Jan. 24, 1710, *ibid.*

62. "Conveyance of land by Andrew Gardner to meundrentten," Feb. 12, 1718, *ibid.*

63. One perpetual lease granted by Philip Livingston to Peter Coole in 1732 was an anomaly. Lease, Mar. 30, 1732, Morristown Historical Park Collection (microfilm), Roll

for life tenure, most of which (18 out of 19) concerned practices at Clermont, are somewhat misleading, because they represented tenurial conditions not at the time of contracting but some years later. One extant tenant list from Clermont refers to 14 of these tenants variously as "very old," "old," or "elderly," suggesting the possibility that they were either widowers or widows and that their original deeds were for two lives. Philip Livingston believed that a tenure of two concurrent lives, by far the most common, was one of several good encouragements that a landowner could offer to attract settlers.[64] He was not alone in this belief. Gulian Verplanck, who owned a large tract in Dutchess and Ulster counties and was active in land development in the middle of the eighteenth century, instructed his heirs to rent "all or any" of his lands "on the best Terms they can giving Leases to the Several Tenants for and During the natural Life of the Respective Tenants and their wives."[65] It is equally significant that some prospective tenants themselves asked for such an agreement, although, if given the option, they would have preferred a fee arrangement or a lease for three lives.[66]

The tenure policy of the Philipsburgh proprietors, from the founder, Frederick Philipse, to the last proprietor, Frederick III, differed radically from that of the other manorial landlords. The Philipses, though as eager as the others for land development, granted neither perpetual nor life-term leases.[67] Generally, leases at Philipsburgh took a verbal, or "parole," form, and occasionally included an obligation bond on the part of a tenant to perform certain conditions.[68] In either case, a lease could be

32, Morristown, N.J. For Clermont tenure practice, see "List of Tenants, Size of Farms and Tenures" (Clermont), Misc. MSS, Livingston, R-W, and also lease indentures in Livingston Manor Papers, both in N.-Y. Hist. Soc.

64. Philip Livingston to Jacob Wendell, Oct. 11, 1737, and Feb. 27, 1740, Livingston Papers, Museum of City of N.Y.

65. Gulian Verplanck's will, July 5, 1750, Gulian Verplanck Papers, Box 8, N.-Y. Hist. Soc.

66. "Notes of Eiphalet Stephens and David Akin's Evidence," Lawsuits, C-F, Kempe Papers; deposition of Gideon Prindle, July 28, 1766, Assorted Legal Manuscripts, 1691–1799, *ibid.*; John Sanders to Mr. Henry Jordice in London, Nov. 26, 1768, Letterbook of John Sanders.

67. Indenture between William Pugsley and Frederick Philipse, June 2, 1761, Philipse Papers, P249, Sleepy Hollow Restorations Lib.; "Evidence on the foregoing Memorial of Fred Philips Esqr," A.O. 12/19, 394.

68. Testimonies of Frederick Philipe III, James De Lancey, Beverly Robinson, John Watts, and John Tabor Kempe on the Philipsburgh lease practice, in "Evidence on Memorial of Fred Philips," A.O. 12/19, 385–405. For a lease in a bond form, see Underhill Barnes's bond of £400 to Adolph Philipse, Apr. 14, 1742, Benjamin Palmer Papers, Box II, N.-Y. Hist. Soc. The bond would be void when the tenant either returned his lease to the landlord or sold his improvements with the consent of the landlord.

terminated by either party at any time, and a person holding this tenure was, legally speaking, a tenant at the will or sufferance of the landlord. This arrangement was likely to favor the landlord more than the tenant, in that the former could control the latter with the threat of eviction. From a strictly legal point of view, it was the least secure and therefore the worst type of leasehold.

We lack the evidence to answer definitively the question of why the manor founder offered such bad lease terms. But the fact that Philipsburgh was populated more rapidly than the other manors, as shall be shown, suggests that it could boast some attractive features. The manor's location on the Hudson River and its proximity to the metropolitan market perhaps outweighed its unfavorable tenure conditions. It is also possible that the landlord and tenants shared some informal understanding that assured the latter they would not be disturbed as long as they performed their obligations.

The drawbacks of tenancy at will, it seems, at least in the Philipsburgh case, were more apparent than real, for one finds a great discrepancy between the legal terms of tenancy at will and the actual status that manor tenants enjoyed. Thus, for example, under these lease terms, tenants were allowed to acquire an equity in the improvements they made on the lands, which "by degrees it became a custom" for them to sell in the market with the consent of the landlord. The improvements could consist of a dwelling house, barn, shed, outhouses, orchard, garden, fences, and fields under cultivation, that is, practically everything other than the soil itself. Under these circumstances, the landlord was in no position to terminate the contract unless he was prepared to compensate the tenant for his improvements. When a lease was sold to another tenant, with all its improvements, the purchaser-tenant gained what might be called a prescriptive right to his leasehold. In one witness's words, "it seemed hard that where a farm had been bought in this way with the Landlords consent that the tenants should afterwards be turned off." The tenant's title to improvements either bought or made by himself provided a shield against the possible arbitrariness of the landlord and immensely enhanced the tenant's sense of security. Also, when a lease changed hands, the landlord benefited from the transaction by receiving a certain portion of the purchase money. Impressed by the secure status of the tenantry on the manor, many contemporary observers agreed that its proprietor "could not turn off a Tenant because he did not like his face." Some even declared that tenancy at Philipsburgh was "something in the nature of copyhold" or "verging very fast towards a copyhold." It might be added, however, that a case testing the respective rights of the two parties never arose in a court of equity.[69]

Because of the transformation of the lease at will into a reasonably good form of tenure, which, in the absence of precedent, contemporaries could not precisely define, Philipsburgh tenants did not seem much concerned about tenure one way or another. In early 1760 Frederick Philipse III gave them the option of taking "a Lease for three lives," which was legally better than a lease "at will," but none of them ever availed himself of the opportunity.[70] This episode goes a long way toward explaining how the tenants perceived their status in relation to the landlord. It establishes that they found the existing arrangement more satisfactory than the new one, even though the latter would qualify them as freeholders for voting purposes. The landlord's proposal, it seems, was not so much a concession to the tenants as an effort to confirm and define precisely what was already existing between them.

Cortlandt Manor contributed another dimension to the diversity of tenurial arrangements. In his will of 1700, Stephanus Van Cortlandt ordered his wife, Gertrude, his eldest son, and the overseers of his children to "take care and see" that his agreement with several manor settlers "be fully observed performed and kept according to the true intent and meaning thereof." There is no way to know the nature of this agreement, but circumstantial evidence suggests that settlement conditions for his tenants had been good. First, Van Cortlandt put special emphasis on the obligations of his heirs and of the overseers toward the tenants, who had been settled at his "great charge."[71] Second, in 1713 Gertrude paid a considerable amount of money (£200) to one John Cornelieus Van Texell, a tenant, in order to obtain quitclaim to a two-hundred-acre tract in the manor; the price (£200 for two hundred acres) of the transaction was much higher than the landlord would have paid had the lease been for years or at will.[72] Third, the manor founder had had to anticipate the day when his manor freeholders would send a representative to the General Assembly by virtue of the manor patent and, hence, the imperative to

69. "Evidence on Memorial of Fred Philips," A.O. 12/19, 393–394, 397–398, 401, 402–405.

70. Frederick Philipse's printed notice, dated Feb. 7, 1760, to his tenants, particularly to James Hunter (on photostat), Philipse Papers, PX2345a, Sleepy Hollow Restorations Lib.

71. Stephanus Van Cortlandt's will, Museum of City of N.Y.; N.Y. Land Papers, II, 245.

72. Quitclaim deed, 1713, Van Cortlandt Papers, V2187, Sleepy Hollow Restorations Lib.

make freeholders out of his tenants by giving them at least a life or longer lease tenure.

While the manor estate was held in common among the heirs, their mother, Gertrude, administered it until her death in early 1724. She seems to have avoided giving leases that might interfere with the heirs' freedom of use or with their disposition of their respective shares in the future. Her intention was to avoid burdening the heirs with tenants holding one, two, or three lives or "fee" leases on what would eventually become their fee simple estate.[73] In the meantime, she honored her husband's agreement with the tenants as directed and, occasionally, hired out lands for a short year term, if such a condition was agreeable to a prospective settler.[74] In the ten-year period following their mother's death, the heirs did nothing on the common property except to make a series of preliminary agreements among themselves with respect to principles and procedures for dividing the manor. Finally, the long-awaited partition of the domain came in the years 1732 to 1734, and with it the transformation from a single to a multiple proprietorship of the land, anticipated by the manor founder, was completed (see the map on p. 183).[75]

The partition broke the long interruption in settlement of the manor as the new owners began to dispose of their shares by selling or leasing or by doing both simultaneously. Starting in 1736[76] with the sale of 1,886 acres by William and Elizabeth (Van Cortlandt) Skinner (as appendix 2 shows), until 1776, about 41,792 acres of land, nearly half of the manor, were sold by eight of the ten original devisees and their descendants. Specifically, the Johnsons sold about 8,937 acres, 93 percent of their share; the Schuylers 6,371 acres, 76 percent; Philip Van Cortlandt 6,259

73. For the same reason, James Alexander, a proprietor of lands in Dutchess County, refused to grant leases for longer than ten years: "I would not Debarr myself or my Children of the Liberty of Selling after that time of ten years." Alexander to Isaiah Ross, Apr. 2, 1746, Alexander Papers, Box 62. See also Rip Van Dam *et al.* to Robert Livingston *et al.*, Nov. 2, 1721, Letters, 1700–1749, Rensselaerswyck MSS.

74. Mrs. Gertrude Van Cortlandt's will, Dec. 16, 1718, in *Abstracts of Wills, on File in the Surrogate's Office, City of New York* (N.-Y. Hist. Soc., *Colls.*, XXV–XLI [New York, 1892–1908]), II, 457, hereafter cited as *Abstracts of Wills;* Account Book of Estate of Gertruyd Van Cortlandt, 1726–1740, N.Y. Pub. Lib.; "A Book of the Estate for Geertry'd Van Cortland alias Beekman," Van Cortlandt Papers, V2302–V2303, Sleepy Hollow Restorations Lib.

75. "Appraisment of all the houses and Lotts of Ground In the Citty of New York," Watts Papers, Vol. 8, N.-Y. Hist. Soc.; Philip Van Cortlandt's petition to Gov. John Montgomery, July 15, 1728, N.Y. Land Papers, X, 66; "Articles of Agreement," Nov. 13, 1730, Cortlandt Manor Papers, 1697–1776, Van Cortlandt Family Papers, N.-Y. Hist. Soc.

76. Deed, the Skinners to Joseph Conklin and John Baisley, Jr., May 21, 1736, Van Cortlandt-Van Wyck Papers, Box 1.

acres, 87 percent; the Skinners 4,333 acres, 48 percent; the Bayards 5,243 acres, 66 percent; the De Lanceys 3,971 acres, 47 percent; the Verplancks 4,653 acres,[77] 60 percent; Stephen Van Cortlandt 2,000 acres,[78] 28 percent. Information concerning the disposition of land by the Milns of Albany is unavailable.[79] The Beekmans kept their entire manor estate under lease until the passing of Gertrude (Van Cortlandt) Beekman in 1777.[80] Out of 65,606 acres of land initially owned by these eight families, 41,767 acres, 64 percent, were sold. Yet some of the land (9,874 acres) went into the hands of their own relatives. For instance, Oliver De Lancey, son of Stephen De Lancey, bought 1,200 acres from his uncle Philip Van Cortlandt's estate in 1757.[81] A year later, Pierre Van Cortlandt, in addition to his small inheritance of the manor land, acquired 3,138 acres more from his father Philip's estate.[82] Sometime in 1740 John Schuyler conveyed 3,696 acres to his brother-in-law, Stephen De Lancey. Gertrude Beekman expanded her manor domain further by purchasing 340 acres from her brother-in-law Andrew Johnston in 1739. Lastly, John Watts, a son-in-law of Stephen De Lancey, bought 1,500 acres from the Bayards before 1776.[83] Thus, the amount of land ac-

77. This figure is based on the will of Philip Verplanck, Oct. 23, 1767, *Abstracts of Wills*, VII, 459.

78. I have arrived at this figure from an examination of the following sources: partition deed among Philip, Johanna, and John Van Cortlandt, Aug. 20, 1791, Deed Book XXIII, 247–250, and Deed Book XVIII, 59–65, Office of the Secretary of State of New York, Albany; Deed Book H, 407–501, Westchester Co. Clerk's Office.

79. All we know about the Milns' land transactions is that they sold Front Lot No. 5 (1,234 acres) to Samuel Bayard soon after the partition of the manor. Lease, Samuel Bayard to John Lent, May 1, 1733, Bayard-Campbell-Pearsall Colls.

80. Gertrude Beekman's will, Feb. 20, 1776, MS No. 12695, N.Y. State Lib.

81. The Estate of Father Philip Van Cortlandt, Van Cortlandt Papers, V1837, Sleepy Hollow Restorations Lib.; "Minutes of the estate of Philip and Stephen Van Cortlandt Esqrs. dec'd," Van Cortlandt Family Papers, N.-Y. Hist. Soc.

82. "Papers Belonging to the Lieutenant Governor, 1757–1759," Van Cortlandt Papers, V1836, Sleepy Hollow Restorations Lib.

83. Deed Book XIX, 109–114, Office of N.Y. Sec. of State; John Watts to Robert Watts, Sept. 2, 1783, Robert Watts Papers, Box 3, N.Y. Hist. Soc. Excluded from this discussion are many other transactions by sale or inheritance among the third-generation proprietors, particularly the De Lanceys. In 1744 Peter Warren, husband of Susannah (a daughter of Stephen De Lancey), who inherited about 1,500 acres of the manor land in 1743, bought about 1,500 acres from his sister-in-law Anne Watts. In the same year, Warren also bought 1,234 acres from his brother-in-law Oliver De Lancey and several years later 912 acres from another brother-in-law, Stephen De Lancey. These purchases of land, which were all rented out, made the Warrens prominent landlords of Cortlandt Manor. Deed Book XIV, 110–111, Office of N.Y. Sec. of State; Peter Warren Papers, 1724–1795, Watts Papers, Vol. 10, and De Lancey Papers, 1647–1804, all in N.-Y. Hist. Soc. The best account of the Warrens' land purchases is Julian Gwyn, *The Enterprising Admiral: The Personal Fortune of Admiral Sir Peter Warren* (Montreal, 1974), 39.

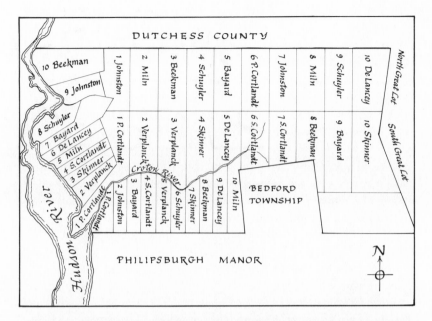

**Sketch of the Partition of Cortlandt Manor among the Heirs of Stephanus Van Cortlandt,**
1732–1734. Sources: Deeds of partition, for the Schuylers, Manuscript No. 12248, New
York State Library, Albany; for the Beekmans, Cortlandt Manor Papers, New-York Historical Society, New York; for Stephen Van Cortlandt, Case for Oversized Manuscripts,
*ibid.*; for the Skinners, Van Cortlandt Papers, V58, V222, Sleepy Hollow Restorations
Library, Tarrytown, N.Y., and Case for Oversized MSS, N.-Y. Hist. Soc.; "Estimate of the
Value in the Manor of Cortlandt, 1733," Van Cortlandt-Van Wyck Papers, 1716–1819,
New York Public Library; "The Return of 10 lots in the South part of the Manor of C. on
the south side of Crooten's River . . . ," May and July 1733, Van Cortlandt Papers, V2193,
Sleepy Hollow Restorations Lib.; "Lotts Drawn by Ger. Beekman 1/10 Manor Cortlandt
1732," *ibid.*, V2066; Samuel Bayard to Mrs. Gertrude Beekman, Feb. 12, 1734, and July 5,
1734, *ibid.*, V2100. (Drawn by Richard J. Stinely.)

quired by settlers other than the Van Cortlandts and their relatives would
be reduced to 31,893 acres, or about 49 percent of the total owned by the
eight original devisees of Stephanus Van Cortlandt. In sum, about 37
percent of the manor was sold to outsiders before 1776.

Some of the reasons for this remarkable disintegration of the original
manorial patent have already been given. Many of the inherited plots
were too poorly situated to support large-scale land development. Most
of the manor proprietors were absentees, and they were aware of the
problems absenteeism would create in the management of their lands. It

seems to have been the consensus among colonial landlords that the land development business without meticulous personal supervision would produce nothing but frustration and pain for an investor.[84] Stephen Skinner, son of William and Elizabeth, probably typified the sentiments of the manor landlords when he asserted in 1768: "I have the lands in this province [New Jersey] that will take up all the time I can spare to attend in that way [the manor]."[85] The manor landlords, with the exception of Philip Van Cortlandt and his son Stephen, and Philip Verplanck, anticipated the liquidation of their holdings by not entailing them.[86]

Moreover, many of them were men of modest means unable to sustain the expense of opening new lands. Families that were primarily engaged in commerce, like the Bayards, were not persuaded of the wisdom of diverting money from trade to land, with its notoriously slow. rental yield. Gentlemen like Stephen Skinner and John Cockran of New Brunswick, a son-in-law of John Schuyler, preferred lending out proceeds from the sale of their manor lands at a 6 or 7 percent interest rate rather than leasing the lands.[87]

Finally, some of the third- and fourth-generation proprietors had to dispose of part of their manor shares in order to satisfy their ancestors' creditors. A case in point was the estate of Philip Van Cortlandt and his son Stephen, respectively second and third manor "lord." Philip was so obsessed with the idea of keeping his paltry manor land intact that he bequeathed it in 1746 to his heirs in entail, in an attempt to reverse the pattern his father had set. So did his son Stephen in 1754. Their heirs later found out, however, that Philip and Stephen together had incurred debts amounting to £13,740. One of the heirs declared in 1759 that "there is an Absolute necessity of disposing of some lands in the manor to pay those persons who are most pressing as also to rid the Estate of a Consuming matter." Following a partial breakup of the entail through

84. Lewis Morris, Jr., to James Alexander, 1735(?), Rutherford Collection, II, N.-Y. Hist. Soc.; Robert R. Livingston to father, Robert, Jr., Apr. 12, 1766, Robert R. Livingston Coll., Box 1, *ibid.*

85. Stephen Skinner to William Skinner, Apr. 2, 1768, Gage Papers, G/Am.

86. Philip Van Cortlandt's will, Aug. 21, 1746, Van Cortlandt Papers, V1837, Sleepy Hollow Restorations Lib.; Philip Verplanck's will, Oct. 23, 1767, *Abstracts of Wills*, VII, 459.

87. John Cockran to Philip Schuyler, Mar. 25, 1772, Schuyler Papers, 1758–1798, Box 24, N.Y. Pub. Lib.; Stephen Skinner to William Skinner, Oct. 23, 1767, Gage Papers, G/Am. From 1718 to 1737, the maximum interest rate allowed by law in New York was 8%. But this ceiling was lowered to 7%, where it remained until the end of the colonial period. See Gwyn, *Enterprising Admiral*, 96.

legislative action, the heirs sold off about 4,250 acres of land, more than half of Philip Van Cortlandt's original share of the manor.[88]

Whatever the long-range disposition of their holdings, many of the Cortlandt Manor proprietors recognized that it was necessary to lease out their land in order to improve it. An increase in the sale and rental value of land depended on the extent to which it was cleared and improved. Moreover, improvements in one area were likely to advance the value of land nearby, even in a state of near total wilderness. For these reasons, most of these landlords inserted detailed descriptions in lease contracts regarding what tenants should do with hired lands. At the same time, the majority of the manor landlords understood not only the aversion of prospective settlers to short-term leases but also the functional relationship between tenure and improvement: the shorter the tenure was, the less attached a tenant would be to the property and the less incentive for him to improve it.[89] Despite the likelihood of policy diversity due to the fragmentation of ownership, the Cortlandt Manor proprietors followed the most common practice of New York landowners by offering a long tenure to farmers.

Of twenty-five extant lease papers of the Beekmans covering the period from 1737 to 1775, twenty-two were for three lives. Of the remaining three, one was for thirteen years, and the other two pertaining to gristmills were for fifteen years.[90] Of the three extant Bayard leases, one

88. Cortlandt Skinner to "Dear Brother," Oct. 25, 1771, William Skinner to Stephen Skinner, 1770, and Stephen Skinner to William Skinner, Oct. 26, 1771, Gage Papers, G/Am; "Minutes of the estate of Philip and Stephen Van Cortlandt," Van Cortlandt Family Papers, N.-Y. Hist. Soc.; Philip Van Cortlandt to Pierre Van Cortlandt, Dec. 12, 1759, Van Cortlandt Papers, V1883, Sleepy Hollow Restorations Lib. Legally, entailed land, even more than land in fee, was not subject to charge for the debts of the deceased. At the debtor's death the entailed estate passed directly to the party next in tail. To prevent that, the other heirs asked the legislature to make the property disposable to satisfy Van Cortlandt's outstanding indebtedness. This type of testamentary problem was frequently solved by legislation in the form of a private bill.

89. Isaiah Ross, who worked for a proprietor of Great Nine Partners Patent in Dutchess County, recommended that "Yu would give a lease of Three Lives or else of 99 years and for the Benefit of the Land I think Either will be to your advantage for such a long Term will Encourage the Said Tenants to build and Improve." Ross to James Alexander, Mar. 26, 1746, Alexander Papers, Box 62; Oliver De Lancey to William Skinner, Jan. 7, 1775, Gage Papers, G/Am.

90. Van Cortlandt Papers, V2189, V1942 (no. 1), V2194, V1960, V1697, V1945, V1942 (no. 2), V2199, V2200, V2066, V2204, V2205, V2188, V2206, V1690, V2207, V2208, V2209, V2190, Sleepy Hollow Restorations Lib.; Mortgage Book C, 252–254, Westchester Co. Clerk's Office; leases in Van Cortlandt-Van Wyck Papers, Box 1. The Beekmans applied the same lease tenure to their lands in Dutchess County. See "Boundaries etc. of the Leases in the Chancellors Allotment in No. 16, Beekmans Precinct," "Uncatalogued Livingston MSS."

was for three lives and the others for two lives.[91] The Schuyler family also offered their renters tenure of either two or three lives.[92] The three extant lease contracts of Philip Van Cortlandt and his sons Stephen and Pierre provided for tenure of one, two, and three lives respectively.[93] On the basis of two extant leases, it can be supposed that Philip Verplanck offered tenure of two or three lives.[94] The Skinners' lease practices are a mystery. We have only a letter written in 1772 by Stephen Skinner in which he refers to a plan to lease a farm in the manor for a rent of £10 on a life term. At least, the Skinners did not seem to shun life-term leases.[95]

By contrast, the De Lanceys usually granted parole (verbal) leases specifying only the amount of rent and not the length of tenure. In one instance, however, they rented out 33 acres of land to a tenant named Nathaniel Close for a ninety-nine-year period in the 1750s.[96] Peter Warren and his wife, Susannah (De Lancey), who in 1769 had twenty-one tenants on their manor estate of 5,336 acres, are known to have given only four tenants a tenure of eleven years. Nevertheless, according to a recent study, the turnover rate of the Warren tenants at will was surprisingly infrequent, suggesting that they "experienced as great security" as those with leases of definite terms.[97]

Stephen Van Cortlandt of New Jersey and his son John of New York City (who actually managed his father's manor lands) too gave rather unpopular leases. John's tenant rolls and letters reveal that out of twenty-eight identifiable tenants, half held leaseholds ranging from five years to a maximum of seventeen years, while the other half were tenants at will.

---

91. Leases, Samuel Bayard to Philip Linnebeker, May 1, 1732, to Peter Win, Nov. 1, 1732, and to John Lent, May 1, 1733, Bayard-Campbell-Pearsall Colls.

92. Philip Schuyler to son Philip Jeremiah Schuyler, Mar. 3, 1796, Schuyler Papers, S941, Sleepy Hollow Restorations Lib.; "Doctor James Perry in account with the Ex[ecu]-tors of Cornelia Schuyler, Aug. 13, 1791," Schuyler Papers, Box 36, No. 2084, N.Y. Pub. Lib.

93. Leases, Philip Van Cortlandt to Solomon Burtis, Apr. 18, 1748, Pierre Van Cortlandt to John Leer, Jan. 27, 1764, Van Cortlandt Papers, V2108, V1684, Sleepy Hollow Restorations Lib.; Stephen Van Cortlandt to Joseph Haight, Apr. 11, 1751, Van Cortlandt-Van Wyck Papers.

94. Philip Verplanck to Benjamin Field, lease, 1742, Philip Verplanck Papers, N.Y. Gen. and Biog. Soc.; memorial of Samuel Tilley, Mar. 8, 1786, A.O. 12/25, 95.

95. Stephen Skinner to William Skinner, Oct. 26, 1771, Gage Papers, G/Am.

96. Uriah Wallace to Nathaniel Close, quitclaim deed, Mar. 7, 1798, Close Papers, N.Y. State Hist. Assoc. John Watts, a son-in-law of Stephen De Lancey, however, gave Peter Syne a lease for a life and Gabriel Carman for two lives. John Watts to Robert Watts and John Watts, Jr., June 2, 1785, Robert Watts Papers, Box 3; "Estimate of part of the Estate and Loss of John Watts . . . 1788," Watts Papers, Vol. 9.

97. Gwyn, Enterprising Admiral, 39, 52.

Tenants with short-term leases could apply for extensions, but the request was rarely granted unless the tenant had performed his obligations to the complete satisfaction of the landlord.[98] Such a policy is hard to explain, but one thing is certain: it engendered apathy in the tenants toward the development of the leasehold. Because the lease was so temporary in nature, the tenants were disposed to exploit rather than expand existing improvements. More often than not, needs for repair were unattended. Instead of trying to find and remove the root cause of unsatisfactory tenant behavior, the short-tempered and haughty John Van Cortlandt reacted with harsh reprimands and threats of eviction. These tactics, however, served only to exacerbate his relationships with his tenants, creating a problem that would seriously menace his father's estate in the future.

## Rent: Theory and Practice

For the landlord, the income from rent was one of the important reasons for leasing his land; but to the tenant, the payments were a burden and an irritation, however light they might have been. The duke de La Rochefoucauld-Liancourt, who was traveling in Albany in 1795, made a shrewd comment on the Rensselaerswyck tenants' perception of the rent problem: "A man, who is obliged to pay every year a ground-rent, soon forgets the moderate terms on which he obtained possession of his estate, feels only the unpleasant compulsion of paying money at a fixed time, and eagerly seizes upon the first opportunity of freeing himself from his incumbrance."[99] What seemed a low and modest rate to the landlord was exorbitant to the tenant; what seemed a fair and mutually agreeable arrangement at the time of initial contracting soon became a matter of contention between the two parties. Because of its basically subjective and controversial nature, involving two legitimate interest groups, it is difficult for the historian to objectify the question.

The problem of gaining an altogether unbiased view is further compounded by the great variety and complexity in the amounts and kinds of rent paid in these manors. As with some of the other conditions on the manors, rents were kaleidoscopic, varying from time to time and from

98. Letterbook and Journal (c) of John Van Cortlandt, 1764–1772, N.Y. Pub. Lib.; Receipt Book of John Van Cortlandt, 1757–1767, and Letterbook and Notebook of John Van Cortlandt, Van Cortlandt Family Papers, N.-Y. Hist. Soc.; Van Cortlandt Papers, V2201, Sleepy Hollow Restorations Lib.
99. Munsell, ed., *Annals of Albany*, IV, 238.

one landlord to another. Such factors as the size, type, and duration of the lease, the location and use of the property, the amount of improvement, the degree of urgency felt by a landlord to clear the lands, and his generosity, all seemed to have contributed to this diversity.[100] Although the records are by no means complete, they clearly show a close relationship between the size of the leased property and the amount of rent charged by the proprietor. It is therefore necessary first to consider farm sizes and then the rent variations among the manors. Leases connected with service industries like milling, blacksmithing, and tailoring, and leases for residential lots or gardening will be excluded from this account.

The sizes of leaseholdings extended from 32 acres possessed by Dirck Gardner of Livingston Manor to 1,223 acres held by John Lent of Cortlandt Manor.[101] Some landlords, notably Philip and Stephen Van Cortlandt of New York and the Skinners of Perth Amboy, parceled and allocated their lands to their tenants fairly equally, while others did not.[102] As table 5.1 shows, Philipsburgh had a spread running from 32 acres to over 400 acres (the largest parcel was 560), with the major concentration of the holdings between 100 and 249 acres. The average individual farm, according to a survey of 228 leaseholds there, was 187 acres. The distribution pattern of leases in Cortlandt resembled that of Philipsburgh, except that the majority of farmers had between 200 and 299 acres and the average holding was 237 acres. Compared with the southern manors, most of the farms in the northern manors of Rensselaerswyck and Livingston were smaller. The former's average tenant holding (including both perpetual leases and leases for years) was 153 acres,[103] and the average on the latter, including the Clermont part, 106 acres. It should be pointed out, however, that Livingston Manor proper, constituting more than 90 percent of the entire manor land, had an average lease of only 84 acres, whereas the sister domain of Clermont averaged 128

---

100. John Watts to Robert Watts, Apr. 10, 1786, Robert Watts Papers, Box 3.

101. Livingston Manor Rent Ledger, 1767–1784, 142, N.-Y. Hist. Soc.; quitclaim deed, Apr. 18, 1771, Samuel Bayard to John Lent, Bayard-Campbell-Pearsall Colls.

102. Advertisement for the sale of North Lot No. 6 in Cortlandt Manor, *N.-Y. Mercury*, Nov. 28, 1757; *ibid.*, Dec. 22, 1766; will of Philip Van Cortlandt, Aug. 21, 1746, Van Cortlandt Papers, V1846, Sleepy Hollow Restorations Lib.; will of Stephen Van Cortlandt, June 7, 1754, *Abstracts of Wills*, V, 173–175; partition deed among the heirs of Elizabeth Skinner, 1768, Deed Book XVIII, 148, Office of N.Y. Sec. of State.

103. It should be noted, however, that there was a sizable difference in acreage between the fee leases and those for years in the period from 1764 to 1783: the former, according to 42 deeds, was 171 acres on the average, while the latter (50 in number) was 135 acres.

Table 5.1. The Size of Leases in the Manors, 1730–1783

| | LEASES | | | |
|---|---|---|---|---|
| Acreage | Cortlandt | Philipsburgh | Rensselaerswyck | Livingston |
| | No.   % | No.   % | No.   % | No.   % |
| 32–49 | | 4   2 | 1   1 | 4   4 |
| 50–99 | | 28   12 | 5   5 | 38   41 |
| 100–149 | 7   8 | 37   16 | 52   57 | 33   35 |
| 150–199 | 12   13 | 73   32 | 20   22 | 11   12 |
| 200–249 | 45   50 | 46   20 | 6   7 | 7   8 |
| 250–299 | 12   13 | 20   9 | 5   5 | |
| 300–349 | 11   12 | 14   6 | 2   2 | |
| 350–399 | 2   2 | 3   1 | | |
| 400–more | 2   2 | 4   2 | 1   1 | |
| | 91   100 | 228   100 | 92   100 | 93   100 |
| Average size in acres | 237 | 187 | 153 | 106 |

Sources:

*Cortlandt Manor*—Sung Bok Kim, "The Manor of Cortlandt and Its Tenants, 1697–1783" (Ph.D. diss., Michigan State University, 1966), chap. 5, tables 3–8; Julian Gwyn, *The Enterprising Admiral: The Personal Fortune of Admiral Sir Peter Warren* (Montreal, 1974), 53.

*Philipsburgh Manor*—"A Plan of the Manor of Philipsburg in the County of Westchester, 1783," in J. Thomas Scharf, ed., *History of Westchester County, New York, Including Morrisania, Kings Bridge, and West Farms* (Philadelphia, 1886), I, 161; "A Map of the Upper part of the Manor of Philipsburgh showing the farm occupants in 1785 prior to sales by the Commrs of Forfeitures and who became purchasers from them . . . ," in the possession of William Slater, surveyor, at Ossining, N.Y.

*Rensselaerswyck*—It was difficult to ascertain the size of leases in Rensselaerswyck, because many deeds prior to 1750 did not give the acreage. As of 1770, a "considerable" number of tenants were on the domain, where the "farms have not yet been surveyed nor the Rents fixed." Catherine Van Rensselaer to John Bleecker and Thomas Hun, 1770, in Letters of Abraham Ten Broeck, 1753–1783, Rensselaerswyck Manuscripts, New York State Library, Albany. Information on the 92 farms was gleaned from the following sources: Rensselaerswyck Rent Ledger, 1768–1787, and "Leases granted by Stephen Van Rensselaer Esquire and his ancestors for Lands . . . , Sept. 1, 1790," Leases, 1766–1797, both in Rensselaerswyck MSS; Van Rensselaer-Fort Papers, 1729–1789, New York Public Library; Claverack Papers, fol. 1, New-York Historical Society, New York; "Lease, Bethlehem," Albany Institute of History and Art, Albany, N.Y.; deeds on Rensselaerswyck in Deed Books 3 to 10, *passim*, Albany County Clerk's Office, Albany, N.Y.

*Livingston Manor*—Livingston-Redmond MSS; "List of Tenants, Size of Farms and Tenures [Clermont]," Miscellaneous Manuscripts, Livingston, R–W, and also Livingston Manor Papers and Livingston Manor Rent Ledger, 1767–1784, all in N.-Y. Hist. Soc.

acres.[104] Since the manorial landlords, with the exception of the Van Rensselaers, did not permit the subletting of part of a farm, or its subdivision among heirs, because they feared possible administrative complications and impoverishment of tenants, it is reasonable to assume that the size of individual leaseholds on the manors remained constant over the years.[105] The Rensselaerswyck tenants, however, were free to sublet and subdivide their farms, and the practice was widespread.[106] The actual individual holdings there were thus likely to have been smaller than the indicated figure of 153 acres.

One cannot help but be impressed by the conspicuous difference in the size of leaseholds between the northern and southern manors. It appears ironic that the proprietors of the little manors should have granted larger amounts of land to tenants than those of the big manors. The Livingstons and the Van Rensselaers apparently subscribed to the notion that "the smaller their farms, the more the land will hould, and the better the Improvements will bee" and that, if a farmer was diligent, 80 to 120 acres in "a fine wheat country," which Albany County was, would afford him a sufficient support for a family of four or five.[107]

104. In the first quarter of the 18th century, Robert Livingston (the founder of Livingston Manor) rarely granted more than 100 acres to a tenant. Deed, Nov. 30, 1727, Livingston to son Gilbert, Columbia County Miscellaneous Manuscripts, N.-Y. Hist. Soc.

105. Beverly McAnear, ed., "Mr. Robert R. Livingston's Reasons against a Land Tax," *Jour. Pol. Econ.*, XLVIII (1940), 88; Frederick Philipse to James Hunter, Feb. 7, 1760, Huguenot Historical Association, New Rochelle, N.Y. In this letter to a tenant, the landlord ordered that "if you have any Person or Persons settled upon [your] Farm . . . you remove them from thence by the First Day of May ensuing, which will be not only for your own Benefit, but your Posterity's; and that you suffer no Person or Persons whatsoever, to settle on said Farm, except it be your Son, whom you design to leave your possession to after your Decease." This evidence contradicts Beatrice G. Reubens's view that "Philipsburgh tenants were free to divide . . . the lease on their farms or to sublease." See Reubens, "Pre-emptive Rights in the Disposition of a Confiscated Estate, Philipsburgh Manor, New York," *WMQ*, 3d Ser., XXII (1965), 439. There was only one instance in which one of the Beekmans' tenants sublet part of his lease. It is impossible to determine whether the tenant had obtained the landlord's prior consent for the transaction, but the Beekmans later confirmed the sublease by giving the subtenant a new lease. Lease, the Beekmans to William Borden, May 1, 1756, Van Cortlandt Papers, V2198, Sleepy Hollow Restorations Lib.

106. Evert Wendell's will, July 23, 1749, Wills, XIX, 40–45, Queens College Lib.; Philip Schuyler's will, June 28, 1748, *ibid.*, XXV, 285; John Mesick's will, Feb. 5, 1774, *ibid.*, XXIX, 468–470; Abraham Witbeck's will, Oct. 22, 1765, *ibid.*, XXXVII, 37–39; Henry Haywood's mortgage to John Duncan, Nov. 10, 1768, and Walter Barrent's mortgage to John Duncan, Apr. 15, 1768, Mortgage Books III, 43, and II, 334, Albany Co. Clerk's Office; Adolph B. Benson, ed., *Peter Kalm's Travels in North America: The English Version of 1770* (New York, 1937), I, 338.

107. Peter Warren to William Johnson, Nov. 20, 1738, *William Johnson Papers*, XIII, 2; Oliver De Lancey to sister Susannah Warren, Feb. 1, 1772, Gage Papers, G/Am; advertisement for the sale of a store in Claverack, *N.-Y. Mercury*, Mar. 11, 1765. Every part of Albany County was not fertile, however. Some western and northeastern sections of Rensselaerswyck were generally "poor and broken" and "clay gravelly and stony." But these

Persuaded by the advantages of small farms, in 1770 Catherine Van Rensselaer, widow of Stephen Van Rensselaer II, instructed her agents to survey "every farm" in the manor that had not already been surveyed and to allocate no more than "120 acres to each Farm unless it should appear that a small allowance ought to be made for broken or bad land, [but] not to exceed 15 acres pr hundred."[108] But the Philipses and the Van Cortlandts had a different plan. Their lands, as one observer put it, were "naturally as bad as [could] be and as full of stones." Another commentator reported that soil in the area with the exception of the narrow strip along the Hudson was "principally" clay, "excellent for pasture" but not well adapted for the cultivation of wheat, and that the terrain was "uneven and hilly." The few veins of light sandy soil that were fit for grain hardly seemed adequate.[109] By means of larger grants of land, the southern landlords perhaps tried to balance off the poor topographical and soil conditions.

The land conditions in Cortlandt and Philipsburgh manors affected not only the type of agriculture their inhabitants developed but also the kinds of rent the proprietors demanded. Until about 1730 the farmers there had cultivated mainly winter wheat, and on the side, they grew oats, rye, Indian corn, buckwheat, and potatoes, exploiting every bit of low land. Their agricultural practices were much the same as those of their counterparts in the north, thus accounting for the province's virtual single-crop economy.

After 1730, however, two notable developments greatly modified this uniform picture. One was the emergence of fertile Albany County as the dominant wheat producer with its rapid expansion of farm population following the end of Queen Anne's War.[110] The southerners, hampered by poor soil and relatively little snowfall to protect the wheat from the region's severe winter frosts, were simply no match for the Albanians in the quantity and quality of their grain production. Almost simulta-

---

parts had not been fully settled until the end of the colonial period. The land in Livingston Manor was "fertile for all kinds of grain," although its face was "very rough and broken." "Remarks on the Town of Livingston" by John Wigram, 1798, and "Description of Town of Rensselaerville," 1798, Land Papers, Book V, 37, Bureau of Waterways; "Major Rutherford's Journal to Princeton, June and July 1765," Duane Papers, Roll 3.

108. Catherine Van Rensselaer to John Bleecker and Thomas Hun, 1770, Letters of Abraham Ten Broeck, 1753–1783, Rensselaerswyck MSS.

109. "Journal of Lord Adam Gordon," in Newton D. Mereness, ed., *Travels in the American Colonies* (New York, 1961), 415; "Geographical Observations on the County of Westchester," 1798, and also Daniel Delavan's report on North Salem, 1798, Land Papers, Book V, 41, 47, Bureau of Waterways.

110. Armour, "Merchants of Albany," 145, 189.

neously, New York City, growing by leaps and bounds, created a tremendous demand for foodstuffs, especially meat and dairy goods.[111] The
farmers in the southern manors believed that their prosperity lay in meeting this urban demand. The adjustment in land usage posed no problem,
because their lands were "perhaps the best calculated for grazing than
any other on the continent."[112] Although the rise of commercial livestock
and dairy husbandry did not completely destroy the older agriculture of
the region, it greatly reduced the tenants' dependence on wheat. The
farmers brought to the metropolis "great numbers" of fat cattle, sheep,
and hogs both on the hoof and in barrels, and "prodigious" quantities of
poultry, fresh butter, and cheese. They could always count on having
their returns within a week.[113] By contrast, the northern frontier tenants
never broke from the system of a single-crop economy dominated by
wheat. Philip Livingston, a wheat merchant-landlord, was biased against
his tenants raising commercial livestock because "it was not so profitable" for him or for the tenants as the staple crop.[114] With most of its
inhabitants owning farms in the country, Albany could not compare with
New York City as a market for livestock. Whatever little demand Albany
burghers might have had for meat products was met by farms in the
nearby countryside or in New England.[115]

The two divergent economic characters of northern and southern
manors were reflected in and partly responsible for the different types of
rent demanded in the second half of the eighteenth century: rents in the
north were paid mostly in winter wheat, and in the south they were paid
in cash. It was not uncommon in the north for frontier local governments
to pay wages and receive taxes and rents in wheat, although the corpo-
rate bodies had no trading interest.[116] In Rensselaerswyck a few tenants
in animal husbandry paid their rent only in pork or lamb instead of

111. New York City's population tripled from 7,248 in 1723 to 21,863 in 1771.
Greene and Harrington, *American Population*, 98, 102.
112. Nathaniel Sackett to Alexander McDougall, Mar. 12, 1777, McDougall Papers
(microfilm), Roll 2, N.-Y. Hist. Soc., which also owns the originals.
113. See the case of one Marlin [Martling?], a Philipsburgh tenant, in *N.-Y. Mercury*,
Dec. 8, 1766.
114. Philip Livingston to Jacob Wendell, Mar. 25, 1741, Livingston Papers, Museum
of City of N.Y.
115. Robert Livingston to son Philip, Oct. 29, 1714, Philip Livingston to father,
Robert, Sept. 19, 1725, Livingston-Redmond MSS, Rolls 6 and 4.
116. "Account of money Received by Robert Livingston of the Tax," 1692, *ibid.*, Roll
1; "Agreement with Dick Wilson for making the highway at the Sand Bergh, 8 September
1686," *ibid.*, Roll 10; Philip Livingston to father, Robert, May 12, 1714, and Feb. 15,
1722, *ibid.*, Roll 5.

grain, and some others paid in both wheat and meat. The northern landlords, however, were not necessarily averse to money payments for rent.[117]

In the Westchester manors, the situation was more diverse. The tenants in the "Upper" part of Philipsburgh were recorded to be paying wheat rent as late as 1749.[118] Perhaps their landlord, Adolph Philipse, preferred the staple crop to money because he could use it in the export trade. Sometime after Adolph's death (1749), which marked the reunion of that part of the manor with the "Lower" in the hands of his nephew Frederick II, cash rent completely replaced wheat. The commutation of rent was caused by several interrelated circumstances. First, cash was becoming more readily available to the Westchester farmers as their traffic in meat and dairy products, which were highly cash convertible, boomed in mid-century.[119] Second, more land was being allocated for grazing and for producing corn for animals, which considerably cut into the available wheat land, with the result that the volume of the wheat crop diminished over the years. The diversification of agriculture rendered grain merely one of many country products and a less important measure of a farmer's income; thus it became a less desirable means of rent payment. A third factor was that both Frederick Philipse II and his son Frederick III, who inherited the domain in 1751, shed themselves of the family's commercial tradition and took on the life-style of gentlemen, depending on a rich income from their real estate and other establishments.[120] The rental from the 145 well-improved farms alone amounted to about £550 annually in the 1750s and £950 in 1760.[121] These Philipses did not have the avid love for wheat that their ancestors had, as was clearly shown by Frederick III's decision in the early 1750s to lease out the two gristmills that his ancestors had founded, expanded, and

117. An examination of 195 Rensselaerswyck leases from 1696 to 1783 shows that the overwhelming majority, 159, were required to pay in wheat, 12 in pork, 19 in pork or lamb and wheat, and 5 in cash. "A list of Indentures, 1696–1744," "Leases granted by Stephen Van Rensselaer Esquire and his ancesters, Sept. 1, 1790," and Rensselaerswyck Rent Ledger, 1768–1789, all in Rensselaerswyck MSS. Isaac J. Truax consistently paid money for his rent although his lease provided for wheat (22 bushels and 2 pecks). See Truax's rent payment record from Apr. 1771 to 1778, Abraham Ten Broeck's Accounts of the Manor, 1763–1787, ibid.

118. "Inventory . . . of the Estates of Mr Adophy Philipse, Deceased, N.Y. Jan 24, 1749," entry on May 21, 1753, Philipse Papers, PX135, Sleepy Hollow Restorations Lib.

119. Reubens, "Pre-emptive Rights," WMQ, 3d Ser., XXII (1965), 441.

120. Hall, Philipse Manor Hall, 97–120.

121. "List of Tenants with the Respective Rents as they are Now Raised, Jan. 10th 1760," Philipse Papers, PA820, Sleepy Hollow Restorations Lib.

personally managed.[122] Since the mills had long functioned as the collection point for wheat rents, Frederick III's decision seems to have been
the probable point at which the commutation began.

The Manor of Cortlandt, opened for the first time to extensive settlement in the 1730s, moved directly into the newly diversified agrarian
economy in which wheat occupied a minor status. Besides, most of the
manor landlords were absentees, and the requirement of a bulky wheat
rent would have raised serious logistical problems for the tenants. Consequently, money became by far the most common means of rent payment, although some landlords, like Philip Van Cortlandt of New York
City, allowed his tenants the choice of either "mony or Country Produce." Similarly, the Beekmans demanded wheat rent from their Dutchess
County tenants who were wheat farmers and cash rent from their Cortlandt Manor tenants who were dairy farmers.[123] Thus, the different
economic circumstances of the tenants and, to some extent, of the landlords brought about different forms of rent.

How varied were the manorial rent rates? From 1735 to 1768 the
yearly rate in Cortlandt Manor was on the average £3 19s. (in New
York money) for a 238-acre farm, or about 4d. per acre. In Philipsburgh,
it was £4 for 184 acres, 5d. per acre, from about 1740 to 1759, and £6
19s. for the same farm, or 9d. per acre, from 1760—the year when there
was a 74 percent rent increase—to 1783. In Livingston Manor, where
wheat was the main rent item, it was nineteen bushels for an 84-acre
farm from 1735 to 1783. Converting grain into money values according
to its current wholesale price at different periods of time, shown by the
graph in figure 5.1, we can estimate that the rent in 1740 was £2 17s.
for the farm, or 8d. per acre, and that in 1769, when wheat was sold at
an all-time high of 7s. per bushel, it was £6 13s., that is, 1s. 7d. per acre.
For Rensselaerswyck wheat rent figures are not available, because until
1764 the manor rent was almost without exception one-tenth of the
entire produce of a farm, regardless of its size. In that year Stephen
Van Rensselaer II introduced a new policy of fixing the exact amount of
wheat rent instead of the tithe, and his widow Catherine and son Stephen

---

122. Advertisement for lease, N.-Y. Gaz.: or, Wkly. Post-Boy, Jan. 6, 1752, Sept. 24,
1753, Oct. 15, 1759; N.-Y. Mercury, Oct. 22, 1759.
123. Lease, Philip Van Cortlandt to Solomon Burtis, Apr. 18, 1748, Van Cortlandt
Papers, V2108, Sleepy Hollow Restorations Lib. Beekman's receipts of rent from the
Dutchess County tenants, particularly Martys Couner, Jan. 31, 1758–Jan. 2, 1760, "Uncatalogued Livingston MSS." It is worthy of note that the Fordham Manor proprietor
imposed a cash rent in the 1740s. Hastings, ed., Ecclesiastical Records of N.Y., IV, 2796,
2837.

Figure 5.1. New York Wholesale Wheat Prices per Bushel, 1684–1773
(in New York Currency)

Sources:
"Walter Webley's Inventory," May 10, 1684, AIN2 (2414), Queens College Library; "City Records," in Joel Munsell, ed., *Annals of Albany* (Albany, N.Y., 1850–1859), IX, 21; *New-York Gazette*, Oct. 17 to Oct. 27, 1726, Oct. 29 to Nov. 26, 1739, and Jan. 7, 1766; Philip Livingston to John D'Witt, July 14, 1740; *William Johnson Papers*, I, 24; Henry Beekman to Gilbert Livingston, Feb. 2, 1749, Beekman Papers, New-York Historical Society, New York; John Pruyn to Jacob Van Schaick, Apr. 24, 1772, Jacob Van Schaick Papers, 1737–1809, New York State Library, Albany; Robert Ray to John Sanders, Apr. 22, 1773, Glen-Sanders Papers, Colonial Williamsburg Foundation Research Department, Williamsburg, Va.; Letterbook of John Van Cortlandt, *passim*, New York Public Library.

III continued the same policy thereafter. From 1764 to 1769 the average rent for a 135-acre farm with a lease for "years," the main form of tenure during the period from 1769 to 1783, was ten bushels, that is, £3 10s. (6d. per acre).[124]

124. The rent rates in these manors are based on the sources listed in the notes for figure 5.2.

In comparative terms, the Cortlandt Manor rent was the lowest, 4d. per acre, and Livingston Manor the highest, 1s. 7d., a spread of almost 500 percent, in the period from 1760 to 1769. Between them were 7d. for Rensselaerswyck and 9d. for Philipsburgh. The moderately high rent at Rensselaerswyck was due to the perpetual tenure, the best of all leases. On the other hand, unusually low rents there were characteristic of leases for fixed terms of years. Be that as it may, the traditional tithe was generally considered "reasonable."[125] The rate at Philipsburgh, relatively high, was related to its advantageous location close to the New York City market and to its highly advanced state of settlement. Conversely, late settlement and undeveloped land seem to have been initially responsible for the low rent in Cortlandt Manor in the 1740s; once fixed, the rate could not be easily changed in subsequent years. The case of Livingston Manor, however, is hard to explain, assuming that my analysis of the extant data is correct. The manor could boast neither the advantageous location of Philipsburgh nor the tenure practices of Rensselaerswyck, and its soil quality was not exceptionally good. Its rent in kind in the 1740s, when wheat was cheaper, matched in cash terms that of the other manors during the 1760s. However, the price inflation for grain in the 1750s and 1760s had the effect of doubling the Livingston rent. Yet the manor proprietor made no rate adjustment in favor of his tenants.[126]

The manorial rents cited above, with the exception of Livingston's, were surely below those prevailing on other plantations in the province. Sir William Johnson, noted for his great success in land development in the Mohawk valley in mid-century, charged a shilling per acre perpetual rent. So did Oliver De Lancey, son of Stephen, for his 6,250 acres near Saratoga. Major Philip Skene, the proprietor of vast lands near Fort Edward, advertised in 1765 for lease of the land at a rent "not to exceed One Shilling, York Currency, per Acre, equal to Seven Pence Sterling." The term was for lives, "renewable for ever."[127] In the 1760s William

---

125. Bond, July 19, 1745, Henry Van Rensselaer to Arent Van Der Carr, Van Rensselaer-Fort Papers.

126. In the first two decades of the 18th century, Robert Livingston, the founder of Livingston Manor, demanded of some of his tenants that they pay rent amounting to a fourth of their produce. Discontented with the high rate, Jacob Vosburgh, one of the tenants, decided to quit the manor. Interestingly, Philip Livingston, son of Robert, thought that the rent was "but a trifle" and that Vosburgh would "never live better then where he is if he would take care and manage it Right." Philip Livingston to father, Robert, Jan. 4, 11, 1724, Livingston-Redmond MSS, Roll 4.

127. Goldsbrow Banyar to Samuel Dunlop, Aug. 28, 1761, and Oct. 18, 1762, Goldsbrow Banyar Papers, Box 6; Thomas Clarke's testimony, 1786, A.O. 12/19, 80–81, 131; Philip Skene's advertisement in N.-Y. Mercury, Mar. 18, 1765.

Smith, Jr., wrote in his promotional tract called "Information to Farmers and Mechanics to remove from Europe to America" that rent between 6d. and 7d. sterling per acre was what immigrants could expect for a durable lease. The rent roll of Kingsborough for the period from 1766 to 1780 indicates that its tenants with life-term leases paid 1s. 2d. per acre. Thus, the going rate in this period was roughly 1s. per acre (province money), which the landlords considered reasonable and promotable.[128] With this situation in mind, Frederick Philipse III felt justified in announcing a 74 percent hike in 1760, which brought his manor rate from 5d. to 9d. per acre, and he could assert that his land even after the raise was "still much lower rented than any Lands in the Province." The tenants naturally would have liked a cheaper rent, as is evidenced by a complaint reportedly from a Philipsburgh tenant in 1769 that the £7 yearly rent for a two-hundred-acre farm (about 8d. per acre) was "extravagant."[129] But at least one group of prospective tenants deemed 9d. annual rent for an acre to be a good bargain, even though the land was wild and remote.[130]

Wheat rent carried an apparent disadvantage, because the burden on the tenants increased correspondingly with an increase in the commodity price. But the adverse effect of inflation was not as serious as it seems. If the rent rate spiraled, the overall income of the farmers also grew proportionally. Cadwallader Colden in 1760 pointed to a 300 percent inflation in the price of all the necessities of life in the previous decade, but since his purpose was to induce the home government to raise provincial officials' salaries, he undoubtedly exaggerated. In negotiating the sale of a farm in 1772, John Van Cortlandt insisted on 30s. per acre, 3s. more than a purchaser was willing to pay, on the grounds that "Country produce is near double to what it was formerly so that Land

---

128. "Information to Farmers and Mechanics," William Smith Papers, Box 3; "Rent Roll of Kingsborough, 1766," Watts Papers, Vol. 5. For further information, see Philip Schuyler's testimony, A.O. 12/30, 126–127; "List of Sundry Farms in the second Nine Partners," Dutchess County Papers, Box 2, N.-Y. Hist. Soc.; "A List of Tenants on Lott No. 8 Belonging to Mrs. Margaret Philipse, 1768," Philipse-Gouverneur Family Papers, fol. 19, No. 159, Columbia University Library, New York; various leases in Schuyler Papers, Box 16, N.Y. Pub. Lib.; Munsell, ed., *Annals of Albany*, VII, 15–18, 20, 51, 53–55, 74–75, 80, VIII, 235, 248–249, 252, on Schaghticoke leases; and Gerlach, *Philip Schuyler*, 61. As early as 1744, the Fordham Manor rent was a shilling an acre. Hastings, ed., *Ecclesiastical Records of N.Y.*, IV, 2796, 2837.

129. Frederick Philipse to James Hunter, Feb. 7, 1760, Huguenot Hist. Assoc.; Halsey, ed., *Journal of Richard Smith*, 5.

130. John Sanders to Henry Jordice in London, Nov. 26, 1768, Letterbook of John Sanders.

must be valued." His statement can be verified by the data on wheat presented in figure 5.1 and further by a comparison of the prices, in New York currency, for such farm produce as flour, beef, and pork in the years 1739 and 1766. In 1739 the price for flour per bushel ranged from 8s. 9d. to 9s., while in 1766 it was 15s.; for beef per barrel, the 1739 price was from £1 15s. to £2, rising to £2 12s. in 1766; and for pork per barrel, the less dramatic increase was from £3 8s. in 1739 to £3 10s. in 1766.[131]

Yet it was the tenants in the southern manors, particularly Cortlandt Manor, with cash rent obligations who benefited most from the inflationary trend. The lease for a life or longer, once contracted, was not subject to alteration until the expiration of the term or unless the two contracting parties agreed. Robert Livingston, Jr., less generous than his father, Philip, and his relatives of the Clermont branch, occasionally increased the rent for new settlers without a formal deed and almost always did so upon the transfer of the lease by sale or on inheritance from father to son.[132] But this was not the case with the other manorial landlords. As tables 5.2, 5.3, and 5.4 show, the rates in Cortlandt Manor remained static from 1750 to 1769—a period of unprecedented inflation. Cortlandt Skinner, son of William and Elizabeth (Cortlandt) Skinner, testified in 1785 that his father had let his manor land at £2 per hundred acres in the 1730s to 1750s and that "the Tenants continued on the land at the same Rent" until he left North America in 1783.[133] The Beekmans, who were painfully aware of the upward trend of commodity prices but were unable to raise the rent on an already granted lease, sought to secure alternative rent rates for new leases for different periods: a lower rate for the first ten years and a higher one for the succeeding years. Thus

131. *N.-Y. Gaz.*, Oct. 29 to Nov. 26, 1739, and Jan. 7, 1766; Cadwallader Colden to earl of Halifax, Aug. 11, 1760, *Colden Letter Books*, I, 10; John Van Cortlandt to Archibald Armstrong, Nov. 4, 1772, Letterbook and Notebook of John Van Cortlandt, Van Cortlandt Family Papers, N.-Y. Hist. Soc.

132. Usually, the rate increase involved 2 to 5 bushels of wheat more than the original amount. See the cases of Philip Couchman, Semon Michel, Andries Lott, Jacob Musher, Coenraedt Ham, Christian Petrie, Johannis Rosman, John Van Tassel, Zachariah Proper, and Abraham Spikerman. Lease to Couchman, Mar. 26, 1771, Livingston-Redmond MSS, Roll 8; leases to Michel, Feb. 1, 1781, to Proper, Mar. 10, 1774, in Livingston Manor Papers, N.-Y. Hist. Soc.; Livingston Manor Rent Ledger, 1767–1784, 102, 60, 108, 5, 64, 123, 48, 80, 137, 57, 16, *ibid.*

133. A.O. 12/13, 37–38. There was no instance of rent increase for the Rensselaerswyck leases. One Jacob Lansing of the manor obtained a durable lease of 12 acres at the yearly rent of 12s. and a couple of hens in 1707. His descendants were paying the same rent in 1796. This is a typical example. See lease, Kiliaen Van Rensselaer to Jacob Lansing, May 1, 1707, Lansing Papers, Box 1, N.Y. State Lib.

Table 5.2.  The Beekmans' Tenants: Annual Rent and Size of Lease for
1752 and 1769, and Rent in Arrears as of 1769
(Rents in New York Currency)

| Name | Acreage | Rent in 1752 | Rent in 1769 | Rent in Arrears[a] as of 1769 |
|---|---|---|---|---|
| | | £  s.  d. | £  s. d. | £  s. d. |
| William Borden | 142 | | 3 10 0 | 26 18 0 |
| Joseph Budd | 220 | 3 10 0 | 3 10 0 | 30 10 0 |
| Mathew Bookhowt | 266 | 2 13 4 | 2 13 4 | ? |
| Jacob Cornell | 143 | 3 10 0 | 3 10 0 | 34 10 8 |
| Ebenezer Clark | 322 | | 4 10 0 | 22 10 0 |
| Amos Fuller | ? | | 4 10 0 | 27  0 0 |
| John Hyat or John Conklin | 331 | 4  5 0 | 4 10 0 | 22 10 0 |
| John Hyat, Jr. | 363 | | 4  5 0 | 3 15 0 |
| Nethenel Hyat | 319 | 3  6 0 | 3  6 0 | 10  7 7 |
| Joshua Hyat | 230 | | ? | ? |
| William Jewell | 266 | 2 13 4 | 2 13 4 | 7 10 0 |
| Jacobus Krankhyt | ? | | 4  0 0 | 56  0 0 |
| Sybout Krankhyt | 50 (plus mills) | | 8 15 0 | 9  0 0 |
| Joseph Lane | ? | | 4  0 0 | 16  0 0 |
| Daniel Lane | 319 | 3  6 0 | 3  6 0 | ? |
| Solomon Lane | 275 | | 3  6 0 | 1 13 0 |
| Lee Lee | ? | | 8  0 0 | 32  0 0 |
| Nathaniel Miller | ? | | 5  0 0 | 35  0 0 |
| Townsend Losse | 192 | | 5  0 0[b] | 30  0 0 |
| Jonathan Odell (Odel) | 300 | 4 10 0 | ? | ? |
| William Ogden | ? | | 5  0 0 | ? |
| Abraham Purdy | 156 | | 3  0 0 | 21  0 0 |
| Joseph Strang | ? | | 2  0 0 | 14  0 0 |
| Joseph Theall | ? | | 4  8 0 | |
| Charles Moore | 143 (plus mills) | | 13  0 0 | 65  0 0 |
| | | | 102  6 8 | 593 15 0 |

Sources:
Van Cortlandt Papers, 1700–1799, Box Miscellaneous Manuscripts, New-York His-
torical Society, New York; Van Cortlandt Papers, *passim*, Sleepy Hollow Restorations
Library, Tarrytown, N.Y.; Van Cortlandt-Van Wyck Papers, New York Public Library.

[a] The problem of arrears in rent is discussed below in this chapter.
[b] Losse received a new lease in 1772 with his rent decreased to £4 for the same premises.

Table 5.3.  The Schuylers' Tenants: Annual Rent and Size of Lease
for 1753 and 1768, and Rent in Arrears, 1768–1774
(Rents in New York Currency)

| Name | Acreage | Rent in 1753 | Rent in 1768 | Rent in Arrears[a] | |
|---|---|---|---|---|---|
| | | £ s. d. | £ s. d. | £ s. d. | as of |
| John Ketchum | 200 | 3 10 0 | 3 10 0 | 49 5 0 | 1773 |
| David Travis | 215 | 3 10 0 | 3 10 0 | 61 5 0 | 1774 |
| Aaron Forman | 206 | 3 10 0 | 3 10 0 | 49 0 0 | 1774 |
| Elisha Turner | 206 | 3 0 0 | 3 0 0 | 97 10 0 | 1774 |
| David Turner | 202 | 3 10 0 | 3 10 0 | 70 0 0 | 1768 |
| John Stevens | 206 | 3 10 0 | 3 10 0 | 72 0 0 | 1770 |
| Robert Galer | 190 | 3 0 0 | 3 0 0 | 42 2 0 | 1774 |
| James Perry | 217 | 2 10 0 | 2 10 0 | 40 0 0 | 1774 |
| Widow Gerow | 202 | 3 10 0 | 3 10 0 | 21 0 0 | 1774 |
| Bartow Underhill | 331 | 3 5 0 | 3 5 0 | 39 0 0 | 1774 |
| | | 32 15 0 | 32 15 0 | 540 2 0 | |

Sources:
Advertisement for the sale of land in Great North Lot No. 4 and Lot South of the
Croton No. 6, *New-York Gazette; and the Weekly Mercury*, Apr. 4, 1768; Schuyler Papers,
Box 10, 19, 23, New York Public Library.

[a] The problem of arrears in rent is discussed below.

in 1761 they provided in their lease to Ebenezer Clark that "£4. 10. 0
shall discharge the rent until 1770" and £5 10s. after that year. In
another lease, Abiel Fuller was to pay £4 until 1770 and £4 15s.
thereafter.[134] Perhaps this dual system was not adequate to insure profitable leasing for the landlords as long as they were not empowered to
raise rent upon the transfer of a lease whenever their interests dictated.[135]
The precautionary measure on the part of the Beekmans, however, was
an exception to the general practices of those landlords, including themselves, who gave life or longer tenure. It is obvious that tenants who held
leases for one, two, or three lives, or forever, and who paid cash rent,

134. Van Cortlandt Papers, V2199 and V2200, Sleepy Hollow Restorations Lib. The
rent adjustment was not always upward. Townsend Losse, a tenant of the Beekmans, for
example, agreed to pay £5 yearly for his lease of 192 acres in 1762. Later, however, he
complained that the rent was too high, and so the proprietor lowered it to £4 in 1772.
Lease, the Beekmans to Losse, Feb. 8, 1772, *ibid.*, V2204.
135. John Watts to Robert Watts, Apr. 10, 1786, Robert Watts Papers, Box 3.

gained doubly from the inflation, first by the mitigation of the rent and second by the increase in profits from marketing their produce.[136]

The position of tenants holding leases at will or for years, even if they paid cash rent, was a less enviable one, for their landlords could legally change the rates at any time; their ultimate defense against the landlords' authority was to quit the lease, a resort that neither they nor the proprietors cherished. The most notorious perpetrator of landlordism was John Van Cortlandt, son of Stephen Van Cortlandt of New Jersey. John, who let his father's land for only several-year terms or at sufferance, frequently raised the rent as soon as a lease expired or changed hands. Captain Annanias Rogers, who possessed two farms, was ordered to pay £10, £2 more than he had previously paid, after his original lease expired. In 1756 Andrew Merrit of Rye hired two farms at the annual rent of £4, £1 more than his predecessor had paid. Michael Mathew could secure in 1760 the renewal of his lease only after promising to pay £6 rent for a farm he had used for £3 for the past five years. John Soulice, who had hired a farm for the yearly rent of £3 10s. in 1754, was told in 1773 that if he wanted to keep it, he would have to pay £35 a year. These are but a few of many examples of rent hikes.[137]

Likewise, as table 5.4 shows, the Warrens raised rents for their tenants with both at-will and year-term leases twice from 1749 to 1775, the first time in 1770 and the second in 1774. The first increase in 1770 brought the rate per acre from the 5d. of 1749 to 1s. 6d., almost as high as the Livingston Manor rent. The second increase four years later resulted in the highest rent among the manors, 2s. per acre. Yet, these hikes did not provoke a mass desertion from the estate. This suggests either that the tenants, despite unprecedentedly high rents, considered the Warrens' lease practices tolerable or that they were prosperous enough to meet their rent obligations.

The Philipsburgh Manor proprietors seem to have leaned backward in handling this touchy rent problem. Just once in the history of the

---

136. Beverly Robinson, one of the proprietors of Philipse's Highland Patent, testified in 1783 that the rents of his tenants were payable in wheat, "but for Temporary Indulgence I took their Rents in Money." If he had demanded wheat from them, these rents, he boasted, "would have produced him £32 more than" his actual income (£99 13s.). Robinson's memorial, Dec. 11, 1783, A.O. 12/21, 158.

137. Receipt Books of John Van Cortlandt, 1757–1762 and 1766–1771, passim, N.-Y. Hist. Soc. Of all the manorial landlords I have studied, John Van Cortlandt fits best the image of the 18th-century Northern Irish landlords who racked their impoverished peasants. "A letter from Ireland," in N.-Y. Gaz., Nov. 3, 1729; "Extract of a Letter from Newry, in Ireland, March 31, 1772," in N.-Y. Gaz.; and Wkly. Mercury, May 25, 1772.

Table 5.4. The Warrens' Land: Annual Rent and Size of Lease,
1749, 1770, and 1774
(Rents in New York Currency)

| Acreage | | Rent in 1749 | Rent in 1770 | Rent in 1774 |
|---|---|---|---|---|
| | | £ s. d. | £ s. d. | £ s. d. |
| **SOUTH LOT FIVE** | | | | |
| Lot 1 | 211 acres | 3  5 0 | 15  6 0 | 15  6 6 |
| 2 | 196 | 4 10 0 | 17  6 6 | 17  6 6 |
| 3 | 227 | 4 10 0 | 15  0 6 | 15  0 6 |
| 4 | 198 | 3 10 0 | 19 16 0 | 19 16 0 |
| 5 | 210 | 4  0 0 | 12 11 0 | 12 11 0 |
| 6 | 174½ | 4 10 0 | 14 10 1½ [a] | 22 10 0 |
| 7 | 203½ | 3 10 0 | 15  5 3 | 15  5 3 |
| 8 | 180¼ | 3 10 0 | 11  0 0 | 23  0 0? |
| 9 | 180¼ | 4 10 0 | 13 10 4½ | 13 10 4½ |
| 10 | 203 | 3 15 0 | 15  5 3 | 15  5 3 |
| 11 | 160½ | 3  0 0 | 12  0 2 | 29  5 9 |
| 12 | 119¼ | 3  0 0 | —— | —— |
| 13 | 105 | 3 15 0 | 7 17 6 | 7 17 6 |
| 14 | 390½ | 3 10 0 | 29  6 6 | 29  5 6 |
| 15 | 341 | 3 10 0 | 22  2 3 | 23  1 0 |
| **FRONT LOT SIX** | | | | |
| Lots 1 and 2 | 279½ | 7  0 0 | 25  0 0 | 32  0 0 |
| Lots 3 and 4 | 242½ | —— | 12  2 6 | 15  0 0 |
| **LOT NINE** | | | | |
| Lot 1 | 136 | 12  0 0 | 13 19 0 | 20  0 0 |
| 2 and 6 | 220 | 6  0 0 | 8  0 0 | 8  0 0 |
| 3 | 233 | 6  0 0 | 17  9 6 | 21  0 0 |
| 4 | 234 | 6  0 0 | 17 10 0 | 17 10 0 |
| 5 | 112 | —— | 8  5 0 | 33  6 0 |
| | 4557½ | 93  5 0 | 323  3 5 | 405 17 1½ |

Sources:
Receipt Book and Account Book of Pierre Van Cortlandt, V1644, V2301, and V1689, Sleepy Hollow Restorations Library, Tarrytown, N.Y.; Gage Papers, G/Am/82, G/Am/89, G/Am/142, G/Am/158, G/Am/170, G/Am/192, *ibid.* (microfilm of the originals at Sussex Archaeological Society, Lewes, Sussex, England); Julian Gwyn, *The Enterprising Admiral: The Personal Fortune of Admiral Sir Peter Warren* (Montreal, 1974), 53.

[a]From the mid-1750s, lots 6 and 12 were leased together.

manor did its landlord exercise his power to raise rents, and he did so only when galloping inflation in the 1750s, fueled by the rampant issuance of paper money, drastically reduced his rental income.[138] Frederick Philipse III spent a great deal of time in persuading his tenants at will of the rationale for a modest rent increase. He finally succeeded in 1760 by pledging that he would not "for the future raise [their] rent."[139] Here one cannot fail to see that the landlord invoked his power with moderation and restraint. Despite the incidence of rent increases, those farmers "at will" and "for years" who contracted leases prior to 1750 and stayed on the farm were able to partake of the benefits of the economic expansion in future years, although their gain was not as much as that of the tenants with a steady tenure.

Attention has so far been centered on the main part of the rent obligations of tenants. In addition, many were obliged to pay two other kinds of rent, namely, fowl, commonly live fat hens, and labor service (the corvée), called the "riding." Without doubt, these were legacies from the feudal past. Again, the picture is complicated and hazy, making sweeping generalizations difficult. Quite a few landlords, among them Frederick Philipse III, Robert Livingston (the founder of Livingston Manor), Philip, Stephen, and John Van Cortlandt of New York, the Skinners, the Schuylers, and the De Lanceys (including the Warrens and Watts), did not follow these old customs.[140] Nor did Kiliaen Van Rensselaer, son of Maria, insert a work requirement in leases until 1707, even though he generally demanded the fowl. The new levy was not retroactive for the old tenants.[141] Moreover, some landlords did not apply these duties uniformly to every lessee. An examination of eight leases granted by

---

138. The propertied class generally entertained apprehensions about the depreciation of the value of currency due to the issuance of paper money. See, for example, Gulian Verplanck's will, July 5, 1750, Gulian Verplanck Papers, Box 8.

139. Frederick Philipse to James Hunter, Feb. 7, 1760, Huguenot Hist. Assoc.; testimonies by Beverly Robinson, James De Lancey, and John Tabor Kempe, Dec. 1784, A.O. 12/19, 393, 398, 403.

140. Robert Livingston's lease to Andrew Gardner, Mar. 25, 1708, Livingston-Redmond MSS, Roll 3; "The Estate of Cornelia Schuyler in acct with Philip Schuyler, 1763–1787," Schuyler Papers, Box 10, N.Y. Pub. Lib.; "Observation" on the case of Frederick Philipse, 1786, A.O. 12/88, 87; Kim, "Manor of Cortlandt," chap. 5.

141. As for the Rensselaerswyck practice before 1707 in this matter, see deeds to Margaret Schuyler in 1689, to Gerrit Teunissen Van Vechten in 1694, and to Volkert Van Vechten in 1705, Deed Book 5: 51–54, 69–70, 146, Albany Co. Clerk's Office; "A list of Indentures, 1696–1744," in Rensselaerswyck MSS. Adding the work provision to the fowls began with Jeronimus Barheyt. Deed to Barheyt, Apr. 15, 1707, Deed Book 5: 40–41, Albany Co. Clerk's Office; deed to Marten Martense Van Alstyn, Aug. 9, 1707, Drawer 1, Albany Inst. of Hist. and Art.

Henry Van Rensselaer of Claverack from 1709 to 1718 indicates that two tenants were required only to pay two and a half schepels of wheat in lieu of the work, in addition to the one-tenth rent; one tenant only chickens; three tenants both wheat substitute and chickens; and two tenants nothing except the main rent. His son John even did away with the wheat substitute for the riding, while keeping the fowl requirement for some of his tenants.[142]

This chaotic example is duplicated in the other manors. Eleven out of 37 agricultural tenants under the Beekmans from 1768 to 1775 enjoyed complete immunity from the supplementary obligations.[143] Of the Rensselaerswyck (proper) tenants who contracted indentures between 1707 and 1744, 10 out of 45 were exempt from the riding. The discriminatory favor seems to have been granted to those who held a relatively high political or economic status in the local community. For instance, Colonel Peter Schuyler, former mayor and one of the most prestigious personalities of Albany, Edward Collins, a noted surveyor, and Captain John Schuyler, a large landholder and Indian trader, all were to pay the fowl but not the work, the performance of which they perhaps considered beneath their station. By the same token, such Beekman tenants as Pierre Van Cortlandt, nephew of the Beekmans, Gilbert Drake, a wealthy merchant and gristmill operator, John Keating, a merchant of New York City, and Isaac Frost, who leased an unusually large tract of 385 acres, did not suffer the "feudal" exactions.[144] Furthermore, tenants working in service industries like milling, tailoring, and shoemaking and those holding a lease for residential and commercial purposes all enjoyed the exemptions, particularly from the work. In Rensselaerswyck, the only additional assignment for tenants in possession of small homesteads and

142. Deed Book 5: 82, 104, 130, 132, 424, Deed Book 6: 104–106, 423–425, Deed Book 8: 334, 386, and Deed Book 10: 98–99, 116–118, Albany Co. Clerk's Office; leases to Casper L. Conyn, Jan. 7, 1715, and to Hendrick Anderson, Sept. 16, 1752, Van Rensselaer-Fort Papers; lease to Henry Cuyler, Apr. 26, 1766, Harmanus Bleecker Papers, Box 2.

143. "List of Tennants in the Manor of C. of Col. Henry Beekman and Wife to May 1769," and lease to John Keating, July 12, 1770, Cortlandt Manor Papers, both in Van Cortlandt Family Papers, N.-Y. Hist. Soc.; Van Cortlandt Papers, V2204, V2205, V2206, V2207, V2208, V2209, V2188, V2190, V2003, Sleepy Hollow Restorations Lib. At least five tenants who took leases from the Beekmans in 1737 were given special treatment, in that "the day's work yearly as mentioned here . . . shall not be accounted for unless it be yearly demanded." This was a conditional exemption, but it is doubtful that the landlord ever demanded it. See Van Cortlandt Papers, V2189, V2198, V2194, V1942, *ibid.*; lease to Dannel De Lamonex, Mar. 25, 1737, Van Cortlandt-Van Wyck Papers.

144. "A list of Indentures, 1696–1744," Rensselaerswyck MSS.

commercial lots along the road from Albany to Watervliet was to "keep the road in repair."[145]

The Livingstons were by far the most consistent in sustaining both customs. Of 479 agricultural tenants listed in the Livingston Manor (proper) rent ledger covering the period from 1766 to 1783, only 8 were exempt from both the work and the fowl requirements, 8 more were exempt only from the former, and one was exempt from the fowl rent alone. The overwhelming majority (384) of its lessees were encumbered by payments of four "live fat hens" and two days' riding "with a waggon, sled or plow and an able Man to drive, with Horses or Oxen," while 75 were subject to the four hens and one day's work. The lighter burden was assigned to those tenants holding less than 60 acres, substantially below the average farm (84 acres) in the manor. The same special treatment was given to three tenants who paid their main rent in flour casks, which the manor landlord in the flour export business very much appreciated.[146] The Clermont record was no better. Out of its 47 tenants as of 1756, only 2 were excused from the supplementary obligations.[147] Why and how these few farmers obtained the rare favor is difficult to answer, but it seems to have had little to do with their economic or political status, contrary to the case with some of the Beekman and Rensselaerswyck tenants. As far as the immunity from the corvée was concerned, it was probably due to either of the following reasons: the leaseholder was a widow or an old man physically unfit for arduous labor, or he was a farmer with a small lease of 30 or 40 acres who, in the opinion of tenant and landlord alike, could not be burdened by the extra charges.[148]

Generally speaking, four hens and one day's work was the standard

145. Leases from Philip Livingston to Epharim Goes, May 9, 1734, and to Evert Evertse, May 1, 1732, Livingston-Redmond MSS, Roll 6; lease, the Beekmans to Jury Brewer, May 1, 1747, Van Cortlandt Papers, V1960, Sleepy Hollow Restorations Lib.; lease, the Beekmans to Caleb Barton, May 1, 1757, Van Cortlandt-Van Wyck Papers. From 1700 to 1744, 34 Rensselaerswyck tenants were nonagricultural. "A list of Indentures, 1696–1744," Rensselaerswyck MSS. See also "A Acct of My Rents, 1st May 1756," "Uncatalogued Livingston MSS," and Livingston Manor Rent Ledger, 1767–1784, *passim*, N.-Y. Hist. Soc.

146. For typical work provisions, see lease, Robert Livingston, Jr., to Broer Decker, Apr. 5, 1765, Livingston Manor Papers, N.-Y. Hist. Soc.; lease to Cornelius Brusie, June 1, 1752, Livingston-Redmond MSS, Roll 7. For Philip Livingston's work policy, see lease to Peter Cool, Mar. 30, 1732, Morristown Hist. Park Coll., Roll 32. For the payment in flour casks, see entries of Abraham, Petrus, Adam Shuts, and Simon Shuts, Livingston Manor Rent Ledger, 1767–1784, 47, 71, 77, 120.

147. "A Acct of My Rents, 1st May 1756," "Uncatalogued Livingston MSS."

148. Elizabeth Shaver paid only £3 rent yearly, and Jacobus Decker, who had a small acreage, paid only 7½ bushels of wheat. Livingston Manor Rent Ledger, 1767–1784.

exaction in Rensselaerswyck proper, Clermont, and some parts of Cort-landt Manor under the Beekmans, the Verplancks, and the Bayards.[149] The landlords allowed tenants either to commute or to substitute other means for these obligations. Even here, Robert Livingston, Jr. (son of Philip), was the least liberal. His commutation fee was 9s. in the 1760s and 12s. in the 1770s for each day of work and a schepel of wheat (worth 6s.) in 1782 for four hens. The Beekmans charged 7s. for the work and 4s. for four hens throughout the period from 1737 to 1782.[150]

Finally, different landlords applied the riding to different uses. The most common one was road repairing. Before 1740 one of the pressing concerns of the Livingston Manor proprietors was expanding and im-proving the primitive roads that Robert Livingston had opened at the turn of the eighteenth century.[151] The provincial government had enacted the first highway act in 1703, directing "respective owners of the Severall Townships Mannors and Lands" to lay out and keep in repair the so-called Kings Highways if and when the projected highways ran by and through their jurisdiction. In the years following, a series of laws with more detailed and specific procedures and plans for highways and back-roads were enacted. Two of these laws, one in 1721 and the other in 1723, ordered the manor inhabitants to repair twice a year (May and October) not only the "General Kings Highway" (the Albany Post Road), with a breadth of four rods, but also "the other Kings Roads," twenty feet broad.[152] This legislative action, inspired by Robert Livingston, the speaker of the General Assembly, enabled him to utilize his tenant labor

149. For the practices of the Verplancks and Bayards, see leases, Samuel Bayard to Philip Linnebeker and Peter Win, 1732, Bayard-Campbell-Pearsall Colls.; lease, Philip Ver-planck to Benjamin Field, 1742, Philip Verplanck Papers, N.Y. Gen. and Biog. Soc.

150. Leases, Robert Livingston, Jr., to John Coenrat Meyer, Apr. 12, 1764, to Lucius Reynolds, Oct. 23, 1765, and to Adam Shuts, Feb. 28, 1770, Livingston-Redmond MSS, Rolls 7 and 8; lease, the Beekmans to Jesse Weeks, Mar. 16, 1775, and Silvanus Hyat's account with the heirs of Gertrude Beekman, 1782, Van Cortlandt Papers, V2190 and V1931, Sleepy Hollow Restorations Lib. In Clermont tenants could pay 2 bushels of wheat for one day's riding. According to the account of rents in 1756, it was commuted at the rate of 6s. Robert Livingston, Jr., of Clermont, to William Snyder, Sept. 8, 1737, and "A Acct of My Rents, 1st May 1756," in "Uncatalogued Livingston MSS." John C. Wagenaer of Livingston paid a certain amount of ashes for 2 days' riding, and Johannis Strevel of the same place transported pig iron for the fowl requirement. Johannes J. Witbeck of Rensse-laerswyck offered geese instead of hens. Livingston Manor Rent Ledger, 1767–1784, 36, 124; Rensselaerswyck Rent Ledger, 1768–1789, 141, Rensselaerswyck MSS. The Living-ston Manor commutation fee for the day work was the same wage rate allowed for that kind of work in the province. See the advertisement by G. Christie in N.-Y. Mercury, June 5, 1758.

151. Deposition of Robert Van Deusen of Claverack, June 13, 1711, Columbia Co. Misc. MSS, N.-Y. Hist. Soc.

152. N.Y. Col. Laws, I, 532–538, 587–588, 795–797, II, 68–78, 156–162.

to develop his estate at no cost to himself. It was probably his reliance on the provincial laws alone to accomplish road work that accounts for the absence of the riding obligation in a lease he granted to Andrew Gardner in 1708.[153] His sons, Philip of the manor proper and Robert, Jr., of Clermont, and his grandchildren, Robert, Jr., and Robert R., however, introduced a manorial counterpart to the provincial highway work requirement by inserting in each individual lease a service provision. This change seems to have occurred because the 1723 law had expired in 1729 and was not renewed until 1742.[154] The nature of the riding was never spelled out in the lease deeds, except that it was for the benefit of the lessor, but there is no question that it was used for road work. In one highly revealing contract of 1737 between Robert Livingston, Jr., of Clermont and his tenant William Snyder, the landlord certified that "as long as" he used the road through Snyder's land, the tenant would be discharged from the "days Riding."[155] But the rent ledger of Livingston Manor proper from 1768 to 1789 shows that its proprietor increasingly diverted some residual work obligations to other purposes. The tenants were ordered to cart firewood, timber, stones, coals, wood, iron ore, and finished iron products to and from forges and foundries at Ancram, Sober, and Maryburgh, and to split and saw logs at the plants. They also worked at one of several manor mills and on the landlord's own demesne.[156]

The lack of evidence about the Van Cortlandt proprietors, namely, the Beekmans, the Bayards, and the Verplancks, makes it impossible to know their use of tenant service, but road repairing was probably the main demand.[157] The proprietors of upper Rensselaerswyck explicitly demanded from the farm tenants work involving the transportation of wood on a wagon or sled driven by two horses, and they required other residents—homesteaders, craftsmen, and those employed in service industries—to repair the road fronting their respective lots. Significantly, the introduction of the corvée for the farm tenants coincided with the time when Kiliaen Van Rensselaer began intensively exploiting the lum-

---

153. Lease to A. Gardner, Mar. 25, 1708, Livingston-Redmond MSS, Roll 3.
154. *N.Y. Col. Laws*, II, 262–270.
155. Lease to W. Snyder, Sept. 8, 1737, "Uncatalogued Livingston MSS."
156. Livingston Manor Rent Ledger, 1767–1784, particularly 14, 36, 68, 69, 80, 92, 107, 119, 136, 148.
157. The Beekman leases, all in print, provided that the obligees were to work "in Such Manner, and at Such Time, and Place" within a certain distance—most commonly 7 miles or rarely 12 miles—of the demised premises as the landlord should direct. Van Cortlandt Papers, V1942 and V2194, Sleepy Hollow Restorations Lib.; lease, the Beekmans to Daniel Field, Dec. 30, 1737, Van Cortlandt Family Papers, N.-Y. Hist. Soc.

ber resources in his domain. According to rent accounts of the manor covering the periods from 1719 to 1744 and from 1749 to 1771, the obligees carried, always off-season, logs, posts, stakes, and wood to designated places.[158]

Considering the pressing shortage of labor in the province, the utilization of tenants by the Van Rensselaers and the Livingstons for purposes other than road work was a clever economic move. The Rensselaerswyck proprietors took care of the manor roads by relying on the provincial highway legislation, which required all the inhabitants to expend each year up to six days' labor for a man without a vehicle or three days with a wagon or sled.[159] Why the second- and third-generation Livingstons and some Cortlandt Manor proprietors did not emulate the Rensselaerswyck example is a mystery. Still, one or two days' road work as demanded by some manorial landlords was hardly onerous compared with the demands imposed by other freehold townships in the province. When the tenants' personal service was used solely for the advantage of the landlord rather than the community as a whole, it could be considered a degrading custom, at least psychologically. Nevertheless, no protest was heard from the farmers against this "feudal" part of the lease system throughout the colonial period, even at the height of the antilandlord riots in the 1750s and 1760s.[160]

The story of rent on the New York manors would not be complete without an examination of actual rent collection, for what the landlords could demand in writing was not the same as what they could command in practice. Defaults in rent payment were most serious on plantations owned by absentee proprietors. Sir Peter Warren, a son-in-law of Stephen De Lancey and owner of about 5,300 acres in Cortlandt Manor, was so afflicted with dilatory tenants that in writing to his brother-in-law and agent Oliver De Lancey in 1750, he was fearful about the future of his estate: " I wrote to you several times about the Rent of the Lands in the Mannor of Cortlandt, which by the Tennants own Concent so long ago as when I was at N. York amounted to near £100 per annum. Surely something ought to be done or Else they will think the Lands their own in

---

158. Rensselaerswyck Rent Ledger, 1719–1744, 1748–1756, and "Het Tiende (Tithes) Book Beginnende 8 ste Febuy, 1758–[1771]," in Rensselaerswyck MSS.

159. N.Y. Col. Laws, I, 795, 797, II, 68–76, 156–162, III, 262–270, IV, 509–510, 1050–1052, V, 374–375, 462–476, 793–801.

160. During the tenant rebellion in Rensselaerswyck Manor in the 1840s, the rebel farmers complained about this aspect of leaseholding as degrading. But such a complaint in an age of egalitarianism is more to be expected. It cannot tell us much about pre-Revolutionary attitudes.

time."[161] De Lancey did everything—"threatnings and perswasions"—short of taking legal action against the tenants in order to force them to pay rents, but it "has had no Effect on Most of them." In explaining to his sister Susannah Warren his "Excessive Trouble" with them, De Lancey wrote on one occasion that "the Fellows that Sr Peter put on Your Lands in Cortlands Mannor . . . are [except a few] of the very worst sort."[162] Records show that in the six years from 1753 to 1758, the agent could collect only about one-fifth of the rents owed to the landlord. Finally, De Lancey, after consultation with his sister, made Pierre Van Cortlandt, who was a resident proprietor, the Warren family agent in the manor in 1758. Thereafter, the situation greatly improved.[163]

The Schuylers, the Beekmans, and John Van Cortlandt experienced difficulties similar to those of the Warrens. All three had agents collecting their rents and supervising the performance of the tenants. The Schuylers retained their cousins the Verplancks as agents, while the Beekmans and John Van Cortlandt employed tenants for the job. As table 5.2 demonstrates, the Beekmans' yearly receivable cash rental was, without counting two tenants whose rents were to be adjusted by their agent, approximately £102 6s. 8d., but back rents as of 1769 had grown to £465 4s. 3d. This means that on the average each tenant had neglected to pay for more than four and a half years. Yet this backlog was mild compared with the performance of the annual work requirement. Of the 25 Beekman tenants who were supposed to render one day's service yearly, 13 had a backlog of 93 days of work; each tenant had somehow evaded the service rent for roughly seven years. The same was true of the fowl requirement. Such tenants as Nathaniel Miller, William Borden, Jacobus Krankhyt, and Ebenezer Clark paid neither cash rent nor the other dues from the very inception of their leases.[164] Still worse were the Schuyler

---

161. Peter Warren to Oliver De Lancey, Aug. 11, 1750, Warren Papers.

162. Oliver De Lancey to Susannah Warren, July 20, 1754, Dec. 20, 1755, and Oct. 4, 1757, Gage Papers, Additional MS 1201.

163. Rent accounts, 1753–1762, ibid., G/Am/82; rent rolls of Oliver and Stephen De Lancey, 1756–1773, and also deed, power of attorney from Oliver De Lancey to Pierre Van Cortlandt, May 10, 1758, Van Cortlandt Papers, V1644, Sleepy Hollow Restorations Lib.; Receipt Book of Pierre Van Cortlandt, 1738–1759, 1760–1766, ibid., V1689; Account Book of Pierre Van Cortlandt, 1762–1763, ibid., V2301. See also the 1771–1775 accounts, Gage Papers, G/Am/129. Prof. Julian Gwyn of the University of Ottawa informed me that "the Warren estate throughout New York at best managed to collect 75% of the rent due, with the average closer to 60%, while a bad year would bring in less than half."

164. "List of Tennants in the Manor of C," Van Cortlandt Family Papers, N.-Y. Hist. Soc. Beekman was also lax in rent collection on his Dutchess County estate. Henry Beekman to Henry Livingston, Dec. 19, 1744, Jan. 7, 1745, and Nov. 7, 1752, Beekman Papers, ibid.

tenants, whose roster by 1774 had shrunk to only ten (see table 5.3). The Schuylers' annual rental income from the manor should have been £32 15s. However, rental payments were over £540 in arrears, which suggests that the Schuylers had not received a farthing from their land for the equivalent of sixteen years! John Van Cortlandt fared no better. The lease tenure of his tenants was short and so were their arrears in rent. But judging from his letters to tenants and his receipt book, peppered with pungent threats warning them to pay their back rent, it is not hard to visualize how uncooperative they were, even though the sources do not yield exact figures on the matter.

The rent collection problem was by no means peculiar to the absentee proprietors. In the early 1750s William Smith, Jr., speaking of Rensselaerswyck and Livingston Manor, which were under the direct supervision of a landlord, stated that rent on these manors "has as yet been neither exacted nor paid."[165] His view, undoubtedly based on rumor, was generally correct according to the pre-1760 records of Rensselaerswyck proper, though the same cannot be said for Livingston Manor. The fairly complete Rensselaerswyck rent ledgers reveal that about three-fifths of its some hundred tenants were chronically delinquent in any given year during the period from 1725 to 1760.[166] In light of this widespread delinquency, it is difficult to believe that the tenants were even conscientious enough to render the tithe rent of one-tenth of their yearly produce as required. Johannis Volckenburgh, a tenant who appears at least on record from 1719 to 1754 to have been unusually punctual, still left as of 1776 arrears of £70, a sum that was probably adequate to cover the preceding twenty years.[167] Jonas Outhout, who held a lease farm called "Turkys" near Cohoes Falls beginning in 1740, as well as other land, was another dilatory tenant. His back rent had piled up so much that in July 1769 Stephen Van Rensselaer II warned him to settle "the many years rent . . . within Eight or Ten days at farthest." Three years later Outhout paid £57, but he owed the landlord still more. It should be noted that

165. Smith, [Jr.], History of New-York (1757 ed.), 199.
166. My estimation of the number of the Rensselaerswyck tenants is based on the following sources: "A list of Indentures, 1696–1744," Rensselaerswyck MSS; N.Y. Col. MSS, XLII, 34, LIX, 19. For those tenants who paid rents, see Rensselaerswyck Rent Ledgers, 1719–1744, 1749–1756, and Book of Tithes, 1758–[1771], all in Rensselaerswyck MSS.
167. See entries on Johannis Volckenburgh in Rensselaerswyck Rent Ledgers, 1719–1744, 1749–1756, Rensselaerswyck MSS; Rensselaerswyck Rent Ledger, 1768–1789, 51, ibid. In 1776 he and his brother Abraham sold their improvements.

these were by no means exceptional cases.[168] Nevertheless, the Van Rensselaers, as a post-Revolutionary put it, "have seldom been reduced"
to take forcible action, such as distressing the defaulters' goods to the
amount of rent due.[169]

Only after the French and Indian War did the situation at Rensselaerswyck radically improve. In the period from 1764 to 1770, the wheat
rent that the patroon collected quadrupled from that of the previous
years, from 350 to 1,251 schepels a year (see figure 5.2). One possible
cause of this change was the expansion of the manor tenantry from 82 in
1712 to about 500 in 1767.[170] Yet, it is doubtful that a large influx of new
settlers into hitherto uninhabited areas like Stephentown and Philipstown near the Massachusetts border and Hellebergh escarpment in the
west had so much impact on the rental volume, for newcomers in this
wilderness were all given some rent-free years. A more important reason
was an unprecedented effort on the part of the proprietor to collect the
rents. Apart from being tired of derelict tenants, he probably began to
realize a dire consequence of his traditional indulgence: the longer he put
off collecting the rents, the harder their collection would become.[171] In
the past his casual attitude toward rent collection had been due to his
generous character, plus the shrewd calculation that he could hold the
tenants' valuable improvements as security for rent. But he now wanted
to avoid, if he could, situations in which he could become involved in
rancorous arguments or costly litigation with his tenants over arrears.

One sure sign of the patroon's determination to collect rents was his
substitution in 1764 of a fixed amount of wheat rent for the old tithe
rent. The new rent policy, which was part of an overall tightening of lease

168. Will of Hendrick (father of Jonas) Outhout, Oct. 11, 1738, Wills, XIII, 363–365,
Queens College Lib.; Stephen Van Rensselaer II to Jonas Outhout, July 25, 1769, Letters
of Abraham Ten Broeck, 1753–1783, and entry on Jonas Outhout, Abraham Ten Broeck's
Accounts of the Manor, 1763–1787, both in Rensselaerswyck MSS. For further informa-
tion on the tenant delinquency, see the cases of Johannes and Peter Cluet, Richard O'Neal,
Stephen Colhamers, Gerrit Seager, Jr., Johannes Salsbury, Coenradt Quant, Hendrick
Cramer, Jan Outhout, Hans J. Gerngross, Molborn Van Hoesen, Baltis Kemble, Stephanus
Kolhamen, and William Magin, Rensselaerswyck Rent Ledger, 1768–1789, ibid.

169. Copy of a letter to be addressed to the tenants, in Stephen Van Rensselaer III to
Abraham Ten Broeck, Feb. 1, 1786, Ten Broeck Family Papers, Box 1, Albany Inst. of Hist.
and Art.

170. "A Acct of the Taxes for People in the City and County Albany Jany 1767 and the
Quotas in the year 1768," Schuyler Papers, Box 18.

171. Henry Beekman asked his agent in Dutchess County to convey the following
advice to his delinquent tenants: "The Longer they Delay the further they git in Debt."
Other colonial landlords must have learned the same lesson. Henry Beekman to Gilbert
Livingston, Jan. 7, 1746, Beekman Papers, N.-Y. Hist. Soc.

Figure 5.2. The Rental Return for Rensselaerswyck (Proper) in Wheat
and Hens, 1725–1770
(Wheat in Schepels)

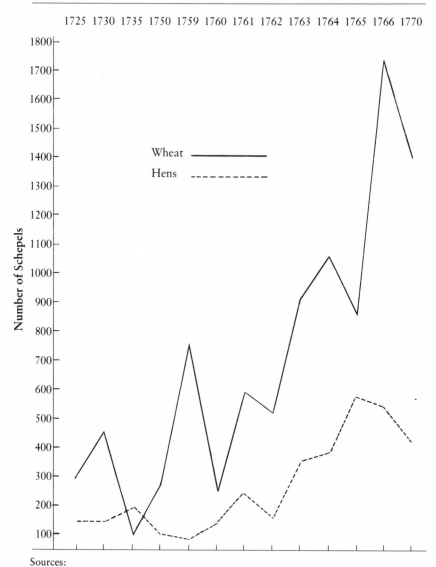

Sources:
    Rensselaerswyck Rent Ledger, 1719–1744, 1748–1756, and Book of Tithes, 1758–
[1771], both in Rensselaerswyck Manuscripts, New York State Library.

arrangements, aimed at the elimination of the managerial task of converting a vague one-tenth of the produce into a concrete figure of bushels and schepels.[172] In fact, the computation of the tithe had often been the occasion of exasperating wrangling between the landlord and tenants, and the task was particularly messy when the rent had been unpaid for many years and records were fragmentary or nonexistent. Coupled with this reform was the increasing pressure, mostly in the form of warnings, that Stephen Van Rensselaer II and, after his death (1769), the executors of his estate, brought to bear upon tenants to pay their dues. It appears from Abraham Ten Broeck's accounts of Rensselaerswyck that Ten Broeck and Philip Livingston, both executors, were more successful than the patroon in collecting back rents, presumably because they took quite seriously their responsibility as administrators of the estate during Stephen III's adolescence and especially because they were hard pressed to obtain funds for cash legacies (at least £3,000) for various heirs as provided by the will of the deceased.[173] As temporary custodians and trustees of the estate, they could afford to be exacting with the tenants. Whenever criticisms of their high-handedness arose, they could find refuge in the dead man's will by pointing out that they were simply performing the responsibility entrusted to them.

In sharp contrast to what is shown in the records of Cortlandt and Rensselaerswyck, the tenants in Livingston Manor (proper) and Philipsburgh seem to have been fairly punctual in meeting their rental obligations.[174] Notwithstanding William Smith, Jr.'s, assertion, Philip Livingston was not only impatient with dilatory tenants but also quite good at compelling them to pay their wheat rent, upon which his export trade

172. Stephen Van Rensselaer II to Isaac Ostrander, Mar. 26, 1768, Deed Book 10: 151, Albany Co. Clerk's Office.

173. Abraham Ten Broeck's Accounts of the Manor, 1763–1787, Rensselaerswyck MSS; Stephen Van Rensselaer II's will, Aug. 30, 1769, Wills, XXIX, 508, Queens College Lib.; Abraham Ten Broeck(?) to Kiliaen Van Rensselaer, May 14, 1771, to Philip Livingston, Oct. 26, 1776, to Abiather Angle, Jan. 15, 1782, and to John T. Visscher, Nov. 26, 1782, William Russell to Ten Broeck, Feb. 8, 1782, and Van Rensselaer's agent to Ten Broeck, Nov. 2, 1781, in Letterbook of Abraham Ten Broeck, 1753–1783 and Letters, 1767–1794, both in Rensselaerswyck MSS.

174. For the Philipsburgh rental situation, I have relied on Frederick Philipse III's testimony in 1784 that the rent had been "very regularly paid him every year." In the absence of contrary evidence, I have no reason to doubt the veracity of this statement, particularly in view of the fact that a large number of Philipse's tenants (about one-fourth of the 287 tenants) faithfully paid their rents during the Revolution to the absentee loyalist proprietor even when the manor itself became a battleground between the opposing armies and most of its farms were deserted. A.O. 12/19, 389; accounts of rents received, 1777 and 1778, Philipse Papers, PA822–823, Sleepy Hollow Restorations Lib.; "An Estimate of the Losses," ibid., PA808, ibid.

largely depended. Though rent records during his proprietorship (1728–1749) are not extant, his correspondence with his manor clerk John D'Witt contains evidence that supports this assessment. In early 1741 he wrote approvingly of D'Witt's management of the plantation: "I wish you may gett in the Remainder. Here are two letters for the Decker's father and son." On another occasion, he wrote, "Pray gett in the Rents ... who are in arrear must expect to have it strainted [distrained?] ... wherefore please to warn by advertisement."[175]

His son Robert, Jr., was also fairly successful in this regard. Data gleaned from the complete rent ledger of Livingston Manor for the period from 1767 to 1774 indicate that the rates of collection varied from one kind of rent to another and from year to year (see table 5.5). In 1767 the landlord could collect only half of the wheat rent and most of the work rent. In the following year he collected most of the wheat rent and less than half of the work rent, neatly reversing the pattern of the previous year. Despite this irregularity in tenant behavior, he could boast of a return of 75.3 percent of the total rents due from 1767 to 1774. Furthermore, the same source reveals an interesting pattern: the poor rental income one year was always followed by a good income the next.[176] This zigzag fluctuation was too constant to be explained in terms of either accident or harvest conditions, which accounted for only the main portion of the rent in both wheat and cash. A more plausible explanation would be that the landlord was willing to indulge some of the tenants one year but was determined to enforce the next.

Many tenants, it seems, would meet their rent responsibilities only if goaded and pressured.[177] Rent default was inherent in the nature of the leasehold system, and a tenant's conscientious fulfillment of his obligation was more an exception than the norm. If a tenant had reasonable assurance that he could get away with nonpayment, he would take advantage of it. In this respect, the poorest tenant was no different from the wealthiest landlord who owed a quitrent or other taxes, for the rich colonial landowners were often remiss in the regular payment of the quit-

175. Philip Livingston to John D'Witt, Mar. 6, 1741, and July 14, 1740, Livingston-Redmond MSS, Roll 9.
176. About one-fourth of the Livingston Manor tenants did not miss a single year's payment during the period under consideration.
177. It is impossible to assess the overall rental performance in the Clermont part of the manor because of the unavailability of its rent ledger, but some scattered evidence suggests that two- to five-year back rents were not uncommon. Robert R. Livingston to Joseph Catchan, May 6, 1770, "Uncatalogued Livingston MSS"; entries on Nicholas Low and Jacob Free, Livingston Account Book, Clermont, 1772–1784.

Table 5.5. Expected and Actual Rent Performance in Livingston Manor, 1767–1774
(Wheat in Schepels, Work in Days, and Cash in Pounds New York Currency)

| Year | Number of Tenants | Schepels of Wheat | | | Hens | | | Days of Work | | | Cash (£) | | | Overall Performance (%) |
|---|---|---|---|---|---|---|---|---|---|---|---|---|---|---|
| | | Expected | Actual | % | Expected | Actual | % | Expected | Actual | % | Expected | Actual | % | |
| 1767 | 266 | 5,058 | 2,696 | 53.3 | 1,000 | 829 | 82.9 | 432 | 359¾ | 83.1 | 111.06 | 85.15 | 76.5 | 73.9 |
| 1768 | 285 | 5,319 | 4,783¾ | 89.9 | 1,008 | 650 | 64.4 | 447 | 190 | 42.5 | 178.11 | 128.00 | 71.9 | 67.1 |
| 1769 | 295 | 5,565 | 4,508 | 81.0 | 1,166 | 999 | 85.6 | 469 | 557½ | 118.0 | 191.11 | 122.00 | 64.0 | 87.1 |
| 1770 | 294 | 5,720 | 3,521 | 61.6 | 1,096 | 1,019 | 92.9 | 477 | 191½ | 40.0 | 202.15 | 146.10 | 74.2 | 67.1 |
| 1771 | 318 | 6,080¼ | 5,308 | 87.3 | 1,132 | 1,039 | 91.7 | 520 | 466¾ | 89.6 | 211.09 | 148.09 | 70.1 | 84.6 |
| 1772 | 327 | 6,454¼ | 4,991¼ | 77.3 | 1,166 | 862 | 73.9 | 527 | 394½ | 74.7 | 165.03 | 109.02 | 66.0 | 72.9 |
| 1773 | 315 | 6,412½ | 5,871½ | 91.5 | 1,215 | 1,037 | 85.3 | 528 | 449½ | 85.0 | 191.03 | 148.16 | 77.4 | 85.8 |
| 1774 | 329 | 6,690 | 5,042 | 75.3 | 1,164 | 798 | 68.5 | 534 | 354 | 66.2 | 167.13 | 89.10 | 53.2 | 65.8 |

Sources:
    Livingston Manor Rent Ledger, 1767–1784, New-York Historical Society, New York.

    Several tenants who were required to pay ducks, turkeys, and flour casks are omitted from this account. Their omission, however, does not materially affect the overall picture.

rent and tried hard to escape from this toll on one pretext or another, although the burden was light indeed compared to the tenants' obligations.[178]

An analysis of the individual renters shows that fairly well-to-do and poor tenants alike indulged in the vice of delinquency. A case in point is Joseph Vail (or Veal). He had settled on a 299-acre farm in 1753 as a tenant of Stephen and John Van Cortlandt. Vail quietly left Cortlandt Manor in 1786, moving to Fishkill in Dutchess County without discharging a large back rent. Several letters from the "surprised" heirs of John Van Cortlandt threatened prosecution, but attempts at collecting the rent were futile until 1790. Despite the arrears, Vail after 1764 owned a freehold of at least 350 acres, free of any encumbrances, in Fishkill; and his personal estate alone, according to a 1779 tax list on the manor, was worth £3,312, making him one of the top property owners in the area. He died in 1794, bequeathing, among other things, five Negro slaves to his heirs.[179] This is just one of many examples in the different manors, especially Rensselaerswyck, where the offense was most contagious. There probably were some tenants who could not honor their contracts because they were too poor. Reporting to Susannah Warren in 1757, Oliver De Lancey said that "half the Tenants in Courtlands Manor Pay their Rent and near the other half so Poor they Cant."[180] The question arises, however, whether the "Poor" tenants were actually poor or just feigning poverty. A plantation manager elsewhere argued from his experience that "the poorer Sort" paid their rents "most redely."[181] Furthermore, that Pierre Van Cortlandt, who became the Warrens' agent in 1758, was effective in collecting the rent from the same tenants in subsequent years brings into question De Lancey's allegations. It appears that

178. James De Lancey to N.Y. council, Oct. 29, 1754, De Lancey Papers, No. 89, Museum of City of N.Y.; Cadwallader Colden to Lords of Trade, Jan. 25, 1762, Colden Letter Books, I, 155–158. For example, the Livingston Manor proprietor neglected to pay his trivial quitrent for his manor from 1721 to 1738. Doc. Hist. N.Y., III, 833.

179. Receipt Book of John Van Cortlandt, N.-Y. Hist. Soc.; Stephen and John Van Cortlandt to Joseph Vail at Fish Kill, May 7 and June 24, 1788, and Oct. 17, 1789, Letterbook of Stephen and John Van Cortlandt, 1771–1792, N.Y. Pub. Lib. For Vail's property holdings, see deed, Jonathan Corey and James Cook to Joseph Vail, Dec. 4, 1764, Deed Book F, 368–370, Dutchess County Clerk's Office, Poughkeepsie, N.Y.; Joseph Vail's will, Dec. 6, 1796, Will Book B, 136–138, Dutchess Co. Surrogate Office.

180. Oliver De Lancey to Susannah Warren, Oct. 4, 1757, Gage Papers, Additional MS 1201.

181. John Meyers to James Duane, Jan. 17, 1793, Duane Papers, Roll 3. Meyer's opinion did not directly relate to our manors or to the period under study, but there is no reason to doubt that the behavior of the manorial tenantry was different from what Meyer described.

it was not the tenants' financial status, but the attitude of the landlord, his willingness or unwillingness to use forcible measures, that largely determined the volume of rent he collected and the rate of collection.

Landlords, of course, had a potential reserve of power at their disposal to counter the delinquency in payments and to force a tenant to perform the terms upon which his lease had been granted. Most of the lease indentures authorized a landlord to enter the leased premises and distrain the goods of a tenant until his rents were paid. This action was supposedly to take place in the space of six or seven months after the day when the rents were due in the case of Rensselaerswyck and only twenty days in the other manors.[182] A tenant without a written deed was liable to similar procedures and even to the harsher penalty of eviction. Individual arrangements were deemed necessary because the colony for a long time had no statutory laws regarding tenant delinquencies and a landlord's right to recovery of rents. It was not until 1767 that the General Assembly passed a law extending to New York three old British parliamentary acts dealing with tenant frauds, and even then, the measure was disallowed by the home authority.[183] Again in 1774 the assembly passed "An Act for the better Security, and more easy recovery of Rents, and renewal of Leases and to prevent Frauds committed by Tenants," which was almost a verbatim reproduction of the British statutes.[184] These belated legislative efforts, clearly inspired by alarmingly widespread rental frauds, were designed to provide an additional legal safeguard to the landed interests that dominated the legislature.

As the large back rents in most of the manors suggest, the manorial landlords were not always prompt to invoke the power provided by their lease contracts. It usually took long and repeated abuse by a tenant before the landlord lost his patience. In general, landlords preferred to take a note or bond from the debtors for the amount of back rent rather

182. Deed Book 5: 40–41, 82, 130, Albany Co. Clerk's Office; lease, Sept. 8, 1737, Robert Livingston, Jr., of Clermont, to William Snyder, Sept. 8, 1737, "Uncatalogued Livingston MSS"; lease, the Beekmans to Daniel Field, Dec. 30, 1737, Van Cortlandt Family Papers, N.-Y. Hist. Soc.; Philip Livingston to Peter Coole, Mar. 30, 1732, Morristown Hist. Park Coll., Roll 32. In one rare instance, a landlord was authorized to invoke the right of distraint if the yearly rent was "behind by the space of two day" after it was due. Robert Livingston's lease to Andrew Gardner, Mar. 25, 1708, Livingston-Redmond MSS, Roll 3.

183. N.Y. Col. Laws, IV, 953–956.

184. Ibid., V, 624–636. In 1724 a law on tenancy was enacted, but it was applied only to certain areas and was aimed specifically at preventing tenants and others from trespassing on lands. And a similar act for the entire colony was passed in 1771, but the home government disallowed it in the following year. Ibid., II, 206–214, V, 204–207; Gov. Burnet to Lords of Trade, Nov. 21, 1724, N.Y. Col. Docs., V, 738.

than distress them.[185] To be sure, the Beekmans in 1748 forced John Lancaster to forfeit his lease because of unpaid rent for seven years.[186] But this seems to have been the only instance of eviction by the Beekmans, although their tenants were notoriously delinquent. Robert Livingston, Jr., despite his quick temper, was equally reluctant to resort to harsh measures until other means of persuasion had been exhausted. In one instance, he distrained the goods of a tenant who owed him fifteen years' rent (£72 13s.).[187] The landlord's evident self-control was testified to by his own tenants. In 1784 Myndert Schut, who had been recently warned of possible eviction for his rent debts, wrote to the landlord: "I received your Letter of wich I can not complain the Demands thereof Being your Just Dew and which I should have Maide you Cettel [settle] fulson [full sum] Long Before now But as you have had Pitte and masse [mercy] on mee so long I Bege and Pray you will Be Plesed to have it a Little Longer."[188] For a tenant named Cornelius Dickerman owing, as of 1772, £33 (120 schepels of wheat, 36 hens, and 16 days' service), Livingston was willing to give a special dispensation: "If the tenant is able to pay bal[ance] of £16. 2, he is to do it. If not I am to forgive it."[189]

As we noted earlier, the Schuylers' tenants were as bad as the Beekmans'. Their landlord would have been justified in taking appropriate measures to obtain restitution. But the Schuylers had counted only on the collection efforts of their Cortlandt Manor agents, the Verplanck family, and on the goodwill of their tenants. One of the tenants, Dr. James Perry, who leased a farm of 217 acres in 1750 at a yearly rent of £2 10s. (less than 3d. per acre) for two lives, confessed to General Philip Schuyler, son of John and Cornelia, in 1786 that he was "ashamed for great neglect in letting it [back rent] . . . amount to such a sum [£37 10s.]" and continued: "Therefore as your Honours Patience has Forbore Prosecuting me for a longtime I hope you will Desist a little longer I am very . . . willing to give a Bond and Security if Required."[190]

Only John Van Cortlandt, agent-manager for his father Stephen of New Jersey, was the exception to the general practices of the manorial proprietors with regard to tenant defaults. To one recently settled tenant

185. Ephraim Rees's bond to Robert Livingston, June 22, 1728, Livingston-Redmond MSS, Roll 4.
186. Lease, May 6, 1749, the Beekmans to Jonathan Odell, Van Cortlandt Papers, V1697, Sleepy Hollow Restorations Lib.
187. Simon Shutt's account, Feb. 1, 1783, Livingston-Redmond MSS, Roll 10.
188. Myndert Schut to Robert Livingston, Jr., Apr. 6, 1784, ibid., Roll 8.
189. Entry on Dickerman, Livingston Manor Rent Ledger, 1767–1784, 17.
190. James Perry to Philip Schuyler, May 9, 1789, Schuyler Papers, Box 23.

he wrote in 1768, "Unless you settle your Rent Immediately on Receipt of this you must Expect to be Compeled shortly." The same day he wrote to another renter a similar threatening letter: " I must now tell you which you may depend on that I shall at Request of the family, replace every person that behaves in such a manner and Desire you will on Receipt of this pay."[191] True to his threats, he evicted at least twelve tenants between 1762 and 1773, either for failing to live up to agreements or for being behind with their rent.[192] Of all the landlords, only Van Cortlandt, with his eccentricities and high-handedness, nearly resembles the stereotype of the haughty and imperious landlord.

How do we explain the extraordinary patience of most of the landlords with their dilatory tenants? As we noted earlier, experience taught the landlords to hold their tenants' valuable improvements as security for arrears in rent. If the amount of back rent grew, so did the improvements, part or all of which the landlords could distrain. An heir of Robert Livingston, Jr., reported in 1790, the year Robert, Jr., died, that "Numbers of our Tenants owe as much back rent as the value of their farms at Sheriff sales."[193] Apparently, Robert, Jr., had kept a close eye on the accumulation of the arrears and had never let them soar to an amount that the tenants' leasehold equity could not cover. This kind of policy was especially judiciously applied in dealing with extremely poor tenants who could not pay rent anyway, although the number of such tenants was few in mid-century. The landlords heeded the old English proverb, "Sue a beggar and catch a louse." Philip Livingston instructed his manor clerk in 1740 not to sue for rent "those that owe small sumes and are poor."[194] Oliver De Lancey reasoned in 1754 that tough measures against the poor without equity in their lease were counterproductive: "All the Letters of Threatnings and perswasions has had no Effect on Most of them. The last Rimidy is to Sue them which I fear will have this Effect that Most of them will leave the Farms as they are very poor."[195]

Indeed, the fear of mass desertion of tenants, whether they were

191. John Van Cortlandt to Benjamin Golden and George Carpenter, Nov. 9, 1768, Letterbook of John Van Cortlandt, N.Y. Pub. Lib.

192. Receipt Book of John Van Cortlandt, *passim*, Van Cortlandt Family Papers, N.-Y. Hist. Soc.; Letterbooks of Stephen and John Van Cortlandt, *passim*, and Journal (c) of John Van Cortlandt, both in N.Y. Pub. Lib.

193. Henry Livingston to brother Walter, Dec. 23, 1790, Livingston-Redmond MSS, Roll 9.

194. Philip Livingston to John D'Witt, July 14, 1740, *ibid.*

195. Oliver De Lancey to Susannah Warren, July 20, 1754, Gage Papers, Additional MS 1201.

poor or not, constituted one of the important deterrents to any possible despotic tendencies of landlords. The existence of vast unsettled land, the necessity to improve it, and the paucity of farmhands resulted in a scramble among landlords for tenants analogous to the intercolonial rivalry for settlers. To compete in the market for tenants, landowners closely watched each other and exchanged information on lease terms. Robert R. Livingston of Clermont wrote in 1762 that "I have lett out" to several farmers "on the same [lease] terms the Patroons of [Rensselaerswyck] lett his as also [John Henry] Lydius," expressing his hope and belief that "great numbers will come on these terms."[196] Sir William Johnson of the Mohawk valley decided in 1767 not to enter into an agreement regarding leases until he knew "how the other Partners will give out theirs."[197] In 1748 George Clarke, holding a large landed estate in the Oblong area, urged his agent to "get tennants as soon as possible by offering better terms than any other lease offered."[198] The competition was not always fair. Sir William Johnson was reported to have discouraged settlers who were committed to another landowner, diverting at least one of them to his own land.[199] Some tenants—cognizant of the economic milieu, which boosted the value of tenantry—employed the threat of leaving their landlord's domain to obtain concessions from him.[200] A manor "lord" in New York, however authoritarian, could not succeed by operating outside the rules of the game played by his fellow landlords and his bargain-minded tenants. No manor could be an impenetrable hermit kingdom with its own distinct political discipline and sociology. Placating the tenantry was thus a prerequisite of a landlord's survival. The alternative was idle land, wild and useless.

    Another constraining element affected a landlord's outlook. As a

196. Robert R. Livingston to son Robert R. Livingston, Jr., Mar. 1, 1762, Robert R. Livingston Coll., Box 1.
197. William Johnson to Goldsbrow Banyar, Jan. 27, 1767, *William Johnson Papers*, XII, 262; Banyar to Samuel Dunlop, Aug. 28, 1761, and Oct. 18, 1762, Goldsbrow Banyar Papers, Box 6.
198. George Clarke to John Chamber, May 10, 1748, John Chamber Papers, Box 1, N.Y. State Lib.
199. Adam Vrooman to James Duane, Dec. 9, 1762, Jan. 12, May 27, June 1, 1765, and Duane to Vrooman, May 25, 1765, Duane Papers, Roll 1; Alexander, *Revolutionary Conservative: James Duane*, 62–63; Philip Schuyler's unsuccessful bid for the Scottish settlers under the Reverend Mr. Clarke in 1764, *N.-Y. Gaz.: or, Wkly. Post-Boy*, Nov. 29, 1764; Gerlach, *Philip Schuyler*, 52.
200. See particularly the case of Edward Clarke's tenants in Cherry Valley in 1766 and 1767. Samuel Dunlop to Goldsbrow Banyar, Aug. 18, 1766, Mar. 6, June 9, 1767, Mar. 17, 1773, Goldsbrow Banyar Papers, Box 6; Kim, "New Look at the Great Landlords," *WMQ*, 3d Ser., XXVII (1970), 606–607.

public man with high standing in local and provincial society, he was naturally concerned about his public image. The gentlemanly ideal to which he aspired included such attributes as honor, kindness, benevolence, and moderation. To be lacking in one of these was to cast odium upon his character and to lose the respect of his peers as well as of common men. Any harsh measure by him, however justifiable it might seem under certain circumstances, would, in the words of a landlord, not only carry "the face of Cruelty" but also bring on him "some Disesteem in the Country."[201] Particularly for those interested in running for an elective office, a bad reputation was something that could not be risked.

Apart from gentlemanly etiquette and economic realism, some landlords felt genuine compassion toward the poor and assumed a paternalistic role. Sir William Johnson, in the course of settling his vast land with downtrodden immigrants, enjoyed happy rewards in witnessing the "rude woods made cultivable" and in providing "sustenance to the poor and distressed." At his deathbed he advised his son to "shew lenity to such of the Tenants as are poor."[202] Other manorial proprietors undoubtedly had similar sentiments.[203]

## Regulations and Obligations Governing the Tenants

Although lease tenure and rent were the core arrangements governing tenant-landlord relationships, several other aspects of the leasehold system also regulated the tenant's economic activity. One important requirement, for example, concerned improvement of the land, such as building a house, planting a fenced orchard and nursery of apple or pear trees, and cultivating the soil. The stipulation was more common in the earlier stage of settlement.

As in other regulations, different landlords imposed different standards with respect to the size and material of the house, the number of trees, and the use of the land. The Bayards, Verplancks, and Livingstons were particularly demanding. Samuel Bayard required each of his tenants

201. Oliver De Lancey to Susannah Warren, Feb. 1, 1755, Gage Papers, Additional MS 1201; Philip Schuyler to Peter Van Schaick, July 7, 1774, Schuyler Papers, Box 2; Henry Beekman to Gilbert Livingston, Dec. 3, 1745, Beekman Papers.

202. William Johnson's will, Jan. 27, 1774, Wills, XXIX, 139, Queens College Lib.; Johnson to John Donell, June 28, 1774, Johnson to Lord Adam Gordon, Feb. 18, 1771, *William Johnson Papers*, XII, 893–894, 1111; *N.-Y. Mercury*, Feb. 25, 1754, on Johnson's advertisement.

203. Myndert Schut to Robert Livingston, Jr., Apr. 6, 1784, Livingston-Redmond MSS, Roll 8.

in the 1730s to build a dwelling house "at least 18 ft. squire, either of Stone or Timber, boarded or shingled without, and plastered within, covered with Shingles." Philip Livingston demanded that a tenant build a house 30 by 18 feet equipped with a brick chimney, with "proper doors and windows," and with a stone cellar that had to be 7 feet deep under the beam floors. However, the Beekmans simply laid down the rule that "no Dwelling-House shall be erected but on a dug Stone-walled Cellar."[204] In the mid-eighteenth century, Robert Livingston, Jr., son of Philip, had his new tenants construct a barn within ten years—most commonly a structure measuring 20 by 40 feet with "outlets on both sides for stables for horses"—but he was the only proprietor who demanded such a thing.[205] Concerning orchards, these proprietors specified that tenants plant within a certain period (no longer than ten years) a fenced orchard of fruit trees—usually 100, rarely 150 or 200—for which two acres would be allocated.[206] Robert Livingston, Jr., and the Beekmans required some tenants to set up a nursery 40 to 50 feet square for the trees.[207] In addition, several landlords put in writing a provision requiring their tenants to clear a specified amount of woodland every year. Robert Livingston, the founder of Livingston Manor, and his son Philip insisted on a yearly improvement of four and eight acres respectively until the entire farm land was cleared, while his grandson Robert, Jr., and his neighbor Kiliaen Van Rensselaer demanded only two acres.[208] The Bayards even had something to say about the use of the land. One of their typical leases in the early 1730s reads as follows:

Lessees stand yearly Bound . . . not to manure any of the Land, so cleared above two crops with Winter Grain, and after that one year with Indian Corn, Oats,

204. Leases, the Bayards to Win and Linnebeker, 1732, Bayard-Campbell-Pearsall Colls.; lease, Philip Livingston to Epharim Brown, Dec. 20, 1744, Livingston-Redmond MSS, Roll 6; Van Cortlandt Papers, V1942, no. 2, V2200, V1942, no. 1, V2198, V2189, V1697, Sleepy Hollow Restorations Lib.

205. Lease, Robert Livingston, Jr., to Andries Janse Reese, June 1, 1752, Livingston Manor Papers.

206. Philip Livingston's instruction to Henry Livingston, July 15, 1747, Livingston-Redmond MSS, Roll 9; lease, Robert Livingston, Jr., to Andries Lott, Oct. 20, 1765, Misc. MSS, Livingston, R-W; lease, Philip Verplanck to Benjamin Field, 1742, N.Y. Gen. and Biog. Soc.; Deed Book 10: 116–118, Albany Co. Clerk's Office; lease, Robert Livingston, Jr., of Clermont, to William Snyder, Sept. 8, 1737, "Uncatalogued Livingston MSS."

207. Leases, Robert Livingston, Jr., to Andries Janse Reese, June 1, 1752, and to Broer Decker, Apr. 5, 1765, Livingston Manor Papers; Mortgage Book C, 252–254, Westchester Co. Clerk's Office.

208. Robert Livingston to Andrew Gardner, Mar. 25, 1708, Livingston-Redmond MSS, Roll 3; Philip Livingston's instruction to Henry Livingston, July 15, 1747, ibid., Roll 9; lease, Robert Livingston, Jr., to Andries Janse Reese, June 1, 1752, Livingston Manor

Flax, or Buck wheat, and, after that to lie Fallow four years, except sown with Flax, on Land first Dunged for that purpose, and so every Four Years to be manured either with Summer or Winter Grain. . . . They shall, after the 1st Ten years setling of the said Farm, leave at least Six Acres of Meadow Ground for Hay not to be plowed up, otherwise than for that Use, and to Dung and Fence the same as Occasion requires.[209]

Another landlord made it mandatory that his tenants sow twenty-four bushels of winter wheat a year.[210]

Many other landlords, such as the Van Rensselaers of Claverack, the Livingstons of Clermont, and the rest of the Cortlandt Manor proprietors, refrained from applying one or the other form of economic regulation. But their total silence on the use and development of the land did not indicate indifference toward this vital matter upon which their prosperity depended. Instead of relying on a written provision, they seem to have let the economics of the leasehold system operate to spur the tenants' industry. They assumed that rents themselves would give the tenantry a sufficient psychological incentive to cultivate more and "raise more than they consume."[211] Furthermore, since the value of the leasehold coincided with the extent of improvements, tenants would find it to their own interest to improve and make good use of the land. After all, the major portion of the improvements belonged to them. It would thus seem that when economic controls were imposed, with the possible exception of a requirement concerning rotating crops, fallowing, and manuring, they were no more restrictive and onerous to the tenantry than any ordinary contractual obligations.

Coupled with the regulation of improvements was the landlord's control over the sale of the lease and the improvements by a tenant. This control took two forms. One required that a tenant secure the landlord's approval before disposing of any improvements; the other, that he should pay to the landlord a certain portion of the sale money, which was known as the "quarter-sale" or "alienation fine or fee." In Livingston Manor (including Clermont), the Claverack part of Rensselaerswyck, and that part of Cortlandt Manor under the Beekmans, when a tenant

---

Papers; lease, Kiliaen Van Rensselaer to Marten Martense Van Alstyn, Aug. 9, 1707, Drawer 1, Albany Inst. of Hist. and Art; Deed Book 7: 45–46, Albany Co. Clerk's Office.

209. Leases, the Bayards to Win and Linnebeker, 1732, Bayard-Campbell-Pearsall Colls.

210. Lease, Robert Livingston, Jr., to Andries Janse Reese, June 1, 1752, Livingston Manor Papers.

211. McAnear, ed., "Robert R. Livingston's Reasons," *Jour. Pol. Econ.*, XLVIII (1940), 88, 89.

wanted to sell his lease, he was required to offer it first to his landlord "at the lowest price."[212] If the landlord declined it, the tenant then was "at liberty to sell it to any other with approbation" of the landlord. At least in appearance, the landlord's assumption of the right of first refusal seems quite unfair, since it interfered with the tenant's economic freedom. But in practice it was not. One famous provincial lawyer argued that the right spelled out in the lease covenant was never intended to authorize the landlord to "prevent a Sale" but only to insure that whatever tenants held the property suited the landlord's "Predilection."[213] The landlord, after all, could not force a tenant to sell his lease. He was simply given a preference of one prospective buyer over another. This option over who was acceptable and who was not on his domain was no different from the screening procedure the New England towns adopted for newcomers.[214] In this connection, it is worthy of note that the Albany city corporation also applied the same right of refusal and consent to its tenant farmers at Schaghticoke.[215] The New York landlords, like the New England town proprietors, had no desire to see their property riddled with troublesome characters. More important, tenants entertained the same apprehension over prospective new neighbors, and were sometimes allowed by their landlord to approve or reject a new tenant.[216]

212. Deed Book 5: 424, 104, Deed Book 6: 423–425, and Deed Book 8: 334, Albany Co. Clerk's Office; advertisements for the sale of the improvements of James Barnard and John King in Philipsburgh, N.-Y. Gaz.; and Wkly. Mercury, Dec. 12, 1768, and May 8, 1769. See also n. 206 above.

213. John Morin Scott held this legal opinion, which concerned a dispute involving Henry Beekman and his tenant named John Trempers of Dutchess County. The tenant was indebted to one Hendrick Meyer. Meyer thought that he could recover the debt and attorney's fee amounting to about £100 only by selling Trempers's lease, but Beekman refused to give his approval to the sale despite the creditor's solicitation. Beekman told Meyer that he intended to keep the lands "for the support of Trempers' wife and family who [would] otherwise become public charge." Interestingly, the frustrated creditor and his lawyer, Egbert Benson, called Beekman's action an "ill judged piece of charity." Whatever the case, Beekman used his right of consent to protect his tenant. See John Morin Scott to Egbert Benson, Apr. 16, 1775, and enclosed documents, "Uncatalogued Livingston MSS."

214. Kenneth A. Lockridge, A New England Town the First Hundred Years: Dedham, Massachusetts, 1636–1736 (New York, 1970), 8.

215. Munsell, ed., Annals of Albany, V, 183–184, VII, 80, 82, 231, VIII, 264, IX, 26, 34, 79, 89.

216. Philip Hermanse to Henry Beekman, Feb. 25, 1774, "Uncatalogued Livingston MSS." In this letter, Hermanse, who had bought a lease from another tenant for £475, asked for the consent of Henry Beekman (landlord), a step that was necessary to complete the transaction. The letter included a statement by Beekman's other tenants certifying that they were "satisfied with Philip Hermanse for a Neighbor." See also Patrick MacArthur to Robert Livingston, Jr., Apr. 25, 1771, Livingston-Redmond MSS, Roll 8. This letter shows that Robert Livingston, Jr., granted permission to a person to settle at a certain section of his manor provided that residents there "would be willing" to accept the newcomer.

Here we can discern a public function of the landlord's right—that of insuring peace and harmony in the community under his proprietorship.

Landlord control over alienation of leasehold property was marked by two other concerns that were private in nature and peculiar to New York landed society. Most of the province's land titles were insecure because of their ill-defined boundaries, with one grant's limits overlapping those of another. Indeed, none of the manors under study was completely immune from boundary disputes. Almost every proprietor lived in fear that saboteurs might be planted by a title challenger in a strategic location on his land and that the tenants might turn conspirators against the estate.[217] This danger was definitely a reason why in the late 1730s Philip Livingston preferred mellow Dutch or German farmers to aggressive and leveling Yankee farmers as settlers on his manor, which at the time seemed vulnerable to encroachment, particularly from Massachusetts land speculators. In the late 1760s his son Robert, Jr., having suffered repeated intrusion by New England settlers in the easternmost section of the domain, temporarily banned his tenants from business dealings (except for daily necessities and sale of their farm produce) with any "stranger" and even from accommodating the stranger or nonresident for longer than forty-eight hours without the landlord's written consent.[218] About that time Stephen Van Rensselaer II, whose ancestors had never exercised the right of refusal and consent, found it necessary to add a new provision to his leases stating that no "sale" of a lease should be made to any persons other than those who "shall take the same by legal conveyance" and register the transaction with the Albany County clerk's office within ten days, and that a lessee should not "Quit or abandone the possession to the prejudice" of the landlord.[219] Understandably, those manorial landlords who felt most uneasy about their land titles were also the most jealous of their right of refusal and consent, which was one means of insuring the integrity of their estates.

Furthermore, a lease sale by a tenant was probably the best and last

---

217. Testimony of David Mathew, Aug. 13, 1784, A.O. 12/30, 121–122. Cadwallader Colden, a proprietor of certain disputed land, was convinced that one effective method to prevent collusion between his tenants and his rival claimants to the land would be the landlord's right of consent to the sale of improvements. Colden to James Alexander, Oct. 20, 1740 (date of its receipt), James Alexander Papers, Box 47.

218. See a newly printed lease, Robert Livingston, Jr., to William Lowry, Apr. 14, 1769, Livingston-Redmond MSS, Roll 8. The new lease policy began in 1767. Peter R. Livingston to father, Robert, Jr., Mar. 2, 1769, ibid.

219. Lease, Stephen Van Rensselaer to Jacob Louck, Jan. 20, 1769, Deed Book 10: 329–330, Albany Co. Clerk's Office.

chance a landlord would have to collect what the tenant owed. With the sale money in his pocket, the tenant would have no good excuse for not paying his debts to the landlord. Moreover, the difficulty of selling a leasehold encumbered by back rents acted as an encouragement to tenants to clear up their debts. We have already noted how delinquent the tenantry were in performing rental obligations. But in the end, the landlord's consent as the final act validating a sale transaction was a "blue chip" that could be used against the possible flight of the tenant with unpaid debts.[220]

Ordinarily, if no special problems were involved, the landlords rather welcomed the sale of a lease. Mrs. Cornelia Schuyler, one of the Cortlandt Manor proprietors, wrote in 1758 to Philip Verplanck, her agent, that "I have no objection to any of my tenants selling their Improvements provided you think It Most beneficial to me of which you are the best Judge, and beg you will Act therein as you think proper."[221] This would have been an understatement for many of the colonial landlords. Their pretension to the alienation fee—an assessment rarely, if ever, implemented until mid-century—was potentially as good a source of profit as rentals. Philip Schuyler, son of Cornelia, asserted that the income from "the frequent transmutations of tenants would exceed the purchase of the fee-simple, though sold at a high valuation."[222]

As in the other aspects of the lease system, quarter-sale rates varied from one landlord to another. Stephen Van Cortlandt of New York, John Van Cortlandt, Oliver and James De Lancey, Robert Livingston, Jr., of Livingston Manor proper, Frederick Philipse III, Robert Livingston, Jr., and his son Robert R. of Clermont, and the Warrens all demanded one-third of the sale price of improvements if the lease in question was being

---

220. There were numerous instances in which landlords collected back rents following the sale of a lease. Abraham Ten Broeck's Accounts of the Manor, 1763–1787, *passim*, Rensselaerswyck MSS. Often the sale of a lease was accompanied by a memorandum certifying that the premises in question were "free and unincumbered of all back rents." Memorandum by Hendrick Van Der Carr to Guy Young, Sept. 21, 1774, Claverack, Van Rensselaer-Fort Papers.

221. Cornelia Schuyler to Philip Verplanck, Apr. 16, 1758, Philip Verplanck Papers, No. 126, N.Y. Gen. and Biog. Soc.

222. Halsey, ed., *Journal of Richard Smith*, 5; testimony of Roger Morris, one of the proprietors of Philipse's Highland Patent, Loyalist Transcripts, XLIII, 240–241; Gerlach, *Philip Schuyler*, 61; Mark, *Agrarian Conflicts*, 67, 71–72. For the complaints about the quarter-sale, see Samuel Peter's testimony, Dec. 13, 1784, A.O. 12/19, 400–401. The first incident of the quarter-sale that I have come across was in 1748 when Philip Van Cortlandt entered an agreement with Solomon Burtis of Cortlandt Manor. See Van Cortlandt to Burtis, Apr. 18, 1748, Van Cortlandt Papers, V2108, Sleepy Hollow Restorations Lib.

sold for the first time. But Stephen Van Cortlandt arrogated only one-fourth when he had to sell the premises under a tenant's possession before the lease tenure expired.[223] John Van Rensselaer of Claverack and the Schuylers of Cortlandt Manor appropriated a quarter of the sale money.[224] In the case of every other sale after the first one, the landlords generally, with the possible exception of Robert Livingston, Jr., and the Claverack proprietor, applied a reduced rate. Robert R. Livingston and Frederick Philipse III, for example, took a fifth and a sixth respectively. The Beekmans, who had never imposed an alienation fee, began in 1775 to demand a tenth of the resale value of improvements, but this new policy was not retroactive, thus leaving unaffected their twenty-two current leaseholders.[225] Records are by no means clear as to the practice at Rensselaerswyck proper, although incidents of lease sale and the landlord's receipt of a certain percentage of the sale money were frequent in the 1760s and 1770s. The fragmentary evidence suggests that those who had bought farmland from the patroon in fee with rental encumbrances, as was the case before 1750, were required to pay half a year's extra rent, while those who had not obtained a deed were obliged to pay a third or a fourth upon the first sale. What the manor proprietors charged upon

223. Lease, Stephen Van Cortlandt of New York to Joseph Haight, Apr. 11, 1751, Van Cortlandt-Van Wyck Papers; lease of John Wilson and Benjamin Golden, Receipt Book of John Van Cortlandt, 1766–1771, N.-Y. Hist. Soc.; Van Cortlandt Papers, VX2108, V1836, and Receipt Book of Pierre Van Cortlandt and Account Book of Pierre Van Cortlandt, Van Cortlandt Papers, V1689, V1644, V2301, *passim*, Sleepy Hollow Restorations Lib.; John Van Cortlandt to Capt. Montross, Apr. 5, 1773, Letterbook of Stephen and John Van Cortlandt, 1771–1792, N.Y. Pub. Lib.; Deed Book H, 501–502, on Henry Scott, Westchester Co. Clerk's Office; "Articles" of agreement between John Robinson and John B. Koens, Oct. 7, 1763, Livingston-Redmond MSS, Roll 7; "Memoranda between Johannis Arkenbregh and Peter Althuyser," Mar. 7, 1753, Misc. MSS, Livingston, A–Z; testimony of Beverly Robinson and Samuel Peters, Dec. 13, 1784, A.O. 12/19, 393, 399; memorial of Samuel Davenport, tenant, A.O. 12/17, 427–430. Compare my view with that of Reubens, "Pre-emptive Rights," *WMQ*, 3d Ser., XXII (1965), 439, and Mark, *Agrarian Conflicts*, 70.

224. Lease, John Van Rensselaer to Johannis Coons, 1770, Claverack Papers; testimony of Philip Schuyler, Mar. 8, 1787, A.O. 12/30, 125; Schuyler Papers, Box 10, on John Stevens.

225. Testimony of Beverly Robinson, A.O. 12/19, 394; lease, Robert R. Livingston to one Hupener, Livingston Account Book, Clermont, 1772–1784. In the 1780s, Clermont lowered the rate to one-sixth of the sale price. See the case of Lot Trip, June 2, 1786, "Uncatalogued Livingston MSS." See also lease, Henry and Gertrude Beekman to Abiel Fuller, Mar. 16, 1775, and to Abel Weeks, Apr. 12, 1775, Van Cortlandt Papers, V2208 and V2209, Sleepy Hollow Restorations Lib. For the quarter-sale practice on nonmanorial patents, see Roger Morris's testimony, A.O. 12/25, 205; John Watts to Henry Livingston, May 11, 1762, *Letter Book of John Watts, Merchant and Councillor of New York, January 1, 1762–December 22, 1765* (N.-Y. Hist. Soc., *Colls.*, LXI [New York, 1928]), 47; Robert R. Livingston's lease to Christean Winne, May 1, 1774, "Uncatalogued Livingston MSS."

subsequent sales is unknown. Practices elsewhere make it seem likely that they asked smaller claims.[226]

Some landlords pursued a different policy. In a contract with a tenant named Solomon Burtis for a life lease in April 1748, Philip Van Cortlandt, the surviving eldest son of Stephanus Van Cortlandt, agreed that if Burtis "Should Incline to Dispose of Said Farme then he must pay me Such a part of Said Disposall *as We Can agre upon.*"[227] This agreement is significant in that the tenant was allowed to have as important a voice as the landlord in determining the rate of the quarter-sale. John Watts, another proprietor of Cortlandt Manor, seems to have exceeded the other manorial proprietors in generosity when he arranged with his tenant Gabriel Carmen in 1772 that the latter be "entitled to one half of the Improvements" upon the expiration of his lease, although the landlord owned the improvements as well as the soil rights.[228]

Tenants, of course, resented the alienation fee, no matter how trivial it might have been. A widow who sold her husband's improvements in Philipsburgh for £1,200 was incensed when the landlord "insisted upon having £400"; she consulted several lawyers in Connecticut upon the occasion but obtained no redress. Although the justification for such a claim by a landlord appears questionable, it is nevertheless true that the tenants agreed to the lease terms voluntarily. Moreover, there were some good reasons for the landlord's claims. After all, most materials with

226. Abraham Ten Broeck's Accounts of the Manor, 1763–1787, particularly on Johannes Becker, Jr., Jacob Wagenea, Gerrit A. Lansing, John Norton, Dirck Cluet, Jeroon Barheyatt, and Gerrit Seager, Rensselaerswyck MSS.

227. Philip Van Cortlandt's certificate dated Apr. 18, 1748, Van Cortlandt Papers, V2108, Sleepy Hollow Restorations Lib.

228. The Carman lease comprised 150 acres of land plus improvements, which Watts had bought from Samuel Bayard and others at different times in 1752. "Estimate of part of the Estate and Loss of John Watts late of New York attainted by an Act of that State, 1788," Watts Papers, Vol. 9; John Watts in London to sons Robert and John Watts in New York, Feb. 29, 1785, and Apr. 10, 1786, Robert Watts Papers, Box 3. The quarter-sale provision was not applied when the conveyance was from father to son or grandson, or within the family. Richard Smith, a visitor to Philipsburgh in 1769, reported his conversation with a manor tenant: "The Tenant for Life here tells me . . . on his demise or Sale, his Son or Vendee is obliged to pay to the Landlord one Third of the Value of the Farm for a Renewal of the Lease." This report, often quoted and accepted by historians, is incorrect on two counts. First, none of the Philipsburgh Manor tenants held lifetime leases, and, second, no fine was imposed on "casting a Descent." For the second point, my argument is based on an investigatory report by the Royal Commissioners of the Loyalist Claims and other sources, such as tenants' own testimonies and statements in their wills. No evidence is available on practices at the manors of Livingston and Cortlandt. Halsey, ed., *Journal of Richard Smith*, 5; Gerlach, *Philip Schuyler*, 61, n. 40; "In the Case of Frederick Philipse Esquire," A.O. 12/88, 90–91; Solomon Horton's memorial, A.O. 12/23, 255–258; John Buckhout's will, Jan. 20, 1774, Wills, XXXVIII, 13–15, Queens College Lib.; Frederick Brown's will, Jan. 12, 1766, *ibid.*, XXV, 403–406.

which the tenants built dwelling houses, outhouses, barns, fences, stables, and other farming appurtenances were extracted from the very soil that belonged to their landlord. Almost every lease indenture allowed a tenant to carry away and use as much timber, wood, stone, and "hayboot, hedgeboot, fireboot and ploughboot" from the commons or the unappropriated lands as was necessary for improvement projects and other domestic uses.[229] This privilege, apart from the right of pasturage, was one of the important benefits of tenancy.[230] Obviously, the first settlers exploited the resources more for improvements than succeeding ones. For this reason, the quarter-sale claim generally was higher at the first sale of a lease and smaller next time. Such flexibility is indicative of the give-and-take of plantation economics as opposed to the rigidity of inherited feudal concepts.

The efforts of manorial proprietors to control their domain's economy extended to the mill industry, particularly to gristmills. Because of the highly valued function of the mills not only for flour manufacturing but also for attracting the staple crop, encouraging settlement, and, above all, bringing in revenue, landlords claimed exclusive jurisdiction over all river streams within the domain suitable for mill sites. The proprietors of Rensselaerswyck, Philipsburgh, and Livingston Manor were most jealous of their rights to mills and mill sites. In Cortlandt Manor, this kind of monopolistic control was difficult to develop, since much manor land was sold off without a restrictive clause on the mill streams in the deeds of sale. Nevertheless, the Van Rensselaers and the Beekmans, as noted earlier, were not wholly averse to the idea of having someone else build and operate mills on a rental basis.[231] This sort of concession was deemed necessary when a landlord did not have sufficient capital to undertake the enterprise himself. The landlords were well aware of the pressing need for the agricultural facility in remote areas. By retaining exclusive rights to the watercourse and by charging reasonable rates for grinding, the Rensselaerswyck and Philipsburgh landlords hoped to mo-

---

229. Samuel Peters's testimony, Dec. 13, 1784, A.O. 12/19, 400–401; "Notes of Eiphalet Stephens and David Akin's Evidence," Lawsuits, C-F, in Kempe Papers, N.-Y. Hist. Soc.

230. For examples, see lease from Robert Livingston to Andrew Gardner, Mar. 25, 1708, Livingston-Redmond MSS, Roll 3; lease, Kiliaen Van Rensselaer to Jeronimus Barheyt, Apr. 15, 1707, Deed Book 5: 40–41, Albany Co. Clerk's Office; bond, Henry Van Rensselaer to Arent Van Der Carr, July 19, 1745, Van Rensselaer-Fort Papers.

231. As noted before, Frederick Philipse III, the last proprietor of Philipsburgh, also joined his fellow manorial landlords by renting out his mills in the mid-18th century. But the Livingstons, particularly of the manor proper, always kept and ran their mills throughout the colonial period.

nopolize the mill business. The patroon's gristmills took as a toll a twentieth part of the grain ground, and both Philipsburgh and Claverack took a fifteenth. These rates compared favorably with the toll of a fourteenth part authorized by township governments in Westchester County for those mills under their jurisdiction.[232]

Still, Jeremiah Van Rensselaer of Rensselaerswyck found it necessary in 1744 to require a tenant to "grind all his grain he consumes on the Patroon's mills."[233] Although it was the first and only recorded instance of this requirement at Rensselaerswyck, the additional precaution was a clear indication that the landlord was determined to insure a milling monopoly in his domain. As long as the mills were conveniently located and tolls were reasonably low, this control was hardly burdensome to tenants. By contrast, the Livingstons of both branches not only maintained a monopoly of grinding facilities but also imposed the feudal custom of a tenth toll. This exploitive practice undoubtedly provoked the ire of their farmers, some of whom indeed ignored the restriction by secretly taking their produce out of the manor to a mill offering cheaper tolls.[234] Evidence on the extent of the violation is not available, however.

Finally, some landlords, notably commercial ones like the Living-

232. "Essays on the Constitution, etc.," Yates Papers, Box 3; Johannes Schank's mill account with Adolph Philipse, Feb. 15, 1751, "Inventory of A. Philipse," Philipse Papers, PX135, Sleepy Hollow Restorations Lib.; John H. Beekman's account, Nov. 19, 1765, Abraham Wendell's account, Jan. 18, 1764, Nanning Fisher's account, Dec. 11, 1771, all with the patroon's mills, in Abraham Ten Broeck's Account of the Manor, 1763–1787, Rensselaerswyck MSS; "Abraham Fonda's Estate account with Henry Van Rensselaer," 1749–1762, Van Rensselaer-Fort Papers; Deed Book E, 244, Westchester Co. Clerk's Office; Fox, *Caleb Heathcote*, 56; "Abstracts from the Town of Westchester, New York," *N.Y. Gen. and Biog. Rec.*, LX (1929), 259. It is worth noting that in 1679 Schenectady township allowed Sweer Teunise, owner of the only mill in town, to collect a ninth part of grain for toll. Van Laer, trans. and ed., *Court Minutes of Albany, Rensselaerswyck, and Schenectady*, III, 189–190.

233. Jury Scherp's lease, Mar. 8, 1744, "A list of Indentures, 1696–1744," Rensselaerswyck MSS.

234. Hendrick Hanse's "account with Robert Livingston," Mar. 2, 1708, to Sept. 3, 1719, Livingston-Redmond MSS, Roll 3; deposition of Garret Van Deusen, Oct. 19, 1744, and lease, Robert Livingston, Jr., of Clermont, to William Snyder, Sept. 8, 1737, "Uncatalogued Livingston MSS"; lease, Robert Livingston, Jr., to Broer Decker, Apr. 5, 1765, Misc. MSS, Livingston, R-W; lease, Robert Livingston, Jr., to Johannis Kool, Jan. 31, 1772, Livingston Manor Papers. It should be noted that the Beekmans, at least on paper, imposed the same toll of one-tenth. Their extant 24 lease papers show that 7 tenants were supposed to use the landlord's mill, though no mills were in existence. It seems that the Beekmans either forgot to cross out the mill provision in the printed lease papers, as they did with a deed for their tenant named Daniel Field, or intentionally kept it in order to help those who had built and were operating the mills. See the Beekman leases, Van Cortlandt Papers, Sleepy Hollow Restorations Lib.; lease to Daniel Field, Dec. 30, 1737, Van Cortlandt Family Papers, N.-Y. Hist. Soc.; the Beekman leases, particularly to Caleb Barton, Van Cortlandt-Van Wyck Papers, N.Y. Pub. Lib.

stons, and probably Frederick and Adolph Philipse as well, tried to control the marketing of grains produced by their tenants. Lease contracts stipulated that the landlord retained the right of preemption or first refusal of all grains harvested over and above the tenants' domestic needs.[235] This was designed to give the landlords a complete monopoly of surplus grains, a goal that the commercial landlords had in mind when they undertook land development. Such an interference with a producer's freedom to sell his crop to his best advantage would appear to eliminate the benefit of competitive bidding and be a clear-cut example of oppression. In reality, however, the right of preemption sometimes also operated in favor of the tenants by presenting a ready market in the landlord's person. It was especially beneficial to those tenants on farms remote from the market.[236] Ultimately, the morality of preemption hinged on whether the landlords, like other grain merchants, offered the true market price for the goods, as was agreed upon in the lease indenture. Records reveal that they did. Both the landlord and the tenant drove a hard bargain; the parties dickered over prices, and sometimes harsh language was exchanged. Philip Livingston, who did not always exercise his preemption right and, when he did, found it challenged by high bidders for his tenants' produce, was prepared to give the farmers the current price, but he and his tenants often disagreed on what the current price was.[237]

In this connection, several letters from Philip Livingston to his manor clerk in the first three months of 1741 are revealing about the way he handled the right of preemption with his tenants. On January 1 he was "inclined to allow" the farmers 3s.—the current market price—per schepel

---

235. The earliest lease indenture allowing a landlord this preemptive right was one between Robert Livingston and Andrew Gardner on Mar. 25, 1708. It reads as follows: "The manor lord and his heirs assigns have the benefit of preemption of all the other corne grain flax hemp or other product . . . over and above what shall be requisit for the support of his [Gardner's] or their private family or familyes Expense and us . . . Livingston his heirs and assigns or any of them *paying for the same what other person or persons shall from time to time offer for the same or according to market prise*" (italics added). The lease is in Livingston-Redmond MSS, Roll 3. See also lease, Robert Livingston, Jr., to Broer Decker, Apr. 5, 1765, Livingston Manor Papers. One Beekman lease stated that the preemptive right would be binding "provided always, landlord or his agent . . . or any of them be then living or abiding within 12 miles of the premises." Lease, the Beekmans to William Jewell, May 11, 1738, Van Cortlandt-Van Wyck Papers. As in the case of the milling requirement, only once did the proprietors of Rensselaerswyck obtain the refusal right of "all grain." "A list of Indentures, 1696–1744," Rensselaerswyck MSS.

236. As late as 1772, when an improved road system made it easy for tenants to reach a nearby market, some of them even hoped that the landlord would buy their wheat "for their relief." John McFarland to James Duane, Mar. 31, 1772, Duane Papers, Roll 1.

237. Philip Livingston to son Robert, Jr., Dec. 1740, Livingston-Redmond MSS, Roll 7.

of wheat. In the same letter he expressed his determination "for the future and now to insist on our Right to have the Refusall of the wheat of our Tenants the price currant if that cant be had I must show them what is Right. Our pay and money is as good as they do gett from others." The next day, after being informed that the "Kinderhook Skippers" already advanced the price to 3s. 3d., he instructed the clerk to "keep pace with them . . . provided [he] cant gett it cheaper." Three days later, he heard the Kinderhook people were giving no more than 3s. and ordered the clerk to adjust the payment accordingly, adding that "I allow that price here [Albany] for the best and nobody gives more." However, the manor tenants wanted more for their wheat. Livingston was furious, calling them "unreasonable," "Brutes," or "Brutish." On February 10 he instructed the clerk to tell them that he did "insist on having their wheat at the price current," with the understanding that they would fix a new price in May or June. Those who refused to accept this offer, he warned, "may leave the mannor."[238] But he soon recovered from his rage. In late February and early March, he sent new directives to the clerk to offer 3s., even though the wheat price was then reported to have gone down to a mere 2s. 9d., due to a government ordinance against the exportation of grain to Dutch and Spanish territory. Why this generosity? Because, he explained, he did not want to "displease the farmers on any account in bargains for wheat" nor did he want to provoke "dispute with the farmers of fixing the price at a future time."[239]

The Livingston Manor tenants employed two common tactics to extort the best price from their landlord. Whenever a rumor was afloat that the landlord was out buying up their crop, they would suddenly withhold it, hoping that the price would rise "still more." Or they would play off the landlord against his rivals for their wheat. In late January 1749 some manor tenants came to Petrus D'Witt, Livingston's clerk, and told him that they would no longer take 4s. per schepel of wheat, since Martin Hoffman, a wheat merchant in Dutchess County, was willing to offer 4s. 6d. The clerk was skeptical because Hoffman had notified him repeatedly in the past two weeks that he intended to give no more than 4s. The clerk made a counterproposal to the tenants that he would also give Hoffman's price, but only if they would bring a certificate under Hoffman's signature confirming their story. The tenants replied that Hoffman would not write the certificate, because he knew that if he did, the land-

238. Philip Livingston to John D'Witt, Jan. 1, 2, 5, 7, Feb. 10, 1741, *ibid.*, Roll 9.
239. Philip Livingston to John D'Witt, Feb. 27, Mar. 5, 6, 1741, *ibid.*

lord would then give the same price, with the result that Hoffman could not "get any wheat out of this Manor." Reporting to Livingston about the conversation with the farmers, the clerk confessed that from his personal experience with Hoffman's usual "underhanded" maneuvers, he had "reason to believe" the story as told by the tenants. Under the circumstances, the clerk hardly knew "what course to take," although a few days before he had been authorized by the landlord to do the same as "our Neighbors," even if the price might be 5s. As the proprietor's wheat procurement agent who had his master's interest at heart, the clerk was disturbed by the possibility of a price war. If he offered Hoffman's alleged price to the tenants, Hoffman would top it with one penny more, and the tenants would ask for more still. It would then be "the same story" all over again.[240]

Whatever the outcome, this episode indisputably establishes that, despite the preemptive right, Livingston could not prevent his tenants from selling their grains to other dealers who outbid him. Because his trade empire was so dependent upon steady procurement of the staple crop, he would have done everything possible to stop the interloping and the tenants' subterfuge. Once or twice he might have obtained grain from his tenants at lower than the market price, but only at the double risk of their withholding it in the future and of losing his tenants, whom he had settled at great expense. As early as 1712, Robert Livingston, who was as much interested in wheat as his son Philip, correctly characterized tenant psychology when he remarked: "Paper money does very well at New York [City] but will not doe among the farmers here, for if you offer it 'tis true they dare not deny it, but then you must never Expect a grain of wheat afterwards from them. Therefore whatever you doe lett it be Silver money."[241] Thus, tenants were more to be pampered than harshly handled if landlords wanted their continued cooperation. Given the temper and canniness of the tenants, it was not, in the final analysis, the preemptive right but rather market conditions and the landlords' willingness to deal honestly with the tenants that determined their success or failure in monopolizing the surplus grain in these manors. It should be added that Robert Livingston, Jr., Philip's son, had the same difficulty as his father.[242] If the most authoritarian and tightfisted landlords like the

240. Petrus D'Witt to Philip Livingston, Jan. 23, 1749, *ibid.*, Roll 6.
241. Robert Livingston to Lawrence Smith, Apr. 2, 1712, *Doc. Hist. N.Y.*, III, 681.
242. James Elliot to Robert Livingston, Jr., June 26, 1765, Livingston-Redmond MSS, Roll 7.

Livingstons were unable to put their "refusal" right into effect, there is no reason to suppose that the others had better luck with it.

Fundamentally, the landlord-tenant relationship was more capitalistic and modern in character than feudal. The landowner and the tenant, two total strangers, met to discuss and bargain the conditions of a lease, the main object of which was to make money for the landlord and to provide a livelihood for the tenant. Their agreement entailed no social and political obligations on the part of the lessee except those concerning a few community affairs. From this point on, it was the tenant who by and large determined the use and disposition of the lease beyond the basic requirements: he decided on what and how much to build, sow, raise, and sell. He sold and bequeathed his improvements as he saw fit. The landlord's oversight of these vital economic activities of the tenant was secondary at best. His right to rents and his right of consent to the sale and descent of the lease bore no relation to feudal tenure. The tenant was bound to him by commercial ties; the ties were severed when the tenant sold the improvements. The only feudal vestige was a provision for one or two days' work, but its practice was not only limited but also often commuted. The fundamental fact and rationale of the lease structure was a rental arrangement in money terms; this was already a capitalistic relationship, wherein land was treated very much like any other commodity of trade.

The language of the lease contracts, such as "Lord Proprietor" and the "right of distraint," conjures up the specter of the feudal past. But interpreting landlord-tenant relations solely on the basis of what is contained in these documents is as absurd as describing colonial political culture in terms of the decrees, instructions, and laws of the British government. Our investigation, therefore, has been directed at the actual workings of the relationship, particularly at how well the tenant performed his rental obligations and how successfully the landlord enforced his will. As we have discovered, the overall rental performance of the manorial tenantry was notoriously poor. This condition was encouraged by the landlords' hesitance to take forcible remedial measures. Judging from these facts and others, it is clear that the farmers were not subjected to oppression and degradation. To use the term "quasi-feudal," as some historians have, to refer to colonial New York in a pejorative sense and to suggest that certain conditions affecting the tenants were oppressive, unfair, and arbitrary, is to deprive that term of its value as a precise word for defining landlord-tenant relations, which, as we have observed, were neither oppressive, nor unfair, nor arbitrary.

# CHAPTER VI

# The Economics and Sociology
# of Tenancy

### Peopling the Manors

Who became a manorial tenant? How did tenants typically perceive their social and economic environment? What did it mean to be a tenant, both economically and psychologically? What role did tenancy play in provincial society? How poor or affluent was the group compared with freeholders? These are questions that no historian has ever attempted to answer, although tenancy was a way of life for many New Yorkers.

Despite all the promotional measures, in the first quarter of the eighteenth century settlement in the New York manors was sluggish. As of 1714, eighty-year-old Rensselaerswyck had only 82 tenants and a total population of 427, an average increase of only one tenant family a year. The same pattern held for its southern neighbor, Livingston Manor, where only 33 tenants—approximately 170 whites—were braving the wilderness in 1716, thirty years after the establishment of the manor. Farther south, Cortlandt Manor had about 17 families in 1712, fifteen years after its founding. By contrast, Philipsburgh boasted on its nineteenth anniversary about 60 tenants with 309 inhabitants, that is, an increase of three households per year on the average. The dismal record of manorial settlement in this period is most noticeable if one compares the populations of the manors to those of the counties in which they were situated. In 1714 the population of Rensselaerswyck, which comprised about half of the known territory of Albany County, was just a quarter of that of the county, even excluding the 1,200 souls of Albany city and

Livingston Manor, and just one-seventh if the city is counted.[1] The same
was true of the manors of Philipsburgh and Cortlandt in relation to Westchester County. Their combined inhabitants (396) in 1712 represented
only one-seventh of the county population (2,485), although the manors
comprised more than half of the area of the county.[2]

Now and then there was a sudden infusion of settlers into these
manors. For instance, from 1716 to 1718, Livingston Manor recruited
seventeen tenant families.[3] About this time, Philip Van Cortlandt, the eldest son of Stephanus, called Governor Hunter's attention to an increase
of inhabitants eligible for militia duty in his manor and Philipsburgh.[4]
These increases, however, were unlikely to have offset the persistent
demographic disparity between the manors and the other parts of the
counties in the following decade. Yet, settlement occurred no more slowly
on manors than on other large patents. In all of Dutchess County, which
was the home of several great patents—Rumbout Patent, Beekman Patent, Great and Little Nine Partners, and Philipse's Highland (or Upper)
Patent—there were in 1715 about a hundred souls, concentrated largely
at Poughkeepsie at the mouth of the Fish Kill. Of all the patentees,
Colonel Henry Beekman was probably the only one who in the next ten
years made some modest efforts at clearing his wild lands by settling a
few Palatine farmers.[5]

The glaringly underpopulated condition of the great estates along
the fertile Hudson River valley drew cynical and pessimistic comments
from royal officials from the earl of Bellomont to Cadwallader Colden.

1. I arrived at the approximate number of the tenant families by dividing the total
number of white inhabitants in the manors by 5.1, which was the average (mean) family
size in Albany County (without including Albany city in my calculation) at the end of the
17th century. Each family unit, I assumed, had a leasehold. N.Y. Col. MSS, XLII, 34, LIX,
19; Doc. Hist. N.Y., III, 905.

2. The extent of Westchester County at the time was estimated to be 307,200 acres.
Robert Bolton, The History of Several Towns, Manors, and Patents of the County of
Westchester (New York, 1905), I, 38.

3. "List of Debtors," Jan. 20, 1710, to Mar. 5, 1718, Livingston-Redmond MSS, Roll
3; "A list of the Inhabitants and Slaves in the City and County of Albany, 1714," N.Y. Col.
MSS, LIX, 19.

4. Van Cortlandt claimed that the number of men eligible for militia duty in the two
manors had grown to 120 and argued for the restoration of an independent Cortlandt
Manor militia company. The Cortlandt company had been absorbed into that of the neighboring Philipsburgh Manor after the death of Philip's elder brother Johannes in 1702.
"Memorandum to Governor Hunter," Sept. 17, 1718, N.Y. Col. MSS, LXI, 57.

5. Helen Wilkinson Reynolds, "Dutchess County before 1830," N.Y. History, XX
(1939), 270; Barnabas Paine to the surveyor general, Dec. 16, 1797, on Armenia town in
Dutchess County, Land Papers, Book V, 35, Bureau of Waterways, New York State Department of Transportation, Albany.

They attributed the phenomenon to the engrossment of the lands by a greedy few and to the concomitant lack of free land, which compelled immigrants as well as natives to desert New York for the neighboring provinces of Pennsylvania and New Jersey. Governor Hunter, chagrined at his difficulty in locating good land for the Palatine settlement, asserted in 1710 that the owners of vast tracts of real estate were keeping the province underpopulated "in hopes of Planting [it] with Tenants of their own." Six years later, he was more to the point: "It is apparent that extravagant tracts of land being held by single persons unimproved is the true cause that this Province does not increase in numbers of inhabitants in proportion to some of the neighbouring ones."[6] Implicit in his complaint was the assumption that all settlers were imbued with antilandlord sentiment and with a penchant for the life of a freeholder. In his report of 1732 on the "State of the Lands in the Province," Colden wrote that the colony was being drained of farmers because the landed magnates "themselves are not, nor never were in a Capacity to improve such large Tracts and other People will not become their Vassals or Tenants." After all, a great many people had uprooted themselves from their native country and ventured the perilous voyage to the new continent, he continued, in order to "avoid the dependence on landlords, and to enjoy lands in fee to descend to their posterity." To illustrate the irreconcilability between the New York land system and the imperatives of settlement, Colden quoted the failure of Captain Laughlin Campbell to erect a manor in the late 1730s. Campbell failed, Colden maintained, because the families he transported absolutely refused to become "his Tenants on any terms."[7] Whether Colden's view in this particular instance is correct is impossible to verify, but it is undeniable that colonial farmers in general preferred the absolute ownership of land to any kind of leasehold system. The yeoman psychology of the settlers was a formidable deterrent to the settlement of the great manors in the first and second decades of the eighteenth century.

In subsequent decades, however, manorial society defied the grim

6. Robert Hunter to Lords of Trade, Nov. 14, 1710, Nov. 12, 1715, Oct. 2, 1716, and Aug. 7, 1718, *N.Y. Col. Docs.*, V, 180, 459, 480, 514. Governors Edward Hyde, Lord Cornbury, and William Burnet entertained similar opinions on this subject. Cornbury to Lords of Trade, June 30, 1704, and Burnet to Lords of Trade, Dec. 20, 1726, *ibid.*, IV, 1112, V, 812.

7. Colden, "State of the Lands in the Province of New York, in 1732," *Doc. Hist. N.Y.*, I, 384; *Colden Papers*, V, 284–285. For Colden's earlier views on this subject, see *ibid.*, 283–286, VIII, 160–164; Kim, "New Look at the Great Landlords," *WMQ*, 3d Ser., XXVII (1970), 581–586.

predictions of the officials and displayed a healthy population increase. The roster of tenants in Philipsburgh jumped from 60 in 1712 to 170 in 1760—a 300 percent growth—to 272 in 1776, and to 287 by 1785. The leveling off from 1776 to 1785 probably indicates that the manor had reached the saturation point.[8] The Livingston Manor tenant body expanded twelve times the original number between 1716 and 1776, from 33 to about 460.[9] Rensselaerswyck proper showed much the same growth pattern, from 82 in 1714 to about 1,000 in 1779, with the most dramatic expansion occurring after 1763 when the northern and northwestern frontiers were at last freed from the persistent French-Indian menace.[10] Figures for Cortlandt Manor and Claverack are not available, but we may safely assume that their development was no slower than their sister manors. The growth rate of the tenantry on the manors is all the more impressive when we compare it with that of the whole provincial population. From 1715 to 1776, New York's white population increased sixfold, from 27,000 to 169,148, which was about the same pace as New Jersey and Connecticut but much faster than Massachusetts. This means that at least the two northern manors, despite their alleged unfavorable "manorial practices," seem to have been more successful in recruiting settlers than the other parts of the province.[11]

What accounts for the demographic expansion of these manors several decades prior to the outbreak of the Revolution? The answer seems to lie in two sets of circumstances and developments, one characteristic

8. Doc. Hist. N.Y., III, 949; "List of Tenants with the Respective Rents as they are Now Raised, Jan. 10th 1760," Philipse Papers, PA820, Sleepy Hollow Restorations Library, Tarrytown, N.Y.; rent roll of Col. Frederick Philipse's estate as of 1776, Loyalist Transcripts, XLI, 581–599; Sleepy Hollow Restorations, Philipsburg Manor, 35, 40; petition of Frederick Philipse to the king, June 11, 1763, C.O. 1071/5, 225, Public Record Office.

9. William H. W. Sabine, ed., Historical Memoirs of William Smith, Historian of the Province of New York, Member of the Governor's Council and Last Chief Justice of That Province under the Crown . . . (New York, 1956), II, 132; "Tax list of the District of the Manor of Livingston," 1779, New York State Library, Albany.

10. A tax list for Rensselaerswyck for the year 1752 indicates that there were 345 taxable inhabitants. We can assume that most or all of them were tenants. See "[Tax List] of the east and west of the Manor of Rensselaerswyck," Feb. 20, 1752, Bleecker, Collins, and Abeel Papers, Box 3, New York Public Library. The figures for 1779 were derived from a tax list of that year for the manor, and include all those who held land for which they were taxed. I excluded 182 people from my estimate on the assumption that they were not holding Van Rensselaer leases. Presumably, they were of Van Balls Patent and Coeymans Patent. Tax list for Rensselaerswyck, 1779, Folder 17, N.Y. State Lib.; "A Map of the Manor of Renselaerswick, 1767," by John R. Bleeker, Doc. Hist. N.Y., III, 916; William B. Fink, "Stephen Van Rensselaer: The Last Patroon" (Ph.D. diss., Columbia University, 1950), 28.

11. Greene and Harrington, American Population, passim. The phrase in quotation marks comes from Turner, Frontier in American History, 80–83.

of the northeastern Atlantic colonies in general and the other peculiar to New York. The first concerns the mounting pressure on land resources in the old settlements from population growth in that period, and the second, the problem of defense on the northern and northwestern frontiers of the province. Several recent studies have demonstrated that New England agricultural communities suffered a land shortage that became critical starting with the maturity of the third-generation colonists, or about a half-century after the founding of a town.[12] This appears to have been true of New York towns as well. For example, with the onset of the eighteenth century, the available land in Kings County on Long Island was felt to be inadequate to support a swollen population. Speaking of the exodus of people from the county, Governor Cornbury remarked in 1708: "Kings County is but small and full of people, so as the young people grow up, they are forced to seek land further off, to settle upon."[13] Subsequently, the land pressure worsened. Probably because of steady out-migration, the county census covering the period from 1703 to 1771 shows extremely slow demographic growth, just 41 percent compared with 446 percent for the whole province.[14]

It was particularly unfortunate for Kings County and other old towns that this problem arose at the very time when most of the fertile provincial lands along the Hudson River had been patented away. Compensatory grants in the northern areas toward Canada might have been a good means to siphon off the excess population, but this outlet was largely closed from the time of the Schenectady Massacre in 1690. Because of its strategic location, New York was fated to be the focal point of battle during the half-century of conflict between the English and French powers. The governors, to be sure, continued to grant vast amounts of land belonging to the Iroquois and made a half-hearted attempt to induce people to settle it, but the real estate remained totally inaccessible except for trappers and fur traders.[15] In 1763 the actual frontier line of the province was no farther than about forty miles north and northwest of

12. Philip J. Greven, Jr., *Four Generations: Population, Land, and Family in Colonial Andover, Massachusetts* (Ithaca, N.Y., 1970), 123, 125–126, 127; Kenneth Lockridge, "Land, Population and the Evolution of New England Society, 1630–1790," *Past and Present* (Apr. 1968), 62–80; Lockridge, *A New England Town*, 147–154; Charles S. Grant, *Democracy in the Connecticut Frontier Town of Kent* (New York, 1961), 98–103.

13. Lord Cornbury to Lords of Trade, July 1, 1708, *N.Y. Col. Docs.*, V, 56; Bellomont to Lords of Trade, Nov. 28, 1700, *ibid.*, IV, 791.

14. Greene and Harrington, *American Population*, 90–91, 95–102. I arrived at this conclusion because the county demographic growth fell far behind the average rate for natural increase of 50 percent every 25 years. Greven, *Four Generations*, 179.

15. George Clarke to Lords of Trade, June 19, 1743, and Dec. 15, 1741, *N.Y. Col.*

Albany; New York was almost as contained as it had been at the end of the seventeenth century.[16] One Albanian, nervous about the French-Indian offensive, lamented in the mid-1740s that Kinderhook, a place about twenty miles south of Albany, "is now a frontier."[17] This fear of invasion, though somewhat exaggerated, was typical of the frontier and unquestionably discouraging to potential settlers. Largely because of the perennial threat of war, the settlement of Rensselaerswyck proper was retarded in the first half of the century. As late as the end of King George's War (1744–1748), the domain lands to the east of the house of Christian Santz (or Shans), about six miles southeast of Albany and beyond Normans Kill to the west, remained in primeval state. The war even visited the manor, with two of the Santzes and four of the Normans Kill inhabitants being killed. The effect of the trauma apparently lingered on, so that for fifteen years only four new settlers came to live eastward of the Santzes.[18] The manor troubles were duplicated in other towns—Schenectady, Saratoga, Half Moon, Hoosick, Schaghticoke, and as far south as Newburgh.[19] In short, frontier conditions oriented New Yorkers inward rather than toward expansion, and the population naturally grew faster in the safer valley of the Hudson to the south than in the north and northwest.[20]

Thus, demographic and military conditions conspired to enhance

---

*Docs.*, VI, 225, 207; William Bayard's testimony, Mar. 14, 1785, A.O. 12/20, 200, P.R.O.; James De Lancey's testimony, 1785(?), A.O. 12/20, 196–198.

16. Robert Livingston to Lords of Trade, May 13, 1701, *N.Y. Col. Docs.*, IV, 873; William Johnson to Goldsbrow Banyar, June 12, 1770, *William Johnson Papers*, XII, 824.

17. Philip Livingston to Jacob Wendell, June 2, 1746, Livingston Papers, Museum of the City of New York; *N.-Y. Wkly. Journal*, Mar. 14 and June 20, 1748.

18. Hendrick Santz's deposition, Aug. 30, 1762, Columbia County Miscellaneous Manuscripts, New-York Historical Society, New York; Christian Santz's administration of his estates, Apr. 4, 1754, AAD4, no. 795, Queens College Library, New York; Philip Livingston to Jacob Wendell, June 2, 1746, Livingston Papers, Museum of City of N.Y.; *N.-Y. Wkly. Journal*, May 19, 1746, May 25, July 6, Aug. 24, 1746, Oct. 12, 1747, Mar. 14 and June 20, 1748.

19. Copybook and Journal of Abraham Yates, 1754–1758, 1–5, Abraham Yates, Jr., Papers, 1607–1825, Box 3, N.Y. Pub. Lib.; Robert Sanders to Jacob Wendell, May 10, July 11, and Sept. 2, 1755, Letterbook of Robert Sanders, 1752–1758, and petition of the inhabitants of the township of Schenectady to James De Lancey, 1756, Schenectady Papers, Box 1 (1600–1759), both in N.-Y. Hist. Soc.; Peter V. B. Livingston to Robert Livingston, Jr., July 22, 1755, Livingston-Redmond MSS, Roll 7.

20. Once the French-Indian menace was removed, the Albany County population showed a remarkable growth that far outstripped the other counties of the province. From 1756 to 1771, the county population grew 245 percent, while that of Dutchess, Westchester, and Ulster counties and of the province itself grew no more than 170 percent. Greene and Harrington, *American Population*, 91, 101–104. For further discussion of the frontier situation in relation to settlement of the province, see Kim, "New Look at the Great Landlords," *WMQ*, 3d Ser., XXVII (1970), 589–592.

the relative value of the large, unsettled Hudson estates that were secure from the enemy and, consequently, to induce potential settlers to overcome their traditional inhibitions toward the manors. At the same time, the stigma attached to the manorial system, as represented by the opinions of the royal officials, was more and more overshadowed by some of the attractive features of leasehold. The difficulties of the province thus redounded to the advantage of the manors. But population growth and land shortages do not themselves explain why a man who could afford a good freehold farm would choose tenancy instead, or why a man picked one manor over another, or why a tenant would hold on to his lease even after he had made enough money to go elsewhere. Ultimately, a tenant's decision, which was his alone, was affected by his economic circumstances, aptitudes, and familial relations, as well as by the location of the manors and the benefits of leaseholding. The ideal of yeomanry undoubtedly still beckoned to him, but as an economic agent he had to be realistic about the options available to him and could not allow himself and his family to perish in the pursuit of a dream.[21]

Fragmentary muster rolls from the years 1758 to 1760 for the manors of Philipsburgh, Cortlandt, and Livingston offer a glimpse of the backgrounds of the manor inhabitants at the time. The documents show the birthplaces of the militiamen but not their places of abode before they moved to these manors. Roughly 43 percent of Philipsburgh tenants were born in New York towns, 27 percent were born overseas, 7 percent in New England and other colonies, and 23 percent on the manor itself. As for Cortlandt Manor, 51 percent were born in New York towns, 12 percent overseas, 18 percent in New England and other colonies, and 19 percent on the manor itself. Significantly, most of the American-born settlers on these southern manors came from Westchester County towns, Long Island, and Connecticut, and seldom from Massachusetts or the northern counties. In Livingston Manor, the foreign-born topped the list of inhabitants with 44 percent, which was followed by 25 percent from New England and other colonies, 24 percent from New York towns, and 7 percent from the manor itself.[22] A heavy representation of foreign im-

21. The persistence of the antitenancy bias was vouched by Warren Johnson, brother of Sir William Johnson, when he stated in 1760 that "the Farmers are very bad and seldom rent, but buy land." "Warren Johnson's Journal, 1760–61," *William Johnson Papers*, XIII, 193. See also Goldsbrow Banyar to Samuel Dunlop, Aug. 28, 1761, Goldsbrow Banyar Papers, Box 6, N.-Y. Hist. Soc.

22. *Second Annual Report of the State Historian*, 880–883, 885–889, 932–944, 863–865, 871–875, 582–584, 598–600.

migrants here was something to be expected in light of Philip Livingston's aggressive recruitment of Germans and Scots.[23] Again significantly, the record registers neither a Long Islander nor a Westchester County man. Especially in light of the long history of the areas, the small proportion of the tenants (militiamen) born on these manors compared with that of tenants of nonmanorial parentage suggests considerable fluidity and instability in the populations of the domains, with considerable out-migration of native-born sons as well as immigration.

## Types of Tenants

Tenancy attracted about five types of settlers. First were desperately poor people whose only assets were their muscles. The manorial lease system with its various promotional features, as discussed in the previous chapter, best met their needs. To start farming on a freehold of modest size, a family needed at least £50 to £60 in the late seventeenth century and £200 to £500 in the middle of the eighteenth century.[24] The majority of the immigrants were from the poorer classes in the old society, and indentured servitude for many was the only means of transporting themselves to the New World.[25] An equal number paid their passage but were not able to buy lands or to subsist when they got here, some so hungry they were willing to work for "Flour or wheat as pay." As one of them admitted, they were in no condition to settle independently on "new lands with empty hands."[26] This perhaps was also true of the ex-servants, with only £10 in their pockets—the maximum compensation upon their discharge from servitude. The fate of the 150 yeoman-minded Palatines who tried to establish themselves on the Schoharie frontier between 1713

23. Philip Livingston to Jacob Wendell, Oct. 17, 1737, May 10, 1739, and Feb. 27, 1739, Livingston Papers, Museum of City of N.Y.; Philip Livingston to John D'Witt, Mar. 5, 11, 1741, Livingston-Redmond MSS, Roll 9.

24. Bellomont to Lords of Trade, Oct. 20, 1699, *N.Y. Col. Docs.*, IV, 588–589; William Smith, Jr., "Information to Farmers and Mechanics," William Smith Papers, Box 3, N.Y. Pub. Lib.

25. See the report on the arrival of the servants from Bristol, *N.-Y. Gaz.*, Oct. 31, 1737; *N.-Y. Mercury*, Oct. 15, 1764. For the indentured servants, see Samuel McKee, Jr., *Labor in Colonial New York, 1664–1776* (New York, 1935), chap. 3.

26. One such group of poor immigrants from Scotland petitioned the government in 1739 and 1740 for "some Allowance" on the ground that they were "unable in their present Poverty to subsist themselves." *Journal of General Assembly*, I, 758, 761. See also George Clarke's speech to the assembly, Oct. 13, 1738, *N.-Y. Gaz.*, Oct. 16, 1738, June 24, July 1, 1728, Nov. 3, 1729, and Apr. 21, 1735; Milton M. Klein, ed., *The Independent Reflector, or, Weekly Essays on Sundry Important Subjects, More particularly adapted to the Province of New-York* ... (Cambridge, Mass., 1963), 82, 85–86; Isaac Vrooman to James Duane, May 4, 1764, James Duane Papers, 1752–1796, Roll 1, N.-Y. Hist. Soc.

and 1716 was a familiar story. Their undertaking, spurred by an aversion to working for the government, was a sheer nightmare, and they finally sold themselves as servants in Pennsylvania for five years.[27] However freedom-loving they were, they could not do without the essential requirements of agriculture—capital, farming instruments, mills, and markets—which the landlords in general provided at the initial stage of settlement.

Even Cadwallader Colden, surveyor general of the province for almost a half-century after 1720 and the most bitter critic of the great landowners, had some kind words for the merits of tenancy: "And as the persons willing to settle and improve lands in the woods on the Frontiers, at a great distance from the Markett, are of the poorest of the Inhabitants, they were desirous to join with Men of Fortune, who, on certain conditions agreed on, where [were] willing to advance money for them, to enable them to settle, to build houses and to purchase other necessaries for improving the Lands, and to support them untill such time as they may be able to support their families by their own labour; which they cannot do in less than three years after they have begun to improve."[28] In 1701 the earl of Bellomont noted that four or five tenants on Livingston Manor, as he was told, were "too poor to be farmers having not the wherewithall to buy Cattle to stock a farm," and that those on Cortlandt and Philipsburgh manors too were "poor families."[29] In any case, with the support of the landlords, such settlers could begin work as farmers with a minimum of deprivation and hardship, which otherwise would have been their lot. The lease system was to a farming family what indentured servitude was to a single man and woman immigrating to America: insurance against the initial hazards of transplantation. If the latter was a promotional instrument of colonization, so was the former. But in one important respect, tenancy was more advantageous, because what a leaseholder invested and raised on the virgin land became his own, whereas the fruits of an indentured servant's labor all went to his master. Of course, the tenant had to pay rent, which in effect earned him the right to keep his improvements. As shall be shown in detail, the value of tenant improvements increased considerably in due course, which in turn

27. Knittle, *Palatine Emigration*, 210; McKee, *Labor in Colonial New York*, 95–97.
28. Colden to Lords of Trade, Mar. 1, 1762, *N.Y. Col. Docs.*, VII, 492; a preamble to an act on leaseholding, passed on July 24, 1724, *N.Y. Col. Laws*, II, 206; John Mason to James Duane, Apr. 5, 1786, Duane Papers, Roll 2; William Smith, Jr., to Mr. Thom, Nov. 14, 1774, William Smith Papers, Box 4; *William Johnson Papers*, XII, 1111, 1023–1024.
29. Bellomont to Lords of Trade, Jan. 2, 1701, *N.Y. Col. Docs.*, IV, 822–833.

boosted the attractiveness of the leasehold system. Yet, ironically, the more the wild manorial lands were taken up and tamed by the first-comers, the narrower the gate of the manors became for succeeding settlers, who had to have enough capital to purchase the valuable improvements. And as the unappropriated manorial lands disappeared—first in Cortlandt Manor and Philipsburgh roughly by 1760, then in Livingston Manor by 1770, and finally at Rensselaerswyck by 1790—the manors' historic function as an asylum for the impoverished came to an end.

The second type of settler, unlike the first, comprised mostly persons with marginal property, including occasionally new immigrants with some cash. Various motives brought these people to the manors. Robert Williams, born at Hempstead, Long Island, had a 50-acre right in Bedford Township but decided in the 1710s to hire a larger tract of 151 acres in northern Philipsburgh. John Garnsey of Litchfield, Connecticut, sold his small farm in town and moved in 1763 to Claverack, where he leased 400 acres from John Van Rensselaer, its proprietor, so that "he might be the better able to provide his family."[30] Probably for a similar reason, Aert Williams sold his land with "improvements and buildings" at Rye for £18 and settled in Philipsburgh in the early 1720s.[31] Concerned about the future livelihood of his eldest son, Volkert, Wynant Van Den Bergh of Albany, a "brickman," leased in the mid-1740s a house and lot in Rensselaerswyck.[32] In 1769 Johannes Miller of the German "Camp" gave up his farm of about 150 acres to son Samuel and obtained for his own support a lease in the nearby Livingston Manor.[33] Peter Van Den Bogert of Poughkeepsie, after he sold his small freehold to liquidate

---

30. Deed Book E, 85, Westchester County Clerk's Office, White Plains, N.Y. See also the cases of Mathias Buckhout and Joseph Tompkins, *ibid.*, 393–394. For further information about Robert Williams, see William Skinner to Samuel Purdie, Feb. 13, 1739, New Jersey Papers, III, N.-Y. Hist. Soc.; *N.Y. Gen. and Biog. Rec.*, XVI, 53–54; A.O. 12/25, 424, 12/19, 577–604. For Garnsey, see petition of Garnsey, Feb. 27, 1773, C.O. 1104/5, 437–440, P.R.O.; Broer Janse to John Casperse, July 26, 1708, Deed Book 5: 70, Albany County Clerk's Office, Albany, N.Y.; deed, John Garnsey of New Lebanon to Jonas and Augustine Odel, Jr., Jan. 10, 1771, Deed Book 8: 419, *ibid.*

31. Deed Book F, 80, Westchester Co. Clerk's Office.

32. Will of Wynant Van Den Bergh, May 8, 1749, Glen-Sanders Papers, Colonial Williamsburg Foundation Research Department, Williamsburg, Va. Obtaining a lease by the worried parents for a son's support was quite common. Will of Philip H. Moyr of Rhinebeck, May 2, 1774, Wills, XXIX, 200, Queens College Lib.; will of William Dietz, Mar. 25, 1782, *ibid.*, XXXIII, 325; will of Jedediah Wing, *ibid.*, XXXVII, 427; will of Adam Van Alen, Oct. 17, 1748, *ibid.*, XVI, 409–411; lease, Robert Teunisson Van Deusen to sons Teewis and Tobias, Feb. 15, 1726, Deed Book 10: 96, Albany Co. Clerk's Office; deed, Jacob Truax to son Andries, Dec. 15, 1769, Deed Book 11: 255, *ibid.*

33. Deed, Johannes Miller to Samuel Miller, Dec. 9, 1769, Deed Book 9: 277, Albany Co. Clerk's Office; Livingston Manor Rent Ledger, 1767–1784, 12, N.-Y. Hist. Soc.

his debts, found it necessary to buy in 1771 an improved lease in the manor.[34] With a design to commercialize his rustic endeavor, Joseph Golden of North Castle bought in 1765 a lease and improvements of 215 acres in Cortlandt Manor, although he then owned a 60-acre freehold in town.[35] Upon coming of age, Underhill Barnes and William Leggett left Westchester Borough for Philipsburgh, and Simon Brady left North Castle for Cortlandt Manor, because their parents' landholdings were too diminished to allow further division for their benefit.[36] Many other individual examples could be given. Handicapped by limited economic resources, these people found a leasehold, improved or not, a viable— and sometimes the only—alternative means of livelihood.

Another commonly found characteristic of this second group of settlers should be noted. The acquisition of a leasehold was for them not only a quest for economic benefits but also a means of remaining geographically close to their parents, siblings, or children. The first-generation colonists were venturesome, since they had braved the treacherous ocean. But subsequent generations, for reasons of either material security or emotional family bonds, did not cherish the thought of moving alone, far away from their kin, to a strange place where family visits might be altogether impractical and the possibility of getting help once in a while would be slight. Thus, the location of a manor could sometimes assume crucial importance for a prospective tenant. That geographical and familial factors influenced tenants is evidenced by the composition of the Livingston Manor tenantry in the mid-eighteenth century. As noted above, Long Islanders and Westchester men were conspicuously absent, while they made up almost half of the tenant population of Philipsburgh and Cortlandt manors. The southerners avoided Livingston Manor not because it offered a bad lease but because it was too remote from them. The

34. Andries Moore to Robert Livingston, Jr., Jan. 28, 1771, and Bartho[lomew] Crannel to Robert Livingston, Jr., May 14, 1773, Livingston-Redmond MSS, Roll 8.

35. Loyalist Transcripts, XXIX, 275; entry on July 30, 1765, Journal (c) of John Van Cortlandt, 1762–1769, N.Y. Pub. Lib.

36. Letter of administration, Apr. 27, 1716, Morristown Historical Park Collection (microfilm), Roll 42, Morristown, N.J.; bond of Underhill Barnes to Adolph Philipse, Apr. 14, 1742, Benjamin Palmer Papers, Box 2, N.-Y. Hist. Soc.; Barnes's will, Dec. 6, 1750, in *Abstracts of Wills on File in the Surrogate's Office, City of New York* (N.-Y. Hist. Soc., Colls., XXV–XLI [New York, 1892–1908]), V, 198, hereafter cited as *Abstracts of Wills; N.Y. Gen. and Biog. Rec.*, XLV (1914), 285. William Leggett's father was mayor of Westchester Borough at one time. For Leggett's tenant status, see the rent roll for 1760, Philipse Papers, PA820, Sleepy Hollow Restorations Lib. For Simon Brady, see John Brady's will, Aug. 14, 1782, Wills, XXXVII, 12, Queens College Lib.; Journal (c) of John Van Cortlandt, N.Y. Pub. Lib., on Simon Brady's lease; and John Van Cortlandt to Joseph Golden, May 24, 1766, Letterbooks of Stephen and John Van Cortlandt, N.Y. Pub. Lib.

rootless and indigent immigrants, however, could not, nor did they have the cause to, exercise such discrimination. The proclivity of American-born colonists to remain near their kin facilitated the rapid growth of the southern manors. In the long run, this helped the other manors too, for the cumulative effect of settlement eventually touched the north. As one contemporary writer observed, a settlement of fifteen or twenty families in wilderness land would be "Incouragement Sufficient for others to settle" in the neighborhood.[37]

Even for an overseas immigrant with some money, it was considered advisable to lease land at the beginning and then to purchase after the settler had a better knowledge of the country and its problems. Significantly, such a precaution was recommended even by Crèvecoeur, who was probably the most articulate colonial romanticizer of the values and virtues of an independent yeomanry. A yeoman farmer himself, Crèvecoeur found nothing demeaning and servile about becoming a tenant. He gave a rosy account of the progress of his onetime neighbor named Andrew, a Scot, from a common laborer to a prosperous leaseholder of a hundred acres in mid-eighteenth-century Pennsylvania. Two advantages of tenancy particularly impressed Crèvecoeur. By leasing the land, the main and most expensive capital investment in farming, Andrew did not have to "disturb" his own money to buy the real estate in fee, and he could instead purchase "a plough, a team and some stock," thus avoiding the large debts that an indigent settler generally incurred at the start. Second, Crèvecoeur was impressed by a provision in Andrew's contract guaranteeing that whatever improvements he made on the land would be appraised by an impartial "jury" of his neighbors and purchased by his landlord whenever he decided to quit the premises. For Crèvecoeur, taking a lease was the best option for Andrew at that particular phase of his adaptation to America.[38] Who among the manorial tenants in New York duplicated Andrew's success is unknown, but we may suppose that many did and that the American-born colonists of marginal means also were drawn to these manors for the kind of material rewards and advantages that Andrew's lease offered.

A third type of settler was the colonial entrepreneur who sought to

37. Robert Livingston, Jr., to James Duane, Nov. 9, 1764, Duane Papers, Roll 1.

38. Crèvecoeur, *Letters from an American Farmer*, 78–91. Crèvecoeur's view of lease-holding was echoed by Mrs. Anne Grant, a keen observer of the Albany County scene in the third quarter of the eighteenth century, when she stated that "every mechanic ended in being a farmer, that is a profitable tenant to the owner of the soil." Grant, *Memoirs of an American Lady*, 264.

exploit the commercial and industrial possibilities of the manors. These men were welcomed as tenants, however, only when a manorial proprietor was himself unable or unwilling to establish and operate such facilities as shops and mills. The Livingston Manor proprietors were all so commercially oriented and so jealous of their captive market that they admitted no competitors. Nor did Adolph Philipse of Philipsburgh, although after his death in 1749 and as Frederick Philipse III withdrew from commercial and milling operations, several merchants moved in to fill the void. One of them, Gilbert Drake of Rye, arrived in the manor in 1749 or 1750 and quickly set up a shop on his leasehold. Probably in partnership with Samuel Drake of the manor and Joshua Delaplaine of New York City, Drake dealt in dry goods and mill and farming utensils, and his business extended to both sides of the Hudson River. In 1767 he took up sawmilling and gristmilling at Cortlandt Manor. Five years later he moved both his business and his family to a 220-acre farm there that he had rented from the Beekmans at the yearly rate of £4. Meanwhile he also dabbled in real estate ventures.[39] Gilbert Drake's counterparts may be found in the other manors as well, though on a smaller scale— Abraham Fonda of Claverack for trade,[40] Robert Van Deusen of the same place for gristmilling,[41] two sons of Evert Wendell, Jr., an Albany merchant-lawyer, for sawmilling in Rensselaerswyck,[42] Joseph Strang of Cortlandt Manor for trade,[43] Jonas and Hendrick Douw and Andries

39. For the activities and career of Gilbert Drake, see "Manor of Philipsburgh, List of officers," *Tarrytown Argus*, Apr. 18, 1903; Philipse Papers, PX135, and Drake's release from the Beekmans, Apr. 27, 1772, Van Cortlandt Papers, V2205, both in Sleepy Hollow Restorations Lib.; *N.Y. Col. Laws*, IV, 78–79, 895–897; "Richard Budd vs Joseph Tompkins," 1771, in Lawsuits, A-B, John Tabor Kempe Papers, N.-Y. Hist. Soc.; Drake's order on Joshua Delaplaine, Apr. 5, 1759, Miscellaneous Manuscripts, T, and Joshua Delaplaine Papers, *passim*, both also in N.-Y. Hist. Soc.; Deed Book G, 663, Deed Book H, 186–187, 272–274, 378–380, Deed Book I, 232–233, Mortgage Book A, 359, Mortgage Book B, 14, all in Westchester Co. Clerk's Office; *N.Y. Gen. and Biog. Rec.*, LVIII (1937), 109.

40. Munsell, ed., *Annals of Albany*, II, 189; Abraham Fonda's will, July 30, 1762, Wills, XXIV, 57, Queens College Lib.

41. Lease, Henry Van Rensselaer to Robert Van Deusen, Sept. 11, 1718, Deed Book 5: 424, Albany Co. Clerk's Office.

42. Evert Wendell to Jeremiah Van Rensselaer, Nov. 22, 1744, Letters, 1700–1749, Rensselaerswyck Manuscripts, N.Y. State Lib.; Wendell's will, July 23, 1749, Wills, XIX, 40–45, Queens College Lib.; Day Book of Evert Wendell, particularly entry on Sept. 22, 1727, N.-Y. Hist. Soc. For Wendell's career, see Armour, "Merchants of Albany," 81–82, 181–182, 196. One of Wendell's sons was Abraham. See also the examples of Andries A. Bratt, Johannes Wendell, and Johannes Van Vechten, Pearson, trans., and Van Laer, ed., *Early Records of Albany and Rensselaerswyck*, II, 247, 271; John Brees Papers, folder 4, on Van Vechten, N.Y. State Lib.

43. Joseph Strang leased a small tract around 1760 for the yearly rent of £2. "List of Tennants in the Manor of C," Van Cortlandt Family Papers, N.-Y. Hist. Soc.; Book H, 264–274, Westchester Co. Clerk's Office.

Witbeck for brewing in Rensselaerswyck,[44] and James Barnard for tavern-and innkeeping in Philipsburgh.[45]

The fourth type of manorial settler was characteristic of Rensselaerswyck. There many Albanians were trapped in tenancy as a way of life due to the geographical and historical circumstances of their city. Despite its powerful commercial and political influence in the county, Albany was a small and compact stockaded town of about seven hundred acres surrounded by huge Rensselaerswyck. Since 1699 it had a satellite colony named Schaghticoke, six square miles in area and lying about twenty miles north on the east side of the Hudson River.[46] Affluent Albanians speculated heavily in the frontier lands in the first half of the eighteenth century, but the tracts they acquired were of little use, being remote and exposed to the French-Indian depredations. The emergence of grain and lumber from a "subsidiary to the dominant role in the economy of the northern frontier of New York" in the first two decades of the century accentuated the demand for land that was conveniently situated and secure from the enemy. The Indian trade continued as the pillar of the city's prosperity for many years to come, but it was definitely on the decline.[47] Land-related businesses, such as commercial farming and saw-milling, thus became a good source of supplementary income or an alternative livelihood for some burghers. People naturally coveted the domain land along the river, although it was available only for rental. It is significant that of 96 leases granted by the patroons from 1689 to 1744, a majority of them, 53, were granted in the period from 1700 to 1720. As of 1720, 32 out of 149 Albany freeholders were also holding manor leaseholds. The freeholder-tenants included great merchant-patricians like Peter Van Brugh (mayor of Albany and father-in-law of Philip Livingston), Myndert Schuyler, Anthony Van Schaick, Hendrick Outhout, and Harmanus Wendell.[48] In 1763 at least 87 of 242 city freeholders were the

44. Lease, Henry Van Rensselaer to Jonas and Hendrick Douw and Andries Witbeck, Oct. 12, 1717, Deed Book 5: 420, Albany Co. Clerk's Office.

45. Advertisement for the sale of Barnard's lease, N.-Y. Mercury, supplement, Mar. 9, 1767.

46. I owe the information about the size of Albany city to Mr. Stefan Bielinsky of the New York State Historian's Office, Albany, N.Y.; Munsell, ed., Annals of Albany, III, 34–35; deed, Henry Van Rensselaer to Albany city, Aug. 30, 1699, Drawer 1, Albany Institute of History and Art, Albany, N.Y. Albany city began to settle Schaghticoke in 1708, but the frontier outpost was deserted whenever war broke out between England and France. Munsell, ed., Annals of Albany, V, 183–184, VII, 12–13, 15–16, 16–18, 20, 51, 54–55, 73–75, 82, VIII, 231, 235, 237, 242–243; Copybook and Journal of Abraham Yates, entry on Sept. 11, 1754, Yates Papers, Box 3; Albany city to James De Lancey, Sept. 11, 1754, N.Y. Col. MSS, LXXIX, 33; Smith, [Jr.], History of New-York (1757 ed.), 199.

47. For land speculation by Albanians, see Armour, "Merchants of Albany," 143–145.

48. Doc. Hist. N.Y., I, 370; Muster Roll, N.Y. Col. MSS, LX, 51; "A list of Inden-

patroon's tenants.[49] The number in both instances would be higher if we were able to track down subtenants, who did not appear on rent rolls of the domain. Not all of these Albanian tenants went in for commercial farming. Cornelius Williamse Van Den Bergh, Jan Gerritze, and Jacob Van Schaick leased "town" lots on the highway connecting their city with Watervliet.[50] Robert Sanders, Mynd Harmens, and Dirck Roseboom, all Indian traders, hired manor land for grazing, presumably because the city's pasture ground was overcrowded.[51] According to the noted Swedish traveler Peter Kalm, many burghers sublet "some greater and smaller lots of ground" in the manor "for kitchen gardens."[52] Henry Cuyler, a merchant, rented seventeen acres of land at Greenbush to build a country mansion. It was these close connections between the manor and Albany that prompted Kalm, writing at mid-century, to remark: "The vast majority, in fact almost everyone [in Albany], carried on a business, though a great many have in addition their houses and farms in the country, close to or at some distance from the town."[53]

Finally, comprising a fifth group were those colonists whose motives or reasons for taking up manorial land cannot be fitted into the categories we have discussed so far. A case in point is Isaac Vrooman of Schenectady, who wanted to lease a "few" acres of woodland in Rensselaerswyck behind his farm in order to prevent a neighbor's cattle from damaging his fence and grain on the field.[54] Others coveted leasehold lands merely for speculation. Twenty-three New Englanders in 1765 together acquired 12,000 acres of lease land known as Stephentown with no intention to

tures, 1696–1744," Rensselaerswyck MSS; Kiliaen Van Rensselaer's letter to an unknown recipient, 1716, on Terck H. Visscher, Letters, 1674–1700, *ibid.*; Rensselaerswyck Rent Ledger, 1721–1733, *ibid.*; Deed Book 5: 307–308, Albany Co. Clerk's Office.

49. "Book of the Freeholders of the City and County of Albany, [1763]," Lawsuits, A–B, Kempe Papers. I have checked the list against the rent ledgers of Rensselaerswyck, wills and deeds of the county residents, and other miscellaneous records relating to the manor tenants.

50. Cornelius Williamse Van Den Bergh's will, Nov. 24, 1706, Wills, AV9, Queens College Lib.; Deed Book 9: 381–383, 10: 190, Albany Co. Clerk's Office. These lots along the highway leading to Watervliet were platted out originally by Kiliaen Van Rensselaer for residential and business purposes. Consequently, they were called "town" lots. A.O. 12/32, 213, 13/16, 206.

51. Lease, Kiliaen Van Rensselaer to Robert Sanders and Mynd Harmens, June 20, 1692, Staats Family Archives, Box 3, N.Y. State Lib.; entry on Dirck Roseboom, Feb. 5, 1777, Abraham Ten Broeck's Accounts of the Manor, 1763–1786, Rensselaerswyck MSS; N.Y. Col. Docs., VII, 615.

52. Benson, ed., *Peter Kalm's Travels*, I, 338.

53. Lease, John Van Rensselaer to Henry Cuyler, Apr. 26, 1766, Harmanus Bleecker Papers, Box 2, 1752–1805, N.Y. State Lib.; Benson, ed., *Peter Kalm's Travels*, II, 615.

54. Isaac Vrooman to Abraham Ten Broeck, Feb. 20, 1767, Ten Broeck Family Papers, Box 3, Albany Inst. of Hist. and Art; Vrooman's lease, June 20, 1769, Rensselaerswyck Leases, 1766–1797, Rensselaerswyck MSS.

settle it themselves.[55] Before 1775 most of them liquidated their rights in the tract with profits ranging from £5 to £42 10s. Some of the second and even third purchasers bought tracts for the same reason. In 1766 James Gray, Jr., "gentleman" of Stockbridge, Massachusetts, and an original lessee, sold part of his share to John Garnsey of Claverack for £10. Five years later Garnsey sold it for £18 to Augustine Odel, Jr., who in turn sold half of the premises for £18 three months later.[56] In 1772 David Pixley of Stockbridge, "gentleman" and an original lessee, disposed of part of his share to Ichabod Turner of Stephentown, "gentleman," for £4, and in the following year Turner parted with half of his purchase for £40.[57] But John Duncan of Schenectady, a merchant and owner of Corry's Bush Patent (10,000 acres) in the Schoharie valley, rented patroon land to sublet for profit. Just three days after he obtained a perpetual lease of 257 acres for a yearly rental of 62 bushels of winter wheat, he subleased 100 acres to Walter Barrant of Schenectady for £12 and an annual rent of 50 bushels of wheat. A few months later, Duncan sublet another 100 acres at the same rent. From these conveyances he could expect a net profit of 38 bushels a year while still holding 57 acres for his own use. Records indicate that he then acquired two more pieces of manor land for a term of years.[58] How common this practice was in the other manors, however, is unknown.

## Equity in Improvements and the New Status of Tenancy

Notwithstanding the heterogeneity of their motives and their backgrounds, manorial tenants in New York shared one thing in common—a desire to better their conditions. They drew two sorts of benefits from their rustic endeavor of leaseholding. One, obviously, was the use of the land. The other, which has been largely ignored by historians, was the

55. For the original tenants at Stephentown, see "Notice of Division" by Benjamin Shelden and others, N.-Y. Gaz.; and Wkly. Mercury, Jan. 23, 1775.

56. Deed Book 8: 315–318, 419, 424–425, Albany Co. Clerk's Office.

57. Deed Book 9: 347, 349, ibid. For land speculation in Stephentown, 1765–1775, see Deed Book 7: 417, Deed Book 8: 130–132, 258–259, 261–262, 296–297, 300–307, 312–313, 315–318, 377, 414, 416–417, 419, 424–426, Deed Book 9: 1, 6, 13–16, 18, 95, 181, 246, 329–331, 342, 344, 347, 349–350, 357, 359, 390–393, 408–409, 411, Deed Book 10: 8–9, 77–78, 100, 104, 115, 118, 183–190, 256, 376, 384–385, 388, 429, and Deed Book 11: 322, ibid.

58. Rensselaerswyck Rent Ledger, 1768–1789, 85, on John Duncan, Rensselaerswyck MSS; Mortgage Book 2: 334, Mortgage Book 3: 43, 292, Albany Co. Clerk's Office; John Duncan to Abraham Ten Broeck, Sept. 22 and Oct. 17, 1769, Ten Broeck Family Papers, Boxes 1 and 3; Duncan's advertisement on "Corry's Bush" Patent, N.-Y. Mercury, Jan. 16 and May 7, 1764.

equity acquired in improvements on the land. Improvements consisted of dwellings, outhouses, barns, stables, fences, orchards, nurseries, cleared fields for ploughing or pasturing, and any other agricultural facilities a tenant might erect. Originally granted by the manorial landlords as a promotional device, what the tenants called their "possession" grew into "something like a custom," with inheritable and marketable property constituting an integral part of tenancy in these manors. Equally important was the retention of this prescriptive right by the tenants even after the lease had expired. The landlords retained title to the soil, but in practical terms, it was no more than a claim to receive rent, for the sale of a lease with improvements transferred the possession of the earth as well as the buildings on a leasehold. The moment an indigent colonist signed a lease and drove his plow into the ground he transformed himself into a propertied man and a copartner in the land with his landlord. Under these circumstances, the landlord was restrained from exercising any "act of absolute ownership."[59]

According to Governor Bellomont, in 1699 the cost of clearing an acre of land "from the woods" was £4 10s. This figure did not include the expenses of planting orchards and of building dwellings and barns.[60] Where the land was rough, densely wooded, or, worse, located on a hillside, the cost of clearing went as high as £50 or more per acre in 1740.[61] Even allowing for the currency inflation and the concomitant increase in the value of labor, a £50 expenditure for clearing an acre still seems exorbitant. According to Bellomont's 1699 estimate, a tenant who cleared ten acres of land built up an equity of £45 in the lease. Even the required planting of fruit trees in orchards eventually turned to his advantage, since a mature apple tree was rated at 7d. A modest tenant dwelling house with three rooms and three fireplaces cost about £40 to build in the 1760s, and a barn of 45 by 50 feet cost about £14 in 1771.[62] Nevertheless, the market value of improvements, like any piece of real estate, was influenced by the length of the lease tenure, the productivity of the soil, the location and size of the farm, and the degree and kind of

59. Beverly Robinson to ?, Dec. 11, 1806, "Family Records," Philipse Papers, PX260, Sleepy Hollow Restorations Lib.

60. Bellomont to Lords of Trade, Aug. 24, 1699, N.Y. Col. Docs., IV, 553–554. According to another land developer, it cost the same amount in the 1760s. James Duane to Mr. S. Chottel, May 21, 1787, Duane Papers, Roll 3.

61. Philip Livingston to Jacob Wendell, Oct. 28, 1740, Livingston Papers, Museum of City of N.Y.

62. Expense of building a house for Isaac Frost in 1768, Journal (c) of John Van Cortlandt, N.Y. Pub. Lib.; John McFarland to James Duane, Dec. 21, 1771, Duane Papers, Roll 1.

improvements. Conrad Van Deusen, a former tenant of Claverack, observed that "Improvements on Leases for Lives" were not "so valuable" as those on perpetual leases, simply because the former was legally less secure than the latter.[63] Furthermore, no two tenant farms in different manors—for instance, Livingston and Philipsburgh—were equal in value even if the other conditions were exactly the same.

There is no simple formula for determining how fast and how much a tenant would typically improve his lease in a certain length of time. Robert R. Livingston of Clermont asserted in about 1752 that a man "seldom sits down a Piece of Land a whole Year, before he is able to dispose of his Improvement for £50, or 100£ and sometimes for much more." He did not indicate, however, whether he was referring to the usual achievement on his manor or somewhere else. Crèvecoeur estimated that his friend Andrew's lease with improvements on 100 acres was worth about £90 after four years of hard work.[64] In 1768 Hendrick Ten Broeck of Claverack sold "all the lease land" of 173 acres for £125 after improving it for the previous five years.[65] In 1773 John Garnsey of the same place, who in ten years built "a good farm, dwelling house and barn and improved 100 acres of upland and meadow" out of 400 acres, claimed the "whole of his Improvements value" to be no less than £600.[66] Cornight Briggs and Solomon Burtis, both of Cortlandt Manor, in 1758 each sold their lease of 250 acres and improvements of ten years' duration for £175 and £80 respectively.[67] It is safe to assume that major improvement projects were carried out in the first and second years of settlement and that further additions were made gradually in subsequent years. Obviously, however, the speed with which a tenant made improvements, and the quality of his work, depended on his diligence, his talents, and his financial strength.[68]

These human and economic factors were responsible for great variations in the value of improvements, as appears in the sixty-five cases of

63. Conrad Van Deusen's testimony on the case of George Finkle, a tenant-loyalist, Sept. 16, 1787, A.O. 12/28, 140.
64. McAnear, ed., "Mr. Robert R. Livingston's Reasons," *Jour. Pol. Econ.*, XLVIII (1940), 90, Crèvecoeur, *Letters from an American Farmer*, 90–91.
65. Deed Book 9: 53–57, Albany Co. Clerk's Office.
66. John Garnsey to Gov. William Tryon, Feb. 27, 1773, C.O. 1104/5, 437–440.
67. "Papers belonging to the Lieutenant Governor," Van Cortlandt Papers, V1836, V1643, Sleepy Hollow Restorations Lib.; Pierre Van Cortlandt's advertisement, *N.-Y. Mercury*, Nov. 28, 1757; lease, Philip Van Cortlandt to Solomon Burtis, Apr. 18, 1748, Van Cortlandt-Van Wyck Papers, N.Y. Pub. Lib.
68. Cadwallader Colden to Gov. Burnet, Aug. 26, 1724, N.Y. Land Papers, IX, 114.

lease sales in the manors from 1749 to 1786 listed in table 6.1.[69] Allowing for the variables, however, there seems to have been a close relationship between the age of a lease and the worth of its improvements: the longer one held a lease, the greater its value. This principle was illustrated on a small scale in the turnover of a 110-acre farm in Clermont, which Bart Steelwell sold for £40 to Samuel Ketchum in July 1771. Five months later Ketchum sold it to Joshua Gifford for £45. Gifford then assigned half of the farm to Joseph Odel for £20 and three years later conveyed the remainder of "his title" to John Sprague for £63.[70] In some cases, the value of improvements grew to an extraordinary amount. "Poesten Farm," a tract of unknown size in Rensselaerswyck proper that had been leased in 1672 by Philip Schuyler, was appraised to have a market value of £1,241 four decades later.[71] A widow of Philipsburgh Manor was reported to have sold "her Husband's Rights" for £1,200 several years before the Revolution. A tenant named Samuel Davenport insisted that in general the possession right of 200 acres on the manor "used to sell for £600 New York Currency" about that time.[72] John Hyat of Cortlandt Manor declared in 1796 that his lease of 230 acres was worth £1,400; he had purchased it for only £62 10s. 9d. four decades earlier. This tremendous increase in the value of Hyat's property cannot be ascribed to the depreciation of New York's currency, which was slight—only about 17 percent—between the mid-1750s and the 1790s.[73] Simon Brady,

69. In addition, I have found at least 40 other cases of lease sales, but the prices are missing.

70. See a note, July 8–Oct. 10, 1774, on Bart Steelwell's farm, "Uncatalogued Livingston Manuscripts," N.-Y. Hist. Soc. Conrad Van Deusen, who had bought a lease of 139 acres in Claverack for £35 in the 1760s, rated it at £100 in 1777. A.O. 12/31, 1–3. See also the transactions of a farm originally leased by William Price in 1742, in "Uncatalogued Livingston MSS." For similar turnovers on other patents, see lease from Oliver De Lancey and Peter Dubois to Johannis Van Deverkin, July 12, 1765, Albany County Misc. MSS, Box 3, N.-Y. Hist. Soc.

71. Deed Book 5: 51–54, 115–116, 124–125, Albany Co. Clerk's Office; "Inventory of the all real Estate as Belonged to Philip Schuyler," Apr. 17, 1711, Schuyler Family Papers, Albany Inst. of Hist. and Art. Besides, during her lifetime Margaret Schuyler held two other large rental farms, including the famous "Schuyler Flats" several miles north of Albany.

72. Testimony of Samuel Peters, formerly of Philipsburgh Manor, Dec. 13, 1784, A.O. 12/19, 400. For Davenport's improvements, see A.O. 12/17, 427–430. But John Bulea of the same place contended that his lease of 200 acres was worth £400. Another tenant named William Underhill appraised his improvements of 200 acres at £500 and still another at £700. A.O. 12/26, 7, 12/27, 417, 12/25, 127. In discussing the value of improvements, we need to keep in mind these variables. To draw a medium figure would be a futile exercise.

73. Lease, Andrew Barton to John Hyat, Nov. 5, 1757, Van Cortlandt Papers, V1945,

Table 6.1. Sale of Improvements on Livingston, Rensselaerswyck, Cortlandt, and Philipsburgh Manors, 1749–1786
(Values in New York Currency)

| Seller | Buyer | Value (£) | Date Sold |
|---|---|---|---|
| | LIVINGSTON MANOR | | |
| John Mckay | Robert Livingston, Jr. | 20 | 1751 |
| Peter Althuyser | Johannis Arkenbregh | 46 | 1756 |
| Daniel Woodworth | Andries Lott | 60 | 1760 |
| John Witbeck | Teunis Snyder | 80 | 1762 |
| John Robinson | John B. Koens | 90 | 1763 |
| Gabriel Brusie | Robert Livingston, Jr. | 150 | 1763 |
| Jacobus Proper | Nicholas Luyck | 29 | 1763 |
| William Krankhyt | Philip Fells | 100 | 1765 |
| Broer Decker | Robert Livingston, Jr. | 72 | 1768 |
| Andries Moore | Robert Livingston, Jr. | 195 | 1771 |
| Jacob the Jew | ? | 125 | 1773 |
| Martin Camel | Dirck Steenberg | 100 | 1783 |
| Albartus Siemon | Robert Livingston, Jr. | 250 | 1784 |
| Hendrick Clapper, Jr. | George Shuffelt | 150 | 1785 |
| Barant Benthuysen | ? | 372 10s. | 1785 |
| Conrad Petri | Jonathan Holcomb | 180 | 1785 |
| Hugh Rea | Robert Livingston, Jr. | 200 | 1786 |
| Andrew Shurts | Teunis Snocks | 150 | ? |
| | RENSSELAERSWYCK | | |
| John Norton | Samuel Heynder | 70 | 1766 |
| Dirck Cluet | Lodowyck Seager | 40 | 1766 |
| Jerom Barheyatt | Corns Jan: Schermerhorn | 36 | 1766 |
| Gerrit Seager | Jacob Cooper | 520 | 1766 |
| John Freeman | Simon J. Cole | 75 | 1766 |
| Johannes Becker | Johannes Eyckerson | 150 | 1768 |
| Hendrick Ten Broeck | Peter Wiesmer | 125 | 1768 |
| Jacob Quackenbush | Jacob Van Schaick | 80 | 1769 |
| Frans Van Valkenburgh | Joseph Hauser | 75 | 1770 |
| William Venton | John Walley | 100 | 1771 |
| Jacob F. Lansing | Philip J. Lerneross | 25? | 1771 |
| Isaac Van Ostrander | Alexander Cummins | 50 | 1775 |
| Samuel Higley | George White | 180 | 1775 |
| Abraham De Forest | John Roff | 200 | 1776 |
| Robert Kenier | Noah Hindman | 200 (in specie) | 1783 |
| Gerrit Seager | David M. De Forest | 35 | 1784 |
| John Beam | Nicholas Stikle, Jr. | 112 (in specie) | 1784 |

Table 6.1 (Continued): Sale of Improvements

| Seller | Buyer | Value (£) | Date Sold |
|---|---|---|---|
| | CORTLANDT MANOR | | |
| Mr. Pelham | Gilbert Totten | 100 | 1749 |
| Abraham Van Woert | Thomas Cromwell | 54 | 1752 |
| Andrew Barton | John Hyat | 62 10s. 9d. | 1757 |
| George Hallet | James Cock | 192 12s. | 1758 |
| William Yeomans | Philip Van Cortlandt | 26 | 1758 |
| Solomon Burtis | Pierre Van Cortlandt | 80 | 1758 |
| Israel Knapp | Pierre Van Cortlandt | 8 | 1758 |
| Cornight Briggs | Pierre Van Cortlandt | 150 | 1758 |
| Joseph Haight | Pierre Van Cortlandt | 175 | 1758 |
| Samuel Fields | Pierre Van Cortlandt | 2 | 1758 |
| John Brady | Richard Crab | 72 | 1758 |
| Jacob Griffin | Samuel Frost | 60 | 1758 |
| Jacob Wright | Henry Wood | 110 | 1758 |
| Thomas Crommel | Joshua Purdy | 84 | 1758 |
| John Willson | "one Write" | 40 | 1759 |
| Mr. Avery | William Pearce | 120 | 1761 |
| Daniel Wright | Daniel Wolsey | 65 | 1762 |
| Jacob Wright | Thomas Powell | 46 10s. | 1763 |
| John Wright, Jr. | Joseph Anthony | 450 | 1764 |
| Daniel Cornel | Joseph Golden | 144 | 1766 |
| John Stevens | Aaron Forman | 90 | 1770 |
| William and Hendrick Lent | Nicholas Bayard | 111 | 1771 |
| Jacob Ryder | ? | 200 | 1772 |
| Benjamin Smith | Samuel Tilley | 300 | 1777 |
| John Krankhyt | John Tompkins | 361 10s. | ? |
| | PHILIPSBURGH MANOR | | |
| ? | Moses Miller | 440 | c. 1765 |
| James Hill | Nathaniel Underhill | 100 | c. 1775 |
| Nehemiah Tompkins | Nathaniel Underhill | 600 | c. 1775 |
| Adrian Leforge | George Fisher | 400 | 1786 |

Sources:

*Livingston Manor*—Livingston-Redmond MSS, Rolls 7 and 8, and the following manuscripts all in the New-York Historical Society: Livingston Manor Papers, Livingston Manor Rent Ledger, 1767–1784; Miscellaneous Manuscripts, Livingston, R–W; Robert R. Livingston Papers, Unclassified; Livingston Account Book, Clermont, Dec. 1772–1784.

*Rensselaerswyck*—Book of Tithes, 1758–[1771], Abraham Ten Broeck's Debit and Credit Accounts of the Manor, 1763–1787, and Rensselaerswyck Rent Ledger, 1768–1790, all in Rensselaerswyck Manuscripts, New York State Library, New York; Claverack

Sources (Continued): Table 6.1

Papers, *ibid.*, AS38, Queens College Library, New York; Deed Book 8: 400–401 and Deed Book 9: 46, Albany County Clerk's Office, Albany, N.Y.
    *Cortlandt Manor*—Account Book of Pierre Van Cortlandt, Van Cortlandt Papers, V2301, V1685, V2108, Sleepy Hollow Restorations Library, Tarrytown, N.Y.; Receipt Book of John Van Cortlandt and Pierre Van Cortlandt to William Bayard, Dec. 10, 1772, Nicholas Bayard Papers, both in N.-Y. Hist. Soc.; Letterbook of John Van Cortlandt, Schuyler Papers, Box 10, and Bayard-Campbell-Pearsall Land Papers, all in New York Public Library; A.O. 12/25, 95, Public Record Office.
    *Philipsburgh Manor*—A.O. 12/25, 127, 113, Public Record Office; Deeds, Dyckman Family Papers, N.-Y. Hist. Soc.

also of Cortlandt Manor, was asked by his landlord in 1792 to pay a bargain price of £550 for a 385-acre farm worth £1,050, including its soil right, because his improvements were "of more value than £500."[74] In 1758 Henry Scot, a tenant of Philip Van Cortlandt and his heirs after 1747, bought two farms of 482 acres for £819 9s., one of which was his leasehold. Four years later, the executors of Scot's will sold the same premises for £1,400, a profit of nearly £600. The difference between the purchase and sale prices within such a short period appears to be related to the unspecified price of improvements, which were not included in the former transaction.[75]

By the end of the colonial period, the tenants' equity in the land had generally grown to the point where it rivaled, and in rare cases exceeded, that of the landlords. In 1806 Beverly Robinson, a former proprietor of Philipse's Highland Patent in Dutchess County, pointedly reminded one of his co-owners that the improvements in the possession of their tenants were "sold for nearly, if not quite, the value" of the soil right belonging to the proprietors. He stated this while discussing ways and means to

---

Sleepy Hollow Restorations Lib.; Pierre Van Cortlandt to son Philip, Mar. 1796, *ibid.*, V1783. For the depreciation of New York's currency from the 1740s to the 1780s, see Gwyn, *Enterprising Admiral*, 57–58, and nn. 140 and 141 on 221.
    74. Journal (c) of John Van Cortlandt, N.Y. Pub. Lib.; John Van Cortlandt to Joseph Golden, May 24, 1766, Letterbooks of Stephen and John Van Cortlandt, *ibid.*; endorsement of the lease deed between the Beekmans and Isaac Frost, Jan. 29, 1773, Van Cortlandt Papers, V2188, Sleepy Hollow Restorations Lib.; Stephen Van Cortlandt to Simon Brady, May 12 and June 21, 1792, Stephen Van Cortlandt to David Montross, June 21, 1792, Letterbooks of Stephen and John Van Cortlandt, N.Y. Pub. Lib.
    75. Deed Book K, 250–252, Deed Book H, 561–562, Westchester Co. Clerk's Office; "Estate of Philip Van Cortlandt, dec'd," Van Cortlandt Papers, V1836, Sleepy Hollow Restorations Lib.; Henry Scot's will, Nov. 2, 1761, *Abstracts of Wills*, VI, 126. Henry Bulyea, together with his son Joseph, bought for £25 the improvements of a 180-acre farm in Cortlandt Manor in the early 1740s and priced the premises at £300 four decades later. A.O. 12/25, 431. See also Kim, "Manor of Cortlandt," 203–205; A.O. 12/26, 17–18.

recover their lands that had been forfeited to the government of New York during the Revolution.[76] With specific reference to the Robinson estate, a former tenant, John Kane, testified under oath in 1783 that "lands on an average" were appraised at "about £5 an Acre whereof he thinks the landlords Interest was worth £3 and the Tenants £2." But another tenant, speaking of his leasehold of 130 acres, thought that "the Land was worth 12£ an Acre whereof his Interest as Tenant worth £8 per acre and Mr. Robinson as Landlord 4£ per acre."[77] Still, a Rensselaerswyck tenant named Jacob Ball, claiming a £560 compensation for his improvements on a hundred acres, argued in 1783 that "sojourners Right" made up "half" the value of the total worth of the farm.[78] The tenant-Loyalists in exile naturally had a tendency to exaggerate their losses, but these comments on the extent of tenant equity cannot be lightly dismissed. It should be noted that John Watts, a Cortlandt Manor landlord, had much the same view as Robinson regarding his tenants' possessions.[79] The landlords' evaluation in this matter is all the more credible, since their own interests would have disposed them to slight the tenants' share in the land. On the other hand, improvements raised the value of the land, too, and thus were one aspect of the lease system that made the tenant-landlord relationship partly symbiotic.

What did mid-eighteenth-century tenant farms look like? Records in this matter are fragmentary, but several "for sale" advertisements in local newspapers give us some idea of the physical contours of these farms. In 1757 John Martlings of Philipsburgh Manor outlined his farm of nearly 200 acres: "All the improvements . . . consisting of a good large dwelling House, having 3 rooms on a Floor; has a large kitchen, a good cellar with a store above it, and a large commodious Barn; besides an orchard."[80] Another tenant named Mrs. James Barnard had these features to boast about her farm in 1768:

Said Farm (situated about 12 miles from the King's Bridge) contains near 300 Acres of land whereof 20 Acres in Orchard, of the choicest graft Fruit, with two

76. Beverly Robinson to ?, Dec. 11, 1806, Philipse Papers, PX260, Sleepy Hollow Restorations Lib.
77. John Kane's testimony, Dec. 1783, A.O. 12/21, 178; testimony of Malcom Morrison, Dec. 21, 1785, A.O. 12/21, 180.
78. Jacob Ball's testimony, n.d., A.O. 12/27, 417.
79. John Watts, discussing his estates in Cortlandt with his sons, admitted that most of his tenants had improvements that were "equal" or "considerable" in value to his own soil right. Watts to sons John and Robert, Jan. 10 and Feb. 27, 1785, Robert Watts Papers, Box 3, N.-Y. Hist. Soc. See also John Watts's memorial, Mar. 22, 1784, A.O. 12/30, 253.
80. N.-Y. Gaz.: or, Wkly. Post-Boy, May 9, 1757.

large Gardens, well stored with a Variety of Peaches, Pears, Plums, Currants, and English Cherries of the best sorts, with several large Beds of Asparagus, all in good Fence, with 200 Acres of Mowing, Plow, and Pasture Lands, together with 80 Acres of woodland, well timbered . . . House has 3 Rooms, a kitchen, and Milk Room of the first Floor; 5 Bed Rooms of the second Floor, a good Cellar, with a thirty Feet Piazza before the whole house, well finished; and in good Repair; a large new Barn and stable, well finished; a horse stand, Hay Loft, Rack and Manger; with several Out Houses, very suitable for a Merchant, Innholder, or private Farmer. For further Particulars, enquire of the widow Barnard, living on the premises.[81]

Not far from the Barnards was a farm of 70 acres belonging to the "property" of the late John King of Philipsburgh. His heirs described it as consisting of "a good Dwelling-House, Kitchen, and Linton(?), a Barn, Shop, an apple and Peach orchard, some fine meadow, and all the Land cleared, but what is sufficient to supply the Place with Firewood."[82] Cornelius Van Den Bergh, a Rensselaerswyck tenant, mentioned these features of his farm in 1772: "A Fine Farm, Six Miles above the City of Albany, about half a mile west from Hudson's River, has a fine brick house with four fire places in it; the house is completely finished and has commodious closets, there is also a good new barn and two good barracks, a stone well and a fine young orchard just beginning to bear apples, an excellent piece of grass land before the door, and exceeding fine plough land; the whole farm is in good fence and has the advantage of a good road to the city."[83]

We will never know which one of these was typical. But, as far as Philipsburgh Manor is concerned, the above examples seem to represent a cross-section of the tenant plantations. While sailing the Hudson River northward in early summer 1749, Peter Kalm was impressed by the panoramic beauty of the country landscape along the east bank about twelve miles from New York City: "As we proceeded we found the . . . [lands] very much cultivated, and a number of pretty farms surrounded with orchards, and fine plowed fields presented themselves to our view."[84] The traveler noticed none of the shacks and dilapidated buildings characteristic of a depressed area. The string of farms that pleased his eyes were in the heartland of Philipsburgh Manor and was cultivated by folk like the Martlingses, the Barnards, and the Kings. We might add that this "delightful prospect" of the country continued until Kalm passed the

81. N.-Y. Gaz.; and Wkly. Mercury, Dec. 12, 1768.
82. Ibid., May 8, 1769.
83. Albany Gazette, June 29, 1772.
84. Benson, ed., Peter Kalm's Travels, I, 326–327.

northwest end of Cortlandt Manor. One can only guess at how surprised the European visitor would have been if he had known that almost all of these farms were held by tenants. That Kalm's view was no mirage is underscored by the testimony of Frederick Philipse III about the pre-Revolutionary condition of the manor: "Many of the Tenants were rich all of them had good Houses and Barns, were in a prosperous and thriving conditions."[85] Another traveler, the marquis de Chastellux, riding several hours through Livingston Manor in the desolate winter of 1780, had this impression of the area to record: "The road was good, and the country rich and well cultivated. We passed several considerable villages, the houses of which handsome and neat, and every object here announces prosperity."[86] Whether the same was true of the eastern and middle parts of the manor, which he did not traverse, is a moot question. Yet, if the tenants in the interior parts of Philipse's Highland Patent and Beekman Patent near Connecticut were reported to be "thriving," their "Buildings in good Order," and their improvements on sale commanding high prices, there is no foundation for believing that conditions elsewhere were any different.[87]

Apart from the physical appearance of the individual farms, the descriptions by Martlings, Barnard, King, and Van Den Bergh offer a rare glimpse of the farmers' optimistic attitude toward the material possibilities of life despite the alleged drawbacks of the leasehold system. Advertisements, like funeral sermons, are well known for deemphasizing the shortcomings and inflating the merits of their subject. Adjectives like "good," "fine," "excellent," "large," and "commodious," lavishly used by the tenants in describing some aspects of their improvements, beckon our caution. But this does not necessarily mean that the tenants did not feel genuine pride in what they owned. The language and tone of the advertisements were hardly the kind that one might expect to hear from the impoverished, downtrodden, and dejected. To the colonial tenantry, a leasehold was a property with a price tag that could be exchanged for cash in the open market.

The increment of improvement value and the consequent enhancement of the tenants' welfare led inevitably to a modification in the popu-

85. "An Estimate of the Losses," Philipse Papers, PA808, Sleepy Hollow Restorations Lib.

86. François Jean, marquis de Chastellux, *Travels in North America in the Years 1780–1781–1782* (New York, 1970 [orig. English ed. publ. London, 1787]), 169.

87. A.O. 12/21, 180; Philip Hermanse to Henry Beekman, Feb. 25, 1774, "Uncatalogued Livingston MSS."

lar perception of tenancy. In the minds of Lords Bellomont and Cornbury
and their contemporaries in the first decade of the eighteenth century, the
institution was fixed as "base," demeaning, and servile. Unworthy of
proud and ambitious men and fit only for those who were objects of pity
and denigration, it was, above all, the station of dejection, poverty, and
vassalage. This was the stereotyped view prevalent in the Old Society,
where racking landlords had subjected peasant masses to feudal exactions "not only in rent, but in respect, regard, and duty."[88] The old
landlord-tenant relationship and the image thereof were founded on the
landlord's exclusive ownership of the improvements as well as the soil.
But once he lost the right to the former, his position deteriorated into a
mere partnership of land with the tenants based wholly on cash rental.
Farmers like the Davenports, the Scots, the Kings, the Van Den Berghs,
the Garnseys, the Ten Broecks, the Maybes, and many others with valuable improvements to boast had no reason to lose a sense of their own
worth. Rather, their easy circumstances were likely to have elicited envy
from the foreign immigrants with all their traces of "Famine, Sickness,
Penury, and Nakedness" crowding the New York City streets or from the
pioneer farmers struggling on the remote frontier.[89] One of the significant barometers of the transformation of New York tenantry was the
increasing use of such favorable nomenclature as "profitable," "rich,"

88. N.-Y. Gaz., June 24, July 1, 1728, Nov. 3, 1729 ("Letter from Ireland"), Apr. 21,
1735; Harry Munro to Sir William Johnson, May 21, 1773, William Johnson Papers, XII,
1023–1024. The phrase in quotation marks comes from Alexis de Tocqueville, Democracy
in America: The Henry Reeve Text as Revised by Francis Bowen . . . , ed. Phillips Bradley
(New York, 1945), II, 196. Tocqueville offered some sharp comments on the contrast
between modern and feudal leaseholdings, comments that have helped me to place the
changing relationships of tenants and landlord in colonial New York in a proper historical
context. Concerning the pride of the manorial tenantry, the example of Johan Jacob Weeger,
a tenant in Rensselaerswyck, is quite revealing. Weeger and his family, consisting of his
parents, wife, two sons, and one daughter, moved to the patroonship in the mid-1750s after
spending several years in Dutchess County. In one of his letters written in 1767, he described
his circumstances to his uncle in Germany: "We are still living [at a place] 3 hours from the
town of Albany at the road to [Hoosick]; there we have a piece of land from [Stephen
Van Rensselaer II], about 150 morgan [about 300 acres], on which we have been free for
10 years. . . . We have good living conditions here in corn and cattle; we have 5 horses, 15
black cattle, 14 sheep, 20 swine, and plenty of wood. . . . I would like to see that the poor
men who are having such hard times over there in Germany, might have the wood we burn
in the fields." As these remarks indicate, Weeger was proud of his material possessions and
of his achievements in the New World. Johan Jacob Weeger to Johannes Weeger in Germany, Sept. 27, 1767, Brunswick Historical Society, Brunswick, N.Y. I am grateful to Mrs.
James V. Marshall, the society's trustee, for providing me with a copy (in English transla-
tion) of the letter.

89. Klein, ed., Independent Reflector, 82.

"thriving," "prosperous," "easy," and "independent" in describing lease-holders.[90] In 1769 John De Lancey, assemblyman from the Borough of Westchester, introduced a bill to qualify for jury duty those Philipsburgh and Cortlandt tenants who held leases at will or for a term of years and whose improvements were valued at £60 or more. Although the primary objective of his move was to mitigate the civic burden of the Westchester County freeholders,[91] that such a scheme, inconceivable in the early decades of the century, was even proposed was symbolic of the changing attitude toward tenancy.

Colonial farmers could hardly have considered the institution of tenancy as "feudal" or degrading, or as a condition that forced a man into permanent peasantry, since the "frequent transmutations of tenants" were so evident. Cadwallader Colden, a proprietor of the so-called Oblong land, wrote in 1740: "This custom of selling possessions [improvements] is become a prevalent trade there." A comment by Robert R. Livingston of Clermont on the rapid turnover of leases has already been noted. Beverly Robinson, speaking of his former Dutchess County estate, stated in 1783 that, on the average, tenant farms changed hands once every nine years.[92] A check of the lease sales from 1709 to 1786 in the manors of Livingston, Rensselaerswyck, and Cortlandt gives an average turnover frequency of 11, 19, and 10 years respectively (see table 6.2).[93] But the available samples are too few to allow any useful generalization in this matter. There must have been many more transactions than are known to us. Besides, the figures in table 6.2 do not include the length of tenure of hundreds of tenants like William White and Martha and Cornelius Esselstyn of Claverack, John Harremse and Underhill Barnes of Philipsburgh, and Peter Haver and Philip Koones of Livingston Manor who lived on their original farms until they died. As a result, the ratio between those who left and those who stayed on cannot be determined.

90. Grant, *Memoirs of an American Lady*, 264; "An Estimate of the Losses," Philipse Papers, PA808, Sleepy Hollow Restorations Lib.; A.O. 12/21, 180; Crèvecoeur, *Letters from an American Farmer*, 90. See also William Smith, Jr.'s, comments, A.O. 12/20, 200.

91. *Journal of General Assembly, 1766 to 1776* (Buel), Nov. 22, 1769; Sabine, ed., *Historical Memoirs of William Smith*, I, 69.

92. Colden to James Alexander, Oct. 20, 1740, James Alexander Papers, Box 47, N.-Y. Hist. Soc.; A.O. 12/21, 163, 12/23, 86–87; Gerlach, *Philip Schuyler*, 61, n. 40; Brantz Mayer, ed., *Journal of Charles Carroll of Carrollton, during His Visit to Canada in 1776, as One of the Commissioners from Congress* (Baltimore, 1876), 57.

93. In one instance, a Livingston Manor farm originally leased by Leendert Meyer in 1763 changed hands three times in 18 years. Lease, Robert Livingston, Jr., to Duncan Cameron, July 21, 1770, Livingston Manor Papers, N.-Y. Hist. Soc.

Table 6.2. Frequency of Lease Turnover on Livingston, Rensselaerswyck, and Cortlandt Manors, 1709–1786

| Tenant's Name | Year Leased | Year Sold | Length of Holding |
|---|---|---|---|
| LIVINGSTON MANOR | | | |
| Bastiaen Spikerman | 1715? | 1766 | 52 |
| Evert Evertse | 1732 | 1741 | 9 |
| John Mckay | 1741 | 1751 | 10 |
| Philip Michel | 1742 | 1767? | 25 |
| Henrick Stiever | 1748 | 1783 | 35 |
| William Vonck | 1748? | 1781 | 33 |
| Zachariah Whitmarsk | 1752? | 1783 | 31 |
| Isaac Fredenburgh | 1753 | 1783 | 30 |
| Jacob Snyder | 1759 | 1783 | 15 |
| Coenradt Hoffman | 1762 | 1782 | 20 |
| John Gardner | 1763 | 1773 | 10 |
| Leendert Meyer | 1763 | 1770 | 7 |
| Timothy Miller | 1764 | 1773 | 9 |
| Broer Decker | 1765 | 1768 | 3 |
| John McCleef | 1765 | 1769 | 4 |
| Ephraim Reynolds | 1766 | 1774 | 8 |
| Kidnie Rudolph | 1766 | 1768 | 2 |
| Andries Schut | 1767 | 1771 | 5 |
| Godfree Snoeck | 1767 | 1773 | 6 |
| Jacobus Witbeck | 1767 | 1770 | 3 |
| Wilhelmus Laaman | 1768 | 1768 | 1 |
| John Peter Snyder | 1768 | 1769 | 2 |
| Mathis Seifer | 1768 | 1771 | 3 |
| Jager Wendell | 1769 | 1786 | 17 |
| Dirck Gardner | 1769 | 1770 | 1 |
| Jury Hoffman | 1770 | 1771 | 1 |
| Philip Parrat | 1770 | 1773 | 3 |
| John Van Tassel | 1770 | 1779 | 9 |
| Arent Williams | 1770 | 1779 | 9 |
| Duncan Cameron | 1770 | 1773 | 3 |
| Anger MacDuffie | 1771 | 1783 | 12 |
| William Shoeck | 1771 | 1783 | 13 |
| Mindert Hse Schut | 1771 | 1773 | 2 |
| Arie Buys | 1771 | 1781 | 10 |
| Solomon Shouten | 1772 | 1773 | 2 |
| Simon Michel | 1773 | 1781 | 9 |
| Albartus Simon | 1773 | 1784 | 11 |
| William Shepherd | 1774 | 1780 | 7 |

Table 6.2 (Continued):  Frequency of Lease Turnover

| Tenant's Name | Year Leased | Year Sold | Length of Holding |
|---|---|---|---|
| LIVINGSTON MANOR | | | |
| Jacob Young | 1774 | 1781 | 7 |
| Jacob Mandevel | 1776 | 1777 | 2 |
| | | Average | 11 |
| RENSSELAERSWYCK | | | |
| Isaac Van Deusen | 1709 | 1745? | 36 |
| Peter Van Buren | 1724 | 1769 | 45 |
| Milborne Van Dousen | 1732 | 1778 | 46 |
| Abraham Defreest | 1734 | 1776 | 42 |
| Jan Outhout | 1752? | 1782 | 30 |
| Johannes Cluet | 1752? | 1784 | 32 |
| Johannes Van Salsbury | 1752 | 1776 | 24 |
| Johannes Boom | 1752? | 1769 | 17 |
| Abraham Frear | 1760 | 1784 | 24 |
| Jacobus Hildenbrandt | 1760? | 1774 | 14 |
| Hendrick Ten Broeck | 1763 | 1768 | 5 |
| John Norton | 1763 | 1766 | 3 |
| Peter Levenson | 1764 | 1773 | 9 |
| Gerrit Seager | 1766 | 1784 | 18 |
| John Partington | 1767 | 1782 | 15 |
| Isaac Ostrander | 1768 | 1775 | 7 |
| Baltis Kemble | 1768 | 1784 | 16 |
| Cornelius C. Van Den Bergh | 1768 | 1776? | 8 |
| Robert Kenier | 1769 | 1783 | 14 |
| Dirck Gardner | 1769 | 1772 | 3 |
| Isaac Hop | 1782 | 1784 | 2 |
| | | Average | 19 |
| CORTLANDT MANOR | | | |
| Mr. Pelham | 1743 | 1749 | 6 |
| John Wright, Jr. | 1747? | 1764 | 17 |
| George Hallet | 1748 | 1758 | 10 |
| Robert Harris | 1748 | 1759 | 11 |
| Jacob Wright | 1748 | 1763 | 15 |
| Andrew Barton | 1749 | 1757 | 8 |

Table 6.2 (Continued):  Frequency of Lease Turnover

| Tenant's Name | Year Leased | Year Sold | Length of Holding |
|---|---|---|---|
| | CORTLANDT MANOR | | |
| Jacob Wright | 1749 | 1758 | 9 |
| Thomas Crommel | 1757 | 1758 | 1 |
| | | Average | 10 |

Sources:

*Livingston Manor*—Livingston-Redmond MSS, Rolls 7 and 8; Livingston Manor Papers, Rent Ledger of Livingston Manor, 1767–1784, Livingston Account Book, Clermont, Dec. 1772–1784, Robert R. Livingston Collection, Unclassified, and Miscellaneous Manuscripts, Livingston, R-W, all in New-York Historical Society, New York.

*Rensselaerswyck*—Book of Tithes, 1758–[1771], Abraham Ten Broeck's Debit and Credit Accounts of the Manor, 1763–1787, and Rent Ledger of Rensselaerswyck, 1768–1789, all in Rensselaerswyck Manuscripts, New York State Library, Albany; Claverack Papers, N.-Y. Hist. Soc.; AS38, Queens College Library, New York; Deed Book 8: 400–401, Deed Book 9:46, Albany County Clerk's Office, Albany, N.Y.

*Cortlandt Manor*—Account Book of Pierre Van Cortlandt, Van Cortlandt Papers, V2301, V1685, V1644, V2108, Sleepy Hollow Restorations Library, Tarrytown, N.Y.; Receipt Book of John Van Cortlandt, N.Y. Pub. Lib.; Schuyler Papers, Box 10, N.-Y. Hist. Soc.

In any event, the information we do have is sufficiently indicative of the marketability of leaseholds.[94] The farmers, it seems, sold their improvements not so much because leaseholding was onerous and degrading, but rather because under the tenant system they grew financially capable of moving to greener pastures, by purchasing either another lease

94. Depositions of William White, William Esselstyn, Cornelius Sharp, and Jeremiah Muller, Oct. 31 and Nov. 24, 1761, and depositions of Hendrick Witbeck and Joris Decker, July 29, 1767, Columbia County Misc. MSS; Underhill Barnes's will, Wills, XX, 389–392, Queens College Lib.; John Harremse's will, Nov. 30, 1739, *ibid.*, XV, 1; Philip Koones's will, Feb. 16, 1769, *ibid.*, XXVII, 333–334; Philip Livingston to John D'Witt, Jan. and Mar. 5, 1741, Livingston-Redmond MSS, Rolls 7 and 9; letter of administration, Apr. 1, 1779, AAD12 (2428), Queens College Lib. Pierre Van Cortlandt, one of the Cortlandt Manor proprietors, regarded settling in Cortlandt Manor as a "priviledge." It was not uncommon for several farmers to scramble for a vacant piece of manorial land. See Account Book of Pierre Van Cortlandt, particularly a comment on William Yeomans (1753–1758), a tenant of Stephen Van Cortlandt of New York, Van Cortlandt Papers, V1689, Sleepy Hollow Restorations Lib.; Zachariah Whitmarsk to Robert Livingston, Jr., Nov. 11, 1752, and Thomas Converse to Robert Livingston, Apr. 15, 1773, Livingston-Redmond MSS, Roll 8; Oliver Parkins to Abraham Ten Broeck, Aug. 28, 1780, and George Bently to Abraham Ten Broeck, Feb. 1781, Letters, 1767–1794, Rensselaerswyck MSS.

or freehold property.[95] In 1715 Peter Drung of Philipsburgh, after some years of tenant farming, bought for £215 a fee simple tract of 220 acres in New Rochelle and moved there.[96] In 1768 Albartus Simon of Livingston Manor bought "William Bevin's" farm while selling his to John D. Snyder; sixteen years later he disposed of the Bevin farm for £250.[97] The sale money would have been sufficient for him to buy 100 to 150 acres in the rapidly developing northern and western frontier region of New York and to start a yeoman life if he desired. In 1784 Dr. James Perry of Cortlandt Manor, a tenant of the Schuylers for the preceding thirty years, stated that he wanted to sell his improvements on 217 acres not because he had suffered "any Oppression" from the family but because he had grown old "not having Strength to carry on the Farm."[98]

It probably never occurred to most buyers that they were paying a large sum of money for a farm that was under feudal obligation to a landlord. A case in point is Asa Douglas, who with his brother Benjamin rented in the early 1740s a farm belonging to Daniel Tracy of Norwich, Connecticut. Mainly interested in raising corn and livestock, Asa made a "considerable" profit when the price of provisions doubled about 1745 and was soon able to buy his brother's right in the lease. In the fall of 1748 he disposed of the lease, his grains, his farm tools, and some livestock, to the value of £1,300 or £1,400 "old Tennor" (worth about £650 to £700 New York money), and removed with his family to a farm that he had purchased in Canaan, Connecticut. Sixteen years later, in 1764, he rented several hundred acres from Robert Livingston, Jr., of Livingston Manor. Always alert to a new opportunity, he moved again

95. Adonijak Strong to James Duane, Mar. 26, 1791, Duane Papers, Roll 3.

96. Jeanne A. Forbes, trans. and ed., *Records of the Town of New-Rochelle, 1699–1828*, 126–129. In 1760 John Tomkins of Philipsburgh bought a 167-acre farm in fee simple in Cortlandt Manor for £359 and moved. Deed Book G, 712–713, Westchester Co. Clerk's Office. Aaron Van Ostrandt in 1765 and Isaac Underhill in 1773 departed from Philipsburgh after their purchase of fee farms elsewhere. Deed Book I, 24–25, and Mortgage Book A, 234, *ibid*.

97. Livingston Manor Rent Ledger, 1767–1784, 40, 141; "Memo: of Leases and agreementts on North and Near it," Miscellaneous Manuscripts, Livingston, R-W, N.-Y. Hist. Soc. Samuel Livingston of Livingston Manor sold his old lease in 1768 and took up a new lease at a lower rent. Livingston Manor Rent Ledger, 1767–1784, 142, 42. Samuel Livingston's lease dated May 1768 is in Misc. MSS, Livingston, R-W. Hendrick Anderson of the same place sold his lease and in 1752 acquired a perpetual lease of 110 acres in Claverack Manor. Lease, Sept. 16, 1752, Van Rensselaer-Fort Papers, N.Y. Pub. Lib.

98. James Perry to Philip Schuyler, Feb. 17, 1784, Schuyler Papers, 1758–1798, Box 19, N.Y. Pub. Lib. For further information on Perry, see "Advertisement" by the Schuylers in *N.-Y. Gaz.; and Wkly. Mercury*, Apr. 4, 1768; Perry's account with the executors of Cornelia Schuyler's will, Nov. 1, 1785, and his correspondence, Schuyler Papers, Box 10, 19, 23.

several years later, this time to Jericho, Massachusetts, a new settlement near Rensselaerswyck, where he lived in the style of a "gentleman." But this did not prevent him from acquiring for £150 two pieces of leasehold property in Rensselaerswyck in 1774 and 1775. To Asa, leaseholding was a means of making money.[99]

As the frequent sales of leases suggest, at least some tenants viewed tenancy as a transitional condition, a short stopover along the way to a better livelihood. Others, however, regarded it as a going concern in itself. Thus, many tenants kept their leases even after they bought a freehold or gained enough financial strength to do so. For instance, Nathan Whitney, a Cortlandt Manor tenant at will of the Warrens, first leased a farm of 204 acres during the early 1740s and paid a yearly rent of £3 10s. By the end of the decade he was able to purchase an 83-acre farm for £85 in Orange County. In 1767 he spent £500 to add 100 acres of well-improved land to his real estate. Four years later he bought another 80 acres of land for £350. By the time of the Revolution, he was worth £5,000![100] Equally significant was the advancement in his social standing. In 1771 he was called "Esquire," replacing "Yeoman" by which he had formerly been addressed in the deeds of sale. "Esquire" and "gentleman," terms used interchangeably at the time, were the hallmark of social respectability, if not of upper-class status. Despite the new acquisitions and his becoming "armigerous," he did not part with the lease that had been his embryonic capital.[101]

The manner in which tenants distributed legacies among their male heirs also helps us to understand the way they perceived leasehold property and, as a corollary, tenancy. Thomas Van Alstyne of Kinderhook owned three farms in 1764, one of which was a leasehold in Claverack.

99. Affidavit of John Carter, Jr., of Canterbury, Mar. 22, 1768, on Asa Douglas, Livingston-Redmond MSS, Roll 10; deeds, mortgage, and bond between Robert Livingston, Jr., and Asa Douglas, Mar. 30 and 31, 1764, ibid., Roll 7; lease, Robert Livingston, Jr., to Joel Chamberlain, Feb. 26, 1783, ibid., Roll 8; Livingston Manor Rent Ledger, 1767–1784, 9; Deed Book 10: 115, 376, Albany Co. Clerk's Office. See also similar record of Ebenezer Haviland, "Esquire," of Westchester. Haviland's will, Dec. 17, 1749, Wills, XVII, 55, Queens College Lib.

100. Whitney's lease was Farm No. 7 of Lot No. 5, for which he paid an annual rent of £3 10s. in the 1750s. See Account Book of Pierre Van Cortlandt, on Nathan Whitney, Van Cortlandt Papers, V2301 and V1689, Sleepy Hollow Restorations Lib.; on Whitney's lease of 203½ acres (Farm No. 7), Warren Papers, N.-Y. Hist. Soc.; Whitney's memorial, n.d., A.O. 12/23, 86–93; Deed Book H, 463–465, 466–468, 469, 471, Westchester Co. Clerk's Office.

101. Besides being a badge of social respectability, the title "esquire" was generally given to an officeholder whose rank was justice of the peace and above. Peter Silvester to John Tabor Kempe, Feb. 25, 1765, Letters, Box 1, Kempe Papers.

He willed the tenant farm to his eldest son, William, on the condition that the heir would pay £100 "still owing on that land," plus £40 to daughter Cathariena. To son Lambarth, the testator bequeathed a farm in Kinderhook. To another son, Peter, he gave his "whole farm" in the town provided that Peter would pay Lambarth £400 within two years, furnish his widow a fourth of the farm income and "a free dwelling," bear his debts, and pay £40 to daughter Maria.[102] In his will of 1763, Thomas Storm, a Philipsburgh tenant since the early 1710s, gave his two sons, Garret and Gores, what he called "my first purchase" (406 acres with buildings and orchards) in Rumbout Precinct in Dutchess County, to son Abraham the "second purchase" in the same precinct, and to another son named Isaac "my Improvement on Phillipses Manor . . . which I now hold under the Honorable Colonel Frederick Philipse."[103] In view of the Dutch custom of equal distribution of inheritance, the testators, it would seem, valued their lease possession as much as a large fee farm of about £500. Moreover, if they had thought of tenancy as a degrading condition to be endured only as a means to a temporary livelihood, they would not have wanted any of their children to repeat the experience. After all, in both of these cases, the father had sufficient financial resources to avoid a mode of living that he did not want either for himself or for his heirs.[104]

102. Will of Thomas Van Alstyne, Nov. 15, 1764, Pearson, trans., and Van Laer, ed., *Early Records of Albany and Rensselaerswyck*, IV, 193–196.

103. Will of Thomas Storm, June 28, 1763, Wills, XXVII, 255–257, Queens College Lib. Information on the size and quality of Storm's leasehold is not available. His yearly rent for his farm, £10 4s. 6d., suggests that it was large, probably 300 acres. Philipse Papers, PA820, Sleepy Hollow Restorations Lib. The tax record on Philipsburgh in 1732 places Storm as the third richest tenant there. "Assessments of the upper part of the Manor of Philipsburgh . . . the 5th day of November, 1732," *Tarrytown Argus*, Apr. 18, 1903.

104. I should note that such examples as Whitney's, Van Alstyn's, and Storm's can be duplicated. See the cases of Abraham Witbeck, Johannes Quackenbush, Robert Sanders, William Ketelhuyn, Jeremiah Muller, Johannis Yates, Dirck Ten Broeck, William Dietz, Tobias Van Deusen, Maas Van Buren, Jacob Mesick, Hendrick Gardineer, Gerrit Teunissen Van Vechten, Aaron Van Alen, Gerrit Van Bergen, and Hendrick Outhout, all of Rensselaerswyck including Claverack; John Griffin, Moses Ward, Charles Warner, Hendrick Post, William Warner, Thomas Wilde (or Willy), Joshua Rich, Isaac Dean, Mathius Vallentine, John Hunter, Solomon Hustis, Peter Van Woert, John Buckhout, John Storm, Graham Bishop, John Tomkins, Gabriel Purdy, William Crawford, James Requau, Thomas Valentine, Michael Chadderton, Frederick Brown, Underhill Barnes, William Davids, Joseph Arser, Nathaniel Underhill, Samuel Dean, Thomas Weeks, all of Philipsburgh; Joseph Sherwood, Gilbert Totten, Silvanus Hyat, Robert Galer, Aaron Forman, Joseph Veal, Joseph Lyon, Joseph Anthony, Abraham Purdy, and Benjamin Ogden, all of Cortlandt Manor; and Bastian Lasher and Johannis Finger of Livingston Manor. Sources (not listed in the order of the tenants' names above) are: Pearson, trans., and Van Laer, ed., *Early Records of Albany and Rensselaerswyck*, IV, 146–148; Mortgage Book 2: 102, and Deed Book 5: 155–156, Albany Co. Clerk's Office; Wills, XVI, 283–285, XX, 389–392, XXIV, 127,

That many tenants were not impatient with their lot is evident also from the speculative activities of some of them. New Hampshire patent records yield evidence that at least twenty-one Cortlandt Manor tenants speculated in land within the jurisdiction of the New Hampshire government. In 1763 fourteen tenants, namely, Silas Smith, Walter Ward, Samuel Frost, William Borden, Joseph Strang, Nathan Whitney, William Horton, John Baily, John Maybe, Samuel Jones, Annanias Rogers, Joseph Veal (Veille, Vail), John Veal, and Bartlet Brundige were granted about 320 acres each in Mansfield, later a part of Stowe, Vermont. The same year, five other tenants, Nathaniel Merrit, Peter Montross, Abel Weeks, Benjamin Green, and Simon Brady, each obtained about the same amount of land there.[105] The next year, Seth Whitney, another tenant, speculated on land in the township of Lincoln, New Hampshire, for which he paid one James Avery £5 for his "expense and labor."[106] These ventures, however, were unsuccessful. The 24,000 acres in Lincoln to Seth Whitney and sixty-two others were forfeited to the governor and council of New Hampshire in 1772 because of the grantees' failure to comply with the conditions of the grant. Peter Montross, Simon Brady, and Abel Weeks sold a part (100 acres) of their rights in Stowe for £5 7s., £5 6s., and £6 7s. respectively at vendues in March and April 1771. And Silas Smith, Joseph Strang, and John Baily sold for an unknown price their rights in Mansfield to Jacob Watson of New York City in the 1780s.[107] But the remaining shares of all the speculators were put to sale by the Stowe and Mansfield town authorities for tax delinquency. To defray town expenses for a division of land and for construction and repair of

---

431–432, XXI, 251–256, 365–367, XXV, 47, 254–257, 403–406, XXVII, 71–74, 167–170, XXIX, 300, 308, 409, XXX, 159, 197–199, XXXI, 99–101, XXXIII, 46–48, 285, 312, 325, 422, XXXV, 253–254, XXXVI, 108–110, 396, XXXVII, 37–38, 46–48, 156, 215, XXXVIII, 13–15, Queens College Lib.; AK3, AM74, Ao1, AU39, Queens College Lib.; Mortgage Book A, 286, Mortgage Book B, 165–166, 227, 235, 256, 301, 335, Mortgage Book C, 8, 9, 86, 98–99, 167, and Deed Book H, 119, 170, 195, Deed Book I, 42, Deed Book K, 60–61, 320, 381, 450–451, and Deed Book L, 106–107, all in Westchester Co. Clerk's Office; A.O. 12/19, 187–190, A.O. 12/22, 213–219, A.O. 12/30, 395.

105. Albert Stillman Batchellor, ed., *State Papers, the New Hampshire Grants, Being Transcripts of the Charters of Townships . . . 1749–1764* (Concord, N.H., 1895), XXVI, 461–464, 514–518; Town Records of Stowe, in two volumes, *passim*, at Town Hall of Stowe, Vt.

106. See receipt of James Avery, Sept. 21, 1764, Whitney Papers, N.-Y. Hist. Soc.; Batchellor, ed., *N.H. State Papers*, XXV, 234–237. Whitney was a tenant of the Skinners of Perth Amboy, N.J. For his rent payment and other business activities, see the Whitney Papers and Whitney-Kipp Papers, N.-Y. Hist. Soc.

107. Isaac W. Hammond, ed., *Town Papers. Documents Relating to Towns in New Hampshire . . .* , XII (Concord, N.H., 1883), 229, 361; Town Records of Stowe, and Mansfield Proprietors Book of Records, Book I, *passim*, both at Town Hall of Stowe, Vt.

bridges and roads, the vendue of "delinquent proprietors' lands" was held from time to time until 1828, when the liquidation of the tenant speculators' rights was completed.[108] The significance of this episode lies in tenants' choosing not to settle the newly acquired lands. Nowhere in the well-preserved town records of Stowe and Mansfield is there an indication that any of them or their relatives moved to the New England towns. It would seem logical that if tenancy was as onerous as some historians have argued, they would have left the manor immediately after securing the land grants. That they did not suggests that they had too much at stake in their existing condition.

In about 1752 a treatise appeared in which Robert R. Livingston of Clermont defended the New York leasehold land system. It was probably the first public challenge made by any provincial to the view that the New England freehold land system embodied the best and the healthiest of socioeconomic arrangements. Livingston argued that individual land-holding there, beginning with small grants, led to smaller and smaller farms due to repeated subdivision of the land among proliferating heirs, finally arriving at a point where the farmers became "incapable" of producing a surplus and "must necessarily be poor." By contrast, the New York proprietors, he continued, by parceling out the lands in a good size, "enable" and, by the rent they charged, "oblige" their tenants to raise "more than they consume." As an additional precaution, they would not suffer a tenant farm to be too much divided, lest "their Tenants should be impoverished."[109] Such an argument, of course, does not prove that freeholding is inferior to leaseholding. Nevertheless, Livingston's point about the economic malaise of mid-century New England agrarian society is well taken. So is his rhapsody over the New York leasehold as a viable economic unit. Recent demographic studies of eastern New England towns have convincingly established that the average family land-holding had by mid-century shrunk to a mere 50 to 70 acres, barely enough for subsistence.[110] This acreage does compare unfavorably with the size of manorial farms, which were 171 acres on the average, roughly

---

108. Town Records of Stowe; Mansfield Proprietors Book of Records, Book II, 33–40, 164–174. See also the land speculation in the Mohawk valley by two Livingston Manor tenants in 1761. There is no evidence that they moved to the frontier until after the Revolution. Deed Book 7: 111–114, Albany Co. Clerk's Office; Livingston Manor Rent Ledger, 1767–1784, 90, 104.

109. McAnear, ed., "Mr. Robert R. Livingston's Reasons," *Jour. Pol. Econ.*, XLVIII (1940), 88–89, 90.

110. Lockridge, *A New England Town*, 149; Greven, *Four Generations*, 126–129, 143, 158, 222–225, 227–228, 247–248.

three times that of their New England counterparts.[111] On the basis of
the statistical evidence compiled here, plus Livingston's comment, one
can claim that most manorial tenants were able to produce considerable
surplus and profit and to enjoy a good living standard. Partly because of
these advantages, a leasehold was a coveted object of land transactions
among farmers, despite its legal encumbrances and restrictions. Ironically, the restrictions on the subdividing of leasehold property were a
blessing in disguise for the welfare of tenant society.

## Tenant Property Holdings

Full understanding of the economic position of the New York tenantry would be possible only if we could study the gross and net annual
income of each individual. But the search for comprehensive data of this
kind has been unfruitful. An alternative approach would be to look at the
property holdings of the group. The numerous extant probate records,
such as letters of administration and wills, however, are inadequate as a
guide, although they provide a general picture of estate conditions. Moreover, the surviving inventories of the estates are too few to be of much
use. The best source of information, the 1779 tax lists in the New York
State Library, contains a nearly comprehensive assessment of each individual estate, both real and personal, in several manors (see tables 6.3
and 6.4). These records do have some minor shortcomings, however. The
appraisal of real estate for the land tax of a shilling on a pound was based
on the 1775 value of land and buildings, excluding mortgages, rents, and
other encumbrances, whereas the appraisal of personal estates for a tax
of 6d. on the pound reflected their "present Value," that is, a 100 percent
inflation over the 1775 price. In order to bring the two categories of
property to the same footing, I have reduced the personalty valuation by
half.[112] Tables 6.3 and 6.4 incorporate this adjustment. Another problem
is that only about one-fourth of the Philipsburgh Manor tenants appear

111. See table 5.1 in chap. 5.

112. Tax lists of 1779 for the manors of Rensselaerswyck, Livingston, Philipsburgh,
and Cortlandt, "pursuant to the act of the Legislature of March 1779," N.Y. State Lib. As
for the tax rates, see John Mckesson to Alexander McDougall, Feb. 16, 1779, Alexander
McDougall Papers (microfilm), Roll 2, N.-Y. Hist. Soc.; George Clinton to John Jay, Feb. 9,
1779, Hugh Hastings, ed., *Public Papers of George Clinton, First Governor of New York,
1777–1795—1801–1804* (New York and Albany, 1899–1914), IV, 554–555. My statement on inflation is based on the "Account of the Value of Several Articles ascertained by
the board of Super[visor]s at their meeting on the 18 June 1782," John N. Bleeker Papers,
Box 3, N.Y. State Lib.

on the tax list. However, since the tenants on the list are a random sample, they can be taken as fairly representative.[113] A more difficult problem is posed by the cases of tenants like Joseph Strang, whose real estate is mentioned but whose personalty is not. Since it is inconceivable that some of these people owned no personalty—Strang, for example, was a merchant in Cortlandt Manor—I have assumed that their movable property was kept somewhere else or had been transferred for safekeeping during the Revolutionary war.[114] In order to keep as much information as possible in the tables, in these cases I have listed the real estate value only; hence the total number of tenants in the personalty category of the tables is smaller than in the realty. (This rule has not been applied to the tenants in Philipsburgh Manor, for which the records are fragmentary.) Moreover, the 1779 tax lists contain no information on lands outside the manorial jurisdiction that tenants may have owned. It should be understood, therefore, that the assessment figures, conservative by nature, are rendered more conservative by this omission. But the assessments at least show the tenants' overall property holdings in manorial lands. Last, the question might be raised whether the real estate value on the lists consisted partly of the landlord's soil right in addition to the improvements claimed by the tenant. Examination of the listed figures, however, in the light of internal evidence and other available information in wills, leaves no doubt that the assessments indicated the value of tenant possessions and not the landlord's interest.[115] The colonial tax

113. Beatrice G. Reubens argued that "just over one fourth of the tenants (seventy-seven) were prosperous enough to be on the land tax list for 1779." Reubens, "Pre-emptive Rights," *WMQ*, 3d Ser., XXII (1965), 440. The implication is that the rest of the tenants were poor and that, therefore, their property was not taxed. The tax list of Philipsburgh Manor makes it clear that the total land tax for the manor was £4,401 11s., but the extant record consisting of the first and last page accounts for only £1,342. Several pages of the record concerning the residue of tax (£3,059 11s.) are missing.

114. See Kim, "Manor of Cortlandt," 178, 185.

115. If a landlord's soil right had been counted, the valuations of the tenants' real estate would have been much higher. The Philipsburgh land in 1775 was worth £4 to £6 per acre because of its proximity to the Hudson River and New York City. But, according to the manor tax list, a 231-acre farm of Benjamin Underhill was assessed at only £300, John Yerks's of 244 acres at £300, Hormer Williams's of 55 acres at £55, Jacob Underhill's of 220 acres at £400, Lewis Angevine's of 190 acres at £400, William Hunter's of 188 acres at £400, William Cornwell's of 227 acres at £400, John Storm's of 207 acres at £500, and John Bishop's of 83 acres at £250. We can therefore definitely establish that the valuations represented only the value of the tenants' possessions. As mentioned above, Samuel Davenport of Philipsburgh claimed that the manor farms of about 200 acres "used to sell for £600" in the pre-Revolutionary period. If so, the official assessments were somewhat conservative. See "A Plan of the Manor of Philipsburgh in the County of Westchester, 1783," in Scharf, ed., *History of Westchester County*, I, 161; "A Map of the Upper Part of the Manor of Philipsburgh," in the possession of Mr. William Slater, Ossining,

Table 6.3. Property Holdings of the Tenants in Four Manors, 1775

| Value (in £ N.Y. Currency) | Tenants' Real Estate | | Tenants' Personal Estate | |
|---|---|---|---|---|
| | No. | % | No. | % |
| **LIVINGSTON MANOR (including Clermont)** | | | | |
| 8–49 | 66 | 14.2 | 6 | 1.7 |
| 50–99 | 102 | 21.9 | 11 | 3.1 |
| 100–199 | 249 | 53.6 | 56 | 15.6 |
| 200–349 | 45 | 9.7 | 156 | 43.5 |
| 350–499 | 1 | 0.2 | 75 | 20.9 |
| 500–699 | 1 | 0.2 | 39 | 10.9 |
| 700–999 | | | 13 | 3.6 |
| 1,000–1,499 | 1 | 0.2 | 3 | 0.8 |
| 1,500–1,999 | | | | |
| 2,000–3,000 | | | | |
| Over 3,000 | | | | |
| Totals | 465 | 100.0 | 359 | 100.1 |
| **RENSSELAERSWYCK (excluding Claverack)** | | | | |
| 8–49 | 251 | 21.1 | 2 | 0.5 |
| 50–99 | 228 | 19.2 | | |
| 100–199 | 235 | 19.8 | 189 | 50.3 |
| 200–349 | 224 | 18.8 | 98 | 26.1 |
| 350–499 | 82 | 6.9 | 30 | 8.0 |
| 500–699 | 75 | 6.3 | 32 | 8.5 |
| 700–999 | 40 | 3.4 | 9 | 2.4 |
| 1,000–1,499 | 30 | 2.5 | 10 | 2.7 |
| 1,500–2,000 | 18 | 1.5 | 3 | 0.8 |
| 2,000–3,000 | 5 | 0.4 | 2 | 0,5 |
| Over 3,000 | 1 | 0.1 | 1 | 0.3 |
| | 1,189 | 100.0 | 376 | 100.1 |
| **CORTLANDT MANOR** | | | | |
| 8–49 | 2 | 2.4 | 2 | 2.9 |
| 50–99 | | | | |
| 100–199 | 6 | 7.3 | 13 | 18.6 |
| 200–349 | 13 | 15.9 | 23 | 32.9 |
| 350–499 | 19 | 23.2 | 12 | 17.1 |
| 500–699 | 15 | 18.3 | 10 | 14.3 |
| 700–999 | 15 | 18.3 | 6 | 8.6 |

Table 6.3. (Continued): Property Holdings

| Value | Tenants' Real Estate | | Tenants' Personal Estate | |
|---|---|---|---|---|
| (in £ N.Y. Currency) | No. | % | No. | % |
| | CORTLANDT MANOR | | | |
| 1,000–1,499 | 8 | 9.8 | 1 | 1.4 |
| 1,500–1,999 | 3 | 3.7 | 3 | 4.3 |
| 2,000–3,000 | 1 | 1.2 | | |
| Over 3,000 | | | | |
| | 82 | 100.1 | 70 | 100.1 |
| | PHILIPSBURGH MANOR | | | |
| 8–49 | | | | |
| 50–99 | 1 | 1.6 | | |
| 100–199 | 6 | 9.8 | 9 | 14.8 |
| 200–349 | 18 | 29.5 | 33 | 54.1 |
| 350–499 | 24 | 39.3 | 11 | 18.0 |
| 500–699 | 10 | 16.4 | 7 | 11.5 |
| 700–999 | 2 | 3.3 | 1 | 1.6 |
| 1,000–1,499 | | | | |
| 1,500–1,999 | | | | |
| 2,000–3,000 | | | | |
| Over 3,000 | | | | |
| Totals | 61 | 99.9 | 61 | 100.0 |
| | ALL FOUR MANORS | | | |
| 8–49 | 319 | 17.7 | 10 | 1.2 |
| 50–99 | 331 | 18.4 | 11 | 1.3 |
| 100–199 | 496 | 27.6 | 267 | 30.8 |
| 200–349 | 300 | 16.7 | 310 | 35.8 |
| 350–499 | 126 | 7.0 | 128 | 14.8 |
| 500–699 | 101 | 5.6 | 88 | 10.2 |
| 700–999 | 57 | 3.2 | 29 | 3.3 |
| 1,000–1,499 | 39 | 2.2 | 14 | 1.6 |
| 1,500–1,999 | 21 | 1.2 | 6 | 0.7 |
| 2,000–3,000 | 6 | 0.3 | 2 | 0.2 |
| Over 3,000 | 1 | 0.1 | 1 | 0.1 |
| Totals | 1,797 | 100.0 | 866 | 100.0 |

Table 6.4. Average Property Holdings of Manorial Tenants Compared with Those of Inhabitants in Freehold Districts, 1775
(Values in New York Currency)

| Value of Realty in £ | | Value of Personalty in £ | |
|---|---|---|---|
| Livingston Manor | 127 | Rykes Patent | 209 |
| Rykes Patent | 148 | German Camp | 242 |
| Pound Ridge | 163 | Salem | 284 |
| German Camp | 233 | Rensselaerswyck Manor | 303 |
| Salem | 244 | Bedford | 314 |
| Rensselaerswyck Manor | 254 | Pound Ridge | 320 |
| Philipsburgh Manor | 355 | North Castle | 323 |
| Bedford | 408 | Livingston Manor | 335 |
| North Castle | 436 | Philipsburgh Manor | 344 |
| Cortlandt Manor | 592 | Cortlandt Manor | 394 |
| Average for manorial tenants | 332 | Average for manorial tenants | 344 |
| Average for inhabitants in freehold districts | 272 | Average for inhabitants in freehold districts | 282 |

practice of not taxing unsettled and undeveloped lands further reinforces this conclusion.[116]

The most obvious characteristic of the 1775 tenant property holdings as a group is their great variation, ranging from £8 for Neal McCarter of Livingston Manor, a laborer,[117] to £7,500 for Volkert P. Douw of Rensselaerswyck, a merchant, a former mayor of Albany, and vice-president of the first provincial congress.[118] Before we examine this wide distribution of wealth, however, some explanation is necessary concerning the situation of the renters who are shown in table 6.3 as having owned less than £99 in real property (36 percent of the total manorial tenants). Significantly, of these 650 tenants, 647 were from Rensselaerswyck and Livingston manors. In the case of Livingston Manor, the 66 tenants with £8 to £49 in real property were mostly artisans, day laborers, and iron-

---

N.Y.; Joseph Orser's claim, A.O. 12/22, 213–219; Samuel Davenport's claim, A.O. 12/17, 427–430.

116. N.Y. Col. Laws, III, 960–962, 996–998, IV, 678–680, 722–724.

117. Deed, July 14, 1761, Deed Book 7: 111–114, Albany Co. Clerk's Office. According to this deed, McCarter was entitled to a fifteenth of a 29,000-acre tract on the Mohawk River. It is a mystery why he did not move to the newly acquired land.

118. N.-Y. Mercury, Nov. 2, 1767; Journal of General Assembly, II, 646; N.Y. Col. Docs., VII, 489; Mary L. D. Ferris, "Colonel Henry T. Van Rensselaer, Master of Millburn," Qtly. Jour. of N.Y. State Hist. Assoc., V (1924), 305.

workers. For example, the cottage and small patch of land owned by Timothy Loomis, a collier at the Ancram iron foundry, were assessed at £12; the house and land of William Trafford, a "hammer Smith," £20 (although his movables were valued at £300); the "small farm" of about five acres owned by Christopher George, a day laborer, at £20; and the dwelling house of Laurence Quackenbush, an artisan, at £20.[119] The realty of recent arrivals was also low in value. Jacob Young, who settled there in 1774 on an eighty-acre farm, is listed for property worth only £30.[120] Many of the Rensselaerswyck tenants who owned realty valued at less than £100 seem to have been either Albanians with a "kitchen garden," pasture land, a town lot, or a house on the road leading to Watervliet, or settlers who came to the wild Hellebergh escarpment, to Stephentown, or to Philipstown in the 1760s and 1770s.[121] The proportion between the Albanians and the new settlers, however, is impossible to determine. The lots of three Albany freeholders, William Hogan, John Spoor, and Jacob Van Schaick, were assessed at £60 each. Johannes Van Schaick, Gerrit Lansing, Gerrit J. Lansing, John Ten Eyck, Wouter Knickerbacker, and Jacob Bogardus, also Albany freeholders, appear to have owned manor lots valued at £15, £20, £30, £40, and £50 respectively. But the tax lists mention nothing about their movable property, indicating that their personalty was probably situated in Albany.[122] The fifty-acre tract that Benjamin Sacket of Stephentown bought for £55 in 1776 was evaluated at £30; the hundred acres that William Russell, also of Stephentown, purchased for £6 10s. in 1771 was assessed at £60; and Samuel Taylor's hundred-acre farm in the Hellebergh, under his cultivation since 1776, was assessed at £40.[123] Like any other community,

119. Loomis's account with Robert Livingston, Jr., Oct. 10, 1783, Livingston-Redmond MSS, Roll 8; Trafford's account with Robert Livingston, Jr., 1766–1767, 1776–1779, Jan. 28, 1783, ibid., and Deed Book 7: 111–114, Albany Co. Clerk's Office; Quackenbush's rent account with his landlord, Livingston Manor Rent Ledger, 1767–1784, 157.
120. Young's account, Livingston Manor Rent Ledger, 1767–1784, 141.
121. Compare the Rensselaerswyck tax list of 1779 with Rensselaerswyck Rent Ledger, 1768–1789, 271, Rensselaerswyck MSS, on William Cummings; ibid., 268, on Jonathan Howard; ibid., 265, on Able Brotherten; ibid., 144, on Adamand Green; ibid., 242, on David Hushton; ibid., 215, on Johannes Snyder; ibid., 111, on Thomas Wood; ibid., 237, on William Snyder; ibid., 163, on John Wards. Jellis Winne, probably an artisan of Albany city, held a small piece of "Corn land" that was assessed at £30, but Winne was not taxed for movables. See Winne's rent payment, Nov. 22, 1765, Abraham Ten Broeck's Accounts of the Manor, 1763–1786, Rensselaerswyck MSS.
122. "Book of the Freeholders of the City and County of Albany, [1763]," Lawsuits, A-B, Kempe Papers; Deed Book 7: 381–383, Albany Co. Clerk's Office; Van Schaick Family Papers, N.Y. State Lib.; N.Y. Col. Docs., VII, 489, on John Ten Eyck. More examples of this sort can be quoted, but space does not allow it.
123. Sacket: Deed Book 10: 186, Albany Co. Clerk's Office. Russell: Deed Book 9: 14;

the manor included a considerable number of inhabitants who relied largely on craftsmanship and service industries for livelihood.[124]

Given the nonagricultural orientation of some of the tenants with less than £100 in realty, it is probably incorrect to lump them all together as "poor." Such a description would be warranted only if a tenant was a farmer and his personalty holding was little or none. It should be noted that at least 40 of 168 "poor" Livingston tenants on the realty side, or 24 percent, had considerable personalty, ranging from Hendrick Shadowick's £153 to Peter Van Den Bogert's £500.[125] The same was true of Rensselaerswyck. The number of marginal property holders, therefore, must have been much fewer than table 6.3 suggests. But their exact numbers are unobtainable because of the absence of vital information about their occupations and about the location and quantity of their property elsewhere.

The majority of the manorial tenants were "fair," or "medium," (£100 to £349) and "substantial" (£350 and more) property owners. Specifically, 294 of the Livingston tenants, or 63.3 percent, owned realty worth £100 to £349; of those holding movables, 212, or 59.1 percent, belonged to this group; and 130 of the manor tenants, or 28.0 percent, held a large but varying amount of movables worth from £350 to £1,000, although only three held that much realty. As table 6.4 shows, the average realty holding for all Livingston Manor tenants, including about 100 artisans, day laborers, and ironworkers, was only £127, very low indeed compared with the tenants in the other manors. This was due in part to the presence of the nonagricultural workers and largely to the smaller size (106 acres on the average) of the Livingston farms. Yet, 359 tenants (77 percent of the manor tenants) had on the average £335 worth of movables, making their average total property value £462. Clearly, they were neither well-to-do nor impoverished.

In Rensselaerswyck, 459, or 38.8 percent, of its 1,189 tenants were medium realty holders (£100 to £349), while 251, or 21.1 percent, were

---

William Russell to Abraham Ten Broeck, Feb. 8, 1782, in Letters, 1769–1794, and Russell's rent account, Rensselaerswyck Rent Ledger, 1768–1789, 265, both in Rensselaerswyck MSS. Taylor: Taylor's rent account, Rensselaerswyck Rent Ledger, 1768–1789, 264, *ibid.*

124. John Waters, a laborer, held a house and lot "near" Albany that was assessed at £30, and John T. Visscher, a clerk by occupation and resident of Albany, had a manor lot worth £10. Mortgage Book 3: 263, Albany Co. Clerk's Office; Abraham Ten Broeck to John T. Visscher, Nov. 26, 1782, Letters of Abraham Ten Broeck, 1753–1783, Rensselaerswyck MSS.

125. Shadowick and Van Den Bogert each had a £80 realty. An extreme example is Jacob Shafer. His personalty was worth £404, but his realty was assessed at only £20.

substantial, owning realty valued at from £350 to £3,000 and over. Of those holding movables in the manor, 287, or 76.4 percent, were medium, and 87, or 23.2 percent, substantial personalty holders. Here, the extraordinary disparity between the numbers of tenants holding the two types of property was primarily caused by the presence of a large number of absentee leaseholders—people from Albany, Schenectady, Stephentown, and Philipstown—who were taxed for their domain land and buildings but not for their personalty situated elsewhere. Thus, that the tax list recorded no personal estate for 813 tenants out of 1,189, or 68.4 percent, does not mean that they owned no other property. Tenants such as John Duncan, a big Schenectady merchant whose real estate in the manor was worth £600, and John Ten Eyck, an Albany Indian trader, very likely owned movables, even though the tax list does not show this.[126] Given these complicated problems, it is impossible to determine the total worth of many of the patroon's tenants. But their real property alone gives some indication of their good financial standing.

Philipsburgh Manor presents a clearer picture. Table 6.3 shows that only one farmer on that manor held a lease of marginal value (£50). The tenant in question was Hormer Williams, who possessed 55 acres and paid a yearly rent of £2 4s. 6d. but whose movables were valued at £300, not an inconsiderable sum. Of 61 tenants under examination, 24, or 39.3 percent, owned between £100 and £349 in realty, and 36, or 49 percent, held realty worth from £350 to £999. As for personalty, 42, or 69.9 percent, owned property worth less than £350, while 19, or 31.1 percent, had holdings valued at from £350 to £999. The total worth—personalty and realty combined—of a Philipsburgh tenant was, on the average, £699. This evidence bears out the observations of landlord Frederick Philipse III that his tenants were "rich" and "thriving."[127]

On Cortlandt Manor, only two renters, Samuel Cole, a tenant of the De Lanceys, and Josiah Ingersoll, a tenant of the Verplancks, can be categorized as poor, if they were farmers.[128] The tax list shows their property to have been worth only £10 and £20 respectively. They were

126. For John Duncan, see n. 58 of this chapter. Ten Eyck was assessed £40 for a lot in the manor.

127. I excluded 27 Philipsburgh tenants from my account because the tax list makes it appear that they held only one kind of property, either personalty (11) or realty (16). For instance, William Pugsley, a lessee of the so-called Upper Mills with several hundred acres is recorded to have £1,000 worth of realty but none in personalty. Benjamin Okeley, however, appears to be owning movables worth £828 but none in realty. It is inconceivable that such affluent tenants were actually deficient in either kind of property.

128. For details of the Cortlandt Manor tenants' property holdings, see Kim, "Manor of Cortlandt," chap. 6.

rather exceptional. According to table 6.3, of 82 tenants, 19, or 23.2 percent, were medium realty owners, holding property worth from £100 to £349, and 61, or 74.5 percent, were substantial property holders, owning from £350 to £3,000 in real estate. On the personalty side, 36, or 51.5 percent, were medium, and 30, or 45.7 percent, were substantial. Twelve of the tenants were recorded to have had no personalty, but circumstantial evidence suggests that they had it somewhere else, where it was not taxable for the manor. For example, the tax list mentions no personal estate for Pierre Van Cortlandt, a wealthy proprietor, because he removed his livestock and valuables to Dutchess County during the Revolutionary war.[129] It is reasonable to assume that many others followed his example. Excluding these twelve tenants from our account, the average personalty for manor farmers comes to £394, and the average realty £592, making the average total property £986. It thus appears that the Cortlandt Manor tenants were the most affluent among the manorial inhabitants in the province.[130]

The economic welfare of the manorial tenants in the 1770s appears most impressive when we compare it with the inhabitants of several other agrarian districts, German Camp (in Albany County), North Castle, Salem, Bedford, Pound Ridge, and Rykes Patent (all in Westchester County), where freehold landownership prevailed. As table 6.4 shows, the manorial tenants, with an average total worth of £676, were economically better off than the average freeholders with £554. Only those in Livingston Manor with £462 fell below the average lot of freeholders, but they were endowed with more personalty than the freeholders. This last point is generally true of other manorial leaseholders, suggesting that they invested heavily in movable property, like livestock, that was absolutely their own.

The conclusion is unmistakable: contrary to common assumptions, tenancy as a way of life did not hamper a man's desire to get ahead economically. A tenant's endeavors were well rewarded despite his dependence on someone else's land. After making due allowance for the fact that tenancy was something less than a freehold, we find that the tenant's status was not as bad as most historians have described it to be.

129. "Memorandum of an Agreement" between Pierre Van Cortlandt and Henry B. Livingston, Apr. 9, 1779, Van Cortlandt Papers, V1758, Sleepy Hollow Restorations Lib.

130. There were a number of well-to-do tenants like Nathan Whitney and Gilbert Drake who are not on the tax list of Cortlandt Manor. It is also possible that I have failed to identify some poor tenants. But their inclusion or exclusion probably will not change the general picture.

We should emphasize again, however, that tenantry in the mid-eighteenth century was most distinguished by its heterogeneity. The group contained the rich as well as the poor, although the latter were surely more numerous in the 1730s and 1740s than in subsequent decades. It also embraced men of different backgrounds, occupations, and aspirations, making it not much different from provincial society itself. Yet, the community of leaseholding, for all its cooperative benefits, could never escape from the tension inherent in the different interests of landlord and tenant. The fact that a tenant was under an obligation to pay rent as a condition for his livelihood was a constant reminder of his inferior status vis-a-vis his landlord's. Rent day was a day of depression for the tenants. Whatever their financial situation, they did not cherish the idea of parting with some portion of their hard-won cash or produce for rent, any more than they liked paying taxes. Some landlords, notably Henry Beekman, tried to cheer up the depressed tenants by giving them hard liquor upon delivery of their rents.[131] It was perhaps an inevitable tendency of human nature that a tenant would forget the "moderate terms upon which he obtained possession of his estate" and feel "only the unpleasant compulsion" of paying rent at a fixed time.[132] But the tension and the nettlesome burden of rent never provoked an open revolt on the part of the tenantry collectively against landlords.

The tenants did not take collective action because they did not perceive themselves as a cohesive interest group. The manorial community was composed of individuals holding varying degrees of equity in improvements and was subject to frequent turnover of its membership. It was not a milieu conducive to the cultivation of class consciousness. Spurred on by the higher standard of expectations in the New World, some tenants, like indentured servants, refused to accept their present lot as their permanent station. Seen as a temporary expedient, tenancy naturally failed to nurture a sense of enduring connection and cohesion among tenants. Furthermore, the well-to-do tenants did not conceive of their interests and status as identical to that of the poor ones. The tenant elite in Claverack and Livingston manors, for example, had an exclusive social club where they clung together, wining, dining, and playing.[133] Inequality in the distribution of wealth, mobility in the tenant society,

131. Henry Beekman to Gilbert Livingston, Jan. 21, 1747, Beekman Papers, N.-Y. Hist. Soc.
132. Munsell, ed., *Annals of Albany*, IV, 238.
133. "Regulations of the Private Club off Claverack Manor and Rolif Jansen Kill," Apr. 26, 1775, Claverack Papers, N.-Y. Hist. Soc.

and, most important, benign lease terms permitting economic advancement, all contributed to producing a stable and peaceful manorial society
in the first half of the eighteenth century.

CHAPTER VII

Agrarian Disturbances,

1751–1757

Prelude

The long reign of peace in manorial society was shattered in 1751 when the eastern section of Livingston Manor was engulfed in violence. Three years later, the disorder spread to Claverack. At times the riotous conditions in the northern manors were so serious that their proprietors, even under the protection of armed guards, became fearful for their lives. Then, in 1757 the disturbances ended as abruptly as they had begun, only to recur almost a decade later.

How do we account for this mid-eighteenth-century phenomenon? The question has intrigued several historians. Irving Mark and Staughton Lynd dealt with the disturbances largely in terms of class conflict between the oppressive landlords and the exploited tenants. Others, like Oscar Handlin and Dixon Ryan Fox, discussed the episode in the sectional context, as the struggle between New York and Massachusetts over land, but could not divorce it entirely from the tenant-landlord conflict.[1] Recently Patricia Bonomi challenged some of their interpretations but left many questions unanswered.[2] For a full understanding

---

1. Mark, *Agrarian Conflicts*, 115–130; Lynd, "Who Should Rule at Home?" *WMQ*, 3d Ser., XVIII (1961), 330–339; Franklin Pope, "The Western Boundary of Massachusetts: A Study of Indian and Colonial History," Berkshire Historical and Scientific Society, *Collections*, I (1892), 27–85; Oscar Handlin, "The Eastern Frontier of New York," *N.Y. History*, XVIII (1937), 50–75; Dixon Ryan Fox, *Yankees and Yorkers* (New York, 1940).

2. Bonomi, *A Factious People*, 200–216.

of the tenant-landlord relationship in this period, we must determine whether the disorders on Livingston Manor and in Claverack in the 1750s resulted from a land dispute or were the outcome of internal social discord. As we shall see, the whole affair was not a rebellion of the tenants against the landlords as such, but was precipitated by the Bay Colony and its land-hungry people. The story of this long and fascinating struggle must begin with the expansionist efforts of Massachusetts.

Throughout the seventeenth century, the Massachusetts Bay Colony had seized every opportunity and pretext to encroach upon the lands of neighboring colonies and patents. Armed with the "sea-to-sea" charter of 1629 and convinced of their righteousness, its people pushed their way into the wilderness. They believed that "every private man" had "a share in the general property." Some of them subscribed to the old idea that land belonged to its cultivator and that absentee ownership was an insult to God's will.[3] Hardy and self-righteous, they were impatient with any obstacles, whether heathen or Christian, standing in the way of their pursuit of virgin land. Having quickly become the most powerful colony in New England, Massachusetts compelled the other colonies to give way to her cupidity.[4] The General Court was always ready to support inhabitants on the move as long as they carried its pride with them and submitted to its authority. Impressed by the Bay Colony's frequent intrusion into neighboring patents, a royal commission reported in 1664 that the province "hath many towns, but not one regularly built" within its "just limits."[5]

Territorial dispute between Massachusetts and New York was anticipated in Charles II's grant in 1664 of New Netherland to his brother the duke of York. The duke's boundary, confirmed in 1674 and 1676, fixed the western limit of Massachusetts at the Connecticut River, but the New Englanders ignored the line, "pretending" that their territory, ac-

---

3. The doctrine of tillers known as *vacuum domicillum* was often invoked against the roving Indians in the 17th century and would linger on into the next century. Chester E. Eisinger, "The Puritans' Justification for Taking the Land," Essex Institute, *Historical Collections*, LXXXIV (1948), 131–143; Gordon M. Day, "The Indian as an Ecological Factor in the Northeastern Forest," *Ecology*, XXXIV (1953), 329–346; Alden Vaughan, *New England Frontier: Puritans and Indians, 1620–1675* (Boston, 1965), 104–105; "The Case of the Inhabitants of New Canaan," Jan. 20, 1773, and petition of William Kellog and others, May 11, 1771, N.Y. Land Papers, XXXIII, 6–7, XXIX, 20; a resolve of the General Court of Massachusetts, Jan. 29, 1757, *Journals of the House of Representatives of Massachusetts* [1715–1760] (Boston, 1919–1964), XXXIII, pt. II, 296–297; Lockridge, *A New England Town*, 83–84.

4. Hutchinson, *History of Massachusetts Bay*, ed. Mayo, I, 129, III, 4.

5. Quoted in William Smith, Jr., *The History of the Province of New-York*, ed. Michael Kammen (Cambridge, Mass., 1972), II, 220.

cording to the 1629 charter, ran all the way "to the south sea" (the Pacific Ocean) on the west. Massachusetts's new charter of 1691, which repeated almost verbatim the description of the western boundary in the old charter, did not remove the ambiguities regarding the boundaries of Massachusetts and New York. In 1757 the Board of Trade, after a thorough examination of the royal charters of these colonies, concluded that the "description of the limits of those grants, is so inexplicit, and defective, that no conclusive Inference can be drawn from them with respect to the extent of territory originally intended to be granted by them."[6] Meanwhile, the New York government had made several grants in the disputed areas—among them Rensselaerswyck and Livingston Manor—some of which covered the distance of twenty to twenty-four miles east from the Hudson River. In 1705 Governor Cornbury awarded the lands between the Westenhook (Housatonic) River and Claverack to Peter Schuyler and eight other New York gentlemen.[7] This grant, commonly known as Westenhook Patent, remained the utmost eastern frontier of New York toward Massachusetts in the first half of the eighteenth century.

Westenhook Patent inevitably became the first stage of dispute between the two provinces. As a precaution against possible Yankee invasion, its proprietors tried in the early 1710s to settle loyal tenants on the fertile lowland of the patent. But the project did not proceed as well as they had hoped, because its distance from the Hudson River appeared to make commercial farming unfeasible and, more important, because potential settlers, like the proprietors, were afraid of the prospect of controversy with the New England colony over the land.[8] In this early period, however, the feared clash did not occur. The rocky Berkshire hills and the Hoosac range gradually rising westward from the Connecticut River had steered land-hungry farmers northward along the river. At the end of the seventeenth century, the line connecting the settlements on the river—Springfield, Northampton, Deerfield, and Northfield—was the western frontier of Massachusetts. Even so, some restless farmers from these towns would have moved westward across the hills and mountains

6. *N.Y. Col. Docs.*, VIII, 224.
7. See "the Names of the Patentees of the Westen Hook," Mar. 5, 1705, Albany County Miscellaneous Manuscripts, Box 3, New-York Historical Society, New York; Westenhook Indian deed, Oct. 2, 1703, Deed Book 4: 272–273, Albany County Clerk's Office, Albany, N.Y. Another Indian deed, dated May 2, 1703, is in Schuyler Papers, Box 2, N.-Y. Hist. Soc.
8. _____ to Peter Fauconier, Apr. 4, 1718, Bleecker, Collins, and Abeel Papers, Box 2, New York Public Library.

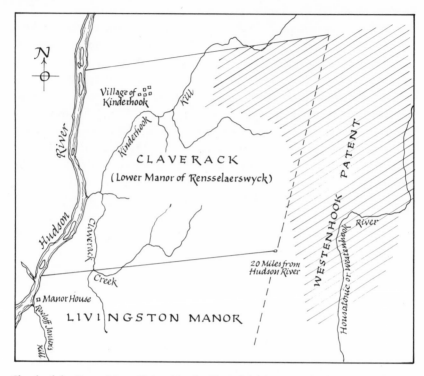

**Sketch of the General Area Claimed by the Westenhook Patentees in the 1710s and 1720s** (Shaded). Adapted from Cadwallader Colden's map, 1771, New York Colonial Manuscripts, Land Papers, 1642–1803, XXIX, 56, New York State Library, Albany. (Drawn by Richard J. Stinely.)

had it not been for Queen Anne's War (1703–1715), which put a damper on expansionist impulses. The French and enemy Indians, descending through the mountain range, sprang a surprise raid on the exposed towns and sheltered themselves in the woods. The inhabitants of Deerfield and Northfield were so frightened of the enemy's onslaught that they deserted their sites at least twice during the war.[9] Thus, the international politics of the region created a buffer between the two provinces.

The picture changed, however, when peace was restored. Frontier farmers resumed the race for new land, and settlement multiplied in every direction. Already by 1716, several bands of people from the an-

9. Josiah Gilbert Holland, *History of Western Massachusetts: The Counties of Hampden, Hampshire, Franklin, and Berkshire* (Springfield, Mass., 1855), I, 161.

cient towns on the Connecticut River were exploring the Housatonic River valley across the Berkshires. The next year, 74 residents of Northampton applied to the General Court of Massachusetts for a grant of an eight-mile-square tract on the west bank of the Housatonic and north of the Massachusetts-Connecticut border line. The legislature rejected the petition, fearing that such an isolated community, if established, would be easy prey for the French and Indians.[10] In November 1719, the Bay Colony proposed to New York that the boundary line be negotiated, but the suggestion was ignored by the latter.[11] In January 1722, the Northampton people renewed their petition for the Housatonic tract, which was quickly joined by more petitions from the towns of Springfield, Westfield, Hadley, and Hatfield. This apparently well-orchestrated campaign by the Connecticut river towns disposed the General Court to review the whole matter of settlement on the Housatonic. Finally, on June 29 of that year, the court granted two townships, Lower Housatonic (later Sheffield) and Upper Housatonic (later Stockbridge), each seven miles square, and ordered a settling committee to admit 120 families into the new towns.[12] The decision of the court was of historic importance because it signaled Massachusetts's first official challenge to New York's claim and, as a corollary, to the Westenhook Patent.

As Lower Housatonic opened for settlement, tension mounted on the New York-Massachusetts frontier. Just a year after the two Housatonic townships were granted, the Albany County authorities moved into the area and attempted in vain to collect quitrents for the lands from the "Inhabitants of No-Mans-land of this Province" (in the language of the Massachusetts General Court), an effort obviously intended to coerce settlers to accept New York jurisdiction.[13] The settling committee of the Massachusetts General Court in turn welcomed even New York Dutch farmers as long as they supported Massachusetts's territorial pretensions. A case in point was a generous grant of land in 1724 to Coenraet Burghardt, Elias Van Schaack, and their relatives, all of Kinderhook. The Yankees had a good reason to be hospitable to the Yorkers.[14] From 1717 to

10. *Journals of Mass. House of Representatives*, I, 232, 243–244.
11. Samuel Shute to governor of New York, Nov. 23, 1719, Daniel J. Pratt, ed., *Report of the Regents of the University, on the Boundaries of the State of New York* (Albany, N.Y., 1884), II, 88–89, hereafter cited as *Report on Boundaries; Journals of Mass. House of Representatives*, II, 69, 187, 262.
12. *Journals of Mass. House of Representatives*, III, 194, IV, 31, 56, 57; Holland, *History of Western Massachusetts*, I, 163.
13. *Journals of Mass. House of Representatives*, V, 53.
14. The exact acreage of their respective grants was unknown. A report in 1736 shows

1721, Burghardt, a mill owner and fur trader, together with Van Schaack, had tried to acquire about four thousand acres of what they believed to be vacant land near their plantations, but they were stopped by Henry Van Rensselaer of Claverack, who claimed that the lands were part of Rensselaerswyck. At the height of the dispute, the irate Burghardt and his partner set fire to a house belonging to a tenant of Van Rensselaer, and for this they were indicted by a grand jury of Albany County. The unfortunate experience transformed them and their descendants into bitter enemies of the landlord for many years to come. They expressed their disaffection with New York by removing themselves to the Housatonic valley in 1731.[15] In return for the favor they received from the Bay Colony, these expatriates worked hard, one might suppose, to advance its expansionist causes.

In the meantime, the General Court further extended the boundary of Massachusetts westward by laying out many more townships on and beyond the Housatonic River. In order to consolidate its territorial claims in the disputed lands or to "prevent Persons from the neighbouring Governments incroaching thereon," the legislature urged grantees to "go and settle."[16] To be sure, the New York government repeatedly protested the encroachment on what it believed to be a part of Westenhook Patent, but the protests fell on deaf ears.[17]

The western expansion of the Bay Colony came to a sudden halt with the outbreak of King George's War (March 1744–October 1748). Again the problem of defending the exposed frontier communities from the French and Indians, and the cost of offensive campaigns, notably against Louisbourg, in which Governor William Shirley of Massachusetts and his people played a major role, taxed the New England colony's

---

that Coenraet Burghardt had 1,600 acres, Elias Van Schaack 800 acres, and Hendrick Burghardt, Sr., and his son 400 acres. *Ibid.*, XXVI, 13; Massachusetts Archives, CXIV, 160, State House, Boston, hereafter cited as Mass. Archives.

15. For Burghardt's career, see *N.Y. Col. Laws*, II, 156–162; Dirck Goes's will, June 1, 1732, Pearson, trans., and Van Laer, eds., *Early Records of Albany and Rensselaerswyck*, II, 172–174; Louis Hasbrouck Sahler, "Isaac Van Deusen and Van Deusen Manor: An Outline," *N.Y. Gen. and Biog. Rec.*, XXVIII (1897), 233–235. For this land dispute with Van Rensselaer, see N.Y. Land Papers, VI, 159, 161, VIII, 35, 43, 56, 156; Minutes of the Court of Sessions, 1717–1723, 23, Albany Co. Clerk's Office; Philip Livingston to father, Robert, Feb. 8, 1721, Livingston-Redmond MSS, Roll 4.

16. Ephraim Williams's memorial, June 1742, Mass. Archives, VI, 46; *Journals of Mass. House of Representatives*, XX, 42, 154–155, 254–255, 365, 384.

17. Petition of the Westenhook proprietors to William Burnet, Apr. 28, 1726, Bleecker, Collins, and Abeel Papers, Box 2; N.Y. Land Papers, X, 4; *Journal of General Assembly*, I, 547; George Clarke to Lords of Trade, May 24, 1739, *N.Y. Col. Docs.*, VI, 143–144; *Journals of Mass. House of Representatives*, IX, 354, X, 53–54, 64, 96, 253, 255, XIV, 203–204, XV, 271, XVI, 109, 190–191.

resources. Her western frontiers trembled, and the exhausted govern-ment turned to Connecticut for military aid. The General Court was forced to rest its territorial ambitions during the war.[18]

But with the restoration of peace, the westward march was resumed. A resolution of the council of Massachusetts in December 1749 admitted that the western expansion was delayed by "Reason of the War" and warned that any further delay in disposing of the lands between Stock-bridge and Pontoosuck (now Pittsfield) and between Sheffield and the Taconic Mountains would have a serious consequence "prejudicial to the Interest of the Province."[19] In this spirit of urgency, the General Court in 1749 and 1750 laid out two more townships "near Hoosuck" and several thousand acres near the "East Branch of Housatonnoc River" for various individuals.[20] Thus, by mid-century her actual western boundary line finally touched the lands claimed by the proprietors of Livingston Manor and Rensselaerswyck including Claverack, and, in the process, Westen-hook Patent became an empty title without land.

The northern manorial landlords were nervous. Massachusetts was closing in on them before they barely recovered their breath from Gover-nor William Cosby's policy in the middle thirties, which had threatened almost every old land title of New York.[21] The activities and thoughts of Philip Livingston of Livingston Manor were perhaps typical of those of the edgy landowners. He saw no "probability" of an early solution to the differences between the two colonies.[22] Nor could he believe that the Bay Colony would cut short her drive at the doorstep of his manor and treat his sprawling estate any differently from the way it had treated Westen-hook Patent. That he was deeply concerned over the boundary contro-versy was clearly manifested in his endeavor to get one of the New York commissionerships on the boundary—a time-consuming job—and to so-licit information from the officials of the two provinces about their re-

18. Philip Livingston to Jacob Wendell, Mar. 3, 1747, Livingston Papers, Museum of the City of New York (unless otherwise specified, all Livingston Papers cited in this chapter are from this repository); *Journals of Mass. House of Representatives*, XX, 317, XXI, 13, 15, 132, 250, XXIII, 15, 24, XXIV, 206, 222, 305; William Shirley to Jonathan Law, Apr. 27, 1745, Charles Henry Lincoln, ed., *Correspondence of William Shirley, Governor of Massachusetts and Military Commander in America, 1731–1760* (New York, 1912), I, 211–212, also 383–384; Hutchinson, *History of Massachusetts Bay*, ed. Mayo, II, 154; Benjamin Doolittle, *A Short Narrative Of Mischief done by the French and Indian Enemy, on the Western Frontiers Of the Province of the Massachusetts-Bay* ... [1743–1748] (Boston, 1750).
19. *Journals of Mass. House of Representatives*, XXVI, 128.
20. *Ibid.*, 13, 132, 158, 178.
21. Klein, "Democracy and Politics," *N.Y. History*, XL (1959), 226–227.
22. Philip Livingston to Jacob Wendell, Jan. 27, 1739, Livingston Papers.

spective positions.[23] Sometime in 1737 he concluded that the future of his estate could not be entrusted wholly to the hands of the government officials, and he decided to take personal measures to ensure its security.

Livingston hit upon a scheme that envisioned the acquisition of lands eastward and at strategic points in Massachusetts, pending the outcome of the intercolonial diplomacy. The tract that he particularly coveted lay between the Taconic Mountains and Sheffield. Several times in 1737 and 1738 he pleaded with his old friend Jacob Wendell, an influential member of the Massachusetts council and a wealthy Boston merchant, to secure the land for him from the General Court.[24] He felt that Massachusetts owed him such a grant as a reward for his "troubles" as chairman of the conference that had fixed the boundary lines between her and New Hampshire in 1731.[25] He took pains to stress that the land in question was "of no great value"—that it was common woodland and "not worth much."[26] Livingston did not want the acreage for its quality, however. We can find a clue to his motives in his characterization of the land as potentially disputable between the two provinces: Livingston was eager to shield the eastern flank of his manor with a Massachusetts title. But he failed. The same motives were present in his frantic efforts to buy lands, preferably in the Housatonic valley and on the Hoosic River adjacent to the manor.[27] Sensing that Colonel John Stoddard of Northampton was the most powerful figure in Western Massachusetts politics, Livingston advised Wendell to bring the colonel into partnership. He wrote in May 1737: "Nothing is likely to be Effected without [Stoddard's] assistance." This strategy had the desired effect. That year Livingston, Stoddard, and Wendell together acquired one of the three townships (24,040 acres) near Stockbridge that had been granted to the town of Boston.[28] Livingston wanted to get more land to the east, however. "I should be

23. Livingston to Wendell, Mar. 7, 1738, ibid.; William Livingston to brother Robert Livingston, Jr., Feb. 4, 1754, Livingston-Redmond MSS, Roll 7.

24. Philip Livingston to Jacob Wendell, Apr. 5, May 23, 1738, Jan. 27, 1739, Livingston Papers. Livingston first revealed his interest in lands at Sheffield in 1736. See Livingston to Israel Williams, May 16, 1736, Miscellaneous Manuscripts, Livingston, N-P, N.-Y. Hist. Soc. Jacob Wendell was born to a Dutch family in the Albany area, moved to Boston probably in the 1720s, and died on September 7, 1761. John M. Wendell to Mrs. Sarah Glen, Sept. 20, 1761, Wendell Papers, ibid.

25. Philip Livingston to Jacob Wendell, Oct. 23, 1737, Livingston Papers; Hutchinson, History of Massachusetts Bay, ed. Mayo, II, 293.

26. Philip Livingston to Jacob Wendell, Oct. 23, 1737, Apr. 5, 1738, Livingston Papers.

27. Gordon, "Livingstons of New York," 90.

28. Philip Livingston to Philip and Jacob Wendell, May 16, 1737, Livingston Papers. Jacob Wendell paid £1,320 for the tract. See deed from Jacob Wendell to Philip Living-

glad to know whether your General Court would dispose of a tract of land. I have a spott in view," he wrote to his Boston friend in late 1738, "which I would willingly buy." In a moment of exuberance, he even conceived of "laying out and settling all the Land from Deerfield westward."[29]

Though daring in conception and ambitious in scope, Livingston's various schemes ran into difficulties. He and Stoddard repeatedly clashed over the method of developing their township near Pittsfield. Livingston insisted on leasing the land and settling it with German and Dutch farmers from New York, while Stoddard was in favor of its outright sale and settlement "all or chiefly" by Yankees. Stoddard even proposed to grant thirty town lots gratis to his people as a means of encouragement.[30] The two men's disagreement surely reflected their different ideas of land economics and the divergent ways of life of Yorkers and Yankees. More important, at stake here was the issue of who would control the area. As Livingston saw it, Stoddard's plan, if followed, would have resulted in Yankee domination of the town and would have nullified the very objective of its acquisition. Another alarming problem was an attempt by Stoddard and his associates, especially Timothy Woodbridge, a teacher of the Stockbridge Indians, to usurp the township. Livingston reported to Wendell in October 1738 that Woodbridge as an agent for Stoddard had gotten an Indian proprietor drunk and then persuaded him to convey to Woodbridge the same township land that the native had earlier sold to Wendell. Livingston was convinced that the Connecticut valley people were "trying to destroy" him and his Boston partner.[31] A much more serious development, however, was the mounting opposition from 1740 to 1742 of the entire population of the Housatonic valley to Livingston's enterprise, which, they feared, aimed at the annexation of the area to New York and at the "ruin of near two hundred farmers" there.[32] In

ston, May 29, 1741, William Williams Collection, III, 305, Berkshire Atheneum, Pittsfield, Mass. For Stoddard's political prominence, see Lincoln, ed., *Correspondence of William Shirley*, I, 209. In 1744 Stoddard was appointed commander-in-chief of the Western Department of Massachusetts.

29. Philip Livingston to Jacob Wendell, Nov. 6, 9, 1738, Mar. 7, 28, June 3, 27, Oct. 29, 1739, Livingston Papers.

30. Philip Livingston to Jacob Wendell, June 3, Aug. 3, 1738, Apr. 21, Oct. 29, 1739, July 21, Oct. 28, 1740, *ibid*.

31. Livingston to Wendell, Oct. 30, Dec. 30, 1738, Mar. 28, Apr. 9, 1739, *ibid*. Reversing his original stand, Livingston now urged Wendell to buy off Stoddard's interest in the township. This, he believed, would be to "our mutual advantage."

32. Petition of the inhabitants of Sheffield, Upper Housatonic, and Stockbridge to William Shirley, June 1742, Mass. Archives, VI, 46.

the face of this hostility from the Yankees, many Dutch farmers who had previously agreed to settle under Livingston were now hesitant.[33]

But the situation was not as bad as it appeared. In the summer of 1740, Livingston began to hear rumors "whispered about" among his coteries that by a new boundary settlement, the Housatonic valley, including his township, would "undoubtedly" fall in New York. In the autumn, his morale was further boosted by a report that the king had ordered Governor Jonathan Belcher of Massachusetts "not to grant any lands on the borders."[34] Livingston, like many fellow colonists, interpreted this as an expression of sympathy on the part of the home government toward New York's case. If the rumors came true, as he firmly believed they would, he had less reason to agonize over the security of his township and manor. Finally, in May 1742, he came to the crucial decision to bank the future of his manorial estate on the boundary settlement and to sell his share of the township. It appears, from his long correspondence with Wendell, that by 1746 he had completely liquidated his share and thus ended his frustrating private campaign against Massachusetts's expansionism.[35] Subsequent events belied Livingston's proleptic calculations, however. The borders remained undetermined, although pressure from the east somewhat eased, thanks to the war. Livingston died in 1749 probably never anticipating that his manor, willed to his eldest son, Robert, Jr., would two years later become one of the foci of the struggle between New York and Massachusetts.

## Conspiracies against Livingston Manor

The beginning of the second half of the eighteenth century was marked by renewed interest on the part of Massachusetts leaders in the opportunities for westward expansion. A couple of circumstances seem to have been mainly responsible for this development. First, the combination of a declining domestic food supply and a growing population required the importation of various kinds of provisions from neighboring

33. These Dutch farmers, mostly from Kinderhook and some from Claverack and Schaghticoke, had asked Livingston not to invite New Englanders to the new township. Livingston gladly accepted the request. Livingston to Wendell, Jan. 15, 1742, Livingston Papers.

34. Livingston to Wendell, Aug. 16, Sept. 8, 1740, *ibid*.

35. Confident that the township would soon be annexed to New York, Livingston proposed to Wendell to join with him to locate the "best spotts" of the town and to obtain grants from the New York government. Livingston to Wendell, May 29, 1742, Apr. 5, 1746, *ibid*.

provinces. This change was reflected in the shifting balance of trade between Massachusetts and New York in favor of the latter to the amount
of £40,000 (New York currency) a year. The grain shortage was so acute
that in April 1749 the General Court established a committee to consider
"some proper Encouragement for improving the natural Advantages of
the Soil and Climate" and to inquire whether the grantees of land had
fulfilled their "conditions of settlement." A contemporary observer called
the attention of the House of Representatives to the fact that the value of
unimproved land in the province was rising about 20 percent annually.[36]
It would not have been difficult for the legislators to discern the cause-
effect relationship between the shortages of land and food.

Another factor in reviving Massachusetts's expansionism was the
humiliating insults the neighboring provinces heaped on the Bay Colony
in the years 1749 to 1751. In 1749 her western towns, namely, Wood-
stock, Somers, Suffield, and Enfield, revolted. The Connecticut government, which had instigated the trouble in the first place, promptly took
the towns under its protection. Coming a few years after the setbacks in
the boundary controversies with New Hampshire and Rhode Island,
which had "divested" Massachusetts of "a great part" of its ancient
lands, the revolt added a fresh wound to its bruised provincial egotism.
Moreover, Massachusetts's efforts in 1750 and 1751 to collect tax arrears
from some inhabitants who were by an order of the king "set off" to
Rhode Island met an "unwarrantable" rebuke from the little colony. The
people from New Hampshire too were daily making inroads on Massachusetts's lands on the east side of the Merrimack River. The days when
the Bay Colony, "by mere dint of power," had its way with its sister
colonies seemed to have gone forever.[37] Its limits were fixed in all direc-

36. In the following June, the General Court again addressed itself to the "great
Danger of a Scarcity of Corn and other provisions in this province." In May, Lt. Gov.
Spencer Phips echoed the sentiment of the legislature by declaring that "among other
Matters that require the Attention of this Legislature, there is nothing more necessary, than
to project some effectual Method for the Encouragement and Increase of the Husbandry of
this Province (that so we may be able to live more within our selves, and depend less upon
our Neighbours for the common Necessaries of Life." *Journals of Mass. House of Representatives*, XXV, 212, XXVI, 14, XXVII, 7–8; *Some Observations Relating to the present
Circumstances of the Province of the Massachusetts-Bay; Humbly offered to the Consideration of the General Assembly* (Boston, 1750), 12; Klein, ed., *Independent Reflector*, 31;
Carl Bridenbaugh, *Cities in the Wilderness: The First Century of Urban Life in America,
1625–1742* (New York, 1938), 332.

37. William Williams, *God the Strength of Rulers and People, And Making them to be
so, to each other mutually* ... (Boston, 1741), 46; Mass. Archives, VI, 65–68, 434;
Hutchinson, *History of Massachusetts Bay*, ed. Mayo, III, 4–6; *Journals of Mass. House
of Representatives*, XXVII, 96–97, 154, 194, 216, XXVIII, 11, 17, 117–118.

tions except westward, and its neighbors had gained strength and, inevitably, a sense of self-importance. Their late challenges were a dramatic
illustration of how low the Bay Colony had sunk in their esteem.

In a pamphlet with the revealing title *Massachusetts in Agony*, published in 1750, a pseudonymous author stated that "poverty and Discontent appear in every Face" and "dwell upon every Tongue," because,
among other reasons, provisions, clothing, and fuel were dear, money
was scarce, and taxes were high. In short, the province was "in a deplor-
able Situation."[38] The colony ought to be ashamed, another writer insisted, for it was gifted in diverse soils and as well "adapted to those
Necessaries of Life" as its neighbors and, therefore, should be able to
support itself. It was equally shameful for Massachusetts's government
officials to let the little neighbors harass it with impunity. In this gloomy
atmosphere, some adventuresome leaders of the colony seem to have
decided to launch a new territorial adventure. Such a course would bring
more arable land, make up for humiliating losses, and demonstrate to
both neighbors and depressed inhabitants that the old New England
power still had muscle to flex. It was this budding expansionist impulse
that the highly moralistic writer detected and probably wanted to warn
against when he quoted Cicero on the title page of his pamphlet: "The
Romans carefully cultivated their own Lands without coveting those of
their Neighbours and by that Means enriched the Republick and enlarged
the Empire with such a Number of Lands, Cities and Nations."[39] But the
successful riot of the Connecticut River towns had perhaps desensitized
the General Court to the immorality of instigating insurgent elements in
a neighboring province in order to advance Massachusetts's territorial
interests. If Connecticut had succeeded, why should the Bay Colony
cringe from following suit? In the early 1750s, the once mighty province
was like a harassed giant determined to solve his problems by lashing out
at the weak who happened to be standing closest to him.

The northern manors standing in Massachusetts's path were fraught
with problems that made the domains easy targets for exploitation. The
most serious was that, no matter how good the terms, leaseholding was
not as desirable as freeholding. The tenants, both rich and poor, were
therefore likely to be tempted by a cause promising the conversion of
leaseholds into freeholds. Another problem was somewhat peculiar to

38. Vincent Centinel, *Massachusetts in Agony: Or, Important Hints to the Inhabitants
of the Province: Calling aloud for Justice to be done to the Oppressed; and avert the
Impending Wrath over the Oppressors* (Boston, 1750), 1.
39. *Some Observations Relating to the present Circumstances.*

the far eastern sections of these manors, which had long been in a state of wilderness because they were so distant from the Hudson River, the common artery of marketing. It was only in the 1740s that settlement there began in earnest. As of 1750, Kakeout (later known as Nobletown, a center of disturbance) in Claverack had no more than a dozen families under its proprietor John Van Rensselaer, and in the vicinity of the Taconic Mountains in Livingston Manor were about twenty families.[40] Thus, eastern New York was a frontier society largely made up of newcomers who did not share much in common with fellow tenants. The new settlers were poor, since they had not sufficiently improved their allotted land, and, in any case, their remote location depressed land values. The worth of their leases appears to have ranged from £15 to a maximum of £50 in Livingston Manor and probably a little more in Claverack, only because leases there were of a durable kind.[41]

Most tenants felt some insecurity simply because of the nature of their tenure. And the poor ones did not have the pride of a property holder that characterized some well-to-do tenants, although rich and poor alike lacked the attachment to the soil that filled the hearts and lifted the spirits of freeholders.[42] Living right next to colonies in which a freehold land system prevailed undoubtedly sharpened their perception of the contrast between the two systems and made their status look worse than it actually was. Moreover, their frequent intercourse with New Englanders exposed them directly to the highly contagious egalitarian culture of that region. One possible countervailing force to this process could have been, in theory, closer communication between tenants and landlord. But their interchanges were infrequent because of the geographical and social distance between them.

A cause requires promoters and supporters, and there were many astute men in western Massachusetts who found in the tenantry of the New York manors and in the unsettled state of the boundaries an ideal combination to be exploited for the good of the Bay Colony and their private interests. None was more active and tenacious than David Ingersoll of Sheffield in converting the tenants into rebels and in educating the General Court about the great potential of the area for Massachusetts's interests.

Ingersoll was born in about 1700 to a distinguished family in West-

40. Depositions of Benjamin Lovejoy, Jockume Van Volkenburgh, and Gabriel Grate, Aug. 27, 28, 1762, Columbia County Miscellaneous Manuscripts, N.-Y. Hist. Soc.
41. Robert Livingston, Jr., to Jacob Wendell, Apr. 12, 1753, Livingston Papers.
42. Crèvecoeur, *Letters from an American Farmer*, 30–31, 43, 61, 65–66.

field that also produced Thomas Ingersoll (David's cousin), a deputy to the House of Representatives from the town in the 1720s and 1730s. A merchant and surveyor by occupation, David Ingersoll occasionally engaged in military contracting and speculated in western lands. In fact, he was the mastermind behind the campaign to obtain the Upper and Lower Housatonic grants in 1722. One report shows that most, if not all, of the settling rights at Stockbridge had "passed through" his hands and that as of 1737 he had 2,800 acres there. Another report in 1736 estimated that he owned 3,200 acres at Sheffield. He was naturally alert to any matters, ranging from the boundary controversy to the country road over the Berkshires, that affected his interests and those of the frontier settlements.[43] Through his heavy involvement in the region's affairs, he forged valuable friendships with a number of political leaders in Massachusetts, such as Joseph Dwight of Brookfield and later of Stockbridge, Oliver Partridge of Hatfield, Ephraim Williams and Timothy Woodbridge, both of Stockbridge, John Ashley of Sheffield, and James Bowdoin of Boston.[44] In his list of friends was also Coenraet Burghardt, a Dutchman from Kinderhook who was once a speculative partner of Ingersoll in the Housatonic lands. It was Ingersoll who, on recognizing the potential utility of Burghardt, induced the Dutchman and his associates to settle in Massachusetts with a generous offer of land. From these expatriates he learned much about the conditions and vulnerabilities of the manors west of the Taconic Mountains.[45] In 1740 he moved his residence from Westfield to Sheffield, an act that would have serious implications for manorial society, and the next year he was elected to the House of Representatives from the district.[46] But the panic that King George's War brought to the frontier community suspended him from this facet of his public career for a while. Despite all of his business successes, his conduct was not above the reproach of dishonesty. The few available records reveal that he was frequently involved in civil suits and was found guilty

43. Committee reports to the General Court, Dec. 10, 1736, and Jan. 6, 1737, Mass. Archives, CXIV, 160, 168–169; ibid., CXVI, 430, 432–433; Acts and Resolves, Public and Private, of the Province of the Massachusetts Bay [1692–1786] (Boston, 1869–1922), XV, appendix X, 289; Journals of Mass. House of Representatives, XVI, 200, IX, 235, XXIX, 147.

44. Bowdoin, a wealthy merchant of Boston, owned, as of 1737, 3,000 acres in Upper Housatonic. Joseph Dwight to Harrison Gray, Mar. 25, 1753, Mass. Archives, VI, 109–112. See also ibid., CXVI, 430, 432–433, CXIV, 168–169, XLVI, 371.

45. Journal of Mass. House of Representatives, XV, 66.

46. Ibid., XIX, 14; deposition of David Ingersoll and Luke Noble on their settlement at Great Barrington, June 29, 1762, Sorted Legal Manuscripts, John Tabor Kempe Papers, N.-Y. Hist. Soc.

of delinquency. Finally, in 1755 the General Court declared him "unworthy to sustain any Office" of trust because of his embezzlement of public funds. In sum, he was an unscrupulous operator bent on lining his pockets even at public expense.[47]

In late 1750, Ingersoll hatched a plot against Livingston Manor. His immediate objective was to rob its proprietor of the manor lands, forty-five or fifty square miles, west of the Taconic Mountains.[48] The lesson of Massachusetts's successful annexation of part of Westenhook Patent was still fresh in his mind. All that past protests of the Yorkers had accomplished was to expose their helplessness. The boundary question remained as uncertain as it had been many decades earlier. The only change on the western frontier was the mushrooming development of towns and settlements of yeoman farmers hostile toward New York landlords and the system they represented. As of 1742, about two hundred families were settled on the Housatonic River, and at the end of King George's War, the population grew rapidly with the fresh influx of land-hungry farmers. Under these conditions, Ingersoll persuaded himself that his new scheme would work just as well as the old one and that he could obtain a lion's share of the spoils.

The contour of Ingersoll's plans was first revealed in his memorial of February 1, 1751, to the General Court. He urged that "province" lands (26,345 acres in his estimation) west and northwest of Sheffield be quickly settled with "good people" or sold to him. Either measure was necessary, he explained, because many "very poor" and "very vicious" Yorkers and Connecticut people were squatting on the lands. In the most significant part of the memorial, he pointed out to the authorities that "some Gentl[emen] of New York Govt are daily inchroaching on the Lands of this Province west of the [Taconic] Mountains and will get footing there if not prevented." The lands he mentioned were inhabited and improved by the tenants of Claverack and Livingston manors and were claimed by their landlords to be within their ancient patents. Ingersoll's statement was significant because no one within or without the government had ever before publicly asserted that the area was Massachusetts's territory.

---

47. As one of the selectmen of Sheffield, Ingersoll defrauded the government to the amount of £42 14s. 8d. *Acts and Resolves of Massachusetts Bay*, XV, appendix X, 378–379, 632; Mass. Archives, I, 287–298a, XLI, 12–14, 69–73, 239–243, XLIV, 185–186; *Journals of Mass. House of Representatives*, XV, 66.

48. "Another Petition of the Proprietor of Livingston Manor," May 31, 1753, *Doc. Hist. N.Y.*, III, 739–740; Oliver Partridge's report, Jan. 15, 1752, Mass. Archives, CXVI, 36.

Probably, he would not have claimed this land as such if he had not been apprised in advance of the position of the legislature on the matter. In any event, two weeks later he petitioned the court again, this time proposing to buy a tract contiguous to Fort Massachusetts (the present site of Adams). But this petition was dismissed, and his first tabled.[49] Undaunted by the setback, he ran for and got elected in the spring to the House of Representatives, undoubtedly with a view to promoting his scheme within the establishment.

At the same time, Ingersoll enlisted "several Gentlemen of Reputed veracity" in western Massachusetts to agitate among the Livingston tenants across the mountains. The Yankees busily disseminated a story that the lands the tenants were cultivating were legally vacant, "not lawfully seized by any person," and lay within the jurisdiction of the Boston government, and that Livingston's right to the tracts was founded on a mere claim and not on a legitimate title. To give credence to the story, they asserted that the Bay Colony authorities had at one time rejected the petition of Robert Livingston, founder of the manor, for the premises.[50] Ingersoll assured the wavering tenants that their leaseholds would soon be changed into freeholds if they would cooperate with him. It would not have been too difficult to convince them of his reliability by pointing out Massachusetts's victory in her past contest with New York over the Housatonic area and Ingersoll's vital role in it. Also, Ingersoll probably called their attention to the prosperity that the Burghardts and Van Schaacks, the Dutch expatriates, were enjoying as a result of their service to Boston.

That Ingersoll's seductive campaign was successful is attested by the refusal of about twenty tenants in the Taconic area to pay their 1751 rents to their landlord, Livingston, and by their joining in October of that year with twenty-six Sheffield residents in petitioning the General Court for a grant of Taconic lands. It appears that most of the area tenants rebelled. According to an official investigation, Ingersoll had a secret understanding with the petitioners that if they succeeded, they would convey at least two thousand acres of the tracts to him. The petition, called Bull's petition, was a product of the collusion among Ingersoll, his town folks, and the Livingston tenants and was couched in language designed to flatter the solons and elicit their sympathy. It stated that the

49. David Ingersoll to the General Court, Feb. 1, 1751, Mass. Archives, XLVI, 237–238.
50. Deposition of Josiah and Abigail Loomis, Nov. 3, 1767, *ibid.*, VI, 415–417.

tenants had been settled under Robert Livingston, Jr.'s, encouragement, but lately had become "very uneasy at present heavy Rents"; that they had "never had the gospel among them as long as they are sensible"; and that since the lands they were improving lay "eastward of the utomost limit of his patent and within the province of the Massachusetts Bay," they were "desirous of the protection" of that colony's authority.[51] Ingersoll also had his ubiquitous hand in another petition (Hopkins's petition), dated May 1751, for land west of Sheffield. The exact location of the tract and the identities of most of the forty-nine petitioners are unknown, but Ingersoll was reported to have made a pitch for five hundred acres in the application for land, and his son William, a surveyor, was a cosigner of the petition. It is clear from the language of the document that the land was claimed by some New Yorkers.[52]

These petitions were not the only immediate pressures on the Massachusetts government to do something about the lands across the Taconic Mountains. In the middle of 1751, it was confronted with the need to find equivalent land for those who were forced to leave the so-called Hop-Lands (about three miles square) in Sheffield that had been allocated for the growing Indian population at Stockbridge.[53] The reactions of the General Court, however, were surprisingly sluggish, due primarily to an obstructionist campaign secretly conducted by Jacob Wendell, a member of the council. Just as with Philip Livingston, Wendell had close personal ties with Robert Livingston, Jr. The Boston merchant depended on the Livingston Manor proprietor for a supply of iron and for food products. He also looked after the welfare of Robert, Jr.'s, son Philip, studying at Harvard College, and another son, Peter, dabbling in trade in Boston. Because of this commercial and personal connection, until his death in 1761 he was willing to act as a watchdog of Livingston's proprietary interest.[54] By covert correspondence, Wendell not only informed the land-

51. Petition of William Bull and 44 others, Oct. 11, 1751, *ibid.*, CXVI, 32–34; a committee report, June 9, 1753, *ibid.*, XLVI, 307–308; Oliver Partridge's report, Jan. 15, 1752, *ibid.*, CXVI, 36; *Journals of Mass. House of Representatives*, XXVIII, 67.

52. Petition of Timothy Hopkins and 48 others, May 1751, Mass. Archives, CXVI, 30; a committee report, June 9, 1753, *ibid.*, XLVI, 308; Robert Livingston, Jr., to Jacob Wendell, May 26, 1753, Livingston Papers.

53. *Journals of Mass. House of Representatives*, XXVII, 152–153, 188, 205, 220, XXVIII, 52, 62.

54. My view here is based on the voluminous correspondence between Robert Livingston, Jr., and Jacob Wendell in Livingston Papers. See also Jacob Wendell to Robert Sanders, Sept. 16, 26, and Oct. 14, 1755, Glen-Sanders Papers, Colonial Williamsburg Foundation Research Department, Williamsburg, Va.; Philip Livingston to brother Robert, Jr., June 30, 1752, and Jacob Wendell to Robert Livingston, Jr., June 9, 1753, Mar. 8, 1755, Livingston-

lord about almost every detail of the General Court's proceedings affecting the manor but also coached him on how to act. Their collaboration won its first victory on January 25, 1752, when the upper house, upon the recommendation from its committee headed by Wendell, rejected a resolution of the lower house approving the Bull petition.[55] Livingston was jubilant at the news communicated by Wendell and responded: "I am really glad to find you had friends Enough in the Council to git that Petition rejected when it came before you for concurrence. I hope you'll be able to do so in Every thing that may prejudice me in my just and peaceable possessions."[56] But this euphoria was short-lived, for Ingersoll, his tenant followers, and his political supporters would persist in their original objectives, sometimes on their own initiative and at other times under the auspices of the civil authorities.

In September 1751, when he first heard of the Bull petition, Livingston was not terribly alarmed, believing that the lands that some of his "uneasy" tenants petitioned for lay between Canaan, Connecticut, and his manor's east line. While discussing the tenants' move with Wendell, the landlord proposed that "if you have a mind with some other friends to put in first [for the lands], I would joyn with you for a proportion be it ¼ or ⅙ or ⅛ just as you may be able to settle that point with some of your leading men."[57] In the middle of November, however, he was shocked to learn that the Bull petition was aimed at forty-five or fifty square miles of his estate west of the Taconic Mountains and that the Massachusetts House of Representatives had ordered Oliver Partridge, deputy from Hatfield, to draw "a general plan" of unappropriated province lands west of the Connecticut River and at the same time to investigate the area and the circumstances of the tenants.[58] Livingston, a man of mercurial temper and aristocratic vanity, was furious with the disloyal tenants and feared that the Massachusetts authorities were intriguing with them to destroy him. At stake, as he saw it, was not just some part of his manor but the entire tenancy system and, as a corollary, his entire

Redmond MSS, Roll 7; Robert Sanders to John Sanders, Sept. 10, 1761, Sanders Papers, Box 7, N.-Y. Hist. Soc.

55. Mass. Archives, CXVI, 36, 37, 38; *Journals of Mass. House of Representatives*, XXVIII, 67, 105, 118, 119. While rejecting the lower house resolve, the council proposed to the house that they establish a joint committee to consider the affair and to inquire into the "quantity and quality of the lands" mentioned in the Bull petition. The lower house agreed.

56. Robert Livingston, Jr., to Jacob Wendell, Aug. 21, 1752, Livingston Papers. This letter was in response to Wendell's letters of May 25 and June 22, which are not extant.

57. Robert Livingston, Jr., to Jacob Wendell, Sept. 14, 1751, *ibid.*

58. *Journals of Mass. House of Representatives*, XXVIII, 68.

property. A measure of his panic was evidenced in his writing on November 18 a letter to each of his four brothers, William, John, Philip, and Peter Van Brugh, all living in New York City, asking for their help and advice. Their response was prompt; they all advised him to lay the problem before the governor and council of New York "as a provincial controversy," since it would be "impossible" for him alone "to contend with a whole government" of the Bay Colony.[59] Livingston could not have agreed with their observations more. But he was soon in for another shock. In early January 1752, he received a letter threatening that his residence and other buildings would be burned, unless he sent £50 to the writer, who signed himself only "WP."[60]

Livingston despaired of getting quick intervention by the New York government on his behalf, for Governor George Clinton was preparing to go home and the assembly was in recess. Though uncertain about who was the real architect of the Bull petition, he knew that the Sheffield people were behind it and that Josiah Loomis, an ore digger for the manor ironworks from Symsbury, Connecticut, was the ringleader of the twenty "insolent" tenants.[61] On January 17, accusing Loomis of being the "promoter and first inventor" of the trouble, Livingston warned him to move off the manor by August 1 and in the meantime not to "put a Plough or hoe or any other tool in the Ground again." Loomis responded with defiance, boasting to his neighbors that the lands were his and that he could be evicted only by force, whereupon Livingston filed an ejectment suit against him and also threatened Michael Halenbeck, a neighbor and tenant-conspirator with Loomis, with a trespass charge.[62] This disturbed several prominent leaders of western Massachusetts, especially Oliver Partridge of Hatfield, who felt that the tenants deserved the en-

59. William Livingston to brother Robert, Jr., John Livingston to brother Robert, Jr., Nov. 25, 1751, Philip Van Brugh Livingston to brother Robert, Jr., Nov. 26, 1751, Philip Livingston to brother Robert, Jr., Nov. 29, 1751, Livingston-Redmond MSS, Roll 7.

60. Gov. George Clinton's Proclamation, Jan. 11, 1752, N.Y. Col. MSS, LXXVII, 30.

61. At the invitation of Philip Livingston, Loomis came to the manor in 1742. Two years later, the manor proprietor gave him permission to build a "small house" for his family and work on a "small piece of land" at Taconic for subsistence. Robert Livingston, Jr., who inherited the domain, let Loomis stay on the farm without a formal lease on the condition that he would dig iron ore. Loomis's house was situated about 18 miles east of the Hudson River. Robert Livingston, Jr., to Jacob Wendell, Oct. 21, 1753, Livingston Papers; affidavits of Thomas Loomis, Timothy Conner, Coenraadt Rosman, and Matthias Van Deusen, all dated Aug. 23, 1753, Livingston-Redmond MSS, Roll 7.

62. Michael Halenbeck had been a tenant for about 30 years on a farm of 60 acres. He was supposed to pay his rent to Gilbert Livingston, the youngest son of the manor founder. Robert Livingston, Jr., to James De Lancey, Feb. 12, 1754, Doc. Hist. N.Y., III, 767; Robert Livingston's deed of gift to Gilbert Livingston, Nov. 30, 1727, Columbia Co. Misc. MSS.

couragement and protection of the Bay Colony. After all, the Yankees
had instigated the trouble, and their interests were closely bound up with
those of the discontented tenants. It was Partridge who several months
before had interviewed the Livingston tenants and persuaded the lower
house to approve the Bull petition. On March 24 he sternly warned Livingston not to harass Loomis and Halenbeck: "In consequence of an order
of Committee of the General Court of the Province of Massachusetts-
Bay, to lay out Equivalents in the Province land, I have begun on the East
side of Tackinick Barrick, and laid out a large Farm which encompasses
the dwellings of Michael Halenbeeck and Josia Loomis, and you may
depend on it the province will assert their rights to said lands." Any legal
steps against the tenants, he menacingly added, would not "turn out to
[Livingston's] advantage."[63] Whether he had the authority to speak for
the General Court or the province is a moot question. His action seems to
have been endorsed by Joseph Dwight, chairman of the committee entrusted with Stockbridge Indian affairs, although Dwight, when confronted by Wendell, denied any knowledge of the incident. The episode
shows the extent to which some influential members of the legislature
became implicated in manor affairs. In any event, Livingston, now mel-
lowed by Partridge's threat, reached a compromise with Loomis and
Halenbeck whereby the tenants would take out new leases subject to the
landlord's pleasure and would bear the cost of the ejectment suit. This
was just a modus vivendi, and Livingston knew it was, for the causes of
the trouble lay not on the west but on the east side of the Taconic
Mountains and the key to a solution was in the hands of Massachusetts.
As long as the boundary dispute was unresolved, the manor, he suspected,
would never be free from encroachment and from tenant rebellions.
Besides, he could gather from the tenor of Partridge's letter that the
General Court was serious about what Partridge said it would do.

Livingston had had many sleepless nights in the months past worry-
ing about the safety of his estate. As he confessed in mid-April to Wendell,
he could hardly think of anything else. Nor did he have time to speculate
on the "inquietude of mortal life, and the constant flux and mutability of
sublunary happiness," which was what his brother William had advised
him to do.[64] To seek help from his government, he traveled to Manhattan

63. Petition of Robert Livingston, Jr., Apr. 16, 1752, Livingston Family Papers, Robert
to William, N.Y. Pub. Lib.; Robert Livingston, Jr., to Jacob Wendell, Apr. 16, 1753,
Livingston Papers. Livingston later called Partridge "the Contriver and promotor of all this
disturbance" in his manor. Livingston to Wendell, Apr. 22, 1754, *ibid*.
64. Robert Livingston, Jr., to Jacob Wendell, Apr. 16, 1752, Livingston Papers; William
Livingston to brother Robert, Jr., Nov. 25, 1751, Livingston-Redmond MSS, Roll 7.

in the early part of April, only to find the town paralyzed because of a smallpox epidemic. Governor Clinton did "not care to see" anyone and was unwilling to convene the council or the assembly. So Livingston left his petition (dated April 16, 1752) with a clerk of the council. In it he asked the governor to do two things: one, to urge the Massachusetts government to suspend all proceedings with respect to the Taconic area until "the true division line be settled between the two Colonies"; the other, to issue orders to the justices of the peace "in and near" the Manor of Livingston to arrest and commit those who "disturb[ed]" his right to the estate.[65] Several days later, the proprietors of Westenhook Patent also presented a petition urging the governor to recover their lands that had been taken by Massachusetts. The governor, however, obliged neither of the parties for almost a year, although he had been advised in May by his attorney general, William Smith, to favor at least Livingston's first request.[66] Clinton's inertia reflected a relative calm in Livingston Manor during the rest of the year.

The Massachusetts General Court, continually prorogued until late November with extremely short sessions (no more than four days) in between, did nothing about the border problem. But some prominent men in the western part of the colony were spoiling for a fight with the landlord in order to test his patience and fortitude and hopefully to plunge the two colonies into a major confrontation. The records bearing on this period show clearly who those provocateurs were. The most active was of course David Ingersoll, now a justice of the peace in Hampshire County. In addition, there were three other local grandees: Captain John Ashley, a deputy from Sheffield and onetime speaker of the House of Representatives; Colonel Oliver Partridge; and Brigadier Joseph Dwight of Stockbridge, a member of the council and a towering political figure in the region who had replaced the late John Stoddard of Northampton in influence and standing.[67]

Especially noteworthy in terms of the escalation of the border con-

65. *Doc. Hist. N.Y.*, III, 727–730.

66. William Smith's report on Livingston's petition, May 25, 1752, *ibid.*, 730–732; surveyor general's report, June 5, 1752, *ibid.*, 733.

67. The most concrete evidence on Brigadier Dwight's support of the rebellious tenants is his letter of Mar. 25, 1753, to Harrison Gray, a deputy from Boston. Mass. Archives, VI, 109–112. Born in 1703 at Hatfield, Dwight married Mary, daughter of Col. John Pynchon of Springfield and granddaughter of William Pynchon. In 1751 he was appointed chairman of the committee on the Stockbridge Indians. From 1753 to 1761 he was a judge of the court of common pleas in Hampshire County. It appears that he owned a considerable amount of land near Stockbridge. L. Hasbrouck von Sahler, "The Dwights of Stockbridge," *N.Y. Gen. and Biog. Rec.*, XXXIII (1902), 15; William Williams to Joseph Dwight, Feb. 26, 1754, Morristown Historical Park Collection (microfilm), Roll 68, Morristown, N.J.

flict was an incident involving one George Robinson, a poor "English-man" from Pennsylvania and the son-in-law of a Livingston tenant, Joseph Pain.[68] Sometime in the spring of 1752, Robinson in vain asked the landlord to rent him a piece of land near his father-in-law in the area west of the Taconic Mountains. Soon Colonel Partridge appeared on the scene and "encouraged" Robinson to "keep possession" of the land for the Bay Colony. This Robinson did by setting up a wigwam, which the landlord quickly had pulled down and its timber burnt. Robinson built it again, only to meet the same treatment, but he was not deterred from doing it a third time. Livingston then had him arrested and committed to the Albany County jail.[69] Robinson could not have done all this—extraordinary for a poor young man—without support from Partridge and the like. The episode tells more about the aggressive attitude of the Massachusetts instigators than about that of the "Englishman."

In Boston, Ingersoll and his friends were hard at work selling their scheme to the legislature. On November 28 they managed to reintroduce the petitions of Bull and Hopkins onto the floor of the lower house.[70] Again, the house was disposed to satisfy the petitioners, while the council was reluctant, due to the influence of Jacob Wendell. Wendell's tactic at this time seems to have been to delay doing anything. But the tide was running against him. Brigadier Dwight, a leading advocate of expansionism, strained every one of his political muscles to counter Wendell. Finally, on December 30, both legislative branches agreed to dispatch a committee to the lands petitioned. The committee, under the chairmanship of Dwight, was ordered to investigate and report by the following May the present circumstances and everything relating to the lands in question, such as the size and value of each settlement, the names of the settlers, and the quantity and quality of the vacant province land "comprehended within the Bounds of the whole Tract," so that the court would be able to convey "the Province's Right to the Settlers on such Reasonable Terms" or to any other purchasers.[71] Though lacking specific reference as to how far the province land would extend, the detailed instructions were the first official declaration of the court's intent to annex some portion of Livingston Manor and even possibly of Claverack.

---

68. Joseph Pain had been a tenant since 1744 or 1745. Robert Livingston, Jr., to Jacob Wendell, Oct. 21, 1753, Livingston Papers.

69. Robert Livingston, Jr., to Jacob Wendell, Apr. 16, 1753, *ibid.*; Robert Livingston, Jr., to James Alexander, Jan. 22, 1753, Rutherford Collection, III, 203, N.-Y. Hist. Soc.

70. *Journals of Mass. House of Representatives*, XXIX, 43.

71. *Ibid.*, XXIX, 111–112.

This action opened a new chapter in the boundary controversy, and, more immediately, had serious repercussions west of the mountains.

Buoyed by the legislative measure, the hawks of western Massachusetts began what Livingston called the "Second Invasion" against his manor. On the night of January 10, 1753, David Ingersoll, a justice of the peace, together with his friend Oliver Partridge, now sheriff of Hampshire County, and five others, came all the way to Ancram to arrest several employees at the ironworks there.[72] This action was obviously designed to revenge the incarceration of George Robinson. Furthermore, Ingersoll particularly resented the actions of about thirty ironworkers who had faithfully followed Livingston's orders directed against the insurgents. But the intruders had to withdraw as quickly as they had come when they were met by armed manufactory workers who had been tipped off about their plan. Afterward a rumor was afloat that the sheriff would return again "speadily" with a reinforcement of a hundred men to apprehend all the woodcutters and colliers at Ancram for cutting trees in what Massachusetts people called "their woods."[73]

The show of force by Ingersoll, though in vain, seems to have pleased the Taconic tenants and indeed made them nearly "as bad as the n. England people." They were spellbound by the man who spoke for the General Court. Ingersoll, variably called by the landlord "wicked man," "audacious man," "madman," "voracious cormorant," "wicked varlet," or "this pest of mankind," kept up his agitation, telling the tenants that he had a commission from the General Court to defend them against Livingston and that they were "fools" to pay rent. "Some" of the tenants in turn pledged to "stand by him in opposition" and saluted the Boston government. Nevertheless, none of them dared to refuse paying rent after the winter of 1751 and to openly disavow their landlord. Apparently, the fate of Robinson convinced them to lay low for the time being.[74]

At no time did Ingersoll and his friends feel as keenly as now the necessity of demonstrating to the tenants that they could deliver on their promises and reward those who were loyal to the Bay Colony. Thus, at the end of February 1753, he, Dwight, and Ashley together contacted "friends" in New York to bail out Robinson, who was subsequently

72. Robert Livingston, Jr., to James Alexander, Jan. 22, 1753, Rutherford Coll., III, 203; *Journals of Mass. House of Representatives*, XXIX, 55, 162.

73. Robert Livingston, Jr., to son Philip, Jan. 23, 1754, Livingston Papers.

74. Robert Livingston, Jr., to William Alexander, Mar. 26, 1753, William Alexander Papers, I, 1717–1756, N.-Y. Hist. Soc.; Robert Livingston, Jr., to Jacob Wendell, Apr. 12, 1753, and Feb. 8, 1754, Livingston Papers.

released. About this time Ingersoll publicized his plan to build a mill on "Tackanick Creek" near Michael Halenbeck's house some miles within the manor. He was also reported to have offered to buy the possessions of at least ten tenants, and he actually bought two at Taconic, one for £13 and the other for considerably more. This was done to procure an interest in the lands, which were expected to be granted soon by the legislature. More important, it was part of his strategy to show to the tenants that from now on their fortunes would fall and rise with his.[75] These measures could not fail to impress them and to stir up in them a strong sense of solidarity with the Bay Colony.

Brigadier Dwight went a step further. On March 25, 1753, he sent Harrison Gray, a deputy from Boston, a long letter that clearly revealed the thinking of the agitators and had a decisive impact on the members of the General Court and on the subsequent turn of events. First, Dwight noted that the tenants, daily pestered by Livingston with writs of trespass, had been asking him if they could have "any encouragement" and "protection." After tersely mentioning the favor that he, Ingersoll, and Captain Ashley had done for Robinson, he declared, "If our court will appoint some attorney" to defend Robinson at the forthcoming trial, "Livingston will soon give up the cause." Behind this zany logic lay his belief that Livingston's "main dependence" for his claim to the manor lands was on the actual possessions of his tenants "for and under him." If the Bay Colony should succeed in taking one tenant's possession away from the landlord, then the others would fall like dominoes, leaving the manor title empty. By way of elaborating on these points, Dwight continued: "Now as this is a valuable Interest of the Province Depending on these Sutes I can't but hope the Government will appear to defend for the men who can't bare to [the?] Expence themselves perhaps the Expence of one Sute only will save the whole Interest which I very much think will be the case or rather that Livingston will give [up] the whole so soon as he sees the Province will Defend it." Dwight sensed Livingston's exhausted emotional condition at the time and perhaps figured that the moment had come for a bold stroke. In fact, in late March, Livingston confessed to his friend William Alexander, "I am at witts End and in a constant dread of the consiquences of this Invasion on my Right." Livingston feared what Dwight anticipated—that the exemplary support of

75. Robert Livingston, Jr., to Jacob Wendell, Apr. 12, 1753, Livingston Papers. Lately, Ingersoll named the Taconic area "Tackanick Bergh."

a tenant would in all probability spawn a general tenant uprising against the landlord.[76]

Dwight also advocated the annexation of all the "province" lands westward of Sheffield and Stockbridge to Hampshire County, so that the county justices could issue "our writts and warrants," should the need arise for them. As an afterthought, he added: "N-York Government have not extended the County of Albany more than Twelve miles of Hudson River." He was of course mistaken, but his suggestion that Massachusetts could expand that far westward was extremely significant. Finally, unless these steps were taken, Dwight warned, the committee appointed the previous December 30 to investigate the land would be "interrupted in their business and even prevented by [Livingston's] Clubb Laws." For any other particulars, he asked Gray to consult Ingersoll, who carried the message.[77]

On April 3, Gray submitted the letter to the General Court, and a debate ensued before a committee that Ingersoll had briefed on "what was transacting by the Dutch etc. and of their imprisoning George Robinson." The court's reaction was both swift and positive. The very next day it resolved that Dwight be directed to hire an attorney to defend Robinson against the action of trespass and that the "Charge of the Defence be borne by the Province." It also accepted Dwight's recommendation that Massachusetts annex all the contested "province" lands—part of Livingston Manor—to Hampshire County. An act to that effect was passed eight days later, thus extending Massachusetts's jurisdictional right to the area over which it had hitherto claimed only territorial right. Translated into legal terms, the rebellious tenants were now the inhabitants of the colony and entitled to its protection.[78] Nevertheless, on the same day (April 12) the bill of annexation became law, the legislature proposed to New York that the boundary problems between the two colonies

76. Robert Livingston, Jr., to William Alexander, Mar. 26, 1753, William Alexander Papers, I.

77. The above discussion is based on Joseph Dwight's letter to Harrison Gray, Mar. 25, 1753, Mass. Archives, VI, 109–112.

78. *Journals of Mass. House of Representatives*, XXIX, 137, 139–140, 164; *Acts and Resolves of Massachusetts Bay*, III, 656. One remaining part of Dwight's recommendation concerning the western limit of Massachusetts was not adopted this time. David Ingersoll's "account of the Time and the Expences that I have been at In Endeavoring to preserve and Defend the Province of Massachusetts Bay from Incroachments on their Western Border from the Government of New York etc., Sept. 1755," particularly the entry on Mar. 1753, indicates that Dwight had Ingersoll handle the legal matters for Robinson. Mass. Archives, VI, 131.

be settled through a meeting of their respective commissioners for the
sake of preserving the "good Understanding" that should "subsist between Fellow Subjects and neighbouring Provinces."[79]

The triumphant Dwight appeared at Sheffield on May 7 with his
two colleagues on the committee and asked Livingston to meet them at
Michael Halenbeck's house at "Taconic" at three o'clock on the following afternoon. His motive for desiring such a meeting is a mystery. Livingston, who was advised in advance by Wendell about their coming,
accepted the request.[80] The conference, though conducted in a "friendly"
atmosphere, turned out to be something other than a forum for serious
and honest exchanges. At one point, Livingston put a question to the
committeemen: why were they sent on "such an Errand" by the legislature while it was soliciting the New York government to settle the boundary question? They answered that they had to carry out their mission
because they had received no rescinding orders; however, they "believed
if their general Court had not been dissolved so soon as it was, they
would have had Orders not to proceed." Their reply was patently dis-
honest and, in the words of Livingston, "entirely frivolous." They could
hardly have forgotten that the act for annexing a certain portion of
Livingston Manor was passed the day before the court was dissolved. But
throughout their conversations with Livingston, the Yankees never mentioned the crucially important legislative measure, either as a fact or as a
justification for their mission. This suggests that the committeemen were
not so much interested in ironing out their differences with Livingston as
in sounding him out and detecting his weaknesses.[81]

Equally revealing was the manner in which the committeemen handled Livingston's invitation to his mansion near the Hudson River. He
told them that if they were interested in checking his titles to the lands in
dispute, he would be glad to show them there. At first, they accepted the

79. Apr. 12, 1753, *Journals of Mass. House of Representatives*, XIX, 125, 164–165.
This resolve was partly a response to Gov. George Clinton's letter dated Mar. 6 protesting
the encroachments on Livingston Manor and Westenhook Patent by Massachusetts. It must
be noted that many people from Massachusetts were moving into the Hoosick area north of
Rensselaerswyck proper while the General Court was making a peace gesture. See petition
of John B. Van Rensselaer and others, proprietors of Hoosick, May 30, 1753, N.Y. Col.
MSS, LXXVII, 39–40. See also *Journals of Mass. House of Representatives*, XXV, 232.

80. Robert Livingston, Jr., to Jacob Wendell, May 26, 1753, Livingston Papers.

81. From hindsight, Livingston felt that the committee called such a conference only to
"quiet" him and "procure an Opportunity of executing their Scheme" without his presence
or interruption. "Another Petition of the Proprietor of Livingston Manor," May 31, 1753,
*Doc. Hist. N.Y.*, III, 744, 748.

offer, but the next morning they asked to be excused from the trip. The change of heart occurred because they became fearful that "the people" —the tenants—might "cast slur on their characters" for succumbing to the landlord's bribery.[82] At this stage of the game, they perhaps could not afford to do anything that would tend to undermine their credibility, which seemed absolutely essential to the success of their scheme. The rebellious tenants, too, were as deceitful and canny as the committeemen. At a meeting attended by those who subscribed to the Bull petition, Livingston asked them why their names were on it. Their reply was that "they could not tell" and that "they had never petitioned for any of [Livingston's] Land but for Lands lying to the Eastward of his East Bounds." Needless to say, this was a sheer lie.[83]

Just before the conference broke up, the landlord asked the committeemen to tell his tenants "to be easy" and to pay "their rents honestly." They agreed and then "desired" him to "forgive" the poor tenants and "take them into favor again." The landlord replied that he would do so only for those who, he thought, had been misled "through ignorance," but he made it clear that he would evict "some few who were ring leaders" of the subversive activities and who "knew better." The committeemen left the conference, however, with the impression that Livingston would be indulgent toward his farmers until the boundary lines were fixed.[84]

The conference was merely a prelude to a stormy confrontation between the landlord on the one side and the rebel tenants and Massachusetts on the other. As soon as the Dwight party returned to Sheffield, they ordered William Ingersoll, son of David, to survey and plot out the lands comprehended in the petitions of Bull and others. With the help of six "New England men" and four sons of Livingston tenants, the surveyor ran the lines on forty square miles of the manor in a week's period. Considering the rugged hills and mountains they had to traverse, the

82. Deposition of Josiah and Abigail Loomis, Nov. 3, 1767, Mass. Archives, VI, 415–417.

83. Robert Livingston, Jr., to Jacob Wendell, May 26, 1753, Livingston Papers. Livingston told the committeemen that David Ingersoll had been "very industrious in seducing" his tenants and dissuading them from the payment of their rents. The landlord asked the committeemen to stop Ingersoll, but no evidence is available as to how they responded to the request.

84. A resolution of Sept. 11, 1753, by the General Court stated that the May conference ended with an agreement that "all proceedings should be Stopt, 'till further Orders were taken by the two Governments." Mass. Archives, VI, 140; *Journals of Mass. House of Representatives*, XXX, 78.

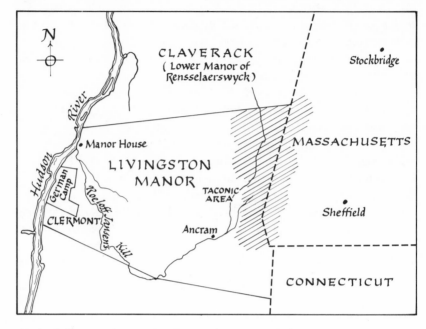

Sketch of the General Area of Violence and Dispute in Livingston Manor, 1751–1757 (Shaded). Adjusted from John Betty's survey map, 1714, in E. B. O'Callaghan, ed., *The Documentary History of the State of New York* (Albany, N.Y., 1849–1851), III, 690. (Drawn by Richard J. Stinely.)

assignment must have been executed in great haste. The survey came as a complete surprise to Livingston because he had not been informed about it at the conference. But he, too, was taking steps. As he had promised, he began weeding out the most obstreperous of his Taconic tenants. The day after the meeting broke up, May 12, he came to Taconic and warned several of them to move out of the manor within a year and prohibited them to plow and sow in the meantime. Among them were Jan Halenbeck, son of Michael, one "Averill," and Robinson, who were both sons-in-law of Joseph Pain, and Josiah Loomis. Speaking for himself and the distressed coconspirators, Jan Halenbeck wrote that day to the committee, still at Sheffield, pleading for help and directions: "Gentlemen it is far worse for us than it was before you come hear. . . . Livingston got . . . much bolder and more sever than he was before. I would pray you Gentlemen to wright me a Leter what to do where Livingston can hold the Land in your opinion or no and where or no you will Releve me or no and If no then I must Remove Immediately."[85] Both the tone and the content of this letter leave no doubt as to how totally dependent the rebel tenants were on their Massachusetts masters for inspiration and direction. As might be expected, the dissidents were advised by the committeemen to reject the ultimatum from the landlord and to defend their possessions, with force if necessary. For a month or so, the tenants, reinforced by the Sheffield people, held their ground, preventing the landlord's "Servants" from approaching them.[86] They plowed and sowed in defiance of the injunction and anxiously waited for "good news" from Josiah Loomis, who had gone with David Ingersoll early in June to appeal their case.[87] On May 9, Jacob Wendell, chairman of a new committee to examine both the report of the Dwight committee and the papers concerning the boundary controversy, informed Livingston: "I saw Mr. Ingersoll and Mr. Loomes in Town this day and suppose they are come doing on these affairs."[88]

Meanwhile, the positions of the two governments during this period seem to have hardened. The New York council refused even to discuss the April 12 resolution of the General Court calling for the mutual appointment of commissioners until the court first answered the question, "What Warrant they had to claim or exercise any Right to Soil or Jurisdiction, Westward of Connecticut River."[89] New York's territorial claim to the west bank of the river, though founded on the 1664 charter for the duke of York, was as unrealistic and inflammatory as Massachusetts's sea-to-sea claim, because it would have brought such old Yankee towns as Northampton, Hatfield, and Deerfield within the boundaries of New York. The Massachusetts legislature interpreted what it called the "majesterial" demand of New York as a rejection of its original proposals.

---

85. Jan Halenbeck to the General Court committee at Sheffield, May 12, 1753, Mass. Archives, VI, 118. Fourteen years after the incident, Josiah Loomis wrote his own account of the sequence in which these events took place. But his story differed substantially from that of Livingston. Loomis contended that Livingston's reneging on his promise not to disturb the rebellious tenants provoked the committeemen to order the survey of the manor land. Loomis was wrong here, because what the committee did was very much in accord with its official assignment. *Ibid.*, VI, 45.

86. *Doc. Hist. N.Y.*, III, 747.

87. James Elliot to Charles D'Witt, June 21, 1753, Livingston-Redmond MSS, Roll 10.

88. Jacob Wendell to Robert Livingston, Jr., June 9, 1753, *ibid.*, Roll 7. Wendell offered the following advice to Livingston: "I heartily wish your General Court would appoint Commissioners from your Government . . . to endeavour the settling the line or agree on some p[er]sons that be appoynted to Settle the same, which would be the best method to settle itt in amicable manner and I think as you are concerned, you would do well to do all in your power to bring your General Court into itt."

89. *Report on Boundaries*, II, 107–108.

On June 12 it declared that the Bay Colony's right to the lands west of the Connecticut River, based on its charter right and actual possession of the lands by its people, "behooves them to go on in settling the Lands." In the spirit of this declaration, the court resolved a week later to establish another committee with "full power" to dispose of the lands at a "reasonable" price.[90] But the most significant action of the legislature did not come until the next afternoon, when it authorized the committee to grant any lands twelve miles east of the Hudson River, thus fully endorsing the earlier recommendation of Brigadier Dwight.[91] This order of course pointed a dagger at the heart of Livingston Manor and Rensselaerswyck (including Claverack) on the east side of the river.

Looking back at this period, Loomis wrote that the actions of the General Court "put such Courage in to us" that he and his coadjutors were able to endure all the "troubles" and "Repeated Law Sutes" that Robert Livingston inflicted upon them.[92] The tenant-insurgents became more daring than ever. The landlord's resort to violence was answered in kind, turning the eastern part of the manor into the scene of frequent armed clashes between the antagonists. In July 1753, Joseph Pain, his son-in-law, and "his company" of twenty people girdled and cut down about 1,200 trees near the Ancram iron furnace. Pain's defense, as described by Livingston, was that he owned the entire manor by virtue of an Indian deed his grandfather had acquired 150 years earlier. He shouted to Livingston's men who came to stop him that he would "distroy the timber as he pleased" and "Robert Livingston kiss his a-s." The incident tells something about the increasing audacity of the rioters.[93]

A more serious incident soon followed. On July 16, Livingston embarked on a punitive expedition with about forty men—his ironworkers and loyal tenants—to the farm of Josiah Loomis, who had lately been made deputy sheriff of Hampshire County by Oliver Partridge. There they cut down winter wheat and destroyed Indian corn and fences on a

---

90. Mass. Archives, IV, 384–385.

91. *Journals of Mass. House of Representatives*, XXX, 35, 53, 55; Mass. Archives, XLVI, 310, 313, 315–316; *Acts and Resolves of Massachusetts Bay*, XV, appendix, VI, 28–29. On Oct. 21, the General Court appointed a committee of three to dispose of the western lands. They were Samuel Wells and James Otis from the lower house and John Chandler from the council.

92. Memorial of Josiah Loomis to the General Court, Dec. 1753, Mass. Archives, XLVI, 321.

93. "Acct of Damage done by Joseph Pain and his company to Robert Livingston, Jr.," Livingston-Redmond MSS, Roll 7; Robert Livingston, Jr., to Jacob Wendell, Oct. 21, 1753, Livingston Papers, Museum of City of N.Y.; Robert Livingston, Jr., to James De Lancey, Dec. 21, 1757, Mass. Archives, IV, 183; *Doc. Hist. N.Y.*, III, 814–817.

five-and-a-half-acre tract. Three days later, Brigadier Dwight and Ingersoll issued a "special warrant" and dispatched Loomis and Samuel Brown
of Stockbridge, another deputy sheriff, to lead a posse to arrest the
landlord and his men. When the attempt was foiled, they turned to a
second target: Robert Van Deusen, an old loyal tenant, and his son
Johannis, who had earlier joined the landlord's expedition.⁹⁴ The raiders
spirited the Van Deusens to the Springfield gaol, where they were charged
with trespassing on Loomis's premises and causing damage to the amount
of £100.⁹⁵ The day after the incident, the Livingston loyalists stormed
several houses of the rebel tenants to catch Loomis and rescue the Van
Deusens, only to learn that the Loomis party was gone. According to a
witness, the landlord's men vented their frustrations on Jacob Spoor, a
Sheffield resident and innocent bystander, by beating him with clubs.⁹⁶

Thus far, Livingston had waged an expensive private war against the
public power of Massachusetts. The New York government, though often asked by the landlord, had never authorized any state protection of
the manor. Officials like William Smith, attorney general, feared such a
measure would impede an accommodation with Massachusetts. Further,
they were not so sure of the extent to which the Bay Colony government
and its agents were involved in the conflict. But the Van Deusen incident
wiped out any doubts and presented a prima facie case for some direct
official action on behalf of the landlord. On July 28, Governor Clinton
issued a proclamation commanding all the law enforcement officers of
both Albany and Dutchess counties to arrest those who had participated
in the kidnapping of the Van Deusens and to prevent the "like Riotous
proceedings for the future" within their authority. The warrant specifically named Josiah Loomis and John Halenbeck, son of Michael, and
three Sheffield inhabitants—William Webb, Joseph Arcourt, and Jonathan Younglow. The governor also sent a strong protest, with a copy of
the proclamation, to Lieutenant Governor Spencer Phips of Massachusetts. Clinton demanded that Massachusetts stop "all proceedings" for

94. Robert Van Deusen was one of the most ancient tenants at Taconic. He settled in
the early 1720s on a farm of about 80 acres near the Livingston Manor-Claverack line. See
"Agreement between Robert Livingston and Hendrick Van Rensselaer," Apr. 19, 1725,
Morristown Hist. Park Coll., Roll 61.
95. "A writ of Israel Williams to the Coroner of the County of Hampshire," July 23,
1753, Livingston-Redmond MSS, Roll 7; Robert Livingston, Jr., to Jacob Wendell, Oct. 21,
1753, Livingston Papers; *Journals of Mass. House of Representatives*, XXXIII, Pt. II,
274–275; Samuel Brown to the General Court, June 8, 1767, Mass. Archives, VI, 364;
Robert Livingston, Jr., to James De Lancey, Nov. 23, 1755, *Doc. Hist. N.Y.*, III, 815.
96. Jacob Spoor's deposition, Sept. 4, 1753, Japheth Hunt's deposition, Aug. 4, 1753,
Joseph Pain's deposition, Aug. 11, 1753, Mass. Archives, VI, 125–129.

the disposition of the Taconic land and extradite to New York for trial all persons concerned in the riots, including local magistrates. In unequivocal and blunt language, he warned Phips that his government would no longer tolerate encroachment on New York lands.[97] The proclamation was most consequential, however, because it not only transformed the hitherto private problems of Livingston into a provincial responsibility but also put the local lawmen at the discretional use of the landlord as a justice of the peace of Albany County.

The elated Livingston quickly assumed personal command of the lawmen to apprehend the troublemakers. On August 6 he sent a copy of the proclamation to his cousin Henry Van Rensselaer of Claverack to be forwarded to one Hendrick, a constable of the district. This document, explained Livingston, would be a sufficient warrant for the constable to arrest Loomis, and the sheriff of the county would be "thereby obliged to take the prisoner in his Goal." He urged Van Rensselaer: "You must Incourage the Constable all you can, to take this man [Loomis]." As a reward for the capture, the landlord promised £3, not an insufficient sum. He stated that he could more easily catch the other rioters if they were kept ignorant of the existence of the proclamation: it was obvious to him that they would flee if they had knowledge of the governor's action.[98] The "New England people," too, unaware of Livingston's imminent move, were out to get the landlord "dead or alive." In a letter dated August 11, Van Rensselaer transmitted to Livingston intelligence that deputy sheriff Loomis had an order to pay 8s. to anyone assisting the plot. Van Rensselaer then introduced Livingston to one William Pandell, who carried the message, as a man willing to "Gitt Josiah Loomis."[99] The landlord gladly accepted the service of Pandell and his two associates with the offer of a bounty. While thanking his Claverack cousin for all these favors several days later, Livingston particularly emphasized the need for the Livingstons and the Van Rensselaers to "consult together," a point he said he had earlier made to John Van Rensselaer, the Claverack proprietor and brother of Henry.[100] The formation of a common front

97. *Doc. Hist. N.Y.*, III, 749–750, 751–752, 756–757; James Alexander to Cadwallader Colden, July 30, 1753, *Colden Papers*, IV, 401–402; N.Y. Col. MSS, LXXVII, 144; *Journals of Mass. House of Representatives*, XXX, 64.

98. Robert Livingston, Jr., to Henry Van Rensselaer, Aug. 6, 1753, Van Rensselaer-Fort Papers, N.Y. Pub. Lib.

99. Henry Van Rensselaer to Robert Livingston, Jr., Aug. 11, 1753, *Doc. Hist. N.Y.*, III, 753.

100. Robert Livingston, Jr., to Henry Van Rensselaer, Aug. 14, 1753, Van Rensselaer-Fort Papers.

was necessary, he continued, lest the two families "might be at a loss" when the Boston committee came out by the end of August or the beginning of September to sell "all our lands." The help that Henry Van Rensselaer rendered to the Livingston cause suggests that the Claverack proprietor was increasingly unnerved by the storm blowing to the south and by Massachusetts's aggressive attitude, although his tenants were quiet, at least in appearance. Under the circumstances, everyone suspected that what had happened in Livingston Manor would be repeated in Claverack.

Livingston could not trap Loomis or the other perpetrators mentioned in the proclamation, but he succeeded in eliminating some of the troublemakers from his domain. By invoking the proclamation, the landlord in August jailed Michael Halenbeck, although he had not been directly involved in the Van Deusen affair. The incarceration of the tenant-dissident was a preventive measure to ensure peace at Taconic. Indeed, from July on, Livingston seemed to be committed to a policy of removing the potential troublemakers from the area once and for all. Jan Halenbeck, Michael's son, was warned to surrender his possessions by the next May and in the meantime not to plow or sow. In late September, Livingston succeeded in capturing Joseph Pain, who had cut down many domain trees and was suspected of having participated in the riot. In line with this exclusion policy, Livingston asked the sheriff of Albany County to set bail for Pain at the "extraordinary" amount of £1,000 New York currency and to refuse Michael Halenbeck the privilege of bail.[101]

The Massachusetts General Court had apparently miscalculated how far Livingston would go to defend his manor. Acting largely on the extremely optimistic recommendations of Dwight, Partridge, and Ingersoll, the solons had hoped that a small encouragement to the rebel tenants would so demoralize the landlord and so encourage the other tenants to be rebellious that he would give up his fight. Instead, Livingston had held his ground and was now mopping up the subversive elements. Another surprising development was the mobilization of police arms by the New York government to deal with the border turbulence. This was a new situation that Massachusetts had never anticipated. At this critical juncture, the General Court strangely kept a low profile. They ordered no retaliatory strike; nor did they press the committee appointed to sell the

101. Robert Livingston, Jr., to Jacob Wendell, Oct. 21, 1753, Livingston Papers; report of the Mass. legislature on Gov. Clinton's letter, Sept. 11, 1753, *Doc. Hist. N.Y.*, III, 756, also 769 (quoted).

disputed lands to begin its work, a step that the rebel tenants would have liked most and that surely would have provoked bloodshed.[102] Their report of September 11 responding to the charges of Governor Clinton, however, pinned the blame for the disorders on his government's refusal to "Join in setling the Line" and upon the arbitrary proceedings of the landlord. In an obvious attempt to drive a wedge between the governor and Livingston, the report asserted that Clinton would never have issued the proclamation or made "such a very Extraordinary and unprecedented demand" for the extradition of the Massachusetts officials for trial in New York if he had been correctly informed about Livingston's conduct. Finally, the legislature again called for a meeting of commissioners from the two colonies sometime in November 1753 to resolve the boundary questions.[103] But it was not about to let down the tenants who had "maintained the Right" of the Bay Colony—the phrase employed by Loomis. Just three days after the proposal was made, the court granted £10 to Loomis "in order to Support him in Carrying on his Action of Trespass" against the Van Deusens. The next day the legislature desired Governor Shirley to write to Governor Clinton as soon as possible, "very particularly" on the Michael Halenbeck affair, conveying its opinion that "the common Rights of any or all his Majesty's Subjects in such Circumstances" had been denied to the man.[104] This legislative behavior was but a corollary of the master-puppet relationship of the court and the rebel tenants. Clearly, the Yankees were determined to press every advantage until the Yorkers proved more accommodating.

The proposed meeting of the boundary commissioners was not held, since the New York council doubted its usefulness and even its constitu-

102. In this connection, one significant episode relating to Jacob Wendell must be noted. He was absent from the roster of a committee of the General Court established on September 6 to write a report on the charges of Governor Clinton, although he had been a ranking member of the various committees concerned with the western frontier settlements and controversies. The lower house "looked upon" Wendell with an "evil eye" for his collusion with Livingston and rejected his nomination by the council on this score. Livingston dubbed the proceeding "Extraordinary" and believed that Oliver Partridge and his clique in the lower house were responsible for Wendell's disgrace. Robert Livingston, Jr., to Jacob Wendell, Oct. 29, 1753, Livingston Papers.

103. *Doc. Hist. N.Y.*, III, 756. The General Court's proposal was in response to the New York government's action appointing commissioners to investigate the problems of boundaries. The commissioners were empowered to "pursue all such steps and methods as to them seem most ADVISABLE" to obtain a "legal settlement of the eastern boundaries with the neighboring provinces." But their authority was severely constricted by a provision that they could *propose* but not actually *make* such a settlement. *N.Y. Col. Laws*, III, 912–916; *Journal of General Assembly*, II, 341.

104. Mass. Archives, VI, 144–145; *Acts and Resolves of Massachusetts Bay*, XV, appendix X, 49; *Doc. Hist. N.Y.*, III, 758.

tionality.[105] Yet, thanks to Clinton's proclamation, Livingston Manor was relatively quiet during the winter months of 1753–1754. Livingston was still nettled by the threat to his life. In the middle of October he was freshly alarmed by a rumor that some Indians at Stockbridge under the supervision of Brigadier Dwight were afield to kidnap him and to take him to Sheffield. But the rioters slunk away, avoiding the vigilant eyes of the constables and the spies that the landlord had planted at Taconic.[106] Jan Halenbeck ran away to Sheffield shortly after he tilled and sowed winter wheat in defiance of the landlord's order. Michael Halenbeck, whom David Ingersoll, at the order of the General Court, had tried in vain to bail out of the Poughkeepsie jail, finally escaped in October and was sheltered at the latter's house. Livingston posted a reward of 20 pistoles for the arrest of the jailbreaker.[107] Joseph Pain was still in jail. The morale of the insurgents was badly shattered. Some of the ringleaders even began to look around for a new settlement outside the manor. Josiah Loomis, Michael Halenbeck, Jan Halenbeck, George Robinson, and one Joseph Orlentt petitioned the General Court in late November to grant a rugged "valley of Land Lying between two Great Mountains," that is, to the east of Taconic and to the west of Sheffield.[108]

## Violence Spreads to Claverack

The year 1754 began on an ominous note. Sometime in the closing days of 1753, David Ingersoll had persuaded Josiah Loomis and Michael Halenbeck to appeal their case to the General Court. In a memorial prefaced with an acknowledgment of their past dependence on the popular body for protection, they begged a like favor for their current hard-

105. The New York council took its traditional position that the disputed lands belonged to the crown and that without the "Royal Direction participation and Concurrence," no agreement between the two colonies on the boundaries would have legal validity. In accordance with this strict legal interpretation, the council believed the appointment of commissioners with plenipotentiary power to be "Derogatory To the rights of the Crown." See the council's "Report on the Papers from Massachusetts Bay," Nov. 16, 1753, *Doc. Hist. N.Y.*, III, 764–766; Gov. Shirley's speech to the General Court, Dec. 5, 1753, *Journals of Mass. House of Representatives*, XXX, 97.

106. Robert Livingston, Jr., to Jacob Wendell, Oct. 29, 1753, Livingston Papers; James Elliot to Charles D'Witt, June 21, 1753, Livingston-Redmond MSS, Roll 10. According to Elliot, who was Livingston's clerk at Ancram, two tenant families, namely, the Ephraim Reeses and Adam Showers, at Taconic were informers for the landlord.

107. Robert Livingston, Jr., to Jacob Wendell, Oct. 21, 1753, Livingston Papers; Mass. Archives, VI, 131; George Clinton to William Shirley, Oct. 1, 1753, *Doc. Hist. N.Y.*, III, 758–759.

108. Petition of Josiah Loomis and others, Nov. 27, 1753, Mass. Archives, XLVI, 320.

ship. Unless "Speedy Relief" was forthcoming, they would soon be "uterly undon." They could be relieved, they suggested, either by sending out a committee to sell the disputed land or "Else by making us a grant of land (somewhere else) so that we may Remove our selves and fameileys on for Refuge."[109] The latter course of action, though feasible and justifiable in the name of humanitarianism, was unacceptable to the legislature because it would deprive Massachusetts of her most useful instruments of westward expansion. Instead, on January 19, 1754, the court appointed a committee to go "as soon as conveniently" to the lands west of the Taconic Mountains and sell the "whole or any part of the Lands" according to its discretion. The court also voted to allow Loomis £5 and Halenbeck £8, "in consideration of their expense and trouble in attending this Court," and ordered John Lydius, who was acting as Massachusetts's unofficial agent in Albany, to bail Pain out of the city jail. These measures resuscitated the spirits of the insurgent leaders. Upon returning from Boston, Loomis and Halenbeck bragged about their successful mission: they each received £10, the court "encouraged" them to "go on in giving [the landlord] all the trouble they can," and a committee would come to lay out a township at Taconic in the coming spring.

Livingston was incredulous and expressed his disbelief to his friend Wendell: "I have a much better opinion of that wise body, than to think that they should be guilty of Encouraging my Tenants to rise up against me under whome and his ancesters they have peaceably lived for many years, and many of them all their lives no it cannot be nor shall I believe it untill I have it from you. I do Suppose that Loomis and Halenbeck have been ordered to say all this and more by those who Encouraged them to go to Boston."[110] The resolution of the General Court as reported by Loomis and Halenbeck confused "many" of the "easy and Quiet" tenants of the manor and made them "shy of coming to [the landlord's] house as usual." The appearance of the committee on the scene, Livingston feared, would instantly turn them into rebels.

On February 12, Livingston entreated James De Lancey, lieutenant governor of New York and a political rival of his brother William Livingston, to order the sheriff of Albany County to raise a "posse Comitatus"

109. Robert Livingston, Jr., to Jacob Wendell, Feb. 8, 1754, Livingston Papers; memorial of Josiah Loomis, Dec. 1753, Mass. Archives, XLVI, 321; votes of the General Court, Jan. 11, 18, 19, 1754, ibid., 338, 347–348; Acts and Resolves of Massachusetts Bay, XV, appendix X, 102; Journals of Mass. House of Representatives, XXX, 138; James Stevenson to Robert Livingston, Jr., Feb. 15, 1754, Livingston-Redmond MSS, Roll 7; Report on Boundaries, II, 143–175.
110. Robert Livingston, Jr., to Jacob Wendell, Feb. 8, 1754, Livingston Papers.

and assist him in apprehending the committeemen "as rioters," although just several days before he had been warned by William that De Lancey did not care "a Groat for you nor your Manor, nor any Man living." Livingston also seems to have written to Thomas Hutchinson, an influential member of the General Court, asking his help to get the Van Deusens discharged from legal action and to "prevent" Ingersoll from "continuing to distill prejudices" into the tenants and from "purchasing their possessions."[111]

The subsequent events (or nonevents) confirmed neither the euphoria of the tenant-insurgents nor the fears of the landlord. For one thing, the committee never showed up to carry out its assignment. For another, the General Court did nothing about Joseph Pain except to protest to New York in April against his bail being set so high.[112] The lethargy of the court was probably due not so much to the abdication of its aggressive intent as to the restraining influence of Governor Shirley, who was weary of intercolonial contention at a time, he wrote, "when a strict Friendship and Union seems more than ever to be necessary" against French Canada.[113] By the spring of 1754, the French and Indian War had unofficially begun, and several colonies were preparing for a congress to be held in Albany for the purpose of dealing with problems of common defense. Shirley's concern for friendly relations with New York grew out of his obsession with the goal of exterminating French power in North America and his understanding of New York's pivotal role in this ambition.

Probably as a result of prodding by Shirley and by moderates like Wendell, the General Court made still another peace gesture. In its resolution of April 19, the legislature authorized the Massachusetts commissioners to the Albany Congress to negotiate with their New York counterparts on the boundary question. With a view to strengthening the Bay Colony's position, it also instructed the delegates to buy up the

111. Robert Livingston, Jr., to James De Lancey, Feb. 12, 1754, *Doc. Hist. N.Y.*, III, 768; William Livingston to brother Robert, Jr., Feb. 4, 1754, Livingston-Redmond MSS, Roll 7.

112. James Stevenson to Robert Livingston, Jr., Feb. 15, 1754, Livingston-Redmond MSS, Roll 7. On Apr. 10, the General Court paid £20 to John Ashley to be used "for the Support of Joseph Pain, now in Albany." *Journals of Mass. House of Representatives*, XXX, 215; *Doc. Hist. N.Y.*, III, 769–771. In the same month, the legislature received a petition from John Halenbeck and his associates for some relief measure. See *Acts and Resolves of Massachusetts Bay*, XV, appendix X, 139.

113. William Shirley to James De Lancey, Apr. 22, 1754, *Doc. Hist. N.Y.*, III, 771; Shirley's speech on the boundary question, Sept. 5, 1753, *Journals of Mass. House of Representatives*, XXX, 64.

claims of the Stockbridge Indians to the lands west of the Connecticut River, particularly the lands west of the Housatonic River.[114] The commissioners from the two colonies met in June and July of 1754 for the first time since the controversy began in 1710. The historic conference, however, was hopelessly deadlocked. New York's initial proposal of the Connecticut River as the eastern boundary was countered by the Bay Colony's insistence on the line twelve miles east of the Hudson River. As a way out of the differences, Massachusetts then proposed a "final" arbitration of the dispute by a third party—"some gentlemen" of the neighboring provinces—only to be rejected by New York. Finally, the New York council, anxious to prevent "Bloodshed among the Borderers," directed her commissioners to put forth a line running from the west side of the Housatonic River at the north line of Connecticut province to a hundred yards west of Fort Massachusetts (presently the town of Adams). But the offer was ignored.[115]

Nevertheless, from the summer through to early December 1754, Livingston had never had a more peaceful period since the trouble started in 1751. To be sure, he was pestered occasionally by threats to his life. An informant told him in July that seven or eight men were plotting to ambush and kill him on the road to Taconic. But by and large he seemed to have the situation under control. This was evidenced by an incident in late July in which he compelled a meek submission from one of the most recalcitrant rebel tenants. On a routine inspection tour, he found about fifteen workmen busily harvesting wheat on Jan Halenbeck's farm at Taconic; about half of the crop was already in when he arrived. The landlord told the people to leave the premises and sarcastically "thanked them for the trouble" in cutting his crop, because Halenbeck had planted it contrary to his order. The farmers "went off quietly." Halenbeck seemed repentant and begged the landlord to be understanding of his poor circumstances. Livingston, "out of compassion," agreed to let the tenant reap his wheat, rye, oats, peas, buckwheat, corn, and hay and to stay in his house until the next May. In return, Halenbeck and his eldest son

114. The Massachusetts commissioners learned in June that some people, "both English and Dutch," had been trying to purchase the lands in question from the Stockbridge Indians. The General Court allocated £1,200 to liquidate the Indian claim, but the money was later diverted to use for the Crown Point expedition. *Acts and Resolves of Massachusetts Bay*, XV, appendix X, 354–355.

115. *Ibid.*, 157–158, 177–178; *Doc. Hist. N.Y.*, III, 769–771, 772–774; James De Lancey's speech, Apr. 24, 1754, *Journal of General Assembly*, II, 379–380, 380–381, 389; Robert Livingston, Jr., to Jacob Wendell, Apr. 22 and May 6, 1754, Livingston Papers; *Report on Boundaries*, II, 132–144. For Wendell's contact with Gov. Shirley, see Robert Livingston, Jr., to Jacob Wendell, Oct. 29, 1753, Livingston Papers.

William gave a note of hand promising to pay "only 200 skiple of good clear wheat" before the next January 20 and to surrender the "possession of the farm." This was a generous deal, insisted Livingston, although Halenbeck and his "wife's side" really did not deserve it. Later in the summer, the landlord sent out his servants to plow the farmland, and the job was done without incident. The sheepish behavior of Halenbeck and his associates was due to their despondency over the unfavorable turn of events. As Jonathan Darby, one of the insurgents, pointed out, they had "from time to time been Encouraged" by several emissaries from the General Court to hold the lands for the Bay Colony, but "nothing Effectual has been done" for them. As long as their patrons were ambivalent, there was not much the abandoned insurgents could do. Asking for "directions" from Governor Shirley in late November, Darby confessed: "My Circumstances are Reduced to this strait that I must Recognize to New York Government or quit the Lands."[116] His comrades, too, were in the same desperate condition. Happy with the "Easey" and docile tenants at Taconic, Livingston could boast to Wendell: "I have all the reason in the world to believe they will continue so, if your folcks will but lett them alone."[117]

The Massachusetts people, particularly Ingersoll, Partridge, and Joseph Dwight, did not leave the tenants alone. Rather, these Berkshire leaders now extended their agitation to 10 or 11 tenant farmers of John Van Rensselaer at Kakeout, fifteen miles straight east of the Hudson River and north of Taconic. Again it was Ingersoll, now a member of the Massachusetts House of Representatives, who played the most active role in the anti-Van Rensselaer agitation. Probably in late November 1754, according to information received by Livingston, Ingersoll had "prevailed on" several Van Rensselaer tenants as well as some at Taconic to assign to him portions of their farms and to give him obligation bonds to pay for his expenses in soliciting grants of their lands from the Massachusetts government. He had also offered £100 to some Stockbridge Indians in order to induce them to accompany him to Boston, claim the sole ownership of the lands, and sell the premises to him and his associates. But the negotiations with the Indians fell through because of objections raised by Timothy Woodbridge, their teacher, who was perhaps

116. Jonathan Darby to Gov. Shirley, Nov. 20, 1754, Mass. Archives, VI, 168.
117. Robert Livingston, Jr., to Jacob Wendell, July 29, 1754, Livingston Papers; note of Jan and William Halenbeck to Robert Livingston, Jr., July 24, 1754, Livingston-Redmond MSS, Roll 7; Robert Livingston, Jr., to James De Lancey, June 23, 1755, Doc. Hist. N.Y., III, 808–809.

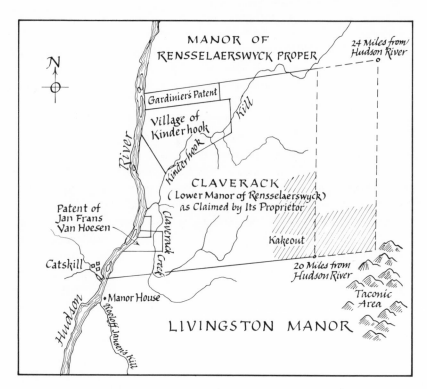

**Sketch of the General Area of Violence and Dispute in Claverack, 1754–1757** (Shaded). Adjusted from Cadwallader Colden's map, 1771, New York Colonial Manuscripts, Land Papers, 1642–1803, XXIX, 56, New York State Library, Albany. (Drawn by Richard J. Stinely.)

becoming disenchanted with Ingersoll's intrigues.[118] Records show that on December 4, 1754, Claverack tenants Robert Noble, Thomas Whitney, Jacob Bacon, Benjamin Lovejoy, and Joseph Elliot, together with 119 others, mostly New Englanders, applied to the General Court for the lands that they claimed to have improved.[119] In another petition of the same date, they also requested the appointment of a commander for the

118. Robert Livingston, Jr., to Jacob Wendell, Dec. 19, 1754, Livingston Papers; Jacob Wendell to Robert Livingston, Jr., Mar. 8, 1755, Livingston-Redmond MSS, Roll 7.

119. The lands in question were in a very fertile section of Claverack 15 to 20 miles east of the Hudson River that had been settled by farmers from Massachusetts and Connecticut. Noble (from Massachusetts) had been there since 1748. Whitney (from Connecticut), Lovejoy (a tavern keeper), Bacon, and Elliot, all were new to the area. Deposition of Henry Van Rensselaer, Feb. 22, 1755, Van Rensselaer-Fort Papers; Jacob Wendell to Robert Livingston, Jr., Mar. 8, 1755, Livingston-Redmond MSS, Roll 7.

district and expressed the desire to build a fort or blockhouse against the enemy Indians and French.[120] The request for garrisoning the area was partly prompted by a recent nearby incident in which a party of provincial soldiers was mauled by enemy Indians.[121] But the plans also seem to have included a secondary target, John Van Rensselaer, whose lands they were scheming to appropriate as freeholders. Both Livingston and Van Rensselaer, it should be noted, understood the plans to be directed primarily against them.[122] In fact, the military establishments were later frequently used by the rebel tenants for their cause. The organization of male inhabitants into regular militia units eventually enabled the insurgents to fight the landlords' forces better. In the thinking of the Kakeout group, the major weakness of the Taconic insurgency lay in its lack of organization.

Almost simultaneously, several New Englanders were busy plotting to acquire the lands "on Tackanic Mountain" for a number of Sheffield people. On December 12, the Taconic tenants met at Ingersoll's house for a "grand" strategy session from which emerged two important resolutions. One called for an active recruiting campaign among fellow tenants, and the other for a united front with the Claverack renters. About this time Ingersoll was also pushing another scheme: enlisting some prominent New Yorkers against the landlords. Among the men contacted was Colonel Martin Hoffman of Red Hook, Dutchess County, who was known to be on bad terms with the Livingston clan. Ingersoll offered him £1,000 for his cooperation, but Hoffman declined.[123]

All these developments came to Livingston as a surprise, for he had "never expected to hear any more trouble" from Massachusetts. As usual in time of crisis like this, he wrote to Wendell pleading for help:

I beg you to do all in your power that your government may not countenance any petitions for lands belonging to me or those settled by any in this government and to keep a watchful Eye on all those that want to make this britch between the 2 governments . . . and hope youll speak to his Excellency your Governor of this

120. Mass. Archives, XLVI, 375, 381; Journals of Mass. House of Representatives, XXXI, 200.

121. Gov. Shirley's message, Nov. 6, 1754, Journals of Mass. House of Representatives, XXXI, 96.

122. When informed that the "New England People had raised a Company of One Hundred Men" at Taconic and "in the Mountains," Livingston asserted that it was designed to "possess themselves of my Lands." Robert Livingston, Jr., to James De Lancey, Feb. 7, 1755, Doc. Hist. N.Y., III, 775.

123. Robert Livingston, Jr., to Jacob Wendell, Dec. 13, 1754, Livingston Papers; Robert Livingston, Jr., to governor of Massachusetts, Jan. 16, 1755, quoted in John Henry Livingston, The Livingston Manor, Order of Colonial Lords of Manors in America, Publi-

matter and convince him that he ought not to pass a grant for those lands which am sure you can Sufficiently do. . . . . I do apprehend if this Engersol and his party should obtain a Grant for my lands that he will have all my tenants to his assistance.[124]

A series of events occurred in January 1755, however, that heightened the tension on the border. The General Court reaffirmed its former resolution to dispose of the disputed lands twelve miles east of the Hudson River and appointed a new committee for the task.[125] Galvanized by what appeared to be a firm commitment by the colony to exert its authority over the disputed area, the Claverack rebels declared that they henceforth owned their land under the Boston government, even though the legislature neglected to vote on the petition of Robert Noble and 124 others for the tract. Late in the month, Ephraim Williams of Stockbridge, a friend of Joseph Dwight, obtained blank militia commissions for several tenant rebels: Michael Halenbeck was made captain and Josiah Loomis lieutenant for a company of about a hundred men, both New Englanders and Taconic tenants, and Noble was made captain for the disputed part of Claverack.[126] Though Governor Shirley had no hand in the appointments, the fact that the commissions were issued in his name bestowed real authority upon their holders and gave the rebel movement a semblance of legitimacy. Meanwhile, at the instigation of "the Boston People," the rebels combed the manors for recruits. On January 27, Hendrick Brusie, Adam Shefer, and Jacobus Van Deusen, all Taconic tenants, visited David Shirts, another tenant, and urged him to join them against the landlord. One of the rewards for his cooperation would be the conversion of his leasehold "for Nothing" into an absolute fee simple estate. Shirts turned them down by saying that "he had nothing to do with the New England People—That he had hired the Lands" from Livingston. But the unconvinced visitors told him to think it over and give them a better answer when they returned in a fortnight.[127]

---

cations, No. 1 (Baltimore, 1914), 21–22; *Doc. Hist. N.Y.*, III, 774–775. For Hoffman's quarrel with the Livingstons, see Philip Livingston to brother Gilbert, Mar. 1744, Misc. MSS, Livingston, N-P; *Journal of General Assembly*, I, 324. Hoffman's obituary is in *N.-Y. Gaz.; and Wkly. Mercury*, Nov. 23, 1772.

    124. Robert Livingston, Jr., to Jacob Wendell, Dec. 19, 1754, Livingston Papers.
    125. Mass. Archives, XLVI, 388–392; *Journals of Mass. House of Representatives*, XXXI, 200, 211; Robert Livingston, Jr., to James De Lancey, Feb. 7, 1755, *Doc. Hist. N.Y.*, III, 774–775.
    126. Robert Livingston, Jr., to Jacob Wendell, Jan. 27, 1755, Livingston Papers.
    127. *Doc. Hist. N.Y.*, III, 774–775.

Both Livingston and Van Rensselaer began to react to the conspirators' menacing moves. Livingston distrained some unfriendly Taconic tenants for rent arrears and intensified his efforts to capture Loomis, who was active again. Van Rensselaer dispossessed a disaffected tenant and had a local constable serve a subpoena on Joseph Elliot, allegedly for his overdue debt to one Peter Helm but really because the tenant had joined Noble. The landlords also kept their friend Abraham Yates, Jr., sheriff of Albany County, in readiness to come down to a trouble spot at a moment's notice and counted on his power to prevent the General Court committee, which was rumored to be on its way in early February, from surveying, platting, and dividing their lands. Livingston advised Yates to "bring more friends along" and to imprison the committeemen "by virtue of the Governour's Proclamation," should they persist in the work.[128]

As is generally true with new converts, the Claverack rebels were most militant, while those at Taconic were content with an auxiliary role. Claverack naturally became the theater of conflict in the subsequent period. In the first week of February 1755, Noble and his party raided the houses of Clark Pixley, the constable who had served the writ on Elliot, and John Morris, Pixley's assistant, planning to carry them both to Sheffield. Though the prisoners made their escape, the incident gave Van Rensselaer an excellent occasion to punish the insurgents and hopefully nip the budding rebellion. On February 11, a quickly assembled posse under Yates, John Van Rensselaer, and his brother Henry, a justice, marched toward the house of Noble in order to apprehend those who had seized the constable. But the expedition ended in a debacle in which the landlord's forces were outmaneuvered and outnumbered by the combined militia companies of the tenants and Yankees under Noble, and, worse still, the sheriff fell into the rebels' hands.[129] The winning party used the occasion to warn the landlord to "leave them alone and not meddle with them untill the [border] controversey should [be] Decided."[130] The sheriff was taken to Sheffield that night, but he bailed himself out the

128. Robert Livingston, Jr., to Abraham Yates, Jr., Dec. 12, 1754, and Jan. 31, 1755, Abraham Yates, Jr., Papers, 1607–1825, Box 1, N.Y. Pub. Lib.; Robert Livingston, Jr., to Jacob Wendell, Dec. 13, 1754, Livingston Papers; William Livingston to brother Robert, Jr., Jan. 10, 1755, Letterbook, 1754–1770 (microfilm), William Livingston Papers, Massachusetts Historical Society, Boston; Abraham Yates, Jr., to James De Lancey, Mar. 29, 1755, Doc. Hist. N.Y., III, 784–785.

129. James Stevenson to Robert Livingston, Jr., Feb. 9, 1755, Doc. Hist. N.Y., III, 776–777; William White, [Jr.]'s, affidavit, Feb. 8, 1755, ibid., 776.

130. Deposition of Henry Van Rensselaer, Feb. 22, 1755, Van Rensselaer-Fort Papers, and also in N.Y. Col. MSS, LXXX, 32.

following day for his appearance in Springfield in May. Twenty-one persons participated in the seizure of the sheriff, among them four Claverack tenants, three Taconic tenants, and the rest, their kin and Massachusetts people.[131]

As Governor Shirley neatly put it, the situation had become "very Serious." Lieutenant Governor De Lancey feared that it might lead to "a civil war between the two governments." On February 17, De Lancey urged Shirley to revoke the militia commissions for Noble and the other New York inhabitants and to accept the temporary jurisdictional line along the Housatonic River proposed earlier by the New York commissioners. Shirley was also under pressure from Dwight, however, who wrote to him on February 13 complaining of the "Riotous and Tumultous Proceedings of Some people of Albany upon our Borders." Concerned as the governor was about a "perfect Harmony" with New York against the French, he nevertheless absolved Massachusetts of responsibility, declaring to the General Court: "No Fault nor Blame be laid upon this Government in this Affair."[132] Shirley's statement of course pleased the solons and the frontier mobs. Indeed, Shirley was so eager to carry his war measures through the legislature that he dared not do or say anything that might antagonize the lawmaking body.[133] As a result, the Boston government quietly ignored the protest from New York, and the border crisis ran its course.

To revenge the humiliation of the Albany sheriff was an absolute necessity for the New York landlords. Otherwise, de facto separation of the rebel strongholds and wholesale disaffection of the loyal tenants would be the likely consequences. Deployment of the sheriff again for the enterprise, however, was out of the question, since he, on bail from a Massachusetts court, was unwilling to risk recapture by the rebels. Instead, Livingston and Van Rensselaer chose to mobilize their district militia. Such a recourse seemed justified in view of the rebels' reliance on their own militia. From the middle of February 1755 on, the manorial militia was continually on patrol pursuing those responsible for the seizure of the sheriff. The insurgents were largely on the defensive, but they never failed to retaliate after being first attacked. On February 18, about

131. Yates's bond was set at £150. Deposition of Abraham Yates, Jr., Feb. 13, 1755, Misc. MSS, No. 10915, N.Y. State Lib.; *Doc. Hist. N.Y.*, III, 778.

132. Gov. Shirley's message, Feb. 24, 1755, *Journals of Mass. House of Representatives*, XXXI, 251; James De Lancey to Shirley, Feb. 17, 1755, *Doc. Hist. N.Y.*, III, 779; Mass. Archives, XLVI, 397.

133. Hutchinson, *History of Massachusetts Bay*, ed. Mayo, III, 66.

125 of Van Rensselaer's men stormed insurgents' houses on the so-called province land and netted William Joyner, Benjamin Trimmou, and Philip Cash on the charge that they were "guilty of riot" at Captain Noble's house a week before. The following night Noble's party of about twenty-five made a futile attempt to seize Joseph Pixley, Van Rensselaer's loyal tenant and the owner of the gristmills and sawmills in the disputed area.[134] A few days later, an unknown number of Livingston men under Lieutenant Dirck Ten Broeck went to Taconic to prevent the reported mustering of a company by Michael Halenbeck. But Ten Broeck was stopped at the gate of Halenbeck's house by about seventeen armed men, who threatened to shoot if they proceeded further. The expedition, nevertheless, was not wholly fruitless, for it captured three armed men from Sheffield who, under the orders of Captain John Ashley, a former member of the Massachusetts House of Representatives, were heading toward Halenbeck's house to "assist" the Taconic rebels. The prisoners were sent to the Albany jail. The insurgents swiftly retaliated: that very evening, Loomis and four "New England men" caught Jury Rosman, one of Livingston's tenants and Ten Broeck's militiamen, on his way to Taconic, after which the sheriff of Hampshire County put him in jail on a warrant issued by Brigadier Dwight. The capture of the three Sheffield inhabitants greatly incensed the townspeople. There was talk among them of joining with the rebel tenants to burn the manor mansion and take the landlord prisoner. A day or two after the incident, Noble appeared at the head of thirty men—some of whom were regular garrison soldiers—presumably to boost the morale of the Taconic rebels. One of the soldiers swore at a rally that he would shoot Livingston on sight.[135] The participation of garrison troops in the insurgency seems to have been approved, around February 22, by the General Court, if not by Governor Shirley.[136]

The threats and increasingly audacious conduct of the Massachusetts party drove home to the landlords anew the need for sharp vigilance. Recent assurance from De Lancey that Governor Clinton's proclamation of 1754 was still in full force was taken by Livingston as an

134. Petition of William Joiner and others, Mar. 25, 1755, Mass. Archives, VI, 186; Joseph Pixley's deposition, Mar. 1755, N.Y. Col. MSS, LXXX, 168.

135. Robert Livingston, Jr., to Jacob Wendell, Mar. 4, 1755, Livingston Papers; Robert Livingston, Jr., to James De Lancey, Mar. 8, 1755, *Doc. Hist. N.Y.*, III, 782.

136. The employment of the garrison for the support of the rebels seems to have been recommended by Brigadier Dwight in his letter of Feb. 13, 1755, to Gov. Shirley. See a committee's report on Dwight's letter, Mass. Archives, XLVI, 397; *Journals of Mass. House of Representatives*, XXXI, 228–229, 233, 251, 256.

authorization for tougher measures against the troublemakers. In early March, Livingston declared to Wendell that he would risk his life to catch them, pull down their houses, and evict their wives and children from his domain. All the bloodshed and misery that might ensue, he continued, should rest on the consciences of the Yankees as the "contrivers and Supporters" of his troubles. But he adopted a wait-and-see attitude, at least for a while, because he entertained the hope that the three-man General Court committee would shortly come out "with orders to Settle peace" on the borders. This hope was based on what he called his "personal knowledge" of two of its members and their "peaceful disposition."[137] But the committee never appeared.

Those who were most upset by the inertia of the Boston legislature were the rebel tenants. On March 25, accompanied by their relatives and other Massachusetts supporters, they presented a petition for protection and relief to the representative body and to Governor Shirley. Like the earlier ones, it pointed out that the establishment of committees from time to time for the disposal of the disputed lands had "encouraged" them to hold their possessions against the claims of the New Yorkers. To their bitter disappointment, the General Court had done "nothing" to make good its numerous resolutions, and, in the meantime, they were "more Exposed to the Cruelty of Mr. Livingston and Rensleaers than ever." Specifically, the landlords daily sent their men after them and apprehended "as many as" they could, circumstances that made it utterly impossible for the poor farmers to "carry on any manner of Bisseness." The petition ended with an impassioned plea for help or "some thing" from the government, without which, they insisted, they would be obliged either to "move off" and surrender their improvements to the "Dutch Claimers" or to "Lye at their tender mercy."[138]

The same day, on behalf of the petitioners, Robert Noble entreated Oliver Partridge, their patron and now the clerk of the Massachusetts

---

137. Robert Livingston, Jr., to Jacob Wendell, Mar. 4, 12, 1755, Livingston Papers; Robert Livingston, Jr., to Abraham Yates, Jr., Mar. 3, 1755, Yates Papers, Box 1.

138. "Petition of Inhabitants of Taughkanick and Province Land," Mar. 25, 1755, Mass. Archives, VI, 189–192. Exactly 70 signed the petition, of whom 10 were from Livingston Manor and 9 from Claverack. See also *Journals of Mass. House of Representatives*, XXXI, 277. Too much has been made by some historians of the ethnic aspect of the conflict, i.e., the Dutch of New York versus the English of New England. They have argued that the Dutch and German farmers were not "inclined to agitation" while the Yankees were disposed to rebel. The divergent characteristics of the two groups, however, seem to reflect their respective economic conditions rather than their ethnicity. The Dutch and Germans, well established economically, were likely to be content with their lot, while the New Englanders, newcomers to New York society and less established in the 1750s and 1760s, were naturally

House of Representatives, to represent once more their case to the government. Noble's letter, a more dramatic version of the plight of the insurgents, clearly highlights the fact that Partridge had been in close touch with them. An important portion of the message reads as follows:

You are not unaquainted how our Houses have been torn down about our Ears, burnt before our Eyes, our Fences thrown Down, our Corn Fields laid waste we have sown but others have reaped, Husbands and heads of Families Carried to Gaol without Law or the Form of It. Wives and Children left in the Wilderness unprovided for as the Ostrich's young under these and such like Difficulties as our hands are feeble. You won't wonder If our hearts faint. . . . They seem to be at their last Gasp one and all ready to Despair and give up all hopes. . . . I can't but think that if the court w'd do, what for us, is in their power we might be made a happy and Free people under the Jurisdiction of This Province.[139]

However, the rebels' hoped-for relief did not come from the General Court until late April 1755.

In the interim, the rebels were subjected to the severest attacks thus far from the landlords. At the request of John Van Rensselaer and on the basis of Abraham Yates, Jr.'s, affidavit concerning the February 11 incident, Lieutenant Governor De Lancey issued on April 2 a proclamation calling for the apprehension of Noble and his associates. Livingston, John and Henry Van Rensselaer, and Abraham Fonda, a justice of the peace and friend of the landlords, had a meeting on April 9 out of which emerged a coordinated plan against the insurgents.[140] From April 13 to

poorer, restless, and envious of their affluent neighbors. The neighbors' Dutchness or Germanness itself, however, played little part in the course of the Taconic revolts. The petition of Mar. 25, 1755, mentioned "the Dutch Claimers," suggesting an ethnic basis for the dispute, but one of the New York proprietors, Robert Livingston, Jr., was not a Dutchman but a Scotsman, and some of the loyal tenants and employees of the landlords, like William White, Cornelius Sharp, Ephraim Reese, and James Elliot, whom the rebels abused, were English. We should recall that the Yankees enthusiastically embraced Dutch expatriates like the Burghardts and Van Schaacks, with whom they cooperated toward a common economic objective against New York. The phrase "the Dutch Claimers" appears to have been employed by the petitioners not so much to represent the border situation truthfully but to excite a possible anti-Dutch bias of the members of the Massachusetts General Court and even of the London government officials (who were expected to hear their case) against the New York landlords. For the historians emphasizing the ethnic dimension of the dispute, see Handlin, "Eastern Frontier," *N.Y. History*, XVIII (1937); Fox, *Yankees and Yorkers*, 142; Bonomi, *A Factious People*, 201.

139. Robert Noble to Oliver Partridge, Sheffield, Mar. 25, 1755, Mass. Archives, VI, 188.

140. Affidavit of Abraham Yates, Jr., Feb. 13, 1755, and Yates to James De Lancey, Mar. 29, 1755, *Doc. Hist. N.Y.*, III, 777–778, 784–785; Robert Livingston, Jr., to Yates, Mar. 3, 1755, Yates Papers, Box 1; Robert Livingston, Jr., to Abraham Fonda, Apr. 9, 1755, Van Rensselaer-Fort Papers.

May 2, a company of forty or fifty armed men raised by the landlords swarmed the borders, captured four tenants (three of Van Rensselaer and one of Livingston), dispossessed several others, pulled down all but two of the die-hard rebels' dwellings, destroyed some of their belongings, and laid waste their farms. Noble's fort-like house was spared because of his wife's pledge that she would persuade her husband "to submit to the Rensselaers and acknowledge their Title," and Jan Halenbeck's house, which Livingston had set aside for his own use, was not demolished.[141] The best prize of the expedition was Loomis, who was hiding with his family at the house of Jonathan Darby.[142] The day (April 14) the raiders at last caught Loomis—"a cunning crafty lying fellow" in Livingston's eyes—the landlord sent off a dispatch to Yates expressing his wish, among others, to keep the prisoner continually in jail "if possible at almost all hazards."[143] But the most serious incident was the killing, at dawn the following morning, of William Reese (or Race), a tenant of Livingston at Taconic for the past thirty years and Noble's associate at the seizure of the sheriff. The hapless fellow was shot while he was trying to escape through the roof of his little house. Coroners of both Hampshire and Albany counties held separate inquests since each jurisdiction claimed Reese to be its inhabitant.[144] He was the first fatal victim of the struggle between Massachusetts and New York, and his death was the climax of the expedition, for the tragedy quickly put an end to it.

Yet, for the other side, Reese's murder became a call for retribution.

141. Sheriff Yates to James De Lancey, Apr. 18, 1755, *Doc. Hist. N.Y.*, III, 787; John McCarthur's "Declaration" before Lt. Gov. Phips, Apr. 28, 1755, Mass. Archives, VI, 204–205; Robert Livingston, Jr., to Jacob Wendell, May 3, 1755, Livingston Papers. The dispossessed tenants were all Livingston's. They were Andries Janse Reese, Jonathan Darby, Christopher Andrews Brusie, Hendrick Brusie, and Jan Halenbeck. See the affidavits of Peter Livingston and others, Nov. 21, 1755, *Doc. Hist. N.Y.*, III, 818–819.

142. Deposition of Josiah and Abigail Loomis, Nov. 3, 1767, Mass. Archives, VI, 615. Loomis was captured "about two hours before the day break."

143. Robert Livingston, Jr., to Abraham Yates, Jr., Apr. 4, 1755, Yates Papers, Box 1. On Apr. 15, Loomis from his prison cell sent a message to Robert Livingston, Jr., proposing a deal. In return for his freedom, Loomis promised to do three things. First, he would "relinquish" his conspiracy with the Boston government "for ever." Second, he would try to use every means in his power to dismiss the action against Jury Rosman, a loyal tenant of Livingston. Last, he would immediately "remove out of and as far from" the manor land as the landlord should desire. At the same time, Loomis declared: "I have not done what I have done of my own head but was advised and Set on by Several of the Great men that belong to Boston." Josiah Loomis to Robert Livingston, Jr., Livingston Papers.

144. Robert Livingston, Jr., to Jacob Wendell, Apr. 18 and May 10, 1755, Livingston Papers; "An Account of the Murder of William Rees," by John Van Rensselaer, Apr. 18, 1755, *Doc. Hist. N.Y.*, III, 788–789; "Anonymous letter to Mr. Gaine," *N.-Y. Mercury*, June 2, 1755. A dispatch from Boston identified the location of Reese's house as Sheffield. *Ibid.*, May 12, 1755.

The violence that the landlords had inflicted upon the insurgents pro-
foundly affected the members of the General Court. The legislature heard
a day-to-day account of the sequence of events leading to the bloodshed
from John McCarthur, a squatter living about twenty miles east of the
Hudson River. His testimony appeared to the solons to confirm what
was discussed and anticipated in the petition of March 25.[145] Asserting
that the distress of the people on the "Province Land" owed very much to
the "Caution" and "forbearance" of the Boston government, the General
Court on April 28 set up a new committee headed by Brigadier Dwight.
As a special favor to the rebel tenants, it ordered the committee to give
them an absolute fee title to their leaseholds at "reasonable Terms" before any sale. The committee was also ordered to execute its task "as
soon as may be" and to make a progress report sometime in May. Furthermore, the legislature recommended to Lieutenant Governor Phips
that he issue a proclamation requiring "all his Majesty's officers civil and
military" to apprehend the "murderers" of Reese and "their abettors"
and that he write to the New York government to help secure them. Phips
complied with the recommendations the same day.[146]

Phips's proclamation was a warrant for a retaliatory strike. On May
6, Noble, Whitney, Jonathan Darby, and about 105 others under the
command of the Hampshire County sheriff raided the Ancram ironworks without meeting any resistance. The raiders captured and carried
to Springfield, James Elliot, Livingston's clerk at the plant, and three
ironworkers who were accused of the Reese killing. Earlier, a German
servant whom Livingston had posted at the dwelling house of Jan Halenbeck was also kidnapped by a white man and an Indian and taken to
Sheffield.[147] Having attained their objectives in Livingston Manor, Noble
and some of his followers marched on to Claverack. There they de-

145. John McCarthur's memorial to Lt. Gov. Phips, Apr. 22, 1755, Mass. Archives,
VI, 191; McCarthur's "Declaration," Apr. 28, 1755, *Doc. Hist. N.Y.*, III, 790–791. The
General Court allowed McCarthur, "now attending this Court on public Business," 30s.
for his trip back home. *Journals of Mass. House of Representatives*, XXXI, 293.

146. See *Journals of Mass. House of Representatives*, XXXI, 277, 293, 294; Mass.
Archives, VI, 199–200, 201–203, XLIV, 165, IV, 478; *Acts and Resolves of Massachusetts Bay*, XV, appendix X, 314.

147. Robert Livingston, Jr., to Jacob Wendell, May 3, 10, 1755, Livingston Papers;
affidavit of Robert Livingston, Jr., May 8, 1755, *Doc. Hist. N.Y.*, III, 792–793; a warrant
to the sheriff of Hampshire County, May 7, 1755, N.Y. Col. MSS, LXXX, 142. According
to Dirck Swart, Livingston's storekeeper, the Ancram workers fled when the invaders
appeared on the scene. Swart to Robert Livingston, Jr., May 6, 1755, *Doc. Hist. N.Y.*, III,
791–792. For the German servant, see Robert Livingston, Jr., to James De Lancey, June
23, 1755, *ibid.*, 809.

stroyed a small fort that Van Rensselaer's tenants had lately erected for their defense against both the insurgents and the French-Indians from Canada. Next their violence was unleashed on three of the loyal tenants of Van Rensselaer in the disputed area—William White, Cornelius Sharp, and Joseph Pixley. White, aged fifty-nine, had settled on the manor in 1729 and was one of the most well-established and respected farmers of the fairly new community.[148] The same was true of his neighbor Sharp, who had taken out his lease about thirty years earlier. Pixley, aged fifty-three, had settled about 1743 and enjoyed prominence in the locale since he owned the only gristmills and sawmills in the vicinity. At one time in May, fourteen of his neighbors guarded him against the Noble gang while he was preparing the mill for grinding. Because of the social and economic standing of these three tenants, their opposition to the insurgency was all the more resented by the Noble partisans. In the dead of the night, Noble's men, disguised as Indians, dragged White and two of his sons out of bed, "pinioned" and carried them "with much ill usage as far as Sheffield, and put them to the cost of nine Dollars and a half" before being discharged. They then vandalized and damaged Pixley's gristmill so that it became "wholly useless." In addition, they killed three horses and two calves in his barn and took many fowl. Sharp too was physically abused.[149]

These operations, which always originated at Sheffield or Stockbridge, kept the loyal and neutral tenants alike in constant terror. Some forty frightened inhabitants at and near Sober, a village where Livingston had recently erected a forge, gathered and lived together at "a small Inclosure" for their mutual defense. During their absence from home, the Noble men pilfered about five hundred pounds of bar iron.[150] Though fairly successful in revenging the earlier setbacks and in terrorizing the inhabitants, the rebels miserably failed to recruit a single tenant to their ranks. The only convert they enlisted was Jacob Knight, a mason indentured to Livingston.[151]

148. Depositions of William White, Oct. 31, 1761, and July 31, 1767, Columbia Co. Misc. MSS.

149. Deposition of Joseph Pixley, May 30, 1755, N.Y. Col. MSS, LXXX, 168; petition of Cornelius Sharp and Joseph Pixley, Nov. 3, 1755, Mass. Archives, IV, 531. That White, Sharp, and Pixley behaved in a manner worthy of their status was attested by the fact that in 1750 they, together with five others, made a monetary contribution to a community project. "Agreement of the Claverack Inhabitants" on the wolf fund, Apr. 3, 1750, Van Rensselaer-Fort Papers.

150. Robert Livingston, Jr., to James De Lancey, May 29, 1755, Doc. Hist. N.Y., III, 801–802.

151. It was reported that in June 1755, Knight joined the Massachusetts provincial

The incarceration of the eight ironworkers and the rampaging by the armed invaders received the blessings of the Dwight committee, which was then surveying and platting the disputed lands. Its work was conducted under the mob's protection.[152] Stung but not demoralized, the manorial proprietors were convinced that "some persons" in the Bay Colony were bent on their ruin "at all Events." On May 8, Livingston hurried down to New York City in order to appeal to his government for help and, more particularly, to see William Shirley, who was reportedly staying there. To Livingston's dismay, Shirley had already left for Boston. But he found James De Lancey, lieutenant governor, and his council taking a grave view not only of the violence directly inspired by the proclamations of the two colonial governments but also of the committee activities on the border. The next day, De Lancey wrote to Shirley proposing an exchange of prisoners held in the two colonies and expressing his willingness to explore "any reasonable methods" for putting an end to the disturbances.[153]

To make doubly sure that his workmen were released from jail, Livingston dispatched his brother William to Springfield with bail money. Another imperative confronting him and his neighbor Van Rensselaer was to stop the work of the Dwight committee, which if unchecked, would be much more consequential to their estates than the sporadic violence by the Noble party. Accordingly, in the middle of the month he sent his cousin Robert R. Livingston of Clermont and William Smith, Jr., a rising star of the New York bar, to western Massachusetts to dissuade the committeemen and to bail out the prisoners.[154]

Shirley could not have agreed more with De Lancey's position. As we noted earlier, he was determined not to let the internecine conflict jeopardize intercolonial cooperation in the military campaign against the French. Coupled with this consideration was his fear that the detention of one of the Ancram ironworkers employed in casting cannonballs for the king's army would do a great disservice to his country.[155] But he also knew that he could not offend in any way the expansionist-minded Gen-

---

army. Dirck Swart to Robert Livingston, Jr., May 6, 1755, and Robert Livingston, Jr., to James De Lancey, June 23, 1755, *ibid.*, 792, 809; Robert Livingston, Jr., to Abraham Yates, Jr., July 16, 1755, Yates Papers, Box 1.

152. William Smith, Jr., and Robert R. Livingston to James De Lancey, May 28, 1755, *Doc. Hist. N.Y.*, III, 803–804.

153. Robert Livingston, Jr., to Jacob Wendell, May 10, 1755, Livingston Papers; De Lancey to Phips, May 12, 1755, *Doc. Hist. N.Y.*, III, 793–795.

154. Robert Livingston, Jr., to Jacob Wendell, May 27, 1755, Livingston Papers.

155. William Smith, Jr., *History of New-York*, ed. Kammen (1972 ed.), II, 184.

eral Court, upon which he was relying for war finances. Thus he found it necessary to walk a political tightrope. In his directives of May 17 and 19 to Brigadier Dwight and two others, all magistrates of the Hampshire County court, Shirley ordered them to free the seven ironworkers simultaneously with the release of the Massachusetts inhabitants now in the Albany jail, provided that the New York prisoners were not "actually concerned" in the murder of Reese. At the same time, he directed the attorney general to enter a *nolle prosequi* in all actions against any New Yorkers, including the Albany sheriff, the Van Deusens, and Jury Rosman. Reporting all these steps to De Lancey, Shirley then urged the New York government to do likewise and to accept the former proposal of the General Court for settlement of the boundary lines by way of third-party arbitration subject to royal approval.[156]

The prisoner exchanges, however, and the stays of prosecution were the only things the two governments were able to achieve.[157] Even these did not come about so easily, because of the Hampshire County magistrates' obstructionism. Basically parochial in political orientation, they had little in common with the governor's far-flung imperial politics. They declared the moment after they finished reading his first directive (dated May 17) that his interposition was of itself "a good reason" for holding the New York prisoners in custody. They also told William Smith, Jr., and his companion Robert R. Livingston, then staying in Springfield, that the prisoners would not go free on bail without further instructions from Boston.[158] Two days later, a new and more peremptory order came that drew grudging submission from them. But they suddenly suspended the order's execution on the pretext that Livingston, according to fresh intelligence provided by Ingersoll, was fortifying the former dwelling house of Jan Halenbeck with three "swivel" guns and thirty or forty armed

156. William Shirley to Israel Williams, Josiah Dwight, and John Worthington, May 17, 1755, Lincoln, ed., *Correspondence of William Shirley*, II, 170–171; *Doc. Hist. N.Y.*, III, 795–798; *Journals of Mass. House of Representatives*, XXXIII, 274–275.

157. Rejecting the Massachusetts proposal, the New York council counterproposed on June 7 that the two governments apply to the king for the "final determination" of the boundary controversy and that the governments would meanwhile exercise their jurisdictions over the borderers as they "actually" had prior to May 1, 1750. But the Bay Colony ignored this suggestion. See minutes of the council, Dec. 20, 1755, Misc. MSS, Livingston; *Journals of Mass. House of Representatives*, XXXII, Pt. 1, 79, 98, 105, 128, 160; William Livingston to brother Robert, Jr., June 20, 1755, Letterbook, 1754–1770, William Livingston Papers, Mass. Hist. Soc. William Livingston, who wrote the counterproposal on behalf of the New York council, privately advised James Alexander, a member of the council, to accept the Massachusetts proposal.

158. William Smith, Jr., *History of New-York*, ed. Kammen (1972 ed.), II, 184.

men to be followed by a hundred more. Matthew Furlong, who had shot Reese, was alleged to be seen among the group. This new development, they informed the governor, gave them cause to fear that unless the guard was extraordinarily heavy, the New York prisoners might escape while "our own people" were still in confinement. Shirley, quite annoyed at their spurious reasoning, "instantly" sent back to Springfield the messenger carrying the report strongly reaffirming his last order. Even so, it took another month before the governor's wishes were fulfilled.[159]

The New York landlords were not entirely happy with the prisoner exchange either. The four men in the Albany jail, whom the Massachusetts side called "our own people" and demanded to be returned, were manorial tenants, three belonging to Van Rensselaer and one to Livingston. Thus, the delivery of these men would be tantamount to acknowledging the Bay Colony's jurisdiction over the disputed area. Despite the ominous legal implications of repatriation, the landlords had to accept what the governors had arranged simply because they had no other alternative.[160] In any event, Livingston was especially glad to bring the workmen back and to resume iron production, for their absence from the furnace had resulted in its blowout, costing him more than £400 for repairs.[161]

## Tranquility Returns

The return of the prisoners to their respective homes in late June 1755 marked the return of tranquility to the troubled manors, although the boundary lines were still as hazy as ever.[162] Livingston ventured in mid-July to go on an unescorted trip across the rebel-infested Taconic Mountains to Boston and stayed away from home for nearly a month. During his travel, Brigadier Dwight, one of the archconspirators against

159. Robert Livingston, Jr., to James De Lancey, June 23, 1755, *Doc. Hist. N.Y.*, III, 809–811; De Lancey to Lt. Gov. Phips, May 12, 1755, *ibid.*, 794; John Halenbake to Mr. Ingersol, May 19, 1755, and affidavit of John Hollambigg, May 22, 1755, *ibid.*, 799–800; Shirley to De Lancey, May 25, 1755, *ibid.*, 801.

160. Robert Livingston, Jr., to James De Lancey, June 23, 1755, *ibid.*, 811. Excepted from the repatriation of the prisoners was Joseph Pain, who was also involved in a civil action. James Stevenson to James Elliot, June 6, 1755, Livingston-Redmond MSS, Roll 10.

161. Robert Livingston, Jr., to Gov. Charles Hardy, Nov. 23, 1755, *Doc. Hist. N.Y.*, III, 815–816.

162. It appears that Loomis was discharged in August separately from the other prisoners. Robert Livingston, Jr., to Charles Hardy, Nov. 9, 1755, *ibid.*, 813; James Stevenson to Robert Livingston, Jr., May 30, 1755, Livingston-Redmond MSS, Roll 8.

the New York manors, wished him "all peace and quietness" while soliciting pig iron from the manor forges.[163] The landlord's correspondence
from July to October lacked any mention of turbulence connected with
the border dispute.

Two factors seem to have contributed to the peace. One was an
unexpected incident that complicated the Dwight committee's work. The
committee had laid out two townships mainly in eastern Claverack and
partly on the "North" side of Livingston Manor for two groups of
people and had presented as "a Gift" a hundred acres each to those
manorial tenants who would hold the lands against their landlords. Its
report, submitted in January 1756 to the General Court, shows that
twelve squatters bought varying amounts of land, roughly at two shillings per acre.[164] While transacting its business, the committee was
visited by some "most respectable" Stockbridge Indians. They complained that it was "not friendly" of the Boston government to dispose of
their lands without appropriate compensation. Anticipating many difficulties ahead because of the natives' opposition, the committee decided
to suspend its work pending further instructions. On June 16, the legislature ordered Dwight to obtain a quitclaim from the Indians with the
maximum offer of £1,500, but that the sum was to be borne by the
grantees of the lands. This last condition, putting a heavy burden on the
borderers, ran counter to the very intent of the resolution that had established the Dwight mission.[165] Whatever the difficulties of the frontiers-
men, the government, plagued by extraordinary war expenditures, was
not disposed to help them financially. Nor were the prospective grantees
willing to accept the "gift" under that condition. The result was that the
deeds the committee drafted in mid-May were never fully executed "by
all parties."[166] The change in the legislature's attitude disheartened the
insurgents and perhaps made them skeptical as to the extent of the help
they could expect from Boston. Under these circumstances they opted to
sit tight while exploring methods to liquidate the Indian claims.

The opponents of the manor landlords suffered another setback. In
early June, charges were brought against David Ingersoll, at the time a
justice of the peace and selectman of Sheffield, that he had defrauded the

163. Robert Livingston, Jr., to Abraham Yates, Jr., July 16, 1755, Yates Papers, Box 1;
Robert Livingston, Jr., to Jacob Wendell, July 22 and Aug. 7, 1755, Livingston Papers.

164. *Doc. Hist. N.Y.*, III, 807; report of the Dwight committee, Jan. 14, 1756, Mass.
Archives, XLVI, 415.

165. *Acts and Resolves of Massachusetts Bay*, XV, appendix X, 354–355; *Journals of
Mass. House of Representatives*, XXXII, 81–82.

166. Mass. Archives, XLVI, 415.

government of £42 14s. 8d. by falsifying a bounty certificate on the killing of wildcats. On August 15, the General Court found him guilty as charged and branded him as unworthy of "any Office or Post of either Honour or Profit within this Government." It then directed the attorney general to begin civil and criminal action against him.[167] The public disclosure of his corruption must have been quite a jolt to those rebel tenants whose insurgency was so closely enmeshed with his conspiratorial scheme. After all, it was he who had masterminded and managed the day-to-day antilandlord campaign; and it was he who looked after their welfare when they were in trouble. They always counted on warm hospitality at his house and sometimes found asylum there.[168] But the crime rendered him untrustworthy as their leader: he had cheated the government, and there was perhaps no reason to believe that he had not cheated them as well or that he would not do so in the future. Shorn of its principal leader during a time of uncertain transition, the insurgency lost its former vigor and aggressiveness.

But the situation was not entirely hopeless for the Massachusetts interest. Brigadier Dwight and Partridge, two other grand patrons, were still willing to assist the insurgents. Besides, the rebel tenants had already risked almost everything they had, and the stakes were too high for them to give up the struggle while there was still hope of their aims being realized. The disgrace of Ingersoll and the June 16 resolution of the General Court only compelled them to rely progressively more on their own resources.

Encouraged by Dwight and Partridge, in the summer months of 1755 some of the rebels started to come back to their old manorial farms and to rebuild their houses. In late October the systematic invasion of the manors by Yankees and former tenants resumed. One evening, a dozen "strange Men" from Massachusetts broke into the house of Johannes Van Deusen at Taconic and threw the tenant and his family out, and Benjamin Franklin, one of the raiders, took occupancy of it. Franklin and his cohorts declared that they were acting under the orders of both the

---

167. In September, Lt. Gov. Phips issued a warrant for the arrest of David Ingersoll. But Oliver Partridge, sheriff of Hampshire County, reported in Feb. 1756 that despite "delligent search," he could not find the criminal. As for the proceedings of the General Court, see Mass. Archives, VI, 287–298a, XLIV, 185–186; *Journals of Mass. House of Representatives*, XXXII, 22–23, 70–71, 147; *Acts and Resolves of Massachusetts Bay*, XV, appendix X, 378–379.

168. Jacob Wendell called Ingersoll and "one" other the "foundation" of all the "Troubles" Livingston had experienced. Jacob Wendell to Robert Livingston, Jr., Mar. 8, 1755, Livingston-Redmond MSS, Roll 7.

General Court and the local magistrates.[169] In early November, another group of about sixty, including Noble, Loomis, and Thomas Whitney, garrisoned the house of Michael Halenbeck and from there launched an operation against the loyal inhabitants in the eastern section of the manors. John Mills, Livingston's carpenter who was repairing a dam near the Ancram ironworks, was warned to clear out since New Englanders would soon demolish the structure.[170] Some of the Claverack rebels stole beehives from the farm of the hated Joseph Pixley. It was also reported that the Sheffield township laid a tax on Van Rensselaer tenants. These incidents were virtually a rerun of what the manorial proprietors and their loyal tenants had undergone just a few months before. They dreaded for their "lives and Estates."[171]

For almost a year, Livingston tried everything short of using violence to recover his Taconic lands. He shunned violent means because they had proved in the past to be counterproductive, begetting only more troubles. In mid-November he somehow managed to obtain from Governor Shirley an extraordinary order against the Sheffield people. Shirley repudiated those who presumed to commit "unlawful violence" in the name of the Massachusetts government, for he feared that such hostilities would again plunge the two provinces into civil war. Besides, he was then heavily dependent upon Livingston for large amounts of provisions and other supplies for his army on the march against French Canada. In no uncertain terms, the governor condemned the Yankees' conduct, calling it a "high Breach of the King's peace," and a "great misdemeanour," and specifically commanded Franklin to leave the Van Deusens' house.[172] However, neither Franklin nor the Taconic rebels at their old tenements obeyed the governor. Franklin's son defiantly told the Livingston men carrying Shirley's order that they "had Bought the Lands and Paid for them from the Committee" and that "Shirley was no Governor" of the Bay Colony "but a Collonel in the Armey" as long as he was absent from Massachusetts. Jonathan Darby, a former tenant of the manor who had

169. Robert Van Deusen to Robert Livingston, Jr., Oct. 29, 1755, and Peter R. Livingston to father, Robert, Jr., Oct. 31, 1755, *Doc. Hist. N.Y.*, III, 812–813.

170. Robert Livingston, Jr., to Gov. Hardy, Nov. 23, 1755, *ibid.*, 814–817.

171. Petition of Cornelius Sharp and Joseph Pixley to Gov. Hardy, Nov. 3, 1755, Mass. Archives, IV, 531.

172. William Shirley to Mr. Franklin, Nov. 16, 1755, Livingston-Redmond MSS, Roll 7; *Journals of Mass. House of Representatives*, XXXII, Pt. II, 316. Livingston was then engaged to furnish 450 cattle to Shirley by Oct. 25, 1755. The landlord was one of the major military contractors during the French and Indian War. Robert Livingston, Jr., to Jacob Wendell, Sept. 25, 1755, Livingston Papers; Jacob Wendell to Robert Sanders, Sept. 16, 26, Oct. 14, 1755, Glen-Sanders Papers.

recently reentered his old house, spoke for several others in the like situation when he asserted that "he would go when he pleased and come when he pleased."[173] To the north in Claverack, Robert Noble and his associates including Josiah Loomis were still perpetrating terror against some loyal tenants, particularly Joseph Pixley.[174] Nevertheless, Shirley was mute after his November order, as was Sir Charles Hardy, governor of New York.

The restraint on the part of the governors was due to two circumstances. One was their preoccupation with the critical problems of the war against the French. The other was the possibility of early determination of the boundary lines through royal intervention. In the summer of 1755, the home government, fully convinced of the futility of intercolonial negotiations, expressed its opinion that nothing but a commission sent from London could resolve the dispute—a formula that had been employed in determining the boundary between Massachusetts and New Hampshire in the 1740s. Subsequently, the governors recommended it to their respective legislatures and urged them to appropriate money for the commission's expenses. Although agreeing with the basic premises of royal determination of the dispute, the budget-conscious General Assembly of New York ignored the recommendation and, when pressed for its answer, asked the governor to tap quitrents for the purpose. The Massachusetts General Court was no less uncooperative, not only because the formula clashed with its own proposal in a fundamental sense but also because the solons feared that a royal commission would favor New York at the expense of the Bay Colony.[175]

Meanwhile, the antilandlord intruders further strengthened their foothold in the area of controversy. By the end of the summer of 1756, they had bought from the Stockbridge Indians the lands laid out for them by the Dwight committee.[176] All they lacked in the way of legitimizing

173. Affidavits of Peter R. Livingston and others, Nov. 21, 1755, *Doc. Hist. N.Y.*, III, 817–819.

174. Joseph Pixley's deposition, Jan. 10, 1756, Mass. Archives, VIII, 294. On the night of Jan. 8, 1756, the Noble people raided Pixley's house. They broke open the door and told the frightened tenant that they would not destroy the house if he would agree to submit to arbitration of a dispute he was having with a Sheffield resident. Pixley gave in to their demand.

175. *Journal of General Assembly*, II, 470–471, 523, 524–525; *Journals of Mass. House of Representatives*, XXXII, Pt. II, 313, 316, 471–472, XXXIII, Pt. I, 128, 142, 149–150; *Report on Boundaries*, II, 145–147; minutes of the council, Dec. 20, 1755, Misc. MSS, Livingston; Lords of Trade to Governor Hardy, Apr. 13, 1756, *N.Y. Col. Docs.*, VII, 79; William Livingston to brother Robert, Jr., Dec. 24, 1755, and Feb. 11, 1756, Livingston-Redmond MSS, Roll 7.

176. An Indian deed to John Halenbeck and 76 others for £261, May 1756, Mass.

their pretension was confirmation of the transactions by the General Court. It was at this crucial moment that the manorial proprietors began legal action against the trespassers, despite the prospect of an eventual royal settlement. In October 1756, Livingston obtained from the Albany County court of common pleas judgments of ejectment against his "rebellious" tenants, namely, Hendrick and Theophilus Brusie, and Andries Reese, brother of the late William Reese. On November 25, Abraham Yates, Jr., accompanied by a large number of Livingston tenants, appeared at Taconic to evict them. While the sheriff was executing the writs, John Van Gelder (a Stockbridge Indian married to a white woman at Sheffield), his two sons, and Benjamin Franklin, all armed, showed up at the house of Hendrick Brusie—about sixteen miles distant from the Hudson River—and threatened that "if they [the posse] touched the House they would kill some of them."[177] Upon this, the sheriff ordered his men to arrest the Van Gelder party. As the sheriff and his men approached them, the old Indian fired and killed Adam Ripenbergh, one of Livingston's loyal tenants. The murderer then rode off but was quickly overtaken and jailed along with his son Lewis and Franklin.[178] Before departing from Taconic, the sheriff evicted the Bruisies and Reese from their possessions and had their houses pulled down.[179] But what steps John Van Rensselaer took to secure his lands are unknown. No evidence is available to show that Noble's followers were expelled from the Claverack area.[180]

In contrast to its past behavior, this time the General Court was

---

Archives, VI, 381–384; an Indian deed to Robert Noble, Thomas Whitney, Japhet Hunt, John McCarthur, and others for 27,026½ acres for £200, May 25, 1756, *ibid.*, 375–379; petition of Truman Powell and others, Aug. 17, 1756, *Journals of Mass. House of Representatives*, XXXIII, Pt. I, 113, 115, 130, 132.

177. The Van Gelders were associates of Noble and others who bought the disputed land from the Stockbridge Indians. Mass. Archives, VI, 384; Gov. Hardy to Lords of Trade, Dec. 22, 1756, *N.Y. Col. Docs.*, VII, 206–208.

178. Robert Livingston, Jr., to Abraham Yates, Jr., Oct. 20 and Dec. 15, 1756, Yates Papers, Box 1; Robert Livingston, Jr., to "Dear Brother," Nov. 26, 1756, Misc. MSS, Livingston, R-W; *N.-Y. Mercury*, Dec. 6, 1756; "Inquisition Indented," Nov. 29, 1756, C.O. 1067/5, 81, Public Record Office; Robert Livingston, Jr., to Jacob Wendell, Mar. 21, 1757, Livingston Papers; *Journals of Mass. House of Representatives*, XXXIII, Pt. II, 241. The Van Gelders and Franklin were indicted by the Albany County grand jury, but the Indians were soon released for a political reason. Franklin died in jail from smallpox in 1756. See Robert Livingston, Jr., to James De Lancey, Dec. 21, 1757, Mass. Archives, IV, 183–184.

179. *Journals of Mass. House of Representatives*, XXXIII, Pt. II, 241.

180. Evidence shows that the Massachusetts militia company under Capt. Noble was, as of Feb. 1757, very active. _____ to Mr. Jonse Woodbeuck, Feb. 1757, Livingston-Redmond MSS, Roll 10.

slow in reacting to the late fray. Massachusetts's Lieutenant Governor Phips was incensed that a committee appointed by the court on January 6, 1757, to investigate the incident failed to meet once in a three-week period. Under his pressure, the legislature finally came up with a resolution (January 29), but it was not vengeful in character.[181] To be sure, it defended the Van Gelders' actions as self-defense, reaffirmed "a Right of Jurisdiction over all Lands" from the Atlantic to the "South Sea," and condemned New York's stubborn refusal to settle the boundary controversy by means of arbitration. Clearly designed to elicit British sympathy for the Massachusetts position, it observed that the New York land system, with its vast tracts of land held by a few elite figures who had no interest in the development of the country, was the reason why a compromised solution of the dispute was all but impossible. Yet the General Court approved an order issued by Phips to restrain the militant Indians at Stockbridge from avenging the imprisonment of the Van Gelders and also asked Phips to employ "every reasonable Measure" to pacify the borderers until the line was determined.[182] In keeping with this pliant posture, the legislature in early February dismissed various petitions by the borderers and former manorial tenants either for grants of contested lands or for the establishment of a separate township from Sheffield.[183] These actions provide more than a hint that the legislature was tiring of the protracted border problems and seeking to maintain the status quo until the government at home announced its rumored momentous decision on the border line.

But the tension still persisted. A piece of intelligence Livingston received in the early spring of 1757 indicated that a company of ninety-seven "vagabonds" had held "a grand councill" with the Stockbridge Indians at Jan Halenbeck's new homestead in Green Kill near Sheffield and that the white men had purchased from the natives about two-thirds of Livingston Manor for £170. They then had sent a petition for a land grant to the General Court, accompanied by the Indian deed, and also had made a mutual pledge to stand by one another to "the last drop of their Blood" and to settle the land the following May with the help of the Indians. As was always the case with the earlier schemes as well, this one involved only four Livingston tenants, all of whom the landlord had already dispossessed for aiding the New England intruders. Why the

181. Lt. Gov. Phips's message, Jan. 6, 26, 1757, *Journals of Mass. House of Representatives*, XXXIII, Pt. II, 232, 288.
182. *Ibid.*, 296–297.
183. *Ibid.*, 241, 270, 274, 312, 313–314, 316.

conspirators bothered to make another Indian purchase when the old ones had failed to receive official sanction is a complete mystery. In any event, on March 21, Livingston wrote to his friend Wendell expressing his hope that the Boston government would stop these "madmen" from their "Diabolical Resolution." He then went off with his militia company to the northern frontier near Saratoga, where he stayed for a little over three weeks.[184]

Exploiting his absence from home, the conspirators busied themselves by marking out farms in the manor for settlement and spreading a story that the landlord had given up his "Cause." Livingston was terribly shaken by the new development. On April 14, the day after his return from the frontier, he wrote to Yates, asking the sheriff to come down to the manor. But it took another urgent letter before the sheriff sent his deputy.[185] On May 7, Livingston, flanked by Thomas Morril, the deputy, and Dirck Wessells Ten Broeck, a justice of the peace, led a "considerable" number of armed men to the house of Jonathan Darby at Taconic, where he was confronted by about thirty armed men.[186] The deputy sheriff stepped forward and commanded the crowd to disperse. Three or four of the rioters went off, but the rest went inside the house and answered the order by shooting at the visitors. In the ensuing gunfight, two men on both sides were wounded mortally, and several others lightly. Outnumbered and outgunned, the rioters began to flee, and the pursuing posse captured three of them. The following day, while patroling the rebel-infested territory, the landlord's force captured two more.[187]

As evidenced in his request of May 10 to the government for fifty armed guards at his mansion house for his protection, Livingston feared

184. The dispossessed tenants were Hendrick and Theophilus Brusie, Andries J. Reese, and Jonathan Darby. Robert Livingston, Jr., to Jacob Wendell, Mar. 21, 1757, Livingston Papers; Robert Livingston, Jr., to brother Peter, Apr. 27, 1757, Rutherford Coll., III. The Stockbridge Indians promised at the meeting to assist the conspirators in settling the lands.

185. It is impossible to ascertain who these men from Connecticut and Dutchess County were. Robert Livingston to James De Lancey, Dec. 21, 1757, Mass. Archives, IV, 184–185; Robert Livingston, Jr., to Abraham Yates, Apr. 14 and 27, 1757, Yates Papers, Box 1. In the last letter, Livingston pleaded: "I must now repeat the same Request and Desire you may come without any Loss of time for its likely that I shall be Invaded in a few days."

186. It was reported that Jonathan Darby, Jonathan Reese, Hendrick Brusie, Andries J. Reese, Joseph Van Gelder, his brother Andries, and Samuel and Ebenezer Taylor were among those at the Darby house. "Proclamation to Arrest Certain Rioters on Livingston Manor," June 8, 1757, Doc. Hist. N.Y., III, 822.

187. The best description of the incident is "An Inquisition Indented Taken on the body of James Burton," May 10, 1757, C.O. 1068/5, 18. See also _____ to John Tabor Kempe, Oct. 14, 1766, Unsorted Legal MSS, Kempe Papers; Doc. Hist. N.Y., III, 821–823.

a reprisal.[188] But it never came. All the routed conspirators could mount was psychological warfare against the landlord and his loyal tenants: they floated a story that they had obtained "Special warrants" to arrest him and "all those" loyal tenants at Taconic. Yet Livingston was not ruffled. He was much more apprehensive that "better Sort of people" in Albany would criticize the manner in which he had prosecuted the Massachusetts intruders. Expressing his uneasiness about this matter in his letter of July 19 to Yates, he went on to state: "I do not mind them [the rioters] at all, trusting that they cannot gitt any new rioters to their assistance and those 30 that are left I know dare not off[er] to come."[189] This was indeed a rare display of optimism. Only two months before, he had been hysterical upon learning that the Van Gelders, who were alleged to be plotting to kill him, had been released from the Albany jail. At that time, his fear of the Indians was such that he even considered hiding somewhere if he were to be unprotected by the government.

How can we account for Livingston's change from a somewhat pessimistic appraisal of his circumstances to an exuberant confidence?[190] For one thing, Lieutenant Governor De Lancey came to his aid by issuing on June 8 a proclamation commanding the lawmen of Albany and Dutchess counties to capture the Taconic rioters.[191] There is no question that the proclamation was a boost to the depressed landlord and a blow to the land-hungry intruders. Equally encouraging was the continuous restraint shown by the Boston government. On June 9, Sir William Pepperell of Maine, at the request of the General Court, protested to Sir Charles Hardy over the late tragedy, but the tone and content of the protest did not fit the image of a government avowedly committed to the defense of its territorial interest. Sir William's epistle blamed the death of the two "unfortunate" persons on Livingston, a man without "any Sense

188. *Doc. Hist. N.Y.*, III, 819–820.

189. Robert Livingston, Jr., to Abraham Yates, Jr., July 19, 1757, Yates Papers, Box 1.

190. Robert Livingston, Jr., to Abraham Yates, Jr., Dec. 15, 1756, and May 15, 1757, *ibid*. The release of the Van Gelders was due to an effort on the part of Sir William Johnson, superintendent of Indian affairs, and the earl of Loudoun, commander-in-chief of the British forces in North America, who were anxious to avoid anything that might offend the friendly Indians at the critical juncture of the war. Charles Hardy to William Johnson, May 16, 1757, *Doc. Hist. N.Y.*, II, 432–433; "Report of a Committee of the Council," July 29, 1757, Misc. MSS, Massachusetts, 1760–1769, N.-Y. Hist. Soc.; *Journal of General Assembly*, II, 497.

191. *Doc. Hist. N.Y.*, III, 821–823; William Livingston to brother Robert, Jr., June 13, 1757, Livingston-Redmond MSS, Roll 7; Robert Livingston, Jr., to James Duane, May 3, 1762, Duane Papers, Roll 2.

of Religion or Humanity," but mentioned nothing about the imprisonment of several borderers. The letter discussed at length what seemed to
be a discriminatory practice on the part of the New York authority in still
detaining Benjamin Franklin, an English subject, while releasing the Indians, although the latter were the principal culprits and the former just
an accessory in the murder of a Yorker the previous November. In any
eve.1t, Pepperell assured Hardy that the Bay Colony would continually
endeavor to "quiet the minds of our people" and, in particular, to keep
"a constant watch over the motion of the Indians at Stockbridge."[192]

The moderate attitude of the Boston government undoubtedly was
influenced by the news that the Lords of Trade, according to the colony's
London agent, had recommended a straight line of twenty miles distant
from the Hudson River as an equitable boundary between the two provinces, as it was between New York and Connecticut. The Massachusetts
General Court accepted the line before the end of April. Having done so,
it could not but discard its erstwhile western expansionism.[193]

Livingston's optimism had another basis. There was a growing rift
between the leadership of the former manorial tenants and their Sheffield
supporters over the disposition of the lands acquired from the Stockbridge Indians. John Ashley, a several-term member of the House of
Representatives from Sheffield, one of the leading instigators and protec-
tors of the tenant rebels, and a friend of Brigadier Dwight and Oliver
Partridge, was furious with Robert Noble and his associates for refusing
to share the spoils with him and with others who had helped the antilandlord cause.[194] According to Ashley's petition of January 1757 to the
General Court, he and "sundry others" had the year before received from
the Dwight committee rights to a township laid out west of Sheffield, but
the actual purchase of the lands from the Indians was made by the Noble
group. In applying to the court for the confirmation of the purchase,
Noble excluded the Ashley people, who were willing to bear appropriate
portions of the purchase price, and admitted "other Persons in their
Room," all against a specific order of the Legislature.[195] Undoubtedly,

192. Sir William Pepperell to Charles Hardy, June 9, 1757, C.O. 1068/5, 16.
193. Exactly when the General Court instructed its agent to express Massachusetts's
consent to the position of the Lords of Trade is unknown. *Report on Boundaries*, II,
148–150.
194. *Journals of Mass. House of Representatives*, XXVII, 152–153, 205; Mass. Archives, VI, 157, XXXII, 493, XLVI, 371.
195. *Journals of Mass. House of Representatives*, XXXIII, Pt. II, 274. But Ashley's
petition was dismissed. See *ibid.*, 312.

Ashley and his friends regarded the sudden assertion of independence by Noble's men, and their complete disregard for the wishes of their Sheffield partners, as an unforgivable sin of ingratitude and treachery.[196] We can surmise from the exceptional silence of Dwight and Partridge during the critical phases of the border dispute in 1757 that they shared their friend Ashley's new antipathy toward the rebels for this betrayal. It was perhaps not a mere coincidence that, beginning with the cleavage between the Noble partisans on the one hand and the western Massachusetts politicos and their associates on the other, the General Court, which had traditionally followed the latter's recommendations, turned apathetic toward the borderers' requests for land grants and protection. The animosity between the two groups had local implications as well. As shown previously, the leadership and overwhelming manpower for the antilandlord campaign had come from Sheffield and sister towns. The inhabitants of these communities and not the rebel tenants initiated both offensive and defensive operations. Now with the disaffection of the Ashley group, the insurgents' strength and vigor were greatly diminished, although they were still strong enough to control the area they had recently named "Nobletown" in Claverack.[197] Well equipped with an extensive spy network at Taconic and beyond, Livingston could not have failed to learn of the dissension in the enemy camp.

In August 1757 the governments of the two provinces received the Board of Trade decision fixing a boundary line of "property and Jurisdiction." This line was to run straight from the point where the southern boundary of Massachusetts met Connecticut to another point that divided New Hampshire and Massachusetts, both points being twenty miles due east of the Hudson River. Actual surveying, however, was left to a future date.[198] The Livingston Manor proprietor was elated at the decision, for it made the eastern limit of New York coterminous with that of the manor as described in his original patent. By contrast, the morale

196. The independent disposition on the part of the insurgents and borderers living farther away from Sheffield was first revealed in their petition in June 1756 to the General Court for a separate district from the town to which they had hitherto paid religious and school taxes. *Ibid.*, Pt. I, 49.

197. "Minutes of Proprietary Meetings of Nobletown," entry on July 19, 1757, Mass. Archives, VI, 407–413; "Petition of inhabitants on the land called Province Land," Oct. 29, 1757, *ibid.*, CXVII, 370; *Journals of Mass. House of Representatives*, XXXIV, I, 177.

198. *N.Y. Col. Docs.*, VII, 223–224, 273–274; *Report on Boundaries*, II, 148–151. The board's decision favored neither Massachusetts's "sea-to-sea" charters nor New York's counterclaim to the west bank of the Connecticut River. It was more of a political solution confirming the pre-1751 settlement situation in the Housatonic River area.

of the rebels and their supporters was shattered. The manor returned to normalcy as it existed before 1751.[199] But John Van Rensselaer, who claimed the eastern bounds of his Claverack estate to be twenty-four miles east of the river, was dissatisfied with the settlement. As De Lancey protested, it would take off four miles from Claverack and Rensselaerswyck proper.[200] Moreover, the action of the Board of Trade had no visible effect on the entrenched insurgents in Nobletown, which fell within the New York jurisdiction. According to Van Rensselaer's report dated December 28, 1758, Massachusetts justices continued to exercise their authority over the townspeople, and New York constables were "afraid to go among them."[201] For many years to come, the proprietor was unable to bring it back under his control for reasons unrelated to the provincial border controversy. But, at least until 1766, the disputed area remained quiet.

In conclusion, the blame for the disturbances in Livingston Manor and Claverack must be placed entirely on the western Massachusetts people and their expansionist-minded General Court. It was they who first instigated the tenants' revolt. Behind virtually every move and at every phase of the insurgency the ubiquitous hand of the Yankees can be discovered. The rebellious tenants were both an instrument of Massachusetts's territorial ambitions, which had some claim to legitimacy based on the early charters, and a pawn in the contest between private speculators in western Massachusetts and the New York landlords. The conflict was over land, not lease terms, though there is no doubt that leaseholding in these manors rendered itself an exploitable issue for the Yankees. Blessed with the best possible leases, the Claverack rioters had no reason to demand better treatment from their landlord. If the grievances connected with the tenant-landlord relationship indeed had been the fundamental issue, the insurgency might have become widespread. But the evidence clearly establishes that the number of rebellious tenant families never exceeded more than twenty-seven, twenty at Taconic and seven at Claverack. As shown above, for all the seductive or terror campaigns on

199. Sometime late in 1757, Jacob Decker, overseer of Livingston Manor, while on a business trip to Taconic, was taken by several insurgents and later indicted by a Massachusetts grand jury. This was an isolated incident, however, and had no visible impact on subsequent developments. Robert Livingston, Jr., to James De Lancey, Dec. 21, 1757, and De Lancey to Gov. Thomas Pownall of Massachusetts, Dec. 26, 1757, Mass. Archives, IV, 185, 180.

200. James De Lancey to Lords of Trade, Oct. 18, 1757, C.O. 1068/5, 29.

201. John Van Rensselaer and Abraham Fonda to Sir Charles Hardy, Dec. 28, 1758, Mass. Archives, IV, 543.

the part of the insurgents and their New England patrons, they were unable to sway others. In Livingston Manor, the rebels constituted only about 5 percent of its approximately four hundred tenant families. They managed to wage a protracted war against Robert Livingston, Jr., not because of internal support but because of the help and encouragement of outsiders. Moreover, the conflict was extremely localized, being confined to the Taconic area claimed by the Massachusetts Bay Colony.

# CHAPTER VIII

~~~~~~

# The "Great Rebellion" of 1766

## Land Titles under Attack

For almost a decade following the 1757 Board of Trade intercession in the New York–Massachusetts boundary controversy, the northern manors were free of violence. Yet the peace was deceptive, for the New York land titles continued to be attacked by a number of people. Other great patents, including Beekman Patent and Philipse's Highland Patent in Dutchess County, found themselves subject to similar challenges at the same time. In the mid-eighteenth century, disputes over rival claims to lands reached epidemic proportions, and almost every "landed property" appeared to be in a "precarious situation."[1] Anne Grant, an acute contemporary observer, noted: "Now that inundation of litigious new settlers, from Massachusetts' bounds, had awakened the spirit of inquiry, to call it no worse, every day produced a fresh law-suit, and all of the same nature, about ascertaining boundaries. . . . And as these great law-suits were matter of general concern, no one knowing whose turn might be next, all conversation began to be infected with litigious cant; and every thing seemed unstable and perplexed."[2] Another observer who was con-

---

1. Henry Cruger Van Schaack, *Memoirs of the Life of Henry Van Schaack, Embracing Selections from his Correspondence during the American Revolution* (Chicago, 1892), 23.
2. Grant, *Memoirs of an American Lady*, 290–291. Henry Beekman mourned in 1751 that "I am dayly kept up with Showers of Law Suets over my lands" in Dutchess County. Beekman to Henry Livingston, Oct. 10, 1751, Beekman Papers, New-York Historical So-

cerned in the Claverack case asserted that "New England Deluges will be the Destruction of the great Patents in this province I have long for-seen."[3]

The so-called Great Rebellion of 1766 began in Philipse's Highland Patent and had a catalytic impact on the course of events in Cortlandt Manor and the other areas. Insofar as it embroiled the eastern part of Claverack, Livingston Manor, and Philipse's Highland Patent, the rebellion was primarily an extension of the controversy over land titles. The landed men became targets of attack not because of their landlordism but because of their claims to certain disputed lands. But the agrarian violence took on the character of a classic tenant-landlord clash when it spread to the Manor of Cortlandt. There a handful of tenants rose up to redress their grievances against the oppressive practices of their landlord. This mixed picture makes it impossible to apply a single theory of causation to the insurgency. For a better understanding of the complex nature of the subject, we will need to examine the conflict over land titles, including that in Dutchess County. We will see that royal officials, such as Cadwallader Colden and William Kempe, were deeply involved in the title disputes and that they helped to create an environment in which resort to violence was the only—and sometimes attractive—alternative for the disgruntled farmers.

The General Court of Massachusetts severed its official ties with Nobletown in Claverack after it became known that the area fell under New York's jurisdiction. But this did not stampede the insurgents into seeking an accommodation with John Van Rensselaer or vacating the area, as the rebels of Livingston Manor had left Taconic.[4] Robert Noble and his associates, their number daily increasing with the stream of land-hungry farmers from the congested New England colonies, successfully held their ground. Soon after the Board of Trade's decision on the boundary, Van Rensselaer won judgments of eviction from the Albany County

ciety, New York. See also Seth Sherwood to Oliver De Lancey, June 25, 1765, John Watts Papers, IX, *ibid.*

3. William Smith, Jr., to Philip Schuyler, Nov. 27, 1772, Schuyler Papers, 1758–1798, Box 24, New York Public Library.

4. It appears that Loomis and the Halenbecks found new homes in the area presently known as Egremont between Sheffield and the Livingston Manor line. John McCarthur joined Noble at Nobletown. The whereabouts of the other Taconic rebels, the Brusies and the Reeses, are unknown. Deposition of Josiah and Abigail Loomis, Nov. 3, 1767, Massachusetts Archives, VI, 415, State House, Boston; Robert Livingston, Jr., to Peter Livingston and James Duane, Mar. 22, 1762, *Doc. Hist. N.Y.*, III, 825–826; petition of William J. Kellog and others, N.Y. Land Papers, XXIX, 20.

court against the intruders, but he was unable to have the verdicts executed.[5] Behind the incapacity of the landlord lay a serious defect in his land title that rendered his claim assailable. Sometime in late 1758, the intruders, though shorn of the vital support of Massachusetts, seized upon this vulnerability in the Claverack title to press their struggle further.

On February 13, 1759, Solomon Bebee and forty-three others submitted a request to the New York government for a grant of land, six square miles, to the south of Rensselaerswyck proper and east of Kinderhook Patent, an area claimed by Van Rensselaer. Noble, Thomas Whitney, and others, who had been active in the rebel movement in the past, were absent from Bebee's list, but there is no question that they were his hidden associates.[6] The petitioners argued that they had purchased the tract for £250 four years ago from the Stockbridge Indians, presuming that it lay within Massachusetts, but had learned since that the "whole or the great part" of it was within New York. Implicit in the argument was the rejection of any prior patent for the land, and, accordingly, of the Van Rensselaer title.

This was not the first time that Van Rensselaer's claim had been challenged. The area east of Kinderhook township had a long history of disputes beginning in the first decade of the eighteenth century. Involved were the Westenhook patentees (who claimed that their land extended to the eastern bound of Kinderhook), the inhabitants of Kinderhook Patent (granted in 1686), Stephen Bayard and his associates with "Wawighnank" Patent of 1743, Coenraet Burghardt and Elias Van Schaack, Johannes Van Deusen and John Van der Pool, and many others. Some other sections of Claverack Manor were also challenged, notably, by the owners of the so-called Van Hoesen Patent (granted in 1669) and by the proprietors of Livingston Manor. The conflicting claims arose because the descriptions of various patents were extremely ambiguous. One group of people, for instance, called Westenhook Patent "the most dark obscure and unintelligible" document that they had ever seen.[7] The same

---

5. Petition of John Van Rensselaer, Dec. 23, 1772, C.O. 1104/5, 315–316, Public Record Office.

6. Petition of Solomon Bebee and others, N.Y. Land Papers, XV, 147. On Feb. 12, 1759, another group, represented by one Josiah Haywood, submitted a petition to the New York government praying for a license to purchase from the Indians what they called vacant lands adjacent to Bebee's location. These petitions were referred to a committee established by the council for review. *Ibid.*, 146.

7. N.Y. Land Papers, VI, 159, VII, 35, VIII, 156, X, 105, 107, 116, 152, 170, XI, 2, 6, 7, 167, XII, 120, 124.

was true for the original 1685 patent of Rensselaerswyck with respect to Claverack. It provided no line linking the northeast boundary of Claverack to its northwest perimeter: the patent indicated only three boundaries or sides beginning "at the Creek by Major Abraham Staats's and so along the [Hudson] River Southward to the south side of Vastrix Island by a creek called Wahankasick stretching from thence with an Easterly Line into the woods 24 English miles to a place called Wawanaquasick and from thence Northward to the head of the creek by Major Abraham Staats' as aforesaid." As Henry Van Rensselaer, proprietor of Claverack and father of John, admitted, the original title contained "some defects and imperfections" in that it did not specify "which or where" the head of the creek by Major Staats's house was, and also failed to identify a closing line from the "head of the creek" to Staats's house.[8] In 1717 David Jamison, a lawyer in New York City knowledgeable in the matter, insisted that Henry Van Rensselaer "has not one foot of all the Land called Claverack for his Patent is not closed and Consequently has nothing but the bare line."[9]

To remedy the shortcomings of the title, Henry Van Rensselaer obtained a patent of confirmation in 1717 that furnished a new line running from Wawanaquasick to the southeast corner of Kinderhook Patent and "from thence northwest by the bounds of Kinderhook to Major Abrahams Falls." The new confirmatory patent, however, did not relieve the Van Rensselaers of disputes in subsequent years. Like the original patent, it still failed to locate the head of Kinderhook Creek. Moreover, Claverack's northeast corner—the key junction—remained unclear, since the Kinderhook boundaries were uncertain.[10] Worse still, the Indian place called Wawanaquasick was nine or twelve miles, not twenty-four miles, due east from the Hudson River.[11] According to a map prepared by Cadwallader Colden in 1771 (see p. 351), five or six different interpretations of the Claverack bounds were possible, the strictest of which would have made the domain a relatively small tract of 23,800 acres.

---

8. Petition of Henry Van Rensselaer, May 23, 1721, *ibid.*, VIII, 156. It should be noted, however, that there were many colonial patents without a fourth, or closing, line, among them the patents of Kinderhook, Schenectady, and Paltz, to name just several. Declaration of Adam Vrooman, surveyor, Jan. 14, 1769, Sorted Legal Manuscripts, John Tabor Kempe Papers, N.-Y. Hist. Soc.

9. Robert Livingston, Jr., to father, Robert, July 3, 1717, Livingston-Redmond MSS, Roll 3.

10. N.Y. Land Papers, VIII, 156; map and exemplification, *ibid.*, XXIX, 56.

11. See the various depositions in 1761 and 1762 on the location of Wawanaquasick in Columbia County Miscellaneous Manuscripts, N.-Y. Hist. Soc.; "Beby and others a[gainst]

Taking advantage of the ambiguities in the patent descriptions, the Van Rensselaer family in the course of time adopted the most liberal interpretation possible, so as to include about 281,600 acres.[12] Their pretension might seem extraordinary and unjustified, but the practice of extending one's land beyond the supposedly granted acreage was a common vice among landowners and even townships.[13] The colonists in general had no moral compunctions about "taking in a little of King George's ground" wherever they could find it. Innumerable boundary and claim disputes thus litter the minutes of colonial equity courts.[14]

In two important respects, the challenge of Bebee and his associates was more menacing to the Claverack proprietor than the earlier ones. First, it was strongly endorsed by the Stockbridge Indians, who, together with other tribes, had recently become more vocal in demanding the restitution of lands that they insisted their ancestors had been cheated out of by the chicanery of white landjobbers. Officials both in the colonies and at home accorded their grievances a sympathetic ear, lest the English interests suffer from the possible disaffection of friendly Indians during the war against the French.[15] More ominously, the Bebee group found as their allies two powerful officeholders, Cadwallader Colden, senior member of the council and surveyor general for many years, and his crony John Tabor Kempe, the attorney general. Though evidence of direct collusion between the officials and the squatters is sketchy, there is enough of it to raise the suspicion that the latter received both moral and material support from Colden and Kempe. If not for this support, the conflict over Claverack could not have escalated as it did in the following decade. If there was one man who contributed most to undermining the Claverack title—for that matter, all the great patents—it was Colden.

Throughout his public career spanning half a century, Colden was

Renselaer, Notes for Reply," n.d., in the handwriting of John Tabor Kempe, Unsorted Legal MSS, Kempe Papers.

12. Map, 1771, N.Y. Land Papers, XXIX, 56; map with an endorsement "New York, Explanation of and Remarks on the Map of V Ranslaer's Pattent etc.," Jan. 25, 1762, C.O. 1070/5, 263.

13. Grant, *Memoirs of an American Lady*, 290–291; Cadwallader Colden to Lords of Trade, Feb. 28, 1761, *Colden Letter Books*, I, 66; Abraham Lott, "Journal of a Voyage to Albany, 1774," *The Historical Magazine*, 2d Ser., VIII, No. 2 (Aug. 1870), 68.

14. I cannot list all the disputes here because of their sheer number. In the course of my research on this subject, I came to believe that most of the large landowners spent a good part of their lives in court and were extremely nervous over the security of their estates. Grant, *Memoirs of an American Lady*, 291.

15. Privy Council's report to the king, Nov. 11, 1761, *The Aspinwall Papers* (Massachusetts Historical Society, *Collections*, 4th Ser., IX–X [Boston, 1871]), I, 441–447, hereafter cited as *Aspinwall Papers*.

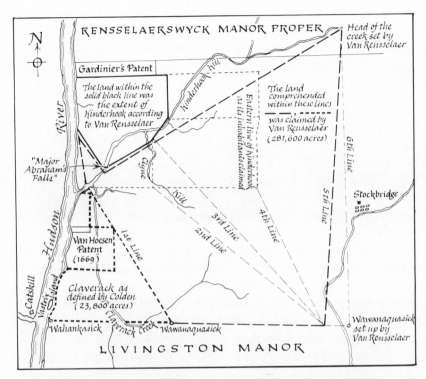

The Confusing Boundaries of Claverack as Described by Cadwallader Colden, 1771. Adjusted from New York Colonial Manuscripts, Land Papers, 1642–1803, XXVIII, 156, XXIX, 56–57, New York State Library, Albany. (Drawn by Richard J. Stinely.)

the most persistent and outspoken critic of the great landowners and the provincial political and economic system they represented.[16] By virtue of their wealth and connections, they were the dominant political influence at the provincial level, if not in county government. As Colden saw it, they were "the principal Demagogues in oppressing the Administration."[17] A seasoned partisan of royal prerogative, he believed that the

16. George Dangerfield, *Chancellor Robert R. Livingston of New York, 1746–1813* (New York, 1960), 16.
17. Cadwallader Colden to William Shirley, July 5, 1749, *Colden Papers*, IV, 122–123; Colden to Lords of Trade, Jan. 25, 1762, *Colden Letter Books*, I, 155–158; Colden to Secretary Popple, Dec. 15, 1727, *N.Y. Col. Docs.*, V, 844–845. For Colden's efforts to broaden royal prerogative power in New York, see Carole Shammas, "Cadwallader Colden and the Role of the King's Prerogative," *New-York Historical Society Quarterly*, LIII (1969), 103–126.

administration's troubles and other ills of the province all stemmed from them and their land titles. The grandees were responsible, he thought, for the alleged slow settlement and improvement of the colony. They had arbitrarily enlarged the boundaries of their patents "so as to take in a much greater quantity of land, than was originally intended." At the same time, they were loath to pay trivial quitrents, thereby depriving the governors of one important source of revenue. For these reasons, he had by 1749 become obsessed with the destruction of the great patents by means of resolute chancery action.

The prospect of redistributing the seized estates at a quitrent of two and a half shillings for every hundred acres enthralled Colden as much as it had the earl of Bellomont five decades before. The increased proceeds from that sector would provide independent means for the administration, which would in turn be able to overcome its traditional weakness against the power of the assembly.[18] Given his vehement hostility toward the great patents, it is not surprising that Colden enthusiastically welcomed the Bebee petition as an opportunity to examine Van Rensselaer's pretensions and to roll back the latter's domain to the smallest possible size under the original patent. Colden held the view that the Claverack domain as defined by its landlord was more than ten times the actual grant, and he was therefore persuaded of the merit of the Bebee case.[19]

Colden publicly committed himself to the anti-Van Rensselaer campaign and became materially interested in its outcome. No evidence better illustrates his partisan involvement than his allowing his daughter Catherine and son Alexander (deputy surveyor general) to join Kempe, Goldsbrow Banyar (deputy secretary of the province), and nine other "children or near Relations" of some members of the council to petition in May 1761 for a grant of 13,000 acres of land east of Kinderhook in the tract that Van Rensselaer claimed. It is especially significant that the petition was submitted to Colden while he was the chief executive officer of the government as president of the council.[20] Further, in order to help

18. Cadwallader Colden, "State of the Lands in the Province of New York, in 1732," *Doc. Hist. N.Y.*, I, 384; Colden to William Burnet, Nov. 1721, *Colden Papers*, VIII, 160–164; Colden to Lords of Trade, Jan. 25, 1762, *N.Y. Col. Docs.*, VII, 486–487; Kim, "New Look at the Great Landlords," *WMQ*, 3d Ser., XXVII (1970), 581–614.

19. C.O. 1070/5, 263; *N.Y. Col. Docs.*, VII, 486. That Colden "countenanced" the application of the Bebee group was clearly evidenced in another petition by the same group dated Apr. 27, 1768. N.Y. Land Papers, XXIV, 117.

20. Petition of Catharine Colden and others, May 27, 1761, N.Y. Land Papers, XVI, 50; Cadwallader Colden to Lords of Trade, May 31, 1765, *Colden Letter Books*, II, 11.

the case of the Bebee group, which he apparently regarded as a driving wedge into the Claverack domain, he had Kempe represent them as attorney and prepare their argument against the proprietor for the anticipated hearing before the council.

No less important in revealing Colden's anti-Van Rensselaer policy was his handling of a petition submitted in 1760 by John Van der Pool and Robert Van Deusen of Albany County for a 2,500-acre tract in the contested area. In their presentation, they explained that Van der Pool and Van Deusen's father, Johannes, had, with a government license, purchased the lands from some Indian owners in 1738 but that the families had neglected to apply for a patent until this time because of the "extreme difficulty" of finding the "true Boundaries" of Westenhook Patent.[21] This explanation is puzzling. The patent's bounds were as ambiguous as they had ever been. If the claimants had no clear idea about the bounds of the land, how and what had they managed to buy from the Indians? Whatever the true explanation, Colden accepted their excuse, and in June ordered his deputy to survey Westenhook Patent at government expense.[22] Judging from his subsequent actions, Colden's real target was Claverack. Under the pretext of surveying Westenhook he expected to "discover" the exact quantity of the land initially granted to the Van Rensselaers and "how far Claverack Manor intruded upon the 'King's lands.'" Once this was accomplished, writs of intrusion or other legal process for determining the true boundary could be issued, and the government would soon be able to recover land usurped by the landlord. In Colden's thinking, this method would be easier and "attended with less popular clamour" than resort to outright "prosecutions" to break the Claverack title on account of its legal defects.[23]

As was the custom in cases concerning conflicting claims to land, copies of these petitions were served on John Van Rensselaer, who was stunned by the appearance of names like Colden, Kempe, and Banyar in one of them. After all, those who were now arrayed against his estate were the most powerful officials of the province. The situation required, as he acknowledged, "more than ordinary attention." In July 1761, he entered

---

The other copetitioners were Catharine Kennedy, Lawrence Read, Augustus Van Cortlandt, Robert James Livingston, William Walton, Jr., Mary Mageletune Nicoll, Matthew Dubois, Josiah Martin, Jr., and William Benson.

    21. Petition of Van der Pool and Van Deusen, Sept. 19, 1760, N.Y. Land Papers, XV, 188.

    22. Warrant for survey, June 17, 1761, *ibid.*, XVI, 61–62.

    23. Cadwallader Colden to Lords of Trade, Jan. 25, 1762, N.Y. Col. Docs., VII, 487.

a caveat with the government against issuing patents until he was heard. A hearing was set for September 3, but when the day arrived, Van Rensselaer pleaded with the government for a postponement of three months on the grounds that "the King's Honour and Justice will be thought to demand greatest caution."[24] In other words, the formidable antagonists made it absolutely necessary for him to collect all possible favorable evidence. The hearing was put off until December 3.

To the exasperation of Van Rensselaer's impatient opponents, he was still not ready when that day came. In a petition dated December 2, he presented two main reasons why he was yet unprepared. One was the initial difficulty of finding a suitable surveyor; another was that certain important documentary proofs would not be available until the following spring. At the same time, he used the occasion to chastise his opponents. Their interpretation of the manor patent, he said, was designed to "squeeze out a vacancy in an old-settled and therefore more valuable part of the province than unassumed Lands on the Frontiers" and thus was founded upon "narrow principles repugnant to the Honor of the Crown." Clearly with a view to drum up support among the large landed interests, he also warned that these "narrow" principles would be "applicable" to many other patents and would "disturb the public Repose."[25]

Kempe, representing the anti-Van Rensselaer groups, delivered an item-by-item rebuttal to the landlord's reasons for further postponement of the hearing. Arguing that if Van Rensselaer was not ready, it was due to his own neglect and that, in contempt of the council, the landlord had provided no proof for his allegations, Kempe called for a prompt resolution of this protracted controversy and pointed to the serious financial plight of his clients—the Bebee group—who could sustain no further expenses "by a new Delay."[26]

Because Claverack was one of the most ancient titles, the controversy swirling around it attracted an inordinate amount of attention. If that manor was to be destroyed, a similar fate was likely to befall other large patents. One group of anxious observers was the old insurgents of Livingston Manor, who, like their northern comrades, had been "wholy putt off by Boston government." In early 1762 they began seriously

24. Petition of John Van Rensselaer, Sept. 1, 1761, N.Y. Land Papers, XVI, 86–87.
25. *Ibid.*, XVI, 105–106.
26. "Argument against the Reasons in Mr. Renselaers Petition for Delay Delivered in Council," Dec. 1761, Unsorted Legal MSS, Kempe Papers.

thinking about "what can be done at New York."[27] The resurgence of
their antimanorial activities was encouraged by two recent developments.
One, of course, was the firm support that Colden and Kempe offered to
the Bebee associates. The other was Colden's proclamation in February
of that year, made in accordance with instructions from the king the
previous December, which, among other things, enjoined "all Persons
whomsoever who have Either wilfully or Inadvertently Seated them Selves
upon Lands reserved or Claimed by the Indians without any Lawfull
authority for so Doing forthwith to remove on pain of being Prosecuted
with the utmost vigor of the Law."[28] This belatedly expressed royal
concern for the Indians' welfare was taken by the Taconic insurgents as a
justification for their renewed attempt on Livingston Manor, for some
part of which they had an Indian deed. Shortly thereafter, they dispatched
a mission to Sir William Johnson, superintendent of Indian affairs, asking for his assistance, but he refused even to talk to them. They then
toyed with the idea of sending an emissary to Sir Jeffery Amherst, commander-in-chief of the British expeditionary forces in North America, to
solicit his favor. Finally, they decided to appeal their cause to Colden.
They also resolved to evict all loyal tenants from the Taconic area in the
spring. Livingston trembled before the specter of renewed violence. In
urging his son-in-law James Duane to do "what may be deemed necessary," he grumbled that he was so "troubled by people . . . that I can't
write scarcely a word." But the insurgents' scheme never got off the
ground, for Colden himself issued a proclamation on March 31, 1762,
commanding the law enforcement agencies of Dutchess and Albany
counties to suppress them. Colden used such forcible measures at the
urgent request of Robert Livingston, Jr.[29]

Colden's pro-Livingston stand did not mean, however, that he was
persuaded of the validity of the Livingston Manor title. In fact, the
lieutenant governor believed that this patent was as defective and irregular as Claverack's.[30] Why then did he defend Livingston? The petition of

27. Robert Livingston, Jr., to James Duane, Feb. 15, 1762, Duane Papers, Roll 1.
28. Deposition of Gideon Prindle, Feb. 28, 1765, Unsorted Legal MSS, Kempe Papers;
king's "Additional Instructions," Dec. 9, 1761, Colden Papers, VI, 101–103.
29. Robert Livingston, Jr., to Peter R. Livingston and James Duane, Mar. 22, 1762,
James Elliot to Robert Livingston, Jr., Mar. 20, 1762, and Cadwallader Colden's proclamation, all in Doc. Hist. N.Y., III, 825–829; Robert Livingston, Jr., to James Duane, Feb.
15 and May 3, 1762, Duane Papers, Roll 1.
30. Cadwallader Colden to [unaddressed], May 10, 1767, Colden Papers, VII, 119–
121; Robert R. Livingston to father, Robert, Jr., Sept. 18, 1767, Robert R. Livingston

the Taconic rebels gave him a rare chance to test the extent to which the Livingston estate encroached upon the king's land, just as the Bebee group's petition had with respect to Claverack. But, given the dominant influence of the Livingstons in the assembly and the limited resources of the governor, Colden perhaps thought it politically inexpedient to take on Livingston Manor in addition to Claverack at that particular time: he wanted to avoid provoking the opposition, under the family's leadership, of a formidable combination of the large landed interests in the province. It was this realistic appraisal of political conditions that probably disposed him to concentrate solely on the most vulnerable of the two patents.[31]

The expected hearing on the Claverack land dispute finally came on October 7, 1762, and was presided over by Governor Robert Monckton, who had assumed his office several months earlier. William Smith, Jr., the attorney for Van Rensselaer, defended the landlord's claim mainly by expounding a liberal construction of the patent and by emphasizing the generous intent of the royal government when it was granted.[32] The argument for his opponents—the Bebee group, the Colden group, and Van der Pool and Van Deusen—was presented by Attorney General Kempe. As before, Kempe was thorough and meticulous in his criticism of the Van Rensselaer patent, countering Smith's defense point by point. He maintained that the patent contained "near 24,000 Acres" and that the landlord thus had "no legal Right" to the disputed lands. He also warned, echoing Colden's favorite argument, that if the government failed now to act decisively against the Van Rensselaer pretension, the rights of the crown could be "continually invaded and the Kings Revenue arising from the Quit Rents greatly injured." But the most significant aspect of the hearing was that Kempe relied almost entirely on the depositions of

Collection, Box 1, N.-Y. Hist. Soc. Colden believed that the Livingston Manor title was void for two principal reasons. First, it was founded on a series of confirmatory patents that had been issued "without advice and consent of Council." Second, the patents had been granted without previous survey. Colden to Lords of Trade, Sept. 20, 1764, N.Y. Col. Docs., VII, 653–655; Colden to William Johnson, Feb. 26, 1769, William Johnson Papers, XII, 699.

31. Cadwallader Colden to Lords of Trade, Jan. 25, 1762, and to the earl of Egremont, Sept. 14, 1763, N.Y. Col. Docs., VII, 486, 549.

32. Another attorney for John Van Rensselaer was James Duane. James Duane to Goldsbrow Banyar, Sept. 27, 1761, Unsorted Legal MSS, Kempe Papers. William Smith, Jr.'s, line of defense is found in "Westen Hook and Renselaer against Beby and others, Notes of argument, 7th Oct 1762," ibid. Smith's basic argument was to establish that Claverack's eastern and northeastern boundaries were 24 miles from the Hudson River. William Smith, Jr., to Philip Schuyler, Sept. 3, 1767, Schuyler Papers, Box 23.

former enemies of the proprietor, like David and William Ingersoll, Luke Noble, John Boghardt, and James Saxton, all of Sheffield, in support of his clients.[33] On the basis of this evidence, one can argue that the new controversy was a continuation of the old. Be that as it may, despite massive evidence in favor of the anti-Claverack groups, on October 20, Monckton and his council dismissed the petition of Bebee and the others on the grounds that it was not sufficiently certain "whether the Lands prayed for as vacant were vacant or not."[34]

The official decision was actually a nondecision in that it neither refuted the claims of the challengers nor defended those of Van Rensselaer. The squatters understood it as "a happy medium" between an absolute rejection of their petition and a grant of the disputed lands to them. It certainly had the effect of quashing for the moment the challenge to the status quo. However, by not taking a clear stand on the issue in contention, the government left the door open for continued agitation. The status of the lands remained "as doubtful as ever."[35] The squatters went about the business of settling and improving their lands unmolested by Van Rensselaer. "The Proprietors Book" of Spencer Township, situated north of Nobletown, indicates that by the end of 1763 a second allotment of the town land had been completed.[36] Undoubtedly, the other towns in the area, like New Canaan east of Kinderhook, also continued to expand (see the map on p. 358). The hardy settlers from New England were determined to stake their lives on these lands, even though they had no "legal Title" except an Indian deed. As one of their spokesmen stated, what worried them most was "not the weakness of their own Title but the [political] Strength" of their opponents. Yet they were thoroughly convinced that the case would ultimately be determined

33. "Beby and others a[gainst] Renselaer, Notes for Reply," Unsorted Legal MSS, Kempe Papers; "Affidavits and Certificates produced as Evidence before the Governour and Council on the Hearing between Bebee and his associates and Mr. Ranselaer," Sept. 9, 1764, Sorted Legal MSS, *ibid.*

34. Jeremiah Van Rensselaer to Henry Van Rensselaer, Jr., Sept. 17, 1761, and John Richard to Henry Van Rensselaer, Jr., Oct. 20, 1762, Van Rensselaer-Fort Papers, New York Public Library; "Proceedings of the Council of the Province of New York relative to the Claims of the Lands called Claverack," Dec. 23, 1772, Jan. 15, Feb. 2, 5, 17, and Mar. 1, 1773, C.O. 1104/5, 315–316.

35. "The Case of the Inhabitants of New Canaan in Kings District in the County of Albany," Jan. 20, 1773, N.Y. Land Papers, XXXIII, 6. See also the petition of Hezekiah Baldwin "for the inhabitants of the township of New Canaan and Spencer," Aug. 27, 1768, *ibid.*, XXIV, 117.

36. "The Proprietors Book . . . of Spencer Township, 1757–1772," MS No. 12379, New York State Library, Albany.

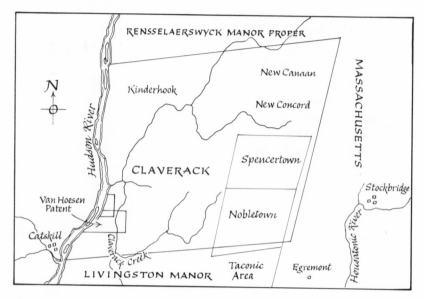

The Squatter Towns in Claverack in the 1760s. Adjusted from Cadwallader Colden's map, 1771, New York Colonial Manuscripts, Land Papers, 1642–1803, XXIX, 56, New York State Library, Albany. (Drawn by Richard J. Stinely.)

in their favor because of the legal maxim stating that "the land belongs to its bona fide tillers."[37] Their optimism was not wholly unrealistic, since their cause was entwined with that of Colden, Kempe, and the like.

Colden could not have agreed more with the squatters' political analysis. His pet view of New York provincial politics was that the major branches of government (council, assembly, and courts), under the firm control of the landed magnates and their allies (lawyers), would never tolerate any measure adversely affecting their land titles. The outcome of the Claverack controversy merely confirmed his thesis. Nevertheless, he was upset by Monckton's decision, which was a jolt not only to his cause but also to his ego, for he had placed his prestige on the line with two of his children in challenging the Van Rensselaer pretensions. Known among the colonists as a "bloody tough" man, Colden would not be easily intimidated by such a setback.[38] Rather, he took this demonstration of the power of the landed interests as proof that his cause against the great patents was all the more justifiable and necessary.

37. "The Case of the Inhabitants of New Canaan," N.Y. Land Papers, XXXIII, 6.
38. John Watts to Robert Monckton, June 1, 1765, Aspinwall Papers, II, 572–573.

From June 1763 to November 1765, Colden, again as acting governor, initiated a series of antiproprietary measures. Because of their impact on the manors, we must give them an extensive examination. In
September 1763, he reminded the earl of Egremont, secretary of state for
the Southern Department, of the standing instruction issued a decade
earlier that required the governor to "enquire" into the state of large
patents and to take, if necessary, "all lawful methods" for revoking any
"exorbitant, irregular and unconditional Grants."[39] But, he continued,
without creating a special fund and appointing an independent judge for
the purpose, the governor could not possibly carry out the mandate.
Hamstrung by the powerful landed grandees, Colden was convinced that
nothing short of direct intervention by the home government would
bring his antagonists to their knees.

This time Colden had reason to hope that his campaign would be
endorsed by his superiors at home. Great Britain had emerged from the
Seven Years' War victorious but with enormous debts—£137,000,000.
In 1764 the British government under the leadership of George Grenville
enacted the Revenue Act. The ministry was reported to be contemplating
a stamp tax and a tax on land and black slaves. These revenue measures
were designed in part to finance tighter control of the colonies, some of
which, in the eyes of British statesmen, had been perverse during the war
in trading with the enemy and flaunting the navigation laws. It occurred
to Colden that the new policy paralleled his own reform objectives—
weakening the antiprerogative elements in New York and obtaining larger
revenue from quitrents. He also probably drew some encouragement
from the noticeable willingness of the British government to redress Indian grievances, especially after London had been stung by the widespread disaffection of Indian tribes from its interest during the French
and Indian War and more recently by Pontiac's Rebellion. One of their
grievances concerned the lands that, they contended, the white men had
years ago stolen from their ancestors.[40] The pro-Indian policy was mani-

---

39. "Representation of the Lords of Trade to the King," July 5, 1753, *N.Y. Col. Docs.*,
VI, 788–791; Cadwallader Colden to earl of Egremont, Sept. 14, 1763, *ibid.*, VII, 549.

40. As for the contemplated land tax, see Robert R. Livingston to father, Robert, Jr.,
June 15 and July 13, 1764, Robert R. Livingston Coll., Box 1, N.-Y. Hist. Soc. The targets
of the Indian grievances were many. Among them were the patents of Claverack, Kayaderosseras (Queensborough), Cannojohary, Oriskene, and a patent granted to Albany city
for the lands at Fort Hunter. In the 1760s, the list expanded to include Philipse's Highland
Patent, Rumbout Patent, and Beekman Patent in Dutchess County. James De Lancey to
Lords of Trade, July 22, 1754, Lords of Trade to Lords Justice, Apr. 22, 1755, William
Johnson to Lords of Trade, July 21, 1755, Sept. 10, 1756, June 5, 1760, and Nov. 13,
1763, Lords of Trade to Cadwallader Colden, July 10, 1764, *N.Y. Col. Docs.*, VI, 850,

fested in the general order from the king in December 1761 requiring
that unextinguished native claims be honored and, more particularly, in
royal orders in 1756 and again in 1764 to vacate the old Kayaderosseras
Patent (256,000 acres) and the Albany city patent at Fort Hunter in favor
of the Mohawk tribe. As for the method, the Board of Trade advised the
governor to apply to the colonial assembly, as Bellomont and Cornbury
had done in 1699 and 1705. Should this method fail, Parliament would
intervene. Colden welcomed the policy with enthusiasm, because the
"effectual redressing" of the Indian complaints, in the words of Sir William Johnson, "strikes at the Interest of some of the wealthiest, and most
leading men in this Province."[41]

Colden's strategy of bringing about a direct confrontation between
the king and the great landowners was first revealed in his intrigue with
the veteran British officers and soldiers of the French and Indian War. By
virtue of a royal proclamation of October 7, 1763, they were entitled to a
bounty of unpatented land—2,000 acres for a lieutenant, 3,000 acres for
a major, and a lesser amount for a soldier—anywhere in British North
America. In New York, however, many of them found it difficult to
locate "a spot free from Indians or patentees claim."[42] Colden saw a
good opportunity in the plight of the officers to resume his attack on the
claim of John Van Rensselaer. With the promise of his support, in the
summer of 1764 he easily persuaded them to submit petitions to him for
a grant of 41,750 acres within the disputed patents of Claverack and
Westenhook. William Smith, Jr., and D. C. Mathews, agents for the
affected patents, quickly entered a caveat against the petitioners.[43] Again,
Kempe defended the challengers in the hearing. But the council turned

---

949, 962, VII, 129, 433, 572–576, 633–634; petition of Muhheckkanunuck or River
Indians, June 29, 1754, N.Y. Land Papers, XV, 110; William Johnson to Colden, Feb. 20,
Mar. 19, and Nov. 6, 1761, and Oct. 9, 1764, *Colden Papers*, VI, 11–14, 17–19, 87, 365;
Colden to Johnson, Mar. 7, 1761, *Colden Letter Books*, I, 70.

41. The quoted remarks were Sir William Johnson's, but Colden would have agreed
with them wholeheartedly. Johnson to Lords of Trade, July 22, 1754, Lords of Trade to
Governor Hardy and James De Lancey, Mar. 19, 1756, and to Colden, July 10, 1764, *N.Y.
Col. Docs.*, VII, 77–79, 633. It should be noted that the development of the new Indian
policy owed much to the efforts of Johnson, who had built his fortune and career on his
friendship with the Six Nations. James De Lancey to Lords of Trade, July 22, 1754, *ibid.*,
VI, 850; Sir Charles Hardy's speech to the General Assembly, July 6, 1756, and Colden's
speech, Oct. 2, 1764, *Journal of General Assembly*, II, 497, 762.

42. John Watts to Robert Monckton, Oct. 11 and Nov. 6, 1764, *Aspinwall Papers*, II,
535, 538.

43. Petition of Lt. John Campbell and others, June 22, 1764, N.Y. Land Papers, XVII,
149. For the other petitions, see *ibid.*, 153, 154, 156, 161, VIII, 32, 33, 37, 108, 129,
XIX, 1, 2, 172. The tract in question was the same one that the Bebee group had earlier
petitioned for. No evidence exists, however, that the squatters had been consulted in

down the petitioners on the same grounds as earlier—that "it did not appear with sufficient clearness that the Lands were vacant." Colden then induced the distraught veterans to "carry their application to his Majesty." For his part, he urged the Board of Trade to favorably consider their case, which was drawn up by the attorney general.[44] It is noteworthy that Colden recommended the appeal procedure to the veterans although not to the squatters in Claverack. He probably calculated that the veterans could serve his purpose better than rustics: the king could not possibly let the warriors down.

Colden's war against Claverack did not end with the veteran officers and soldiers. In the early spring of 1765, the Board of Trade directed Colden to assist Lords Ilchester and Holland (Henry Fox, the father of Charles James Fox) and their associates, who had earlier received a royal mandamus for 60,000 acres, in locating their lands in New York.[45] Their preference was for land on either the Mohawk or the Hudson rivers between New York and Albany. In his May report to the Board of Trade, Colden called its attention to Claverack as a possibility for the English gentlemen, while insisting that there was "no Land on the Mohawk River" not already patented or claimed by the Indians. The way in which he described the history and current state of the disputed Claverack Patent leaves no doubt as to his design. To assure that the controversial land was large enough to satisfy every challenger, he pointed out that Van Rensselaer's right was only 23,000 acres out of the pretended 170,000 acres. As further inducement, he dangled what seemed to be an irresistible bait: "If some Persons could obtain a Grant . . . of that large Tract claim'd by Ranslaer, they could make considerable proffits of it by pedling it out in small Tracts to poor People."[46] As might be expected, the English nobles did as Colden hoped, locating their lands in Claverack.[47]

Meanwhile, Colden fanned out his offensive to several other patents

---

advance by the veteran officers or by Colden about their move. Caveat, June 24, 1764, *ibid.*, XVII, 151.

44. In his correspondence with the home government, Colden made it appear that the veterans had initiated all these actions. On the contrary, I would argue that he was the principal plotter and that they were merely following his suggestions. Colden to Lords of Trade, Oct. 11, 1764, and May 31, 1765, *Colden Letter Books*, I, 377–378, II, 8–12.

45. N.Y. Land Papers, XVIII, 1; Lords of Trade to Cadwallader Colden, Mar. 6, 1765, *N.Y. Col. Docs.*, VII, 707–708.

46. Cadwallader Colden to Lords of Trade and earl of Hillsborough, May 31, 1765, and to Lords of Trade, June 7, 1765, and Colden to William Johnson, May 31, 1765, *Colden Letter Books*, II, 5–9, 13–14, 12.

47. *Journal of the Commissioners for Trade and Plantations from January 1764 to December 1767* . . . (London, 1936), 218.

as well. Sometime in 1764, he and Sir William Johnson sent two Mohawk Indians to London at government expense so that they could present their case against Kayaderosseras Patent.[48] In October when the assembly rejected his request for a bill vacating the patent, Colden ordered the attorney general to enter a *scire facias* against it. The titles of Hardenburgh (about 150,000 acres) in Ulster and Orange counties were also earmarked for prosecution. He was particularly venomous against "an enormous claim" of the Minisink proprietors, who were reported to be harassing the "really poor industrious Farmers."[49] According to his account, after these squatters had improved the lands and defended them against the "Savages" and "as soon as" the peace arrived, these "avaricious ingrossers" (the patentees) tried to rob them of "their lands and all the Fruits of their Labour." On their behalf, in late 1764 Colden recommended the actual settlers to the Board of Trade for the "Kings protection and favour." Subsequently, he ordered Kempe to sue the proprietors for the usurpation of the king's land.[50]

Yet, Colden was skeptical that his prosecution of the great patents would be successful, given the proprietary orientation of the supreme court, which functioned as the appellate bench in common law cases. Overcoming this legal impediment seemed essential, and he reasoned that the task could be accomplished only by allowing an appeal on the merit of a cause from that jurisdiction to the governor as chancellor in the council and ultimately to the king in the privy council. How much importance he attached to the appeal procedure can be surmised from his suggestion in November 1764 to the Board of Trade that the "validity" of any patents and their "true " boundaries might be "judicially determined; especially if the Right of Appeal to his Majesty in his Privy Council be supported."[51] At the same time, he must have been well aware of the difficulties ahead, for the landlords had been waging a battle

---

48. "Account of Expenses for the Two Mohawk Indians Returned from London," May 1765, *Colden Papers*, IX, 193.

49. Cadwallader Colden to earl of Hillsborough, May 31, 1765, *Colden Letter Books*, II, 5–8.

50. Cadwallader Colden to Lords of Trade, Nov. 1764 and Apr. 13, 1765, *ibid.*, I, 403, 477–479. But before the writ was issued, the Minisink proprietors submitted to Colden's blackmail by taking out a new patent for the disputed land at the official rate of quitrent. Colden proudly reported to his superiors about his achievement: "This is one Instance of what may be done by vigorous measures when at any time they become requisite." Colden to Lords of Trade, June 7, 1765, *ibid.*, II, 14. For the history of the Minisink Patent, see Armand Shelby LaPotin, "The Minisink Patent: A Study in Eighteenth Century New York" (Ph.D. diss., University of Wisconsin, 1974).

51. *Colden Letter Books*, I, 404.

against the court of chancery for decades. They detested it as an instrument of prerogative that could be used to inquire into their patents and to recover arrears in quitrents.

Possibly with the thought of setting a precedent, Colden intervened in the civil suit of *Forsey v. Cunningham.* On October 31, 1764, he issued a writ for the defendant, ordering the chief justice to bring the proceedings before him, although the case had been decided for the plaintiff. Such a challenge to the finality of a jury verdict merely by gubernatorial fiat was unprecedented. The suit itself was of minor consequence, but the issue of appeal was not. Many colonial lawyers publicly denounced Colden's move as an attack on the jury system. But the great proprietors perceived it more correctly as a thrust at their land titles. According to Colden, "They know what must be the consequence in suits depending between them and other the Kings Tenants, or the consequence of Informations of Intrusion, which may be justly brought against them etc. in case the merits of the Case be brought before the King and Council."[52]

In April 1765, several months before the arrival of a new governor, Colden made another move against the landed interest. He urged the Board of Trade to disallow an act of 1762 pertaining to quitrents and to the partition of large patents that he had earlier approved only with "reluctancy" and "many amendments."[53] Those holding large tracts in joint tenancy badly wanted this piece of general legislation in order to remove legal obstacles to dividing land as a preliminary step toward its settlement. But Colden argued against the act on the grounds that it would only make it easier for proprietors to defraud the king by liberally extending boundaries. Since his appointment as surveyor general, Colden

52. *Ibid.,* I, 396–397, 406, 420, 446–447, 452, 455, 457–458, 459, 462, 468, 470; John Watts to Robert Monckton, Nov. 6, 10, and Dec. 10, 1764, William Smith, Jr., to Robert Monckton, Nov. 5, 1764, *Aspinwall Papers,* II, 536–537, 542–543, 545–546, 539–542, also, 547, 549–550, 552–553, 554–558. The best account of the legal aspects of the Forsey-Cunningham controversy is Herbert A. Johnson, "George Harison's Protest: New Light on Forsey versus Cunningham," *N.Y. History,* L (1969), 61–82. See also Milton M. Klein, "Prelude to Revolution in New York: Jury Trials and Judicial Tenure," *WMQ,* 3d Ser., XVII (1960), 439–462; Julius Goebel, Jr., "The Courts and the Law in Colonial New York," in David H. Flaherty, ed., *Essays in the History of Early American Law* (Chapel Hill, N.C., 1969), 265–270; Mark, *Agrarian Conflicts,* 100–102. Very significantly, John Watts, one of the Cortlandt Manor proprietors, argued that Colden's efforts in the matter of appeal were "more detested" by the colonists than the Stamp Act. *Aspinwall Papers,* II, 579–580.

53. John Watts to Robert Monckton, Dec. 29, 1763, *Aspinwall Papers,* II, 506–507; Colden to Lords of Trade, Apr. 13, 1765, *Colden Letter Books,* I, 477–479; Kim, "New Look at the Great Landlords," *WMQ,* 3d Ser., XXVII (1970), 593–595.

had consistently maintained this position. Nonetheless, his renewed criticism of the legislation at this particular time—after three years of silence —was significant. It must have seemed pointless to him to allow the partition of the "irregular" patents while he was trying at the same time to prosecute them.

Colden's antiproprietary campaign, coupled with the unextinguished Indian claims, if unchecked, would have seriously endangered the ancient land titles. Since none of the patents was completely free of defects and conflicting claims, and able to stand close scrutiny, the proprietors in general were extremely nervous. In 1764 John Van Rensselaer found it necessary to hire one Mr. Hansen of London as his agent—quite an expensive proposition—to defend his claim at the seat of the empire.[54] The following year, Stephen Van Rensselaer of Rensselaerswyck proper leased out on unusually liberal terms a 50,000-acre tract, an area that came to be known as Stephentown, to twenty-three western Massachusetts families. The patroon thus hoped to avert the kind of violent confrontation with the Yankees that had convulsed the Claverack domain. In June the Minisink proprietors succumbed to Colden's threat by taking out a new patent for the disputed area at a higher quitrent.[55] In September the Kayaderosseras proprietors offered a quitclaim on some part of their land to the Indians as a gesture of compromise.[56]

The apparent indifference of other individual landowners, however, was belied by their fierce collective endeavor to protect their interests. A dramatic illustration of this was the formation of an alliance in 1763 between the two traditional antagonists, John Van Rensselaer and the proprietors of Westenhook Patent. Faced with a common menace to their overlapping claims to the area east of Kinderhook, they agreed to "compromise" their old differences and unite their two titles for the sake of mutual defense.[57] In general, the landed men in the province believed

---

54. *Journal of the Commissioners for Trade, 1764 to 1767*, 22.

55. Samuel Ten Broeck to Abraham Ten Broeck, Mar. 24, 1767, Ten Broeck Family Papers, Box 3, Albany Institute of History and Art, Albany, N.Y. For Stephentown settlers and deeds, see Deed Books 9 and 10, *passim*, Albany County Clerk's Office, Albany, N.Y.; *N.-Y. Gaz.; and Wkly. Mercury*, June 23, 1775; Cadwallader Colden to Lords of Trade, June 7, 1765, *Colden Letter Books*, II, 13–14.

56. William Johnson to Lords of Trade, Sept. 28, 1765, *N.Y. Col. Docs.*, VII, 765; Gen. Thomas Gage to earl of Hillsborough, Aug. 17, 1768, Clarence Edwin Carter, ed., *The Correspondence of General Thomas Gage with the Secretaries of State, 1763–1775* (New Haven, Conn., 1931–1933), I, 184.

57. "Copy of Agreement between Collo. Rensselaer and the Westenhook Patentees, 1763," Miscellaneous Manuscripts, Westenhook, N.-Y. Hist. Soc.; A.O. 12/30, 120–123, 46–47, 125–126, P.R.O.

that the precedent of revoking a crown grant would "render all Property insecure." Through the assembly, council, courts, and newspapers, they articulated their irritation with Colden and with the increasingly vocal Indian complaints. They opposed the "old man" in everything he did and advocated. They also publicly ridiculed, scorned, and humiliated him. Finally, they succeeded in blocking him in the matter of appeals.[58] In the course of just three years as acting governor, he turned himself into a hated and forlorn political figure, estranged from his own council and briefly even from Kempe. The language of opposition was always couched in the traditional rights of Englishmen and general welfare of the people, but this rhetoric should not obfuscate the underlying issue of contention, the survival of the ancient titles.

At the end of 1765, with the arrival of Sir Henry Moore, the new governor, Colden retired to his country estate without achieving his major objective. Yet, the impact of his reform efforts and of British pro-Indian policy was deeply felt in provincial society. In rejecting the recommendation of the Board of Trade that Kayaderosseras Patent be vacated, the anxious assembly warned in October 1764 that "an easy Attention to Indian claims of Lands long since patented, has a natural tendency to excite new and repeated complaints, from a People who rendered themselves Indigent."[59] The domino effect that the assembly anticipated would follow from the pro-Indian measure was also expected to follow from Colden's antiproprietary policy. In fact, the distinction between the alleged white and Indian victims of the great patents is immaterial, since, with few exceptions, it was the white victims—land-hungry people from New England—who transformed the dormant Indian grievances into a hot political and social issue. Encouraged by the official disfavor toward the great patents, landjobbers and squatters sought out the Indian proprietors to vouch for fraudulent land deals perpetrated by whites, and pored over old, dusty patents, deeds, and other land papers to find any title irregularities and defects. A contemporary summed up this rising contentious spirit: "In the Land Fever contagion now prevalent we must expect applications where there is the least prospect of a vacancy." He and others blamed New Englanders for this turn.[60]

58. *Journal of General Assembly*, II, 764, 806; O'Callaghan, ed., *Calendar of Historical Manuscripts*, II, 752, 755, 757; Cadwallader Colden to William Johnson, Nov. 19, 1764, Colden to Lords of Trade, Jan. 22, 1765, *Colden Letter Books*, I, 406, 446–447, 452.

59. *Journal of General Assembly*, II, 764.

60. James Hamilton to William Johnson, Mar. 19, 1754, *William Johnson Papers*, I, 396–398; William Johnson to Cadwallader Colden, Feb. 20, 1761, *Colden Papers*, VI,

The Yankee farmers were aggressive, leveling, self-righteous, and, above all, tenacious, but their challenge to the powerful landed magnates would not have persisted as long as it did had they not been encouraged by signs of actual or imagined official endorsement. Whether armed with Indian deeds or not, they and some of their New York supporters were deluded by the governor's antiproprietary rhetoric and activities and the king's pro-Indian statements into thinking that their cause was basically identical with Colden's cause and with the crown's. Colden had always argued that the prerogative was "oppressed by the great landowners." So were they, they imagined. Excited by a sense of legitimacy, the small farmers became ever more defiant. In 1765 when John Van Rensselaer brought ejectment actions in the supreme court against several squatters in New Canaan and Spencertown, the "proprietors" of the latter town solemnly resolved at their meeting of November 28 that "we will Defend our Lands against other claimers" and chose Ensign John Dean as the agent to "represent our case at New York or Else where in Defence of our Lands."[61] Two months earlier, Samuel Monrow, the principal organizer of squatters against the Philipse's Highland Patent who was subsequently incarcerated on charges of instigating the Wappinger Indians, protested his confinement to Kempe by asserting that the attorney general had "no Legal Authority for such a Prosecution," and then threatened:

I shou'd glad of your Imediate answer, as I have all my Proceedings ready to send home to the King and Council as well as the Lords Comissionrs of Trade, this Step I would not Chuse to take if matters can be Settl'd here without Prejudice to either Party, for if the affair is Represented in its proper light, its no more than Probable that some of his Majesty's officers may be Remov'd from their Employment in this Colony as their Proceedings is absolutely contrary to his Majesty's Proclamation of 1761 which was Republished here by order of his Honor the Lieutenant Govenor [Colden].[62]

However, the provincial system through which the squatters tried to obtain justice repeatedly proved to be unresponsive to their "legitimate"

---

11–14; Catharyna Brett to William Johnson, Aug. 26, 1762, *ibid.*, 190–192; Henry Moore to earl of Shelburne, Dec. 22, 1766, *N.Y. Col. Docs.*, VII, 885–886; William Smith, Jr., to Philip Schuyler, Mar. 21, 1767, and Nov. 27, 1772, Schuyler Papers, Boxes 23 and 24; Grant, *Memoirs of an American Lady*, 290–291.

61. "The Proprietors Book . . . of Spencer Township, 1757–1772," MS No. 12379, 11, N.Y. State Lib.

62. Samuel Monrow to John Tabor Kempe, Oct. 3, 1765, Unsorted Legal MSS, Kempe Papers.

demands. When they thought that they had exhausted legal means, only one alternative appeared open to them—violence, which they finally took with reluctance.

## Squatters versus Proprietors in Dutchess County

The so-called Great Rebellion of 1766 began not in Claverack or Livingston Manor but in Philipse's Highland Patent and the adjoining area in Dutchess County. Here, as elsewhere, the conflict between farmer and landlord was primarily over land. The question of lease tenure remained a secondary issue for a long time. As in the two northern manors, the rebel strongholds lay in the easternmost section of the patent, where title disputes were endemic. The history of the contention over the area seems to hold the key to the origins and nature of the rebellion.

Underlying the controversy in the mid-eighteenth century was the ambiguous eastern terminus of Philipse's Highland Patent (granted in 1697) and Beekman Patent (granted in 1703). These patents were supposed to extend to the Connecticut boundary, defined in the 1683 agreement as a line running at a distance of twenty miles at all points from the "serpentine" course of the Hudson River. The agreement also provided for a compensatory tract to be granted by Connecticut to New York for the lands the latter surrendered on Long Island Sound. If the colonies had followed up the agreement with surveying and other necessary measures for a final settlement, the eastern borders of the patents would have been spared subsequent troubles. Meanwhile, Connecticut gave two grants near the border, one to New Fairfield in 1707 and the other to Ridgefield the following year. Settlers with deeds from the towns pushed their way across the boundary, thus encroaching upon some sections of the great estates. To further complicate the situation, the two colonies drew up a new agreement in 1725, under which a straight line was drawn from a set point in the north twenty miles from the river to another point in the south at an equal distance from the river.[63] Finally confirmed in 1731, this partition (the present boundary of the states of New York and Connecticut) moved the boundary at some places a mile or so westward

---

63. William Kempe to Mr. Fargreaharson, c. 1753, Kempe Papers, Box 14 (on Oblong). For the discussion of the Oblong question, I am indebted to Dr. Philip J. Schwarz, who kindly let me read his paper "Faction, Fraud, and Fragmentation: The Connecticut–New York Boundary Dispute, 1725–1735," delivered at the Duquesne History Forum, Oct. 1973. See also *Report on Boundaries*, I, 58–62.

and at most places a mile or two or more eastward according to the turns of the Hudson River, thus creating the compensatory tract of about 62,000 acres known as the Equivalent Lands or the Oblong.[64]

Scarcely had the cession occurred when several rival groups sprang up, each pretending to some portion or even the whole of the Oblong. One group was headed by the duke of Chandos (James Brydges) and Sir Joseph Eyles, powerful English politicos who received a patent from the crown for the entire tract on May 15, 1731, the day after the transfer took place. Challenging this royal patent was a group organized by the Equivalent Land Company, including the Ridgefield proprietors and such provincial leaders as George Clarke, William Smith, Sr., Cadwallader Colden, and James Alexander, that held a provincial patent (June 8, 1731) for 50,000 acres of the tract.[65] In addition, the owners of Philipse's Highland Patent and Beekman Patent considered the "Hoveout land" or "Cast out Land," consisting of about 12,000 acres that the company had left out of the Oblong, to be theirs. Finally, there were the people of New Fairfield, who claimed "a prior grant" of 10,000 acres of the Oblong, which, for the most part, would have taken in the lands claimed by the company but also extended to some part of the Hoveout (see the sketch on p. 369).[66]

By dint of their "Riches, power and Influence in the Country," the Equivalent Land Company patentees soon emerged as the de facto owners of the 50,000 acres, ruining every attempt on the part of the English claimants to make good the royal patent.[67] By the 1740s, the colonists assumed that the holders of the royal patent had dropped their claim. A number of poor people, or, in the words of James Alexander, "Run-

64. Cadwallader Colden stated that the boundary was about 21 miles from the Hudson River with some variations at different points. *N.Y. Col. Docs.*, IV, 628–630; *Report on Boundaries*, I, 230–231.

65. Patent to Thomas Hyat and others, June 8, 1731, Patent Book 11: 4–18, Office of the Secretary of State of New York, Albany; James Alexander to Cadwallader Colden, June 23, July 3, 7, 1731, Mar. 23, Apr. 24, 30, 1732, *Colden Papers*, II, 20–21, 23, 59, 62, 61.

66. William Kempe to Mr. Fargreaharson, c. 1753, Kempe Papers, Box 14; Charles Clinton to George Clinton, Dec. 18, 1752, George Clinton Papers, William L. Clements Library, Ann Arbor, Mich.

67. The English patentees tried to bring a chancery action against the Equivalent Land Company in 1735. Two years later, Francis Harrison, their agent, also endeavored to stop the surveying and other proceedings of the company. All these actions turned out to be futile. After that, the English claim remained dormant. "Answer of the Proprietors of the Equivalent Lands to the Attorney Generals Bills in Chancery before Governor Cosby," in "New York and Connecticut Boundary, Oblong Papers, 1733," No. 1, BV-N.Y. State-Boundaries, N.-Y. Hist. Soc.; petition of Francis Harrison, May 3, 1737, N.Y. Land Papers, XII, 82; Lords of Trade to Queen Caroline, Aug. 28, 1735, *N.Y. Col. Docs.*, VI, 34–35; *Colden Papers*, II, 128–131, 23, 24–26, 60–61, 62, 65–71, 71–72, 132–133, 140–141;

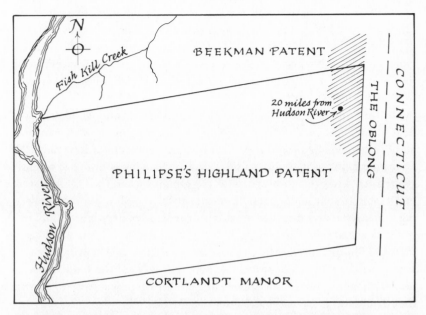

**Sketch of the Location of "Hoveout"** (Shaded). Adjusted from "Hampton Map of the Upper Patent of Philipsburg, 1757," Manuscript No. 11068, New York State Library, Albany. (Drawn by Richard J. Stinely.)

aways and thieves" who had settled under the English title, were the worst victims of this turn of events. Some of them attorned themselves to the company as tenants at will, and many others, thrown out by violence, moved into what they considered to be the vacant part of the Hoveout, hoping that they would be left alone. But the land they picked out was that claimed by the Philipses and the Beekmans. To make their situation worse, in the period from 1750 through 1752, William Smith, Sr., one of the Oblong patentees and the attorney general, and three others including Governor George Clinton took out patents for 8,000 acres of the Hoveout.[68] Undoubtedly, this also cut into the claims of Fairfield people such as Samuel Monrow and the Beekman and Philipse proprietors.

---

Lewis Morris to James Alexander, Aug. 9, 25, 1735, Rutherford Collection, II, 127–129, N.-Y. Hist. Soc.; James Alexander to Cadwallader Colden, Feb. 21, 1732, James Alexander Papers, Box 47, N.-Y. Hist. Soc.; "Advertizement," *N.-Y. Gaz.*, Oct. 25, 1731, Nov. 8, 1732, Feb. 5, 1733.

68. James Alexander to Cadwallader Colden, Mar. 23, 1732, *Colden Papers*, II, 59; William Kempe to Mr. Fargreaharson, c. 1753, Kempe Papers, Box 14; N.Y. Land Papers, XIV, 65, 70, 78, 68, 156; Vincent Mathews to George Clinton, Dec. 18, 1752, Clinton Papers.

Already in 1743, Henry Beekman was taking steps to protect his estate in the Oblong area either by giving the willing squatters leases or by evicting the recalcitrant ones.[69] But from about 1749 on, frequent violence riddled his back land, where a "Drove of Banditt Rovers" made "great Havek" and harassed his loyal tenants. He wrote his agent Henry Livingston to tell "our Tennants, that if any Incrochment hapen to be made, they must Destroy the same, So Soon it be don and will defend and Bear them harmless." The squatters, apparently united with Monrow and "his party," answered the landlord with "Showers of Law Suets."[70] In the meantime, the squatter ranks were swollen by an influx of recently evicted tenants from those parts of the Oblong where proprietors were more interested in selling land "as fast as they could" rather than collecting a meager rental income. Jonathan Brown, a country lawyer and one of the new Fairfield claimers, and Monrow cajoled some tenants of Beekman and Philipse on the Hoveout to join their party with a promise of fee farms. In 1752 Brown asserted publicly that he held the land "under a new fairfield Right and not under Philips." Beekman was upset: "So that they Trump up more and more tytells against us."[71]

The picture changed in November 1752 when William Kempe, the newly appointed attorney general and a friend of the duke of Newcastle, arrived with a commission from the English patentees to reassert their nearly forgotten title to the Oblong.[72] He was quick to acquaint several of the New York patentees with his mission and urged that they make some concessions. But the proposal met with "great contempt." The

69. The first reference to Beekman's trouble with the squatters appears in his letter to Gilbert Livingston dated Dec. 12, 1743, touching on his ejectment suit against Samuel Monrow. Beekman Papers, N.-Y. Hist. Soc. According to William Kempe's account of the New Fairfield right, Monrow, Jonathan Brown, and three or four others held some kind of lease of "a gore of land [that] lyes betwixt Mr. Philips Patent and the Oblong." The grantors of the lease were the original purchasers of the New Fairfield township named "one Minor and Michell," from whom descended all the rights to the disputed land. See Kempe's notes on the Fairfield claims, Kempe Papers, Box 6. This clarification of Monrow's status is helpful in understanding the causes of the 1766 rebellion in Dutchess County, because he became the "first projector" or the "first Cause" of the upheaval. Depositions of Ebenezer Weed and James Birdsell, Aug. 6, 1766, in Irving Mark and Oscar Handlin, eds., "Land Cases in Colonial New York, 1765–1767: The King v. William Prendergast," *New York University Law Quarterly Review*, XIX (1941–1942), 177, 190.

70. Henry Beekman to Henry Livingston, Jan. 16, Aug. 16, 31, Dec. 8, 1749, Feb. 10 and Dec. 29, 1750, Mar. 20 and Oct. 10, 1751, Beekman Papers.

71. Henry Beekman to Henry Livingston, Apr. 7, 1752, Dutchess County History Society, *Year Book*, VI (1921), 38.

72. William Kempe obtained the office through the duke of Newcastle, secretary of state for the Southern Department. Catherine Snell Crary, "The American Dream: John Tabor Kempe's Rise from Poverty to Riches," *WMQ*, 3d Ser., XIV (1957), 177; George Clinton to Sir Henry Clinton, Jan. 19 to 23, 1752, Clinton Papers.

story of the breakdown of the negotiations rapidly traveled to the country. The "harassed and oppressed" squatters in the Hoveout—the Fairfield
claimers and the former tenants of the English—saw in this a glimmer of
hope: with the help of the powerful official and his political connections
at home, they might defeat the provincial landowners and achieve their
ultimate goal, the acquisition of freeholds. Indeed, they were then so
desperate that they would have allied with the devil to defend the lands in
which they had invested so much sweat. Kempe's New York office was
soon swamped with visitors and letters from these farmers inquiring
about his intentions and begging for his "protection." Relating affairs to
one of the English proprietors in the spring of 1753, he stated, "There
was scarce a day for 4 months together that I had not 6 or 7 of them with
me." Kempe realized that these men, who actually possessed the land and
were willing to fight all the New York landowners—the Philipses and the
Beekmans included—provided him with an excellent opportunity to establish "a footing there." From this common interest against the provincial patents, a defense pact developed between Kempe and twenty-eight
or more squatters. Under the agreement, they would hold their possessions as tenants at will with no rental obligations to Sir Joseph Eyles and
the other English patentees, and in return Kempe would defend them free
of charge "if they should be served with ejectments." In addition, Kempe
"encouraged several people" who had been evicted elsewhere to resettle
the Hoveout upon his "assurance of assistance and protection." He was
more interested in this land of about 10,000 acres than any other part of
the Oblong because he privately believed that it belonged neither to the
Philipses and Beekmans nor even to his English clients.[73] Significantly,
one of these tenants, Mathew Fuller, had been "most active" in the anti-
Beekman agitation in the late 1740s, and at least three of them, namely,
Thomas Gage, Philip Philipse, and Elisha Calkin, would appear as lieutenants of Samuel Monrow in the 1766 rebellion.

As conflicting claims continued to arise in the area, some hitherto
loyal Beekman tenants became rebellious and refused to pay their rents.
Worse still for Beekman, in early 1753 the Philipse heirs of Highland
Patent began an ejectment suit against squatters including four Beekman
tenants. The chagrined landlord remarked: "So that now their is oppen
ware proclamed. and Each Side shoe Title."[74] Basically a man of mild

73. William Kempe to Mr. Fargreaharson, c. 1753, Kempe Papers, Box 14.
74. Henry Beekman to Henry Livingston, Jan. 9, 1753, Beekman Papers; Jonathan
Prosser, Sr., and 17 others to John Tabor Kempe, Nov. 10, 1763, Dutchess County Misc.

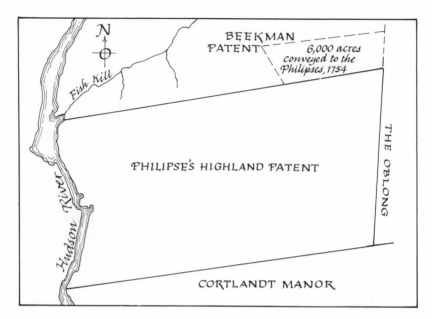

The Beekman Conveyance of 6,000 Acres to the Philipses, 1754. Adjusted from "Hampton Map of the Upper Patent of Philipsburg, 1757," Manuscript No. 11068, New York State Library, Albany. (Drawn by Richard J. Stinely.)

temper, Beekman submitted to the concatenation of pressures. To spare himself further trouble, he yielded to the Philipses in 1754 a stretch of land of about 6,000 acres in the southeastern corner of his domain (see the map above). This conveyance largely explains why his estate re-mained quiet in subsequent years.[75] Meanwhile, the other New York proprietors reacted to the new threat with vigor, either by legal means or by force, whichever seemed to be appropriate to the given situation. But each time, Kempe stood by his new allies. His tough stand surely won him their cheers and, more important, many new converts to the English cause. For instance, in June 1756 one John Wright of the Oblong, upon

MSS, Box 2 (Apr. 16, 1696–Dec. 1772), N.-Y. Hist. Soc.; Patent Book 14: 312–315, Office of N.Y. Sec. of State.

75. For Beekman's gentle disposition, see Beekman to Gilbert Livingston, Dec. 3, 1745, Beekman Papers. In this letter, while discussing the controversy over militia commis-sions in Dutchess County, he stated, " I would act the conscious peacefull part, for it seem that the Sead of Discord is very prevellant, and would reather suffer small Indignity than Inflame the Community." "Hampton Map of the Upper Patent of Philipsburg, 1757," MS No. 11068, N.Y. State Lib. For the acreage of the Beekman conveyance, see the memorial of Beverly Robinson, Dec. 11, 1783, A.O. 12/21, 148, 160, 161; Patent Book 15: 351–355, Office of N.Y. Sec. of State.

learning that some New York patentees had rented his possession out to someone else, wrote to Kempe soliciting his advice and protection. In the same letter, he also conveyed the wishes of his neighbor named Jacob Doty to "come under the old England patent if there by any Encouragement of his being protected."[76] It appears that Kempe acted directly as the guardian of the squatters and also, through his support of their leader, Samuel Monrow, provided help with many other problems.[77]

But when Kempe died in July 1759, the high hopes of the squatters were shattered as suddenly as they had risen. In the next few years, bereft of their patron, they were subject to merciless persecution by the New York proprietors, who lost no time in pressing their claims. It was not, however, on the 50,000-acre tract controlled by the Equivalent Land Company or on the 8,000-acre patent of William Smith and others where the difficulties persisted, but in the easternmost part of Philipse's Highland Patent, including the small strip of land the Philipse heirs had acquired from Beekman.[78] More specifically, the contested area was in and around the Hoveout, which William Kempe had considered to be vested in the crown and thus vacant and which the Philipses and the Beekmans claimed.

Shortly after the death of William Kempe, the heirs of Frederick Philipse II—Philip Philipse, Roger Morris,[79] and Beverly Robinson—began an effort to consolidate their holdings in the eastern part of their patent known as Lot Numbers 6, 7, 8, and 9 (see the map on p. 374). In 1760 they had Alexander Colden, deputy surveyor general, survey a narrow strip of the controverted land amounting to 4,402 acres and one other small gore of 221 acres. On March 22, 1761, they obtained a patent for these tracts, thus extending their domain all the way to the Oblong at every point.[80] This was done of course at the expense of the squatters (and the New Fairfield claimers) who had been there for the past thirty years, although one of the government's excuses for issuing the patent was to quash the Philipses' pretension to the Oblong proper.

76. John Wright to William Kempe, June 29, 1756, William Kempe Papers, N.-Y. Hist. Soc.

77. Samuel Monrow to William Kempe, Mar. 19, 1754, and Mar. 27, 1755, ibid.

78. This suggests that the squatters on the first two tracts who had attorned to the English patentees made some sort of accommodation with the provincial landowners.

79. Maj. Roger Morris, by his marriage to Mary Philipse in Jan. 1758, became a proprietor of the Highland Patent. G. D. Scull, ed., The Montresor Journals (N.-Y. Hist. Soc., Colls., XIV [New York, 1881], 56), hereafter cited as Montresor Journals.

80. Most, if not all, of the first tract (4,402 acres) was annexed to Robinson's Lot No. 7. This Lot 7 became the center stage of the riots in 1765 and 1766. N.Y. Land Papers, XVI, 22–24; Philipse-Gouverneur Land Titles, fol. 13, Columbia University Library, New York; A.O. 12/21, 148–149.

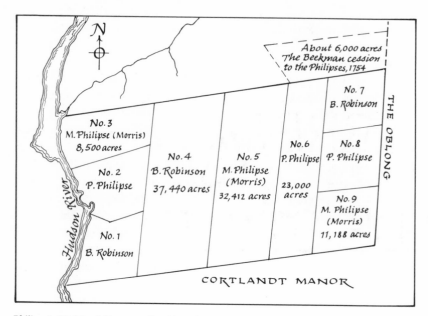

Philipse's Highland Patent as Partitioned among the Philipse Heirs, 1757. Adjusted from "Hampton Map of the Upper Patent of Philipsburg, 1757," Manuscript No. 11068, New York State Library, Albany. (Drawn by Richard J. Stinely.)

Several days later, Beverly Robinson started an ejectment action in the supreme court against Samuel Monrow, whose farm worth £500 straddled both Robinson's Lot Number 7 and the former Beekman tract north of the lot.[81] This suit was followed by five more in that year by the Philipse heirs, all directed against Monrow's associates in the Hoveout. As might be expected, the trials ended with the squatters' defeat. The triumphant Philipses told them to buy "their farms paying mony Down" or "remove immediately." No evidence is available, however, to show that they complied with the demand or that the landowners took any forcible actions against the squatters.[82]

The appearance of stubbornness notwithstanding, it seems that the

81. "Mr. Robinson's Instructions in order to Draw Information," 1765, Unsorted Legal MSS, Kempe Papers; *Beverly Robinson* v. *Samuel Monrow*, Philipse-Gouverneur Land Titles, fol. 7. Monrow had been in possession of the premises since 1733. See Samuel Monrow to John Tabor Kempe, Oct. 8, 1765, Unsorted Legal MSS, Kempe Papers.

82. Minute Book of the Supreme Court of Judicature, 1756–1761, 250, Hall of Records, New York; petition of Thomas Gage and 37 others to the king, Feb. 27, 1764, Dutchess Co. Misc. MSS, Box 2.

basic objective of the distressed farmers during late 1762 and early 1763 was to reach some sort of accommodation with the proprietors. That they tried this course is seen in their bitter complaint against Robinson in 1764 that he "would not Lease the Land to the inhabitants who had lived on it for Near 30 years past" and "whereas if he had gave us the privileges of tenants on Reasonable terms we should have been his tenants." What these "reasonable terms" were is difficult to say, but the squatters would almost certainly have demanded the inclusion of a provision guaranteeing their right to improvements on the soil. Failing to realize their modest wishes, the squatters became as uncompromising as their opponent. From late 1763 on, their frozen position was that the land they were cultivating was vacant, since it "has not as yet Ever been Disposed of or granted to any the Kings Letters patent."[83] In other words, they refused to recognize the Philipses' claim based on the original patent of 1697 or the new patent of 1761 for the Hoveout.

At this stage, the squatters were not entirely without hope that they might be able to redress their grievances within the framework of the provincial system. In November 1763, a group led by Stephen Willcocks (or Willcox) in Beekman Precinct requested John Tabor Kempe, son of William, to investigate their predicament and stressed that their land had been claimed by both the Philipses and Henry Beekman. However, they neglected, perhaps deliberately, to mention the Beekman cession to the Philipses a decade earlier. In February 1764, another group, headed by Thomas Gage, addressed the king, Colden, and Kempe condemning Robinson's gross abuse of their rights and begging the "favor of Justice."[84] The timing and pattern of this petitioning suggest that Willcocks and his associates had been misled by the antiproprietary activities of the colonial officials into believing that they were entitled to the same governmental protection as the squatters in Claverack and Minisink. Colden ignored the petitions, although he sympathized with their case.[85] In practical terms, however, he was in no position to do anything in their favor. In

83. Petition of Jonathan Prosser, Sr., and 17 others to John Tabor Kempe, Nov. 10, 1763, Dutchess Co. Misc. MSS, Box 2.

84. See nn. 82 and 83 above. Willcocks's farm included in the Beekman cession of 1754 to the Philipses was worth £720, not an inconsiderable amount. See a note by Beverly Robinson, 1766, Unsorted Legal MSS, Kempe Papers.

85. In his account of the causes of the "Great Rebellion" of 1766, Colden argued that the Philipses and the Livingstons had "harassed the Farmers in their neighborhood with expensive and ruinous lawsuits." It is extremely significant that Colden noted the landowners' disputes with their *neighboring* farmers and not with *their farmers*. Colden to Mr. Conway, June 24, 1766, *Colden Letter Books*, X, 115.

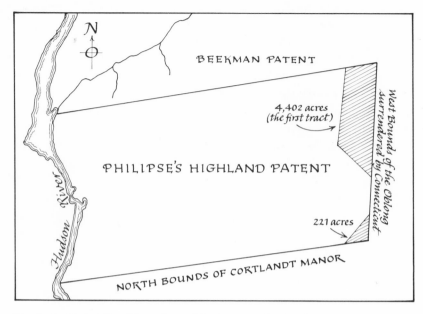

Sketch of a Plot of Two Tracts Covered in the Patent for the Philipse Heirs, March 27, 1761. Adjusted from New York Colonial Manuscripts, Land Papers, 1642–1803, XVI, 24, New York State Library, Albany. (Drawn by Richard J. Stinely.)

the first place, the patenting of the disputed lands to the Philipses in 1761 was done under his authority, and he was therefore legally and morally bound to defend his action. Moreover, being one of the provincial proprietors of the Oblong himself, he was well aware of the repercussions that might follow if he recognized the rights of the squatters (and the New Fairfield claimers), who were the former adherents of the rival English patentees. Colden's own interests were at stake no less than the stability of land titles in the area. If the circumstances had been slightly different, however, he might have backed their cause.

After this frustrating experience, the distraught farmers finally lost faith in the provincial system of justice and found hope in an appeal to the king, a remarkable parallel to Colden's conclusion with respect to land reform. In the spring and early summer of 1764, their major quest was for a means of transforming their interests into an imperial issue worthy of royal attention. This transformation they soon achieved by merging their sagging cause with that of the Wappinger Indians at Stockbridge, Massachusetts, who were the original owners of the lands east of the Hudson River from New York City to "about the middle of Beekman's Patent."[86] The credit for this alliance must go to Samuel Monrow for inducing Daniel Nimham, the thirty-eight-year-old chief of the tribe, to challenge the Philipse titles and to appoint Monrow in November as the sole guardian of the tribal "interests in land." Monrow's task could not have been too difficult, however, since the Indian sachem was already angry with the white men who had taken his ancestral lands, causing his people to be addicted to an "idle strolling life" and barely capable of supporting themselves.[87] Furthermore, Nimham was encouraged by Colden's proclamation in 1762 in accordance with his majesty's instruction, which promised relief for the unextinguished Indian claims in New York. Indeed, Nimham in that year had tried to hold Governor Monckton to the royal promise by complaining about the fraudulent practices of a proprietor of Rumbout Patent (west of Beekman Patent) against the tribal land, but his case received only passing notice.[88]

In August 1764, Nimham issued, on the advice of Monrow, an "advertisement" in which he declared himself to be "the Rightful owner" of Philipse's Highland Patent, except 5,000 acres thereof, and expressed his determination to prosecute, "agreeable to his majestys laws" or even "by application to his majesty," all occupants of the area who did not have a legal conveyance from him.[89] In the next few months, Monrow and his party mounted an intensive public-relations campaign in Dutchess and Westchester counties and even in Connecticut. Copies of Colden's 1762 proclamation on the Indian land claims were nailed up at different places in the patent in order to give "colour" to Nimham's charges, and Monrow made inflammatory speeches constantly harping on the theme that

86. Deposition of Daniel Nimham, Aug. 2, 1762, Columbia Co. Misc. MSS. By this time, the numbers of the Wappingers had been reduced to about 227. See "Statement of a Controversy between Daniel Nimham et al and Philipse Heirs, Mar. 9, 1765," N.Y. Land Papers, XVIII, 128; Philipse-Gouverneur Land Titles, fol. 13, no. 45.

87. An agreement regarding the guardianship of Samuel Monrow, Nov. 17, 1764, Unsorted Legal MSS, Kempe Papers; William Johnson to earl of Shelburne, Jan. 15, 1767, N.Y. Col. Docs., VII, 892.

88. Catharyna Brett to William Johnson, Aug. 26, 1762, Colden Papers, VI, 190–192; Calendar of Council Minutes, 1668–1783, New York State Library Bulletin, No. 58 (Albany, N.Y., 1902), 459; attorney general's report, Aug. 2, 1762, Chalmers Collection, II, 26, N.Y. Pub. Lib. Irving Mark mistakenly treats Nimham's complaint as if it concerned Philipse's Highland Patent. The land in question was Nimham's deceased father's home in Rumbout Patent. Mark, Agrarian Conflicts, 131–132.

89. "Nimhams Advertizement," Aug. 17, 1764, Unsorted Legal MSS, Kempe Papers. In 1767 Nimham argued that his ancestors had granted only 17,480 acres to Adolph Philipse. Philipse-Gouverneur Land Titles, fol. 13, no. 45.

378 Landlord and Tenant in Colonial New York

Adolph Philipse "had never purchased the Land" from the natives for his patent of 1697. The squatters' leader also solicited and obtained financial and moral support from Dr. Charles Peck of Danbury, Connecticut, Captain John Johnson, merchant and gristmill owner in Peekskill, Benjamin Palmer, a rich innholder and landowner of Pelham Manor, and some officials of Dutchess County, such as Jacobus Teroross, a judge of the court of common pleas, and John Akin, a justice of the peace. According to Peter Pratt, a spy planted by the landlords, Monrow often "amused" his audience by such quips as "Philipse Patent is Dated in 1697 and is bounded upon Beekman [Patent] Dated 1703 the older bounded on the younger."[90]

But Monrow's major efforts were directed at the regular tenants in Lots 6, 7, and 8, whose disaffection from the landlords was deemed most vital to the cause of the squatters and Indians. By November, many of his followers had taken out new leases for their lands from Nimham "for 999 years upon very Reasonable Terms"—two peppercorn rent. At meetings attended by a hundred persons or more, he repeatedly threatened the Philipse tenants with eviction should they refuse to do likewise. In a formal "Advertisement" issued in the name of Monrow and Nimham on December 22, the loyal tenants were given about a three months' grace period to make up their minds and were "desired not to pay" any back rents to Robinson and Philipse in the meantime. "All those that Do not Encline to take Leases before that Day," continued the threat, "may Depend on being removed according to his majesties King George's procklimation with the utmost Rigor of Law."[91] As the advertisement suggests, Monrow did not have much luck in winning these tenants over to his side, even though the virtually perpetual lease he offered was far better than the ones they typically held, which were at will or for a term of years.[92] The loyal tenants were fearful of the Indians and squatters, but

90. Peter Pratt to Beverly Robinson and Philip Philipse, Dec. 29, 1764, and deposition of Gideon Prindle, Feb. 28, 1765, Unsorted Legal MSS, Kempe Papers; Philipse-Gouverneur Land Titles, fol. 13. As for John Johnson, see a deed from Johnson to Gilbert Bloomer, May 9, 1769, McKesson Papers, Box 4, N.-Y. Hist. Soc.; Johnson's "advertizement," N.-Y. Gaz.; and Wkly. Mercury, Feb. 13, 1775. Benjamin Palmer's lease of 400 acres from Nimham, Dec. 19, 1765, Benjamin Palmer Papers, Box 1, N.-Y. Hist. Soc. In 1761 Palmer bought Minifords Island in Pelham Manor for £2,730 and tried to turn it into a "trading town." Benjamin Palmer to an unknown recipient, 1777, ibid.; Isaiah Bennett to Beverly Robinson, Oct. 12, 1763, Unsorted Legal MSS, Kempe Papers.

91. John Ganoong and 28 others to Philip Philipse and Beverly Robinson, Nov. 21, 1764, Unsorted Legal MSS, Kempe Papers.

92. For Robinson's lease terms, see his memorial, Dec. 11, 1783, and testimony of his tenant named Malcom Morison, Dec. 21, 1785, A.O. 12/21, 159, 180; lease, Beverly

they were still more afraid of retaliation by the landlords. Besides, being basically timid souls, they were unwilling to exchange the modest equity in their improvements and their sense of security for the uncertain promise of deliverance from their existing economic arrangements. Thus, on November 21, twenty-nine of them, explaining their "great concern and uneasiness" caused by Monrow's threat, pleaded with Philip Philipse and Robinson for "protection and advice": "We . . . beg you will send us by the bearer hereof your Direction how we shall act in the affair and whether we may Depend upon you to protect and Defend us in our possessions against those Intruders and Disturbers of our peace."[93] In subsequent months, however, the tenants' relationships with the conspirators would improve as the landlords' power diminished in the disputed area.

Predictably, the Philipse heirs' reaction was legal retribution. In late December 1764, they brought ejectment suits against fifteen Indian tenants.[94] But instead of panicking the conspirators, these actions rather had the effect of coalescing them into a tighter organization. At a meeting on December 27, twenty-nine of the most active conspirators signed "the Articles of Combination," which was reportedly drafted in New York City. The articles provided, first, that Isaac Perry, holding an Indian lease, would enter as defendant in trial for all others, present and future Indian lessees; second, that the group would raise a defense fund for that purpose; and, third, that they would establish a six-man standing committee to be appointed by Nimham and Monrow to conduct day-to-day operations. Their secret strategy, however, was that Nimham, not Perry, would stand trial as the "defendant for the whole" crew and that his attorney, Samuel Johnson of Connecticut, would try to obtain an order of the supreme court to "remove the case home" for trial. Should this maneuver fail, Nimham and Monrow would then "appeal" their case directly to the king, possibly with the assistance of Sir William Johnson.[95] This decision, without doubt, reflected their disillusionment with the provincial court system, which they believed was hopelessly in the control of the large landowners.

Robinson to Nathan Burdsell, Apr. 20, 1754, File No. 6332, Dutchess County Clerk's Office, Poughkeepsie, N.Y.

93. John Ganoong and others to Philip Philipse and Beverly Robinson, Nov. 21, 1764, Unsorted Legal MSS, Kempe Papers.

94. "King v. Daniel Nimham," Dec. 9, 1764, File No. 1072, Dutchess Co. Clerk's Office; Minute Book of Supreme Court, 1762–1764, 229, 349, 455; *ibid.*, 1764–1767, 73–74.

95. "The Articles of Combination," Dec. 27, 1764, Unsorted Legal MSS, Kempe Papers; Peter Pratt to Beverly Robinson and Philip Philipse, Dec. 29, 1764, *ibid.*

While the trial was pending in the supreme court, both the Philipses and Nimham in February and March 1765 presented their cases to the governor and council. On March 6, 1765, the council after a brief hearing not only upheld the Philipses but also ordered the attorney general to arrest and prosecute four of the tenants and advisers of the Indians— Samuel and Daniel Monrow, Joseph Crow, Jr., and Stephen Willcocks— for the high misdemeanor of "Disinherison," or deprivation of the inheritance, of the crown. On the very next day, Samuel Monrow was put in the New York City jail, where he would stay until late 1767. The supreme court shortly thereafter issued judgments against all fifteen Indian tenants for want of plea from them.[96] Sir William Johnson politely "declined" to give Nimham and his white tenants "any assistance or Encouragement" on the ground that he was "not sufficiently acquainted with the Affair."[97] This series of setbacks, accentuated by the absence of Monrow, the architect of conspiracy, so demoralized them that they failed even to execute their pet plan of appealing to the crown.

Meanwhile, the triumphant Philipses, armed with the writs of possession, threw out the unrepentant Indian tenants without compensation for their improvements (replacing them with the proprietors' own choices) and permitted the contrite to stay as tenants at will. The ease with which the landlords recruited rentees suggests that lease terms in Philipse's Highland Patent were not particularly onerous and that the leaderless dissidents were in such a state of disarray that new settlers were unafraid of them. Peace returned to the disputed area, but it was fragile at best because the farmers still believed in their just right to the land. Nevertheless, this uneasy peace might have lasted and the discontents been contained if the established political order in the colonies had remained an object of respect.

96. "Report of Committee on Controversy between Daniel Nimham et al and Philipse Heirs," Mar. 6, 1765, N.Y. Land Papers, XVIII, 142; "A Geographical, Historical Narrative or Summary of the Present Controversy between Daniel Nimham ... and ... Legal Representatives of Colonel Frederick Philipse . . . ," Lansdowne Manuscripts, Vol. 707, fol. XXXI, 15–16, Library of Congress (transcripts; originals at British Library); Samuel Monrow to John Tabor Kempe, May 5, 1767, Unsorted Legal MSS, Kempe Papers; Minute Book of Supreme Court, 1764–1767, 73–74. Interestingly, Cadwallader Colden took a position that the Wappingers had "no right to interpose in the Disputes among the Christians." Colden to William Johnson, Mar. 15, 1765, Colden Letter Books, I, 474. But Nimham's later statement on the council proceedings of Mar. 6 gives the distinct impression that the natives counted on Colden's support for their cause. Philipse-Gouverneur Land Titles, fol. 13, no. 45; "Daniel Horsmanden, Judges warrant, Mar. 17, 1765," Unsorted Legal MSS, Kempe Papers.

97. Roger Morris to William Johnson, Aug. 12, 1765, Johnson to Morris, Aug. 26, 1765, William Johnson Papers, IX, 820–821, XI, 884–886, 911–912.

## Uprisings of the Country "Sons of Liberty"

The resistance to the Stamp Act of 1765 was a watershed in the emergence of American disaffection with the British empire. The paralysis of governmental machinery that resulted from the violent opposition to the new taxes created an environment in which the socially disgruntled were tempted to try extralegal means to redress their grievances. Country farmers knew about, and some even participated in, the "Greatest Mob" rampaging in New York City in the first week of November.[98] In the face of mobocracy, government officials were frightened and helpless, the hated stamps were shipped back, the courts and customhouses were shut up, British soldiers were kept off the streets, and lawyers dared not issue writs. Judge Robert R. Livingston, staying in the city, observed on November 20 that "people begin already to take advantage of" the situation "to refuse payment."[99] Ordinary men did not have a sophisticated understanding of the subtleties of constitutional arguments and disagreements.[100] In this political milieu, suffused by the rhetoric of opposition ideology, a liberty from one particular piece of legislation was perceived by them as a license to oppose the entire legal order. The "common people are [of the] opinion that there is no Law and very freely Say So upon account of the Ditestable Stamp Act," an observer noted. On another level, the breakdown of authority accompanying the endemic disorders impressed some people with the notion that "every thing which had the appearance of resisting Government might be undertaken with impunity."[101]

The reign of near-anarchy awakened the former squatters in Dutchess County from the apathy or despair into which they had lapsed since March. Sometime in the second week of November, they were ready again for a confrontation with the Philipses. Led by Samuel Monrow, Jr. (son of the incarcerated guardian of the Wappingers), John Kane, a "rich" merchant, William Finch, a laborer, Philip Philipse, a former English tenant, William Prendergast, a former squatter, Dr. Joseph Crane, and others, they published an "advertisement" calling for a meeting of the

---

98. Nicholas Gouverneur to an unknown recipient, Nov. 3, 1765, Morristown Historical Park Collection (microfilm), Roll 19, Morristown, N.J.; Robert R. Livingston to Robert Monckton, Nov. 8, 1765, *Aspinwall Papers*, II, 559–567.

99. Robert R. Livingston to father, Robert, Jr., Nov. 20, 1765, Livingston-Redmond MSS, Roll 7.

100. Crèvecoeur, *Letters from an American Farmer*, 207–208.

101. Isaac Vrooman to James Duane, Jan. 6, 1766, Duane Papers, Roll 1; Henry Moore to Secretary Conway, Apr. 30, 1766, *N.Y. Col. Docs.*, VII, 825.

inhabitants in the Hoveout to be held on November 21. The manifesto declared that the purpose of the meeting was to force "the landlords to give Leases for three Lives" at a reasonable rent adjusted by disinterested persons; that the signers were determined to bring about the reinstatement of all those evicted by the proprietors; and, finally, that every tenant of the South Precinct (as Philipse's Highland Patent was then called) must attend the meeting or suffer the loss of his "estates."[102] Conspicuously absent from the manifesto was any reference to the possessors' inherent right to the land, and absent also was any mention of the Indian claim. The avowed objectives of the new campaign were the restoration of old possessions and the improvement of tenant leases. The squatters were skeptical, however, of the prospect of getting voluntary cooperation from the regular tenants: hence, the use of intimidation against the latter.

At the appointed time, several mass meetings were held in the Hoveout (Robinson's Lot Number 7). The number of participants varied from a hundred to two hundred. Many regular tenants, especially from the eastern part of the Philipse domain, came to the meetings in order not to draw upon themselves the wrath of the Monrow party. Thus, some were "spectators"; but others, like Silas Washburn and Edward Ganoong who in 1764 had asked for the landlords' protection from the fury of the Nimham associates, actively participated in the insurgency, either because of force of circumstances or because they agreed with the new program of the rebels.[103] Although the regular tenants seem to have outnumbered the former squatters at these meetings, leadership was squarely in the hands of the latter. Two examples are sufficient to prove this. Prendergast was elected as their "captain" at the nomination and insistence of Samuel Monrow, Jr. A majority plan calling for either direct negotiations with Robinson or arbitration was quashed by the Monrow party, which refused

102. Deposition of Gideon Prindle, July 28, 1766, Sorted Legal MSS, Kempe Papers; depositions of Seth Covel, Moses Mead, Simeon Covel, Nathan Cole, and Aaron Mead, June 30, 1766, depositions of John A. Dakin (dated Aug. 1, 1766) and William Hill (dated Aug. 12, 1766), *ibid.*; Mark and Handlin, "King v. Prendergast," *N.Y. Univ. Law Qtly. Review*, XIX (1941–1942), 189.

103. Silas Washburn (blacksmith by occupation) held a 380-acre, and Edward Ganoong a 144-acre, farm. Both were tenants of Philip Philipse in Lot No. 6. See "Morgan's Field Book, 1762," N.-Y. Hist. Soc.; depositions of George Huson (Nov. 26, 1765), Aaron and Moses Mead (June 30, 1766), Sorted Legal MSS, Kempe Papers. For Washburn and the Ganoongs, see John Ganoong and others to Beverly Robinson and Philip Philipse, Nov. 21, 1764, Unsorted Legal MSS, *ibid.*; Samuel Peter's deposition, June 7, 1766, Lawsuits, Unsorted P-U, *ibid.*

anything short of the landlord's unconditional acceptance of their original terms in the advertisement.[104]

For the first time, a confederacy between the regular tenants and former squatters was born, and as the title disputes merged with a classic antilandlord movement, the character of the agrarian conflict somewhat changed. The insurgents pledged to stand by each other with their "Lives and fortunes" against the landlords and warned people not to pay rent except "their just Debts." In the next two days, they organized into several bands, evicted at least five of those loyal tenants whom the landlords had several months earlier planted at the expense of the Indian tenants, and reinstated the latter with "equitable Title." They "terrified" loyal tenants, constables, justices of the peace, and Robinson, who fled (on November 21) from his country mansion to New York City, not because of any actual brutality on the part of the insurgents but because of the mere "appearance" of the mob, about two hundred strong, armed with pistols, swords, and clubs. Remarkably, until late May 1766, only one incident of property destruction occurred—the burning of a barn belonging to a justice of the peace.[105] For a "mob," the rebels were unusually well disciplined, suggesting that the word may not apply. It was Prendergast's declared policy that his men should not commit "mischief" or "abuse any person but be very civil."[106] Before the year was over, eastern Dutchess County was firmly in their control. Yet, they were unable to exact concessions from the landlords. The stalemate persisted until the eruption of riots in the Manor of Cortlandt the following April. In the meantime, the Dutchess rebels were idle wasting "too much Time" in meetings and neglecting their fields.[107]

104. Deposition of Gideon Prindle, July 28, 1766, Sorted Legal MSS, Kempe Papers; Mark and Handlin, eds., "King v. Prendergast," N.Y. Univ. Law Qtly. Review, XIX (1941–1942), 179. For an identification of the cleavage between a radical faction composed of the former Indian tenants under Samuel Monrow, Jr., and a moderate faction composed of the regular Philipse tenants, see deposition of James Livingston, sheriff of Dutchess County, in Mark and Handlin, eds., "King v. Prendergast," ibid., 190–191; deposition of Seth Covel, Jr., June 30, 1766, Sorted Legal MSS, Kempe Papers.

105. Mark and Handlin, eds., "King v. Prendergast," N.Y. Univ. Law Qtly. Review, XIX (1941–1942), 175, 177–179, passim. See also depositions of James Covey, Jr., Felix Holdridge, Ebenezer Weed, and Simeon Bundy, Nov. 21–23, 1765, Sorted Legal MSS, Kempe Papers; "Notes of Eiphalet Stephens and David Akin's Evidence," Kempe Papers, Lawsuits, Unsorted C-F, ibid.

106. Deposition of Gideon Prindle, July 28, 1766, Sorted Legal MSS, Kempe Papers; testimony of Samuel Towner, Mark and Handlin, eds., "King v. Prendergast," N.Y. Univ. Law Qtly. Review, XIX (1941–1942), 189.

107. Testimony of Gideon Crowfoot, Mark and Handlin, eds., "King v. Prendergast,"

Unlike the agrarian disturbances in Dutchess County, the riots in Cortlandt Manor had uncomplicated beginnings. There the rebels seem to have had no clear platform or organization; theirs was simply an outburst of long-simmering discontent against an autocratic landlord and his harsh practices. In that sense, the Cortlandt Manor riots fit the classic pattern of tenant-landlord conflict that one can find in Europe.

In April 1766, violence engulfed the estate of Stephen Van Cortlandt of New Jersey. It is amazing that this estate, situated in the northeastern section of the manor near Connecticut and managed by the impetuous and haughty John Van Cortlandt, the eldest son of Stephen, had thus far been peaceful.[108] As we have seen in a previous chapter, the manager charged exceptionally high rents, raised them frequently, granted short-term leases or leases at will, often refused to renew tenure, and evicted many tenants for minor irregularities—all practices in sharp contrast with those of the other manor proprietors. Adding to his tenants' irritation was the harsh and nasty language he used in scolding them for defaults in lease performance, however trivial. Some of his tenants now seized upon the breakdown of law and order and the rioting in Dutchess County to defy him.

The incident that provoked violence was an effort on the part of John Van Cortlandt to retrieve back rents and to remove two tenants, Daniel Cornel and Isaac Wright. Cornel, a tenant at will, owed £50 to the landlord by the end of 1763. In the middle of January 1764, the irate Van Cortlandt instructed his agent-tenant, Joseph Golden, who also owned sixty acres of freehold in the nearby town of North Castle, to order Cornel either to surrender his lease or to pay his back rent.[109] Two months later, Cornel emptied his pocket by paying £38 18s. 9d., a large portion of his rent arrears, to the landlord.[110] At the same time, he seems to have entreated Van Cortlandt to let him retain his lease, the improvement of which was worth £190. But Van Cortlandt was adamant. In

---

N.Y. *Univ. Law Qtly. Review*, XIX (1941–1942), 193. See also Bonomi, *A Factious People*, 220–222; Mark, *Agrarian Conflicts*, 134–136.

108. Stephen Van Cortlandt of Second River (now Belleville) died in Aug. 1765. John Van Cortlandt to John William Hoffman, Sept. 15, 1765, Letterbook of John Van Cortlandt, N.Y. Pub. Lib.

109. John Van Cortlandt to Joseph Golden, Jan. 19, 1764, *ibid*. For Golden's freehold in North Castle, see Loyalist Transcripts, XXIX, 275.

110. Entry on Mar. 30, 1764, Journal (c) of John Van Cortlandt, 1764–1772, N.Y. Pub. Lib.

June 1765, Golden, having paid the landlord £48, a part of the improvement money on Cornel's lease, took over the premises.[111]

The case of Isaac Wright was somewhat different from that of Cornel. Wright had hired a farm for a tenure of fifteen years in May 1748.
His lease stipulated that he would pay an annual rent of £3 after five
years. When the term expired in 1763, the landlord refused to renew it,
alleging that Wright had failed to pay during the past three years rents
amounting to £9.[112] The real reason, however, was that Van Cortlandt
had been approached by one Simon Brady, who was willing to pay £20
yearly, £17 more than Wright. Thus he removed Wright in favor of
Brady.[113]

The victims of landlordism were naturally bitter, but legally there
was nothing they could do about the situation. Meanwhile, they barely
subsisted on their savings and on the sympathy of their friends, seeking
new employment or settlement. In late 1765 and the first month of 1766,
mass demonstrations and great turbulence swirled around them: a sustained struggle of the Sons of Liberty in urban centers of British North
America, a popular uprising in Schenectady against its obnoxious town
charter,[114] and the ongoing movement of the Dutchess rebels. The proven
effectiveness of mob action was a lesson that the desperate men and their
friends in Cortlandt Manor, as elsewhere, could not miss, and which, in
turn, emboldened them to use the same weapon. Daniel Cornel, his
brother Richard (probably a resident of Dutchess County), Isaac Wright,
Joseph Tidd, Daniel Chapman, Captain Joshua Bishop, all inhabitants of
the manor, met on February 28 at the house of Daniel Brundige to discuss strategies against the landlord and his favorite tenants. From there
merged a resolution: solicit help from the Dutchess rebels and in the meantime withhold any action. Help from the north was available by April 10,
when Cornel, Wright, and seventeen others including five Dutchess men
assaulted Joseph Golden, turned him out of his possessions, and put
Daniel Cornel back on his old farm.[115] During the riot, which lasted for

111. Entry on July 30, 1765, ibid.
112. Receipt Book of John Van Cortlandt, Van Cortlandt Family Papers, N.-Y. Hist.
Soc.
113. Journal (c) of John Van Cortlandt, N.Y. Pub. Lib.
114. Isaac Vrooman to James Duane, Jan. 6, 1766, Duane Papers, Roll 1.
115. "A List of the Persons Concerned in the Riots on Cortlandt's Manor taken from 4
Informations," Lawsuits, C-F, Kempe Papers; John Van Cortlandt to Joseph Golden, May
24, 1766, Letterbook of John Van Cortlandt, N.Y. Pub. Lib.; Pierre Van Cortlandt to a

an hour, Cornel was most violent in physically abusing Golden.[116] The next day, John Van Cortlandt rushed to John Tabor Kempe and paid him £3 4s. to prosecute "Cornel and the Ryetors that Dispos[ses]sed Joseph Golden."[117] A week passed without incident. Then, on April 17, about the same number of rioters, joined by William Prendergast, attacked the next target, Simon Brady, and threw him "out of the possession of his House and Farm"; the former lessee, Isaac Wright, was reinstated.[118] The alarmed attorney general quickly issued a bench warrant for the arrest of the rioters. On April 19, Wright, Bishop, and Bartlet Brundige (another of Van Cortlandt's tenants), "three of the principals" in the riots, were rounded up by John Thomas, sheriff of Westchester County, and his deputies, and sent to the New York City jail.[119] That the lawmen carried out the arrest without encountering any resistance suggests that the rebel movement in the manor was badly organized, weak, and limited in scope. It was probably for that reason that the rioters had turned to the Dutchess insurgents for help in the first place.

Government officials and landed magnates perhaps considered this crackdown a sufficient warning against further violence. It was reported that Captain Bishop became "faint" when he was haled before a legal authority, and this incident led Pierre Van Cortlandt, the only resident proprietor of the manor, to hope that now "affairs may be in a better situation."[120] Subsequent events, however, proved otherwise. The punitive measure seems to have made the manor and Dutchess rioters more united and determined.

During the early stages of the rioting, the Dutchess men were reluctant to associate themselves with the manor tenants. According to the testimony of Moss Kent, a Dutchess County inhabitant and witness picked by the Philipses, the Prendergast party had "looked on [the] Cortlandt mannor rioters to be wrong and would not connect themselves with

---

relative, Apr. 1766, and to Mr. Travis, Apr. 22, 1766, Van Cortlandt Papers, V2098, Sleepy Hollow Restorations Library, Tarrytown, N.Y.

116. "The King against Daniel Cornel and others," Lawsuits, C-F, Kempe Papers.

117. Journal (c) of John Van Cortlandt, N.Y. Pub. Lib.

118. "The King against Daniel Cornel and others," Lawsuits, C-F, Kempe Papers; John Van Cortlandt to Joseph Golden, May 24, 1766, Letterbook of John Van Cortlandt, N.Y. Pub. Lib.

119. "The King vs. Joshua Bishop and Isaac Wright, Apr. 19, 1766," Minute Book of Supreme Court, 1764–1767, 141; N.Y. Col. Docs., VII, 826, 886.

120. Pierre Van Cortlandt to Mr. Travis, Apr. 22, 1766, Van Cortlandt Papers, V2098, Sleepy Hollow Restorations Lib.

them."[121] Kent did not explain why this was so. The cleavage reveals something about the different origins and nature of the agrarian unrest in the two areas. The Dutchess insurgency, despite its manifesto of November, was under the influence of the squatter ideology, and its primary objective was to protect "the equitable title" of the true possessors of the land; the Cortlandt rising, on the other hand, was merely an outburst against the abuses of landlordism.[122] Nevertheless, the Dutchess farmers forged a united front with the Westchester men in the first week of April, indicating that the former had changed their tactics and even their objectives. After almost half a year of waiting for a word from the Philipses, they may have come to the conclusion that the only way to break the protracted stalemate with the proprietors would be to get whatever help they could from the elements who were dissatisfied with the existing social and economic order and apply maximum pressure on the provincial government. The "common Talk among them," according to a witness, was that they were "going to do Justice and relieve the oppressed" and that "it was high Time the great men such as the Att[orne]y Gen[eral] and the Lawyers should be pulled down." They assumed and hoped "all the Tenants between New York and Albany" would join the mob.[123] Inspired by the newly adopted radical views and hopes, they agreed to support "those of the Mannor of Cortlandt" and "defend the Whole." At the same time, they boasted of their strength by declaring that they were joined by the " Inhabitants of some other Counties, and by great numbers [5 or 6,000] of the Connecticut People bordering on West Chester." Now hoisting the flag of "levellers," they had indeed come a long way from the small beginnings of a squatter-interest insurgency.[124]

On April 21, just two days after the imprisonment of the manor rioters, Prendergast called a meeting at which the Dutchess rebels unani-

121. Mark and Handlin, eds., "King v. Prendergast," N.Y. Univ. Law Qtly. Review, XIX (1941–1942), 175–176.
122. The Dutchess County insurgents were still scheming with Nimham. This was evidenced in the enlistment of Bartlet Brundige, a Cortlandt Manor rioter, as an interpreter and adviser to the sachem in the middle of April. Henry Moore to earl of Shelburne, Dec. 22, 1766, N.Y. Col. Docs., VII, 886; "Geog. Hist. Narrative," Vol. 707, fol. xxxviii, 30, and fol. xlii, 37, Landsdowne MSS.
123. "Notes of Eiphalet Stephens and David Akin's Evidence," Lawsuits, C-F, Kempe Papers; Mark and Handlin, eds., "King v. Prendergast," N.Y. Univ. Law Qtly. Review, XIX (1941–1942), 176; Henry Moore to Secretary Conway, Apr. 30, 1766, N.Y. Col. Docs., VII, 825; "King against Elisha Cole," June 13, 1767, Sorted Legal MSS, Kempe Papers, particularly testimony of Samuel Peters.
124. N.Y. Col. Docs., VII, 825; testimony of Simeon Bundy, in Mark and Handlin, eds., "King v. Prendergast," N.Y. Univ. Law Qtly. Review, XIX (1941–1942), 176.

mously approved a scheme to liberate the prisoners by force. Eight days
later a group perhaps three hundred strong and led by Prendergast, William Finch, and Samuel Monrow, Jr., gathered near the house of Joseph
Golden at North Castle.[125] Their second objective, after the release of the
prisoners, was to secure from John Van Cortlandt "a grant foreover of
his Lands" or to "pull down his House in Town." Though never mentioned in their public announcements, freeing Samuel Monrow, Sr., the
old Indian guardian still confined in the city jail, was probably upper-
most in their minds. On their march to the city, they expected to be met
at King's Bridge—the bridge connecting Manhattan Island and Westchester County—by several other companies that were "coming down the
North [Hudson] River road to join them." Before starting the march from
North Castle, Samuel Monrow, Jr., warned the terrified Mrs. Golden to
remove all her household goods because he "believed the mob on their
return would pull down" her house too.[126] In the late afternoon of that
day, the Westchester and Dutchess insurgents arrived at the bridge as
planned. Their numbers had increased to five hundred. There Prendergast
began calling his followers the "Sons of Liberty" as a tactic to identify
their movement with the one by that name in the city. The rebellious
group, which a year or so earlier had expressed an absolute faith in the
king as their protector, now dressed themselves up as liberty men, an
inconsistency that did not bother the desperate folk. They apparently
"expected to be assisted by the poor people" of New York. To solidify
the unity of the rebels, Prendergast proclaimed: "If any Person or persons
offended us . . . the Sons of Liberty, . . . we should take them to the first
convenient Place of mud and water, and there duck them as long as we
think proper from thence we should take them to a white oak tree, and
there whip them as long as we think proper, and thence take them out of
the County and there kick their Arses as long as we think fit."[127] The
mob huzzahed the speech. After a brief rest, they proceeded toward the
city that night.

Meanwhile, the city residents had become aroused by rumors that
the rioting farmers would "set the City on Fire in several different Places

125. "Notes of Eiphalet Stephens and David Akin's Evidence," Lawsuits, C-F, Kempe
Papers. The information about the gathering of the insurgents was provided by Benjamin
Randolph of Cortlandt Manor. N.Y. Council Minutes, XXVI, 4, N.Y. State Lib.; Proclamation of Gov. Henry Moore, in N.-Y. Gaz., May 5, 1766.
126. N.Y. Col. Docs., VII, 825; Montresor Journals, 363; N.-Y. Gaz., May 5, 1766.
127. Montresor Journals, 363; Mark and Handlin, eds., "King v. Prendergast," N.Y.
Univ. Law Qtly. Review, XIX (1941–1942), 175, 183; testimony of Samuel Peters, June 7,
1763, Unsorted Legal MSS, Kempe Papers.

at the same time."[128] Most upset by the country "Sons of Liberty" were, ironically enough, such leading members of New York City's Sons of Liberty as John Van Cortlandt himself, John Morin Scott, an attorney who later was to sit on the bench at the trial of Prendergast, and Peter R. Livingston, the heir apparent to the lordship of Livingston Manor.[129] Their reaction led Captain John Montressor of the British army to re-mark sarcastically that the "Sons of Liberty [are] great opposers to these Rioters as they are of opinion that no one is entitled to Riot but them-selves."[130] Governor Henry Moore acted quickly to meet the threat. He ordered both the regular troops and the city's militia units to be "in readiness" and to take "every other precaution." The rebels, upon enter-ing the city the next day, April 30, sent a committee of six to negotiate with the governor, but he flatly refused to meet with them and ordered the militia to attack the main body. He then issued a proclamation offer-ing a reward of £100 for the apprehension of the rebel chief, £50 for William Finch, and the same amount for Monrow. He also commanded the civil officers of Dutchess and Westchester counties to exert themselves to put down other rioters. The rebels, unable to enlist any support in town, fled before a shot was fired.[131]

The rout of the rebels marked the end of the riot in Cortlandt Manor. A week after the showdown between the governor and the rebels, Joseph Golden happily reported to John Van Cortlandt that he had returned to the leasehold from which he had been expelled a month be-fore. John Thomas, now a judge of the county court, also informed Van Cortlandt that Simon Brady had been restored to his farm.[132] As the manor returned to normalcy with the aid of the very authority that he, as a prominent leader of the Sons of Liberty, had tried to disrupt, the landlord vigorously sought to dislodge the troublemakers among his tenants. On May 24, 1766, he directed Golden to use every means to distrain cattle owned by Augustine Rogers, who owed a back rent of

---

128. *N.Y. Col. Docs.*, VII, 825.

129. Thomas Jones, *History of New York during the Revolutionary War*, ed. Edward Floyd De Lancey (New York, 1879), I, 109. John Van Cortlandt was one of the radical leaders of the city Sons of Liberty and was later elected to the New York provincial congress. William Smith, Jr., wrote that Van Cortlandt was "formerly violent for Liberty and against Independency for which he is now one of the most intemperate Advocats." Sabine, ed., *Historical Memoirs of William Smith*, II, 118.

130. *Montresor Journals*, 363.

131. N.Y. Council Minutes, XXVI, 5; *N.-Y. Gaz.*, May 5, 1766; *Montresor Journals*, 365.

132. John Van Cortlandt to Joseph Golden, May 24, 1766, Letterbook of John Van Cortlandt, N.Y. Pub. Lib.

£10, and those of Bartlet Brundige, who owed £39 5s. 4d., including four years' rent and bond. Besides, Golden was empowered to terminate the two leases. To make sure that Golden understood his instructions, Van Cortlandt emphasized at the end of the letter that "you will not fail seizing the cattle of Brundige to secure the Rent." Finally he added his hope that "all the Good Tenants are well."[133]

For a closer look at the Cortlandt Manor upheaval, we are fortunate in having available a complete list of the rioters, as drawn up by John Tabor Kempe. Kempe's tally of the thirty-seven active participants is presented in table 8.1, in which the list is broken down more specifically, showing those who acted against Golden on April 11 and those who acted against Brady on April 17. Several salient facts emerge from this roll of the rioters. First, almost half of the men who participated in the first action were also involved in the subsequent one. Second, of the thirty-seven, eight were drawn from two families, the Cornels and Wrights, whose grievances against Van Cortlandt had caused the rioting; and seven families—the Cornels, the Wrights, the Tidds, the Brundiges, the Comes, the Ganons (or Ganoongs), and the Bishops—together supplied nineteen persons, more than half of the manpower. Furthermore, seven out of thirty-seven came from outside the manor. Significantly, of the twenty-four tenants of the landlord in the entire manor, only four—Rogers, Brundige, Wright, and Cornel—were active; the rest, 83 percent, were bystanders, undoubtedly with some interest in the outcome of events. Van Cortlandt therefore had these meek tenants in mind when he expressed his hope in his letter of May 24 that "all the Good Tenants are well."

In terms of the large manorial context, it should be noted that the disturbance was confined to the estate of John Van Cortlandt; other parts of the manor were not affected at all. This point cannot be overemphasized. Irving Mark, in his classic work *Agrarian Conflicts in Colonial New York, 1711–1775,* stated that "the Westchester men . . . threatened to pull down the city homes of Pierre Van Cortlandt and of Lambert Moore."[134] He based this statement on a remark found in the diary of Captain Montressor that they would "pull down Mr. Cortlandt's house in town and also one belonging to Mr. Lambert Moore."[135] It could not possibly have been Pierre Van Cortlandt to whom the officer referred, for

---

133. Entry on Nov. 6, 1766, in John Van Cortlandt's Journal (c), *ibid.*, shows that his agent distrained and sold 13 sheep owned by Brundige for the back rent of £5.

134. Mark, *Agrarian Conflicts,* 139.

135. *Montresor Journals,* 363.

Table 8.1. John Tabor Kempe's List of the Cortlandt Manor Rioters

*Those responsible for the dispossession of Joseph Golden on April 11*

| | | |
|---|---|---|
| Daniel Cornel | Yeoman | Cortlandt |
| Richard Cornel | Yeoman | Cortlandt |
| William Cornel | Laborer | Cortlandt |
| Isaac Wright | Yeoman | Cortlandt |
| Isaac Wright, Jr. | Laborer | Cortlandt |
| Robert Wright | Laborer | Cortlandt |
| Joshua Bishop | Yeoman | Cortlandt |
| Joseph Tidd | Yeoman | Cortlandt |
| Daniel Chapman | Yeoman | Cortlandt |
| Comfort Chadwick | Yeoman | Cortlandt |
| John Cross | Yeoman | Cortlandt |
| James Barker | Yeoman | Cortlandt |
| Richard Satterly | Yeoman | Cortlandt |
| Nathan Brundige | Yeoman | Cortlandt |
| William Derbyshire | Laborer | Cortlandt |
| Samuel Ruff | Laborer | Cortlandt |
| Silas Bayley | Laborer | Cortlandt |
| Edward Ganoong | Yeoman | South Precinct, Dutchess Co. |
| John Quitterfield | Yeoman | South Precinct, Dutchess Co. |
| Thomas Baxter | Laborer | South Precinct, Dutchess Co. |
| William Finch | Laborer | South Precinct, Dutchess Co. |
| Abrahm Sluff | Cordwainer | South Precinct, Dutchess Co. |

*Those responsible for the dispossession of Simon Brady on April 17*

| | | |
|---|---|---|
| William Prendergast | Yeoman | South Precinct, Dutchess Co |
| Isaac Wright | Yeoman | Cortlandt |
| Jonathan Wright | Yeoman | Cortlandt |
| William Wright | Yeoman | Cortlandt |
| Robert Wright | Laborer | Cortlandt |
| Daniel Cornel | Yeoman | Cortlandt |
| Richard Cornel | Yeoman | Cortlandt |
| William Cornel | Laborer | Cortlandt |
| Joseph Tidd | Yeoman | Cortlandt |
| Joseph Tidd, Jr. | Yeoman | Cortlandt |
| Solomon Tidd | Yeoman | Cortlandt |
| Bartlet Brundige | Yeoman | Cortlandt |
| Daniel Brundige | Yeoman | Cortlandt |
| Thomas Comes | Yeoman | Cortlandt |
| Solomon Comes | Yeoman | Cortlandt |
| Joshua Bishop | Yeoman | Cortlandt |
| John Bishop | Yeoman | Cortlandt |
| Augustine Rogers | Yeoman | Cortlandt |
| Comfort Chadwick | Yeoman | Cortlandt |

Table 8.1 (Continued): Cortlandt Manor Rioters

| James Barker | Yeoman | Cortlandt |
| John Gonoong | Yeoman | South Precinct, Dutchess Co. |
| Isaac Gonoong | Yeoman | South Precinct, Dutchess Co. |

Sources:
"A List of the Persons Concerned in the Riots in Cortlandt's Manor taken from 4 Informations" and "The King against Daniel Cornel and others, Apr. Term, 1766," Lawsuits, C–F, John Tabor Kempe Papers, New-York Historical Society, New York.

Pierre did not own a house in the city until January 1775, when he bought a house and lot for £2,000 on the east side of Bowery Lane there.[136] If the tenants had grievances against Pierre, they would have attacked his home at Croton on the Albany Post Road about thirteen miles west of the scene of rioting (see the sketch on p. 393). Throughout the turmoil, however, Pierre remained at the Croton home keeping himself posted about what was happening. In response to a request from a relative for information about the manor situation, he wrote:

The Last mob or Ryot here In the Manor was when, Pendegrass and Bishop Took out of possession, one [Simon] Brady *on Co[usin] John [Van] Cortlandts land* and put in Isaac Wright, Since which have heard nothing from the Eastward only am Creditedly Inform'd that Pendgrass publicly Said by way of proclamation, that he bid Diffiance to any officer or person that should molest or Disturb any his men at their perril and that he wod Vindicate them at all Events, and believe his Interest here in the manor is more than generally Expected. . . . [137]

This letter, written shortly after the second manor riot, makes it clear that John Van Cortlandt's estate was the only part of the manor that was affected.

Had disaffection in Cortlandt Manor been widespread, Pierre Van Cortlandt would indeed have been a principal target of the rioters, as Mark claimed. For he was both a landlord in his own right and the agent of a number of the other manor proprietors, including the Beekmans, the De Lanceys, the Warrens, Peter Kemble, and Philip Van Cortlandt, the

136. Deed, Richard Varick to Pierre Van Cortlandt, Jan. 5, 1776, Van Cortlandt–Van Wyck Papers, N.Y. Pub. Lib.; Stokes, comp., *Iconography of Manhattan Island*, VI, 150–151.
137. Pierre Van Cortlandt to a relative, Apr. 1766, Pierre Van Cortlandt to Mr. Travis, Apr. 22, 1766 (italics added), Van Cortlandt Papers, V2098, Sleepy Hollow Restorations Lib.

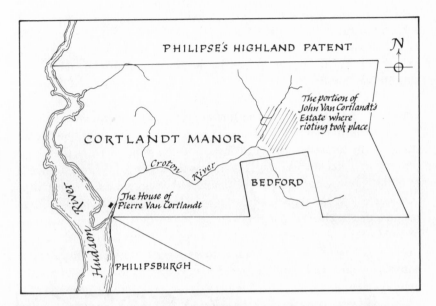

Sketch of the Area of Rioting in Cortlandt Manor, 1766. Adjusted from a map in the Cadwallader Colden Papers, New-York Historical Society, New York. (Drawn by Richard J. Stinely.)

eldest son of Stephen Van Cortlandt (Pierre's older brother).[138] That such was not the case is hardly surprising, however, in view of the liberality of most lease terms in the manor and the overall prosperity of the tenants.

The Dutchess rebels overreached themselves. The anticipated general uprising of what they called "oppressed" people, that is, the tenantry, the poor, and the alienated, did not materialize. Yet, their reeling back in the face of the firm stand of Governor Moore and the city militia did not crumble their insurgency as it did the Cortlandt Manor riots. Nor did the news of the repeal of the Stamp Act, which arrived in New York in early May, and the subsequent restoration of order weaken their movement. Regrouped on their home ground, they were still strong, but seemed to be content with pursuing their original limited objectives in the Highland Patent. They were strong enough to exact a promise from Samuel Peters, a justice of the peace of the county, "not to do anything against any of their party"; to impose their "Law" on the inhabitants; to evict proland-

138. See chapter 5, above.

lord tenants out of their possessions; and to free one John Way, a prisoner
for rent debt, from the Poughkeepsie jail. During the last-mentioned
incident, which occurred on June 6, 1766, the "confederates" assembled
in front of the jail were estimated by the petrified sheriff, James Livingston, to be "about 500" and by a frightened creditor-landlord "about 7
or 800"—discrepancies in the head count that probably depended on the
degree of one's fear. Reporting this and other critical circumstances to
the governor the next day, the sheriff confessed that it would "be impossible," with the little assistance he could draw upon from the peace
officers, to "execute his office."[139] It was then clear to the royal officials
that the "Conspirators can not be suppressed without the aid from a Military Force." At the request of Governor Moore, General Thomas Gage,
commander-in-chief of the king's forces in North America, on June 19,
ordered Major Arthur Browne of the Twenty-Eighth Regiment, then on
its way to New York from Albany, to help the county civil magistrates
enforce the laws and restore order. The next day, Moore issued a proclamation ordering the arrest of Prendergast and six of his lieutenants.[140]

Landing at Poughkeepsie on June 26, Major Browne was told by
Beverly Robinson and the sheriff that some of the "principal" rioters had

139. N.Y. Council Minutes, XXVI, 53, 54. Staughton Lynd has argued that the "armed
tenants" in Dutchess County numbered 2,000, and Irving Mark put the figure at 1,700. My
examination of the sources indicates that the Dutchess County insurgents never exceeded
300, even at the height of their movement. Simeon Bundy, a loyal tenant evicted by the
rioters, deposed in early June of 1766 before the attorney general that their number was
about 500 and that the "conspiracy has extended itself among so many persons in the said
County . . . that the Sheriff with the Force of the County, he may procure to assist him, will
be insufficient to suppress them." Samuel Peters, a justice of the peace, estimated his abusers
to be 400 strong. The veracity of these figures given by the victims of mob violence is
questionable because, apart from the discrepancies in number, they were interested in
inflating the rebel strength not only to justify their inaction but also to obtain a reinforcement from the provincial government. The problem of ascertaining the number of rebels is
complicated further by the fact that the insurgents, too, as Governor Henry Moore pointed
out, "industriously propagated exaggerated accounts of their numbers" so as to "spread
Terror." Probably the most accurate account comes from Moss Kent (a witness picked by
the landlords), who observed during the trial of William Prendergast that "the persons that
might [be] properly called Mobmen were about 300 the rest only Spectators." Lynd, "Who
Should Rule at Home?," WMQ, 3d Ser., XVIII (1961), 335; Mark, Agrarian Conflicts,
143; Mark and Handlin, eds., "King v. Prendergast," N.Y. Univ. Law Qtly. Review, XIX
(1941–1942), passim, particularly 167, 175; deposition of Simeon Bundy, June 1766,
Sorted Legal MSS, Kempe Papers; deposition of Samuel Peters, June 7, 1766, Lawsuits,
Unsorted Legal MSS, ibid.; Moore to Secretary Conway, Apr. 30, 1766, N.Y. Col. Docs.,
VII, 825.

140. N.Y. Council Minutes, XXVI, 54; Henry Moore to Gen. Thomas Gage, June 19,
1766, Gage to Maj. Art Browne, June 19, 1766, Gage Papers, Clements Lib. A copy of
Gov. Moore's Proclamation is in Livingston-Redmond MSS, Roll 12. The requisition of
troops was "approved" by the General Assembly as well. Gage to Secretary Conway, June
24, 1766, Carter, ed., Correspondence of Gage, I, 95.

already begun to "repent." Impressed by this report and by "the countenance of the inhabitants" there, he confidently predicted to his superior that the "appearance of the Regiment" would be sufficient to "frighten" the insurgents into submission.[141] As it turned out, the execution of his assignment was not that easy since some of his antagonists were prepared to fight. Upon hearing of the arrival of the redcoats, Prendergast vowed: "Let them come as soon [as] they will we will soon dispatch them" and that "they never should cross the mountains." Silas Washburn, captain of a rebel company, told his men to "kill every son of a Bitch." Some of the insurgents declared that "they would spend their blood before they would yield."[142] The next morning, British troops under the direction of the sheriff embarked on a march toward Quaker Hill in the Hoveout, where the rebels were reported to be gathering.[143] But the advance was uneventful until June 28, when several sharp skirmishes occurred in Fredericksburgh (Robinson's Lot Number 7), wounding three soldiers, two of them critically.[144] The bold challenge to his majesty's army by what appeared to them a bunch of "peasants" and, much worse, the resulting casualties among their comrades instantly galvanized the regulars: they were no longer bound by General Gage's restrictive order "not to repel Force by Force unless in case of absolute necessity." In the judgment of Major Browne, the moment "the Sons of Liberty" fired upon the king's troops they turned into "Traitors." With vengeance, the soldiers pursued the insurgents. By the end of that month, "above Sixty of the mob" had surrendered, and the resistance crumbled for all intents and purposes.[145] By the time General Gage's dispatch of July 2 arrived urging Major Browne to give them "a good Dressing," Prendergast, too, put himself at the

---

141. Maj. Art Browne to Gen. Gage, June 26, 1766, Gage Papers, Clements Lib.

142. Testimonies of Jeremiah Huson, Malcolm Morison, and Samuel Peters, "King against Elisha Cole," June 13, 1767, Sorted Legal MSS, Kempe Papers.

143. Prendergast was a resident at the foot of Quaker Hill in the middle of the Oblong. "An Act for the more easy collecting . . . Quit Rents in the Oblong Patent," N.Y. Col. Laws, V, 669–670; testimony of Moss Kent, June 13, 1767, "King against Elisha Cole," Sorted Legal MSS, Kempe Papers.

144. Maj. Art Browne to Gen. Gage, June 30, 1766, Gage Papers, Clements Lib.; deposition on Gideon Prindle in "King v. John Kane," July 28, 1766, Sorted Legal MSS, Kempe Papers; "Notes of Eiphalet Stephens and David Akin's Evidence," Lawsuits, C-F, ibid. One of the badly wounded soldiers died on Aug. 1. Pennsylvania Journal; and the Weekly Advertiser (Philadelphia), Aug. 17, 1766. The epithet "peasant" was used by Capt. John Clarke, who led a company against the insurgents in Albany County, and not those in Dutchess County. But there is no question that Maj. Browne's soldiers shared Clarke's disdain for the rebellious farmers. Capt. John Clarke to Gen. Gage, Aug. 17, 1766, Gage Papers, Clements Lib.

145. Gage to Browne, June 19, 1766, and Browne to Gage, June 30, 1766, Gage Papers, Clements Lib.; Boston-Gazette, and Country Journal, July 14, 1766.

mercy of the British, while most rebel leaders fled to the Connecticut towns of Danbury, New Fairfield, and Newton.[146]

## "Those troublesome Banditti" in Claverack and Livingston Manor

In striking contrast with Philipse's Highland Patent and Cortlandt Manor, the northern manors with a long history of boundary disputes and small farmer agitation were relatively quiet throughout the spring months of 1766. During the preceding ten years, the Claverack squatters had effectively fought off John Van Rensselaer's efforts to evict them, despite their repeated defeats in litigation. Writs and warrants of the Albany County authority stopped short of Spencertown and Nobletown, each comprehending seven square miles.[147] Conditions at Livingston Manor were somewhat different. There, the Loomises, the Halenbecks, Reese, and others had not been able since 1762 to establish a foothold and renew their struggle. While the Philipse domain was in upheaval, "nothing" exciting was going on in Livingston Manor. In the middle of February 1766, Robert Livingston, Jr., was happy to announce to his son-in-law, James Duane, that he had at last surmounted the chronic depression and insomnia that had taken from him "all comfort or Enjoyment of any Satisfaction in this world" and that his health had never been better and "freer of pain for many years past than this winter." Besides, his domestic industries, forges and mills, were all going well.[148]

---

146. Gage to Browne, July 2, 1766, Gage Papers, Clements Lib. Moore's proclamation of June 20 named Prendergast, Jacobus Gonsales, Silas Washburn, James Secord, Elisha Cole, Isaac Perry, and Micah Vail as guilty of "High Treason." As of Aug. 6, 1766, the rebel leaders, except the first two, were reported to be hiding in Connecticut. Samuel Monrow, Jr., and Stephen Crane joined them. Gov. Moore to Gov. William Pitkin of Connecticut, July 21 and Aug. 6, 1766, Connecticut Historical Society, *Collections*, XIX (1921), 14–15, 26–27; *N.-Y. Mercury*, Aug. 25, 1766. Another leader, Stephen Willcocks, left the country for an unidentifiable destination. Reed Ferris to Robert R. Livingston, Mar. 17, 1773, "Uncatalogued Livingston MSS," N.-Y. Hist. Soc. In the summer of 1766, more than 60 of the Dutchess farmers were indicted for their riotous activities, found guilty, and "variously punished with fines, imprisonment, and pillories." In August, William Prendergast, tried in a specially impaneled oyer and terminer court, was convicted of high treason and sentenced to death. But, in December, the king, acting on the recommendations of the court and of Gov. Moore, pardoned the rebel leader. Mark, *Agrarian Conflicts*, 145–150; Julius Goebel, Jr., and T. Raymond Naughton, *Law Enforcement in Colonial New York: A Study in Criminal Procedure (1664–1776)* (New York, 1944), 87–89.

147. "Proceedings of the Council of the Province of New York, relative to the claims of the Lands called Claverack . . . ," C.O. 1104/5, 315–316; William Smith, Jr., to Philip Schuyler, Apr. 15, 1765, Schuyler Papers, Box 9; "Petition of Robert Noble and [62] others to his Excellency Sir H. Moore," July 1, 1766, Miscellaneous Manuscripts, Rensselaerswyck, N.-Y. Hist. Soc.

148. Robert Livingston, Jr., to James Duane, Dec. 28, 1765, and Feb. 17, 1766, Duane Papers, Roll 1.

This happy feeling was soon dissipated, however, when Livingston discovered in early March that a new plot against his estate was being hatched by the same old conspirators across the Taconic Mountains.[149] Anxiety seized him again since he knew from past experience what kind of trouble he might have to face, especially when the country was in uproar over the Stamp Act and authority was paralyzed. In early May, he received the ominous information that a group from the Taconic area, along with "some" of his "tenants," was intending to pay him "a visit." Panicked, he turned to his cousin Robert R. Livingston of Clermont (justice of the supreme court) for "advice and assistance on the occasion." The cousin quickly responded: "If they should come . . . give up nothing, for if you give any thing by compulsions of this sort you must give up every thing." As for the strategy of dealing with potential trouble, the Clermont gentleman suggested: "I would let the mob go on their own way and as soon as they had separated get a warrant and take up those that are most dangerous and guilty, and carry them to Albany Gaol. I can't think they dare offer any Insult to your Person or Injury to your property especially if you have a few armed men to defend you, and if they should chance kill any person in the Fray every man of them is guilty of murder and then the Government must interpose even if they should be obliged to raise men for the purpose."[150]

It was not until around June 19 that the anticipated "visit" took place. About two hundred insurgents with "sticks" showed up at Robert Livingston, Jr.'s, manor seat with "some Proposals," but they were dispersed by a contingent of forty armed men led by Walter Livingston, son of the proprietor.[151] From there they went to the house of Henry Van Rensselaer, brother of John, several miles away. Disappointed to find him absent, they denounced him and left a message for him to meet them at "their Rendezvous" the next day or they would return. On the same day, a party of "twelve or fifteen" under Robert Noble, one of the "chief Instigators," descended on Peter Witbeck, a tenant of John Van Rensselaer, and demanded surrender of his property. When he refused, they gave him a grace period of eight days at the end of which he

149. Peter R. Livingston to father, Robert, Jr., Mar. 31 and Apr. 7, 1766, Livingston-Redmond MSS, Roll 8.

150. Robert R. Livingston to Robert Livingston, Jr., May 14, 1766, *ibid.*

151. Entry on June 28, 1766, *Montresor Journals*, 375–376. I found Capt. John Montresor's estimation of rebel strength on different occasions very exaggerated. Throughout the rebellion of 1765 and 1766 he drew some sadistic pleasure from the plight of the great whig landlords. For the visitors at Livingston's mansion, I had to rely on his figure because it was the only available source. See also *Boston-Gaz., and Country Journal*, July 14, 1766.

would either join their party or suffer the destruction of his house and grain. Robert Abraham Van Deusen, another tenant at Claverack, was less lucky. His place was raided several hours later by a group of "sixty or seventy" headed also by Noble. When he refused to surrender his possession, they kicked the door down, "pulled him out by the Hair of his Head, beat his Son, turned out his Wife and Children, threw out his Goods and destroyed a part of them, tore off the Roof of his House and then went away." Significantly, during the day of rampage none of the loyal tenants of Livingston Manor was harassed and abused. The pattern of the mob activities suggests that the Claverack squatters and the old rebels of Livingston Manor were allied this time as before and that the former played a leading role in these incidents.[152]

A counteroffensive from the landlords came swiftly. Their behavior in subsequent weeks leads to the suspicion that they, particularly John Van Rensselaer, welcomed the mob-initiated violence, for it provided them with an excellent pretext for retaliatory action and eventually for government intervention on their behalf. Indeed, the Claverack proprietor had every reason to be unhappy—probably more so than the squatters—with the status quo, which put over half of his domain beyond his control and which he had so far failed to break by legal means.[153] Obviously, the longer he permitted the squatters to hold the disputed lands, the harder it would be for him to dislodge them. Such a situation, he may have figured, would also render his claim tenuous in the eyes of the imperial authority that had yet to decide on the rival claims of the veteran officers and the powerful English claimants. Under these circumstances, the mobilization of the British army to suppress the Dutchess rebels, coming simultaneously with the outbreak of disturbances in Claverack, appeared as a timely blessing to Van Rensselaer. If the Philipse heirs were entitled to military protection, he must have reasoned, he was too. But in his case, he needed more than just protection and a restoration of order. He needed to repel his inveterate antagonists, the squatters, and recover the disputed lands. Van Rensselaer could not have overlooked the possibility of making use of British arms for that end. However, the government aid that both he and Robert Livingston, Jr., desperately wanted would be available only if bloodshed occurred. It was this grisly

152. Deposition of Robert Van Rensselaer and Harmanus Schuyler, July 2, 1766, Misc. MSS, Rensselaerswyck.
153. For John Van Rensselaer's efforts to evict the squatters by legal means, see William Smith, Jr., to Philip Schuyler, Apr. 15, 1765, Schuyler Papers, Box 9.

conclusion that seems to have disposed the worried landlords to seek a violent confrontation with the troublemakers.

On June 20, Albany was buzzing with the story of General Gage's express orders to the Twenty-Eighth Regiment to arrest Prendergast and the other leaders of the Dutchess rebels. That same day, Robert Van Rensselaer of Claverack, son of John, was in Albany with his father's tenants, Witbeck and Van Deusen, to lay their problems with the Taconic rebels before the county justices of the peace. On June 21, Harmanus Schuyler, sheriff and a relative of the Van Rensselaer family, was directed by the Albany magistrates to apprehend Robert Noble, Michael Halenbeck, and twenty-seven others. In the early morning of June 26—the day the army regulars landed at Poughkeepsie—the sheriff mustered about 130 or 140 armed men from all over the county at a Claverack church.[154] From there, the sheriff's party, including Walter Livingston and Robert Van Rensselaer, marched toward the house of Noble, about sixteen miles away from the Hudson River. Meanwhile, about sixty farmers from Nobletown and adjacent communities gathered at their leader's house in response to a report that John Van Rensselaer was coming with an armed posse "in order to destroy" the town and "kill" all its inhabitants.[155] Noble and 30 of his followers "armed with Clubs" met the sheriff's party at a railed fence across a road leading to the house. Schuyler ordered him to take down the fence or surrender. When Noble refused to do either, the sheriff pulled down one of the rails and tried to grab the rebel leader, only to be assaulted by Noble's men. Suddenly, firing started from both sides and lasted for three-quarters of an hour, leaving one dead and seven wounded on the lawmen's side and three dead and "several" wounded on the squatters'. Thomas Whitney, the former tenant-rebel of Van Rensselaer, was one of the rebel fatalities. Noble was wounded in the back, the sheriff found his hat and wig shot off, Robert Van Rensselaer's horse was killed under him, and Henry Van Rensselaer was shot in the arm. Despite their overwhelming strength in arms and numbers, the posse accomplished only to capture one rioter; all but 25 of the sheriff's party

154. Deposition of Robert Van Rensselaer and Harmanus Schuyler, July 2, 1766, Misc. MSS, Rensselaerswyck. The account that follows in the text is largely based on this lengthy deposition. See also "Copys of the Justices Warrant against Noble and others," June 21, 1766, ibid.; "The King against Alexander McCarthur, Daniel McCarthur, Thos. Johnson and Levi Stockwell," Albany, Aug. 25, 1766, MS No. 16277, N.Y. State Lib.

155. Some of those who came to Noble's house were from Massachusetts towns like Sheffield, Egremont, and Stockbridge. Depositions of Johannis Mtocksin (July 2 and Aug. 18, 1766), Jacob Spoor (Aug. 18, 1766), and James Smith (July 1, 1766), ibid.; testimony of James Smith, July 23, 1766, Mass. Archives, VI, 327.

deserted rank the moment firing started, and the rest, discouraged, opted to withdraw without even recovering the body of their fallen comrade. In this sense, the expedition was a dismal failure. In another sense, however, it was a splendid success for the manorial landlords inasmuch as the bloody contest and the inability of local authority to subdue the mob furnished them with a clear justification for military intervention by the government.[156]

As initially planned, the sheriff and Robert Van Rensselaer that afternoon rode to Poughkeepsie to apply to Major Browne for "aid" before he set out on his mission against Prendergast. To their chagrin, they found the commander uncooperative. Several days later, they were in New York City to report to Governor Moore about what had happened, and asked for his assistance. Almost at the same time, Noble and sixty-two inhabitants of Nobletown and Spencertown submitted a lengthy petition to the governor discussing the hardships and violence they had endured for their refusal to accept tenancy under Van Rensselaer and beseeching him to put a stop to further "effusion of blood." Simultaneously and significantly, they had the Stockbridge Indians, from whom they had bought the disputed lands, appeal to Governor Francis Bernard of Massachusetts for intervention.[157] As Robert R. Livingston of Clermont had predicted, Governor Moore and the council were most eager to support the landlords' cause. On July 2 and 3, Moore not only asked General Gage to help the civil authorities of Albany but also issued an unprecedented proclamation ordering all peace officers of the province— and not just those of one or two counties—to apprehend Noble and his associates. On July 2, General Gage in turn authorized Major Browne to give the magistrates of Albany County "all the aid in your Power" should they apply for it. For logistic and other reasons, the arrival of the troops was delayed until July 24 or 25.[158]

---

156. "Petition of Robert Noble and [62] others to his Excellency Sir H. Moore," July 1, 1766, and deposition of Robert Van Rensselaer and Harmanus Van Rensselaer, July 2, 1766, both in Misc. MSS, Rensselaerswyck; N.-Y. Gaz.: or, Wkly. Post-Boy, July 3, 1766; Boston Gaz., and Country Journal, July 14, 1766; "Declaration" of Nathan Beach, Oct. 26, 1767, Mass. Archives, VI, 395–396.

157. Petition of Robert Noble and others to Gov. Moore, July 1, 1766, Misc. MSS, Rensselaerswyck; petition of Stockbridge Indians, July 1, 1766, Mass. Archives, XXXIII, 393, 393a. On behalf of the people of Nobletown, Spencertown, and New Canaan, the Indians wrote to Volkert Douw, mayor of Albany, not to prosecute "those people who only defended themselves." See their letter, June 30, 1766, British Library Additional Manuscript 22697 (transcript), Library of Congress.

158. Gen. Gage to Maj. Arthur Browne, July 2, 1766, and Henry Van Rensselaer and John Ten Eyck to Gov. Moore, July 10, 1766, Gage Papers, Clements Lib.; Moore's

Captain John Clarke of the Sixty-sixth Regiment and about a hundred soldiers with two fieldpieces quickly learned how frustrating it could be to subjugate the Noble party, which refused to fight, took advantage of thick woods and extensive terrain, and, above all, had the sympathy of the Yankees. Worse still, they were hamstrung both by General Gage's order "not to be led out of this Government into that of Massachusetts" and by the control of civilian magistrates.[159] Between July 26 and 28, troops swept through Nobletown, demolishing at least seven houses, burning barns, plundering "Every thing they could lay their Hands upon," and destroying livestock and goods. On the last day of operations, they penetrated into the town of Egremont "within the Province of Mass. Bay." It appears from numerous testimonies that the Nobletown settlers suffered almost a total loss of their property except the crops in the fields. The psychological trauma from these savage attacks is beyond calculation. The community, which had only a short time before rubbed off its primitive traces, turned into a ghostly place as its people ran away to seek asylum in the woods and across the provincial border. Egremont alone received, as of July 31, about fifteen to twenty refugee families from Nobletown.[160] Yet, Clarke's mission was far from accomplished. In his report of July 29 to a superior, he admitted that "the Mob is rather increased than quelled." The armed insurgents, he explained, were "inhabitants on the back parts of Renselaers [Claverack] Manor 16 and 20 or More miles" from the Hudson River. To his dismay, he was unable to capture them because the country was "open and very extensive," and they posted their spies "at every corner." He tried excursions by night, which "answered once" but not a second time. In the face of the elusive enemy, he sadly concluded that the artillery were "not in the least wanted." As

proclamation, July 3, 1766, *Doc. Hist. N.Y.*, III, 830–832; Robert Livingston, Jr., to Henry Van Rensselaer, July 24, 1766, Van Rensselaer-Fort Papers, N.Y. Pub. Lib.

159. Gen. Gage's instructions to Capt. John Clarke, July 19, 23, 1766, Gage Papers, Clements Lib. For the number of troops sent to Claverack, see Gage to duke of Richmond, Aug. 26, 1766, Carter, ed., *Correspondence of Gage*, I, 102.

160. Petition of William Kellog and others, Egremont, July 30, 1766, to the General Court, Mass. Archives, VI, 334–336; *Boston Gaz., and Country Journal*, Aug. 18, 1766. Some squatter families went to Sheffield and Great Barrington. Hendrick Houghtaleing, a Nobletown resident, estimated his property loss to be £400 of New York money. He was captured by the regulars, but soon escaped. Declaration of Hendrick Houghtaleing, Oct. 26, 1767, Mass. Archives, VI, 374. Houghtaleing's neighbor named Isaac Andrews later reminisced about his losses: "They [the troops] carried away all that I had in the House Beds and Chests of Cloaths and Sadlars tools Three or four Saddlers and all my Provisions, my Oxen Cows Sheep Hoggs and Fowls." Andrews to William Williams, Feb. 27, 1773, William Williams Papers, I, 12, Berkshire Atheneum. See also the losses of William Beavens, Beavens's petition, May 21, 1767, Mass. Archives, VI, 355.

an alternative, he suggested burning and destroying everything including
the crops that were about to be harvested. But, in the final analysis, if
Massachusetts refused to help "suppress these licentious proceedings,"
he predicted, "they must continue."[161]

Scarcely were the squatters dispersed and tranquility restored in the
area when a dispute developed between Robert Livingston, Jr., and the
Van Rensselaers about how they should henceforth best utilize the military. Representing the viewpoint of Livingston, John Ten Eyck of Livingston Manor, a justice of the peace, recommended on July 29 and 30 that
Captain Clarke leave only twenty-five of his men "on the borders between the manor of Livingston and Claverack" to keep in awe some few
insurgents still skulking in the woods. Ten Eyck assumed that most of the
rioters were now demoralized and that therefore just a small contingent
would be adequate to maintain the "quiet and repose of this part of
the Country."[162] This argument immediately drew a strong objection
from Sheriff Harmanus Schuyler, who seemed more concerned about the
Van Rensselaer interest than other properties. He declared:

I cannot conceive with what Propriety Mr. Ten Eyck can be of opinion that the
Rioters are mostly Quelled, as he well Knows that on the 27th Inst a Party of 9 or
10 in arms attempted to take and Kill Robert Abraham Van Dusen, nor can he be
Ignorant that a Large Number in Indian Dress and armed were seen on the 28th
within five Miles of where the Troops lay that Preceedg Night Mr. Hogeboom
and Mr. Van Ness also give Information of 10 or 12 of them in one Place and
about 40 in another being assembled on the same day.[163]

Citing this information as well as the fact that "none of the Principal
Rioters" was captured, he wrote to Captain Clarke that "all the Troops
under your Command" should stay at Claverack until further notice
from the governor and General Gage. Philip Schuyler, son-in-law of the
Claverack proprietor and a member of the assembly, who came there the
last day of the month to bolster the antisquatter campaign, went further

161. Capt. John Clarke to Lt. Col. Maitland, July 29 and Aug. 1, 1766, Gage Papers,
Clements Lib. Several days later, Capt. Clarke repeated his wishes to obtain an order to
burn and destroy the crops. Clarke to Maitland, Aug. 5, 1766, *ibid.*

162. John Ten Eyck to Capt. John Clarke, July 29, 30, 1766, *ibid.* Apparently, the
letter of July 29 was written after Ten Eyck and Livingston had a heated argument with
Schuyler and the Van Rensselaers. Concluding his recommendation, Ten Eyck added: "If
you should find it necessary to employ your men otherways I beg that you will apply to
another Justice of the peace as I am too much fatigued to return." Later he indeed quit the
captain's company when he found his recommendations rejected.

163. Harmanus Schuyler to John Clarke, July 30, 1766, and depositions of Robert A.
Van Deusen and Evert Knickerbacker, July 28 and Aug. 1, 1766, Gage Papers, Clements
Lib.

than his namesake. "Anxious" for the security of his father-in-law's estate, he asked the captain to get reinforcements. The officer was mystified by the request because he firmly believed that a hundred troops were "enough" for his assignment: "Unless he [Schuyler] means to protect every mans house by placing a few men in each I can't conceive what foundation he has for the demand."[164] As noted above, the Van Rensselaers were not so much interested in the restoration of tranquility as in the expulsion of the entrenched squatters and vindication of their land titles. For that latter end, the Schuylers advocated not only a large, sustained military operation but also the removal of the company headquarters from the Livingston Manor–Claverack border to Claverack proper. For precisely the same reason, the sheriff hoped to have the operation directed also at the settlers in Spencertown and New Canaan about "sixteen or twenty miles" north of Nobletown, although they had not been involved in and thus were not responsible for the disturbances of June 19.[165] The employment of the military by the Van Rensselaers to decide the pending land-claim controversy was an abuse of justice. Disorder at Claverack, though at first provoked by the squatters, was perpetuated by the proprietor. Robert Noble and his associates were perhaps on sound ground when they argued that John Van Rensselaer, by exploiting the breakdown of law during and after the Stamp Act crisis while at the same time acting under the "pretense of Law," resorted to violence in order to attain his economic objectives.[166]

The dispute between the Schuylers and Ten Eyck was settled in favor of the former, due probably to the influence of William Smith, Jr., and Philip Schuyler with Governor Moore.[167] More troops under Sir Edward Pickering and fresh supplies came. The search and harassment operation resumed, this time, however, avoiding the mistake of chasing the rebels from "one part of the County to another," which "always ended in disappointment." The new tactics relied on the element of surprise. The

164. John Clarke to Lt. Col. Maitland, Aug. 1, 1766, *ibid.*
165. Clarke to Maitland, Aug. 5, 1766, *ibid.*
166. Declaration of Robert Noble and others, Oct. 30, 1767, Mass. Archives, VI, 390–391A. One anonymous writer charged that these "Mighty Men" were using the military to support their land titles, which were "good for Nothing." *Boston Gaz., and Country Journal,* Aug. 25, 1766. The same view was echoed by a New York writer. See a "letter from a Gentleman . . . to his Friend in Providence," *N.-Y. Gaz.: or, Wkly. Post-Boy,* Aug. 21, 1766.
167. For the friendship between Smith and Schuyler and the role that Smith played in defending the Van Rensselaer interest at the level of provincial government, see Schuyler and Smith correspondence in Schuyler Papers and William Smith Papers, N.Y. Pub. Lib. See also Gerlach, *Philip Schuyler,* 68–73.

redcoats would swiftly move and maneuver in such a way—"by way of Feint"—as to fall upon their antagonists where and when they least expected it. They also guarded the crops on the ground to force the rebels to either "surrender or abandon the country," since they could not subsist without reaping the harvest.[168] As the sheriff recommended, Clarke sent a detachment of fifty to Spencertown on August 5, with orders "as much as possible" to distress and harass its inhabitants, who were reported to be harvesting. In addition, on August 10 and 11, the troops secured Kinderhook Road and Claverack Road, the two main arteries leading to Massachusetts from Spencertown and Nobletown.[169]

Yet all these measures, though resulting in the apprehension of some rebels and greater security at the manors, did not destroy the insurgency. The root cause of the army's frustration was not the woods that "always received" the rebels but the moral and material aid that the government and people of the Bay Colony funneled to them. After Governor Moore's proclamation of July 3 left the squatters with no illusions about where his sympathies lay, they had again turned to their erstwhile "protector and supporter," the Massachusetts government. As early as mid-July, Nobletown sent William Kellog, a town leader, to Governor Francis Bernard and his council to explain their predicament and to solicit assistance. Shortly after the arrival of British troops in Claverack, Kellog found it necessary to write a letter to the governor reaffirming as "the truth" whatever he had said on the previous occasion. To show that the government had a moral obligation to help his people, Kellog declared: "It was by the doing of the Government of Massachusetts Bay that the Inhabitants of Noble Town settled Those Lands we actually settld by order and under the patronage of said Government and purchased Those Lands of the General Courts Committee and received privileges and did Duty in the County of Hampshire for some Time." Moreover, to stir the governor's humanitarian conscience, he emphasized that the settlers would be ruined "unless some kind of patron who is able to help us will interpose for our relief." They would be greatly obliged if the General Court were to annex the contested area to Massachusetts, to which "we do most properly belong." Such a measure, he was quite sure, would

168. Gen. Gage to John Clarke, Aug. 4, 1766, and Clarke to Lt. Col. Maitland, Aug. 5, 1766, Gage Papers, Clements Lib.

169. John Clarke to Gen. Gage, Aug. 17, 1766, *ibid.* Capt. Clarke frequently sent detachments on search-and-destroy missions to Egremont in the middle of August. Memorial of Levy Stockwell, Nov. 28, 1766, Mass. Archives, VI, 343; *Boston Gaz., and Country Journal*, Aug. 25, 1766.

"still our enemies and we should be able to maintain the ground." Finally, explaining why these disturbances occurred, he argued: "It is pretended That now we are rioters and a mob but all is for the Lands. This is the bone of contention."[170]

After they were "Driven as Sheep by wolves" from their homes, the Nobletown people again appealed on July 30 to the Massachusetts government for "some effectual method to put a stop to these oppressive usages."[171] The neighboring town of Egremont, flooded with refugees, endorsed their case and asked the governor to direct how to proceed with the newcomers, who were, in the words of its selectmen and overseers of the poor, "originally descended from this Province." While the House of Representatives was still in recess, Governor Bernard and the council assured the Egremont town leaders on August 7 that they might count on being refunded for "any expence" for the support of the refugees. Representing the case of the squatters as "deserving compassion," Bernard pressed Governor Moore of New York not only to let them return to harvest their grain but also to prohibit the Albany sheriff and the troops from molesting them until the final adjudication of the boundary line by the king.[172] This official pledge of support could not but boost the morale of the insurgents, although it fell short of what they had hoped. At least, they were assured of food and shelter for their families and spared from either submitting to the New York landlords or forsaking their farms permanently. Equally important, Governor Bernard's action stamped their cause with the color of legitimacy and helped rekindle in the Massachusetts inhabitants the spirit of comradery with the squatters that had been lost since 1757. Thus encouraged, they together patrolled the contested lands and dared to fire at the redcoats. Their menace was such that Van Deusen and Witbeck, the two abused loyal tenants, still could not go home, and Captain Clark took necessary precautions while marching, as if he were "in a Indian country."

By August 16, the British troops had arrested thirty-two rioters,

---

170. William Kellog to Gov. Francis Bernard, July 25, 1766, Mass. Archives, VI, 328–329.

171. Petition of the inhabitants of Nobletown, July 30, 1766, *ibid.*, 334–336.

172. Petition of Ephraim Fitch and others of Egremont to Gov. Francis Bernard, July 31, 1766, *ibid.*, 333; John Cotton, deputy secretary of Massachusetts, to the selectmen of Egremont, Aug. 7, 1766, enclosed in John Clark's letter to Gen. Gage, Aug. 19, 1766, Gage Papers, Clements Lib.; Gov. Henry Moore to earl of Shelburne, Feb. 24, 1767, *N.Y. Col. Docs.*, VII, 911. Gov. Bernard also transmitted to the Board of Trade all the petitions of the Nobletown people and his comments favoring their case. Gov. Moore rejected Bernard's protest and at the same time urged the Bay Colony to extradite the rioters to New York.

twenty of whom were from the Egremont and Taconic area and the rest
from Nobletown and Spencertown. Ostensibly for the purpose of apprehending "some more of the mob," the following morning Captain Clarke
moved his headquarters several miles eastward to a tavern belonging to
one Isaac Spoor, who was in business under a Massachusetts license. The
tavern stood at the foot of a mountain and, the officer understood, was
about four hundred yards away from the New York–Massachusetts border.[173] But the premises were claimed by the Yankees to be within their
jurisdiction, since it was three miles east of the twenty-mile line from the
Hudson River and only about four miles west of Great Barrington, or
Lower Sheffield. The troop deployment was obviously a maneuver of the
desperate Claverack proprietor, who in spite of the military effort found
himself no closer to firm control of the disputed lands than he had been a
month earlier. He knew that the army would have to leave sooner or
later and that with the majority of the insurgents still at large, he would
be unable to defend his estate.[174] One can almost suspect that he brought
the troops this far hoping to provoke a violent incident with the Yankees,
violent enough to warrant further police action until all traces of rebellion were completely destroyed. This suspicion deepens when one con-
siders that the new location of the headquarters was no more conducive
to catching "more of the mob" than the old, given the type of insurgency
the army confronted.

According to a Boston newspaper account, the appearance of the
redcoats "alarmed the whole country."[175] Hardly had the troops en-
camped when Captain Clarke was visited by the "Chief men" of Berkshire
County including Elijah Williams, sheriff, and Elijah Dwight, justice of
the peace. The delegation, protesting the encroachment on Massachusetts
territory, requested the officer to remove his quarters "west of the mountain" or face "a great many Difficulteys." To impress him with the solidarity between the squatters and the province, a selectman of Egremont
showed him Bernard's instruction authorizing the support of the refugees
from Claverack. The session, lasting well into midnight, was frequently
interrupted by the shouting of 350 squatters and 40 Stockbridge Indians
who came there to uphold the authority of the sheriff. At one point, the
unruly crowd appeared to be getting out of hand, and the frightened
soldiers, their bayonets fixed, tensed for battle. Bloodshed was averted

173. John Clarke to Lt. Col. Maitland, Aug. 5, 1766, and to Gen. Gage, Aug. 17,
1766, Gage Papers, Clements Lib.
174. Clarke to Gage, Aug. 19, 1766, *ibid*.
175. News from Boston dated Sept. 8, 1766, in *N.-Y. Mercury*, Sept. 15, 1766.

only by the swift interposition of the sheriff and Captain Clarke. Clarke must have realized that he was violating General Gage's strict order not to pursue the insurgents into Massachusetts "unless attended by the Civil Magistrates" of that Province. The next morning, an intelligence report had it that "a great many men" in arms were ready to pay another visit to the camp. His common sense dictated that he withdraw. Yet, his pride told him not to give the appearance of a precipitate retreat from the threat of the "peasants." He needed a face-saver, which, to his relief, the county magistrates were willing to provide. Colonel Israel Williams, a justice, and others "importuned" him to retire west of the mountain so as to dispel "the fears of the people" and promised that "their people" would not "Interfear upon the Troops." Although they flatly refused to honor the proclamation of Governor Moore and the warrants for the arrest of Noble and his associates, their demeanor and entreatment were good enough for Captain Clarke to do what he had to do. In the name of putting the minds of the inhabitants at ease, he moved the troops west of the mountains that morning. This was a severe jolt to Robert Van Rensselaer, who had accompanied the officer all this time.[176] But the worst was yet to come. A week later, General Gage called off the entire operation and ordered Captain Clarke to rejoin the corps because, "The Country being in peace, the Civil Officers will have no further occasion" for military assistance.

Harmanus Schuyler, the Albany County sheriff, and the Van Rensselaers could not have disagreed more with General Gage's appraisal of the situation. Peace surely came to the area, but it was the kind of peace the landlord would rather not have had. For all the wanton destruction of property and the dispersal of the insurgents, the disputed lands remained out of his reach.[177] For one thing, the squatters were as defiant as ever. For another, the Albany County lawmen, who had repeatedly betrayed

176. William Henry Ludlow's affidavit, Aug. 27, 1766, HM1506, Henry E. Huntington Library, San Marino, Calif.; Gen. Gage to duke of Richmond, Aug. 26, 1766, Carter, ed., *Correspondence of Gage*, I, 102–103; John Clarke to Gage, Aug. 19, 1766, Gage Papers, Clements Lib. General Gage, while calling back the troops from Claverack, complimented Capt. Clarke for having moved "west of the mountain." He then added, "It is not our Business to ascertain exact Limits only to assist the Civil Power to put the Laws in Force and to preserve the peace." Despite his alleged reason for ordering the troop withdrawal, his action was probably prompted more by the strong protest of Gov. Bernard against the activities of the regulars than by the conditions in the country. Gage was well aware of the steps that the Massachusetts governor had taken to support the insurgents.

177. The property losses of 51 Nobletown people alone were estimated to be £2,231 16s. of Massachusetts money, about £44 per person. William Kellog to Gov. Bernard, May 27, 1767, Mass. Archives, VI, 358–360.

their incompetence, were still a broken reed. As soon as the fife and drums of the troops faded away, the area reverted to its condition prior to their arrival. Isaac Andrews of Nobletown, who was "effectually impoverished," quit the place to take up a seafaring life so that he would not be hounded by his creditors.[178] Some may have followed his example. But most of the squatters came right back to rebuild and stay. The military intervention in Claverack was an exercise in futility that served neither the landlord nor the Noble party.

Elsewhere, order was restored and the rights of the landlords preserved. In the middle of September, General Gage reported, "Every thing now wears the Face of Quiet." He noted ruefully, however, that the riotous spirit was "too high" among the people to be "as yet quite evaporated."[179] The military power had proved successful in suppressing the manifestations of that spirit but had not eradicated its deep-rooted causes. This was so because the task of the military had stopped short of meddling with the land disputes that had given birth to the conflict. As long as these problems were unresolved, the proprietors continued to be harassed. Beverly Robinson, whose Lot Number 7 in Highland Patent was the major stage of agitation, complained scarcely a month after the trial of the rioters that "it seems my Troubles are not yet at an End." His new troubles began when Jonathan Brown and his associates reinvoked the New Fairfield claim and managed to "seduce" some of the former Indian tenants and some of the squatters who had become tenants of Robinson to take new leases under them.[180] In December came the eruption of fresh disturbances in the area as Nimham and his people, who had lately returned from London, were again "forcibly turning some poor people out of Possession of their Houses." The Indian behavior was directly attributable to a report from the Board of Trade to the king that was favorable to the Nimham claim. In substance, the report stated that the action of the New York government against Samuel Monrow, the ally of the Indians, carried with it "unreasonable Severity, the Colour of great Prejudice and Partiality and of an intention to intimidate these Indians from prosecuting their claims" and that "there is foundation for further examination" into the case of the Wappingers.[181] Roughly coinciding

178. Isaac Andrews to William Williams, Feb. 27, 1773, Williams Papers, I, 12, Berkshire Atheneum.
179. Gen. Gage to duke of Richmond, Sept. 13, 1766, Carter, ed., *Correspondence of Gage*, I, 107–108.
180. Beverly Robinson to James Duane, Sept. 9, 1766, Duane Papers, Roll 1.
181. In late June 1766, Nimham and his small party had sailed to England in order to appeal their case to the king. Petition of the Wappinger Indians to Sir William Johnson, May 29, 1766, *William Johnson Papers*, XII, 97–98; earl of Shelburne to Johnson, Oct.

with the return of Nimham to Stockbridge and probably encouraged by the good news he brought from home, "those Pests of Society"—the Indian purchasers across the Taconic—again revealed ambitions against Livingston Manor. The excitable proprietor of the manor was petrified.[182] More bad news came from New York City in late January or early February 1767, when the earl of Shelburne, the new secretary of state for the Southern Department and an architect of the pro-Indian policy, chastised both Governor Moore and General Gage, and particularly the sheriff of Albany, for what the official deemed to be excessive use of military power in civil affairs.

Most ominous of all was a rumor in Albany about that time that the crown, persuaded of the merit of the French-Indian War veterans' case, had ordered the governor to "prosecute Mr. Renselaer for an Intrusion on the Lands at Claverack as the King's soil." The rumor proved to be true by June.[183] Colden must have been elated at this order, for it was a clear vindication of his past assault on Claverack. To the provincial landed magnates, the court appeared "determined to have a part of that Tract." Robert R. Livingston of Clermont best expressed their reaction: "Madness seems to prevail on the other side of the water; melancholy and dejection on this. The order to try the Renslaers Title seems to be a Fire that endangers every neighbour." As if to confirm the dire prediction, the Livingstons learned that Cadwallader Colden had "furnished twelve folio pages" against their manor title.[184] Not the least alarming to both Livingston and Van Rensselaer were the persistent efforts on the

---

11, 1766, *ibid.*, V, 394–395; *N.-Y. Mercury*, July 7, 1766; Henry Moore to earl of Shelburne, Dec. 22, 1766, and "Report of the Lords of Trade on the Petition of the Wappinger Indians," Aug. 30, 1766, *N.Y. Col. Docs.*, VII, 885–886, 868–870.

182. John Schuyler, Jr., Walter and Robert Livingston, and James Duane to father, Robert, Jr., Dec. 29, 1766, and Feb. 2, 1767, Livingston-Redmond MSS, Roll 8. In this instance, Livingston was probably overreacting to the news that the Nobletown inhabitants had written a petition to Sir William Johnson entreating him for help. The petition, dated 1766, was destroyed by the fire at the New York State capitol in 1911. See Richard E. Day, comp., *Calendar of the Sir William Johnson Manuscripts in the New York State Library* (Albany, N.Y., 1909), 338–339; Mark, *Agrarian Conflicts*, 150.

183. William Smith, Jr., to Philip Schuyler, Feb. 1767, Schuyler Papers, Box 23. On Apr. 13, 1767, the king ordered Gov. Moore to bring suit against John Van Rensselaer at the crown's expense. He also ordered that if the judgment was in favor of the proprietor, the attorney general of the province "do prosecute an appeal" to the Privy Council. C.O. 1073/5, 25, 72–73; Gov. Moore to earl of Shelburne, Aug. 22, 1767, *N.Y. Col. Docs.*, VII, 950; N.Y. Land Papers, XXXIII, 18.

184. Peter R. Livingston to father, Robert, Jr., Sept. 5, 1767, Livingston-Redmond MSS, Roll 8; Robert R. Livingston to father, Robert, Jr., of Clermont, Sept. 18, 1767, Robert R. Livingston Coll., Box 1. See also Bonomi, *A Factious People*, 209; Gerlach, *Philip Schuyler*, 72–73.

part of the settlers of Spencertown, Nobletown, New Canaan, and Taconic to obtain Massachusetts's protection.[185]

Nevertheless, by dint of their influence and power, the landed men weathered the storms quite well. On March 11, the governor and council, after two days of hearings on the Wappingers versus the Philipse heirs, unanimously declared that "the original Indian Title" to the lands comprehended in Philipse's Highland Patent had long since been "extinguished" by purchases "honestly and fairly made" and that the "complaints of the Indians, to which they have been wholly excited by white persons, with a View to Countenance and Support their own illegal Pretensions to the Lands is Vexatious and unjust, and as such ought to be, and is hereby accordingly dismissed."[186] This decision, which defied the wishes of the imperial government, gave the coup de grace to the Nimham claim and, by implication, also to the claims of the other Stockbridge Indians upon which the alleged rights of the Claverack and Taconic squatters were founded. In May it was reported that "those troublesome Banditti" at Taconic with Indian deeds had "at last" abandoned their plot against the Manor of Livingston.[187] To the further relief of the provincial landed interests, the supreme court trial of John Van Rensselaer ended on November 5, 1767, in favor of the landlord.[188]

But for Van Rensselaer it was a hollow victory because the verdict did little to change the real picture. Ironically, in the next few years almost everything he did turned sour, and his fortune continuously skidded downhill. Shortly after the trial, he warned the squatters to either "give up their claim to their possessions" or accept tenancy. His tough warning was neutralized by the encouragement to sit tight that John

185. Petition of William Kellog and others, June 1767, Mass. Archives, V, 362–363a, also 373, 417–420; "The Proprietors Book . . . of Spencer Township, 1757–1772," MS No. 12379, 11–12, N.Y. State Lib.

186. *N.-Y. Mercury*, Mar. 23, 1767; Gov. Moore to earl of Shelburne, Jan. 13, 1767, *N.Y. Col. Docs.*, VII, 890; Sir William Johnson to earl of Shelburne, Apr. 1, 1767, *ibid.*, 913–914, also 915–916; John Tabor Kempe to Johnson, Mar. 17, 1767, Letters, A-Z, Kempe Papers; Moore to Johnson, Mar. 17, 1767, *William Johnson Papers*, XII, 281.

187. Shortly after the hearing, the Stockbridge Indians asked Sir William Johnson to intercede on their behalf, but to no effect. Johnson to Gov. Moore, "Papers relating to N.Y., 1764–68," British Lib. Additional MS 22679 (transcript), Lib. of Congress; Walter and Robert Livingston to father, Robert, Jr., May 30, 1767, Livingston-Redmond MSS, Roll 8.

188. *N.-Y. Gaz.; and Wkly. Mercury*, Nov. 14, 1768; "King against John Van Rensselaer Esq.," memorandum, Sorted Legal MSS, Kempe Papers; Gov. Moore to earl of Shelburne, Aug. 22, 1767, *N.Y. Col. Docs.*, VII, 950; "Attorney General's Report to the Govr and Council, assigning the Reasons why no Writ of Error was brought in the prosecution for Intrusion to his Claverack Estate," Feb. 10, 1773, Claverack Papers, Folder 3, N.-Y. Hist. Soc.

Tabor Kempe, the attorney general, and Peter and Henry Van Schaick of Kinderhook offered them. Kempe himself, it will be remembered, had some years before been interested in the tract, served as the squatters' defense lawyer during the Bebee controversy, and had recently employed many of them as witnesses for the crown.[189] The Van Schaicks, leading rivals of the Van Rensselaers in local politics, were then trying to extend the Kinderhook township boundary at the expense of the Claverack-Westenhook proprietors. In 1770 Van Rensselaer was opposed by the neighboring communities over the appointment of highway commissioners and militia officers for Claverack district, an opposition not unrelated to the conflicting land claims.[190] The same year, some people from Van Hoesen Patent, with which Van Rensselaer had been having a boundary dispute since 1765, physically assaulted him.[191] In 1771 Nobletown inhabitants again challenged his claim by presenting a new petition to the New York government. This was followed by several more from his traditional enemies, all aiming at certain parts of the contested lands.[192] His proprietary status was as uncertain as ever since, in accordance with the king's order, Kempe was preparing to appeal the court decision to the crown in Privy Council. To make his affairs still gloomier, William Tryon, the new governor (July 9, 1771–April 6, 1774), a man who is best remembered for vigorous suppression of the North Carolina Regulators, entertained some reservations about Van Rensselaer's title, believing that "the Crown had not fair play on the Trial for the Intrusion."[193]

The proprietor was sensible of a thorny path ahead of him now that even the governor was taking his opponents' side. Almost seventy years

189. John Munro to John Tabor Kempe, Mar. 10, 1769, Letters, A-Z, Kempe Papers; "Copy of Mr. Munro's List of Evidences on the part of the Crown and their places of abode," Sorted Legal MSS, *ibid.*

190. "Proprietors Book . . . of Spencer Township," MS No. 12379, 13, N.Y. State Lib.; Cadwallader Colden to Sir William Johnson, Jan. 28, 1770, *Colden Papers*, VII, 164–165; Johnson to Henry Van Schaick, Mar. 26, 1770, *William Johnson Papers*, XII, 807; *Journal of General Assembly*, II, 809; Sabine, ed., *Historical Memoirs of William Smith*, I, 80; N.Y. Land Papers, XXVIII, 157, 155, XXXII, 136; Richard Treat of Spencertown to John Tabor Kempe, Nov. 6, 1766, Unsorted Legal MSS, Kempe Papers.

191. William Smith, Jr., to Philip Schuyler, Feb. 21, 1765, June 5, 1769, and Apr. 17, 1770, and Jeremiah Van Rensselaer to Philip Schuyler, Jan. 22, 1770, Schuyler Papers, Box 23.

192. Petition of William Kellog and others, inhabitants of Nobletown, May 11, 1771, N.Y. Land Papers, XXIX. For the other petitions, see *ibid.*, XXIV, 117, XXVII, 107, XXVIII, 51, 54, XXX, 27, 44, 48, 77; Sabine, ed., *Historical Memoirs of William Smith*, I, 104.

193. Petition of Lt. Alexander McDonald, Jan. 12, 1773, C.O. 1104/5, 384–385; William Smith, Jr., to Philip Schuyler, June 17, 24, 1769, and Nov. 27, 1772, Schuyler Papers, Box 24.

of age, he was genuinely exhausted emotionally and financially after two decades of controversy and violence. He had come to the point where he felt he could no longer afford another round of litigation, which, even if he might win, would be "attended with an Expence almost ruinous to his Estate and destruction of his Peace."[194] In late November 1772, Tryon made an overture to the proprietor: surrender about 66,000 acres of the disputed land to the crown, and, in return, the government would grant a confirmatory patent for the remainder (about 120,000 acres) of Claverack Manor. Simultaneously, Van Rensselaer learned from several sources that the governor was "determined" to give some portion of the tract to the squatters. Under the circumstances, the deal seemed to the landlord to be the best that he could expect, and he accepted it a month later. We can assume that he took that step after consulting his Westenhook allies, because he had already in 1769 conveyed most of the surrendered land to them in accordance with the 1763 agreement (see the map on p. 413). On February 24, 1773, he received a confirmatory patent (see the sketch on p. 414).[195] The squatters of Spencertown and Nobletown were displeased with it since it bargained away the "greater part" of the former and a "considerable part" of the latter to Van Rensselaer. The controversy with the squatters therefore continued, but it was soon overshadowed by the War of Independence.[196]

To sum up, the causes of the "Great Rebellion" were complex. On the surface, the rebellion everywhere appeared to be directed against the landlords and the lease systems they represented. But a closer look reveals that the conflict in the northern manors, like the one in the 1750s, revolved around conflicting land claims. As the rebel spokesman, William Kellog of Nobletown, pointed out, the "bone of contention" was land and not the prevailing lease conditions. The same was true of the insurgency in Philipse's Highland Patent until early 1765. The farmers there

194. James Duane to Robert Livingston, Jr., May 17, 1769, Livingston-Redmond MSS, Roll 8; petition of John Van Rensselaer, Dec. 23, 1772, N.Y. Land Papers, XXXII, 138.

195. "Deed of Surrender to the Crown of sundry parcels of Land formerly claimed by Colonel John Van Rensselaer as part of his Claverack Est.," C.O. 1104/5, 287–312, also 343–382; William Smith, Jr., to Philip Schuyler, Nov. 27, 1772, Schuyler Papers, Box 24; minutes of council meeting, Dec. 23, 1772, Misc. MSS, Box 4, Kempe Papers; William Smith, Jr., to John Van Rensselaer (draft), Nov. 27, 1772, Sabine, ed., *Historical Memoirs of William Smith*, I, 129, also 133–134, 137; Gov. William Tryon to earl of Dartmouth, Mar. 3, 1773, C.O. 1104/5, 253–258.

196. N.Y. Land Papers, XXXIII, 597–599, XXXIV, 75–76, 82; Philip Schuyler to Peter Van Schaick, July 7, 1774, Schuyler Papers, Box 2; Simeon Rowlee, Robert Meeker, and Truman Powell to the legislature of New York, Jan. 23, 1789, Columbia County Misc. MSS, N.-Y. Hist. Soc.

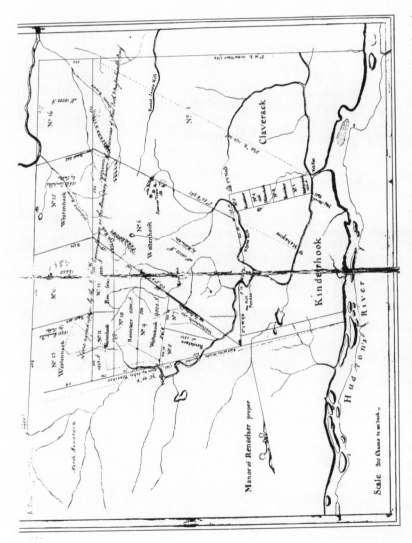

**Allotments of Land between Van Rensselaer and the Westenhook Proprietors. Source: New York Colonial Manuscripts, Land Papers, 1642–1803, XXXIV, 75, New York State Library, Albany.**

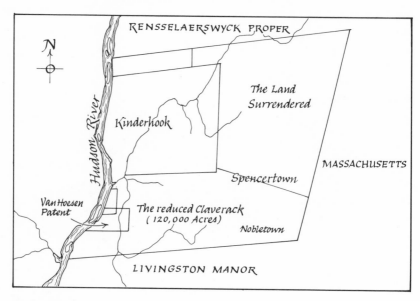

**Sketch of the Land Surrendered by John Van Rensselaer, 1772–1773.** Adjusted from "Deed of Surrender," C.O. 1104/5, 287–312, 343–382, Public Record Office. (Drawn by Richard J. Stinely.)

were embittered because the Philipses had tried to engross the lands they had occupied and cultivated for many years. The squatters refused to become the tenants of the proprietors. Once allied with the regular tenants of the Philipses and John Van Cortlandt, what was basically an antiproprietary movement took on more of the character of a tenant rebellion for better lease terms. But this merger should not be allowed to blur the fact that the squatters firmly held its leadership throughout and that they never abandoned their squatter claims to their possessions. Their alliance with the regular tenants was, it seems, a marriage of convenience that they hoped to exploit for the advancement of the squatter interest.

The only classic antilandlord campaign connected with tenancy was manifested in Cortlandt Manor. But, contrary to common interpretation, the rioting was extremely limited and short-lived and was the result of difficulties between John Van Cortlandt and a handful of his tenants. It had, we may speculate, the potential of setting in motion a tidal wave of antirent agitation—if the colonial tenantry had lived under unbearable oppression and hardship. But none of the tenants in Rensselaerswyck proper and Philipsburgh, and few in Cortlandt, Livingston Manor, and Claverack joined the rebel ranks. As it turned out, the Cortlandt Manor phenomenon was no more than a diversion in the noisy title disputes.

The title disputes lay at the bottom of the Great Rebellion. But they would not have persisted as long as they did and would not have escalated into armed conflict if colonial officials like William Kempe and Colden, and if the home government itself, had not been involved. Kempe, governed mainly by greed, saw to it that the Dutchess squatters were encouraged to reject the claims of the New York proprietors. Colden, through his tenacious antiproprietary campaign and his attack on the Van Rensselaer patent, created a milieu in which challenging an ancient title would look honorable and just. British authority supported Indian grievances against the great patents, leading the squatters to believe that their cause was identical with that of his majesty. The net effect of all these activities was to undermine the sanctity of the land titles and to intensify the land disputes. When legal and political recourse was unfruitful, the squatters turned to violence during the Stamp Act controversy.

The rebellion of 1766 in New York was not a class conflict between the rich and the poor or between oppressor and oppressed, despite the rhetoric of the squatters. Not even the poor in New York City identified their interests with those of the rebellious farmers or sought in any way to aid them. Nor did many of the participants and abettors in the rioting conceive of themselves as being involved in class warfare. The squatters were clearly devoted to freehold property for themselves, and they violently resisted the efforts to subject them to leasehold status. However, there is no evidence that they rejected in principle the large landowner-tenant arrangement. They were fighting for their own property in good middle-class fashion. Prendergast, one of the principal leaders of the rebellion, reportedly refused the offer of friends to help him escape from jail, saying that "if he should escape without any other inconveniences, it would be attended with the Loss of his Property in the Government, which would reduce his Family to poverty and Want." His friends agreed with this reasoning and thereupon abandoned their schemes for his release.[197] Their concern for property was as great as that of the landlords they were opposing. The rebels of 1766 were, in short, neither social revolutionaries nor a jacquerie but simply petty landed bourgeois.

197. N.-Y. Gaz., Sept. 29, 1766.

# Appendixes

## Appendix 1: Genealogies

### VAN RENSSELAER

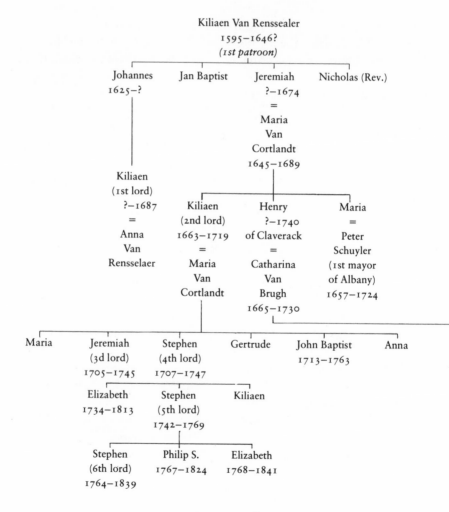

Kiliaen Van Renssealer
1595–1646?
*(1st patroon)*

Johannes 1625–?　　Jan Baptist　　Jeremiah ?–1674 = Maria Van Cortlandt 1645–1689　　Nicholas (Rev.)

Kiliaen (1st lord) ?–1687 = Anna Van Rensselaer

Kiliaen (2nd lord) 1663–1719 = Maria Van Cortlandt

Henry ?–1740 of Claverack = Catharina Van Brugh 1665–1730

Maria = Peter Schuyler (1st mayor of Albany) 1657–1724

Maria　　Jeremiah (3d lord) 1705–1745　　Stephen (4th lord) 1707–1747　　Gertrude　　John Baptist 1713–1763　　Anna

Elizabeth 1734–1813　　Stephen (5th lord) 1742–1769　　Kiliaen

Stephen (6th lord) 1764–1839　　Philip S. 1767–1824　　Elizabeth 1768–1841

Van Rensselaer Genealogy (Continued):
Children of Henry (?–1740) and Catharina Van Brugh

| Maria 1690–? | Catarine 1692–? | Anna 1696–? | Elizabeth 1700–? | Helena 1702–? | Johannes 1708–? | Henry, Jr. 1712–? | Kiliaen 1717–1781 |
|---|---|---|---|---|---|---|---|
| = | = | = | = | = | = | = | = |
| Samuel Ten Broeck | Johannes Ten Broeck | Peter Douw | John Richards | Jacob Wendell | Engeltie Livingston | Elizabeth Van Brugh | (1) Ariantje Schuyler |
| | | | | | | | = |
| | | | | | | | (2) Maria Low |

Source: Kiliaen Van Rensselaer, *The Van Rensselaer Manor* (Baltimore, 1929), 40–46.

# LIVINGSTON

Robert Livingston = Alida (Schuyler) Van Rensselaer
1654–1728     1656–1729

Philip
1686–1749
=
Catrina
Van
Brugh

Gilbert
1690–1746
=
Cornelia
Beekman

Robert, Jr.
(of Clermont)
1688–1775
=
Margaret
Howarden

Robert, Jr.
1708–1790
=
Maria
Thong

Peter
Van
Brugh
1710–
1793

John
1714–
1788

Philip
1716–
1778

Henry
1719–
1772

William
1722–
1790

Peter R.
1737–
1794

Walter
1740–
1797

Robert C.
1749–
1794

John
1750–
1822

Henry
1753–
1825

Mary

Alida

Catherine

[Judge] Robert R.
1718–1775
=
Margaret Beekman

Robert R.
1746–
1813

John R.
1755–
1851

Henry B.
1750–
1831

Edward
1764–
1836

Source: Patricia Joan Gordon, "The Livingstons of New York, 1675–1860: Kinship and Class" (Ph.D. Diss., Columbia University, 1959), 152, 219, 220.

## PHILIPSE

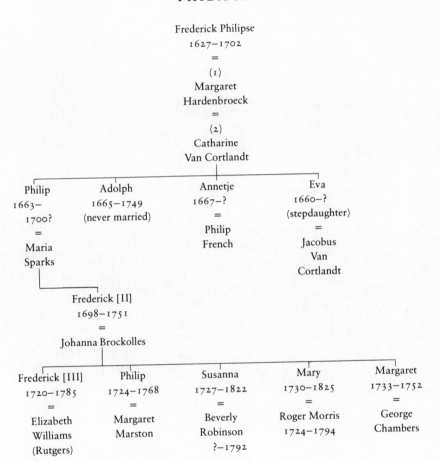

Source: Philipse Genealogical Research Report, Sleepy Hollow Restorations Library, Tarrytown, N.Y.

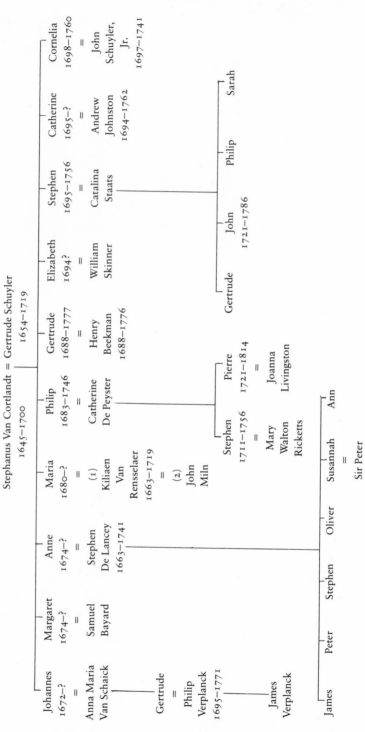

VAN CORTLANDT

Stephanus Van Cortlandt = Gertrude Schuyler
1645–1700                    1654–1719

Source: *The Journal of the Reverend Silas Constant, Pastor of the Presbyterian Church at Yorktown, New York* . . . (Philadelphia, 1903), 424–430.

# Appendix 2: Land Transactions in Cortlandt Manor

Table A.1. Land Transactions between the Original Proprietors and Settlers in Cortlandt Manor, 1733–1776

| Purchaser | Original Home of Buyer | Status | Year of Purchase | Acreage | Price Paid £ s. d. |
|---|---|---|---|---|---|
| ANDREW JOHNSTON ESTATE | | | | | |
| Gertrude Beekman | N.Y. City | Landlord | 1739 | 340 | |
| Peter Burr | Cortlandt | Yeoman | 1742 | | |
| Ephraim Hayward | Cortlandt | Yeoman | | | |
| Zachariah Hubbell | Cortlandt | Yeoman | | | |
| Isaiah Treadwell | Cortlandt | Yeoman | 1742 | 5,135[a] | 2,619 4 5 |
| Simon Dackin | Dutchess Co. | Yeoman | | | |
| Elisha Johnson | Dutchess Co. | Yeoman | 1742 | | |
| Caleb Hall | Mass. | Yeoman | | | |
| Caleb Hall | Cortlandt | Yeoman | 1745 | | |
| Pelatia Haws | Cortlandt | Yeoman | 1745 | 335 | 167 10 0 |
| Joseph Travis | Cortlandt | Tenant | 1748 | 121½ | 121 0 0 |
| Caleb Hall | Cortlandt | Yeoman | 1748 | 115 | 115 0 0 |
| Eleazer Yeomans | Cortlandt | Tenant | 1748–1760 | 326 | 500 15 0 |
| Richard Curry | Dutchess Co. | Yeoman | 1750–1753 | 432½ | 475 0 0 |
| Israel Kniffen | Cortlandt | Yeoman | ? | 202 | 225 0 0 |
| Joseph Lee | Cortlandt | Tenant | 1753 | 102 | 132 0 0 |
| Jeremiah Drake | Cortlandt | Yeoman | 1756 | 134 | 268 0 0 |
| James Lent | Cortlandt | Yeoman | 1760 | 88 | 200 0 0 |
| Hackaliah Brown | Cortlandt | Yeoman | 1762–1772 | 342½ | 691 11 0 |
| John Seeley | Conn. | Yeoman | 1763 | 210 | 500 0 0 |
| Levi Baily | Cortlandt | Tenant | 1773 | 318¾ | 832 10 0 |
| Patrick Cumins | Cortlandt | Tenant | c. 1775 | 303¼ | |
| John Greens | N. Castle | Yeoman | 1772 | 229¾ | |
| Peter Corne | Cortlandt | | 1773 | 202 | |
| | | | | 8,937¼ | |
| JOHN SCHUYLER ESTATE | | | | | |
| Stephen De Lancey | N.Y. City | Landlord | 1762 | 3,696 | ? |
| David Travis | Cortlandt | Tenant | 1766 | 215 | 433 5 0 |
| Jeremiah Travis | Cortlandt | Tenant | 1766 | 192 | 384 0 0 |
| James Guion | Cortlandt | Yeoman | 1767 | 190 | 380 0 0 |
| Frances Lent | Cortlandt | Yeoman | 1768 | 200 | 900 0 0 |
| Hendrick Lent | Rykes Patent | Tenant | 1768 | 300 | 750 0 0 |
| Andrew Gerow | Cortlandt | Tenant | 1768 | 109 | 196 4 0 |
| Aaron Forman | Cortlandt | Tenant | 1768 | 205 | 404 0 0 |
| Aaron Forman | Cortlandt | Tenant | c. 1768 | 111 | ? |
| Joseph Lyons | Cortlandt | Tenant | 1768 | 203 | 403 0 0 |
| Jacob Underhill | Cortlandt | Yeoman | 1769 | 220 | 410 0 0 |
| John Lee | Cortlandt | Yeoman | 1773 | c. 200 | 436 10 0 |

Table A.1. (Continued): Land Transactions in Cortlandt Manor

| Purchaser | Original Home of Buyer | Status | Year of Purchase | Acreage | Price Paid £ s. d. |
|---|---|---|---|---|---|
| | JOHN SCHUYLER ESTATE | | | | |
| John Petrue | Cortlandt | Yeoman | 1765 | 260 | 525 7 0 |
| David Becker | Cortlandt | Yeoman | 1766 | 5 | 17 0 0 |
| William Bailey | Cortlandt | Yeoman | 1772 | 265 | 1,076 15 0 |
| | | | | 6,371 | |
| | PHILIP VAN CORTLANDT ESTATE | | | | |
| Henry Scott | Cortlandt | Tenant | 1757 | 480 | 819 8 0 |
| John Tomkins | Philipsburgh | Tenant | 1757 | 241 | 361 10 0 |
| Cornright Briggs | Cortlandt | Tenant | 1758 | 125 | 450 0 0 |
| Samuel Fields | Cortlandt | Tenant | 1758 | 125 | 450 0 0 |
| John Duncan | Schenectady | Trader | 1757 | 500 | 590 0 0 |
| Oliver De Lancey | N.Y. City | Gentleman | 1757 | 1,200 | 1,719 7 0 |
| Moses Knapp | Cortlandt | Tenant | 1759 | 250 | 525 0 0 |
| James Russel, Jr. | Cortlandt | ? | 1760 | 100 | ? |
| Pierre Van Cortlandt | Cortlandt | Shopkeeper | 1758–1762 | 3,138 | 1,197 10 0 |
| David Weeks | Cortlandt | Miller | 1761 | 100 | |
| | | | | 6,259 | |
| | WILLIAM SKINNER ESTATE | | | | |
| John Beasley, Jr. | Cortlandt | Tenant | 1736 | | |
| Joseph Conklin | Cortlandt | Tenant | 1736 | 1,886 | 360 0 0 |
| Harmanus Gardenier | Cortlandt | Yeoman | c. 1737 | c. 400 | |
| Daniel Gerow | N. Rochelle | Yeoman | 1755 | 200 | 250 0 0 |
| John Pinkney | Cortlandt | Tenant | 1765 | 123½ | 339 12 6 |
| Michael Michael | Cortlandt | Tenant | 1765 | 219½ | 811 2 6 |
| Seth Whitney | Cortlandt | Tenant | 1765–1768 | 246 | 671 9 2 |
| John Veal | Cortlandt | Tenant | 1765 | 233¾ | 818 2 6 |
| John Travis | Cortlandt | Tenant | 1765 | 127 | ? |
| John Bowton | ? | Yeoman | 1770 | 314 | 314 0 0 |
| Gilbert Drake | Philipsburgh | Tenant | 1767 | 204 | 700 0 0 |
| Joseph Strang | Cortlandt | Tenant | 1767 | 76 | 296 3 4 |
| Ezekiel Hawley | Cortlandt | Yeoman | 1772 | 58 | 58 0 0 |
| John Ambler | Cortlandt | Yeoman | 1773 | 136 | 314 5 0 |
| Thaddeus Weed | Cortlandt | ? | 1775 | 110 | 354 0 0 |
| | | | | 4,333¾ | |
| | SAMUEL BAYARD ESTATE | | | | |
| Samuel Brown | Rye | Yeoman | 1743 | c. 1,000 | 392 0 0 |
| Hackaliah Brown | Rye | Yeoman | 1743–1760 | c. 600 | c. 300 0 0 |
| John Gedney | Manor of Scarsdale | Yeoman | 1743 | 608½ | 160 0 0 |

Table A.1. (Continued): Land Transactions in Cortlandt Manor

| Purchaser | Original Home of Buyer | Status | Year of Purchase | Acreage | Price Paid £ s. d. |
|---|---|---|---|---|---|
| | | SAMUEL BAYARD ESTATE | | | |
| James Woods | N.Y. City | Yeoman | 1743 | 120 | |
| Thomas Smith | Cortlandt | Carpenter | 1760 | 167 | 250 10 0 |
| Nathaniel Newman, Jr. | Westchester Co. | ? | 1760 | 113 | 118 17 1½ |
| Joseph Benedict | Cortlandt | Tenant | 1760 | 454½ | 500 10 0 |
| Benjamin Griffin | Westchester Co. | Yeoman | 1760 | 106 | 131 0 0 |
| Jacob Newman | Westchester Co. | Yeoman | 1760 | 114 | 139 6 1½ |
| Jonathan Brown | Westchester Co. | Yeoman | 1760 | c. 1,000 | 1,073 18 6 |
| Lewis Palmer | Cortlandt | Tenant | 1765 | 162 | |
| Thomas Thorn | Cortlandt | Tenant | 1761 | 50 | |
| Thomas Barker | Cortlandt | Tenant | 1771 | 300 | |
| John Leverick | Cortlandt | Cooper | 1773 | 106 | 341 5 0 |
| Abraham Wright | Cortlandt | Tenant | 1774 | 100 | |
| Joseph Ogden | Cortlandt | Tenant | 1775 | 15 | |
| William and Hendrick Lent | Cortlandt | Tenant | 1771 | 111 | |
| James Van Horne | N.Y. City | Merchant | 1743? | 116 | |
| | | | | 5,243 | |
| | | STEPHEN DE LANCEY ESTATE | | | |
| Andrew Miller | Cortlandt | Tenant | 1761 | 200 | 365 5 0 |
| John Maybee | Cortlandt | Tenant | 1761 | 248 | 496 0 0 |
| Three unidentifiable persons | | | 1761 | 728 | 1,460 0 0 |
| Epenetus Townsend | Cortlandt | Priest | 1769 | 60 | |
| Denton Smith | Cortlandt | Tenant | 1769 | 115 | 230 0 0 |
| Levi Baily | Cortlandt | Tenant | 1769 | 227 | 510 11 0 |
| Nathaniel Delivan | Cortlandt | Yeoman | 1769–1773 | 151½ | 361 10 0 |
| John Delivan | Cortlandt | Tenant | 1769 | 124 | 310 17 0 |
| Robert Weeks | Cortlandt | ? | 1769 | | |
| Joseph Osborn | Cortlandt | Tenant | 1769 | 482 | 424 4 0 |
| Samuel Scribner | Cortlandt | ? | 1771 | ¾ | 0 10 0 |
| Mathew Delivan | Cortlandt | Tenant | 1773 | 89 | 152 11 6 |
| Cornelius Steenrod | Cortlandt | Millwright | 1773 | 5½ | 50 0 0 |
| John Patrick | Cortlandt | Yeoman | 1773 | 116 | 186 8 0 |
| Abraham Delivan | Cortlandt | Yeoman | 1773 | 23 | 81 10 0 |
| Timothy Van Scoy | Cortlandt | Tenant | 1773 | 59¾ | 83 13 0 |
| Jacob Keeler | Cortlandt | Tenant | 1773 | 109 | 219 0 0 |
| Benedict Carpenter | Scarsdale | Yeoman | 1773 | 105¾ | |
| Halsey Wood | Cortlandt | Yeoman | 1773 | 73 | 100 0 0 |
| Daniel Lobdill | Cortlandt | Tenant | 1773 | 123 | 184 17 0 |
| John Lobdill | Cortlandt | Yeoman | 1774 | 160 | 251 12 0 |
| Gabriel Purdy | Cortlandt | Tenant | 1773 | 265¾ | 531 0 0 |
| Caleb Smith | Cortlandt | Yeoman | 1773 | 218 | 240 7 0 |

Table A.1. (Continued): Land Transactions in Cortlandt Manor

| Purchaser | Original Home of Buyer | Status | Year of Purchase | Acreage | Price Paid £ s. d. |
|---|---|---|---|---|---|
| STEPHEN DE LANCEY ESTATE | | | | | |
| David Brown | Cortlandt | Tenant | 1773 | c. 20 | |
| Ephrain Lockwood | Cortlandt | Tenant | 1773 | 111 | 178  8 0 |
| David Ogden | Cortlandt | Tenant | 1771 | 156 | |
| | | | | 3,971 | |

[a] In 1743 Hayward, Hubbell, Treadwell, Dackin, and Johnson surrendered their shares to Peter Burr and Caleb Hall for £1,700. Two years later, Burr conveyed his moity to Pelatia Haws for £1,300.

Sources:

*Andrew Johnston Estate*—Deed Book G, 359–361, 401, 402, 403, Deed Book H, 171–181, 342–345, 376–378, 425–426, 427–428, Deed Book I, 66–67, 70–72, 179–180, 210–211, Deed Book K, 8–9, 21–22, 284–286, Westchester County Clerk's Office, White Plains, N.Y.; Deed Book 14, 293–294, Office of the Secretary of State of New York, Albany; Van Cortlandt Papers, V1644, V2066, Sleepy Hollow Restorations Library, Tarrytown, N.Y.; MS No. 12695 (4), New York State Library, Albany.

*John Schuyler Estate*—Deed Book H, 232–234, 448–449, 449–451, Deed Book K, 246–247, Mortgage Book B, 281, Westchester Co. Clerk's Office; Deed Book 19, 110, Office of N.Y. Sec. of State; Schuyler Papers, Box 10, 19, 23, New York Public Library; Schuyler Papers, Sleepy Hollow Restorations Lib.

*Philip Van Cortlandt Estate*—Miscellaneous Land Papers, Box 1, Van Cortlandt-Van Wyck Papers, N.Y. Pub. Lib.; Van Cortlandt Papers and "Minutes of the estate of Philip and Stephen Van Cortlandt Esqrs decd, 1760," by Philip Van Cortlandt, both in New-York Historical Society, New York; Deed Book K, 250–252, Westchester Co. Clerk's Office.

*William Skinner Estate*—Misc. Land Papers, Box 1, Van Cortlandt-Van Wyck Papers, N.Y. Pub. Lib.; Deed Book G, 223–224, 596–597, 599–600, 601–602, 602–604, 663–664, Deed Book H, 266–269, 563–565, Deed Book I, 115–116, 368–369, Westchester Co. Clerk's Office; Deed Book 18, 142–146, 455–456, Office of N.Y. Sec. of State; Whitney-Kip Family Papers, Whitney Papers, and Cortlandt Manor Papers, all in N.-Y. Hist. Soc.; Van Cortlandt Papers, V1681, Sleepy Hollow Restorations Lib.; *New-York Gazette; and the Weekly Mercury,* Oct. 31, 1768.

*Samuel Bayard Estate*—Deed Book G, 312–313, 477–478, 693–695, Deed Book H, 106–108, 277–280, 320–325, 481–483, Deed Book I, 36–37, Westchester Co. Clerk's Office; Bayard-Campbell-Pearsall Land Papers, Misc. Land Papers, Box 1, Van Cortlandt-Van Wyck Papers, and American Loyalist Transcripts, XVII, 137, XXIX, 17, all in N.Y. Pub. Lib.; Philip Van Cortlandt (son of Pierre) to William Bayard, Nov. 8, 1773, and Apr. 10, 1773, Nicholas Bayard Papers, and "Droughts of Front Lot No. 5," Cortlandt Manor Papers, both in N.-Y. Hist. Soc.; Book of Wills B, 295–298, Westchester County Surrogate Office, White Plains, N.Y.

*Stephen De Lancey Estate*—Deed Book H, 375–376, 388–390, 391–397, 401–402, 459–460, 513–514, 518–520, 555–558, 558–559, 560–561; Deed Book I, 5–6, 21–22, 40–45, 130–132, 162–163, 177, 180–181, 183–185, 250–251, 321–322, Westchester Co. Clerk's Office; Deed Book 19, 432–433, Office of N.Y. Sec. of State; Van Cortlandt Papers, V1644, Sleepy Hollow Restorations Lib.

# A Note on Sources

※※※※

## Manuscripts

Except for those topics covered in the first two chapters, I have relied almost entirely on primary sources for this study. These sources, however, are scarce and fragmentary, and, worse still, those that have survived have often been tucked away by well-meaning archivists under the rubric of "miscellaneous papers," since they concerned neither famous men nor great events. The difficulty of getting at the manuscript sources undoubtedly has had much to do with the dismal state of the historiography of manorial society. Few secondary works on colonial manors, landlords, and tenantry are available, and I have had to overcome research problems by following the maxim, "If you look hard enough for it, you will surely find it."

Of the various depositories of documents, the Sleepy Hollow Restorations Library, Tarrytown, New York, has by far the richest collections on the families and the landholdings at Cortlandt and Philipsburgh manors. The number of Van Cortlandt and Philipse papers concerning leases, deeds, wills, rent accounts, and other manorial affairs runs to several thousand. The sources were locked in the Rockefeller Estate Office and closed to the general public until 1975. I was privileged, however, to read the precious collections in 1964 and again in 1969. In addition, the library has other materials on microfilm, on photostat, and in typescript. Noteworthy among these are: Public Records Office materials, including Colonial Office Series 5, Treasury Series 1, and High Court of Admiralty Series 1, all on twenty-two rolls of microfilm, and the Gage Papers, on two rolls of film, from the originals at the Sussex Archaeological Society, Lewes, Sussex, England. The Gage Papers were especially valuable for furnishing information on the estate owned by Sir Peter Warren and his heirs in Cortlandt Manor.

In reconstructing the story of tenant-landlord relations in the southern manors, I found it necessary also to consult sources in other libraries. Among them, the following collections at the New-York Historical Society were most helpful: the Van Cortlandt Family Papers, in 41 volumes, which includes the Cortlandt Manor Papers, 1697–1776, John Van Cortlandt's Receipt Books, 1757–1762 and 1766–1771 (two volumes), John Van Cortlandt's Letterbook and Note Book, and John Van Cortlandt's Daybooks, 1758–1786 (15 volumes); the Peter Warren Papers, 1724–1795; the Watts Papers, 9 volumes; the Robert Watts Papers, 3 boxes; the Whitney Papers; the Whitney-Kip Papers; the Benjamin Palmer Papers, 1679–1945; and the Stephen and Oliver De Lancey Papers, 1647–1804. Equally important materials at the New York Public Library are the Schuyler Papers, 1758–1798, 32 boxes, particularly boxes 10, 19, 23; the Bayard-Campbell-Pearsall Collections, 1732–1827; the Van Cortlandt-Van Wyck Papers, 1667–1912, 6 boxes, especially box 1 and 4; the Journal (c) of John Van Cortlandt, 1764–1772; the Letterbooks of Stephen and John Van Cortlandt, 1762–1769 and 1771–1792; and the Account Book or Ledger of Gertruyd Van Cortlandt, 1726–1740. The Verplanck Papers at the New York Genealogical and Biographical Society too provided an insight into the lease practices of the Verplanck family.

For Rensselaerswyck and its operations, I consulted the huge collection of Rensselaerswyck Manuscripts at the New York State Library, Albany, which survived the fire at the state capitol in 1911. It came as a complete surprise to me that this record, touching on many aspects of provincial and local affairs, has never been systematically utilized by scholars. The collection includes the manor's rent ledgers, 1719–1744, 1748–1756, 1758–1771, 1768–1789; Letters, 1674–1700, 1700–1749, 1767–1794; "Abraham Ten Broeck's Accounts of the Manor, 1763–1787"; and "Letters of Abraham Ten Broeck, 1753–1783." I also benefited from the Staats Family Archives, 4 boxes, and the Lansing Papers in the same library, which are illuminating about local elections and about certain administrative aspects of the manor. Concerning Rensselaerswyck, I also studied the following sources: at the New York Public Library, the Van Rensselaer-Fort Papers, 1729–1789, 3 boxes, which contain useful information about activities of the Claverack branch of the Van Rensselaer family; at the Albany Institute of History and Art, the Ten Broeck Family Papers, 4 boxes; and, at the New-York Historical Society, the Claverack Papers and John Van Rensselaer Papers, especially "Notes of Evidence" in the trial of the king versus John Van Rensselaer, 1768, which dramatized the complexity of conflicting land claims in the Claverack area.

Of the four major manors, Livingston Manor is most abundantly blessed with records. Its proprietors not only wrote profusely but also kept most of their correspondence and duplicate copies of their indentures. The major collection is the Livingston-Redmond Papers at the Franklin Delano Roosevelt Library, Hyde Park, New York. I used the microfilm edition on 13 rolls. This priceless collection covers almost every facet of the activities of the manor and its proprietor during the colonial period. Still, for the purpose of investigating lease practices there and in the Clermont section of the manor, I consulted numerous records at other depositories. At the New-York Historical Society, they were the Rent Ledger of Livingston Manor, 1767–1784; the Livingston Account Book, Clermont, 1761–

1781 and 1772–1784; the Livingston Manor Papers; Miscellaneous Manuscripts, Livingston, A–Z; and the Robert R. Livingston Collection. At the New York Public Library, I used the Gilbert Livingston Papers and, at the Museum of the City of New York, the Livingston Papers, particularly the correspondence between Philip Livingston, the second proprietor of the manor, and Jacob Wendell, a Boston merchant, in the 1730s and 1740s. I should also note that about 85 boxes of "Uncatalogued Livingston Manuscripts," New-York Historical Society, were a mine of information on the lease practices of both the Clermont and Beekman estates in Dutchess County. A large portion of the records, mostly in a crumpled condition, would be valuable to social historians of post-Revolutionary New York. For future reference, the New-York Historical Society archivist has kindly set aside under separate title a box of papers that are cited in this book.

Much of our traditional misunderstanding of the mid-eighteenth century disturbances on the New York manors has been due to the tendency of historians to look only at the materials at the New York libraries, a tendency that is related to their assumption that the disturbances stemmed from internal tension within the manorial system—particularly from the strained relationship between landlords and tenants. However, I was impressed more by the intrigues and agitation of outsiders as I examined the following records: the Massachusetts Archives, volumes IV, VI, XLVI, and CXIV, at the State House in Boston, which detail the conspiratorial schemes of several western Massachusetts land speculators against Livingston Manor and Claverack and show also the dependence of some New York tenants on the speculators. The Abraham Yates, Jr., Papers, 1607–1825, 4 boxes, New York Public Library, and the Livingston Papers at the Museum of the City of New York, particularly the correspondence between Robert Livingston, Jr., the third proprietor of Livingston Manor, and Jacob Wendell, further underscored the importance of external forces. I was also able to learn a great deal about the nature and progress of the "Great Rebellion" of 1766 from reading the Thomas Gage Papers at the William L. Clements Library, University of Michigan, Ann Arbor, especially the reports from Major Arthur Browne and Captain John Clarke, commanders of the two British army detachments to suppress the riots in Dutchess and Albany counties. The James Duane Papers, 1752–1796, in 10 boxes and on 3 rolls of microfilm at the New-York Historical Society, reveal Robert Livingston, Jr.'s, innermost thoughts as well as his actions when his estate was threatened by New Englanders.

The complicated land disputes that preceded the rebellion are highlighted by several sources. The William and John Tabor Kempe Papers, letters and legal papers, both "Sorted" and "Unsorted," 1752–1777, in 16 boxes, along with the Philipse's Highland Patent Papers (including "Field books of Benjamin Morgan's surveys of Philip Philipse's lot No. 6 made in 1762 and 1771") in 2 volumes, Dutchess County Papers, 1696–1806, and the Beekman Papers, in one box, all at the New-York Historical Society, were helpful in understanding the Oblong and the "Hoveout" land controversy. The Philipse-Gouverneur Land Titles, numbers 13 and 14, at the Columbia University Library and "A Geographical, Historical Narrative or Summary of the Present Controversy between Daniel Nimham . . . and Legal Representatives of Colonel Frederick Philipse . . .", a transcript at the

Library of Congress (originals in the Lansdowne Manuscripts, Volume 707, 24–51, pp. 1–55, British Library) reflect the Philipse family's position in these affairs.

For tenants' property holdings and status, I have consulted, at the New York State Library, the "Tax Lists" for the year 1779 of various districts in New York. Though conducted at a time of soaring inflation, the tax assessment of the real estate was based on the 1775 valuation of the property, thus making these lists a valid source regarding the distribution of wealth in the pre-Revolutionary period. "[Tax List] of the east and west of the Manor of Rensselaerswyck," Feb. 20, 1752, in the Bleeker, Collins, and Abeel Papers, New York Public Library, helped me to understand the general contours of tenant property and also the tenant population of the manor. Absolutely indispensable in studying these subjects have been the many volumes of testaments, land deeds, and patents at public archives in New York, which show generally how much and what kind of wealth the manorial tenantry owned and occasionally how the social group perceived both their own status and their relationship to their landlords. I might add that these sources were also useful in identifying each of the tenants in these manors. They are: Deed Books A–K, 1690–1783, and Mortgage Books A–D, Westchester County Clerk's Office, White Plains, N.Y.; Deed Books 1–11, Albany County Clerk's Office, Albany, N.Y.; Deed Books 1–2, Dutchess County Clerk's Office, Poughkeepsie, N.Y.; Wills, 1665–1800, formerly in the Surrogate Office, City of New York, and now at Queens College Library; Deeds and Mortgages, 1641–1841, 43 volumes, and Patent Books, 1664–1786, 17 volumes, at the Office of Secretary of State of New York, Albany; and New York Colonial Manuscripts, Land Papers, 1642–1803, 63 volumes, at the New York State Library.

Supplementing the above are the American Loyalist Papers, 1783–1790, in the Audit Office Series, Classes 12 and 13, in the Public Record Office. Transcripts of the records running to 60 volumes are at the New York Public Library. Volumes 17 to 24, 32, and 41 to 46 concern the loyalists from New York. I examined both the transcripts and the microfilm edition of the originals at the Library of Congress. Since the loyalist claims tended to be exaggerated, I treated the material with caution. Nevertheless, a careful reading of this material was very rewarding, since the investigations of the parliamentary commissioners into the loyalist claims also covered landlords' lease policies and problems, the conditions of tenants' improvements in some of the manors and large patents, and the colonial land situation in general.

County politics in relation to the manors and their landlords and the governance structure of the estates are two subjects that have received scant attention from historians, while at the same time, the landed men's influence on the provincial political scene has been fully elaborated. The Minutes of the Court of Sessions in Albany County, 1685–1689, 1712–1723, and 1763–1782, all in three volumes, at the Albany County Clerk's Office, and the court of sessions records for Westchester County, 1657–1697, in Deed Book D, 17–139, at the Westchester County Clerk's Office are required reading for a study of local politics. Unfortunately, the records are not comprehensive. Informative also were the New York Colonial Manuscripts, 1638–1800, in 103 volumes, which contain the court of sessions minutes (though fragmentary), and the New York Council

Minutes, 1668–1783, 28 volumes, in the New York State Library, even though more than half of the sources were partially scorched or completely burned in the 1911 fire.

Since manorial life was much influenced by outside political, social, and economic forces, a study of these forces is of prime importance. I have examined the following sources: the William Blathwayt Papers (both originals and microfilm edition), at the Colonial Williamsburg Foundation Research Library, Williamsburg, Va., an excellent source on Stephanus Van Cortlandt, Leisler's Rebellion, and the earl of Bellomont; the William Smith Papers, New York Public Library, full of incisive comments on such diverse topics as the colonial landlords' attitudes and strategies toward land development, land politics, boundary disputes, economic conditions, and agrarian disturbances; the James Alexander Papers, 1710–1800, New-York Historical Society, useful in understanding lease practices and problems in Dutchess County and settlement policy of land speculators in the province; the Goldsbrow Banyar Papers, 1745–1815, at the same library, revealing, among other things, Edward Clarke's estate situation in Cherry Valley and his tenants' temperament in the 1760s; and the Van Schaick Family Papers, 1715–1831 (especially "A Memorandum Book of Business" owned by John G. Van Schaick), the Harmanus Bleecker Papers, 1752–1805, and the John Chamber Papers, all at the New York State Library, which include expositions of the advantages and disadvantages of the various lease tenures practiced in the colony.

## Printed Sources

It is a truism that no student of Colonial New York can afford to ignore E. B. O'Callaghan and B[erthold] Fernow, eds., *Documents Relative to the Colonial History of the State of New-York . . .*, 14 volumes (Albany, N.Y., 1853–1887). This series and also E. B. O'Callaghan, ed., *The Documentary History of the State of New York*, 4 volumes (Albany, N.Y., 1849–1851), include a multitude of letters, reports, and comments by public and private figures on almost every aspect of provincial life. Volume III of the *Documentary History* (1850) has 232 pages of papers relating to Livingston Manor, half of which concern agrarian unrest in that area in the 1750s.

My endeavor at tracing the controversies surrounding the legal status of the manors in the administrative and judicial organization of the province was greatly assisted by *The Colonial Laws of New York from the Year 1664 to the Revolution*, 5 volumes (Albany, N.Y., 1894–1896); *Journal of the Votes and Proceedings of the General Assembly of the Colony of New York, 1691–1765*, 2 volumes (New York, 1764–1766); *Journal of the Votes and Proceedings of the General Assembly of the Colony of New York, from 1766 to 1776* (Albany, N.Y., 1820); *Journal of the Legislative Council of the Colony of New-York, 1691–1765 . . .*, 2 volumes (Albany, N.Y., 1910); Dixon Ryan Fox, ed., *The Minutes of the Court of Sessions (1657–1696), Westchester County, New York* (Westchester County Historical Society, *Publications* [White Plains, N.Y., 1924]); Joel Munsell, ed., *Annals of Albany*, 10 volumes (Albany, N.Y., 1850–1859), and *Collections on the History of Albany, from Its Discovery to the Present Time*, 4 volumes (Albany, N.Y., 1865–1871), both of which contain Albany city's Common Council minutes; A. J. F. van Laer, ed., *Minutes of the Court of Albany, Rensselaers-wyck and Schenectady, 1668–1685*, 3 volumes (Albany, N.Y., 1926–1932); Victor Hugo Paltsits, ed., *Minutes of the Executive Council of the Province of New York: Administration of Francis Lovelace, 1668–1673*, 2 volumes (Albany, N.Y., 1910).

An essential guide for understanding provincial land problems in general is the letters of Cadwallader Colden, long-term surveyor general of New York. These are printed as follows: *The Colden Letter Books, 1760–1775* (New-York Historical Society, *Collections*, IX–X, [New York, 1876–1877]) and *The Letters and Papers of Cadwallader Colden* (New-York Historical Society, *Collections*, L–LVI, LXVII–LXVIII [New York, 1917–1923, 1934–1935]). But one should read Colden's observations critically because of his well-known bias against the provincial land system and landed interests. The Indian interest in New York land, particularly on the frontier, is most extensively discussed in James Sullivan *et al.*, eds., *The Papers of Sir William Johnson*, 14 volumes (Albany, N.Y., 1921–1965).

On various aspects of provincial and manorial society, I was enlightened by the following collections of private memoirs and letters, some of which were written by contemporary observers and others by those involved directly in manor affairs: J. Franklin Jameson, ed., *Narratives of New Netherland, 1609–1664*, Original Narratives of Early American History (New York, 1909); Jaspar Dankers and Philip Sluyter, *Journal of a Voyage to New York and a Tour in Several of the American Colonies*, trans. and ed. Henry C. Murphy (Long Island Historical Society, *Memoirs* [Brooklyn, N.Y., 1867]); Daniel Denton, *A Brief Description of New-York (1670)*, with a bibliographical note by Victor H. Paltsits, Facsimile Text Society, Publication No. 40 (New York, 1937). A. J. F. van Laer, trans. and ed., *Correspondence of Jeremias Van Rensselaer, 1651–1674* (Albany, N.Y., 1932) and *Correspondence of Maria Van Rensselaer, 1669–1689* (Albany, N.Y., 1935), contain particularly vivid commentaries on the difficulties faced by the patroons during the transitional period following the English conquest of New Netherland. In addition, useful are John Miller, *New York Considered and Improved*, ed. Victor Hugo Paltsits (Cleveland, Ohio, 1903); Carl Bridenbaugh, ed., *Gentleman's Progress: The Itinerarium of Dr. Alexander Hamilton* (Chapel Hill, N.C., 1948), which is peppered with some gossipy comments on several New York landlords; and Milton M. Klein, ed., *The Independent Reflector, or Weekly Essays on Sundry Important Subjects, More particularly adapted to the Province of New-York . . .* (Cambridge, Mass., 1963). [Anne] Grant, *Memoirs of an American Lady: With Sketches of Manners and Scenery in America, As They Existed Previous to the Revolution* (New York, 1809), contains highly perceptive observations of the cultural, social, and economic scene of the Albany area in the pre-Revolutionary period. G. D. Scull, ed., *The Montresor Journals* (New-York Historical Society, *Collections*, XIV [New York, 1881]), has interesting but often biased observations on the disturbances during and after the Stamp Act controversy in New York. Clarence Edwin Carter, ed., *The Correspondence of General Thomas Gage with the Secretaries of State, 1763–1775*, 4 volumes (New Haven, Conn., 1931–1933), is a good source on the political and social conditions in the years 1765 and 1766. J. Hector St. John [Michel Guillaume St. Jean de Crèvecoeur], *Letters from an American Farmer . . .* (London, 1782), is probably the most outspoken romanticization of what eighteenth-century America offered; yet the work has some favorable views on tenancy. "Journal of Lord Adam Gordon," in Newton D. Mereness, ed., *Travels in the American Colonies* (New York, 1961); Francis W. Halsey, ed., *A Tour of Four Great Rivers, The Hudson, Mohawk, Susquehanna and Delaware in 1769, Being the Journal of Richard Smith of Burlington, New Jersey* (New York, 1906); and the "Journal of Isaac Norris, during a Trip to Albany in 1745 . . . ," in the *Pennsylvania Magazine of History and Biography,* XXVII (1903), are also worth consulting.

There are public documents of other colonies that deserve special mention. *The Journals of the House of Representatives of Massachusetts* [1715–1760] (Boston, 1919–1964), and the *Acts and Resolves, Public and Private, of the Province of the Massachusetts Bay* [1692–1786], 21 volumes (Boston, 1869–1922), yielded valuable information on the boundary disputes between New York and Massachusetts, which had important effects upon the local disturbances in Albany County in the 1750s and 1760s. I read the above along with Daniel J. Pratt, ed., *Reports of the Regents of the University, on the Boundaries of the State of New York* (Albany, N.Y., 1884), II, which contains many official writings on the boundary negotiations. In order to determine the extent of land speculation by New Yorkers in the New Hampshire and Vermont areas in the middle of the eighteenth century, I also spent much time scanning Albert Stillman Batchellor, ed., *State Papers, the New Hampshire Grants, Being Transcripts of the Charters of Townships, . . . 1749–1764,* 40 volumes (Concord, N.H., 1895), and Isaac W. Hammond, ed., *Town Papers. Documents Relating to Towns in New Hampshire . . . ,* 22 volumes (Concord, N.H., 1883).

I am very much in debt to William Smith, *History of the late Province of New-York, from its Discovery to the Appointment of Governor Colden, in 1762 . . . ,* 2 volumes (New York, 1830 [orig. publ. London, 1757]). For all its shortcomings reflecting Smith's misanthropic traits, his whiggish frame of reference, his narrow legislative-defense focus, and his vindictiveness toward his personal enemies, the work is still the best contemporary account of the colonial history of New York. It offers insights into the defense and land questions and the lease practices in Livingston and Rensselaerswyck manors.

Finally, I must note my reliance on several newspapers from the period 1740 to 1776. Advertisements in these papers for the sale of real estate by both manorial proprietors and tenants revealed much about the quality of land, the degree of its improvement, tenants' perception of their estates, the conditions for sale, and the identity of the present occupants of different tracts. Some reports covered the progress of the 1766 riots. The following papers were most useful: *Albany Gazette; Boston-Gazette, and Country Journal* (Edes and Gill), 1756–1793; *New-York Gazette* (Bradford); *New-York Weekly Journal* (Zenger), 1733–1749; *New-York Journal; or, The General Advertiser* (Holt), 1766–1776; *New York-Mercury,* 1752–1768, changed to *New-York Gazette; and the Weekly Mercury* (Gaine), 1768–1783; *Pennsylvania Journal; and the Weekly Advertiser* (Philadelphia); and *Tarrytown Argus.*

# Index

DATE DUE

MAR 1 0 1988

JAN 3 0 1995

HIGHSMITH 45-220